D0011307

ECUADOR
& THE GALÁPAGOS ISLANDS

BEN WESTWOOD

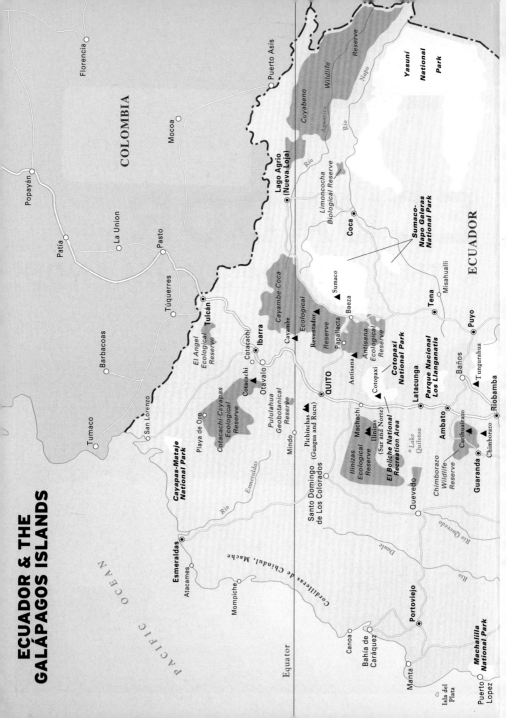

ECUADOR & THE GALÁPAGOS ISLANDS

PACIFIC OCEAN

COLOMBIA

ECUADOR

Equator

Cities and towns

Florencia
Popayán
Patía
La Unión
Mocoa
Pasto
Túquerres
Barbacoas
Tumaco
San Lorenzo
Puerto Asis
Puerto Loja)
Lago Agrio (Nueva Loja)
Tulcán
El Angel Ecological Reserve
Cotacachi
Ibarra
Otavalo
Cotacachi-Cayapas Ecological Reserve
Pululahua Geobotanical Reserve
Playa de Oro
Cayapas-Mataje National Park
Esmeraldas
Atacames
Mompiche
Río Esmeraldas
Cordilleras de Chindul, Mache
Santo Domingo de Los Colorados
Mindo
Pichincha (Guagua and Rucu)
QUITO
Machachi
Illinizas Ecological Reserve
El Boliche National Recreation Area
Illinizas (Sur and Norte)
Lake Quilotoa
Quevedo
Chimborazo Wildlife Reserve
Chimborazo
Guaranda
Carihuairazo
Ambato
Latacunga
Cotopaxi
Cotopaxi National Park
Parque Nacional Los Llanganatis
Baños
Tungurahua
Riobamba
Puyo
Tena
Misahuallí
Antisana
Antisana Ecological Reserve
Cayambe
Cayambe-Coca Ecological Reserve
Reventador
Papallacta
Baeza
Sumaco
Sumaco-Napo Galeras National Park
Coca
Limoncocha Biological Reserve
Cuyabeno Wildlife Reserve
Yasuní National Park
Río Napo
Río Aguarico
Río Daule
Río Quevedo
Quevedo
Portoviejo
Bahía de Caráquez
Canoa
Manta
Isla del Plata
Puerto López
Machalilla National Park

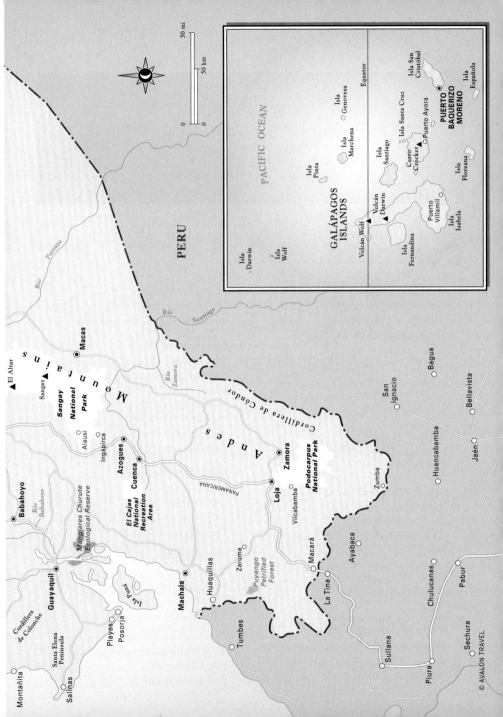

Contents

Discover Ecuador & the Galápagos Islands

I first came to Ecuador in 1998, fresh from university and eager for South American adventures. As I flew over the Avenue of Volcanoes south of Quito, the young woman sitting next to me proudly pointed out the perfect cone-shaped peak of Cotopaxi to the east and, on the other side of the aircraft, majestic Chimborazo looming to the west. Barely 20 minutes later, we were flying over the sodden marshland and rice fields of the coastal plains before touching down in hot, humid Guayaquil. I was immediately struck by Ecuador's incredible contrasts, and it wasn't long before I was bouncing on a bus through the banana plantations into the mountains and rainforests beyond to see it all firsthand.

Instead of asking "Why go to Ecuador?," you should ask yourself, "Why haven't I been there already?" This is a country where you can wake up gazing at the Pacific, drive through the Andes past 5,000-meter-high volcanoes, and reach the Amazon rainforest before sundown. The locals call Ecuador "four countries in one," and it's no exaggeration. The contrasts you encounter in an area roughly the size of Britain or the U.S. state of Colorado are astonishing, and the people of Ecuador are just as diverse as the landscapes – Shuar Indians hunting with blowpipes, poncho-wearing artisans plying their wares in Andean markets, and salsa-dancing señoritas tearing it up on urban dance floors.

As varied as the terrain and the people is the wildlife. Ecuador is one of the world's most biodiverse countries, with 1,600 species of birds and 25,000 species of plants, more than the total number of species found in North America. All this diversity on the mainland doesn't even take into account the unique ecosystem of the Galápagos Islands, frequently voted the world's best tourist destination. Nowhere else on earth can you view wildlife so utterly unconcerned by humans. Come face to craggy face with giant tortoises, snorkel with nonchalant sea turtles and playful sea lions, watch the hilarious mating dance of the blue-footed boobies, or go scuba diving with whale sharks and hammerheads.

After experiencing all these wonders, you may be reluctant to leave – and you're in good company. The first evening I spent in Ecuador, the boss of the language institute where I was working told me with a knowing look: "A lot of people come down here, fall in love, and end up staying." I laughed it off at the time, but it wasn't long before I became one of those people. Perhaps you'll be next.

Planning Your Trip

▶ WHERE TO GO

Quito

Ecuador's capital has scenery as breathtaking as its elevation of nearly 2,850 meters. The second-highest capital in the world is also one of Latin America's best-preserved colonial cities, with beautiful churches, plazas, and museums as well as dramatic views from the surrounding hills. A few kilometers to the north you can stand with a foot in each hemisphere on the Equator at Mitad del Mundo.

Northern Sierra and Western Andean Slopes

The hills north of Quito contain much for hikers and shoppers alike. The thriving indigenous communities ply their wares in the colorful markets of Otavalo and Cotacachi, while the surrounding hills and mountains offer excellent trekking opportunities. The Andes drop down to dense cloud forest and rushing rivers to the northwest around Mindo, where bird-watchers can tick off countless

A Guayaquil woodpecker feeds in the cloud forests around Mindo.

IF YOU HAVE...

- **ONE WEEK:** Visit Quito, Baños, Cotopaxi, Cuenca, Otavalo, and do the Devil's Nose train ride.

- **TWO WEEKS:** Add Mindo, Lake Quilotoa, and either the Galápagos Islands or a rainforest trip via Coca or Tena.

- **THREE WEEKS:** Add Ingapirca, Cajas National Park, Loja, Vilcabamba, and Zaruma.

- **FOUR WEEKS:** Add Guayaquil, Machalilla National Park, Bahía de Caráquez, and Canoa.

---

species and adrenaline seekers can zip across the forest canopy.

Central Sierra

South of Quito, the spectacular Avenue of the Volcanoes contains eight of Ecuador's 10 highest peaks, including Cotopaxi and Chimborazo. Just as spectacular are the shimmering turquoise waters of Lake Quilotoa and the hikes around it on the surrounding loop trail. Take a dramatic train ride from Riobamba along the famous Nariz del Diablo (Devil's nose) and relax in the hot springs of Baños, Ecuador's most idyllic spa town.

Southern Sierra

This region's relative isolation makes for a delightful step back in time. The colonial center of Cuenca rivals Quito for its churches, plazas, and museums but has a pace as gentle

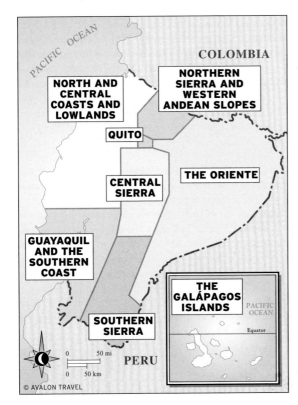

© AVALON TRAVEL

neighboring countries. Options range from luxury lodges to basic rainforest camps and from primary forest east of Coca to secondary forest near Puyo. For a more action-packed adventure, go rafting, kayaking, and canyoneering near Tena.

North and Central Coasts and Lowlands

Resorts such as Atacames fill up with partyers in high season, while surfers opt for quieter spots like Mompiche, which also has the region's newest luxury hotel. The most popular backpacker resort is surfer hangout Canoa farther south. Ecotourism is also on offer in the mangroves near Bahía de Caráquez and the protected tropical dry forest of Machalilla National Park. Isla de la Plata is deemed the "poor man's Galápagos" for its birdlife, and the whale-watching is spectacular off Puerto Lopez June–September.

Guayaquil and the Southern Coast

Ecuador's biggest city has a beautiful riverside *malecón*, a regenerated center, and excellent nightlife. West of the city, the gleaming high-rises and beaches of the Santa Elena Peninsula attract more affluent visitors, while backpackers and surfers head north to Montañita. To the south, through the banana plantations, head up to the idyllic hilltop town of Zaruma.

The Galápagos Islands

The unique ecosystem of the archipelago

as its people. Ingapirca is Ecuador's best set of Inca ruins, and Cajas National Park is one of the country's most rugged hiking spots. The award-winning eco-city of Loja leads to the idyllic Valley of Longevity at Vilcabamba, popular with retired folk and backpackers alike. Horse-riding, hiking, and bird-watching await in Podocarpus National Park near the Peruvian border.

The Oriente

Whether you want to canoe through flooded rainforests, hike at night to tarantula holes, go bird-watching from the top of the rainforest canopy, or stay with indigenous people, the Ecuadorian rainforest offers unforgettable experiences and is more accessible than in

that fascinated Charles Darwin, inspiring his monumental theory of evolution, is one of the world's natural treasures. Where else can you snorkel with sea lion pups and marine turtles, sunbathe with iguanas, or scuba dive with whale sharks? The bird-watching is also among the world's best—everything from blue-footed boobies to red-chested frigates and waved albatrosses to the tiny finches that inspired Darwin's theory. The landscapes are otherworldly too—blackened lava flows and steaming volcanoes are a geologist's dream.

► WHEN TO GO

Ecuador's climate is as diverse as its landscape. On the coast, the tropical seasons are most easily defined: *invierno* (winter) is hot and wet with fierce sunshine broken by torrential rain. *Verano* (summer) is cooler, cloudier, and mostly dry. The Galápagos's climate mirrors that of the coast but with less rain and humidity. In the highlands, it's wettest February–April, but seasons are less defined, with showers most of the year. It tends to be warmest and driest June–September and coldest around Christmas. The Oriente is hot and wet year-round with the driest period around December and the wettest June–September.

High season is particularly busy on the beach and runs from Christmas through Carnival (usually February) and Easter with another brief high season in July–August. The best time for traveling around Ecuador is probably just outside the high seasons in May and November, but if hustle and bustle is your thing, go in high season but expect to pay more.

Ecuador is a great destination for water sports, both on Andean rivers and on the coast.

▶ BEFORE YOU GO

Passports, Tourist Cards, and Visas

Travelers to Ecuador will need a passport that is valid for at least six months beyond the date of entry. A tourist card (also called a T-3) is issued on entry and must be returned on leaving Ecuador. Stays of up to 90 days are permitted without a visa and can sometimes be extended a further 90 days. Travelers must also be able to show "proof of economic means" (a credit card is usually good enough) and a return or onward travel ticket out of Ecuador.

Vaccinations

All visitors should make sure their routine immunizations are up to date. The U.S. Centers for Disease Control and Prevention recommend that travelers be vaccinated against hepatitis A, typhoid fever, and in cases of close contact with locals, hepatitis B. Rabies vaccinations are also recommended for those venturing into rural areas. Proof of yellow fever vaccination is necessary when entering Ecuador from Peru or Colombia, but it is a good idea no matter where you arrive from.

Transportation

Ecuador has two international airports: Mariscal Sucre International Airport, which is moving east of Quito to El Quinche, and José Joaquin Olmedo International Airport in Guayaquil. You can get just about anywhere within Ecuador from either city in under an hour by plane (from $60 one-way) or in a day by bus or car.

Ecuador's public transportation network is comprehensive, and roads have improved in recent years, but it's not always the quickest way to get around. If your time is limited, consider flying between larger cities instead of taking all-day (or all-night) buses, or renting a car. Renting a taxi and driver for the day is more expensive than buses but quicker and more direct.

Guayaquil's waterfront and artistic district in Las Peñas are models of regeneration.

Explore Ecuador & the Galápagos Islands

► THE BEST OF ECUADOR

Ecuador is so compact that, if you plan it right, you can see a decent chunk of the country in just two weeks. This itinerary takes in the highlights of the mountains as well as a trip to the rainforest. If you have an extra week, include a visit to the Galápagos Islands.

Day 1

Fly to Quito and spend the day touring the churches, plazas, and museums of Old Town, including a trip up to either El Panecillo, La Basílica, or Itchimbía for great views. Spend the night in New Town and enjoy the international restaurants and nightlife. If you decide to add a trip to the Galápagos, book it now if you haven't already.

Day 2

Tour the New Town, including the archaeological treasures of Casa de la Cultura and Guayasamín's famous artistic work, La Capilla del Hombre. Take an afternoon excursion to the equator at Mitad del Mundo.

Day 3

Take a bus to Quilotoa via Latacunga. Spend the afternoon hiking around the spectacular extinct volcanic Lake Quilotoa and enjoy home-cooked food while staying with an indigenous family.

Day 4

Spend the day hiking and cycling around

Llamas thrive in Cajas National Park near Cuenca.

INDIGENOUS PAST AND PRESENT

Ecuador is full of vibrant indigenous cultures and remnants of history that spans thousands of years. Time your visit right and you can catch an outstanding local fiesta or two, such as Latacunga's **Mama Negra** (early November) or Imbabura's **Inti Raymi** (June). There are large indigenous markets every day of the week in the Andes.

QUITO AND VICINITY

- In Old Town, visit the **Itchimbía Cultural Center,** the preserved colonial home of María Augusta Urrutia, and the Centro Cultural Metropolitano.

- In New Town, visit the **Casa de la Cultura** and **La Capilla del Hombre,** Guayasamín's famous artwork dedicated to the suffering of indigenous people.

- Stop by the **artisanal market** at **Parque El Ejido** or in **La Mariscal.**

- The area near Otavalo, two hours north of Quito by bus, is rich with indigenous culture. Visit crafts villages such as **Ilumán** and **Peguche.** Bargain at the markets, like the famous one in **Otavalo's Plaza de Ponchos,** and sample a traditional plate of *cuy*. Visit **Laguna Cuicocha,** the waters of which are renowned for their healing properties by local indigenous people.

LATACUNGA

- Latacunga, south of Quito, is the starting point for the **Quilotoa Loop** into the Andean hinterlands. Browse the sheep's hide paintings in **Tigua** and the animal market in **Zumbahua** before gazing on the spectacular **Laguna Quilotoa.** Stay with indigenous people in the villages of **Chugchilán** and **Isinlivi.**

- If you're in this region on Thursday, stop by the market at Saquisilí.

CUENCA AND VICINITY

Ecuador's third-largest city has great cultural offerings.

- Don't miss the shrunken heads in the **Museo del Banco Central** and the ruins of the Inca city **Pumapungo** behind the museum.

- Beyond the city limits, take in the well-preserved Inca ruins at **Ingapirca** and the indigenous villages of **Gualaceo, Chordeleg,** and **Cañar.**

SARAGURO

- Visit the indigenous community of Saraguro, south of Cuenca. Stay at **Hostal Achik Wasi** and go **hiking** in the surrounding hills with indigenous guides.

traditional woven hammocks for sale

Locals believe Lake Cuicocha is sacred.

Cotopaxi National Park and enjoy wonderful views of the volcano. Head to Baños and enjoy a thermal bath in the early evening.

Day 5

Cycle the route along the Pastaza Valley from Baños toward Puyo, stopping at several waterfalls along the way. Alternately, go white-water rafting or hike to the foot of active volcano Tungurahua. Take the bus to Riobamba and spend the night.

Day 6

Take the early morning train to Alausí and travel along the dramatic Devil's Nose switchbacks. Spend the night in Alausí or head south to stay near Ingapirca.

Day 7

Tour the Inca ruins of Ingapirca in the morning and travel to Cuenca, spending the afternoon taking in its colonial center. End your day with the evening session at the hot springs in Baños.

Day 8

Spend the morning hiking around the rugged hills and deep lagoons of Cajas National Park. Return to Cuenca in time to catch a late-afternoon flight to Quito.

Day 9-12

Spend a minimum of four days at an Amazon lodge via a flight to Coca or Lago Agrio. Alternately, take a bus to Tena with an optional stopover at the hot springs at Papallacta. Visit a nearby Kichwa community in secondary rainforest and take in some rafting on the upper Napo. Remember that getting to the rainforest will be at least half a day on both ends, so consider extending your stay by a day and forgoing Day 13's activities.

Days 13-14

Head back to Quito and go straight to Otavalo, ideally in time for the Saturday textile market. Stock up on indigenous clothing and carvings. Extend your stay by a day with hikes to nearby lakes such as Cuicocha and Mojanda before going back to Quito in time for your flight.

WILDLIFE WONDERS

Ecuador's incredible biological diversity can keep you busy for months. Travel through terrain teeming with wildlife: quetzals in the cloud forest, howler monkeys in the Amazon, and giant tortoises in the Galápagos Islands.

QUITO

In Quito, whet your appetite at the **Botanical Gardens** and New Town's **Vivarium** as well as the **Quito Zoo** in nearby Guayllabamba. To get an early start on **birding,** stay at the **Hostería San Jorge** in the Pichincha foothills.

WESTERN ANDEAN SLOPES

Head up to the **Mindo** area in the **cloud forest** for some world-class bird-watching. Stay either in Mindo or nearby comfortable lodges such as **Tandayapa** and **Bellavista** that cater to birders. Reserves such as **Maquipucuna** and **Yanacocha** are also packed with life.

CENTRAL SIERRA

Book a day tour up into the foothills of the **Antisana Ecological Reserve,** where the South American condor – the largest flying bird in the world – still soars. Alternately, visit **Cotopaxi National Park** for another chance to spot this magnificent creature.

THE AMAZON

Take a four-day or preferably five-day tour of the Amazon. Stay at a lodge such as **Napo Wildlife Center** and experience the incredible diversity of the rainforest: pink dolphins, parakeets, alligators, and anacondas. Get the adrenaline pumping at night with walks to tarantula holes and canoe rides to spot the eyes of caimans peeking from the water.

THE GALÁPAGOS ISLANDS

What could possibly beat the Amazon forest for wildlife enthusiasts? One of the few places on earth is the Galápagos archipelago. Naturalists and photographers are thrilled because the species have no fear of humans: Whether you take a land-based tour with day excursions or a cruise, opportunities to get up close and personal with wildlife are all around, including snorkeling with sea lions off **Floreana,** scuba diving with sharks at **León Dormido** on San Cristóbal, and grumbling with giant tortoises at **Charles Darwin Station** on Santa Cruz.

GUAYAQUIL

Head up to **Machalilla,** where you can hike in the coastal dry forests, watch whales off the coast (June–September), or simply relax on the beach at **Los Frailes.** If you haven't had your fill of bird-watching, head to **Isla de la Plata** to see blue-footed boobies or farther up the coast to the mangroves around **Bahía de Cáraquez,** which are teeming with frigate birds.

Frigate birds inflate their chests to the size of basketballs.

▶ GALÁPAGOS EXPEDITION

There are simply not enough superlatives to describe the Galápagos. For scientists, visitors, divers, writers, and photographers alike, this archipelago 970 kilometers west of the Ecuadorian mainland is the ultimate experience in wildlife watching—and the creatures watch you as much as you watch them. This truly unique ecosystem contains a bewildering array of species, most of them endemic, and the lack of natural predators means that they have almost no fear of humans.

A tour of at least five days is recommended, and seven or eight days is even better, as it takes a half-day each way to get to and from the islands. Most travelers visit the isles on package tours, but it's increasingly easy to do it yourself, staying in the three main ports and taking day trips and shuttles between islands. Highlights of any tour include the Charles Darwin Research Center on Santa Cruz, Post Office Bay and Devil's Crown on Floreana, León Dormido on San Cristóbal, Pinnacle Rock on Bartolomé, Punta Suárez on Española, Sierra Negra on Isabela, and Punta Espinosa on Fernandina.

Giant tortoises gave the Galápagos Islands their name.

When to Go

The high tourist season is December–April, peaking at Christmas, Carnival, and Easter; there is another July–August high season. If you are planning to travel to the islands during these months, be sure to book your tour well in advance. Also note that many boats are dry-docked for repairs and maintenance during September–October.

During the dry season (June–November), the islands become more barren as dormant vegetation awaits the rains. The ocean is also considerably colder and rougher. Rains alternate with hot and sunny days during the wet season (January–April); the islands turn green, and the waters are calmer and warmer.

Perhaps the best time to visit is just before and after the high season in May–June or November.

Planning Your Trip

In simple terms, the farther you are from the Galápagos, the more you pay. Cruises, land tours, and diving tours can all be arranged in your home country or through a travel agency in Ecuador. Keep in mind that when booking a tour from abroad, a deposit of at least $200 per person, via wire transfer or Western Union (no credit cards by Internet or phone), is usually required.

Many travel agencies in Quito and Guayaquil advertise tours, and shopping around is the way to go. Holding out for last-minute deals may save you 5–50 percent, but be aware that it may leave you stranded as well. Some travelers with time on their hands even fly to the Galápagos, book into a cheap hotel for a few days, and try to get on a last-minute cruise, saving even more than 50 percent in some cases; but there are no guarantees.

Sally Lightfoot crabs are an unexpected highlight of the islands.

Transportation

Transportation to the islands is generally not included in the price of a tour. Flights to the Galápagos depart from Quito and Guayaquil daily. There are two airports in the Galápagos: one on Baltra, near the central island of Santa Cruz, and one on San Cristóbal. Make sure you're flying to the correct island to begin your tour. Prices are about $350 return from Guayaquil and $400 from Quito.

If you are traveling to the islands without being booked on a tour, Puerto Ayora is the best place to arrange a budget tour. Note that getting from Baltra to Puerto Ayora is a journey in three stages involving two bus rides and a ferry ride. There are daily ferry shuttles from $25 per person one-way to the other two main ports—Baquerizo Moreno on San Cristóbal and Puerto Villamil on Isabela.

Tour Boats and Guides

Tour boats are organized into five classes— economy, tourist, tourist superior, first, and luxury. Economy-class boats are very basic, and are appropriate for those on a very limited budget or time frame; tourist- and tourist superior-class boats are the most common

in the islands, with a bit more comfort and better guides; first class and luxury tours offer air-conditioning, gourmet food, and service that match those in the finest hotels on the mainland, and guides are qualified scientists. Prices vary widely, but all prices should include food, accommodations, transfers to and from your boat, trained guides, and all shore visits.

Land-based tours are increasingly common and are especially popular with those suffering from seasickness. There is more flexibility in some ways, but many of the islands (for example Fernandina, Española and Genovesa) are excluded from land-based itineraries, and precious time is spent traveling to and from sites every day.

A good guide is the most important factor in your visit. All Galápagos guides are trained and licensed by the National Park Service and qualify in one of three classes, in ascending order of quality. When booking a tour, ask about your guide's specific qualifications and what languages he or she speaks.

Diving

The underwater riches found here include manta rays, marine iguanas, and active volcano vents, to name just a few. At last count there were over 60 marine visitor sites throughout the archipelago, many on islands closed to visitors above the surface. Wolf and Darwin Islands are sure to be highlights of any diving expedition.

However, note that diving here is not for beginners. Many dives are in open water, and the most interesting marine life usually keeps to areas of strong currents—up to 3.5 knots in places. A wetsuit is essential, and in the cold season a wetsuit with a hood, booties, and gloves becomes necessary. Many companies require a certain level of experience: an open water certification, a minimum number of dives, and sometimes a medical certificate.

blue-footed boobies

Note that new regulations state that every boat must be registered either as a cruise boat or a dive boat, but not both. This means that divers either have to join a live-aboard (which are expensive) or do a land-based tour and take day trips. Most large Galápagos tour agencies can book dive trips.

Sample Itineraries
CRUISES
For cruises, there are basically three itineraries: northern, southern, and western. Five-day tours include one of these areas, and eight-day tours include two; it's only possible to experience all three areas on the more expensive and rarer two-week tours. Note that the western itinerary has fewer departures and is mainly available on eight-day tours because distances are greater. Most tours start off in Santa Cruz, but you can also start in San Cristóbal. Always check the exact itinerary and the class of boat before booking.

Five-Day Northern Cruise
- **Day 1:** Baltra airport, Bachas Beach
- **Day 2:** Bartolomé, Santiago, and Rábida
- **Day 3:** Genovesa
- **Day 4:** Plaza, Santa Cruz (Charles Darwin Station, Tortuga Bay)
- **Day 5:** Baltra

Five-Day Southern Cruise
- **Day 1:** San Cristóbal (Isla de Lobos, Kicker Rock)
- **Day 2:** Plaza, Santa Fe
- **Day 3:** Española (Punta Suárez, Gardner Bay)
- **Day 4:** Floreana (Post Office Bay, Punta Cormorant, Devil's Crown)
- **Day 5:** Santa Cruz (Charles Darwin Station), Baltra

Eight-Day Cruise Option 1
- **Day 1:** San Cristóbal (Isla de Lobos, Kicker Rock)
- **Day 2:** San Cristóbal (highlands, Punta Pitt)
- **Day 3:** Floreana (Post Office Bay, Punta Cormorant, Devil's Crown)
- **Day 4:** Santa Cruz (Black Turtle Cove), Bartolomé
- **Day 5:** Genovesa
- **Day 6:** Santiago
- **Day 7:** Plaza, Santa Cruz (Charles Darwin Station)
- **Day 8:** Baltra

Eight-Day Cruise Option 2
- **Day 1:** Baltra, Rábida
- **Day 2:** Isabela (Vicente Roca Point), Fernandina (Punta Espinoza)
- **Day 3:** Isabela (Tagua Cove, Urbina Bay)
- **Day 4:** Isabela (Elizabeth Bay, Moreno Point)
- **Day 5:** Isabela (Wetlands, Wall of Tears, Tortoise Breeding Station)
- **Day 6:** North Seymour, Santa Cruz (Charles Darwin Station)
- **Day 7:** Española (Punta Suárez, Gardner Bay)
- **Day 8:** San Cristóbal (Interpretation Center and La Galapaguera)

ADRENALINE RUSH

It's no surprise that there are plenty of thrills to be had in a country that boasts such dramatically changing terrain, where rolling plains rise sharply through foothills to 5,000-meter-high mountains only to drop down again to tropical rainforest. Whether you want to zoom downhill on a bike, kayak through river rapids, or scale a peak with an ice axe, there's enough to give adrenaline junkies their fix. Note that climbing mountains should not be attempted lightly, and you need sufficient time to acclimate to peaks over 4,000 meters:

- Go on an exhilarating full-day **downhill bike ride** near Quito in the **Intag Valley.** Follow this with a **hike** in the **Lagunas de Mojanda** and **climb Fuya Fuya**, excellent practice for higher peaks.

- **Hike** around the base of the volcano, and do some **cycling** in **Cotopaxi National Park.** If you want to scale the peak, you will need to spend a couple of days here.

- From Riobamba, **hike** to the **Collanes** plain at the foot of El Altar for Ecuador's most impressive volcanic panorama – the jagged peaks of Obispo, Monjes, and Tabernacle loom over Laguna Amarilla as glacier ice tumbles down the slopes. Camp up here for one night in the thatched *chozas*.

- At **Chimborazo National Park** choose among **hiking, cycling,** or **climbing.** The peak is more technical to climb and so requires longer preparation and more experience.

- The **Inca Trail to Ingapirca** takes two nights and ends at Ecuador's foremost Inca buildings. From here, take a bus to Cuenca and do some **hiking** in **El Cajas National Park.**

- In **Baños,** do some **cycling, rafting,** and **hiking,** or simply unwind in the thermal baths. Alternately, head south to do some **horseback riding** and **trekking** in **Podocarpus National Park,** where you can camp among glacial lakes or hike through verdant forests.

LAND-BASED TOURS

Land-based tours restrict you to sites within a day's travel of three populated areas: Puerto Ayora on Santa Cruz, Baquerizo Moreno on San Cristóbal, and Puerto Villamil on Isabela. A five-day land-based tour can take in two of these islands, while an eight-day tour can take in all three plus a few day trips to nearby islands such as Seymour Norte, Plaza, Floreana, Santa Fé, and Bartolomé. Other islands are strictly off-limits to day trips.

Five-Day Land Tour

- **Day 1:** San Cristóbal (Isla de Lobos, Kicker Rock)

- **Day 2:** Ferry to Santa Cruz (Charles Darwin Station, Tortuga Bay, highlands)

- **Day 3:** Day trip to Bartolomé

- **Day 4:** Day trip to Floreana, Plaza, or North Seymour

- **Day 5:** Bus to Baltra

Eight-Day Land Tour

- **Day 1:** San Cristóbal (Isla de Lobos, Kicker Rock)

- **Day 2:** Ferry to Santa Cruz (Charles Darwin Station), ferry to Isabela

- **Day 3:** Isabela (Sierra Negra trek)

- **Day 4:** Isabela (Las Tintoreras, Tortoise Breeding Center, Wall of Tears)

- **Day 5:** Ferry to Santa Cruz (highlands, Tortuga Bay)

- **Day 6:** Day trip to Bartolomé

- **Day 7:** Day trip to Floreana, Plaza, or Seymour Norte

- **Day 8:** Bus to Baltra

▶ SUN AND SURF

Ecuador's coastline is less visited by foreign travelers than by locals, but miss it and you're missing a huge chunk of the country. Here you'll find beautiful beaches, some of which are backed by mangroves and dry forest. The surfing here attracts enthusiasts from all over the Americas, and the seafood is the mouth-watering highlight of Ecuadorian cuisine.

Mompiche, Canoa, and Montañita all have world-class surfing.

Day 1

Start in the regenerated center of Guayaquil, Ecuador's largest city. Walk along the riverside *malecón* up to the artistic district of Las Peñas and marvel at the urban iguanas in Parque Bolívar. Take an afternoon excursion to Parque Histórico across the river and gain insight into rural life as well as a glimpse of coastal wildlife.

Day 2

Take an early bus to Montañita and spend the day surfing, sunbathing, and socializing in this vibrant backpacker hangout. For a more active day, hike up to the waterfalls and forests of Dos Mangas in the hills behind the town.

Day 3

Take a bus to Puerto Lopez and spend the day in Machalilla National Park. Visit the museum and archaeological site in the hills around Agua Blanca before visiting one of Ecuador's most stunning beaches: Playa los Frailes. As an alternative to Puerto Lopez, stay in nearby Puerto Rico and enjoy some delicious seafood at La Barquita or Alandaluz.

Day 4

Take a day trip to Isla de la Plata, dubbed the poor man's Galápagos for its birdlife. Hike around the island and cool off with some snorkeling. If you're visiting June–September, substitute this with a whale-watching trip to see dozens of humpbacks breaching.

Day 5

Head north to Bahía de Cáraquez and enjoy the gentle pace of this clean, friendly eco-city. Take an excursion to the nearby mangroves and Isla Corazón, which has a large colony of frigate birds.

Day 6

Spend the day in the nearby resort of Canoa. Go surfing or take a kayaking excursion. Alternately, learn about the workings of an organic farm by visiting Rio Muchacho.

Day 7

Head north to the fishing village of Mompiche. Blow your budget on the luxurious Royal Decameron Hotel on the hill or rough it with the surfers in the laid-back village.

Day 8

If you're in the mood for a party, continue north to Atacames, where the beach bars pump out music until the early hours. Don't miss *encocado* (seafood cooked in coconut) for dinner at the beachfront restaurant Marco's. For a quieter break, stay at Playa Escondida or Súa.

QUITO

Ecuador's capital is a city that scales many heights, not least in terms of elevation. The second-highest capital in the world after Bolivia's La Paz, Quito sits at 2,850 meters above sea level in a valley hemmed in by mountains, including the twin peaks of Volcán Pichincha. Quito's dramatic geographical position has led to its long thin shape: spread out over 50 kilometers long, but just eight kilometers wide.

Quito (pop. 1.6 million) is an intriguing mix of old and new: colonial squares and concrete office blocks, traditional markets and modern malls, indigenous artisans and fashion-conscious professionals—and this diversity allows visitors to have the best of both worlds. The *centro histórico* (historic center) delivers a delightful trip back in time to the colonial era with narrow cobbled streets, elegant plazas, and spectacular churches. New Town, on the other hand, looks firmly forward and is so cosmopolitan that parts of it are nicknamed *gringolandia*. With a vibrant cultural scene, great nightlife, a vast array of hotels, travel agencies, and the country's best range of restaurants, it's no surprise that Ecuador's political capital is also its tourism hub.

Much of the population of Ecuador's second-largest city lives in *barrios* (neighborhoods) or shantytowns, either up the slopes of the mountains or spread north and south of the city center. The people themselves are historically more conservative than in the rest of Ecuador; the capital has always clung to traditional, conservative values, in contrast to the outward-looking merchants of Guayaquil. However, a new generation, a large student population, and

HIGHLIGHTS

◖ La Compañía: The epitome of gaudy golden grandeur, this extravagant chapel is the most dazzling of all Quito's many beautiful colonial churches (page 29).

◖ La Basílica del Voto Nacional: The tallest church in Ecuador with its armadillo gargoyles is a striking sight, and even more spectacular are the views from its spires over Old Town (page 34).

◖ Casa de la Cultura: From Valdivia figurines to giant *bahía* statues and a majestic Inca sun mask, this is easily Ecuador's best museum (page 36).

◖ Capilla del Hombre: Oswaldo Guayasamín's final work, the Chapel of Man, is an awe-inspiring and humbling tribute to the indigenous peoples of the Americas (page 40).

◖ Mitad del Mundo and Museo de Sitio Intiñan: Take the obligatory photo with a foot in each hemisphere (supposedly), then test out the real Equator a few hundred meters away at nearby Museo de Sitio Intiñan (pages 69 and 70).

© AVALON TRAVEL

LOOK FOR ◖ TO FIND RECOMMENDED SIGHTS, ACTIVITIES, DINING, AND LODGING.

modern businesses have all injected a healthy dose of open-mindedness. Most importantly, visitors will find Quiteños helpful, welcoming, and justifiably proud of their city.

Quito's residents have plenty to be proud of: In 1978 it was the first city in the world to receive World Heritage Site status from UNESCO. Although there have been problems with upkeep, in recent years a multimillion-dollar regeneration program has left the city in better shape than ever. A new feeling of cleanliness and security pervades Old Town, with an increased police presence and a burgeoning cultural and nightlife scene. Interior patios have been tastefully renovated, and street artists have replaced beggars and hawkers. New Town is also increasingly well-kept,

although it has some way to go to solve its security problems.

HISTORY

According to a pre-Inca legend, the city of Quito was founded by Quitumbe, son of the god Quitu, in honor of his father. The valley that would eventually cradle Ecuador's capital was originally occupied by the Quitu people, who united with the Cara from the north to form the Shyris nation around A.D. 1300. In 1487 the Incas took over and turned the city into an important nexus of their northern empire, known as the Quitosuyo. Within 100 years the empire fell to infighting, leaving room for the newly arrived Spanish to start almost from scratch.

The city of San Francisco de Quito was founded by Sebastián de Benalcázar on December 6, 1534, and named in honor of fellow conquistador Francisco Pizarro. Benalcázar quickly set about appointing government officials, distributing land to his men, and constructing churches. Originally, Quito consisted only of the present-day section known as Old Town, bounded by the Plaza de San Blas to the north, the Pichinchas to the west, and the Machangara ravine to the east. An art school was founded in 1535 and helped the city become a center of religious art during the colonial period, with its own style, the Quito School.

Since its founding, Quito has been an administrative rather than a manufacturing center. A population boom in the mid-20th century, aided by the discovery of oil, brought thousands of immigrants who spread their homes and businesses into today's New Town, as well as farther south of Old Town and west up the slopes of Pichincha. By the mid-1980s, these makeshift *suburbios* housed as much as 15 percent of the city's population and had acquired most of the services that the older areas took for granted. An earthquake in 1987 damaged numerous structures and left others in ruins, and the eruption of Guagua Pichincha in 1999 showered Quito in ash but otherwise left the city unscathed. Today, the city is officially home to about 1.8 million residents, but the real number is likely higher.

CLIMATE

Quito is famed for its springlike climate, and most of the year daytime temperatures fluctuate 10–21°C. As you would expect in a city at an elevation of 2,850 meters, cloud cover and the time of day have a big effect on the temperature. Mornings tend to be chilly, but it can heat up considerably around midday, when you will likely take off the sweater. Don't leave it in the hotel, though, as temperatures drop quickly on rainy afternoons and in the evenings. Locals say that the city can experience all four seasons in a single day, and that isn't far off the mark.

The dry season in the capital lasts June–September, with July–August seeing the least precipitation. This is also the warmest time of year. A shortened dry season runs December–January, which is also the coldest time of year. The most rain falls February–April and, to a lesser extent, October–November. Afternoons tend to be rainier, so sightseeing early is a good idea.

More of a consideration than the weather is the elevation, which will leave you breathless and light-headed for a couple of days. Dizzy spells, headaches, and fatigue can also occur. It is best not to overexert yourself and to minimize caffeine and alcohol in favor of plenty of water and light food. After two or three days, you'll be used to the elevation.

ORIENTATION

Quito extends over 50 kilometers north–south, and about eight kilometers across. Luckily for first-time visitors, the capital is easily divided into zones: one for historical sights (Old Town); one for visitor services, restaurants, and accommodations (New Town); and then everything else. The city's long, narrow geography makes it quite easy to get around.

A new system of street numbers was implemented in Quito in 2000, with letters prefixing the normal hyphenated numbers (e.g. "Foch E4-132"). Most addresses also give the nearest cross street, so the full address would be "Foch E4-132 y Cordero."

Old Town

Quito's historical heart sits at the northern flank of El Panecillo (Little Bread Loaf) hill, whose statue of the Virgin is visible from most of the neighborhood. This area, also called Quito Colonial or *centro histórico* (historic center), is roughly bordered by 24 de Mayo to the south and Parque La Alameda to the north. Most of the sights are situated within a few blocks of the central Plaza de la Independencia, the original core of the city.

Steep, narrow streets characterize this part of Quito, and cars barely fit in lanes designed for horse and foot traffic. Wrought-iron balconies hang over ground-level storefronts selling household wares, clothing, and shoes.

QUITO

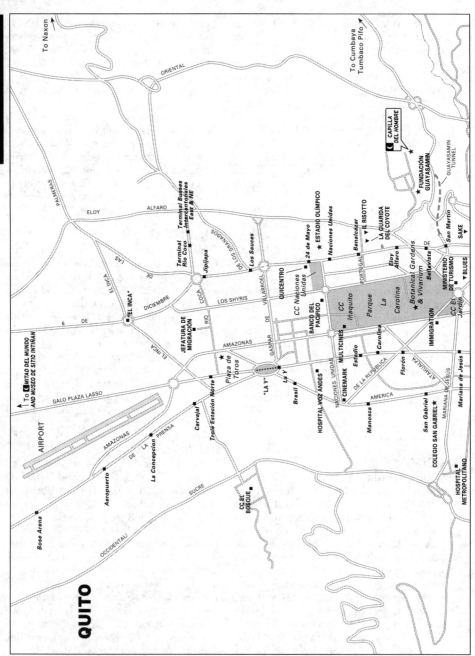

QUITO

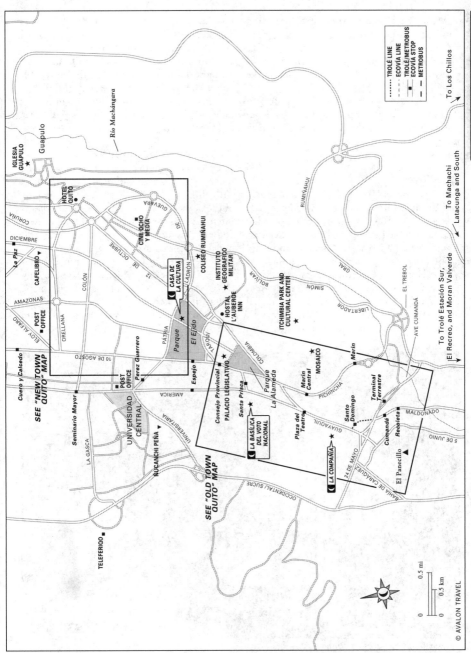

TROLÉ LINE
ECOVIA LINE
TROLÉ/METROBUS
ECOVÍA STOP
METROBUS

To Los Chillos

To Machachi

Latacunga and South

To Trolé Estación Sur,
El Recreo, and Moran Valverde

EL TREBOL

LIBERTADOR

AVE CUMANDÁ

GRAL. RUMIÑAHUI

RUMIÑAHUI

SIMÓN BOLÍVAR

5 DE JUNIO

MALDONADO

Río Machángara

Guápulo

IGLESIA GUÁPULO

HOTEL QUITO

CINE OCHO Y MEDIA

CORUÑA

DICIEMBRE

La Paz

CAFELIBRO

AMAZONAS

ELOY ALFARO

POST OFFICE

COLÓN

ORELLANA

12 DE OCTUBRE

DE GUEVARA

CALDRÓN

COLISEO RUMIÑAHUI

CASA DE LA CULTURA

INSTITUTO GEOGRAFICO MILITAR

HOSTAL L'AUBERGE INN

ITCHIMBIA PARK AND CULTURAL CENTER

Parque El Ejido

PATRIA

TAJOUI

COLOMBIA

Cuero y Caicedo

SEE "NEW TOWN QUITO" MAP

Seminario Mayor

LA GASCA

10 DE AGOSTO

AMÉRICA

Perez Guerrero

Pérez Guerrero

POST OFFICE

Espejo

UNIVERSIDAD CENTRAL

UNIVERSITARIA

ÑUCANCHI PEÑA

Consejo Provincial

PALACIO LEGISLATIVO

Santa Prisca

MOSAICO

Parque La Alameda

Marin

Marin Central

PICHINCHA

Terminal Terrestre

LA BASÍLICA DEL VOTO NACIONAL

SEE "OLD TOWN QUITO" MAP

OCCIDENTAL/SUCRE

Plaza del Teatro

GUAYAQUIL

Santo Domingo

Cumandá

Recoleta

BAHIA DE CARÁQUEZ

LA COMPAÑÍA

24 DE MAYO

El Panecillo

TELEFÉRICO

0   0.5 mi
0   0.5 km

© AVALON TRAVEL

Most visitors come for the outstanding churches, convents, museums, and plazas that are key to Quito's status as a UNESCO World Heritage Site. Other visitors are content to wander the cobbled streets that evoke Ecuador's colonial past.

There are many wonderful viewpoints to take in Old Town's impressive skyline—from the gothic spires of the Basílica to the top of El Panecillo or the green spaces of Parque Itchimbía.

New Town

Northeast of Old Town, Parque La Alameda and El Ejido form a buffer between past and present. New Town is a world away from the colonial cobbled streets of the historic center. The Mariscal Sucre area is the hub and aptly nicknamed *gringolandia* for its abundance of hotels, restaurants, tour operators, shops, Internet cafés, bars, and discos. This area, enclosed by Avenidas Patria, Orellana, 10 de Agosto, and 12 de Octubre, is alive with backpackers and also doubles as the city's

main area for nightlife, heaving with partyers on weekends. North and east of La Mariscal are quieter neighborhoods such as La Floresta and González Suárez as well as Quito's largest park, Parque Carolina. To the east, high above this park, is one of the highlights of the city, artist Oswaldo Guayasamín's famous work, La Capilla del Hombre (Chapel of Man).

Other Neighborhoods

The section of Quito north of New Town hosts much of the capital's industry and sparkles with shiny high-rises that house a large part of the city's businesses. These areas are of less interest to visitors. Modern shopping centers and chic restaurants cater to the middle and upper classes that live in this area or in the fast-growing Valle Los Chillos and Tumbaco valleys, both to the east, which also have growing expat retirement communities. The dramatic beauty of the steep old neighborhood Guapulo spills down below Avenida 12 de Octubre and the lofty Hotel Quito. More residential

La Basílica del Voto Nacional

© QUITO TURISMO

neighborhoods occupy the lower slopes of Pichincha west and north of New Town.

SAFETY

Unfortunately, this most dramatic and historic of South American cities is not without its problems. Quito has rising crime rates, and although you shouldn't be alarmed, bear in mind that there is more crime against visitors here than in any other region of Ecuador. The high concentration of foreigners sadly has led to an increased number of criminals targeting them, so you must take precautions.

One of the diciest areas is the visitor-filled Mariscal Sucre neighborhood of New Town, sometimes simply called "La Mariscal." Increased police presence has recently improved the situation, but the neighborhood still harbors many thieves. Walking alone at night should be avoided; take a taxi to and from your hotel, preferably booked in advance. Don't get into an unmarked cab, and check for the orange license plate and registration number on the side of the vehicle, as "express kidnappings" (a robbery using a vehicle) have been reported.

Watch for pickpockets and bag-slashers on public transport and in Old Town in general. Pay particular attention in crowded areas and when exiting tourist spots like churches. Keep all bags and cameras in front of you, and don't leave your wallet in your back pocket. Don't go into any parks after dark. Beware of people "accidentally" spilling liquids on you and other diversionary tactics.

The trolleybus services (Trole, Ecovia, and Metrobus) are perhaps the worst for pickpockets, and it is guaranteed there will be several thieves on crowded services. It's simple: either keep your valuables well-hidden, or don't take them on the bus at all. Better yet, if you're going sightseeing, take a taxi. A ride from New Town to Old Town costs just $2–3.

The area around El Panecillo is not safe, so take a taxi to get there and back (the driver will usually wait for about $8 round-trip). At the *teleférigo* (cable car), assaults and muggings have been reported on the hike to Rucu Pichincha, although there are now police patrols on the weekend. Do not attempt this climb alone, and ideally don't take valuables.

PLANNING YOUR TIME

If the elevation doesn't make your head spin, the amount to see in Quito probably will. Quito can be a little overwhelming, and you simply can't see it all in a couple of days. You might even consider getting straight on a bus and going down in elevation to a quieter town (Otavalo, Mindo, or Baños) to get your bearings if you've just arrived in South America.

If you only have a couple of days here, spend one each in Old Town and New Town. Start at **Plaza Grande** and take in the cathedral, the presidential palace, **La Compañía,** and Plaza San Francisco before enjoying the views over the city at **El Panecillo** or **La Basílica.** In New Town, don't miss the **Museo del Banco Central,** the **Guayasamín Museum,** and the **Capilla del Hombre.** You may have time to visit the Equator at the **Mitad del Mundo,** or take an extra day to combine this with a hike to **Pululahua** for a little bird-watching and crater-viewing. The *teleférigo* (cable car) ride west of New Town offers the most spectacular views over the city at 4,000 meters.

Most visitors stay in New Town, mainly because there are so many visitor amenities. However, staying in Old Town is increasingly possible and offers a more authentic experience. It really depends on what you want: to hook up with kindred spirits for tours and to socialize at night, stay in New Town; for quieter and more cultural experiences, stay in one of the historic hotels in Old Town. Wherever you stay, it's only a short cab or bus ride between the two districts.

Sights

Quito's Old Town is what makes the city famous, containing a huge number of colonial churches and religious buildings set around elegant plazas. The walls and ceilings are decorated with elaborate paintings and sculptures, and altars are resplendent with gold leaf.

Flash photography is prohibited in most churches and historical museums to protect the fragile pigments of the religious paintings and statues. Keep in mind that opening hours fluctuate regularly; those provided here are the latest available. Several churches are currently undergoing extensive renovation work, but all are open.

OLD TOWN

Quito's Old Town is cleaner, safer, and a joy to wander around following a multimillion-dollar regeneration in the past decade. Gone are the beggars and street vendors, replaced with police and horse-drawn carriages carting visitors around churches, which are beautifully lit at night. A system called Pico y Placa regulates traffic congestion by restricting the entry of certain license-plate numbers at peak hours. It has improved the traffic situation, although the narrow streets still struggle to accommodate Quito's cars. Cars are prohibited completely 9 A.M.–4 P.M. Sunday, making it the most pleasant day for sightseeing.

The municipality of Quito has put together excellent **guided maps** to historic walks through Old Town, available at tourist offices. Even better are the **multilingual tours** given by municipal police from the tourist office.

Plaza Grande and Vicinity

This ornate 16th-century plaza is the political focal point of colonial Quito. Officially called the Plaza de la Independencia, it features a winged statue to independence atop a high pillar. The surrounding park is a popular gathering place with regular music, mime, and dance performances.

On the plaza's southwest side, the **Catedral**

is actually the third to stand on this site (mass 6–9 A.M. daily). Other visits are available through the museum located on Venezuela (tel. 2/257-0371, 9:30 A.M.–4 P.M. Mon.–Sat., $1.50). Hero of independence Antonio José de Sucre is buried here. Behind the main altar is the smaller altar of Nuestra Señora de Los Dolores, where, on August 6, 1875, president Gabriel García Moreno drew his last breath after being attacked with machetes outside the presidential palace. He is now buried here also, as is the country's first president, Juan José Flores.

Next door, formerly the main chapel of the cathedral, the **Iglesia El Sagrario** (10 A.M.–4 P.M. Mon.–Fri., 10 A.M.–2 P.M. Sat.–Sun.) was begun in 1657 and completed half a century later. The walls and ceiling of the short nave are painted to simulate marble—even the bare stone is speckled black-and-white. Impressive paintings and stained glass windows decorate the center cupola. Bernardo de Legarda, the most outstanding Quiteño sculptor of the 18th century, carved and gilded the baroque *mampara* (partition) inside the main doorway.

A long, arched atrium to the northwest lines the front of the handsome **Palacio Presidencial** (10 A.M.–5 P.M. Tues.–Sun., free tours when the government is not in session), also known as El Carondelet. The ironwork on the balconies over the plaza, originally from the Tuileries Palace in Paris, was purchased just after the French Revolution. Current president Rafael Correa opened the doors of the palace to daily visitors in 2007, and it's worth making a line for the guided tours of the interior that leave every hour or so.

The **Palacio Arzobispal** (Archbishop's Palace) on the northeast side leads to a three-story indoor courtyard housing a number of small shops and eateries. Cobbled courtyards, thick whitewashed walls, and wooden balconies make it worth a look. The plaza's colonial spell is broken only by the modern **City Hall** to

President Rafael Correa has opened up the Palacio Presidencial to the public.

the southeast. The church of **La Concepción** (10 A.M.–4 P.M. Mon.–Fri., 10 A.M.–2 P.M. Sat.–Sun.) stands at the corner of Chile and García Moreno. The attached convent is Quito's oldest, dating to 1577, and is closed to visitors.

At the corner of Benalcázar and Espejo, the **Centro Cultural Metropolitano** (tel. 2/295-0272, 9 A.M.–4:30 P.M. daily) houses the collection of the **Museo Alberto Mena Caamaño** (tel. 2/295-0272, ext. 135, 9 A.M.–5 P.M. Tues.–Sun., $1.50), which includes colonial and contemporary art and a set of wax figures depicting the death throes of patriots killed in 1810 by royalist troops. The cultural center also includes lecture rooms, the municipal library, and gallery space for temporary art exhibits.

◖ La Compañía

La Compañía (9:30 A.M.–5 P.M. Mon.–Fri., 9:30 A.M.–4 P.M. Sat., 1:30–4 P.M. Sun., $3) is one of the most beautiful churches in the Americas and certainly the most extravagant. Seven tonnes of gold supposedly ended up on the ceiling, walls, and altars of "Quito's Sistine Chapel," which was built by the wealthy Jesuit order between 1605 and 1765. The church has been restored from the damage caused by the 1987 earthquake and a raging fire in 1996. It is a glorious example of human endeavor but at the same time borders on opulence gone mad.

Even the outside is overwhelming, crammed with full-size statues, busts, and sculpted hearts. The interior has eight side chapels, one of which houses the guitar and possessions of Quito's first saint, Santa Mariana de Jesús—her remains are under the main altar. Some of the more expensive relics, including a painting of the Virgin framed with gold and precious stones, are locked away in a bank vault between festivals. One of the more eye-catching objects in La Compañía is a painting depicting hell, where sinners—each labeled with one of the deadly sins—receive excruciating punishments.

Across Sucre from La Compañía is the **Museo Numismático** (tel. 2/258-9284, 9 A.M.–1 P.M. and 2–5 P.M. Tues.–Fri., 10 A.M.–1 P.M. and 2–4 P.M. Sat.–Sun., $1), which traces the

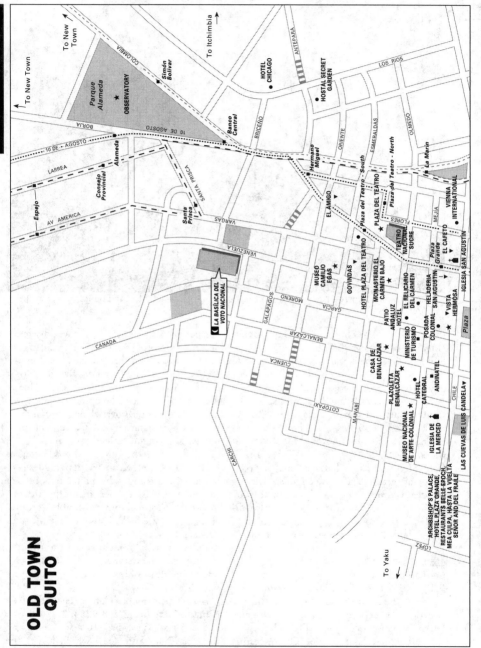

OLD TOWN QUITO

To New Town

To New Town

To Itchimbia ↑

Parque Alameda

OBSERVATORY

Simón Bolívar ★

COLOMBIA

Banco Central

HOTEL CHICAGO

HOSTAL SECRET GARDEN

ANTEPARA

LOS RIOS

OLMEDO

BRICEÑO

10 DE AGOSTO

10 DE AGOSTO

BORJA

LARREA

Consejo Provincial

Espejo

AV AMERICA

Alameda

Santa Prisca

SANTA PRISCA

VARGAS

VENEZUELA

CANADA

GALAPAGOS

GARCIA

MORENO

BENALCAZAR

CUENCA

COTOPAXI

MANABI

CARCHI

Hermano Miguel

ORIENTE

ESMERALDAS

La Merín

MEJIA

FLORES

EL AMIGO

Plaza del Teatro - South

Plaza del Teatro - North

TEATRO NACIONAL SUCRE

VIENNA INTERNATIONAL

Plaza Grande

EL CAFETO

LA BASÍLICA DEL VOTO NACIONAL

MUSEO CAMILO EGAS ★

GOVINDAS ▼

HOTEL PLAZA DEL TEATRO

MONASTERIO EL CARMEN BAJO

PATIO ANDALUZ HOTEL

POSADA COLONIAL

MINISTERIO DE TURISMO

CASA DE BENALCAZAR ★

PLAZOLETA BENALCAZAR

HOTEL CATEDRAL

ANDINATEL

EL RELICARIO DEL CARMEN

HELADERIA SAN AGUSTIN

IGLESIA SAN AGUSTIN

VISTA HERMOSA ▼

Plaza

CHILE

MUSEO NACIONAL DE ARTE COLONIAL

IGLESIA DE LA MERCED

LAS CUEVAS DE LUIS CANDELA ▼

ARCHBISHOP'S PALACE, HOTEL PLAZA GRANDE, RESTAURANTS BELLE EPOCH, MEA CULPA, HASTA LA VUELTA SEÑOR AND DEL FRAILE

LOPEZ

To Yaku ↓

QUITO

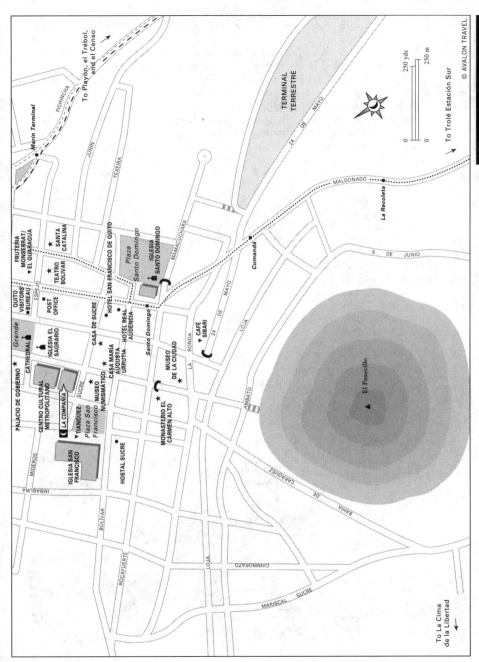

© AVALON TRAVEL

history of Ecuador's various currencies, from shell currency to the adoption of the U.S. dollar. An inflation chart shows just how bad the economic situation used to be, before dollarization stabilized it in the last decade. Also housed here is the national music library, where there are often free concerts in the evenings. On the opposite side of García Moreno from the museum is the **Casa de María Augusta Urrutia** (García Moreno 760, between Sucre and Bolívar, tel. 2/258-0107, 10 A.M.–6 P.M. Tues.–Sat., 9:30 A.M.–5:30 P.M. Sun., $2), a wonderfully preserved 19th-century mansion. Doña María passed away in 1987, and her house is a virtual window on the past, with three inner patios and luxurious accoutrements from all over the globe, as well as a gallery of Victor Mideros's paintings.

Heading east on Sucre brings you to the **Casa de Sucre** (Venezuela 513 at Sucre), once home to Simón Bolívar's southern counterpart. The building has been preserved in its original state from the early 1800s, and the collection focuses on military history.

Plaza San Francisco and Vicinity

Turn right up the hill past La Compañía to one of Ecuador's most beautiful squares. This wide cobbled expanse is a highlight of the city, dominated by the wide facade of the **Iglesia San Francisco** (8 A.M.–noon and 3–6 P.M. daily), the oldest colonial edifice in the city and the largest religious complex in South America. It was begun on the site of an Inca royal house within weeks of the city's founding in 1534. The first wheat grown in Ecuador sprouted in one of its courtyards, and Atahualpa's children received their education in its school.

Two white spires flank a glowering stone facade, which sets the perfect mood for the interior. Inside, it's easy to imagine yourself in the 16th century, with the musty odor drifting up from the creaking wooden floorboards. Thick encrustations of gold cover almost every surface, and seeing the carved roof alone is worth a visit. Notice how many of the design motifs come from indigenous cultures, including the smiling and frowning faces of sun gods, repeated several times, and harvest symbols of

© BEN WESTWOOD

Plaza San Francisco is one of Quito's most beautiful squares.

flowers and fruit. At the time of this writing, the altar of the church was still undergoing a long and painstaking multiple-year restoration. Don't miss the choir rooms upstairs at the back of the church, adorned by statues of monks and the original wooden ceilings (enter through the museum).

To the right of the main entrance, the **Museo Fray Pedro Gocial** (tel. 2/295-2911, 9 A.M.–5:30 P.M. Mon.–Sat., 9 A.M.–12:30 P.M. Sun., $2) houses one of the finest collections of colonial art in Quito, dating from the 16th–19th centuries. Guided tours are included in English, Spanish, and French. A highlight is the seven-meter-high portrait of the Franciscan family tree on the stairs leading up to the choir room. On the other side, the **Capilla de Catuña** (8 A.M.–noon and 3–6 P.M. daily) also has colonial art on display. The story goes that this chapel was constructed by an indigenous man named Catuña who promised to have it completed in a certain amount of time. When it became obvious that he wasn't going to come close to his deadline, he offered his soul to the devil in exchange for help getting the job done. Catuña finished but had a sudden change of heart, begging the Virgin Mary to save him from his hasty agreement. Sure enough, a foundation stone was discovered missing during the inauguration, negating his deal with the devil.

The Tianguez café and gift shop downstairs is a great place to overlook the plaza with a coffee and a snack.

Plaza Santo Domingo and Vicinity

Down the hill southeast of Plaza San Francisco is the elegant Plaza Santo Domingo. A statue of Sucre pointing to the site of his victory on the slopes of Pichincha decorates the square. Crowds often surround performance artists in front of the **Iglesia Santo Domingo** (7 A.M.–noon and 3–6 P.M. daily), which was begun in 1581 and finished in 1650. Four clock faces and an off-center tower decorate the stone facade. Despite the stained glass behind the altar, the

© BEN WESTWOOD

The historic street, La Ronda, has been completely regenerated with bars, cafés, and live music.

decoration, much of which was completed in the 19th century, is a little muddled, although the baroque filigree of the Chapel of the Rosary to one side is stunning. The attached **Museo Fray Pedro Bedon** (tel. 2/228-2695, 9 A.M.–4:30 P.M. Mon.–Fri., 9 A.M.–1 P.M. Sat.–Sun., $1) has obligatory tour guides to take you through the reserved chapels.

Nearby is one of the best-preserved colonial streets in Old Town. Also called Calle Juan de Díos Morales, **La Ronda** was nicknamed for the evening serenades (*rondas*) that once floated through its winding path. The narrow lane is lined with painted balconies, shops, tiny art galleries, and cafés. It's reached most easily via Guayaquil, sloping down from the Plaza Santo Domingo. This used to be a dangerous area, but an extensive regeneration has left it safe and one of the most popular evening haunts for Quiteños and visitors to soak up the atmosphere with a drink and some traditional music. It is well guarded and completely a pedestrian-only zone.

Museo de la Ciudad and Monasterio El Carmen Alto

Just up from La Ronda is Museo de la Ciudad (García Moreno and Rocafuerte, tel. 2/228-3882, 9:30 A.M.–4:30 P.M. daily, $3). One of Old Town's best museums, it traces the history of the city from precolonial times to the beginning of the 20th century. It is set in the old Hospital San Juan de Díos, founded at the order of King Philip in 1565. The collection includes Inca burials, photographs, clothing, religious and scientific artifacts, scale models of the city at different periods, and a large painting depicting Francisco de Orellana's descent of the Amazon. Tours in English, French, Italian, and German can be arranged for an extra charge.

The Monasterio El Carmen Alto, opposite the museum at Rocafuerte and García Moreno, was the home of Santa Mariana de Jesús from 1618 to 1645. Abandoned children were once passed through a small window in the patio to be raised by the nuns; adjacent, there is a small store that allows visitors to purchase cookies, chocolate, honey, creams, and herbs (9–11 A.M. and 3–5 P.M. Mon.–Fri.). The church is only open for 7 A.M. mass. The **Arco de la Reina** (Queen's Arch) over García Moreno marks the original southern entrance to Quito's center and once sheltered worshippers from the rain.

NORTH AND EAST OF PLAZA GRANDE
Iglesia de la Merced and Vicinity

The entrance to one of Quito's most modern churches, Iglesia de la Merced (6:30 A.M.–noon and 12:30–6 P.M. daily), completed in 1742, is on Chile, just up from the corner of Cuenca. The 47-meter tower houses the largest bell in town. Enter the high-vaulted nave, decorated with white stucco on a pink background, from the Plaza. The church is dedicated to Our Lady of Mercy, whose statue inside is said to have saved the city from an eruption of Pichincha in 1575. To the left of the altar is the entrance to the **Monasterio de la Merced,** housing Quito's oldest clock, built in London in 1817; a new clock face was recently installed. There

are many paintings by Victor Mideros depicting the catastrophes of 1575.

Across Mejía is the **Museo Nacional de Arte Colonial** (Cuenca and Mejía, tel. 2/228-2297, 9 A.M.–1 P.M. and 2–4 P.M. Tues.–Fri., 10 A.M.–2 P.M. Sat., $2), home to Quito's finest collection of colonial art. Works by renowned artists Miguel de Santiago, Caspicara, and Bernardo de Legarda make up part of the collection, which has been extensively renovated.

A few blocks away, the colonial mansion and beautiful courtyard of **Casa de Benalcázar** (Olmedo 962 at Benalcázar, tel. 2/228-8102, 9 A.M.–1 P.M. and 2–5 P.M. Mon.–Fri., free) is worth a visit. It was built in 1534, the year of Quito's refounding.

◖ La Basílica del Voto Nacional

Walk eight blocks northeast from Plaza Grande on Venezuela for the best view of Old Town from within its boundaries. Even though construction began in 1892, the Basílica (9 A.M.–5 P.M. daily, $2) is still officially unfinished. However, its two imposing 115-meter towers make this the tallest church in Ecuador. Notice that the "gargoyles" are actually a menagerie of local animals, including armadillos. After appreciating the stained glass and powerful gilt statues in the nave, ride the elevator up to take in the fantastic views. Climb up unnerving stairs and metal ladders to the roof on the northern steeple or, even more unnerving, a higher point on the east tower. Tread carefully.

Iglesia San Agustín and Vicinity

East of Plaza Grande, the Iglesia San Agustín (Chile and Guayaquil, 7 A.M.–noon and 1–6 P.M. daily) contains no surface left unpainted, including the likenesses of saints that line the arches against a pastel background. A black Christ occupies a side altar. The adjoining **Convento y Museo de San Agustín** (Chile and Flores, tel. 2/295-5525, 9 A.M.–12:30 P.M. and 2:30–5 P.M. Mon.–Fri., 9 A.M.–1 P.M. Sat., $1) features a feast of colonial artwork on the walls and surrounds a palm-filled cloister. Ecuador's declaration of independence was signed in the *sala capitular* on August 10, 1809; don't miss the incredible carved benches and altar. Many of the heroes who battled for independence are buried in the crypt.

Plaza del Teatro and Vicinity

This small plaza at Guayaquil and Manabí is surrounded by restored colonial buildings, including the **Teatro Nacional Sucre,** one of Quito's finest theaters. The gorgeous building, erected in 1878, also has a wonderful restaurant called Theatrum on the second floor above the lobby. The theater hosts frequent plays and concerts, including opera, jazz, ballet, and international traveling groups. Tucked in the far corner is the renovated **Teatro Variedades,** reborn as an elegant dinner theater. Next door is the popular **Café Teatro.**

Enter the **Monasterio El Carmen Bajo** (Venezuela between Olmedo and Manabí, 8 A.M.–noon daily, free) through huge wooden doors that date to the 18th century. Whitewashed stone pillars support a two-story courtyard inside, surrounded by nuns' quarters and schoolrooms.

Teatro Bolívar

Scorched by a fire in 1999, only two years after an extensive restoration, the opulent Teatro Bolívar (Pasaje Espejo 847 y Guayaquil, tel. 2/258-3788, www.teatrobolivar.org) is being restored yet again. The 2,200-seat theater was built in 1933 by a pair of American theater architects, and it incorporates elements of art deco and Moorish styles. The theater is on World Monuments Watch's 100 Most Endangered Sites list and is currently open during restoration. Your ticket price will help fund the ongoing work, and you can make an additional donation.

Santa Catalina

The newly opened **Convent Museo Santa Catalina** (Espejo and Flores, tel. 2/228-4000, 8:30 A.M.–5 P.M. Mon.–Fri., 8:30 A.M.–12:30 P.M. Sat., $1.50) is housed with the church of the same name. The remains of assassinated president Gabriel García Moreno

rested here secretly for many years before being buried under the cathedral. Many of his personal effects are on display, and his heart is buried in the private chapel. There is also a wide-ranging display of religious art and artifacts. A guided tour is included in the price and is recommended because the collection is spread among many rooms.

ABOVE OLD TOWN
El Panecillo

Old Town's skyline is dominated by a 30-meter statue of the Virgin of Quito on the hill at the southern end. The close-up view of the Virgin with a chained dragon at her feet is very impressive, and although she's nicknamed the "Bailarina" (Dancing Virgin), she's actually preparing to take flight. You can climb up inside the base (9 A.M.–5 P.M. Mon.–Sat., 9 A.M.–6 P.M. Sun., $1) to an observation platform for a spectacular view of the city. Note that the neighborhood on the way up is dangerous so take a taxi and ask the driver to wait. The area at the top of the hill has security until 7 P.M. A taxi ride costs about $3–4 one-way, $8 round-trip including a short wait.

Itchimbía Park and Cultural Center

The old Santa Clara market building—imported from Hamburg in 1899 and brought to the highlands, by mule, in sections—has been transported from Old Town and rebuilt in all its glass-and-metal glory on top of a hill to the east. The structure is now a cultural center (tel. 2/295-0272, ext. 137, 9 A.M.–5 P.M. daily, $1) hosting occasional exhibitions, but the more common reason to come here is the view. The vicinity is more pleasant than El Panecillo, if not quite as spectacular, and not as hair-raising as climbing the Basílica. The center is surrounded by a 34-hectare park that is being reforested and laced with footpaths. It is beautifully lit up at night, and the views are great by day too. Just below on Samaniego is the restaurant Mosaico, along with several happening new spots for drinks and elite elbow-rubbing that justify their prices every evening at sunset. A taxi from Old Town costs $3.

La Cima de la Libertad

In the foothills of Pichincha to the west of Old Town stands this military museum and monument to Sucre's decisive victory over the royalist forces at the Battle of Pichincha on May 24, 1822. At the **Templo de la Patria,** an expansive mosaic of the independence struggle by Eduardo Kingman competes with the view of the city and snowcapped volcanoes on clear days. The **Museo de las Fuerzas Armadas** (tel. 2/228-8733, 9 A.M.–5 P.M. Mon.–Fri., 10 A.M.–4 P.M. Sat.–Sun., $1) displays a modest collection of historical military tools and weapons as well as a scale model depicting the battle. Not many visitors make it up here; there are occasional buses, or take a taxi from Old Town (from $5).

BETWEEN OLD TOWN AND NEW TOWN
Parque la Alameda

Ornamental lakes and a monument to Simón Bolívar hold down opposite ends of this triangular park. In the center stands the oldest **astronomical observatory** in South America, inaugurated in 1864 by then-president García Moreno. If you've visited observatories in North America and Europe, it may come up short, but it's still worth a visit. The beautiful old building also houses a museum (tel. 2/257-0765, 9 A.M.–noon and 2:30–5:30 P.M. daily, $1) filled with books, photos, and antique astronomical tools, including a brass telescope that still works. Visitors can sometimes view the stars on clear nights; call ahead for a schedule and information on occasional astronomy lectures. Many of the large trees found here were planted in 1887, when the park began as a botanical garden.

Palacio Legislativo

Just north of Parque la Alameda at Gran Colombia and Montalvo, drop by when this arm of Ecuador's government is out to lunch and you can peek through the fence to see Oswaldo Guayasamín's infamous 1988 mural titled *Imagen de la Patria.* The huge work, depicting and protesting injustice in Latin America, caused a stir during its unveiling at a formal ceremony of ambassadors and dignitaries. An evil-looking face with a helmet labeled CIA caused the U.S. ambassador to storm out of the room. Copies of the mural are available in the Guayasamín Museum.

◖ Casa de la Cultura

On the northern edge of Parque El Ejido, this curved glass building looks rather like a convention center, but don't let that dissuade you from visiting the best collection of museums in Ecuador. The Casa de la Cultura (tel. 2/222-3392, www.cce.org.ec, 9 A.M.–5 P.M. Tues.–Fri., 10 A.M.–4 P.M. Sat.–Sun., $2) was remodeled in 2005. The centerpiece of the complex is **Museo del Banco Central,** a world unto itself and easily Ecuador's most impressive museum. The collection includes more than 1,500 pieces of pre-Inca pottery, gold artifacts, and colonial and contemporary art, all labeled in English and Spanish.

The first hall is the massive **Sala de Arqueología,** which contains archaeology from Ecuador's long line of indigenous cultures: Figurines from the Valdivia, animal-shaped bottles from the Chorrera, one-meter-high statues known as *gigantes de la bahía* (bay giants), and Manteña thrones are just a few of the vast array of pieces.

A vault downstairs protects a dazzling collection of gold pieces: masks, breastplates, headdresses, and jewelry, many decorated with motifs of cats, serpents, and birds. The highlight is the majestic Inca sun mask, the symbol of the museum.

Upstairs is the **Sala de Arte Colonial,** which contains a massive 18th-century altar and a large collection of paintings and polychrome carvings from the Quito School. There are adjacent rooms dedicated to republican and contemporary art, the highlight being several paintings by renowned artist Oswaldo Guayasamín. The Casa also contains collections of furniture and musical instruments.

The **Agora,** a huge concert arena in the center of the building, hosts concerts (admission cost varies by event). There's also a *cine* showing art and cultural films most evenings.

The old building on 6 de Diciembre, facing the park, houses occasional exhibits and a bookshop that sells its own publications. Next door is the **Teatro Prometeo,** open for evening performances.

Parque El Ejido

Avenidas Patria, 6 de Diciembre, 10 de Agosto, and Tarquí form the wedge filled by Quito's most popular central park. It's all that remains of the common grazing lands that stretched for more than 10 kilometers to the north. The park played its part in one of the most infamous moments in Ecuador's history when liberal president Eloy Alfaro's body was dragged here and burned following his assassination. These days, the most heated things get is during a game of *Ecuavolley* (the local version of volleyball) in the northwest corner of the park most evenings and weekends; a children's playground takes up the northeast corner. You can also often see people playing an Ecuadorian version of a French game of *boules*. On weekends, the area near the arch at Amazonas and Patria becomes an outdoor arts and crafts market; paintings line the sidewalk along Patria, and Otavaleños and other artists sell textiles, antiques, and jewelry.

NEW TOWN

New Town is where most visitors, particularly backpackers, stay in Quito and go out in the evenings. The commercial artery of this sector is **Avenida Amazonas,** and the busiest area lies just off the avenue in the blocks around Plaza Foch. Here you'll find all the visitor amenities: hotels, restaurants, bars, Internet cafés, banks, shops, and travel agencies. It's not nicknamed *gringolandia* for nothing, and the contrast with Old Town is striking; this sector has a decidedly international feel, which may or may not suit you. On the plus side, you can meet plenty of kindred spirits in the bars and cafés, and the nightlife is particularly raucous Thursday–Saturday. The biggest concentration

of quality international cuisine in Ecuador is also here, and there are several 24-hour coffee shops for night owls. However, if you want to escape the hordes of foreign visitors and have a more authentic Andean experience, you may be tempted to spend your time elsewhere.

Museo Jacinto Jijón y Caamaño

The family of a prominent Ecuadorian archaeologist donated his private collection of colonial art and archaeological pieces to the Universidad Católica after his death. Now it's on display at the Museo Jacinto Jijón y Caamaño (tel. 2/299-1700, ext. 1242, 9 A.M.–4 P.M. Mon.–Fri., $0.60), located within the university compound on the third floor of the main library building. Enter off 12 de Octubre near Carrión—ask the guard to point you in the right direction. Nearby in the Central Cultural block is the extensive **Weilbauer** collection.

Museo Amazónico

The small **Abya Yala** complex (12 de Octubre 1430 at Wilson, tel. 2/396-2800) contains a bookstore with the city's best selection of works on the indigenous cultures of Ecuador. Shops downstairs sell snacks, crafts, and natural medicines, while the second floor is taken up by the small but well-organized Museo Amazónico (8:30 A.M.–12:30 P.M. and 2–5 P.M. Mon.–Fri., $2). Guided tours are available in Spanish to take you past stuffed rainforest animals, stunning Cofán feather headdresses, and real Shuar *tsantsas* (shrunken heads). The pottery depicting lowland Kichwa gods, each with its accompanying myth, is particularly interesting, as are photos of oil exploration and its environmental impact.

Mindalae Ethnic Museum

Run by the Sinchi Sacha Foundation, which promotes indigenous cultures, fair trade, and responsible tourism, the Mindalae Ethnic Museum (Reina Victoria and La Niña, tel. 2/223-0609, 9:30 A.M.–5:30 P.M. Mon.–Sat., $3) has five floors with comprehensive collections of ethnic clothing, artifacts, and ceramics from all regions, plus a shop and a restaurant.

QUITO

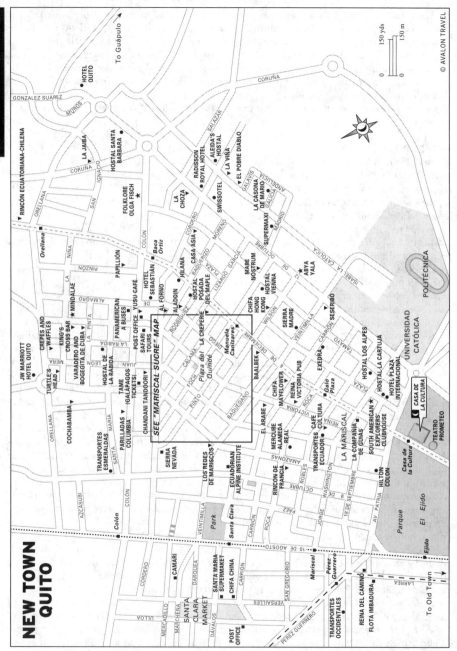

NEW TOWN QUITO

To Guápulo

GONZALEZ SUÁREZ

HOTEL QUITO

CORUÑA

RINCÓN ECUATORIANA-CHILENA

LA JAIBA

HOSTAL SANTA BARBARA

CORUÑA

RADISSON ROYAL HOTEL

ALEIDA'S HOSTAL

LA VIÑA

EL POBRE DIABLO

FOLKLORE OLGA FISCH

LA CHOZA

GALAXY'S

LA CASONA DE MARIO

SWISSOTEL

SUPERMAXI

Orellana

CASA ASIA

HILANA

Baca Ortiz

HOTEL SEBASTIÁN

AL FORNO

HOSTAL POSADA DEL MAPLE

MARE NOSTRUM

HOSTAL VIENNA

ABYA YALA

PAPILLÓN

JW MARRIOTT HOTEL QUITO

CREPES AND WAFFLES

KING'S CROSS BAR

MINDALAE

VARADERO AND BODEGITA DE CUBA

PANAMERICANA BUSES

YUSU CAFÉ

ALADDIN

CHIFA HONG KONG

SIERRA MADRE

TURTLE'S HEAD

POST OFFICE SAFARI TOURS

SESERIBÓ

Plaza del Quinde

LA CREPERIE

Manuela Cañizares

TAME (GALÁPAGOS TICKETS)

HOSTAL DE LA RABIDA

COCHABAMBA

BAALBEK

EXEDRA

HOSTAL LOS ALPES

CHANDANI TANDOORI

PARILLADAS COLUMBIA

SEE "MARISCAL SUCRE" MAP

EL ARABE

CHIFA MAYFLOWER

VICTORIA PUB

Galo Plaza

HOSTAL LA CARTUJA

HOTEL PLAZA INTERNACIONAL

TRANSPORTES ESMERALDAS

SIERRA NEVADA

LOS REDES DE MARISCOS

MERCURE ALAMEDA REAL

REINA VICTORIA

CAFÉ CULTURA

LA COMPAÑIA DE GUÍAS

SOUTH AMERICAN EXPLORERS' CLUBHOUSE

CASA DE LA CULTURA

TEATRO PROMETEO

ECUADORIAN ALPINE INSTITUTE

RINCÓN DE FRANCIA

TRANSPORTES ECUADOR

HILTON COLON

Casa de la Cultura

Parque El Ejido

Park

Santa Clara

CAMARI

SANTA MARIA SUPERMARKET

CHIFA CHINA

SANTA CLARA MARKET

POST OFFICE

Mariscal

Pérez Guerrero

Colón

REINA DEL CAMINO

TRANSPORTES OCCIDENTALES

FLOTA IMBADURA

To Old Town

To Guápulo

POLITÉCNICA

UNIVERSIDAD CATÓLICA

MUROS

CORUÑA

ORELLANA

SAN IGNACIO

ORELLANA

COLÓN

NIÑA

PINZÓN

LA ALMAGRO

LA PINTA

LA RÁBIDA

JUAN LEÓN MERA

AZCASUBI

SANTA MARIA

ORELLANA

COLÓN

VEINTIMILLA

SANTA CLARA

CARRIÓN

ROCA

PÁEZ

JORGE WASHINGTON

ROBLES

18 DE SEPTIEMBRE

DE

AV. PATRIA

10 DE AGOSTO

REINA VICTORIA

DIEGO DE ALMAGRO

6 DE DICIEMBRE

FOCH

CALAMA

PINTO

BAQUEDANO

RODRÍGUEZ

LIZARDO GARCÍA

JOSÉ CALAMA

WILSON

VEINTIMILLA

CARRIÓN

TAMAYO

MAYO

PLAZA

AMAZONAS

DE OCTUBRE

ANDALUCÍA

GARCÍA

MADRID

ISABEL LA CATÓLICA

GALICIA

CORDERO

MORENO

BAQUERIZO

COLÓN

ULLOA

MERCADILLO

MARCHENA

DARQUEA

SAN GREGORIO

CORDERO

CARRIÓN

VERSAILLES

DÁVALOS

PÉREZ GUERRERO

LARREA

N

0   150 yds
0   150 m

© AVALON TRAVEL

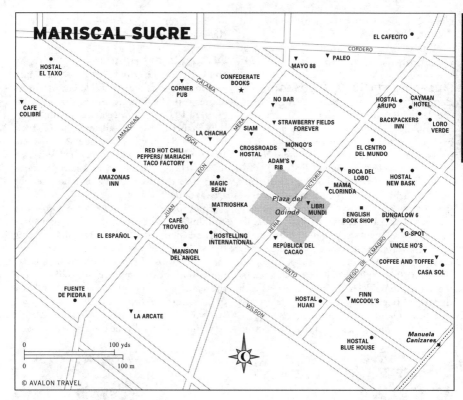

MARISCAL SUCRE

EL CAFECITO
CORDERO
PALEO
MAYO 88
HOSTAL
EL TAXO
CORNER
PUB
CALAMA
CONFEDERATE
BOOKS
★
NO BAR
HOSTAL   CAYMAN
ARUPO   HOTEL
CAFE
COLIBRÍ
AMAZONAS
STRAWBERRY FIELDS
FOREVER
BACKPACKERS
INN   LORO
VERDE
FOCH
LA CHACHA
MERA
SIAM
RED HOT CHILI
PEPPERS/ MARIACHI
TACO FACTORY
LEON
CROSSROADS
HOSTAL
MONGO'S
EL CENTRO
DEL MUNDO
ADAM'S
RIB
AMAZONAS
INN
MAGIC
BEAN
VICTORIA
BOCA DEL
LOBO
MAMA
CLORINDA
HOSTAL
NEW BASK
JUAN
MATRIOSHKA
Plaza del
Quinde
LIBRI
MUNDI
ENGLISH
BOOK SHOP
BUNGALOW 6
CAFÉ
TROVERO
REINA
G-SPOT
EL ESPAÑOL
HOSTELLING
INTERNATIONAL
REPÚBLICA DEL
CACAO
DIEGO DE ALMAGRO
UNCLE HO'S
COFFEE AND TOFFEE
CASA SOL
MANSION
DEL ANGEL
PINTO
FUENTE
DE PIEDRA II
WILSON
HOSTAL
HUAKI
FINN
MCCOOL'S
LA ARCATE
Manuela
Canizares
0   100 yds
0   100 m
HOSTAL
BLUE HOUSE
© AVALON TRAVEL

NORTH OF NEW TOWN
Parque La Carolina

If you want to escape the concrete of New Town without actually leaving the city, the nearest place to do so is Quito's largest park, which stretches from the intersection of Orellana and Eloy Alfaro almost one kilometer east to Naciones Unidas. It's popular with early-morning joggers, and the *laguna* has two-person paddleboats for rent.

Natural history is the focus of the dusty **Museo de las Ciencias Naturales** (Rumipamba 341 at Los Shyris, tel. 2/244-9824, 8:30 A.M.–4:30 P.M. Mon.–Fri., $2), at the east end of the park. Here the Casa de la Cultura administers displays on zoology, botany, and geology, including a huge collection of dead spiders and an anaconda

skeleton. Fans of creepy-crawlies will enjoy the **Vivarium** (Amazonas 3008 at Rumipamba, tel. 2/227-1820, 9:30 A.M.–5:30 P.M. Tues.–Sun., $2.50), with more than 100 live reptiles and amphibians. The collection includes poisonous and constrictor snakes from the Oriente. You can have your photo taken with a six-meter-long python ($3) if that appeals. If you're more into flora than fauna, visit the **Jardín Botánico** (between Ciencias Naturales and Shyris, 9 A.M.–5 P.M. daily, $3), which showcases Ecuador's vast array of flora, including some 500 species of orchids in the greenhouses.

For a modern shopping experience, there are three large **shopping malls** surrounding the park: El Jardín (Avenida de La República and Amazonas), Iñaquito (Amazonas and Naciones

QUITO

Unidas), and Quicentro (Naciones Unidas and Avenida de Los Shyris).

Note that Parque Carolina, like most of Quito's parks, is not safe after dark.

Museo Fundación Guayasamín

East of Parque Carolina, up a steep hill in the Bellavista neighborhood, the former home of Ecuador's most famous artist has been converted into the Museo Fundación Guayasamín (Bosmediano 543, tel. 2/244-6455, 10 A.M.–5 P.M. Mon.–Fri., $3). Pre-Columbian figurines and pottery fill the first building, while Oswaldo Guayasamín's paintings and an impressive collection of colonial art wait farther on. Guayasamín's large-scale paintings are alternately tender and tortured but are always deeply emotive. The balcony outside has a café. In the gift shop, ask to see the many unique pieces of jewelry designed by the master himself. The artist is buried beneath the Tree of Life in the gardens of his house just above the museum.

To get to the museum, take a bus bound for Bellavista from Parque Carolina (marked "Batan–Colmena") or hail a taxi ($2).

◖ Capilla del Hombre

You can't see everything in Quito, but whatever you do, don't miss Oswaldo Guayasamín's masterwork. Completed three years after his death in 1999 by the Guayasamín foundation, the Chapel of Man (Calvachi and Chavez, tel. 2/244-8492, www.capilladelhombre.com, 10 A.M.–5:30 P.M. Tues.–Sun., $3) is dedicated to the struggles endured by the indigenous peoples of the Americas before and after the arrival of the Spanish.

Huge paintings fill the open two-story building, which is centered on a circular space beneath an unfinished dome mural portraying the millions of workers who died in the silver mines of Potosí, Bolivia. Other works cover topics both heartening and wrenching, from the tenderness of a mother and child's embrace in *La Ternura* to the gigantic *Bull and Condor,* symbolizing the struggle between Spanish and Andean identities. In the center of the ground

Iglesia de Guápulo dates from the 17th century.

© QUITO TURISMO

the *teleférigo* (cable car)

floor burns an eternal flame. Guided tours are offered in English and Spanish.

Visitors receive a discount on entrance fees if they visit both the chapel and the Guayasamín museum in the same day, although this is only possible Tuesday–Friday. The chapel is a 10-minute walk up the hill from the museum.

Guápulo

Take the precipitous Camino de Orellana down the hill behind the Hotel Quito—or the footpath from the park and playground—to reach this hillside neighborhood. Narrow cobbled streets are lined with shops, cafés, and homes, including lavish walled-in residences favored by ambassadors, a world away from Quito's New Town. At the center is the 17th-century plaza fronting the beautiful **Iglesia de Guápulo,** built between 1644 and 1693 on the site of an even older convent. The sparkling church can be seen from far above and houses a collection of colonial art, including crucifixes and a pulpit carved by Juan Bautista Menacho in the early 18th century.

Teleférigo (Cable Car)

Quito's most dizzying tourist attraction is the *teleférigo* (cable car) ride (tel. 2/225-0825, 10 A.M.–7 P.M. Sun.–Thurs., 10 A.M.–10 P.M. Fri.–Sat., $4), which climbs up the slopes of Pichincha. Completed in 2005, it departs from above Avenida Occidental, where a tourist center with restaurants, a café, and a small theme park has been built. The 2.5-kilometer ride takes about 10 minutes. After a big rush of visitors in its first year, the *teleférigo* has recently lost popularity, but the breathtaking views over the city and the Andes from 4,050 meters make it worth the trip. It's busiest on the weekend, when there is also more security. From the top, you can hike three kilometers to Rucu Pichincha, but don't do this walk alone because robberies have been reported. *Teleférigo* shuttles run from Rio Coca y 6 Diciembre (Ecovia) and Estación Norte (Trole).

Entertainment and Events

Quito has a thriving nightlife scene centered around Plaza Foch, Reina Victoria, and Calama in Mariscal Sucre. These blocks heave with locals and visitors Thursday, Friday, and Saturday evenings. Historically, things don't really get going until after 11 P.M., but a new law prohibits alcohol sales after midnight Monday–Thursday and after 2 A.M. Friday–Saturday. This has compelled young people to go out earlier, although many establishments stay open later regardless. Most of the dance clubs and discos include a small cover charge (usually $3–5), which includes a drink. Many bars have happy hours 5–8 P.M. to bring in the crowds earlier, and several have ladies nights with free drinks before 10 P.M.

After hours, there are a couple of cafés that stay open 24 hours, but late-night alcohol sales are officially banned. Most bars, discos, and even many restaurants are closed on Sundays.

Note that as well as being the most popular nightlife spot, at night Mariscal Sucre is also the most risky area for foreign visitors. Walk just a couple of blocks away from the main drag and the police presence is replaced by groups of thieves looking for an opportunity. You can reduce the risk by taking a taxi to and from your hotel, even if it's only a few blocks away. Don't take valuables, credit cards, or more cash than necessary (you're unlikely to spend more than $30, unless it's a big celebration).

NIGHTCLUBS AND DISCOS

By far the most popular spot in Mariscal is the American- and British-run **Bungalow 6** (Calama and Almagro, tel. 8/519-4530, 8 P.M.–midnight Mon.–Thurs., 8 P.M.–2 A.M. Fri.–Sat., cover $5). Recently expanded to three floors, this friendly place is where Quito's college crowd mixes on the dance floor with backpackers. It gets very busy downstairs on the weekend after 11 P.M., but there's always a quieter spot upstairs for a drink. Ladies night is Wednesday.

Elsewhere, the discos in Mariscal are decidedly hit and miss. If you're looking for total mayhem, try out the meat market of **No Bar** (Calama and Juan León Mera, tel. 2/245-5145, 8 P.M.–midnight Mon.–Thurs., 8 P.M.–2 A.M. Fri.–Sat., cover $5). Somewhere among the gyrating bodies is a pool table.

For a more Latin American experience, **Seseribó** (Veintimilla and 12 de Octubre, tel. 2/256-3598, 9 P.M.–2 A.M. Thurs.–Sat., cover $5–10) has been offering *pura salsa* for more than a decade. It occasionally has live music too. Another popular *salsateca* is **Mayo 68** (Lizardo García 662 at Juan León Mera, tel. 2/290-6189, 9 P.M.–2 A.M. Thurs.–Sat.).

One of the few late-night bars in Quito is **Blues** (República 476 at Pradera, tel. 2/222-3206, www.bluesestodo.com, 10 P.M.–6 A.M. Thurs.–Sat., cover $7–15), spinning a mix of electronic and rock with international DJs and live rock bands on Thursdays to a style-conscious crowd.

BARS, PUBS, CAFÉS, AND *PEÑAS*

Quito's sizable expat population from Europe and North America can't do without their draft beer, and a few decent pubs have been doing great business in the city for years. Perhaps the best ales can be found at the **The Turtle's Head** (La Niña 626 at Juan León Mera, tel. 2/265-5544, 4 P.M.–midnight Mon.–Thurs., 4 P.M.–2 A.M. Fri.–Sat.), a few blocks from the main drag. Even though the Scottish owner has moved on, the legacy of microbrew beers lives on. They also have pool, darts, and food. Nearby **King's Cross Bar** (Reina Victoria and La Niña, tel. 2/252-3597, 5 P.M.–midnight Mon.–Thurs., 5 P.M.–2 A.M. Fri.–Sat.) sometimes features a good selection of ales.

One block from the center of the Mariscal scene, Irish-run **Finn McCool's** (Almagro N24-64 at Pinto, tel. 2/252-1780, www.irishpubquito.com, 5 P.M.–midnight Mon.–Thurs., 5 P.M.–2 A.M. Fri.–Sat.) has developed into the most popular expat pub, attracting a multinational crowd for pool, foosball, and pub food. The **Reina Victoria Pub** (Reina Victoria 530 at Roca, tel. 2/222-6369, 5 P.M.–midnight Mon.–Thurs., 5 P.M.–2 A.M. Fri.–Sat.), located in a 100-year-old house, is west of the main drag. Although it has seen better days, the quiet British- and American-run pub atmosphere is ideal for relaxing with an ale and a plate of English fish-and-chips in front of the fireplace. The aptly named **Corner Pub** (Amazonas and Calama, tel. 2/290-6608, 2 P.M.–midnight Mon.–Thurs., 4 P.M.–2 A.M. Fri.–Sat.) is a newer bar that has quickly become popular with expats and visitors. For a trip back to the 1960s, visit Beatles bar **Strawberry Fields Forever** (Calama and Juan León Mera, tel. 9/920-0454, 5 P.M.–midnight Mon.–Thurs., 5 P.M.–2 A.M. Fri.–Sat.), adorned with memorabilia, a menu of cocktails named after Beatles songs, and a *Yellow Submarine*–themed restroom. It attracts a creative Bohemian crowd and is a welcome break from the Mariscal madness.

Jazz and the occasional singer or poetry reader attracts an arty crowd to **Café Libro** (Leonidas Plaza and Wilson, tel. 2/223-4265, www.cafelibro.com, noon–2 P.M. and 5 P.M.– midnight Mon.–Sat.). Well-stocked bookshelves and photos of writers decorate this literary place. **Ghoz Bar** (La Niña 425 at Reina Victoria, tel. 2/255-6255, www.ghoz.com, 5 P.M.–midnight Mon.–Thurs., 5 P.M.–2 A.M. Fri.–Sat.) is Swiss-run and offers darts, pool, foosball, and pinball upstairs. On the first floor, there's a wide selection of quality beers, board games, and a kitchen that whips up a good set meal—Swiss food, of course—for $4–7.

Elsewhere in Mariscal, there are plenty of attractive restaurants that double as great places for a drink. Standing out from the crowd is the colorful glass-encased **Boca del Lobo** (Calama 284 at Reina Victoria, tel. 2/254-5500, 5 P.M.– midnight Mon.–Thurs., 5 P.M.–2 A.M. Fri.– Sat.). Chic and stylish with rather surreal decor and an eclectic Mediterranean menu, it's a great place to indulge. **La Bodeguita de Cuba** (Reina Victoria 1721 at La Pinta, tel. 2/254-2476, noon–4 P.M. and 5 P.M.– midnight Mon.–Fri., noon–midnight Sat.– Sun.) is a Cuban restaurant with live music Thursday–Saturday.

Gay bars are harder to find and in a conservative culture, the Internet is probably the best source of information; www.quitogay.net has useful recommendations. The best-known are **Bohemio** (Baquedano and 6 de Diciembre, tel. 2/221-4127, 10 P.M.–3 A.M. Fri.–Sat.), also known as El Hueco, and **Matroishka** (Pinto and Juan León Mera, tel. 2/227-5617, 8 P.M.– midnight Wed.–Thurs., 8 P.M.–2 A.M. Fri.– Sat.). Take a taxi to and from these bars.

There is a certain herd mentality to going out in Mariscal, and it's not for everyone. If you want a quieter evening, head to La Floresta, where ◖ **El Pobre Diablo** (Isabel la Católica E12-06 at Galavis, noon–3 P.M. and 7 P.M.–midnight Mon.–Thurs., 7 P.M.–2 A.M. Fri.–Sat.) is still one of the best places for live music in Quito. There are bands playing a range of jazz, blues, and world music several times a week, particularly on Wednesdays and Saturdays. The diverse cocktail menu, fusion food, and sophisticated crowd make for a great atmosphere. In the neighborhood of Guápulo is **Ananké** (Camino de Orellana 781, tel. 2/255-1421, 6 P.M.–midnight Mon.–Sat.), a funky little spot with great views from both floors by day, and DJs and chill-out rooms upstairs by night. The pizzas are a specialty, and there's also a branch on Almagro at Pinto in Mariscal.

Live folk music happens at **Ñucanchi Peña** (Universitario 496 at Armero, tel. 2/225-4096, 9 P.M.–midnight Wed.–Thurs., 9 P.M.–2 A.M. Fri.–Sat.).

Alternatively, Quito's Old Town also has a few good spots to go out. The best are along the regenerated **La Ronda,** which is lined with restaurants, cafés, and bars, several of which offer live music on the weekend. One of these is **Café Sibari** (La Ronda 707, tel. 2/228-9809, 11 A.M.–midnight Mon.–Sat.) which has performances every night.

Wherever you go out, you cannot help but notice that Ecuadorians' dancing skills leave the rest of us looking like we have two left feet. You can do something about this— take the plunge and get some classes at one of these **dancing schools: Academia Salsa and Merengue** (Foch E4-256, tel. 2/222-0427), **Ritmo Tropical Dance Academy** (Amazonas N24-155 at Calama, tel. 2/255-7094, ritmo-tropical5@hotmail.com), **Tropical Dancing School** (Foch E4-256 at Amazonas, tel. 2/222-0427), and **Son Latino** (Reina Victoria N24-211 at Lizardo García, tel. 2/223-4340). Prices at all of these schools start at about $6 pp per hour for one-on-one or couples lessons.

CINEMA

There are plenty of cinemas around the city showing mainstream releases a few months after they appear in the United States. Most showings are available in English with Spanish subtitles or dubbed into Spanish; check the language before buying your ticket. The *El*

Comercio newspaper has a daily cinema schedule. Cinemas include **Multicines** (in the CC Iñaquito, Naciones Unidas and Amazonas, tel. 2/226-5061 or 2/226-5062; at the CC **El Recreo** on Maldonado in south Quito, www.multicines.com.ec) and **Cinemark** (Naciones Unidas and América, tel. 2/226-0301, www.cinemark.com.ec); ticket prices are $4.

For a more artistic lineup, look to **Ocho y Medio** (Valladolid N24-353 at Vizcaya, tel. 2/290-4720), an alternative theater in La Floresta neighborhood. Pick up its monthly program at many hotels and restaurants.

THEATERS AND CONCERTS

The *El Comercio* newspaper runs information on theater performances and music concerts. When possible, buying advance tickets is a good idea. The **Casa de la Cultura** (6 de Diciembre N16-224 at La Patria, tel. 2/290-2272, www.cce.org.ec) is the city's leading venue for theater, dance, and classical music. The colorful, indigenous-themed **Jacchigua Ecuadorian Folklore Ballet** (tel. 2/295-2025, www.jacchiguasecuador.com) performs here at 7:30 P.M. Wednesday. Another good option

for ballet and contemporary dance is Ballet Andino Humanizarte at **Teatro Humanizarte** (Leonidas Plaza N24-226 at Lizardo García, tel. 2/222-6116).

Quito has several excellent theaters. The 19th century **Teatro Sucre** (Plaza del Teatro, tel. 2/257-0299, www.teatrosucre.com) is Ecuador's national theater and one of the best. The **Teatro Bolívar** (Espejo 847 at Guayaquil, tel. 2/258-2486, www.teatrobolivar.org) is still under restoration following a devastating fire but should return to its former glory in the near future following substantial government investment.

The **Teatro Politecnico** (Ladrón de Guevara and Queseras) is the best place for classical music, hosting the National Symphony. The **Patio de Comedias** (18 de Septiembre 457 at Amazonas, tel. 2/256-1902) is a good spot to catch a play Thursday–Sunday in a more intimate atmosphere.

Quito's biggest rock and pop concerts take place at the **Coliseo Rumiñahui** and **Estadio Olímpico.** Many big-name acts from North and South America play at these prestigious venues. A good website for tickets to upcoming events is Ecutickets (www.ecutickets.ec).

Shopping

CRAFTS AND GALLERIES

New Town has the richest pickings for shoppers—almost every block in the Mariscal district has some sort of crafts shop or sidewalk vendor. Take your time, shop around, and compare quality. There are also a few standouts in Old Town.

Hungarian-born Olga Fisch came to Ecuador to escape the war in Europe in 1939. She became a world-renowned expert on South American crafts and folklore; during her lifetime, she was sought by the Smithsonian Institution and collectors worldwide for her advice. **Folklore Olga Fisch** (Colón E10-53 at Caamaño, tel./fax 2/254-1315, www.olgafisch.com, 9 A.M.–7 P.M. Mon.–Sat.) was her house until her death in 1991. The first floor is filled

with gorgeous but pricey ceramics and textiles from all over the continent. Out back in what was once a storeroom is a restaurant called El Galpon. There are outlets of Fisch's shop in the Hilton Colón, the Swissôtel, and the Patio Andaluz in Old Town.

La Bodega (Juan León Mera and Carrión, tel. 2/222-5844) has been in business for over 30 years and stocks high-quality artisanal works that include adorable ceramic Galápagos creatures and jewelry. For suede and leather, try **Aramis** (Amazonas N24-32 at Pinto, tel. 2/222-8546), where they can make clothes or handbags to order.

Mindalae (Reina Victoria 17–80 at La Niña, tel. 2/223-0609) is also operated by the non-profit Sinchi Sacha Foundation. It houses a shop selling indigenous crafts and a small restaurant. The **Camari Cooperative** (Marchena and 10 de Agosto, tel. 2/252-3613, www.camari.org) provides a place for indigenous and fair-trade groups from throughout Ecuador to sell their crafts. The store features a wide selection with good prices and quality.

Excedra (Carrión 243 at Tamayo, tel. 2/222-4001) serves as an art gallery, folklore and antique outlet, and tea room. It's an offbeat little place with a nice selection of crafts. Beautiful, high-quality wool textiles for less money than you'd think are the specialty at **Hilana** (6 de Diciembre 1921 at Baquerizo Moreno, tel. 2/250-1693).

The most popular place to buy paintings is **Parque El Ejido Art Fair** (Patria and Amazonas), open all day Saturday–Sunday. Most paintings for sale are imitations of more famous works, but there's a good range and excellent value. Haggling, of course, is advised.

Professional browsers could spend hours on Juan León Mera and Veintimilla, where half a dozen highbrow crafts and antiques stores and art galleries cluster within two blocks of Libri Mundi. Try **Galería Latina** (Juan León Mera N23-69, tel. 2/222-1098, www.galerialatina-quito.com) for Tigua hide paintings and other quality works; or stop by the weekend arts-and-crafts market in the park by Avenida Patria. **Galería Beltrán** (Reina Victoria 326, tel. 2/222-1732) has a good selection of paintings by Ecuadorian artists.

In Old Town, one of the best options is **Tianguez** (underneath the Iglesia San Francisco, Plaza San Francisco, tel. 2/223-0609, www.tianguez.org, 9 a.m.–6 p.m. daily), which is run by the Sinchi Sacha Foundation, a nonprofit set up to help support the people of the Oriente. The store, which also has an outdoor café on the Plaza San Francisco, features an excellent selection of quality handicrafts from around the country for surprisingly low prices. Profits from the masks, ceramics, Tigua hide paintings, jewelry, and weavings go to fund their programs to benefit indigenous communities.

Hugo Chiliquinga (Huachi N67-34 at Legarda, tel. 2/259-8822) is considered by many to be the best guitar maker in Ecuador. He makes and sells guitars, but he may have a waiting list, since he has an international reputation.

BOOKS

Libri Mundi (Juan León Mera N23-83 at Wilson, tel. 2/223-4791, www.librimundi.com, 8:30 a.m.–7:30 p.m. Mon.–Fri., 10 a.m.–6 p.m. Sat.) is probably the best bookstore in Ecuador. Along with a wide range of titles in Spanish, it sells new and a few used English, German, and French foreign books at a markup. Libri Mundi also has branches in the Plaza del Quindé, Centro Comercial Quicentro, and in Cumbayá.

For great deals on secondhand books, have a free cup of tea at the friendly English-run **English Bookshop** (Calama and Almagro, 10 a.m.–6:30 p.m. daily). **Confederate Books** (Calama 410 at Juan León Mera, tel. 2/252-7890, 10 a.m.–6 p.m. Mon.–Sat.) also has a wide range of used books. **South American Explorers** (Jorge Washington and Leonidas Plaza, tel./fax 2/222-5228, quitoclub@saexplorers.org, www.saexplorers.org, 9:30 a.m.–5 p.m. Mon.–Fri., 9:30 a.m.–noon Sat.) has a good selection of guidebooks and a book exchange.

MAGAZINES AND NEWSPAPERS

Foreign magazines fill the shelves at **Libro Express** (Amazonas 816 at Veintimilla, tel. 2/254-8113, 9:30 a.m.–7:30 p.m. Mon.–Fri., 10 a.m.–6 p.m. Mon.–Sat). Street vendors all along Amazonas also stock a few foreign publications. Bookshops in expensive hotels sell foreign magazines and newspapers, but be sure they don't try to mark up the newspapers over the printed price.

SPORTING EQUIPMENT

If you're looking for a mask and snorkel (or even a wetsuit) for your Galápagos trip, you'll find them—along with a whole store full of modern sporting equipment—at **KAO Sport** (Ed. Ecuatoriana, Almagro and Colón, tel.

2/255-0005 or 2/252-2266). Other KAO branches are located in many of the city's *centros comerciales.*

JEWELRY AND ACCESSORIES

Marcel G. Creaciones (Roca 766, between Amazonas and 9 de Octubre, tel. 2/265-3555, fax 2/255-2672) carries a good selection of Panama hats. For exclusive jewelry designs, stop by the **Museo Fundación Guayasamín** (Bosmediano 543, tel. 2/244-6455, 10 A.M.–5 P.M. Mon.–Fri.) or **Ag** (Juan León Mera 614 at Carrión, tel. 2/255-0276, fax 2/250-2301). Many small leather-working shops in New Town can make custom clothes, boots, bags, and other accessories for surprisingly reasonable prices; try **Zapytal** (Pinto 538 at Amazonas, tel. 2/252-8757).

MARKETS

Vendors have been moved off the streets, making driving and walking around the city much easier, if a little less colorful. For street-side shopping in Old Town, go to Ipiales (clothing and shoes), Calle Cuenca between Mejía and Olmedo (crafts and bazaar items), San Roque (food and furniture), and Plaza Arenas ("recycled" stolen goods, clothes, and hardware). Note that there are a lot of pickpockets, so watch your wallet, and ideally don't take valuables and cameras when you go to a market.

On weekends, the north end of **Parque El Ejido** becomes an outdoor art gallery with a selection of paintings, sculpture, and jewelry. **La Mariscal** artisan market in New Town occupies half of the block south of Jorge Washington between Reina Victoria and Juan León Mera. Just about every indigenous craft in Ecuador makes an appearance daily. Quality is variable, and haggling is obligatory.

Local produce is the main draw to New Town's **Mercado Santa Clara** (biggest market on Wed. and Sun.), along Ulloa and Versalles just south of Colón. Every Friday, a fruit and vegetable market fills Galaviz between Toledo and Isabel La Católica, where children sell baskets of spices and wealthy shoppers hire elderly basket carriers to tote the day's purchases.

Boutiques, supermarkets, and movie theaters find a home in Quito's many *centros comerciales* (malls). Close your eyes and you could be in North America. Major malls include **El Bosque** (Al Parque and Alonso de Torres), **El Jardín** (República and Amazonas), **Iñaquito** (Amazonas and Naciones Unidas), **Multicentro** (6 de Diciembre and La Niña), **CC Nu** (Naciones Unidas and Amazonas), and **Quicentro** (6 de Diciembre and Naciones Unidas); and in the south, the **El Recreo** trolley terminus and **Quitumbe** bus terminal.

Sports and Recreation

CLIMBING AND MOUNTAINEERING
Climbing Companies

A few of the many tour companies in Quito specialize in climbing—they have the experience and professionalism to get you back down in one piece should anything go wrong. Prices for these climbing tours vary from $70 per person for easier climbs, such as the Pichinchas, to $190 per person for a two-day ascent of Cotopaxi.

Andean Face (Pasaje B 102, Jardines de Batán, tel. 2/243-8699, www.andeanface. com) is a Dutch-Ecuadorian company specializing in climbing. The **Compañía de Guías** (Jorge Washington 425 at 6 de Diciembre, tel. 2/255-6210, tel./fax 2/250-4773, guisamonta-nia@accessinter.net, www.companiadeguias. com) is a guide cooperative whose members speak English, German, French, and Italian. **Ecuadorian Alpine Institute** (Ramírez Dávalos 136 at Amazonas, Of. 102, tel. 2/256-5465, www.volcanoclimbing.com) has well-organized, professionally run climbs and treks, and spans all experience levels. **Safari Tours** (Edificio Banco de Guayaquil, 11th Fl., Reina Victoria y Colón, tel. 2/255-2505, fax 2/222-3381, tel./fax 2/222-0426, www.safari.com. ec) has highly recommended climbing trips to any peak in the country, plus a range of other tours. **Sierra Nevada** (Pinto 637 at Cordero, tel. 2/255-3658 or 2/222-4717, fax 2/255-4936, www.hotelsierranevada.com) is a small, dependable operator that also offers rafting, the Galápagos, and Amazon trips.

Climbing and Camping Equipment

Quito has by far the best selection of outdoor gear merchants in the country. Everything from plastic climbing boots and harnesses to tents, sleeping bags, and stoves is readily available, although not always of the highest quality or best state of repair. Needless to say, check all zippers, laces, and fuel valves before you head off into the wild. Large-size footgear (U.S. size 12 and up) may be hard to locate. Gear is both imported (at a high markup) or made in Ecuador.

For climbing gear for sale or rent, try **Altamontaña** (Jorge Washington 425 at 6 de Diciembre, tel. 2/255-8380) or **Antisana Sport** (tel./fax 2/246-7433) in the El Bosque Shopping Center, also good for large-size hiking boots. Other places to buy camping gear include **Camping Cotopaxi** (Colón 942 at Reina Victoria, tel. 2/252-1626), **The Explorer** (Reina Victoria 928 at Pinto, tel. 2/255-0911), and **Los Alpes** (Reina Victoria 2345 at Baquedano, tel./fax 2/223-2326). **Equipos Cotopaxi** (6 de Diciembre N20-36 at Jorge Washington, tel. 2/225-0038) makes its own sleeping bags, backpacks, and tents for less than you'd pay for imported items. The various **Marathon Sports** outlets in the Centros Comerciales El Bosque, El Jardín, Iñaquito, San Rafael, and Quicentro stock light-use sportswear at decent prices.

BIKING

The **Aries Bike Company** (Av. Interoceanica Km. 22.5, Vía Pifo, La Libertad, tel. 2/238-0802, www.ariesbikecompany.com) offers 1–14-day biking and hiking tours all over Ecuador. The guides speak English, Dutch, and Spanish.

Biking Dutchman (Foch 714 at Juan León Mera, tel. 2/254-2806, www.bikingdutchman. com) runs well-reviewed day trips to Cotopaxi, Papallacta, and the Tandayapa-Mindo area. The 30-kilometer descent down Cotopaxi is guaranteed to raise your blood pressure. There are two-day trips to Cotopaxi and Quilotoa as well as the upper Amazon, and tours of up to eight days are offered.

Once every two weeks on Sunday, a long north–south section of road through Quito is closed to cars and open only to cyclists, skateboarders, skaters, and walkers.

RAFTING AND KAYAKING

Yacu Amu Rafting (Foch 746 at Juan León Mera, tel. 2/290-4054 or 2/254-6240, fax 2/290-4055, www.yacuamu.com) is the leader in white-water trips out of Quito. The year-round day trips down the Toachi and Blanco Rivers offer more rapids per hour than anywhere else in Ecuador ($79 pp Toachi, $89 pp Quijos)—plus cold beer at the end of every trip. Two-day trips cost from $219 pp, and five-day trips on the Upano are offered August–February. Customized itineraries are possible, as are kayak rentals and kayak courses.

HORSEBACK RIDING

Sally Vergette runs **Ride Andes** (tel. 9/973-8221, www.rideandes.com), offering top-quality riding tours through the highlands. From the foothills of Imbabura to cattle roundups near Cotopaxi, the trips use local horse wranglers, support vehicles, and healthy, happy animals. Guests stay in some of the country's plushest haciendas along the way. The options range from $98 pp for two people on a one-day tour to an eight-day circuit of Cotopaxi for $1,860 pp. You must have some riding experience for the longer tours, but it's worth it to experience the scenery from atop a horse.

Astrid Müller of the **Green Horse Ranch** (tel. 8/612-5433, www.horseranch.de) offers riding trips starting in Pululahua Crater from

TOUR COMPANIES

Quito has more tour companies than ever, and many of them are excellent. For a price, they offer expertise and local knowledge that you can't find elsewhere and provide a rewarding experience that would be difficult to replicate independently. Taking a guided tour also takes the worry out of traveling: Accommodations, food, and logistics are all sorted out for you. Bear in mind that not all operators in Quito have good reputations: Some overcharge and are underqualified. The following are recommended for their quality, professionalism, and value.

- **Dracaena** (Pinto E4-353 and Amazonas, tel./fax 2/254-6590, www.amazondracaena.com) is best known for its 4-5-day Cuyabeno trips.

- **Enchanted Expeditions** (De Las Alondras N45-102 at Los Lirios, tel. 2/334-0525, fax 2/334-0123, www.enchantedexpeditions.com) covers the entire country, with a focus on the Galápagos – the boats *Cachalote* and *Beluga* receive frequent praise.

- **Metropolitan Touring** is the largest tour operator in the country and was the first to organize high-quality Galápagos trips

in the 1960s. Since then, the company has branched out to include just about every kind of tour in Ecuador, including hacienda stays, community visits, city and market tours, and train trips. It has branch offices throughout the country, including a main one in Quito (De los Palmeras N45-74 at Las Orquideas, tel. 2/298-8200, www.metropolitan-touring.com). Information and bookings are available in the United States through Adventure Associates (13150 Coit Rd., Suite 110, Dallas, TX 75240, U.S. tel. 800/527-2500, U.S. fax 972/783-1286, www.adventure-associates.com).

- **Nuevo Mundo Travel and Tours** (18 de Septiembre E4-161 at Juan León Mera, tel. 2/250-9431, www.nuevomundotravel.com) was started in 1979 by a founder and former president of the Ecuadorian Ecotourism Association. Its tours and facilities are therefore among the most environmentally conscious in Ecuador – the company doesn't even advertise some of them to minimize impact on the destinations. Along with the usual Galápagos and Oriente tours, several unique options include shamanism

$75 pp for one day, $195 pp for two days, and up to $1,620 pp for a nine-day tour in the highlands and cloud forests. These are for people of all experience levels, and the prices include food, accommodations, and transportation to and from Quito. Multilingual guides accompany all trips.

SPECTATOR SPORTS

Watching a **soccer** match (called *fútbol* or football outside the United States) in Ecuador is quite an experience. Witnessing the fervor of the fans firsthand can be exhilarating. The best place to go in Quito is the **Estadio Atahualpa** (6 de Diciembre and Naciones Unidas) when the national team plays. Take the Ecovia to the Naciones Unidas stop to get there. The Casa Blanca, which is the stadium of Liga de Quito,

the city's most successful club, has home games several times per month. Buy tickets ahead of time at Casa Blanca at the "Y" junction, and take the Metrovía bus to the Ofelia terminal. **Bullfights** are held year-round on publicized dates at the **Plaza de Toros** (Amazonas and Juan de Azcaray), just south of the airport; Take the trolley north to La Y. The festival of the founding of Quito during the first week of December is an especially popular time for bullfights. Smaller evening bullfights are sometimes held at the remodeled Plaza Belmonte near San Blas.

CITY TOURS

The **tourist information office** (tel. 2/257-0786, 9 A.M.–2 P.M. daily) on the Plaza Grande in Old Town offers four daily tours ($6–15

programs and one-month Spanish courses combined with environmental studies.

- **RainForestur** (Amazonas N4-20 at Robles, tel./fax 2/223-9822, www.rainforestur.com) has received praise for its Cuyabeno trips and rafting in Baños, but there's also a full slate of other options.

- **Safari Tours** (Foch E4-132 at Cordero, tel./fax 2/222-0426, tel. 2/255-2505, fax 2/222-3381, www.safari.com.ec) is one of the most frequently recommended operators in the country and can take you just about anywhere in Ecuador to climb, hike, bird-watch, camp, or mountain bike. Safari has a complete Galápagos database and can book last-minute spaces or make reservations online.

- **Sangay Touring** (Amazonas 1188 and Cordero, tel. 2/255-0180, www.sangay.com) is a British- and Ecuadorian-run agency that has been offering tours around the country since 1992. Sangay recently split off a sister company, Guide2Galapagos (www.guide-2galapagos.com) to handle island bookings.

- **Surtrek** (Amazonas N23-87 at Wilson, tel. 2/223-1534, fax 2/250-0540, www.surtrek. org) offers a wide range of Galápagos and Amazon tours as well as trekking, climbing, cycling, and rafting.

- **Tropic Journeys in Nature** (Republica E7-320 at Almagro, tel. 2/222-5907, in the U.S. tel. 202/657-5072, www.tropiceco.com) is run by Andy Drumm, a fellow of the Royal Geographic Society and the president of the Amazon Commission of the Ecuadorian Ecotourism Association. These trips have won awards for socially responsible tourism and are especially strong in the Oriente, where they introduce travelers to the Huaorani, Cofán, and Achuar.

- **Via Natura** (Av. Del Parque Oe7-154, CC Dicentro, 3rd Fl., tel. 2/600-5011, www.vianatura.com) offers tours to the Galápagos on the yacht *Monserrat* and at the Casa Natura hotel in Puerto Ayora. Additionally, personally tailored tours are offered throughout Ecuador, with everything from boutique luxury to ecotourism and adventure tours.

pp) of Quito's municipal highlights, as well as two nightly tours (6–9 P.M., $8–20 pp). The pricier tours include admission fees and transportation.

What better way to enjoy newly spruced-up Old Town than in **horse-drawn carriages,** which depart from the Plaza Grande next to the Government Palace 6 P.M.–midnight daily. It's best in the evening when there is less traffic.

CLASSES
Art and Dance

The **Academia Superior de Arte** (Jorge Washington 268 at Plaza, tel. 2/256-4646, class locations may vary) offers drawing and painting courses as well as tai chi and martial arts classes.

Overcome your inhibitions on the dance floor by signing up for Latin and Caribbean dance classes—including salsa, merengue, *cumbia,* and *vallenato*—at the following recommended schools: **Academia Salsa and Merengue** (Foch E4-256, tel. 2/222-0427), **Ritmo Tropical Dance Academy** (Amazonas N24-155 at Calama, tel. 2/255-7094, ritmotropical5@hotmail.com), **Tropical Dancing School** (Foch E4-256 at Amazonas, tel. 2/222-0427), and **Son Latino** (Reina Victoria N24-211 at Lizardo García, tel. 2/223-4340). Prices at all of these schools start at about $6 pp per hour for one-on-one or couples lessons.

Learning Spanish

Ecuador is quickly becoming one of the best places to learn Spanish in Latin America. Not only do Ecuadorians—at least those who live

QUITO

in the mountains—speak slowly and clearly in comparison to their quick-talking, slang-tossing neighbors, but competition among dozens of schools keeps prices low and quality up—and it's a great place to travel.

Dozens of Spanish schools in Quito offer intensive Spanish instruction. With such intense competition, it's worth your while to shop around for one that fits your needs perfectly. Tuition usually includes 4–7 hours of instruction per day, either in groups or one-on-one (four hours daily is usually plenty). Costs range $6–9 per hour. An initial registration fee may be required, and discounts are often possible for long-term commitments. Make sure to get a receipt when you pay, and check to see if any extras are not included in the hourly rate. South American Explorers (SAE) members often receive discounts of 5–15 percent.

Many schools draw business by offering extras such as sports facilities and extracurricular activities. Some will house you (for a fee) or arrange for a homestay with a local family (typically $10–25 per day for full board, $9–15 for lodging only). Don't sign any long-term arrangements until you're sure of both the school and the family.

The following schools have received many positive reviews:

- **Amazonas** (Ed. Rocafuerte, 3rd Fl., Jorge Washington 718 at Amazonas, tel./fax 2/250-4654, www.eduamazonas.com)
- **Bipo and Toni's** (Carrión E8-183 at Plaza, tel. 2/255-6614, www.bipo.net)
- **Cristóbal Colón Spanish School** (Colón 2088 at Versalles, tel./fax 2/250-6508, www.colonspanishschool.com)
- **Guayasamín Spanish School** (Calama E8-54 near 6 de Diciembre, tel. 2/254-4210, www.guayasaminschool.com)
- **Instituto Superior de Español** (Darquea Terán 1650 at 10 de Agosto, tel. 2/222-3242, www.instituto-superior.net)
- **La Lengua** (Ed. Ave María, 8th Fl., Colón 1001 at Juan León Mera, tel./fax 2/250-1271, www.la-lengua.com)
- **Simón Bolívar** (Foch E9-20 at 6 Diciembre, tel. 2/254-4558, www.simon-bolivar.com)
- **South American Language Center** (Amazonas N26-59 at Santa María, tel. 2/254-4715, www.southamerican.edu.ec)

Accommodations

As Ecuador's capital and tourism hub, Quito has an enormous range of accommodations, from bargain basement to lavish luxury. Most are found in New Town, although Old Town has more historic hotels.

Reservations are a good idea at busy times, such as holidays, especially Christmas and Easter. Book by phone or fax whenever possible. A tax of up to 22 percent will be added to bills in the more expensive hotels, and a separate charge may be tacked on for paying by credit card.

UNDER $10

The constant stream of backpackers through Quito means that competition is fierce and there is a huge range of budget accommodations. Most are very good value and are concentrated in New Town. Luckily, Quito keeps most of its room-by-the-hour seedy motels separate from the main tourist areas of Mariscal and Old Town (if you must know, they are found near Parque Carolina).

New Town

French Canadian–run **El Centro del Mundo** (Lizardo García 569 at Reina Victoria, tel. 2/222-9050, www.centrodelmundo.net, $6 dorm, $8 s, $15 d) is one of the most popular backpacker crash pads and has rock-bottom prices. The small rooftop patio features cooking facilities, and the cable TV is always on in the cushion-strewn common room. Note that it gets pretty raucous on the free rum-and-coke nights. Breakfast and Internet access are included. **The Backpacker's Inn** (Juan Rodriguez E7-48 at Reina Victoria, tel. 2/250-9669, www.backpackersinn.net, $6.50 dorm, $11 s, $16 d) is a quieter budget option with simple, decent guest rooms, a laundry area, free Internet, and TV in the lounge. **Hostal New Bask** (Lizardo García and Diego de Almagro, tel. 2/256-7153, www.newhostalbask.com, $6 dorm, $16 s or d) is another quiet option with a homey atmosphere, excellent-value guest rooms, and a small lounge.

Hostal Blue House (Pinto and Diego de Almagro, tel. 2/222-3480, www.bluehouse-quito.com, $8–9 dorm, $18 s, $24–30 d) is a very popular new backpacker hostel with a kitchen, a bar, free Internet, and breakfast included. A cozy option is **El Cafécito** (Cordero 1124 at Reina Victoria, tel. 2/223-4862, www.cafecito.net, $7 dorm, $10–15 s, $25 d), which has guest rooms above a popular café. The small and inviting **Hostal Posada del Maple** (Juan Rodriguez E8-49 at 6 de Diciembre, tel. 2/290-7367, www.posadadelmaple.com, $9 dorm, $19–21 s, $26–33 d, breakfast included) is an attractive place with balconies and a plant-filled courtyard. Breakfast is big, and there's a comfortable TV room. **Hostal Huauki** (Pinto E7-82 at Diego Almagro, tel. 2/604-3734, www.hostalhuauki.com, $6 dorm, $8–15 s, $20 d) is a little corner of Japan in a converted 1940s residence with comfortable guest rooms and a very good sushi restaurant.

Old Town

Most of Old Town's options are in the mid- and expensive range, but **Hostal Sucre** (Bolívar 615 at Cuenca, tel. 2/295-4025, $4–10 pp) bucks the trend. It's astonishing that such a cheap place is right on Plaza San Francisco with views of the square. For these prices and location, you can't expect more than cheap, shabby guest rooms, but the view and the friendly atmosphere make it a worthwhile choice.

Hidden away on a quiet street northeast of Old Town is Aussie-run backpacker favorite

Secret Garden (Antepara E4-60 at Los Rios, tel. 2/295-6704, www.secretgardenquito.com, $9 dorm, $24–30 s and d). Set on five floors in a UNESCO World Heritage–listed building, TV is shunned for music and murals. The rooftop terrace has an impressive view, and there are big breakfasts and organic food. It's a great place to meet other travelers in a relaxed setting.

$10-25

You are spoilt for choice in this category in New Town. All hotels below offer guest rooms with private baths unless otherwise noted.

New Town

Hostal El Vagabundo (Wilson E7-45, tel. 2/222-6376, $13 s, $22 d) is another dependable budget option with a small café and table tennis. The **Loro Verde** (Rodriguez 241 at Almagro, tel. 2/222-6173, www.hostaloroverde.com, $15 s, $28 d, breakfast included) is as colorful and chirpy as its name ("green parrot"). On a corner of Mariscal's main artery, the **Amazonas Inn** (Pinto 471 at Amazonas, tel. 2/222-5723, $14 s, $26 d) is a friendly hotel with comfortable if compact guest rooms with cable TV.

You don't have to stay in Mariscal; a few blocks uphill from New Town is a neighborhood called La Floresta. Not to be confused with La Casona in Old Town, **La Casona de Mario** (Andalucia 213 at Galicia, tel./fax 2/223-0129 or 2/254-4036, www.casonademario.com, $10 pp) is run by a friendly Argentine in a comfortable house with a garden, a kitchen, a patio, and laundry facilities. Also in La Floresta is **Aleida's Hostal** (Andalucia 559, tel. 2/223-4570, www.aleidashostal.com.ec, $17–21 s, $30–36 d), a friendly family-run guesthouse with large guest rooms.

Old Town

The **Vienna International** (Chile and Flores, tel. 2/295-9611, $20 s, $40 d) offers good service with guest rooms around an interior patio. Just before the southbound Plaza del Teatro *trole* stop, the **Hotel Plaza del Teatro**

(Guayaquil 1373 at Esmeraldas, tel. 2/295-9462 or 2/295-4293, $12 pp) is a great value. The plush reception area leads to charming if slightly worn guest rooms.

$25-50

All hotels in this category and up include breakfast in the price unless otherwise indicated.

New Town

A small rise in price brings you into the realm of charming old guesthouses with all the amenities and a healthy dose of character. **Hotel Plaza Internacional** (Leonidas Plaza 150 at 18 de Septiembre, tel. 2/252-4530, tel./fax 2/250-5075, www.hotelplazainternacional.com, $25 s, $32 d) is the attractive colonial home of two former presidents. Staff speak English, French, and Portuguese. **Hostal El Arupo** (Juan Rodriguez E7-22 at Reina Victoria, tel. 2/255-7543, $30 s, $45 d) is an attractive renovated house with colorful rooms, and nearby **Cayman Hotel** (Juan Rodriguez 270 at Reina Victoria, tel. 2/256-7616, www.hotelcaymanquito.com, $34 s, $53 d) has a similar offering with a huge fireplace, a large garden, and a good restaurant inside a renovated house. **Jardín del Sol** (Calama E8-29 at Almagro, tel. 2/223-0941, www.hostaljardindelsol.com, $30 s, $45 d) has decent guest rooms, some with balconies. The rear guest rooms are quieter.

Wooden floors and a cozy atmosphere await visitors to the **Casa Sol** (Calama 127 at 6 de Diciembre, tel. 2/223-0798, www.lacasasol.com, $48 s, $68 d), a cheery spot with a tiny courtyard owned by *indígenas* from Peguche, near Otavalo. They have a TV room and a book exchange in front of a fireplace.

Old Town

A former colonial home, the **(Hotel San Francisco de Quito** (Sucre 217 at Guayaquil, tel. 2/228-7758, tel./fax 2/295-1241, www.sanfranciscodequito.com.ec, $30 s, $48 d) is the pick of Old Town's mid-range options, with a fountain and ferns filling the courtyard and a rooftop patio with great views. Tucked upstairs facing La Concepción Church is the renovated

Posada Colonial (García Moreno and Chile, tel. 2/228-1095, $26 s, $36 d), with comfortable guest rooms that have classic decor and tall ceilings. **Hotel Catedral** (Mejia 638 at Benalcázar, tel. 2/295-5438, www.hotelcatedral.ec, $31 s, $55 d) has recently been upgraded with more comfortable guest rooms, cable TV, a sauna, and a steam room. **Hotel Real Audiencia** (Bolívar 220 at Guayaquil, tel. 2/295-2711 or 2/295-0590, www.realaudiencia.com, $33 s, $52 d) has stylish guest rooms, black-and-white photography on the walls, and a great view of Plaza Santo Domingo.

$50-75
New Town

Thick fur rugs in front of the fireplace add to the Old World feel of **Hostal Los Alpes** (Tamayo 233 at Jorge Washington, tel./fax 2/256-1110, www.hotellosalpes.com, $67 s, $80 d). The bright and clean **Hostal de La Rábida** (La Rábida 227 at Santa María, tel./fax 2/222-2169, www.hostalrabida.com, $71 s, $91 d) has an immaculate white interior and stylish carpeted rooms. There's a fireplace in the living room and a peaceful garden out back.

(Fuente de Piedra II (Juan León Mera and Baquedano, tel. 2/290-0323, $56) is a place to treat yourself. This colonial-style mid-range hotel is elegantly furnished with attentive service, Wi-Fi, and a gourmet restaurant. A sister hotel is at Tamayo and Wilson.

$75-100
New Town

A nine-story building is home to the **Hotel Sebastián** (Almagro 822 at Cordero, tel. 2/222-2300, fax 2/222-2500, www.hotelsebastian.com, $82 s, $94 d, not including breakfast), which uses organic vegetables in its restaurant; the building boasts one of the best water-purification systems in the country.

(Café Cultura (Robles 513 at Reina Victoria, tel./fax 2/222-4271, www.cafecultura.com, $100 s, $122 d) is set in a beautifully restored colonial mansion, formerly the French cultural center. The hotel is lovingly decorated with dark wood, paintings, and a grand staircase in the center of it all. Guest rooms are individually styled, and the baths are huge, with tubs for relaxing after a hard day's sightseeing. There's a gourmet café downstairs, a small private garden out back, a library full of guidebooks, and three stone fireplaces for those cold Quito nights. Breakfast is not included in the room price.

$100-200
New Town

The lavishly decorated **Mansion del Angel** (Wilson E5-29 at Juan León Mera, tel. 2/255-7721, $150 d) has 10 beautifully appointed guest rooms with crystal chandeliers, antiques, and attentive service, plus luxurious private baths and a buffet breakfast. Book well in advance.

The huge **Hotel Quito** (González Suárez N27-142 at 12 de Octubre, tel. 2/254-4600, fax 2/256-7284, www.hotelquito.com, $111 s, $148 d, not including breakfast) boasts one of the best views in Quito, high on a hill above Guapulo. The guest rooms are rather bland, but there is plenty to keep you busy—a casino, a swimming pool, a spa, and a gourmet restaurant.

The 415 guest rooms and suites of the **Hilton Colón** (Amazonas 110 at Patria, tel. 2/256-0666, fax 2/256-3903, U.S. tel. 800/HILTONS—800/445-8667, www.hiltoncolon.com, $161 s or d, not including breakfast) tower over the Parque El Ejido, and it's probably the most popular spot for visitors who have unlimited budgets. Facilities include an excellent gym, a 10-meter pool, a reading room, a casino, and shops.

Mariscal now has its very own slice of boutique chic in the shape of the **Nu House** (Foch E6-12, tel. 2/255-7485, www.nuhousehotels.com, $145 s, $160 d). This wood-and-glass building rises high over the main plaza. Guest rooms have huge windows and dramatic color schemes, and there's a new spa.

The newest and perhaps largest luxury hotel in Quito is the **JW Marriott Hotel Quito** (Orellana 1172 at Amazonas, tel. 2/297-2000, fax 2/297-2050, www.marriott.com, $162 s or d). This glass palace contains 257 guest rooms and 16 suites, a business center, an outdoor heated pool, a health club, and a Mediterranean restaurant.

Old Town

Once a family home, **El Relicario del Carmen** (Venezuela and Olmedo, tel. 2/228-9120, www.hotelrelicariodelcarmen.com, $105 s, $135 d) has been meticulously renovated and made into a comfortable retreat for travelers who want to stay in the colonial part of the city. The abundant artwork and stained glass windows are particular highlights.

Patio Andaluz (García Moreno and Olmedo, tel. 2/228-0830, www.hotelpatioandaluz.com, $200 s or d) is the fruit of a massive project that restored a 16th-century colonial home with two interior patios, spacious guest rooms, and split-level suites. There is an excellent restaurant on the first-floor patio with carved stone pillars, and service is understandably top-notch.

OVER $200
New Town

Uphill from the Hilton Colón to the east, the **Swissôtel** (12 de Octubre 1820 at Cordero, tel. 2/256-7600, fax 2/256-8079, http://quito.swissotel.com, $250 s, $265 d) has 277 wheelchair-accessible guest rooms and a private health club, along with Japanese and Italian restaurants, a casino, and a gourmet deli.

Old Town

Quito's first hotel and still one of its best is **Plaza Grande** (García Moreno and Chile, tel. 2/251-0777, U.S. tel. 888/790-5264, www.plazagrandequito.com, $500 s or d) on the main square. It has 15 suites, three restaurants, a ballroom, champagne and brandy bars, chandeliers, and luxurious guest rooms with marble bathroom floors and jetted tubs.

LONGER STAYS

Most **hotels** will arrange a discount for stays of a few weeks or more. For example, the **Residencial Casa Oriente** (Yaguachi 824 at Llona, tel. 2/254-6157) offers apartments with

QUITO

or without kitchens for $115–140 per month with a minimum stay of two weeks. Spanish lessons are available, and English, French, and German are spoken. **Alberto's House** (García 545, tel. 2/222-4603, www.albertoshouse.com) has guest rooms with shared or private baths from $70 per week, $180 per month.

To have a more authentic cultural experience, a **family stay** is a great way to practice your Spanish and get to know Ecuadorian culture from the inside. It is often just as affordable as a budget hotel as long as you are willing to make a longer commitment. Check at the South American Explorers (SAE) Quito Clubhouse for the latest list; stays can also easily be arranged through language schools. SAE is also a reliable source of information on **apartments** for rent, or try the classified ads in the local newspapers.

Food

Quito has the widest range of international restaurants in Ecuador as well as many excellent local eateries. Here you will find the biggest diversity of world cuisine: from Asian curries to Italian pasta, Mexican fajitas to Argentine steaks, and there are plenty of cheap cafés, fast food joints and $2 set-menus for those on a tighter budget. Many restaurants outside New Town close by 9 or 10 P.M. and throughout the city many are closed on Sundays. Note also that it's surprisingly difficult to find an early breakfast in New Town as most places open at 8 A.M.

OLD TOWN
Bakeries, Cafés, and Snacks
There are plenty of cozy little bakeries to pop into between sights in Old Town. At the entrance of San Agustin Monastery is **El Cafeto** (Chile and Guayaquil, no phone, 8 A.M.–7:30 P.M. Mon.–Sat., 8 A.M.–noon Sun.), specializing in coffee and hot chocolate served with *humitas,* tamales, empanadas, and cakes. In the courtyard of the Centro Cultural Metropolitano, **El Búho** (Jose Moreno and Espejo, tel. 2/228-9877, 11 A.M.–7 P.M. Mon.–Thurs., 11 A.M.–9 P.M. Fri.–Sat., noon–5 P.M. Sun., $3–6) is a quiet spot for a snack with a range of soups, salads, sandwiches, and pasta.

Old Town has several great ice cream parlors. **Frutería Monserrate** (Espejo Oe2-12, tel. 2/258-3408, 8 A.M.–7:30 P.M. Mon.–Fri., 9 A.M.–6:30 P.M. Sat.–Sun., $2–5) serves extravagant helpings of fruit salad and ice cream

as well as cheap lunches and sandwiches. **Heladería San Agustin** (Guayaquil 1053, tel. 2/228-5082, 9 A.M.–6 P.M. Mon.–Fri., 9 A.M.–4 P.M. Sat., 10 A.M.–3 P.M. Sun., ice cream $1.50) claims to be the oldest in the city, having made *helados de paila* sorbets in copper bowls for 150 years.

Ecuadorian
Old Town has plenty of places for cheap set meals, but quality varies widely. On Plaza Grande, there is a small food court on Chile with a range of restaurants offering well-prepared local specialties. Just down the hill from Plaza Grande, **El Guaragua** (Espejo Oe2-40, tel. 2/257-2552, 10 A.M.–9 P.M. Mon.–Thurs., 10 A.M.–11 P.M. Fri.–Sun., entrées $3–6) is one of several restaurants offering local specialties from chicken stew to fried pork chops with beans. With live music Thursday–Saturday and 360-degree views over the colonial city, the **Vista Hermoso** (Mejía 453 at García Moreno, tel. 2/295-1401, entrées $6–10) offers pizzas, snacks, and cocktails on its rooftop terrace. Bring a jacket at night.

On Plaza San Francisco, under the arches below the monastery is the ideally situated café **Tianguez** (Plaza San Francisco, tel. 2/295-4326, www.tianguez.org, 10 A.M.–6 P.M. Mon.–Tues., 10 A.M.–11 P.M. Wed.–Sun., entrées $3–5). After browsing the eclectic gift shop, choose from traditional snacks such as tamales and well-presented entrées such as *fritada* and *llapingacho.*

FOOD
MARKETS AND
SUPERMARKETS

The most economical spot to buy food is the **Santa Clara Market** (Ramírez Dávalos between Carrión and Antonio de Marchena, 7 A.M.-3 P.M. Mon.-Fri., 7 A.M.-noon Sat.-Sun.), two blocks from 10 de Agosto. This place has countless small food stands and meals to go along with a few inexpensive markets.

For a more comfortable shopping experience, head to **Supermaxi,** the city's biggest supermarket, with branches at La Niña and Yanes Pinzón, one block off 6 de Diciembre, as well as in the Centros Comerciales El Bosque, Iñaquito, Multicentro, América, El Jardín, and El Recreo, among others. The biggest **Megamaxi** branch is at 6 de Diciembre and Julio Moreno. **Mi Comisariato** is in the Centro Commercial Quicentro, at García Moreno and Mejía, and at Nuñez de Vela and Ignacio San María. They're all open 9 A.M.-7 or 8 P.M. Monday-Saturday and close earlier on Sunday. The **Santa María** stores (8 A.M.-8 P.M. daily) are a little cheaper; there are two in the north on Versalles and in Centro Commercial Iñaquito, as well as in the center at Venezuela and Sucre.

International

Part of colonial Quito's recent renaissance is an upsurge in high-end eateries. For a gourmet meal, look no further than the cozy cellar setting of **◖ Las Cuevas de Luis Candela** (Benalcázar 713 at Chile, tel. 2/228-7710, 10 A.M.-11 P.M. daily, entrées $7-10), which has been attracting Quito's wealthy patrons since the 1960s. Paella and fondue bourguignonne are just two of the specialties. **Theatrum** (Manabi N8-131, tel. 2/257-1011 or 2/228-9669, www.theatrum.com.ec, 12:30-4:30 P.M. and 7-11 P.M. Mon.-Fri., 7-11 P.M. Sat.-Sun., entrées $10-15), on the second floor of the Teatro Sucre, is another of the city's most

elegant dining experiences, serving extravagantly presented gourmet dishes such as barbecued octopus, crab ravioli, and rabbit risotto in a stylish setting. **Mea Culpa** (Chile and García Moreno, tel. 2/295-1190, 12:30-3:30 P.M. and 7-11 P.M. Mon.-Fri., entrées $10-20), which overlooks the Plaza Grande, has a strict dress code, so leave your sneakers and jeans at home if you want to try out the special fare, such as ostrich with brandy and apple.

Beneath the Itchimbía Cultural Center is **◖ Mosaico** (Samaniego N8-95 at Antepara, tel. 2/254-2871, 11 A.M.-11 P.M. daily, entrées $9-12), which is best for drinks at sunset, when the views of Old Town are unbeatable from the mosaic-inlaid tables on the terrace. Arrive early to secure a table, because this stylish spot fills up quickly with Quito's elite. The limited menu lists Greek dishes, sandwiches, and desserts. Cheesecake is a particular specialty. A taxi from Old Town is $2.

Vegetarian food is harder to come by in Old Town than in Mariscal, but **Govindas** (Esmeraldas 853, tel. 2/296-6844, 8 A.M.-4 P.M. Mon.-Sat., entrées $2-3) is 100 percent meat-free and has a wide range of lunches such as vegetable risotto and plenty of fresh yogurt and granola for breakfast.

NEW TOWN
Asian

Hundreds of inexpensive *chifas* fill the city, but most are barely adequate. **Chifa Mayflower** (Carrión 442 at 6 de Diciembre, tel. 2/254-0510, www.mayflower.com.ec, 11 A.M.-11 P.M. daily, entrées $3-7) has received good reviews from celebrity chefs and is one of seven in a small Quito chain, which includes branches in the El Bosque, El Jardín, Quicentro, and El Recreo malls. Portions of fried rice and noodles are large, and there are plenty of veggie dishes.

For sushi, expect to pay out. **Tanoshii** (in the Swissôtel, 12 de Octubre 1820 at Cordero, tel. 2/256-7600, 12:30-3 P.M. and 7-11 P.M. daily, entrées $10-20) is one of the best in town, with excellent teppanyaki and sashimi. **Sake** (Rivet N30-166, tel. 2/252-4818, 12:30-3 P.M. and

6:30–11 P.M. daily, entrées $15–25) is also very good.

Mariscal offers several restaurants offering Asian specialties that you would struggle to find anywhere else in Ecuador. For curries, you can't beat **◖ Chandani Tandoori** (Juan León Mera and Cordero, tel. 2/222-1053, noon–10 P.M. Mon.–Sat., noon–5 P.M. Sun., entrées $3–5). Everything from *dopiaza* to korma, tikka masala, and *balti* is done well here, served with saffron rice or naan bread. For Vietnamese, Thai, and Asian fusion specialties, head to **◖ Uncle Ho's** (Calama and Almagro, tel. 2/511-4030, noon–11 P.M. Mon.–Sat., entrées $5–8). Choose from a wide range of rolls, soups, and curries. It's a good place for a drink too, and friendly Irish owner Kevin is usually the life and soul of the party.

For something a little different, try Mongolian barbecue at **Mongo's Grill** (Calama E5-10 at Juan León Mera, tel. 2/255-6159, noon–11 P.M. Mon.–Sat., entrées $3–8), where sizzling meat and vegetables are cooked in front of you. The buffet lunch is a particularly good value, and it's a good place for cocktails later on.

Cafés, Bakeries, and Snacks

El Cafécito (Cordero 1124 at Reina Victoria, tel. 2/223-4862, entrées $3–7) is a good option for breakfast as well as Italian and Mexican dishes later on. Candles and crayons for coloring your place mat and a fireplace add to the cozy ambience. **The Magic Bean** (Foch 681 at Juan León Mera, tel. 2/256-6181, 7 A.M.–11 P.M. daily) is another great option for breakfast with fresh Colombian coffee, crepes, and a wide range of juices. Branches of the **Coffee Tree** (Plaza del Quindé, Foch and Reina Victoria, Plaza de los Presidentes, Washington and Amazonas, 24 hours daily) are always an option when nowhere else is open, but the food is nothing special.

The best option for breakfast and after hours is **◖ Coffee and Toffee** (Calama and Almagro, tel. 2/254-3821, 24 hours daily, entrées $3–6), which serves a variety of breakfasts prepared in the open kitchen and served on sofas and armchairs. Choose from the cozy brick interior or a seat on Calama watching the world go by. There's free Wi-Fi too. Another good option for breakfasts and snacks is **El Español** (Juan León Mera and Wilson, tel. 2/255-3995, 8 A.M.–9 P.M. Mon.–Fri., 8 A.M.–6 P.M. Sat.–Sun., entrées $3–6), a chain delicatessen with great sandwiches and high-quality cured hams and cheeses.

Chocoholics should head to **República del Cacao** (Foch and Reina Victoria, tel. 2/255-3132, 9 A.M.–11 P.M. daily), where you can consume it in all its varieties: truffles, cakes, ice cream, cocktails, and hot drinks.

Burgers and Steaks

Burgers, grilled plates, and barbecue are the specialties at **Adam's Rib** (Calama and Reina Victoria, tel. 2/256-3196, noon–11 P.M. Mon.–Sat., $6–8). A similar offering is found at slightly cheaper prices at **The Texas Ranch** (Juan León Mera 1140 at Calama, tel. 2/290-6199, noon–11 P.M. Mon.–Sat., $4–7). For very cheap burgers with trimmings galore, ignore the dubious name and try **G-Spot** (Almagro and Calama, no phone, 11 A.M.–11 P.M. daily, entrées $1.50–$3).

Cuban

The cuisine of this Caribbean island has become quite popular in Ecuador. There are two good places at the north end of Mariscal. **Varadero Sandwiches Cubanos** (Reina Victoria and La Pinta, tel. 2/254-2757, noon–4 P.M. and 7 P.M.–midnight Mon.–Sat., entrées $5) has sandwiches, and things heat up at night with live music by the bar. **La Bodeguita de Cuba** (Reina Victoria 1721 at La Pinta, tel. 2/254-2476, noon–4 P.M. and 7 P.M.–midnight Mon.–Sat., entrées $4–6) is popular for its Cuban *bocaditos* (appetizers) as well as the live Cuban music on Thursday nights.

Ecuadorian

Amidst the dozens of international restaurants, a few eateries offering local specialties stand out. **La Choza** (12 de Octubre 1821 at

Cordero, tel. 2/223-0839, noon–4 P.M. and 7–10 P.M. Mon.–Fri., noon–4 P.M. Sat.–Sun., $2–4) is a popular mid-price place serving appetizers such as *tortillas de maíz* and entrées like the tasty *locro de papas*. For larger portions, try **Mama Clorinda** (Reina Victoria 1144 at Calama, tel. 2/254-4362, 11 A.M.–10 P.M. Mon.–Sat.), where you can get *llapingachos* and a quarter of a chicken for $6, or try a half guinea pig (*cuy*) for $10.

French

Gallic cuisine tends to be served in the most upscale of Quito's foreign restaurants. **Rincón de Francia** (Roca 779 at 9 de Octubre, tel. 2/222-5053, www.rincondefrancia.com, 12:30–3 P.M. and 7–11 P.M. Mon.–Fri., 12:30–3 P.M. Sat., entrées $15–20) is among the best restaurants in the city. Make reservations and dress well. Specialties include oysters, steak in brandy, and fruit melba.

For a more economical dip into French fare, **La Crêperie** (García 465 at Almagro, tel. 8/222-6274, 5 P.M.–midnight Mon.–Sat., entrées $3–5) is one of the longest-running restaurants in the city, and it's often packed on Friday nights for live music. Crepes, of course, are the mainstay, but the cheese fondue ($18 for 2 people) is also hard to beat.

Italian

As the city has spread north, several classy restaurants have followed the business-lunch crowd up Eloy Alfaro. One of the best is the **Il Risotto** (Eloy Alfaro and Portugal, tel. 2/222-6850, noon–3 P.M. and 5 P.M.–11:30 P.M. daily, entrées $7–16), with a great view of the city from the main dining room northeast of the Mariscal. Good service and generous portions make the prices more bearable, as does the delicious tiramisu. For more economical pizza and pasta, try **Le Arcate** (Baquedano 358 at Juan León Mera, lunch and dinner daily, entrées $6–14), which offers over 50 varieties of wood-oven pizzas (the "Russian" has vodka as an ingredient) for $6–9. Equally good is **Al Forno** (Moreno and Almagro, tel. 2/252-7145, noon–3 P.M. and 6:30–11 P.M.

Mon.–Sat., entrées $6–14) with an equally wide range of pizzas. The calzone is particularly mouthwatering. More central in Mariscal is **Tomato** (Moreno and Almagro, tel. 2/290-6201, 10 A.M.–1 A.M. daily, entrées $4–8).

Mexican

A plate of fajitas at **Red Hot Chili Peppers** (Foch and Juan León Mera, tel. 2/255-7575, noon–10:30 P.M. Mon.–Sat., entrées $5–8) will easily fill two people. It's a tiny place with a big TV and graffiti covering the walls, and it just may serve the most authentic Mexican food in town. Next door, **Mariachi Taco Factory** (Foch and Juan León Mera, tel. 2/255-3066, noon–10:30 P.M. Mon.–Sat., entrées $5–8) is busier, and they have karaoke later (which may or may not be a good thing).

Middle Eastern

Shawarma (grilled meat in warm pita bread with yogurt sauce and vegetables) is becoming more and more popular in Ecuador, and Middle Eastern restaurants are springing up left, right, and center. In Mariscal, **El Arabe** (Reina Victoria 627 at Carrión, tel. 2/254-9414, 10 A.M.–9 P.M. Mon.–Sat., 11 A.M.–7 P.M. Sun., entrées $6–8) is a long-established popular spot. The patio at **Aladdin** (Almagro and Baquerizo Moreno, tel. 2/222-9435, 10:30 A.M.–midnight daily, entrées $2–4) is always packed at night. The water pipes and 16 kinds of flavored tobacco probably have something to do with it, along with the cheap falafel and *shawarma*.

Seafood

Two restaurants stand out in this category: **Mare Nostrum** (Tamayo 172 at Foch, tel. 2/252-8686, noon–10 P.M. Tues.–Sat., entrées $8–17) claims to have "70 ways of serving fish." Boat models, suits of armor, low lighting, and dark wood beams in a castle-like building set the stage for delicious cream soups and *encocados* served in half a coconut shell. The same owners run **Las Redes de Mariscos** (Amazonas 845 at Veintimilla, tel. 2/252-5691, noon–10 P.M. Mon.–Sat., $5–8), which has an extensive wine list and specializes in large bowls of *ceviche*.

Vegetarian

Being vegetarian tends to attract quizzical looks around Ecuador, but in Quito there are several good options. **El Maple** (Foch 476 at Almagro, tel. 2/223-1503, noon–9 P.M. daily, entrées $3–5) has everything from pasta and curry to burritos and stir-fries. Lunch is great value at $3.50.

Although there are animals on the menu, **The Magic Bean** (Foch 681 at Juan León Mera, tel. 2/256-6181, 7 A.M.–10 P.M. daily, entrées $5–7) is still a vegetarian restaurant at heart. Salads, pizzas, pancakes, fresh juices, and Colombian coffee—served inside or on the covered patio—have made this place one of the more popular gringo stopovers in New Town.

Other International

For a tangy Swiss fondue, try **Paleo** (Cordero E5-48 at Juan León Mera, tel. 2/255-3019, lunch and dinner Mon.–Sat., entrées $6–12), which also serves great raclette. **La Paella Valenciana** (Republica and Almagro, tel. 2/222-8681, noon–3 P.M. and 7:30–11:30 P.M. Mon.–Sat., noon–3 P.M. Sun., entrées $10–20) is one of the best places for a wide range of Spanish entrées and tapas.

One of the most enticing restaurants in Mariscal is the colorful, glass-encased patio of █ **La Boca del Lobo** (Calama 284 at Reina Victoria, tel. 2/254-5500, 5 P.M.–midnight Mon.–Sat., entrées $7–14). The decor is flamboyantly eclectic, with birdcages and psychedelic paintings, and the menu focuses on Mediterranean specialties—marvel at how many ways they can cook mushrooms. The cocktail menu is another highlight. This place attracts a higher class crowd and is also gay-friendly.

If you want the exact opposite of La Boca del Lobo (i.e., down-to-earth home cooking), try the Irish bar **Mulligans** (Calama E5-44, tel. 2/254-0876, 11 A.M.–midnight Sun.–Thurs., 11 A.M.–2 A.M. Fri.–Sat., entrées $3–6), where the order of the day is fried food such as chicken wings and fish and chips washed down by pitchers of draft beer with soccer on the big screen.

Information and Services

VISITOR INFORMATION

The **Corporación Metropolitana de Turismo** (Quito Visitors Bureau) is the best tourist information bureau in Ecuador and an excellent source of information on Quito, with maps, brochures, leaflets, English-speaking staff, and a regularly updated website. The main office is at the Palacio Municipal (Plaza de la Independencia, Venezuela and Espejo, tel. 2/257-2445, 9 A.M.–6 P.M. Mon.–Fri., 9 A.M.–5 P.M. Sat.). There are also branches in Mariscal (Reina Victoria and Luis Cordero, tel. 2/255-1566), the airport (tel. 2/330-0164), the Museo Nacional del Banco Central (6 de Diciembre and Patria, tel. 2/222-1116), and at Quitumbe bus terminal.

The Quito Visitors Bureau works with the Tourism Unit of the Metropolitan Police (tel. 2/257-0786) to provide **guided tours** of the city. These well-informed officers are clad in blue-and-red uniforms (and look rather like airline pilots). Tours of Old Town range $6–15 pp, and a tour of Mitad del Mundo costs $40.

The main office of Ecuador's **Ministerio de Turismo** (Eloy Alfaro N32-300 at Tobar, 3rd Fl., tel. 2/239-9333, 8:30 A.M.–12:30 P.M. and 1:30–5 P.M. daily), near the Parque La Carolina, is also helpful and can assist with hotel reservations. It has maps, and some staff speak English.

Outside the tourist offices, a good source of information is **South American Explorers** (SAE, Jorge Washington 311 at Plaza, tel./fax 2/222-5228, quitoclub@saexplorers.org,

CONSULATES IN QUITO

- **Argentina:** Ed. Banco de los Andes, 5th Fl., Amazonas 477 between Robles and Roca, tel. 2/256-2292, 9 A.M.-1 P.M. Mon.-Fri.

- **Bolivia:** Ed. Torres Viscaya II, 1st Fl., César Borja Lavayen and Juan Pablo Sanz, tel. 2/245-8863, 8 A.M.-4 P.M. Mon.-Fri.

- **Brazil:** Ed. España, 10th Fl., Amazonas 1429 at Colón, tel. 2/256-3141, 9 A.M.-3 P.M. Mon.-Fri.

- **Canada (Australia):** Amazonas 4153 at Unión Nacional de Periodistas, tel. 2/245-5499, 9 A.M.-noon and 2:30-5:30 P.M. Mon.-Fri., appointment required, Australians also welcome; the Australian consulate is in Guayaquil.

- **Chile:** Sáenz 3617 at Amazonas, 4th Fl., tel. 2/224-9403, 8 A.M.-5 P.M. Mon.-Fri.

- **Colombia:** Atahualpa 955 at República, 3rd Fl., tel. 2/245-8012, 8:30 A.M.-1 P.M. Mon.-Fri.

- **Costa Rica:** Isla San Cristobal N44-385 at Guepi, tel. 2/225-2330, 8 A.M.-1:30 P.M. Mon.-Fri.

- **Cuba:** Mercurio 365 at El Vengador, tel. 2/245-6936, 9 A.M.-1 P.M. Mon.-Fri.

- **Denmark:** Ed. Gabriela 3, 3rd Fl., República de El Salvador 733 at Portugal, tel. 2/243-7163, 9:30 A.M.-1:30 P.M. and 3-5 P.M. Mon.-Fri.

- **France:** 18 de Septembre 115 at Leonidas Plaza, tel. 2/294-3840, 8:30 A.M.-1 P.M. and 3-5:30 P.M. Mon.-Fri.

- **Germany:** Ed. Citiplaza, 14th Fl., Naciones Unidas and República de El Salvador, tel. 2/297-2820, 8:30-11:30 A.M. Mon.-Fri.

- **Guatemala:** Ed. Gabriela 3, 3rd Fl., República de El Salvador 733 at Portugal, tel. 2/245-9700, 9 A.M.-1 P.M. Mon.-Fri.

- **Ireland (consulate):** Yanacocha N72-64 at Juan Procel, tel. 2/357-0156, 10 A.M.-1 P.M. Mon.-Fri.

- **Israel:** Ed. Plaza 2000, 9th Fl., 12 de Octubre and Salazar, tel. 2/397-1500, 10 A.M.-1 P.M. Mon.-Fri.

- **Italy:** La Isla 111 at Albornoz, tel. 2/256-1077, 8:30 A.M.-12:30 P.M. Mon.-Fri.

- **Japan:** Ed. de Corporacion Financiera Nacional, Juan Mera N30 and Patria, tel. 2/256-1899, 9 A.M.-noon and 2-5 P.M. Mon.-Fri.

- **Mexico:** 6 de Diciembre 4843 at Naciones Unidas, tel. 2/292-3770, 9 A.M.-1 P.M. Mon.-Fri.

- **Netherlands:** 12 de Octubre 1942 at Cordero, tel. 2/222-9229, 8:30 A.M.-1 P.M. and 2-5 P.M. Mon.-Fri., by appointment only.

- **Paraguay:** Ed. Torre Sol Verde, 8th Fl., 12 de Octubre and Salazar, tel. 2/223-1990, 8:30 A.M.-2:30 P.M. Mon.-Fri.

- **Peru:** República de El Salvador 495 at Irlanda, tel. 2/246-8410, 9 A.M.-1 P.M. and 3-5 P.M. Mon.-Fri.

- **Spain (consulate):** La Pinta 455 at Amazonas, tel. 2/256-4373, 8:30 A.M.-noon Mon.-Fri.

- **United Kingdom:** Ed. Citiplaza, 14th Fl., Naciones Unidas and República de El Salvador, tel. 2/297-0800, http://ukinecuador.fco.gov.uk, 8:30 A.M.-12:30 P.M. and 1:30-5 P.M. Mon.-Thurs., 8:30 A.M.-1:30 P.M. Fri.

- **United States:** Avigiras and Guayacanes, tel. 2/398-5000, http://ecuador.usembassy.gov, 8 A.M.-12:30 P.M. and 1:30-5 P.M. Tues.-Fri.

- **Venezuela:** Ed. Cedatos, 8th Fl., Amazonas N30-240 at Eloy Alfaro, tel. 2/255-7209, 9 A.M.-12:30 P.M. and 2-4 P.M. Mon.-Fri.

www.saexplorers.org, 9:30 A.M.–5 P.M. Mon.–Wed. and Fri., 9:30 A.M.–8 P.M. Thurs., 9:30 A.M.–noon Sat.). The SAE puts most of its energy these days toward paying members, making the annual fee ($60 pp, $90 per couple) a solid investment for those who plan to stay in Ecuador more than a month or travel through many countries in South America. Nonmembers can get free maps and advice here too. With branches in Ithaca (New York), Lima, Cuzco (Peru), and Buenos Aires, the club stocks a wealth of information readily accessible to members by mail, email, fax, or in person. You can store equipment, peruse the library, and help yourself to tea and coffee in the lounge. An SAE membership card entitles you to discounts at many hotels, tour agencies, and Spanish schools in Quito and around the country. The biggest perk of membership is access to countless trip reports written by members giving the lowdown on destinations throughout the continent. The SAE also has a good volunteering database.

VISAS

Tourist-visa extensions beyond the standard 90 days are the main reason most travelers end up at the **Ministerio de Relaciones Exteriores** (Carrión E1-76 at 10 de Agosto, tel. 2/299-3200, www.mmrree.gob.ec, 8:30 A.M.–1:30 P.M. Mon.–Fri.) Go early and be ready to wait. Unfortunately, you can only extend your visa on the day before or on the actual day it expires, which makes it a stressful process. If you can, go the week before to be sure of the procedure. All nontourist visa holders (student, cultural, volunteer, or work visas) must register within 30 days of arrival at the same office; otherwise you have to pay a $200 fine.

MAPS

The hike up Paz y Miño is worth it for the commanding view of the city from the **Instituto Geográfico Militar** (IGM, tel. 2/250-2091, 8 A.M.–4 P.M. Mon.–Fri.). Here you can get general tourist maps of Ecuador, as well as topographical maps for hiking. While you wait for the staff to process your map order (bring a book), consider a show at the planetarium.

The IGM often closes early on Fridays, and visitors must surrender their passports at the gate to enter.

The Quito **Visitors Bureau** (Plaza de la Independencia, Venezuela and Espejo, tel. 2/257-2445, 9 A.M.–6 P.M. Mon.–Fri., 9 A.M.–5 P.M. Sat.) can supply decent maps for visitors as well as specialist walking tour maps.

POST OFFICES AND COURIERS

Quito's main **post office** is in New Town (Eloy Alfaro 354 at 9 de Octubre, tel. 2/256-1218, 8 A.M.–6 P.M. Mon.–Fri., 8 A.M.–noon Sat.). The Express Mail Service (EMS, tel. 2/256-1962) is at this office. There is also a branch post office one block east of the Plaza de la Independencia in Old Town (Espejo between Guayaquil and Venezuela, tel. 2/228-2175, 8 A.M.–6 P.M. Mon.–Fri.).

If you're sending something important, using an international courier service is preferable. There is a branch of **FedEx** (Amazonas 517 at Santa María, tel. 2/227-9180), and **DHL** has several offices throughout the city, including on Eloy Alfaro and Avenida de Los Juncos (tel. 2/397-5000), Colón 1333 at Foch (tel. 2/255-6118), at the Hilton Colón, and at the airport.

TELECOMMUNICATIONS
Telephone

You're never far from a *cabina* offering telephone service. The national companies **Andinatel** and **Pacifictel** no longer have a monopoly—together with Claro (Porta), Movistar, and Alegro, they both run competing offices. Movistar and Claro also have pay phones everywhere, and each type requires its own brand of prepaid card. The most convenient offices in Mariscal are at Juan León Mera 741 at Baquedano, and on Reina Victoria near Calama.

Internet Access

Internet access is even easier to find than a phone booth. Internet cafés are everywhere, particularly in Mariscal. Expect to pay $1 per hour and to have access at most cafés 8 A.M.–9 P.M.

QUITO EMERGENCY TELEPHONE NUMBERS

Police	101
Fire Department	102
Red Cross	131
Emergency	911

daily, possibly later on weekends. Although connection rates and computer quality vary widely, most cafés have fax service, scanners, printers, and Internet phone programs, allowing foreign visitors to call home for a fraction of the cost of a regular phone connection. The term *café* may be misleading, however, because many offer only water and snacks.

Listing Internet cafés in Quito is an inherently futile gesture because they open and close so fast. In New Town, the block of Calama between Juan León Mera and Reina Victoria has a handful. The increasing number of hotels with free Internet access and Wi-Fi often makes a visit to a Internet café unnecessary.

MONEY
Banks and ATMs

ATMs for most international systems (Plus, Cirrus, Visa, and MasterCard) can be found at major banks along Amazonas and around the shopping centers. These tend to have limits on how much you can withdraw per day (usually $500), so if you need to, say, pay cash for a Galápagos trip, you'll have to go to a bank branch. It's best to take a taxi straight to the travel agency if you withdraw a large amount of money. **Banco del Pacífico** has its head office on Naciones Unidos at Los Shyris, and there is a branch at Amazonas and Washington. **Banco de Guayaquil** is on Reina Victoria at Colón,

and on Amazonas at Veintimilla; **Banco de Pichincha** is on Amazonas at Pereira, and on 6 de Diciembre. **Banco Bolivariano** is at Naciones Unidas E6-99.

Exchange Houses

Since the introduction of the U.S. dollar, exchanging other currencies has become more difficult, and many exchange houses have closed. Try to bring U.S. dollars traveler's checks, as rates are poor for Canadian dollars, British pounds, and even the euro. Exchanging those currencies outside Quito, Guayaquil, and Cuenca is difficult if not impossible. If you really have to, try one of the large banks listed above.

Credit Card Offices

Visa (Los Shyris 3147, tel. 2/245-9303) has an office in Quito, as do **American Express** (Ed. Rocafuerte, 5th Fl., Amazonas 339 at Jorge Washington, tel. 2/256-0488) and **MasterCard** (Naciones Unidas and Shyris, tel. 2/226-2770).

Money Transfers

Western Union (8 A.M.–6 P.M. Mon.–Fri., 9 A.M.–5 P.M. Sat.–Sun.) has many locations around the city, including on Av. Del República and on Colón—check www.westernunion.com for a list of offices worldwide. The company charges $52 for a same-day transfer of $1,000, plus local taxes. It'll cost you $25 to transfer any amount to and from other places in the Americas, and $35 to and from Europe, at the **Banco del Pacífico** (Amazonas and Jorge Washington); you are also expected to cover the cost of contacting your home bank. If that much cash makes you itch, you can change it into American Express traveler's checks at the main branch of the Banco del Pacífico (República 433 at Almagro). This transaction costs $10 to change up to $1,000, and 1 percent of the total for additional amounts.

HEALTH
General Concerns

Unless you're traveling from an equally high city such as La Paz, you will certainly feel the effects of Quito's **elevation** within the first few hours of arriving. At best, you will feel a bit breathless and light-headed, but dizzy spells, headaches, and fatigue are also common. It is best not to overexert yourself, to minimize caffeine and alcohol intake, and consume plenty of water and light food. After two or three days, you'll more or less be used to the elevation.

Don't let the cool climate at this elevation fool you into thinking that you don't need to bother with sunblock. The **sun** is far stronger up here, so slap it on. The **smog** from the traffic can leave you with a sore throat, particularly because Quito's location in a valley seems to trap all the pollution.

Like everywhere in Ecuador, you may suffer from stomach problems. Minimize the risks by avoiding salad, unpeeled fruit, ice, pork, and shellfish. Don't eat on the street or from bus vendors.

Hospitals and Clinics

The **Hospital Metropolitano** (Mariana de Jesús and Occidental, tel. 2/226-1520) is the best hospital in Quito and is priced accordingly. The American-run **Hospital Voz Andes** (Villalengua 267 at 10 de Agosto, tel. 2/226-2142) is cheaper and receives the most business from Quito's foreign residents. It's described as fast, competent, and inexpensive, with an emergency room and outpatient services. To get there, take the *trole* north along 10 de Agosto just past Naciones Unidas.

The 24-hour **Clínica Pichincha** (Veintimilla E3-30 at Páez, tel. 2/299-8700) has a laboratory that can perform analyses for intestinal

parasites. Women's health problems should be referred to the 24-hour **Clínica de la Mujer** (Amazonas N39-216 at Gaspar de Villarroel, tel. 2/245-8000).

Private Doctors

Dr. John Rosenberg (Foch 476 at Almagro, tel. 2/252-1104, jrd@pi.pro.ec) is a highly recommended general practitioner who speaks English and German. He is the doctor for the U.S. Embassy and performs house calls. **Eduardo Larrea** (Centro Medico Metropolitano, 3rd Fl., Suite 311, tel. 2/226-7652 or 9/919-4665) also speaks English.

Carlos Ribadeneira (Mariana de Jesús and A St., tel. 9/448-9115) is a gynecologist who speaks English.

Renato León (Ascazubi and 10 Agosto, tel. 2/223-8342 or 2/255-2080) is a tropical disease specialist who speaks English and does parasite lab tests more quickly and cheaply than the hospitals.

Roberto Mena (Coruña and Isabel la Católica, tel. 2/256-9149) comes very highly recommended for quality dental work. He speaks English and German.

OTHER SERVICES
Laundry

Wash-and-dry places are common in New Town: There are several on Foch, Pinto, and Wilson between Reina Victoria and Amazonas. A few may even let you use the machines yourself. Laundry services are available in many hotels, and the receptionists in more expensive ones can point you toward a dry cleaner (*lavaseca*).

Getting There and Around

GETTING THERE AND AWAY
Air

The **Mariscal Sucre International Airport** (tel. 2/294-4900, www.quiport.com) is north of New Town beyond the intersection of 10 de Agosto, Amazonas, and De la Prensa. At the time of this writing, it remains Quito's main airport, but it will be replaced, most likely in 2012, by a new airport at El Quinche, 18 kilometers east of the city. This new facility, costing over $500 million, will host all national and international flights on a 1,500-hectare site and will accommodate over 5 million passengers per year.

Until the new airport opens, from Mariscal it's straightforward to get to and from the airport. Buses marked "Aeropuerto" head down 9 de Octubre, 12 de Octubre, and Juan León Mera. You can also take the trolley along 10 de Agosto and then transfer onto the Rumiñahui connecting bus (*alimentador*) from the Estación Norte, or onto the Metrobus on América, which stops at the airport. Be wary of pickpockets on these services, however. From the airport, take pretty much any bus heading south (left) to reach both New Town and Old Town.

A taxi ride from the airport during the day should cost about $3 to New Town and $5 to Old Town, but to get these prices you need to flag down a cab outside the terminal parking lot. Taking a taxi directly in front of the terminal costs a few dollars more.

Services at the airport include tourist information, a post office, late-night money exchange, duty-free shops, Andinatel phone service, and a few restaurants and cafés.

Once the new airport is built, it will be far more time-consuming to get to Quito. A taxi will take about 50 minutes, and a shuttle bus service will probably be offered, although that has not yet been confirmed.

INTERNATIONAL AIRLINES IN QUITO

- **Air France and KLM:** Ed. World Trade Center, Suite 401, 12 de Octubre N24-562 at Cordero, tel. 2/252-4201, shared offices

- **American:** Av. Patria and Amazonas, tel. 2/226-0900

- **Avianca:** Coruña 1311 at San Ignacio, tel. 2/223-2015

- **Continental:** Ed. World Trade Center, Suite 1108, 12 de Octubre and Cordero, tel. 2/255-7170

- **Copa:** República de El Salvador 361 and Moscu, tel. 2/227-3082

- **Delta:** Ed. Renazzo Plaza, 3rd Fl., Los Shyris and Suecia, tel. 2/333-1691 or 800/101-060

- **Iberia:** Ed. Finandes, Eloy Alfaro 939 at Amazonas, tel. 2/256-6009

- **Icelandair:** Diego de Almagro 1822 at Alpallana, tel. 2/256-1820

- **Japan Airlines:** Amazonas 3899 at Corea, tel. 2/298-6828

- **LAN:** Amazonas and Pasaje Guayas, tel. 2/255-1782

- **Lufthansa:** Ed. Harmonia, Amazonas N47-205 at Río Palora, tel. 2/226-7705

- **Taca:** República de El Salvador N34-67 at Suecia, tel. 2/225-4662

- **TAME:** Amazonas 13-54 at Colón, tel. 2/245-2657 or 800/500-800

- **United:** Ed. Almirante Colón, Av. Republica de El Salvador, tel. 2/225-4662

TAME (Amazonas and Colón, tel. 2/396-6300) has flights from Quito to Baltra in the Galápagos ($350–400 round-trip) and to the following destinations for $50–80 one-way: Coca, Cuenca, Esmeraldas, Guayaquil, Lago Agrio, Loja, Machala, and Tulcán. **Icaro** (Palora 124 at Amazonas, tel. 2/245-0928) is sometimes marginally cheaper and has daily flights to Coca, Cuenca, Manta, and Guayaquil. **Aerogal** (Amazonas 7797 at Juan Holgún, tel. 2/225-7202) flies to Guayaquil and the Galápagos and also has daily flights to Cuenca. The newest line is **VIP** (Foch and 6 de Diciembre, tel. 2/396-0600), which has smaller planes to Coca, Lago Agrio, and seasonally to Salinas. **SAEREO** (Indanza 121 at Amazonas, tel. 2/330-1152) has a daily flight to Macas.

National Buses

Quito has replaced its dilapidated old bus station at Cumandá with two brand-new terminals. The biggest terminal, Quitumbe, in the far south of Quito, is a joy to visit; security and cleanliness are both excellent. This terminal serves all long-distance routes traveling west, east, and south as well as services to the north to Esmeraldas via Santo Domingo. Those traveling to other destinations north and northwest need to head for either the new Carcelén terminal or La Ofelia terminal, both in the far north of Quito.

Trole, Ecovia, and Metrobus have extended their services to all three main bus terminals, running until midnight on weekdays and until 10 P.M. on weekends.

A few private bus companies have their own small departure terminals. **Panamericana Internacional** (Colón and Reina Victoria, tel. 2/255-1839) has service to Guayaquil (8 hours, $10), Machala and Huaquillas (13 hours, $11), Cuenca (10 hours, $10), Manta (9 hours, $10), Portoviejo (9 hours, $10), and Esmeraldas (6 hours, $9). **Flota Imbabura** (Larrea 1211 at Portoviejo, tel. 2/223-6940) has service to Cuenca, Guayaquil, and Manta. **Ecuatoriana** (Jorge Washington and Juan León Mera, tel. 2/222-5315) runs plush buses to Guayaquil. **Reina del Camino** serves Manabí from Pedernales to Puerto López, including Manta and Portoviejo, from its terminal (18 Septiembre and Larrea).

The new northern terminal at Ofelia, which is only for county buses, is where **Coop Pichincha** serves Guayllabamba and El Quinche; **San José de Minas** serves the northwest (Nanegal, Minas, Chontal, Cielo Verde); **Flor de Valle** goes to Cayambe, Pacto, and Mindo; **Transportes Otavalo** doesn't go to Otavalo—only Minas and Pacto; and **Malchingui** and **Cangahua** run buses to various locations. Ofelia is the end of the Metrovia city bus route, and dozens of connections spread out from here into the northern parishes. The terminal is clean, organized, and well signposted. The Mitad del Mundo buses come through here—use your existing bus ticket and pay just $0.15 extra for the transfer.

Rental Cars and Motorcycles

Renting a car may be a good way to get out of the city, but take into account the convenience and cheapness of buses as well as the many vagaries of driving in Ecuador. It's definitely not the way to see the city.

Small cars start at $50 per day. Several major car-rental companies operate in Quito:

- **Avis:** at the airport, tel. 2/601-6000, www.avis.com.ec
- **Bombuscaro:** at the airport, tel. 2/330-3304, www.bombuscarorentacar.com
- **Budget:** Colón 1140 at Amazonas, tel. 2/223-7026, www.budget-ec.com
- **Hertz:** at the airport, tel. 2/225-4257, www.hertz.com

Other options include **Safari Tours** (Foch E4-132 at Cordero, tel. 2/255-2505, fax 2/222-3381, tel./fax 2/222-0426, www.safari.com.ec), which has some 4WD vehicles and drivers available to head into the mountains, and it can arrange larger cars and buses for groups. **Ecuadorian Alpine Institute** (Ramírez Dávalos 136 at Amazonas, Suite 102, tel. 2/256-5465, fax 2/256-8949, eai@

ecuadorexplorer.com, www.volcanoclimbing. com) has 4WD vehicles as well.

For motorcycles, try American-owned **Ecuador Freedom Bike Rental** (Juan León Mera N22-37 at Veintimilla, tel. 2/250-4339, www.freedombikerental.com), which has recently opened in Mariscal, offering a range of motorcycles as well as mountain bikes for rent. Guided tours or self-guided tours with a GPS unit are available. Always wear a helmet and be careful.

Trains
Quito's **Chimbacalle train station** (Sincholagua and Maldonado) is a few kilometers south of Old Town. The trolley is the easiest way to reach it, and the Chimbacalle stop is right at the station, which is a delightful step back in time.

At present there are services from Quito to Boliche, Machachi, and Latacunga (4 hours, $10). The route is being extended to Riobamba to link up with the Devil's Nose route and will continue all the way to Guayaquil by the end of 2013.

GETTING AROUND
Local Buses
If you traveling a relatively simple route, local buses can be useful. The routes are rather complicated, so it's best to take short journeys along the major roads, especially Amazonas and 10 de Agosto. It's a good idea to ask a local at the bus stop which bus number goes to your destination. For more complex journeys, you're better off taking the trolley systems or a taxi.

Any of 10 de Agosto's major crossroads, including Patria, Orellana, and Naciones Unidas, are likely places to find a bus heading south to Old Town or north as far as the turn to Mitad del Mundo. "La Y," the meeting of 10 de Agosto with América and De la Prensa, is a major bus intersection, as is Parque Huayna Capac at 6 de Diciembre and El Inca. The flat fare is $0.25. Have it ready, and take care with your belongings on crowded buses.

Trolley Systems
Quito's network of three electric trolley buses is the best of its kind in Ecuador: It is cheap, clean, fast, and well-organized. The buses are

© BEN WESTWOOD

Quito's train service will soon run all the way to Guayaquil.

BUSES FROM QUITO TERMINALS

FROM QUITUMBE

Ambato	2.5 hours	$2.70
Atacames	7 hours	$8
Baños	3 hours	$3.70
Coca	9 hours	$10
Cuenca	9 hours	$12
Esmeraldas	6 hours	$7
Guaranda	5 hours	$4.50
Guayaquil	8 hours	$8
Lago Agrio	9 hours	$8
Latacunga	1.5 hours	$1.70
Macas	7 hours	$8
Puyo	5 hours	$5
Santo Domingo	3 hours	$3
Tena	5 hours	$6

FROM CARCELÉN

Atacames	7 hours	$8
Esmeraldas	6 hours	$7
Ibarra	2.5 hours	$2.50
Los Bancos (indirect to Mindo)	2 hours	$2.50
Otavalo	2 hours	$2.50
Tulcán	5 hours	$5

FROM OFELIA

Cayambe	1.5 hours	$1.50
Mindo (direct)	2 hours	$2.50
Mitad del Mundo (via the Metrobus line)	1.5 hours	$0.40

separated from ordinary traffic to avoid delays. Flat fare for all services is $0.25, payable at kiosks or machines on entry. Cars pass every 5–10 minutes.

El Trole (5:30 A.M.–11:30 P.M. Mon.–Fri., 6 A.M.–10 P.M. Sat.–Sun.) runs north–south from Estación Norte north of New Town near La Y, south past stops at Mariscal and Colón, through Old Town past Chimbacalle train station, to the new southern bus terminal at Quitumbe. It takes about an hour to get to Quitumbe from New Town. The main *trole* thoroughfare, 10 de Agosto, reserves a pair of center lanes for the service, detouring down Guayaquil and Maldonado in Old Town, then continuing on Maldonado south of El Panecillo.

The **Ecovia** (6 A.M.–10 P.M. Mon.–Fri., 6 A.M.–9:30 P.M. Sat.–Sun.) is similar, but without the overhead wires. It also runs north–south from its northern Río Coca terminal along 6 de Diciembre past La Casa de la Cultura to La Marín near Old Town. Most trolleys turn around at La Marín, where there are interchanges with many country bus routes to the south and the valley; an extension continues past the exit of the old Cumandá bus terminal to Avenida Napo.

The third line, called **Metrobus** (5:30 A.M.–10:30 P.M. Mon.–Fri., 6 A.M.–10 P.M. Sat.–Sun.), runs from La Marín in Old Town up Santa Prisca and along Avenida América, La Prensa, and north to both the Ofelia and Carcelén terminals, where there are connections to the northern highlands, cloud forest, and northern coast. It takes about 40 minutes to get to these terminals from New Town.

If you want to bypass Quito by traveling between Carcelén in the north and Quitumbe in the south, there is now a direct shuttle service.

It all seems too good to be true, and in one sense, it is: Unfortunately, all of the trolley lines are notorious for highly skilled **pickpockets,** and foreign visitors are easy targets. If you're going sightseeing with your camera, avoid crowded services and consider taking a taxi. Don't take valuables or large amounts of cash on the bus, and if possible, avoid traveling at peaks times in morning or late-afternoon rush hour.

For further information on the trolleybuses, visit www.trolebus.gov.ec.

Taxis

Digital meters are required in taxis by law. Many drivers will pretend that the meters are out of order ("*no funciona*"), in which case you should offer to find another cab. Saying this has a strange tendency to fix malfunctioning meters instantly, although many drivers will refuse to use them, even though that's illegal. Meters start at $0.35, with a $1 minimum charge, and run except when the cab is stopped. Rides within Old Town and New Town shouldn't be more than $2.50 during the day. Prices increase at night, but shouldn't be more than double. Drivers are particularly reluctant to use the meter for longer trips to the bus terminals. Rates tend to vary from $5 to Carcelén and Ofelia to $8 to Quitumbe.

Freelance yellow cabs prowl the streets, and various small taxi stands exist all over the city, especially in front of expensive hotels. These have a set price list for destinations and are usually more expensive than a metered ride. Note that prebooking a taxi from your hotel is by far the best option because the hotelier will use a reliable company. Otherwise, never take an unmarked cab, and in the case of yellow taxis, check for the orange license plate as well as the company name and registration on the side of the cab and on the windshield. The driver should also have an ID. Don't be afraid to ask for this ("*identidad*") before getting in. All these precautions will minimize the risk of being a victim of crime, which has become more common in Quito taxis in recent years.

Radio taxis can be called at a moment's notice or arranged the day before. Try the **Central de Radio Taxi** (tel. 2/250-0600 or 2/252-1112) or **Taxi Amigo** (tel. 2/222-2222 or 2/222-2220). Both are reliable and available at any hour. **Taxis Lagos de Ibarra** (Asunción 381 at Versalles, tel. 2/256-5992) sends five-passenger taxis to Ibarra for $8 pp, or to Otavalo for $7.50 pp. **Sudamericana Taxis** (tel. 2/275-2567) sends cabs to Santo Domingo or stops along the way, such as La Hesperia or Tinalandia, for $15 pp.

Vicinity of Quito

CALDERÓN

Just nine kilometers from Quito's northern suburbs, artisans in this tiny town craft figures out of a varnished bread dough called *masapan.* This technique, unique to Ecuador until Play-Doh came along, originated with the annual making of bread babies for Day of the Dead celebrations in November. Artisans in Calderón developed more elaborate and lasting figures, adding salt and carpenter's glue, and the villagers gradually created new techniques. With the introduction of aniline dyes, the *masa* became colored.

Today, Calderón is filled with artisan's shops and private houses that turn out the figurines by the hundreds. Tiny indigenous dolls called *cholas* stand in formation on tables and shelves next to brightly painted parrots, llamas, fish, and flowers. Each flour-paste figure is molded by hand or rolled and cut with a pasta maker

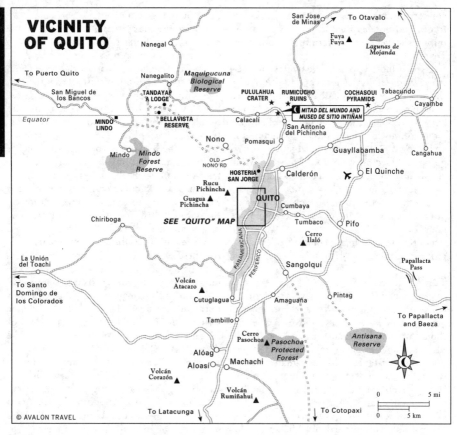

VICINITY OF QUITO

Nanegal

San Jose de Minas

To Otavalo

Fuya Fuya ▲

Lagunas de Mojanda

To Puerto Quito

Nanegalito

Maquipucuna Biological Reserve

PULULAHUA CRATER ★

RUMICUCHO RUINS ★

COCHASQUI PYRAMIDS ★

Tabacundo

San Miguel de los Bancos

TANDAYAPA LODGE ●

MITAD DEL MUNDO AND MUSEO DE SITIO INTIÑAN

Cayambe

Equator

MINDO LINDO ■

BELLAVISTA RESERVE

Calacalí

San Antonio del Pichincha

Mindo

Mindo Forest Reserve

Nono

Pomasqui

Guayllabamba

Cangahua

OLD NONO RD

HOSTERIA SAN JORGE ●

Calderón ○

El Quinche

Rucu Pichincha ▲

QUITO

Guagua ▲ Pichincha

SEE "QUITO" MAP

Cumbayá ○

Chiriboga

Tumbaco ○

Pifo ○

Cerro Ilaló ▲

La Unión del Toachi

PANAMERICANA

PERIFERICO

Sangolquí ○

Papallacta Pass

To Santo Domingo de los Colorados

Volcán Atacazo ▲

Cutuglagua ○

Amaguaña ○

Pintag ○

To Papallacta and Baeza

Tambillo ○

Cerro Pasochoa ▲

Pasochoa Protected Forest

Antisana Reserve

Alóag ○

Aloasí ○

Machachi ○

Volcán Corazón ▲

Volcán Rumiñahui ▲

To Latacunga

To Cotopaxi

© AVALON TRAVEL

0   5 mi

0   5 km

and pastry cutter. They are then dried, painted, and varnished. The figures make unusual, inexpensive gifts and are popular as Christmas ornaments. Models of Nativity scenes, Santa Claus figures, and decorated trees are sold along the main street. Buses for Calderón leave regularly from the Ofelia terminal.

GUAYLLABAMBA AND VICINITY

Past Calderón, on the road to Cayambe and Otavalo, this small town on the river of the same name is home to the best zoo in the country.

Quito Zoo (tel. 2/236-8898, 8:30 A.M.–5 P.M. Tues.–Fri., 9 A.M.–4 P.M. Sat.–Sun., $4), which opened in 1997, is now considered one of the most spacious zoos in Latin America. The largest collection of native fauna in the country occupies the 12-hectare spread, including several animals rescued from the illegal fur trade. The focus is on mammals such as spectacled bears, wolves, monkeys, and pumas; this is also your best chance to see the elusive jaguar, so difficult to spot in the wild. Macaws, parrots, eagles, Andean condors, and toucans represent native birds, and a dozen Galápagos tortoises complete the collection. The zoo is three kilometers from the center of town—take a taxi ($1.25), or it's a long 40-minute walk uphill. Tours are available for $5.

El Quinche

Six kilometers away, through the dry, eroded landscape south of Guayllabamba, is the village of El Quinche. The town's ornate church and sanctuary dedicated to the Virgin of Quinche draw crowds of pilgrims from Quito in search of the Virgin's blessing year-round, and especially at processions honoring the Virgin held on November 21. The shrine is thought to grant special protection to truck and taxi drivers. From here, you can follow the road south to Pifo, then west into Quito's valley suburbs and up into the city.

El Quinche will be on the tourist map from 2012, when Quito's new airport is expected to open just outside town. Visit www.quiport.com for further information.

◖ MITAD DEL MUNDO

You can't come to a country that's named after the Equator and not stand with a foot in each hemisphere; a visit to "The Middle of the World" complex is the most popular day trip near Quito. La Mitad del Mundo tourism complex (tel. 2/239-5637, 9 A.M.–6 P.M. Mon.–Fri., 9 A.M.–8 P.M. Sat.–Sun., www.mitad-delmundo.com, $3) lies just beyond the village of **Pomasqui,** 14 kilometers north of the city.

The centerpiece is a 30-meter-high monument topped by a huge brass globe; a bright red line bisecting it provides the backdrop for the obligatory photo. However, whisper it quietly—the real Equator is actually a few hundred meters away.

It costs an extra $3 to go inside the monument, but it's well worth it for the excellent **ethnographic museum.** Ascend to the top in an elevator for impressive views over the surrounding valley, and then descend the stairs through nine floors of colorful exhibitions on a dozen of Ecuador's diverse indigenous cultures, filled with clothing and artwork. Tours are available in English and Spanish.

The rest of the complex has an assortment of attractions, some more interesting than others. The **France building** is the best, with a well-presented exhibition on the expedition led by Charles Marie de La Condamine

© BEN WESTWOOD

Take a photo at Mitad del Mundo with a foot in each hemisphere.

to plot the Equator in the mid-18th century. Another highlight is the intricate model of colonial Quito in the **Fundación Quito Colonial** ($1.50). The three-square-meter model took almost seven years to build and has labeled streets. Models of Cuenca, Guayaquil, and various old ships are also part of the display. There is also a **planetarium** with 40-minute presentations in Spanish ($1.50), artwork in the **Spain building,** and a small exhibition on insects in the **Ecuador room.** The **Heroes del Cenepa** monument near the entrance is dedicated to the soldiers killed in border clashes with Peru in 1995.

On the weekend, the square hosts colorful music and dance performances, and it's a very pleasant place to relax over lunch or a snack in the cluster of cafés.

Tourist agencies offer package tours to Pululahua and Rumicucho. **Calimatours** (tel. 2/239-4796 or 2/239-4797), with an office inside the Mitad del Mundo complex, has tours leaving 10 A.M.–1 P.M. for $8 pp.

To get here, take the Metrobus on Avenida América to the Ofelia terminal and catch the connecting Mitad del Mundo bus.

◖ Museo de Sitio Intiñan

If you've come all this way to stand on the Equator, it's a bit of a shock to hear that the Mitad del Mundo complex was built in the wrong place by a few hundred meters. Understandably, this is kept rather quiet, and you could easily miss the excellent **Museo de Sitio Intiñan** (tel. 2/239-5122, www.museointinan.com.ec, 9:30 A.M.–5 P.M. daily, $3). Located about 300 meters east of the Mitad del Mundo complex, its name means "Museum of the Path of the Sun" in Kichwa, and the family that owns and operates it has done a great job with the collection, which includes displays on local plants and indigenous cultures. However, the real reason to come here are the experiments that you are invited to participate in to prove this really is the site of the Equator—flushing water in opposite directions on either side of the line, walking along the line and feeling the strong gravitational pull

The Equator is actually at Museo de Sitio Intiñan.

on either side, and the nearly impossible task of balancing an egg on the Equator (you get a certificate if you can do it).

Pululahua Crater and Geobotanical Reserve

About five kilometers north of Mitad del Mundo, the 3,200-hectare Pululahua Reserve ($5 pp) sits inside an extinct volcanic crater. Pululahua bubbled with lava thousands of years ago, but these days the main activity is that of farmers who reside in its flat, fertile bottom. The reserve was officially created in 1978 to protect the rich subtropical ecosystem within one of the largest inhabited craters in South America and possibly the world.

Regular buses and taxis take the road from the base of Mitad del Mundo's pedestrian avenue toward the village of Calacalí. Along the way, a dirt lane leaves the road to the right, after the gas station, and climbs to the lip of the crater at Moraspungo. You can also hike to Pululahua up a road between San Antonio de Pichincha and Calacalí, passing the Ventanilla

The dramatic descent into the Pululahua crater makes a great hike.

viewpoint; this becomes a path that continues down into the crater.

El Crater (Pululahua, tel./fax 2/243-9254, from $91 s or d) is a hotel that perches on the edge of the crater. The panoramic view from the large windows justifies the prices of its restaurant (lunch and dinner daily, entrées $9–12). There's also a smaller café that sells drinks and snacks.

A few hours' hike will bring you to the bottom of the crater and left up the Calacalí road to a very basic **hikers refuge,** where you can spend the night; the stay is included with your admission to the reserve. Bring your own food, because there aren't any restaurants in the crater, and bring your own bedding. Hike over the rims to rejoin the paved road to Calacalí (10–15 kilometers, 3–4 hours), where you can catch a bus back to the Mitad del Mundo. It's also possible to circle the crater rim on foot. **Horseback tours** of the crater are available through Astrid Müller's **Green Horse Ranch** (tel. 9/971-5933, ranch@accessinter.net, www. horseranch.de) in Quito.

Rumicucho Ruins

Often tacked onto the end of tours of the area, the modest pre-Inca Rumicucho Ruins (7:30 A.M.–5 P.M. daily, $1 pp) consist of a series of rough stone walls and terraces on a small hilltop with a commanding view of the windswept surroundings. To get here, take 13 de Junio (the main drag) northeast from San Antonio de Pichincha, then turn right at the Rumicucho sign. It's quite hard to find, so ask around locally or take a taxi.

THE PICHINCHAS

The twin peaks that give the province its name tower over Quito, dominating the landscape as much as the city's history. It was on the flanks of these volcanoes that Ecuador won its independence in 1822. Both are named Pichincha, which is thought to come from indigenous words meaning "the weeper of good water." **Rucu** (Elder) is actually shorter (4,700 meters) and nearer to the city, while **Guagua** (Baby) stands 4,794 meters high and has always been the more poorly behaved of the two.

MEASURING THE EARTH

By 1735, most people agreed that the earth was round, but another question remained: *how* round was it? Some scientists theorized that the rotation of the earth caused it to bulge outward slightly in the middle, while others found that idea ridiculous. With explorers setting out daily to the far corners of the globe, it became more and more important to determine how much, if any, the earth bulged in the middle, since navigational charts off by a few degrees could send ships hundreds of kilometers in the wrong direction.

To answer the long-standing debate, the French Academy of Sciences organized two expeditions to determine the true shape of the earth. One team headed north to Lapland, as close to the Arctic as possible. The other left for Ecuador on the equator. Each team was tasked with measuring one degree of latitude, about 110 kilometers, in its respective region. If the length of the degree at the equator proved longer than the degree near the Arctic, then the earth bulged. If they were the same length, it didn't.

The Ecuadorian expedition was the first organized scientific expedition to South America. At the time, Ecuador was part of the Spanish territory of Upper Peru. It was chosen because of its accessibility – much easier to visit than alternate locations along the equator in the Amazon basin, Africa, and Southeast Asia. The Ecuadorian expedition was led by academy members Louis Godin, Pierre Bouguer, and Charles Marie de La Condamine.

With them came seven other Frenchmen, including a doctor-botanist, Godin's cousin, a surgeon, a naval engineer, and a draftsman.

Tensions hampered the expedition from the start, as Bouguer and La Condamine quickly learned they did not get along. Bouguer was stern, stoic, and accused of being paranoid about competitors, while La Condamine, a protégé of Voltaire, was comparatively easygoing. This personal rivalry sparked numerous quarrels as the extroverted, enthusiastic La Condamine effectively assumed leadership of the expedition.

The group arrived in Cartagena, Colombia, in 1735. There they were joined by two Spaniards, both naval captains under secret orders from the king of Spain to report back on the French expedition and conditions in the Spanish territories. In March 1736 the party sailed into Ecuador's Pacific port of Manta and soon traveled via Guayaquil to Quito. Quiteños received the earth measurers with delight, and dances and receptions filled the days following their arrival. As the festivities continued, Pedro Vicente Maldonado, an Ecuadorian mapmaker and mathematician, was chosen to join the historic expedition.

Eventually, the group got down to business. For the sake of accuracy, it was decided that the measurements would be made in the flat plains near Yaruquí, 19 kilometers northeast of Quito. As the work progressed, troubles mounted. The French and Spanish, unused to the elevation and the cold of the Sierra, began

---

Climbing Rucu is easier and more accessible, requiring no special equipment. Unfortunately, the trail to Rucu has been plagued by robberies in recent years. The opening of the *teleférigo* (cable car) has led to increased security, but it is wise to inquire locally about the current situation. Currently there are security patrols on the route from Cruz Loma on the weekend but not during the week.

Guagua sat quiet following an eruption in 1660 until October 1999, when it blew out a huge mushroom cloud of ash that blotted out the sun over Quito for a day and covered the capital in ash. Although things seem to have calmed down, you should still check for the latest update on Guagua, which is officially highly active.

Private transportation—preferably a 4WD vehicle—is almost essential to reach Guagua, the farther peak. The starting point is the pueblo of **Lloa,** southwest of Quito. A dirt road leaves the main plaza and heads up the valley between the Pichinchas, ending in a shelter maintained by the national civil

to fall ill. Soon the group suffered its first death: the nephew of the academy's treasurer, one of the youngest team members.

As the mourning scientists wandered the plains with their strange instruments, local residents grew suspicious. Rumors began circulating that they had come to dig up and steal buried treasure, maybe even Inca gold. The situation became so tense that La Condamine and a fellow member of the expedition were forced to travel to Lima to obtain the viceroy's support. They finally returned in July 1737 with official papers supporting their story. The measurements continued, and by 1739 the goal of determining the true shape of the earth was in sight. Then disastrous news arrived from the academy: The Lapland expedition had succeeded. The earth was flattened at the poles. The verdict was already in.

As La Condamine tried to keep the expedition from disintegrating, more bad luck struck. The party surgeon, Juan Seniergues, became involved in a dispute over a Cuencan woman and was beaten and stabbed to death at a bullfight in the Plaza de San Sebastián by an angry mob sympathetic to his local rival, the woman's former fiancé. The rest of the group sought refuge in a monastery. In the confusion, the team botanist, Joseph de Jussieu, lost his entire collection of plants – representing five years' work, this loss eventually cost him his sanity as well. The team draftsman was then killed in a fall from a church steeple near Riobamba. La Condamine had to fend off accu-

sations from the Spanish crown that he had insulted Spain by omitting the names of the two Spanish officers from commemorative plaques he had already erected at Oyambaro.

Finally, in March 1743, the remaining scientists made the last measurements, confirming the Lapland expedition's findings and bringing the expedition to an end. Even though they had come in second, the group's efforts did lay the foundation for the entire modern metric system. Some members decided to stay on in Ecuador – two had already married local women – while others traveled to different South American countries. Most went back to Europe. La Condamine, accompanied by Maldonado, rode a raft down the Amazon for four months to the Atlantic Ocean. From there, the pair sailed to Paris, where they brought the first samples of rubber seen in Europe and were welcomed as heroes. Maldonado died of measles in 1748, while La Condamine enjoyed the high life in Paris until his death in 1774.

In 1936, on the 200th anniversary of the expedition's arrival in Ecuador, the Ecuadorian government built a stone pyramid on the equator at San Antonio de Pichincha in honor of the explorers and their work. This pyramid was eventually replaced by the 30-meter-tall monument that stands today at Mitad del Mundo. Busts along the path leading to the monument commemorate the 10 Frenchmen, two Spaniards, and one Ecuadorian who risked their lives – and sanity – for science.

defense directorate. Park here, pay the entry fee ($1), which goes toward the guardian's salary, and don't leave anything of value in the car. Sleeping space for 10 people costs $5 pp per night, including running water and cooking facilities.

Another hour's hike will bring you from the shelter to the summit. The west-facing crater is pocked by smoking fumaroles, active domes, and collapsed craters. A rocky protrusion called the Cresta del Gallo (Rooster's Crest) separates the old inactive side to the south from the

newer active area to the north. Several climbing tour operators in Quito offer this trip.

HOSTERÍA SAN JORGE

Four kilometers up the road from Cotocollao to Nono in a 93-hectare mountain reserve is Hostería San Jorge (Vía Antigua a Nono Km. 4, tel. 2/224-7549, www.hostsanjorge.com. ec, $67 s, $73 d), run by the friendly and enthusiastic George Cruz. The traditional country house, once owned by former Ecuadorian president Eloy Alfaro, offers wonderful views of the Quito valley from 3,000 meters up the Pichincha foothills. Gardens, a lake, and a spring-fed swimming pool and hot tub surround the guest rooms warmed by fireplaces on chilly evenings. It is a good place to acclimate, and the owners offer a wealth of activities, including birding in the backyard and treks on pre-Inca trails to the coast. The Mindo and Nono areas are within mountain-biking distance. You can get here by taxi or call for pickup.

SANGOLQUÍ

Corn is king in this town southeast of Quito. A 10-meter statue of a cob, called "El Choclo," greets visitors in a traffic circle at the entrance. In late June, festivities mark the end of the harvest. During the fourth and final day, bullfights become venues for raging displays of machismo as alcohol-numbed locals try to get as close to the bull as possible without getting killed—unsurprisingly, someone usually gets injured. The central plaza area has been beautifully restored, and the town hosts an excellent indigenous market on Sundays and a smaller one on Thursdays. To get here, take a "Sangolquí" bus from the local terminal at Marin Bajo.

PASOCHOA PROTECTED FOREST

The densest, most unspoiled stretch of forest close to Quito is the Pasochoa Protected Forest (open daily, $5 pp), 30 kilometers southeast of the city. A long sloping valley preserves the original lush wooded state of the area surrounding Quito. The reserve ranges 2,700–4,200 meters in elevation, the highest point being Cerro Pasochoa, an extinct volcano. Primary and secondary forest topped by *páramo* supports 126 species of birds, including many hummingbirds and a family of condors.

Loop paths of varying lengths and difficulty lead higher and higher into the hills, ranging 2–8 hours in length. It's also possible to climb to the lip of Cerro Pasochoa's blasted volcanic crater in six hours. Campsites and a few dorm rooms with showers and cooking facilities are available near the bottom. Free guided tours are sometimes available.

To get here from Quito, take a bus marked "Playón" from the south end of the Plaza La Marín below Old Town to the village of Amaguaña (30–40 minutes, $0.60). Hire a pickup ($5–8) from the plaza in Amaguaña to the turnoff for the reserve, which is marked by a green sign facing south one kilometer toward Machachi on the Panamericana. From there, a dirt road leads seven kilometers up a rough, cobbled road to the reserve. Drivers may agree to come back for you, or you could catch a ride down with the reserve personnel in the evening. Take a phone card, and you can call from the cell phone at the entrance for a taxi to pick you up.

Some tour operators in Quito offer group day trips to Pasochoa.

NORTHERN SIERRA AND WESTERN ANDEAN SLOPES

Ecuador's northern highlands, which stretch from Quito to the Colombian border, contain spectacular mountain scenery and picturesque towns inhabited by thriving indigenous communities. With so much on offer for hikers and shoppers alike, it's no surprise that this is one of the country's most popular regions for visitors. Many of the highlights are just a few hours from Quito, but it may surprise you how easily you can leave the beaten path and find yourself in rural areas and nature reserves far from the tourist crowds.

Otavalo's textile market, one of the most spectacular in South America, is the biggest draw in the region, and many of the smaller villages around Otavalo specialize in particular crafts, so there are rich pickings on offer for those seeking handmade clothing, jewelry, and ornaments. For nature lovers, several spectacular

lagoons are close by—notably Laguna Cuicocha and Lagunas de Mojanda, and this region also contains some impressive peaks—Imbabura, Cotacachi, and snow-capped Cayambe.

Farther north, the quiet colonial "White City" of Ibarra is larger but less visited. Fewer visitors make it up to Tulcán unless they're crossing to Colombia, but the town's famous topiary cemetery is another highlight of the region.

Parks and nature reserves offer hiking, camping, and mountaineering. The Cotacachi-Cayapas and Cayambe-Coca Ecological Reserves spill from the highlands into the coastal lowlands and the Oriente, respectively. Many smaller private reserves, such as Intag and Cerro Golondrinas, are tucked into the corners of the larger ones. After a long hike, ease those aching limbs in hot springs that

© RUNA TUPARI

HIGHLIGHTS

◖ Mindo: This sleepy town, nestled in the cloud forest, teems with toucans, hummingbirds, quetzals, and butterflies. Adrenaline seekers can fly across the forest canopy on zip-lines or plunge down the river rapids (page 78).

◖ Textile Market: Otavalo's textile market, held every Saturday, is one of the best on the continent – patterned ponchos, sweaters, embroidered shirts, handmade jewelry, and felt hats are all on sale, so haggle away (page 90).

◖ Lagunas de Mojanda and Fuya Fuya: Explore these three beautiful lagoons high above the valley in the shadow of jagged mountains. Nearby Fuya Fuya is excellent practice for climbing more challenging peaks (page 98).

◖ Laguna Cuicocha: This 200-meter-deep crater lake in the shadow of Volcán Cotacachi is one of Ecuador's most stunning sights. Hike around it or take a boat through the canal between two volcanic cones in the center (page 102).

◖ Tulcán's Municipal Cemetery: With its extraordinary topiary works, this graveyard has been called "so beautiful, it invites one to die" (page 117).

LOOK FOR ◖ TO FIND RECOMMENDED SIGHTS, ACTIVITIES, DINING, AND LODGING.

bubble up from the hillsides. The best example is at Chachimbiro, northwest of Ibarra.

Some of the region's most beautiful scenery is found at Mindo, a small town on the western Andean slopes. It is a bird-watcher's paradise surrounded by cloud forest, waterfalls, rushing rivers, and an incredible diversity of birds and butterflies.

PLANNING YOUR TIME

The northern Sierra is the most compact Andean region covered in this book, and its highlights can easily be seen in under five days. If you want to visit a remote private reserve or get off the beaten track, give yourself at least a week.

Otavalo makes the best base, with Ibarra a

viable alternative. **Otavalo's textiles market** and other indigenous markets fill a day, while hikes to **Laguna Cuicocha,** part of the gigantic Cotacachi-Cayapas Ecological Reserve, and **Lagunas de Mojanda** take a day or two. The area around Ibarra can fill another couple of days, and if you want to do some climbing in the region, factor in an extra couple of days. Farther north is the chilly, otherworldly expanse of **El Angel Ecological Reserve.** At the Colombian border, **Tulcán's municipal cemetery** is one of the most beautiful in South America and worth a few hours.

The cloud forests around **Mindo** are a great way to spend a day or two, or they can easily be seen briefly as a day trip from Quito.

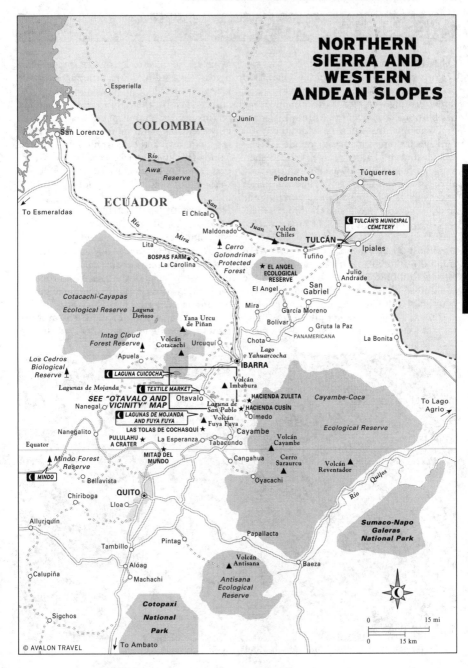

NORTHERN
SIERRA AND
WESTERN
ANDEAN SLOPES

Esperiella

COLOMBIA

Junín

San Lorenzo

Río
Awa
Reserve

Piedrancha

Túquerres

ECUADOR

To Esmeraldas

Río

Mira

El Chical

Lita

BOSPAS FARM
La Carolina

Maldonado

Cerro
Golondrinas
Protected
Forest

San

Juan

Volcán Chiles

TULCÁN

Tufiño

TULCÁN'S MUNICIPAL
CEMETERY

Ipiales

Julio
Andrade

EL ANGEL
ECOLOGICAL
RESERVE

El Angel

San
Gabriel

Cotacachi-Cayapas
Ecological Reserve

Laguna
Doñoso

Yana Urcu
de Piñán

Mira

García Moreno

Bolívar

Gruta la Paz

La Bonita

Intag Cloud
Forest Reserve

Volcán
Cotacachi

Urcuqui

Chota

PANAMERICANA

Lago
Yahuarcocha

Los Cedros
Biological
Reserve

Apuela

IBARRA

Lagunas de Mojanda

LAGUNA CUICOCHA

Volcán
Imbabura

Nanegal

TEXTILE MARKET

SEE "OTAVALO AND
VICINITY" MAP

Otavalo

Laguna de
San Pablo

HACIENDA ZULETA

HACIENDA CUSÍN

Olmedo

Cayambe-Coca

To Lago
Agrio

Nanegalito

LAGUNAS DE MOJANDA
AND FUYA FUYA

Volcán
Fuya Fuya

Cayambe

Ecological Reserve

Equator

LAS TOLAS DE COCHASQUÍ

PULULAHU
A CRATER

La Esperanza

Tabacundo

Volcán
Cayambe

MITAD DEL
MUNDO

Mindo Forest
Reserve

MINDO

Bellavista

Cangahua

Cerro
Saraurcu

Volcán
Reventador

Volcán
Antisana

Río

Quijos

Chiriboga

Lloa

QUITO

Oyacachi

Alluriquín

Sumaco-Napo
Galeras
National Park

Tambillo

Pintag

Papallacta

Calupiña

Alóag

Machachi

Volcán
Antisana

Baeza

Sigchos

Cotopaxi
National
Park

Antisana
Ecological
Reserve

© AVALON TRAVEL

To Ambato

0   15 mi

0   15 km

Western Andean Slopes

NORTHERN SIERRA

◖ MINDO

Set in a tranquil valley at an ideal elevation of 1,250 meters, surrounded by dense cloud forest teeming with birdlife, this small village has blossomed in recent years into Ecuador's best hub for bird-watchers. More than 400 bird species found in the surrounding forest include toucans, barbets, golden-headed quetzals, and hummingbirds galore, and there are also 250 species of butterflies and 80 species of orchids. Mindo isn't all about watching the trees, however; you can also fly through them on canopy zip-lines if you want a more action-packed trip.

Almost 21,000 hectares of forest, from tropical rainforest to *páramo,* fall within the **Mindo-Nambillo Protected Forest,** to the east and south of town. The rushing Mindo, Nambillo, and Cinto Rivers drain the area, and there are several waterfalls near Mindo. It's relatively easy to explore parts of the forest alone, but for a better-quality experience, particularly for bird-watchers, hiring a local guide is recommended.

Mindo is still a relatively low-key place and retains a village atmosphere with few cars. However, more and more hotels are springing up in town and the surrounding area, and Mindo fills up on the weekend with day-trippers from Quito, so consider coming during the week for a quieter experience.

Recreation and Tours

Mindo is filled with knowledgeable **bird-watching guides** who can lead you through the forests at dawn to see toucans and quetzals and also up to leks where brilliant crimson-colored Andean cock-of-the-rock males compete for females. Most guides charge small groups $50 for half-day trips and $100 for a full day. Vinicio Pérez, owner of the **Birdwatchers House** (Colibries, tel. 2/217-0204 or

Zip-lining across the canopy in Mindo is exhilarating.

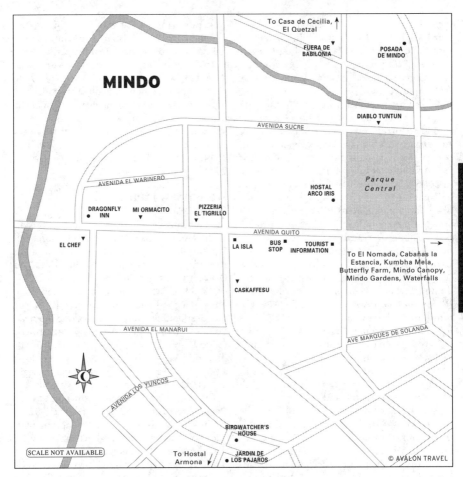

9/947-6867, vinicioperez@birdwatchers-house.com), is highly recommended. Other recommended guides include Marcelo Arias at **Ruby Birdwatcher's Place** (tel. 9/340-6321), Danny Jumbo (tel. 9/328-0796), and Julia Patiño (tel. 8/616-2816). For extended bird-watching tours in Mindo and elsewhere in Ecuador, contact **Andean Birding** (Salazar Gómez E-1482 at Eloy Alfaro, tel. 9/418-4592, www.andeanbirding.com) in Quito.

A German-Ecuadorian couple owns seven hectares of land uphill from Mindo called **Mindo Lindo** (tel. 9/291-5840, www.mindolindo.com), which offers easier access to the cloud forest than other properties in town. They charge $4 pp to use the trails and $20 pp for accommodations.

Southeast of town is the best access point into the **Bosque Protector Mindo-Nambillo** cloud forest. The road leads past several sets of accommodations before splitting. Take the left fork to reach the butterfly farm **Mariposas de Mindo** (www.mariposasdemindo.com, 9 A.M.–6:30 P.M. daily, $5), which breeds 25 species, including the brown owl eye and the Peleides blue morpho, the latter with a wingspan of 20 centimeters. The tour follows the life cycle from eggs to caterpillars to pupae to butterflies. Come in the early morning and you may see them hatch.

Where the road forks, walk up to the right to reach two sets of canopy-tour operators. The second company you come to, **Mindo Canopy Adventure** (tel. 8/542-8758, www.mindocanopy.com) was actually the first to bring their expert knowledge of zip-lines from Costa Rica in 2006. The company is fully accredited and has an excellent safety record. There are a total of 13 lines ranging up to 400 meters in length and 120 meters in height. You can spend 1.5 hours zipping across all 13 for $10 or do three lines for $5. Try out the "superman" or "butterfly" poses for extra fun. There is also a new "extreme Tarzan" swing, a 40-meter-long pendulum. The newer company, local-run **Mindo Ropes and Canopy** (tel. 9/172-5874, www.mindoropescanopy.com), offers 10 zip-lines for $10. A taxi from town costs $3.

If you haven't had your fill of adrenaline kicks, an unusual alternative to rafting is **tubing**—tumbling down the river rapids in an inflatable tube. This can be arranged with any of the agencies in Mindo ($8 pp).

About one kilometer up the hill from the canopy companies is a more relaxed way to travel across the treetops. The **La Tarabita** ($5 pp) cable car cruises 150 meters above a river basin, and on the far side there are trails leading to seven **waterfalls.** Although the paths are not well marked, you're unlikely to get lost because the route is circular. The entire circuit takes about two hours, and it gets muddy in places. Bring boots and waterproof clothing as there is regular rainfall. Access to the waterfall trails is included in the cost of the cable car. There is another waterfall on the opposite side, **Tambillo** ($3 pp), where you can swim or slide downstream. Walking up to La Tarabita and the waterfalls takes about an hour from town, so consider taking a taxi ($7).

A recommended tour operator that can organize all of these activities, including transportation, is **La Isla** (Av. Quito, tel. 2/217-0181, www.laislamindo.com), which has an office on Mindo's main street.

In Mindo, it's worth heading up to **El Quetzal,** a hotel north of town on 9 de Octubre, to see how chocolate is made. For $3.50 you get an hour-long explanation of the process and a free brownie, hot chocolate, or ice cream. West of town, **Mindo Lago** organizes an evening walk to listen to frogs (tel. 9/709-3544, www.mindolago.com.ec, 6:30 P.M. daily, $3.50).

Accommodations
IN MINDO
In the center of Mindo, the cheapest option is the **Hostal Arco Iris** (9 de Octubre, tel. 2/390-0405, $9 pp) on the plaza. On the main Avenida Quito, as you arrive in town, **The Dragonfly Inn** (Quito and Sucre, tel. 2/217-0426, $27 s, $46 d), a new wooden cabin–style hotel, is a good mid-range choice, with balconies overlooking a garden patio along the river. For a more intimate setting, **⊂ Caskaffesu** (Sixto Durán Ballén, tel. 2/217-0100, $16 s or d), run by an American-Ecuadorian couple, is a very good deal with cozy guest rooms, a leafy courtyard, and a good restaurant.

On the northern edge of town, **Casa de Cecilia** (north of 9 de Octubre, tel. 2/217-0243, $6.50–7.50 pp) is the best budget option, with guest rooms in two rustic cabins on the edge of a roaring river. Next door, **El Quetzal** (north of 9 de Octubre, tel. 2/217-0034, www.elquetzaldemindo.com, $17 pp, breakfast included) has three guest rooms and lots of chocolate made on the premises. **Posada de Mindo** (Vicente Aguirre, tel. 2/217-0199, $20 pp) has spotless new cabins with a good restaurant attached.

Walking southwest of the main street along Colibries are two great-value mid-range options. On the right, **Jardín de Los Pájaros** (Colibries, tel. 2/217-0159, $14 s, $26 d, breakfast included) has comfortable guest rooms, a balcony lounge, and a small heated pool. Across the street, **The Birdwatcher's House** (Colibries, tel. 2/217-0204, www.birdwatchershouse.com, $15 pp) has stunning photographs in the guest rooms, hummingbirds in the gardens, and an outdoor jetted tub. Farther down the street, another rustic place adjoining the soccer field is the friendly **Hostal Armonia** (Colibries, tel. 2/217-0131, $14 pp), which is packed full of orchids and has private cabins with hot water. Nonguests can visit the impressive orchid garden ($2). The **Hostal Rubby** (tel. 2/217-0417 or 9/193-1853, $8–16 pp) has two classes of rooms and is in the process of moving to the edge of town.

VICINITY OF MINDO

Walking east of town toward the reserve, there are plenty of pleasant cabins set in the forest. The first is **Cabañas la Estancia** (tel. 9/878-3272, www.mindohosterialaestancia. com, $15 pp), with spacious cabins across a rickety bridge set in landscaped gardens with an outdoor restaurant, a swimming pool, and even a waterslide. Camping is available (from $3 pp). Deeper in the forest is **Kumbha Mela** (tel. 9/405-1675, dorm $16 pp, cabin $21 pp) with cabins and guest rooms nestled in extensive gardens. There's a good restaurant, a pool, and a private lagoon.

Past the Butterfly Farm is one of the best options in town, ◖ **Mindo Gardens** (tel. 9/722-3260, www.mindogardens.com, $50–65 s or d, breakfast included), with comfy, brightly colored cabins on a 300-hectare private reserve of forest and waterfalls. There's a restaurant right on the Río Mindo, and the cabins have private baths with hot water.

Near the Mindo Gardens Lodge, **El Monte Sustainable Lodge** (tel. 2/217-0102, www.ecuadorcloudforest.com, $96 pp) is run by American Tom Quesenberry and his Ecuadorian wife, Mariela Tenorio. They offer three wooden cabins at the edge of the Río Mindo with hot water, private baths, and thatched roofs. Rates include all meals and birding guides for the hiking trails nearby. To reach the lodge, cross the river on a small cable car.

Food

Eating out in Mindo is far more varied than it used to be, and the main street, Avenida Quito, is lined with restaurants. The best of these is **El Chef** (Quito and Colibries, tel. 2/390-0478, 8 A.M.–8 P.M. daily, entrées $4–7), where the set lunch is great value at $2.50 and the specialty is thick, juicy barbecued steak. Other options on Avenida Quito include **Mi Ormacito** (Av. Quito, no phone, lunch and dinner daily, entrées $4–5) for seafood, and the pizzeria **El Tigrillo** (Av. Quito, no phone, lunch and dinner daily, entrées $4–7) for Italian. Most of the best options are off the main street, however. For a more refined dining experience, try **Caskaffesu** (Sixto Durán Ballén and Quito, tel. 2/217-0100, 8 A.M.–10 P.M. daily, entrées $4–8) with steak, fish, and vegetarian dishes. East of the center is the best pizza in town, made in front of you in a wood-burning clay oven at **El Nómada** (Av. Quito, tel. 2/390-0460, noon–9 P.M. daily, entrées $6–9). North of town, **Fuera de Babilonia** (9 de Octubre, tel. 9/475-7768, 7:30 A.M.–9:30 P.M. daily, entrées $4–5) is great for seafood and local specialties like steamed trout. It is a funky little place with indigenous artifacts and misshapen tables, and it is a good place to hang out after dinner for a few drinks and listen to music. Nightlife in Mindo is limited, but on the weekend a few discos open in the center, including **Diablo Tuntun** (north end of Parque Central, no phone, 8 P.M.–2 A.M. Fri.–Sat., $1).

Information

There's a **Centro de Información** (8:30 A.M.–12:30 P.M. and 1:30–5 P.M. Wed.–Sun.) on Avenida Quito near the plaza. Ask for a list of members of the local naturalist guides association. Alternately, staff at **La Isla** (Av. Quito, tel. 2/217-0181, www.laislamindo.com) farther down the street are very helpful and knowledgeable.

Getting There

The road from Quito to Mindo runs west from Mitad del Mundo. It joins the old road just north of Mindo and continues west to Los Bancos and Puerto Quito. An eight-kilometer road connects Mindo to the main highway.

Direct buses from Quito with the **Flor del Valle** cooperative leave at 8 A.M., 9 A.M., and 4 P.M. Monday–Friday; 7:40 A.M., 8:20 A.M., 9:20 A.M., and 4 P.M. Saturday; and 7:40 A.M., 8:20 A.M., 9:20 A.M., 2 P.M., and 5 P.M. Sunday. Daily buses return from Mindo to Quito at 6:30 A.M., 1:45 P.M., and 3 P.M. Monday–Friday; 6:30 A.M., 2 P.M., 3:30 P.M., and 5 P.M. Saturday, with extra buses at 3 P.M. and 4 P.M. Sunday.

If you miss the bus from Quito, take a taxi to Carcelén terminal and take the first bus to Los Bancos, which drops you on the main road at the top of the hill above Mindo, where you can catch a taxi (from $1). Leaving Mindo, take a taxi to the main road and flag down any Quito-bound bus.

MAQUIPUCUNA BIOLOGICAL RESERVE

Less than three hours from Quito, more than 4,500 rugged hectares purchased by the Nature Conservancy in 1988 protect the Maquipucuna Biological Reserve ($10 pp), one of the last remaining chunks of cloud forest in northwestern Ecuador. Most of this privately owned and managed reserve is undisturbed primary forest, ranging from a low-elevation (1,200-meter) subtropical zone to cloud forest at the base of 2,800-meter Cerro Montecristi. It's surrounded by another 14,000 hectares of protected forest.

Temperatures range 14–24°C, allowing thousands of plant species to thrive in a wide range of climates. More than 330 species of birds include the cock-of-the-rock and the empress brilliant hummingbird. The reserve is also the first place where spectacled bears have been reintroduced into the wild. Wander farther afield and chances are you'll stumble across a burial mound or a *culunco*—a half trail, half tunnel between the Andes and the Oriente—left by the pre-Inca Yumbo people.

Next to the open-air Thomas Davis Ecotourism Center, at 1,200 meters elevation, the reserve has 10 guest rooms (tel. 2/250-7200, www.maqui.org, $73–96 s, $134–184 d, includes three meals) with shared or private baths.

To get to the reserve, take a bus from Quito's Ofelia station to Nanegal, the nearest village to Maquipucuna. From Nanegal, you'll have to hire a truck or taxi ($10) to take you to Marianitas, which is four kilometers from the reserve entrance.

For more information, contact the Fundación Maquipucuna in Quito (Baquerizo Moreno 238 y Tamayo, tel. 2/250-7200, www.maqui.org).

YANACOCHA

The old Nono–Mindo road offers great birding along most of its length. One particularly good spot is the 964-hectare Yanacocha reserve ($5 pp) of elfin *Polylepis* forest in the Pichincha foothills, which protects wildlife from agricultural expansion in the region. Take a turnoff to the left (south) 18 kilometers from Quito and drive up to the gate. The entry fee helps the Fundación Jocotoco (www.fjocotoco.org) protect special bird areas around Ecuador. Twenty-two species of hummingbirds have been spotted in the vicinity, including the endangered black-breasted puffleg, which only lives in this region and has recently been adopted as the emblem of Quito.

TANDAYAPA LODGE

Iain Campbell, a geology expert turned birding guide, runs this luxury birder lodge along the old Nono–Mindo road. He bills Tandayapa (Reina Victoria 1684 at La Pinta, Ed. Santiago 1, Dep. 501, tel./fax 2/244-7520, www.tandayapa.com, $126 s, $213 d, all meals included) as "the only lodge in the world designed by birders, owned by birders, and run for birders by birders." You can tell it's the real thing: 4 A.M. breakfasts are no problem, and they've already planted 30,000 trees in the immediate area to help combat deforestation.

The 12 guest rooms all have private baths with hot water. They're in a single building with a fireplace, a bar, and a balcony overlooking the cloud forest, making it easy to start your day with new sightings. They've seen 18 species of hummingbirds from the balcony feeders alone, and a total of 320 species of birds on their trails. Many species are "staked out," meaning the guides know where they are on a regular basis. Three–five-day packages that include guides and transportation are available.

To reach Tandayapa, either head up the old Nono–Mindo road (now called the Ecoruta Paseo del Quindé) or take the new road and get off the bus at the turnoff at Km. 52. It's seven kilometers to the lodge from there (11 kilometers from Nanegalito).

BELLAVISTA CLOUD FOREST RESERVE

British ecologist and teacher Richard Parsons started the reserve with 55 hectares of prime cloud forest near the town of Tandayapa in 1991, where he built a four-story thatched-roof lodge looking out over the moss-covered treetops. The ground floor of the geodesic dome—one of most distinctive accommodations in Ecuador—encloses the living and dining rooms, while guest rooms upstairs have private baths, hot water, and balconies with hummingbird feeders. Interested ornithologists and friends have helped increase the size of the reserve to 700 hectares, and three comfortable houses plus a research station for students and scientists have all been added. The reserve includes four waterfalls and 10 kilometers of trails where birders can search the premontane cloud forest (1,400–2,600 meters elevation) for the tanager finch, giant antpitta, and white-faced nunbird that frequent nearby streams.

Visits are arranged through the reserve's office in Quito (Jorge Washington E7-23 at 6 de Diciembre, tel./fax 2/223-2313, www.bellavistacloudforest.com). Private guest rooms ($66 s, 102 d or $98 s, $166 d with meals) are available in the dome buildings, and upstairs are dorms ($32 pp or $55 pp with meals). For more privacy, choose one of the three newer houses for the same rates. Campsites ($6 pp) are available, as is hostel-style lodging in the research station ($18 pp). Day trips from Quito ($115 s, $190 d) include guides, transportation, and two meals; 2–3-day packages are also possible.

Transportation can be arranged from Quito, or take a public bus to Nanegalito from the terminal at Ofelia. Any bus to Pacto, Puerto Quito, San Miguel de los Bancos, or Mindo passes Nanegalito. Ask in Nanegalito about renting a pickup truck ($15) to travel the last 15 kilometers to the reserve. If you're driving yourself, head for Mitad del Mundo and Calacalí on the new road to Esmeraldas, and then turn left at Km. 52, just across a bridge (look for the "Bellavista" sign). Follow this road six kilometers to the village of Tandayapa, then uphill another six kilometers to the reserve. You can also continue on the road to Esmeraldas through the town of Nanegalito to Km. 62, then turn left and follow signs along the ridge for 12 kilometers to Bellavista. The third access is at Km. 77, just one kilometer from the Mindo entrance; the road to the reserve is 12 unpaved kilometers.

Quito to Otavalo

LAS TOLAS DE COCHASQUÍ

On the road from Quito to Otavalo, northwest of Tabacundo, are the ruins of 15 flat-topped pre-Inca pyramids at Cochasquí (8:30 A.M.–4:30 P.M. Tues.–Sun., $3), one of Ecuador's most important archaeological sites. Built by the Cara people at an elevation of 3,100 meters in A.D. 900, this eight-hectare site reached its peak around 1200 with an estimated local population of 70,000. Its strategic hilltop position indicates that it was either a fortress or an observatory—excavations have revealed platforms thought to be calendars on top of pyramid 14. Two circular platforms represent the sun and moon, and the shadows thrown by upright stones are thought to have marked the best times to plant and harvest. The site was abandoned long before the Spanish conquest

THE LANGUAGE OF THE INCAS

More people speak Kichwa (also written *Quechua*) today than in the 16th century when the last Inca died. The language is currently experiencing a revival, encouraged by President Rafael Correa, who learned the language as a student. Indeed, some indigenous groups have recently stated a preference for their people to be referred to as "Kichwa" rather than "indigenous."

Many Kichwa words have become commonly used in English, including *condor, gaucho, jerky, llama, puma,* and *quinine*. South American Spanish is so full of Kichwa words, particularly words concerning food and clothing, that many nonindigenous locals are not even aware of their origin. Examples include *papa* (potato), *choclo* (corn), *chompa* (sweater), and more amusingly, *chuchaqui* (hangover).

Also known as *runasimi*, "the language of the people," Kichwa is pronounced similarly to Spanish, with the addition of glottal stops popped in the back of the throat and indicated by apostrophes (as in *hayk'aq*, meaning "when"). The consonant "q" is exaggerated until it sounds almost like the "g" in "guitar," and "th" is aspirated toward the sound of "t" alone. The stress is always on the next-to-last syllable.

- *ama sua, ama llulla, ama quella* – Don't steal, don't lie, don't be lazy (traditional Inca greeting)

- *quampas hinallantaq* – To you likewise (traditional response)

- *napaykullayki* – greetings

- *alli tuta manta* – good morning

- *alli p'unshaw* – good afternoon

- *alli tuta* – good evening

- *allichu* – please

- *imamanta* – What's up?/What's happening?

- *yupay chany* – Thanks for everything.

- *alli shamuska* – You're welcome.

- *tayta/mama* – sir/madam

- *wayki* – brother, friend (said to another man of the same age)

- *allinllachu kanki?* – How are you?

- *allimi* – fine

- *ima shuta kanki?* – What is your name?

- *ñuca...shutimi kani* – My name is…

- *maymanta shamunki?* – Where are you from?

- *Ñuca...-mi-manta kani* – I am from…

- *allilla* – good-bye

- *kavakama* – see you later

and rediscovered only in 1932. Three decades passed before excavations began into the earth-covered hills; one mound was found to contain 400 skulls, probably from ceremonial sacrifices.

The ruins are no comparison to Mexico's Chichén Itzá, and many of the pyramids are little more than large overgrown mounds, but the hilltop setting is dramatic with spectacular views over Quito, Cotopaxi, the Ilinizas mountains, and Antisana on clear days. Shamans still come here to absorb the site's "special energy,"

and festivals are held at the solstices (June 22 and December 22) and equinoxes (March 21 and September 23).

Visitors must be accompanied by a guide, and tours (included in the entrance fee) leave hourly. An outdoor scale model of the site makes it easier to visualize, and two small museums display artifacts found nearby; there are also traditional buildings with medicinal gardens. Campsites are available uphill of the ruins, and hiking up and over to the Lagunas de Mojanda makes a stunning six-hour trip.

Getting There

Take a bus to Otavalo from Quito's Carcelén terminal by way of Tabacundo (most buses take this route), and ask the driver to drop you off at the new tollbooths beyond Guayllabamba. From the cement sign for the ruins ("Pirámides de Cochasquí"), it is eight kilometers up a cobbled road to the site. If you plan on walking, bring water—it can be a hot two hours up-hill. Alternately, get off the bus at Tabacundo or Cayambe, take a taxi ($10 per hour) and arrange a pickup time. There are also guided tours available from operators in Quito.

CAYAMBE

The quiet little town of Cayambe (pop. 17,000) is overshadowed by the eponymous volcano that dominates the valley. Surrounded by the heavily cultivated pastures of old haciendas, Cayambe is the regional center of Ecuador's flower industry (the country's fourth largest export) and is also well-known for its cheese and *bizcochos* (a type of buttery cookie). Market day is Sunday; the traditional market plaza is several blocks up the hill from the church.

The **Inti Raymni** festival merges with the **Fiesta de San Pedro y Pablo** (Festival of Saints Peter and Paul) on June 28–29 and is celebrated with gusto in Cayambe and throughout the province. It's particularly important here because San Pedro is the town's patron saint. During the festival, the streets are filled with indigenous groups representing their communities. There may be more roosters suspended from poles than you'd ever expect to see. This is for the *entrega de gallo* (delivery of the rooster), a reminder of a colonial tradition in which hacienda workers gave the *patrón* (owner) a ceremonial gift of a rooster every year.

Outside festival time, there's not a huge amount to do in Cayambe, and the town has seen visitor numbers drop since most Quito–Otavalo buses bypass the town north of Tabacundo. Cayambe is pleasant enough, however, with a leafy **Parque Central** and the **Museum de la Ciudad** (8 A.M.–5 P.M. Wed.–Sun., free) with a small archaeological collection. It's also a good base for climbing Cayambe or Saraurcu to the east, or for visiting the ruins at Cochasquí to the west.

Accommodations and Food

In town, **Hotel El Refugio** (Terán and 10 de Agosto, tel. 2/236-3700, $8 s or d) has small, basic guest rooms. On the Parque Central, **Aroma** (Bolívar and Rocafuerte, no phone, 7 A.M.–9 P.M. daily, entrées $2–3) is a good choice for filling Ecuadorian meals. For more comfort, **Hotel La Gran Colombia** (Avenida Natalia Jarrín, tel. 2/236-1238, $15 s or d) is about 0.5 kilometers south of the city center. Guests enjoy TV, private baths, and a children's playground out back. The hotel's restaurant is popular with locals. Another 0.5 kilometers farther out is the **Hostería Mitad del Mundo** (Natalia Jarrín 208, tel. 2/236-0226, $7 pp), which boasts a covered pool, a sauna, and a steam room (not included, $4 pp). The clean rooms have private baths, hot water, and TVs.

By far the most interesting place to stay near Cayambe is ◖ **Hacienda Guachala** (tel. 2/236-3042, www.guachala.com, $44 s, $59 d), a 400-year-old estate straddling the equator 10 kilometers south of town. From the old saddles in the entrance hall to the 18th century murals in the chapel, this hacienda is steeped in history. It dates from 1580 and claims to be the oldest hacienda in Ecuador. La Condamine's globe measurers lodged here in 1743, and two centuries later the hacienda was inherited by Neptalí Bonifaz Ascázubi, who was elected president of Ecuador but then disqualified for being of Peruvian nationality. It was opened as a hotel in 1993.

An underground spring feeds the sun-heated pool, and you can browse through hundreds of pictures from the early 20th century in the photographic museum. The 30 guest rooms are simple and comfortable, there are three dining rooms, and horses and bicycles ($10 per hour) are available for exploring the surrounding countryside.

Getting There

Buses from Quito to Otavalo and Ibarra no

NORTHERN SIERRA

longer pass directly through Cayambe, so you can either change at Tabacundo or take a direct bus from Quito's Ofelia terminal (80 minutes, $1.50). From Otavalo ($0.70) it takes 45 minutes.

CAYAMBE-COCA ECOLOGICAL RESERVE

The second-largest Andean reserve in Ecuador, the Cayambe-Coca Ecological Reserve ($2 pp) stretches from the snowy heights of Cayambe down the eastern face of the Cordillera Oriental. The reserve's 4,000 square kilometers stretch across four provinces and range in elevation from 600 to 5,790 meters (the top of Cayambe). Three major peaks and more than 80 lakes dot the incredibly varied landscape, from alpine tundra to tropical forest. Most visitors come to climb the spectacular but difficult peak of Cayambe, but there is an enormous area to explore on foot, including a great multiday hike from the Andes down into the eastern rainforest. The park boasts some 900 species of birds, including the condor, mountain toucan, and Andean cock-of-the-rock.

Artifacts found in Cayambe-Coca provide evidence of a prehistoric migration from the Amazon to the Andes. Today, about 600 Cofán *indígenas* live in a handful of communities near the northeastern corner of the reserve. Visits to the area can be arranged through the Fundación Sobreviviencia Cofán through their Quito office (Mariano Cardenal N74-153 at Joaquín Mancheno, tel. 2/247-4763, www.cofan.org).

Descendants of the Caranqui people inhabit the southern, tropical part of the reserve as high as Oyacachi, where their ancestors fled after a massacre at the hands of the Inca at Lago Yahuarcocha.

Volcán Cayambe

The snow-capped top of Ecuador's third-highest peak (5,790 meters) is a unique and beautiful spot: It is not only the highest point in the world on the Equator but also the coldest, and it is the only place in the world where temperature and latitude reach zero simultaneously.

The name Cayambe means "water of life" in Kichwa, and the rivers that rush down from this wide, white mountain certainly give life to the surrounding valleys. Ironically, though, Cayambe also takes lives. It has the reputation of being a dangerous climb, especially since three famous Ecuadorian climbers were killed by an avalanche in 1974 on the mountain's slopes. Climbers Edward Whymper, Jean-Antoine Carrel, and Louis Carrel were the first to summit the volcano's northeast peak in 1880, but their route wasn't repeated until 1974 by Quito's San Gabriel Climbing Club.

Cayambe is recommended only for advanced climbers. Although it's only a seven-hour climb from the refuge to the summit, there are many obstacles—an ever changing network of crevasses, unusually high winds, strong snowstorms, and occasional avalanches. The Bergé-Oleas-Ruales refuge (4,600 meters) offers the services of a permanent guardian, a cooking stove, and hot showers for $16.50 pp per night. It's owned by the San Gabriel Climbing Club and is administered by Alta Montaña in Quito (tel. 2/252-4422 or 9/873-6181). Snacks, water, soda, and beer are for sale.

The IGM *Cayambe* and *Nevado Cayambe* 1:50,000 maps cover the mountain.

Cerro Saraurcu

One of the few nonvolcanic peaks in Ecuador, Cayambe's smaller sister, Cerro Saraurcu (4,676 meters), isn't climbed nearly as often as Cayambe. The "Corn Mountain" (from the Kichwa *sara,* meaning "corn") is also known, more ominously, as Devil Mountain in both Kichwa (Supaiurcu) and Spanish (Cerro del Diablo). Even so, it's an impressive and comparatively straightforward climb, aside from the terrible approach through kilometers of boggy *pantano* (marshland).

The IGM *Cangahua* and *Cerro Saraurcu* 1:50,000 maps cover the area.

Oyacachi Trail

One of the country's best hikes crosses the entire southern part of the reserve from

Cayambe, by way of Cangahua and Oyacachi, to El Chaco in the Oriente. The partly cobbled trail dates back to pre-Inca times and is probably the route that Gonzalo Pizarro used on his ill-fated trip to find the gold of Eldorado. It is strenuous with rough terrain; due to weather it is only easily passable November–March.

Trucks and buses leave hourly from Cayambe for Cangahua, the starting point for a full day's hike to Oyacachi (3,200 meters). If you just want to enjoy the **hot springs** at Oyacachi, buses leave Cayambe at 8 A.M. Saturday–Sunday, returning at 3 P.M. During the week, you will probably have to spend the night. There are now several small hostels ($10 pp) in Oyacachi, or you can camp near the hot springs across the river.

In Oyacachi, horses are available for trips as far as Cedro Grande (1–2 days) for about $10 per day, and guides can be hired for $20 per day plus food. To go farther, you'll probably have to pack all your supplies yourself, because the going gets rougher and the rivers widen. Forests nearby hide red-crested cotingas, gray-breasted mountain toucans, and the shining sunbeam hummingbird.

The trail east to El Chaco follows the left side of the Río Oyacachi. You'll have to cross a few rivers along the way. When the bridges are in good condition, that is no problem, but in places you need to cross using cables or a climbing harness and pulley. You have to ford the Ríos Cariaco, Chaupi, and Santa María during the descent to El Chaco (horses can go only as far as the Río Cedro). From the El Chaco end, the road continues toward the Río Santa María, which is much appreciated by kayakers who enjoy paddling the lower Oyacachi River. The entire hike from Oyacachi to El Chaco takes 2–3 days. Enquire at **Waterdog Tours** (Calle Ierac and Texaco, tel. 9/352-2152, www.waterdogtours.com) in El Chaco for rafting and kayaking trips.

The IGM *Oyacachi–Santa Rosa de Quijos* 1:50,000 map covers most of the hike.

Getting There

You can enter the Cayambe-Coca Ecological Reserve from a few different directions. From the west, the route that climbs Volcán Cayambe via Juan Montalvo and the Piemonte guard post is the most direct. Alternately, a recently paved road leads from the town of Cayambe through Olmedo and east to the Guaybambilla guard post and Laguna San Marcos. Here, at 3,400 meters, there is an interpretive center, paths, and campsites. Alternately, follow the road from Chota in the north through Pimampiro and Nueva América to hike to Lago Puruanta. This beautiful lake, high in the *páramo*, is one of the unspoiled jewels of the Ecuadorian Andes.

From the east, the La Virgen guard post is a few kilometers before Papallacta by the road from Quito to Baeza. From here, Laguna Sucos is a 45-minute hike. Beside the springs at Papallacta is the newest entry route, leading up to the guard post in the *páramo*, on the new road that crosses the reserve to Oyacachi. Between Baeza and Lago Agrio, the El Chaco and Aguarico guard posts provide access to the more difficult and less explored eastern section of the reserve. Volcán Reventador and San Rafael Falls are both found along this stretch of road.

HACIENDA ZULETA

This venerable estate (Vía Cayambe-Olmedo, tel. 6/266-2182, www.zuleta.com, from $194 pp all-inclusive) was owned by former Ecuadorian presidents Leónidas Plaza and Galo Plaza Lasso, the latter from the 1940s until 1987. Family members still take an interest in all operations, including guided tours. The original farmhouse, nine kilometers north of Olmedo on the road from Cayambe, dates to 1691. It was later augmented with workshops and a chapel when the Spanish crown deeded the entire region to the Jesuits.

Zuleta is best known for the signature Zuleteño embroidery, in which intricate, colorful designs are sewn onto white cloth shirts, napkins, and wall hangings. The hacienda's Galo Plaza Lasso Foundation oversees a condor rehabilitation project as well as the women's community embroidery project.

Andean peaks loom beyond the grass fields, eucalyptus, and native forests that fill the 1,800-hectare spread. Tree-lined lanes and an enormous cobbled central plaza set the stage for home-cooked meals of organic vegetables, fresh trout, and dairy products straight from the farm. Guided tours on horseback, mountain bike, and foot can take you to indigenous villages on steep mountainsides, where endangered spectacled bears are returning. You can also explore some of the countless mounds and pyramids left by the pre-Inca Caranqui people.

One-day to two-week horseback-riding programs are available. The Hacienda's own breed of horses (Zuleteños) are strong and well adapted to the elevation. Zuleta is a working farm that employs more than 100 workers from the community, including 20 who are learning English and specializing in tourism.

A minimum stay of two nights is recommended, and the rates include all meals, snacks, refreshments, farm visits, and taxes. There are discounts for longer stays and for families. Reservations are required for the 15 comfortable guest rooms. German, French, English, and Spanish are spoken.

Otavalo and Vicinity

Despite its modest size, Otavalo (pop. 43,000) hosts the biggest textiles market in Ecuador and one of the most famous in South America. The market is a permanent fixture in the Plaza de Ponchos, but every Saturday the stalls spread out across the town, and thousands of locals and visitors mix it up in a festival of buying, selling, and haggling.

The unique local indigenous group, the Otavaleños, dominate the town, and much of the local population is dedicated to making and selling textiles, handicrafts, jewelry, and ceramics. Their textiles and indigenous music are carried around the world. There is so much to buy that shopaholics may consider leaving a trip to Otavalo until the end of their Ecuador visit to avoid dragging their purchases around the rest of the country.

Otavalo is not just about shopping, however, and there's plenty to keep you occupied in the vicinity. The setting of the town is very attractive, nestled at 2,530 meters in the verdant Valle del Amanecer (Valley of the Sunrise) between two dormant volcanoes: Cotacachi to the northwest and Imbabura to the east. Both peaks offer climbing opportunities, and there is great hiking around several stunning lakes close to town.

Otavalo is one of the oldest towns in Imbabura Province and was a market town long before the Incas arrived. After the Spanish conquest, exploitation of the local craftspeople pervaded, and they were forced to work in sweatshops in terrible conditions. Independence did little to improve matters with the equally oppressive *huasipungo* system, in which indigenous people labored in exchange for access to tiny farm plots. In the 19th century, mass production switched to factories, but handmade products remained popular. It wasn't until 1964 that the exploitation was outlawed by the Agrarian Reform Law and indigenous people were given land and control over their choice of work. Since then, textiles have become the product of choice, earning the Otavaleños global fame and quality of life that is worlds apart from most other indigenous groups in South America. It's easy to see that there is wealth here, with the younger generation driving shiny new 4WD vehicles blasting contemporary music in the streets in the early evening. The indigenous heritage is still dominant in Otavalo, however, and locals wear their distinctive hats, ponchos, embroidered shirts, and blouses with pride.

Sadly, the large number of visitors has led to occasional robberies, although far less frequently than in Quito. Never leave your hotel room unlocked, and be careful of bag-slashers and pickpockets in the crowded Saturday

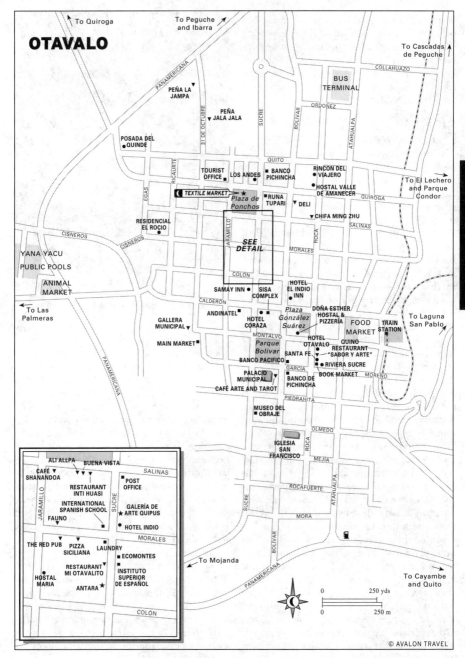

OTAVALO

To Quiroga
To Peguche and Ibarra
To Cascadas de Peguche

COLLAHUAZO

PANAMERICANA

BUS TERMINAL

ORDOÑEZ

PEÑA LA JAMPA

PEÑA JALA JALA

SUCRE

BOLÍVAR

ATAHUALPA

POSADA DEL QUINDE

QUITO

RICAURTE

31 DE OCTUBRE

TOURIST OFFICE   LOS ANDES   BANCO PICHINCHA

RINCON DEL VIAJERO

HOSTAL VALLE DE AMANECER

To El Lechero and Parque Condor

EGAS

TEXTILE MARKET

RUNA TUPARI

QUIROGA

Plaza de Ponchos

DELI

CHIFA MING ZHU

SALINAS

RESIDENCIAL EL ROCÍO

CISNEROS

CISNEROS

JARAMILLO

SEE DETAIL

ROCA

MORALES

YANA YACU PUBLIC POOLS

COLÓN

ANIMAL MARKET

SAMAY INN   SISA COMPLEX

HOTEL EL INDIO INN

To Las Palmeras

CALDERÓN

ANDINATEL   HOTEL CORAZA

Plaza González Suárez

DOÑA ESTHER HOSTAL & PIZZERÍA

FOOD MARKET

TRAIN STATION

To Laguna San Pablo

GALLERA MUNICIPAL

MONTALVO

Parque Bolívar

HOTEL OTAVALO

QUINO RESTAURANT "SABOR Y ARTE"

MAIN MARKET

SANTA FE

BANCO PACIFICO

RIVIERA SUCRE

BOOK MARKET

MORENO

PALACIO MUNICIPAL

GARCÍA

BANCO DE PICHINCHA

CAFÉ ARTE AND TAROT

PIEDRAHITA

MUSEO DEL OBRAJE

OLMEDO

PANAMERICANA

IGLESIA SAN FRANCISCO

ROCA

MEJÍA

To Mojanda

ROCAFUERTE

ATAHUALPA

SUCRE

MORA

BOLÍVAR

PANAMERICANA

To Cayambe and Quito

0   250 yds
0   250 m

© AVALON TRAVEL

Detail:

ALI ALLPA   BUENA VISTA

SALINAS

CAFÉ SHANANDOA

POST OFFICE

JARAMILLO

RESTAURANT INTI HUASI

SUCRE

INTERNATIONAL SPANISH SCHOOL

GALERÍA DE ARTE QUIPUS

FAUNO

HOTEL INDIO

MORALES

THE RED PUB   PIZZA SICILIANA   LAUNDRY

ECOMONTES

RESTAURANT MI OTAVALITO

INSTITUTO SUPERIOR DE ESPAÑOL

HOSTAL MARIA

ANTARA

COLÓN

market. You should also be careful on the bus between Otavalo and Quito. When exploring the area's trails and more remote locations, it's better to travel in groups or on guide-led tours because lone hikers have occasionally been robbed. On the whole, however, the streets of Otavalo are safe at night.

SIGHTS
◖ Textile Market

The town's biggest draw, and the reason you probably can't find a hotel room on Friday night, is the Saturday textile market. Vendors from town and surrounding villages set up shop well before dawn. By 8 A.M. the animal market is under way, and soon the Plaza de Ponchos is packed with a brightly colored, murmuring throng of vendors and visitors haggling over every imaginable type of textile and craft. The market has become so successful that it is now open daily, and there's a wider choice of wares any day of the week than in other market towns. The Saturday market is still the biggest, though, and it's worth experiencing the hustle and bustle even if you don't intend to buy anything.

In Otavalo, clothing is made in the traditional way.

© CHRIS O'CONNELL

Anything made out of wool, cotton, or synthetic yarn can be found here in all shapes and sizes, including for infants. Clothing is the most popular buy: Thick wool and alpaca sweaters keep out the cold and come in interesting patterns; pajama-style thin cotton trousers come in every color imaginable; embroidered shirts, blouses, skirts, and wool mittens are popular; and rather less traditional is a huge range of T-shirts with Ecuadorian-themed designs. Carpets and blankets are often covered in llama designs, and wall hangings, woven with abstract patterns, are popular. The traditional hats made of felt or wool are another good buy as well as handbags and cloud-soft alpaca teddy bears. The best (and most expensive) ponchos, worn by the Otavaleños themselves, are made of thick wool dyed blue with indigo imported from abroad, and with a collar and gray or plaid fabric on the inside. Other ponchos are made of synthetic materials like Orlon, which is less expensive but brighter.

Long cloth strips called *fajas,* used by *indígenas* in the Sierra to tie back their hair, hang next to their wider cousins called *chumbis.* Many of these belts are woven in La Compañía, on the other side of Lago San Pablo. A single belt woven on a traditional backstrap loom (stretched between a post and the waist of the seated weaver) can take as long as four days to complete. Jewelry similar to that worn by indigenous women is spread out on tables: necklaces of black or red beads interspersed with earrings of turquoise and lapis lazuli. Other treasures include raw fleece, yarn, and dyes, textiles from Peru and Bolivia, painted balsawood birds, and even novelty shrunken heads (fake, of course).

For the Saturday market, it's best to spend Friday night in town, but make a reservation because hotels fill up fast. Alternately, get up early Saturday morning to take the bus from Quito. Bargaining is expected, even in the many stores in town, and foreigners are naturally offered rather inflated prices, so haggle away, but don't be too pushy; if you get 30

THE *INDÍGENAS* OF OTAVALO

Otavaleños are a special case among indigenous groups. Their unusual financial success and cultural stability allow them to travel and even educate their children abroad while still keeping a firm hold on their traditions at home.

Although many of Otavalo's residents are white or mestizo (mixed race), more than 40,000 Otavalo *indígenas* live in the town and the surrounding villages. Their typical outfits makes Otavaleños easily recognizable. "They walk, sit, and stand with exquisite grace," wrote Ludwig Bemelmans in the early 20th century. "The men have historic, decided faces, and the women look like the patronesses at a very elegant ball." Women traditionally wear elaborately embroidered white blouses over double-layered wool skirts, white underneath and black or dark blue on top. Shawls ward off the sun, provide warmth at night, or carry babies. Necklaces of gold metal or red beads (once coral, now usually colored glass or plastic) are worn around the neck, and their long, black hair is tied back in a single braid and wrapped in a woven *faja.*

Men also wear their long black hair braided in a *shimba,* often to the waist. (Their hair is such an important symbol of ethnic identity that *indígenas* of any ethnic group aren't required to cut it off when they enter the army). Blue wool ponchos are worn in all types of weather over white calf-length pants and rope sandals. A straight-brimmed felt fedora tops it off.

The history of the Otavaleños' famous weavings started before the arrival of the Incas, when the backstrap loom had already been in use for centuries. The Incas, appreciating the fine work, collected the weavings as tributes. Specially chosen women dedicated their lives to weaving fine textiles, some of which were burned in ritual offerings to the sun. On their arrival, the Spanish forced the Otavaleños to labor in workshops called *obrajes.* Despite the terrible conditions, the Otavalo *indígenas* became familiar with new weaving technology and learned how to produce textiles in mass quantities.

In the early 20th century, Otavalo's weavers caught the world's attention with a popular and inexpensive imitation of fine woven cloths from Asia called cashmere. The 1964 Agrarian Reform Law turned weaving into a profitable industry for the local people, who were now able to weave in their own homes. Today, the clack and rattle of electric looms turning out rolls of fabric can be heard in the smallest towns. Most private homes have an antique treadle-operated sewing machine along with a freestanding manual loom. Many weavers, though, still go through the entire process of hand-cutting, washing, carding, dying, and weaving wool over a period of days. Some backstrap looms are still in use; weaving a blanket on one can take over a week. Men traditionally operate the looms, either full-time or after finishing the day's work in the fields, while women perform the embroidery. Families start training children as young as age three to weave.

Most important, Otavaleño weavers have been able to hold onto their roots while keeping their business feet firmly in the present. Otavalo's *indígenas* own most of the businesses in town, as well as many stores throughout Ecuador and in other countries in South America. They travel extensively abroad in the Americas, Europe, and Asia to sell their products. The election of Otavalo's first indigenous mayor in 2000 shows how strong the native presence is in the Valley of Sunrise – organized indigenous strikes can bring the entire region to a standstill – and gives hope to other more downtrodden groups.

This success and visibility attracts both admiration and envy. Spend some time here and you'll see that Otavaleños have learned to straddle the fine line between making a profit and selling out their culture, and they seem to have come out ahead for their efforts.

NORTHERN SIERRA

percent off the starting price, you're doing well. Prices peak when the tour buses from Quito are in town, usually 9 A.M.–noon, so either shop very early or linger late for the best deals.

For a very different market experience, get up early and visit the **animal market,** held on Saturday morning starting at sunrise. Everything from cows, piglets, guinea pigs, puppies, and kittens (not for eating, thankfully) are for sale here. It's an animal rights campaigner's nightmare, and you're unlikely to make a purchase, but it's an interesting experience nevertheless. To get here, head west on Morales or Calderón and cross the bridge, passing the stadium. The market is straight ahead across the Panamericana.

Other Sights

Outside the market frenzy, the most attractive and historic part of Otavalo is at the south end of town. **Parque Bolívar** is dominated by the statue of brave Inca general Rumiñahui, who valiantly resisted the Spanish invaders and remains a symbol of indigenous pride. On the west side of the park is the main church, San Luis, and two blocks east on Calderón and Roca is a more attractive church, El Jordán. A block south is the **Museo del Obraje** (Sucre 6-08 at Olmedo, tel. 6/292-0261, 8 A.M.–12:30 P.M. and 3–5 P.M. Mon.–Sat., $2), which showcases the textiles that have made the area famous. It also offers courses in weaving and other handicrafts.

In the center of town, the **SISA** complex (Calderón 409 between Bolívar and Sucre, tel. 6/292-0154) has a handicrafts shop, a bookstore, an art gallery, a bar, and a restaurant on two floors. The name is an acronym for Sala de Imágen, Sonido y Arte (Image, Sound, and Art Space), and it also means "flower" in Kichwa. Live music is performed on weekend nights.

Mirador El Lechero and Parque Condor

Otavalo is surrounded by great hiking opportunities. The walk to El Lechero and Parque Condor is the closest to town and is easily done independently. It's quite a steep climb,

takes over an hour, and is poorly signposted, so ask for directions if you get lost; don't do the hike alone. Head southeast out of town on Piedrahita. The road quickly steepens into a series of switchbacks to Mirador El Lechero. This tree is renowned locally for the magical healing powers of the milky liquid contained in its leaves (hence its name, "the milkman"). From here you will have great views of Otavalo, Laguna de San Pablo, and Imbabura.

Parque Condor (tel. 6/292-4429, www.parquecondor.org, 9:30 A.M.–5 P.M. Tues.–Sun., $3 pp) is a short continuation of the Lechero hike and a rare opportunity to see condors, hawks, eagles, owls, and other birds of prey at close quarters. The birds are well cared for, and they fly freely for half an hour each morning at 11:30 A.M. and each afternoon at 4:30 P.M. It's quite a hike to do round-trip, so consider taking a taxi from Otavalo to the park ($4 one-way) and then walk back, which also reduces the risk of getting lost.

ENTERTAINMENT AND EVENTS
Nightlife

Nightlife is low-key in Otavalo most of the week but gets going on the weekend, particularly on Saturday when the locals celebrate a hard day's trading. You can catch live Andean music at several *peñas* in town, but locations change frequently, so ask around. Currently, the most popular places are **Peña Jala Jala** (31 de Octubre, tel. 6/292-4081, 7 P.M.–2 A.M. Fri.–Sat.) and **Peña La Jampa** (31 de Octubre, tel. 6/292-7791, www.lajampa.com, 7 P.M.–2 A.M. Fri.–Sat.), both northwest of Plaza de Ponchos. Grab a high-octane pitcher of *canelazo* (hot cinnamon tea with *aguardiente*), sit back, and enjoy.

For a more international vibe with pitchers of beer and rock music, head to **The Red Pub** (Morales between Jaramillo and Sucre, tel. 6/292-7870, 4 P.M.–midnight Mon.–Thurs., 4 P.M.–2 A.M. Fri.–Sat.), a little slice of Britain in the Andes, or nearby **Fauno** (Morales between Jaramillo and Sucre, tel.

6/292-1611, 2 p.m.–midnight Mon.–Thurs. and 2 p.m.–2 a.m. Fri.–Sat.).

Festivals
Inti Raymi, the Inca festival of the northern solstice, has been absorbed into the Roman Catholic **Festival of San Juan** held in late June. Boats of every description dot Lago de San Pablo, and people cheer local favorites in bullfights.

Yamor, the region's best-known celebration, takes place close to the equinox, traditionally during the first weeks of September. In Otavalo, the Inca festival of Colla-Raymi, a harvest celebration of the earth's fertility, has been combined with the festival of San Luis Obispo, the patron saint of the harvest. Yamor is a two-week-long party with parades, marching bands, bullfights, cockfights, colorful costumes, and dances, all fueled by a special *chichi de yamor* made from seven different grains and drunk only during the festivities. Things can get very boisterous, so be careful late at night.

In *la entrada de ramos* (entrance of the branches), food and animals—from bread and fruit to live guinea pigs—are displayed, recreating a ritual presentation of food to the landowner dating to colonial times. A highlight is the appearance of the *coraza,* often played by a patron of the festivities. The only participant on horseback, the *coraza* wears an elaborate costume with a three-cornered hat and silver chains covering his face.

SHOPPING
In addition to the markets, throughout Otavalo are stores where you can browse in a less frantic atmosphere among huge selections of woven goods. **Antara** (Sucre near Colón) sells handmade Andean musical instruments. For more work by local artists, try the **Galería de Arte Quipus** (Sucre and Morales), which specializes in oil paintings and watercolors. You can buy, sell, or trade books at **The Book Market** (Hostal Riviera Sucre, Roca and García Moreno), which has a good selection of works in several languages. All day Saturday, the **produce market** overflows with food,

household items, and clothes in and around the Plaza 24 de Mayo.

RECREATION AND TOURS
Although many of the areas around Otavalo can be explored independently, there are several agencies in town that organize tours to watch the production of crafts and textiles and see how the artisans live. Most agencies also offer hiking, driving, biking, and horseback trips of varying lengths and itineraries. All the agencies in town offer tours in English.

The agency that provides the most authentic indigenous experiences in the region is **Runa Tupari** (Plaza de los Ponchos, Sucre and Quiroga, tel. 6/292-2320 or 6/292-5985, www.runatupari.com). The company can set up homestays ($27 pp including meals and transportation) with 15 families in five small communities near Otavalo, where visitors live with and learn from traditional families, who benefit financially from the arrangement. Runa Tupari also sells products from various local community projects. Day tours ($27 pp) are to weaving villages as well as hikes to Cuicocha, Lagunas de Mojanda, and Fuya Fuya. Also offered are a shamanic medicine tour ($40 pp), horseback riding in Cotacachi-Cayapas National Park ($40 pp), and an excellent downhill bike ride into the Intag Valley ($65 pp). For climbers, there are ascents of Imbabura and Cotacachi (one day $70 pp, two days $150 pp). Multiday tours of the region are also available.

Another reputable agency in town is **Ecomontes Tour** (Sucre and Morales, tel. 6/292-6244, www.ecomontestour.com), which offers many of the activities and community tours described above and can also arrange rainforest trips, Galápagos cruises, and climbing in other parts of Ecuador. They also have an office in Quito (J. Mera N24-91 at Mariscal Foch, tel. 2/290-3629).

ACCOMMODATIONS
Otavalo has a lot of accommodations, mainly budget and mid-range with some top-end haciendas outside town. During the week there is usually plenty of availability, but the best hotels

NORTHERN SIERRA

fill up fast on Friday and Saturday nights, so consider booking ahead, or try to arrive before Friday if you're staying for a few days.

Under $10

The **Residencial El Rocío** (Morales between Ricaurte and Egas, tel. 6/292-0584 or 6/292-4606, $6 pp) offers some of the cheapest basic guest rooms in town, with more attractive cabins across the Panamericana ($12 pp) for those who want quiet and a parking space.

$10-25

The **C Hostal Valle del Amanecer** (Roca and Quiroga, tel. 6/292-0990, www.hostal-valledelamanecer.com, $10–12 pp) is the most pleasant budget place in town and has the feel of a backpacker hub with its cobbled, plant-filled courtyard, outdoor fireplace, hammocks, and friendly service. There is a restaurant and bikes for rent. This hostel is also your best bet for direct transportation to the community of Playa de Oro in Esmeraldas Province. On the same street, **Hostal Rincón del Viajero** (Roca 11-07, tel. 6/292-1741, $10–12 pp, breakfast included) is another hospitable option for budget travelers, with artwork on the walls, a TV lounge with a fireplace, a rooftop terrace with hammocks, a games room, and a restaurant.

If you want to stay near the Plaza de Ponchos, bear in mind it can get noisy. Right on the Plaza, **Hostal Los Andes** (Roca and Juan Montalvo, tel. 6/292-1057, $10 s, $15 d) is one of the cheapest options, with simple guest rooms overlooking the market. **Hotel Indio** (Sucre and Morales, tel. 6/292-0060, $15 pp), half a block up from the Plaza, is better, with colorful guest rooms and an open-air courtyard. The best value close to the market is probably the family-run **Samay Inn** (Sucre and Colón, tel. 6/292-2871, $10 pp), with firm beds, cable TV, and small balconies. The owner is opening a sister hotel on the eastern edge of town. Half a block south, guest rooms at the **Hotel Coraza** (Calderón and Sucre, tel./fax 6/292-1225, $17 pp, breakfast included) are very comfortable.

Many of the city's best mid-range hotels are

situated south of the Plaza de Ponchos, along Roca one block southeast of Parque Bolívar. The colonial-style **C Hotel Otavalo** (Roca 504 at Juan Montalvo, tel. 6/292-0416, www.hotelotavalo.com.ec, $22 s, $44 d) offers great value, with a spacious peach-colored interior and immaculate guest rooms. **Hotel Santa Fe** (Roca and García Moreno, tel. 6/292-3640, $15 s, $30 d) also has excellent quality guest rooms furnished in pine and eucalyptus along with a good restaurant. On the corner, **Hotel Riviera Sucre** (Moreno 380 at Roca, tel./fax 6/292-0241, $15 s, $26 d) is another great option, with an open courtyard, a large garden, a lounge area, and spacious, colorful guest rooms.

$25-50

The renovated colonial **Doña Esther** (Montalvo 444 at Bolívar, tel. 6/292-0739, www.otavalohotel.com, $28 s, $40 d) is the best value in this range. Owned by a Dutch family, it has a verdant courtyard and a great restaurant with Mediterranean specialties. The **Hotel El Indio Inn** (Bolívar 904, tel. 6/292-2922 or 6/292-0325, $36 s, $53 d, breakfast included) has elegant guest rooms, cable TV, private parking, and a restaurant.

Otavalo's most distinctive hotel is the **C Posada del Quinde** (Quito and Miguel Egas, tel. 6/292-0750, www.posadaquinde.com, $44 s, $67 d, breakfast included), formerly known as Ali Shungu, at the northwest corner of town. The new owners continue to offer one of the best lodging options in town. The staff are very helpful, and the hotel is intricately decorated; each wall is lined with colorful masks, dolls, and weavings, and leafy plants fill all the corners. At the back are a gift shop and a patio overlooking the flower garden. The restaurant is very good (and open to nonguests), and there is live Andean music on the weekend.

FOOD

Otavalo has a sweet tooth: The freezers of most stores are stocked with freshly made sorbet (*helados de paila*), and you're never far from a bakery. One of the best is on the south side of the Plaza de Ponchos. **Café Shenandoah** (Salinas 5-15, no phone, 7:30 A.M.–9 P.M. daily, $1.50) has been serving homemade fruit pies for more than 30 years. Choose from 10 flavors that include lemon, passion fruit, and blueberry. Next door, **Alli Allpa** (Salinas 5-09 at Sucre, tel. 6/292-0289, 7:30 A.M.–9 P.M. daily, entrées $3–5) is an endearing little café offering meat and vegetarian options and a good-value set lunch ($3.50). Upstairs, **Buena Vista** (Salinas and Sucre, tel. 6/292-5166, 10 A.M.–10 P.M. Wed.–Mon., entrées $4–6) is a good place to watch the market from the balcony over a coffee and a chocolate brownie (the specialty) or feast on lasagna, trout, or steak from the wide-ranging menu. On the same street, for a more upscale meal, try **Inty Huasi** (Salinas, tel. 6/292-2944, 8 A.M.–10 P.M. Tues.–Sat., 8 A.M.–5 P.M. Sun.–Mon., entrées $5–7) for well-presented meat and seafood dishes.

For Ecuadorian specialties, the best place in town is 【 **Mi Otavalito** (Sucre and Morales, tel. 6/292-0176, 8 A.M.–11 P.M. daily, entrées $5–7). A cozy cellar-like atmosphere, waitresses in traditional indigenous dress, artwork and artifacts on the walls, and an imaginative menu complete a very pleasant dining experience. Try the pork chops in orange sauce or the *trucha Otavalito* (trout in garlic sauce). Another good place for local specialties is **Quino Restaurant Sabor y Arte** (Roca near Montalvo, tel. 6/292-4094, 10 A.M.–11 P.M. daily, entrées $5–8), an intimate, colorful little restaurant with seafood specialties such as *ceviche* as well as mulled wine to warm the bones.

For international food, Otavalo has a good selection of high-quality establishments. For the best Mexican in town as well as delicious tomato soup, hot chocolate, crepes, and desserts, head to 【 **The Deli** (Quiroga and Bolívar, tel. 6/292-1558, www.delicaferestaurant.com, 9:30 A.M.–9 P.M. Sun.–Thurs., 9:30 A.M.–11 P.M. Fri.–Sat., entrées $4–8), a little gem of a café one block from the market.

For something more unusual, try the crepes at 【 **Café Arte and Tarot** (García Moreno and Bolívar, no phone, 8 A.M.–10 P.M. daily,

entrées $3–5), an eclectically decorated place on the main square. The most popular seat in the house is a toilet seat in the café upstairs!

The best of the many *chifas* is the **Chifa Ming Zhu** (Roca and Salinas, tel. 9/771-0381, lunch and dinner daily, entrées $3–6), which is popular with locals for its generous portions of noodles, fried rice, sweet-and-sour dishes, and soups.

INFORMATION AND SERVICES

The **tourist office** (Quiroga and Jaramillo, tel. 6/292-7230, 8:30 A.M.–1 P.M. and 2:30–6 P.M. Mon.–Fri., 9 A.M.–2 P.M. Sat., 9 A.M.–noon Sun.) is at the corner of Plaza de Ponchos.

Banco Pichincha (Bolívar and García Moreno; Sucre and Quiroga) has ATMs. **Banco del Pacífico** (Sucre and García Moreno) on the Central Plaza will change traveler's checks. You can also try **Vaz Money Exchange** (Sucre and Colón), which handles many foreign currencies, traveler's checks, and Western Union money transfers. Some tour agencies change cash and traveler's checks as well. The **post office** (8 A.M.–7 P.M. Mon.–Fri., 8 A.M.–1 P.M. Sat.) is on the corner of Sucre and Salinas.

Most hotels do laundry, or you can try **Lavandería** (Morales and Sucre, no phone). Internet cafés have sprung up all over town, and there are several lining Sucre south of the Plaza de Ponchos, including **C@ffe Net** (tel. 6/292-0193). The local **hospital** (Sucre, tel. 6/292-0444) is northeast of town, and the **police station** (tel. 101) is on Avenida Luis Ponce de León at the northeast end of town.

Spanish Lessons

Instituto Superior de Español (Sucre 11-10 at Morales, tel. 6/299-2424, www.instituto-superior.net) is recommended for Spanish classes. One-on-one instruction ($7 per hour) is offered for speakers of English, German, and French, and the school can arrange homestays and tours for students. Another option is the **Mundo Andino Spanish School** (Salinas 404 at Bolívar, tel./fax 6/292-1864, www.mundoandinospanishschool.com), which offers 4–7 hours of classes per day ($5 per hour) and homestays with local families.

GETTING THERE AND AROUND

Otavalo's **bus terminal** (Atahualpa and Ordoñez) is on the northeast corner of town, where you can catch buses to Quito (2 hours, $2.50) and Ibarra (40 minutes, $0.40) every 15 minutes, as well as to nearby villages such as Ilumán, Carabuela, Peguche, and Agato. You can also catch any bus heading north along the Panamericana and ask the driver to let you off at the appropriate intersection, then walk. Coming back is even easier—just flag down any bus heading south.

Taxis, which congregate at the bus terminal, plazas, and parks, charge about $1 for short journeys around town, $3 for attractions on the edge of town (Peguche waterfalls and El Lechero are two examples), and from $10 per hour for more out-of-the-way locations like Lagunas de Mojanda.

LAGUNA DE SAN PABLO

The nearest lake to Otavalo is the huge Laguna de San Pablo that you pass on the way from Quito. At the foot of **Volcán Imbabura,** surrounded by pastoral hamlets, it' a beautiful spot and popular on weekends with locals, who go sailing and waterskiing.

The road surrounding the lake is ideal for a day's bike ride or hike. The festivals of **Corazas** (Aug. 19) and **Los Pendoneros** (Oct. 15) are celebrated in the tiny shoreline villages, which specialize in crafts such as woven reed mats. The walk from Otavalo south to the lake takes about an hour, or walk via El Lechero and Parque Condor. The bus from Otavalo marked "Araque" follows this road (catch it in front of the market on Atahualpa), or simply take any bus south toward Quito and get off when you pass the lake after about 10 minutes.

Accommodations and Food

A billboard along the Panamericana points down a dirt road to the **Hostería Puertolago**

Volcán Imbabura dominates the valley around Otavalo.

© CHRIS O'CONNELL

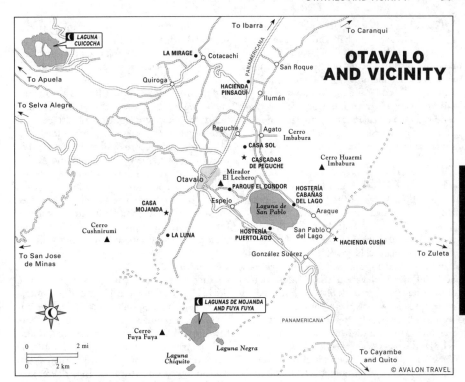

OTAVALO AND VICINITY

© AVALON TRAVEL

(tel. 6/292-0920, www.puertolago.com, $91 s, $103 d) on the southern shore of the lake. Meticulously mowed grounds surround a main building housing a nautical-motif bar, a restaurant, and an atrium with a wide window over the lake. Well-appointed guest rooms have fireplaces; rowboats and kayaks are available by the hour or the day, as are motorboats and paddleboats. Day or night lake tours ($5.50 pp) are available. A taxi from Otavalo costs $3.

The comfortable **Hostería Cabañas del Lago** (Lago San Pablo, tel. 6/291-8108, www.cabanasdellago.com.ec, cabins $85 d), around on the eastern shore, caters to family groups and has two restaurants specializing in trout. Foot-powered paddleboats and motorboats are available for rent on the weekend. The two-person cabins have fireplaces and private baths.

HACIENDA CUSÍN

Outside the town of San Pablo del Lago is one of the most famous and luxurious country inns in South America. Built in 1602, the Hacienda Cusín (San Pablo del Lago, tel. 6/291-8013, fax 6/291-8003, www.haciendacusin.com, www.mythsandmountains.com, rooms $90 s, $120 d, cottages $120 s, $150 d, breakfast included) is one of the oldest in the country, named after a young local warrior who fought bravely against the Inca. Situated in a wide, scenic valley just south of Imbabura at 2,400 meters elevation, the hacienda is a relaxing, Old World type of place where llamas and sheep graze in the shadow of avocado trees. Old stone walls topped with moss encircle a hectare of gardens, which bloom continuously in the mild climate. Hummingbirds inhabit the forests of bougainvillea, belladonna, orchids, and foxglove.

Choose from 15 garden cottages or 25 guest rooms, all with private baths and garden views; some have bathtubs and fireplaces. This main colonial building is decorated with antiques and tapestries and houses the games room and a library graced by French windows. The restaurant seats 40 under a beamed ceiling, and food is served on carved wooden plates in front of a log fire. Horses are available to rent, and there are trails into the hills and fields.

◖ LAGUNAS DE MOJANDA AND FUYA FUYA

Half an hour south of Otavalo by car, a cobbled, winding road leads up to three stunningly beautiful lakes in the shadow of dark jagged mountains. Laguna Grande (also known as Caricocha), Laguna Negra (Huarmicocha), and Laguna Chiquita (Yanacocha) sit amid *páramo* at 3,700 meters elevation, some 1,200 meters above Otavalo. The peak of Fuya Fuya (4,263 meters) to the west is the highest point in the region and is a popular four-hour climb as acclimation practice for higher peaks. The first lake is by far the biggest, at two kilometers wide, and there is a hiking trail around it. A dirt road extends part of the way around the lake, and trails lead east and south to the other smaller lakes.

A taxi from Otavalo costs $10 one-way. Take a taxi driver's phone number or arrange a pickup time because this is a remote area. Be aware that there have been occasional robberies, so it's best to come here in a group or take a guided tour.

Casa Mojanda

The American- and Ecuadorian-run Casa Mojanda hotel (tel. 6/299-1010 or 9/973-1737, www.casamojanda.com, dorm $61 pp, $110 s, $183 d, breakfast and dinner included) is an ecologically and socially minded place with excellent views, five kilometers south of Otavalo at an elevation of 2,980 meters. On the road to the Lagunas de Mojanda, the hotel clings to the edge of a valley facing Cotacachi and the Cerro Cushnirumi, one of the few undisturbed tracts of Andean cloud forest in Ecuador. All the buildings were constructed using the *tapial*

(rammed-earth) process in a simple, tasteful style with whitewashed walls, wood, terraces, and hammocks. Casa Mojanda prides itself on good environmental practice and has won eco-tourism awards.

The airy main building houses the dining and living rooms, and there is a separate library building. There are eight guest cottages and two 10-bed dormitories. Outside is a small amphitheater that faces the valley, an outdoor hot tub with a great view, and an organic garden that supplies the restaurant. Nearby there are hiking trails, and you can go cycling, horseback riding, or kayaking. The owners also oversee the nonprofit Mojanda Foundation, working for environmental protection and the social welfare of surrounding communities.

La Luna

Farther up the road from Casa Mojanda to the Lagunas de Mojanda is the budget *hostería* La Luna (Vía a Lagos de Mojanda, tel. 9/315-6082, www.lalunaecuador.com, dorm $7 pp, $16–19 s, $24–32 d) with private guest rooms and campsites ($3.50 pp). The main building has a small restaurant and bar, and there is live Andean music on Saturdays. To get here, take the first left past the Casa Mojanda and head downhill a few hundred yards, then over the bridge. A taxi from Otavalo costs $4.

PEGUCHE

A small indigenous villages near Otavalo, Peguche (pop. 4,000) is renowned for its artisanal wares, particularly weavings and musical instruments. Various homes and workshops around town specialize in rugs, blankets, tapestries, and scarves. If you're looking for fine tapestries, stop by the home-workshop of **José Cotacachi** (tel. 6/269-0171, www.josecotacachi.com). From the Central Plaza of Peguche, take the sidewalk to the right of the church and turn right at the end of the street to reach the showroom. Or visit **Artesania El Gran Condor** (Central Plaza, tel. 6/269-0161, www.artesaniaelgrancondor.com), another good textile workshop run by José Ruiz Perugachi.

On the musical side, **Ñanda Mañachi** (tel. 6/269-0076), just a couple of blocks north of the plaza, is an interesting place to visit—they give demonstrations of how several types of panpipes are made and played. A variety of instruments, including *flautas* (reed flutes) and *rondadores* (Andean panpipes), are on sale.

Cascadas de Peguche

Perfect for cooling your feet after a day's hike, the small waterfall at forested Cascadas de Peguche park is just south of the town. Pass under two white arches to the signed park entrance, where there is a small interpretive center (8:30 A.M.–5 P.M. daily). There is no entrance fee, but you are asked to make a small donation.

Follow the path through eucalyptus-scented forest; to the right there is a small bathing pool, and farther along are the falls. There is a bridge across the river and lookout points on each side. Past the right-side lookout, you can squeeze through a small cave to see another smaller waterfall. The waters from these falls plunge down the valley into Laguna San Pablo.

© BEN WESTWOOD

Cascadas de Peguche

From Otavalo, the 45-minute walk to Cascadas de Peguche begins by following the railroad tracks north out of town. Follow the road when it leaves the tracks up and to the right, and look for the sign at the park entrance. A taxi from Otavalo costs $3, or you can take a bus to Peguche and walk down. Note that robberies have occasionally been reported at the falls, so don't go alone or at night.

Accommodations

Peguche offers a few options for those who want to stay outside Otavalo but remain nearby. Just up the hill from the entrance to the Cascada de Peguche is ◖ **La Casa Sol** (Peguche, tel. 6/269-0500, Quito tel. 2/223-0798, www.lacasasol.com, $60 s, $72 d, breakfast included). With the same indigenous owners as its namesake in Quito's New Town, the 10 guest rooms and two suites were built using traditional materials and methods. Balconies and terraces offer great views over Peguche and the Otavalo Valley, staff are friendly, and the hotel is involved with local educational projects.

Peguche Tío Hostería (Peguche, tel./fax 6/269-0179, $10 pp) is housed in an unusual circular wooden building with a lookout tower. Inside you'll find a dance floor, a restaurant, and a library. The 12 guest rooms outside near the gardens all have hot water, fireplaces, and private baths. The hotel is frequently closed, so be sure to make reservations in advance.

Straddling the railroad tracks farther into town is the **Hostal Aya Huma** (tel. 6/269-0333, www.ayahuma.com, $18 s, $29 d). It's well equipped with fireplaces, hammocks, a book exchange, Spanish classes, a vegetarian restaurant, live Andean music on Saturday nights, and a beautiful garden. Entrées in the restaurant, which serves all meals, are around $5. Follow the signs through town, or ask for directions.

AGATO, ILUMÁN, AND CARABUELA

About four kilometers northeast of Otavalo, just east of Peguche, is Agato, another village where artisans are known for their traditional-style

ILUMÁN'S NATIVE HEALERS

Ilumán is known for its *curanderos* (native healers), who can be hired to cure or curse. Residents have passed down knowledge of natural remedies and spiritual cures here for centuries, treating everything from back problems to cancer. In 1988 there were 85 registered faith healers in Ilumán, eight of them women, but according to locals, only a small percentage were genuine. Dozens of Ecuadorians come to Ilumán daily to be cured or to pay for black magic, and even a few foreigners seek the wisdom of the healers every year.

Curing rituals are a blend of ancient wisdom, folklore, and modern faith. Invocations in Kichwa to Mama Cotacachi and Taita Imbabura, the old gods of the volcanoes, are sent up alongside prayers in Spanish to the Christian God and Jesus. *Curanderos* spit water and blow cigarette smoke on the patient, or rub the patient with special stones. A candle is passed over the patient's body, then lit to learn about the patient by studying the flickering flame. Cures can take the form of prayers or medicinal herbs like eucalyptus, poppies, and lemon, either rubbed on the patient's body or drunk as a tea.

Less public are the *brujos*, practitioners of the black arts. Traditionally working only at night, these wizards will cast malignant spells for jilted lovers or failing businesspeople – for the right price, of course. Rumor has it that their powers extend even to murder.

weaving and fine embroidery. A great place to observe the process is the workshop of master weaver **Miguel Andrango** and his family (Agato, tel. 6/269-0282). You can watch the artists weaving wool on backstrap looms while others create intricate embroidery on the finished cloth. Miguel has woven fine ponchos and blankets for 60 years and continues to teach younger weavers who will carry on the traditions. Many of their high-quality textiles are for sale. Practically anyone in town can give you directions to the workshop, and many area tours stop by as well. Look for a sign to the right of the Panamericana, just past Peguche, or ask in Peguche for the road toward Agato. There are local buses to Agato from Otavalo's train station.

Ilumán, a small town noted for its felt hats and weavings, is a little farther up the Panamericana from Peguche, across from the entrance to Pinsaqui. Follow the cobbled road uphill straight toward Imbabura, and turn right when it levels out to reach the center of town and the plaza. South of the plaza on Bolívar is a sign for Carlos Conteron's **Artesanías Inti Chumbi** workshop (near Bolívar, tel. 6/294-6387). The couple at this workshop presents backstrap-loom weaving demonstrations and sells textiles and beautiful indigenous dolls.

Throughout Ilumán there are workshops specializing in the colorful felt fedoras worn by the area's *indígenas*.

IlumÁn is also famous for its *curanderos* (healers) and *brujos* (sorcerers). There are about 30 of them working in town, mixing indigenous and Christian rituals and herbal medicines to drive out evil spirits. Ask around in town to locate one, but be prepared for an intense experience and likely to get covered in spit, which is all part of the ritual. Buses from Otavalo go straight to the town center.

On the west side of the Panamericana, close to IlumÁn, Carabuela is another weaving village. Local specialists include Don José Carlos de Torre, who spends months making each of his exquisite ponchos.

These villages can be visited independently, but for a better experience and to ensure weavers are expecting you and ready to give demonstrations, book a five-destination village tour with **Runa Tupari** (Plaza de Ponchos, Otavalo, tel. 6/292-2320 or 6/292-5985, www.runatupari.com).

HACIENDA PINSAQUÍ

An equestrian theme pervades this hacienda just north of Otavalo, on land that has been in the family of owner Pedro Freile for centuries. Hacienda Pinsaquí (tel. 6/294-6116, www.haciendapinsaqui.com, $105 s, $139 d) began in 1790 as a textile workshop that supported as many as 1,000 workers at one time. Simón Bolívar was a repeat guest on his way between Ecuador and Colombia during the struggles for independence.

The 30 guest rooms and suites feature thick walls, canopy beds, fireplaces, and tiled floors, and some suites contain hot tubs. Across the railing from the main hall and its fountain is a 120-seat restaurant and lounge with huge walk-in fireplaces reminiscent of Elizabethan houses in England. There are a variety of hiking and horseback day tours. Take a taxi from Otavalo ($4–5), or take a bus to Ibarra and get off just after the turnoff to Cotacachi.

Northwest of Otavalo

COTACACHI
Across the Río Ambi gorge from the Panamericana, the small town of Cotacachi (pop. 13,000) is said to have been created during an earthquake when Volcán Imbabura and Volcán Cotacachi made love. If that creates a rather complicated mental image, the town itself is quite a simple place, and far quieter than Otavalo. The main reason to come here is for the leather goods, which you can smell long before you browse the stores of the main streets. From Bolívar, follow 10 de Agosto to the market on Rocafuerte. Just about anything that can be made out of suede or leather is available or can be crafted to order—bags, saddles, jackets, boots, vests, and purses. The quality is generally high, and prices are reasonable (some bargaining is possible on larger purchases). The main market day is Saturday.

As in Otavalo and elsewhere in the province, the biggest celebration is at the end of June. Thousands of people pack the streets for the **Fiesta de San Juan** (June 24), during which local men dance and drink at night in the main plaza until their wives drag them home. On the last day, though, it's the women's turn to carouse while their husbands watch over them.

Sights
The **Museo de las Culturas** (García Moreno, tel. 6/291-5945, 9 A.M.–noon and 2–5 P.M. Mon.–Fri., 1–5 P.M. Sat., 10 A.M.–2 P.M. Sun., $1) is a small but well-done museum one block off the main square. Set in a colonial-style building dating from 1888, it houses displays on local music, festivals, and arts, with descriptions in English. Guided tours are available.

The area around Abdón Calderón Plaza has several restored colonial buildings that are worth a look.

The **crafts market,** in the Parque San Francisco (10 de Agosto and Rocafuerte), two blocks south of Bolívar, is modest during the week but larger on Saturday and Sunday.

Accommodations and Food
For the budget-minded, **Tierra Mia** (Bolívar 12-26 at 10 de Agosto, no phone, $7 pp) has small basic guest rooms with private baths. **Hostal Mindales** (Bolívar and 9 de Octubre, tel. 6/291-6990, $15 s, $25 d) has better guest rooms for slightly higher prices. Next to the museum is the **Inn Land of the Sun** (García Moreno 13-67 at Sucre, tel. 6/291-6009, $60 s, $71 d, breakfast included). Inside a spacious colonial building is a bright three-story courtyard with sky-blue balustrades. Flowers spill over the edges, and old musical instruments grace the walls. All guest rooms have private baths.

Cotacachi has a few good restaurants. **La Marqueza** (10 de Agosto and Bolívar, tel. 6/291-5488, lunch and dinner daily, entrées $6–8) is a smart place with tasty local fare. The **Leñador** (Sucre 1012 at Montalvo, lunch and dinner daily, tel. 6/291-5083, entrées $5–8) caters to all tastes with huge servings and specializes in grilled meat.

Just outside of Cotacachi is **La Mirage Garden Hotel and Spa** (10 de Agosto, tel. 6/291-5237, fax 6/291-5065, www.mirage.com.ec, $362, breakfast and dinner included), a luxury hotel designed in the style of an old hacienda. La Mirage was accepted into the prestigious international Relais & Châteaux association in 1997, making it the only member in Ecuador. Five hectares of spectacular gardens, brimming with bougainvillea and exotic flowers and pollinated by eight species of hummingbirds, are maintained by full-time gardeners. Oriental rugs and tiled floors decorate the whitewashed buildings. There's a gym, a gift shop, a small private chapel used occasionally for weddings and baptisms, and a comfortable bar with a roaring fire and large sofas. Each of the 23 palatial guest rooms features a high-canopy bed, an antique writing desk, a fireplace, and cable TV. Hiking, biking, horseback riding, and birding are possible in the surrounding countryside beneath Volcán Cotacachi. The spa has hot tubs, a steam room, and a solar-heated indoor pool as well as staff trained in massage, aromatherapy, facials, and reflexology; a traditional shaman is available from a local community. La Mirage's restaurant is excellent, with a huge selection of wines from around the world. Transfers to La Mirage are available from Quito. In the United States, make reservations through the Latin American Reservation Center (U.S. tel. 800/327-3573, U.S. fax 863/439-2118, www.larc1.com).

Getting There

Frequent buses run to Otavalo (25 minutes, $0.25) and Ibarra from the bus station (Sucre and 10 de Agosto). Trucks run to Laguna Cuicocha ($5), and you can arrange to have them pick you up later.

COTACACHI-CAYAPAS ECOLOGICAL RESERVE

Northwest of Cotacachi, the huge Cotacachi-Cayapas Ecological Reserve ($2 pp) stretches over 2,000 square kilometers from the cold Andean *páramo* over the western edge of the Andes and well into the humid tropical

rainforests in Esmeraldas province. Elevation ranges from 4,939 meters (the top of Volcán Cotacachi) to just 30 meters above sea level in the lowlands. The park, part of the Chocó bioregion, extends far along the old Ibarra–San Lorenzo rail line and west over the Cordillera de Toisán to the headwaters of rivers flowing into the Pacific.

Cotacachi-Cayapas is defined by water. The Ríos Bravo Grande, Agua Clara, San Miguel, and Santiago all drain the reserve's lower regions, and waterfalls like the Salto del Bravo and the Cascada de San Miguel are a few hours upstream by boat from the San Miguel guard post. The Andean part of the reserve is dotted with trout-stocked lakes, including Lagos Yanacocha, Sucapillo, and Burrococha at the foot of Yana Urcu de Piñan (4,535 meters).

Home to a range of rich habitats, the reserve is a naturalist's dream. All four species of monkey indigenous to western Andean tropical forests swing through the trees here, including black howlers, and nutria (river otter) tracks often turn up on the banks of the muddy rivers. One of Ecuador's three species of tapir hides in the underbrush, along with the occasional jaguar, ocelots, and river otters. The rare Andean spectacled bear inhabits the Cordillera de Toisán and the Andean forests on the flanks of Cotacachi.

Access

From Cotacachi, a road leads west through the town of Quiroga to a park entrance gate near Laguna Cuicocha. Pay the $2 pp entrance fee (although staff are frequently absent during the week). A guard post near Lita, halfway along the route between Ibarra and San Lorenzo, offers entrance into the reserve's lower-elevation cloud forests. Boats are available from Borbón, near San Lorenzo, to travel upriver to the San Miguel guard post, but security is a problem in this region, so it's preferable to access the park from the highlands.

◀ Laguna Cuicocha

This stunning crater lake is one of the most beautiful and frequently visited in Ecuador.

At the foot of Volcán Cotacachi, 3,070 meters up in the Andean *páramo,* the azure waters of 200-meter-deep Laguna Cuicocha shine brightly with twin volcanic cones at the center. It's considered sacred by many locals, and every year at summer solstice people take purification baths here. A trail leads around the entire lake and takes 4–6 hours. It makes for a spectacular hike with wonderful views of Cotacachi, Imbabura, and snowcapped Cayambe. Looking down, you can see the caldera dropping steeply down into the depths of the lake. Bring water, sunscreen, and sturdy boots. On the weekend there are frequent boat trips ($2 pp), although the islands, Teodoro Wolf and Yerovi, are off-limits due to scientific research.

The park entrance is supposedly staffed 8 A.M.–5 P.M. daily ($2 pp if the guards are there), and a **visitors center** (9 A.M.–4 P.M. daily) overlooks the water with exhibits on the ecology, geology, and human history of the lake.

Close by, the best lodging available is **Hostería Cuicocha** (tel. 6/264-8040 or 9/920-4786, $40 s, $70 d, breakfast and dinner included).

Buses run regularly from Otavalo to Cotacachi and Quiroga. From Cotacachi, take a left at the last traffic light in town on 31 de Octubre and follow the road west through the town of Quiroga to the park entrance gate near the Laguna Cuicocha. It's better to take a bus to Quiroga, where you can hire a private truck ($5) from the main plaza or tackle the two-hour uphill hike on foot. Take the taxi driver's number or arrange a pickup time ($10 round-trip). Note that robberies have occasionally been reported, so traveling with a group is advisable.

Volcán Cotacachi

The 4,939-meter climb up Mama Cotacachi, first done in 1880 by Edward Whymper, Jean-Antoine Carrel, and Louis Carrel, is fairly straightforward and nontechnical, and the lower part is worth hiking even if you don't intend to reach the summit. The top can be tricky (some climbing experience and a helmet

RUMBLINGS OF LOVE

In such a fertile region, it's no surprise that local folklore has assigned genders to the two volcanoes that loom over Otavalo. Cotacachi (4,939 meters) is the *mama* and Imbabura (4,609 meters) the *taita* (Kichwa for father). Many locals revere the two peaks as gods that govern the valley and ask for *taita*'s blessing for an abundant harvest of the crops planted on his flanks. The couple's nuptials supposedly gave birth to the smaller peak of Yana Urcu, but it doesn't end there. A sprinkling of snow on Cotacachi means that she has been visited by her lover during the night, while rain in the region is reputed to be Imbabura urinating on the valley. Imbabura's bad behavior extends further, according to lesser-known folktales. One explanation for why Cotacachi has only occasional snow while Cayambe is permanently white is that Imbabura is a notorious womanizer and now prefers the more beautiful, taller peak, while Cotacachi presumably gazes moodily on. Luckily, the love triangle has not been explosive enough to cause either volcano to erupt. However, all three peaks are officially dormant, not extinct, so let's hope there are no rumblings of discontent in the near future.

are advised because of the loose rock), so it's a good idea to do this on a guided tour from Otavalo, unless you are an experienced climber.

Yana Urcu de Piñan

This mountain, the supposed love child of Imbabura and Cotacachi, is climbed far less often than its parents, mainly because the approach can take up to three days. It rises from the *páramo* in a less-visited region of the reserve near the Gualaví guard post north of the Volcán Cotacachi. One route runs south from the Juncal bridge, where the Panamericana passes over the Río Chota north of Ibarra. It can also be approached from the south near the Hacienda El Hospital. Reserve personnel at the entrance may be able to help you plan a route. The ascent itself, up the southeast ridge, is relatively simple and should take 5–6 hours. The hike northwest from Irunguichu (four kilometers west of Urcuquí) to the **Piñan Lakes** at the base of the mountain is a beautiful way to spend three or more days, described in the *West of Ibarra* section.

LOS CEDROS BIOLOGICAL RESERVE

The largest privately owned reserve in Ecuador, protecting 6,400 hectares of humid rainforest and cloud forest, Los Cedros is tucked against the southwestern corner of Cotacachi-Cayapas, whose southern flank and watershed it helps protect from human intrusion. The Centro de Investigaciónes de los Bosques Tropicales (Tropical Forest Research Center) runs this remote nonprofit biological reserve 70 kilometers from Otavalo, founded in 1991 by North American José DeCoux and named after the cedar trees once found in abundance here. Three river systems tie together three mountain ridges within the reserve, drenched by up to 350 centimeters of rain per year.

Preliminary studies have found more than 200 species of birds in the reserve, including the Andean cock-of-the-rock and the spectacular golden-headed quetzal. Troops of brown-headed spider monkeys, endemic to the region, share the branches with white-throated capuchins and howler monkeys. Botanists will appreciate the 400 known species of orchids found amid ferns and palms galore. At night, huge, silent moths of every color and pattern crowd light bulbs like rush-hour commuters at subway turnstiles.

The reserve is set up primarily for researchers and volunteers, but a 100-meter canopy walkway and lodge are available. There is also a network of trails ranging 2–7 hours. The driest months, best for visits, are July and September. Volunteer opportunities are broad, including nature tourism and various programs on environmental and health education developed with local communities. Volunteering costs $280 for two weeks or $450 per month, including lodging and food. For short-term visitors, there is a minimum stay of three nights, costing $50 pp per night. Contact the center (tel. 2/286-5176, jose@reservaloscedros.org, www.reservaloscedros.org) for more information.

Reaching Los Cedros is half the adventure. Buses with Transportes Minas run from Quito's Ofelia bus station to El Chontal (3.5 hours, $2.50) four times daily, but you need to take the 6 A.M. bus to be sure of arriving at the reserve before dusk. It's a six-hour hike from El Chontal to the reserve, or mules can be arranged for riding or hauling luggage.

INTAG CLOUD FOREST RESERVE

The 505-hectare private Intag Cloud Forest Reserve (tel. 6/299-0001, www.intagcloud-forest.com) begins west of Laguna Cuicocha, as the land drops quickly from Andean *páramo* to cloud forest, where the Cayambe-Cotacachi Reserve ends. It is owned and operated by Carlos Zorilla and his wife, Sandy, and like Los Cedros it has been opened to the public to help cover operating costs. Intag's mission is not only to preserve the area's ecosystem but also to bring local communities directly into the conservation picture through educational programs and projects. The reserve ranges 1,850–2,800 meters in elevation—70 percent of the acreage is primary or secondary cloud forest. Some areas receive up to 250 centimeters of rain during the October–May wet season.

The bird-watching is outstanding, offering occasional glimpses of the plate-billed mountain toucan or the white-rimmed brush-finch, as well as more than 20 species of hummingbirds. Carlos occasionally works as an interpretive guide. Hiking trails ranging 1–5 hours in length lead into primary and secondary forests, and there's a waterfall less than 10 minutes from the cabins.

Facilities at Intag include a main building with an attached dining area and a library nearby. Simple but comfortable guest cabins feature sun-heated showers and solar lights. Much of the organic vegetarian food is grown nearby in a part of the reserve dedicated to sustainable agriculture, and the coffee is roasted on the farm. The atmosphere is very informal, and guests are encouraged to pitch in with washing dishes, milking the cows, and feeding the chickens.

To help fight the destruction of the surrounding forests, the Zorillas founded the Organization for the Defense and Conservation of the Ecology of Intag (DECOIN, tel./fax 6/264-8593, www.decoin.org) in 1995. Through the group they've successfully organized resistance to government-funded mining projects that would have destroyed even more of the cloud forest, and they have organized a local organic coffee growers' association as well as a province-wide environmental congress. At the time of writing, the region is once again under threat from government mining projects.

Staying at the reserve costs $45 pp per day. Because the number of visitors is strictly controlled, reservations are a must. Minimum group size is eight people, and a two-night minimum stay is required. No walk-ins, please—remember, this is also their home.

APUELA, NANGULVÍ, AND GUALIMÁN

Apuela is an isolated village at 2,000 meters elevation on the western edge of the Cordillera Occidental and serves as a good starting point for even more remote destinations northwest of Otavalo. The bus ride to get here, through the cloud forests of the western Andes, is spectacular in itself. The road to Apuela starts to the left of the Cotacachi-Cayapas entrance gate near Laguna Cuicocha, heading up and over into the Río Intag valley. Accommodations with shared baths are available in Apuela at the cheap **Residencial Don Luis** (tel. 6/264-8555, $5 pp), a few blocks from the main plaza. **Pradera Tropical** (tel. 6/264-8557, $4 pp), near the school, has simple cabins.

The area around Apuela is worth exploring. The clean, quiet hot springs at the **Piscinas Nangulví** ($1.50) are next to six new triple guest rooms (tel. 6/264-8291, $10 pp) about seven kilometers from the town center. There's also a restaurant with cheap set meals ($2.50). Accommodations in cabins with private baths are also available near the hot springs at the pretty **Cabañas Río Grande** (tel. 6/264-8296, $20 pp). Flowers surround each cabin's porch, and the restaurant is good and inexpensive. Reservations are recommended, especially on weekends. Buses from Otavalo may take you all the way to the hot springs—ask first—or catch one from Apuela bound for García Moreno.

On a plateau above Nangulví are the pre-Columbian ruins at the **Gualimán** archaeological site, where you'll find pre-Inca burial mounds, a run-down pyramid, and a small museum, with breathtaking views all around.

Four buses leave from Otavalo to Intag daily, passing through Apuela and close to Gualimán (3 hours). Ask the driver to drop you off. For more information on the Intag valley, call tel. 6/264-8291 or visit www.intagturismo.com.

NORTHERN SIERRA

Ibarra and Vicinity

Half an hour northeast of Otavalo is the capital of Imbabura province, Ibarra (pop. 150,000), nicknamed "La Ciudad Blanca" (The White City) because of its wealth of whitewashed colonial buildings. Ibarra is far more cosmopolitan than Otavalo; here the locals prefer T-shirts and jeans to ponchos, and an Afro-Ecuadorian population from the nearby Chota Valley adds diversity. At a slightly lower elevation of 2,225 meters, the city is also a little warmer than Quito and Otavalo.

Ibarra's status as the commercial hub of the province is clear when you step off the bus and walk toward town past the large *Mercado Amazonas* market, which spills over several blocks, selling everything from food to electronic goods and clothing. Continue to Ibarra's historic center, however, and you will find stately squares overlooked by grand churches and colonial buildings sheltering garden courtyards. Not nearly as many visitors come to Ibarra as to Otavalo, but the city is growing as a tourist draw, and the reopening and expansion of the train service will surely increase Ibarra's popularity in the near future.

Ibarra was founded in 1606 under the name Villa de San Miguel de Ibarra. It served early on as the administrative center for the textile *obrajes* (workshops) of the Otavalo region. Disaster struck in August 1868, however, when an earthquake left the city without a single building standing and killed more than 6,000 residents. It took a long time to recover, but today Ibarra is a thriving city with proud, friendly inhabitants. You can take in the historic center in a couple of hours, and be sure to eat at the most famous ice cream store in Ecuador. The streets in the city center are safe to walk at night, but be careful in the area around the train station and the markets. Volcán Imbabura looms large over the city, and on sunny days the towering snow-capped peak of Cayambe is clearly visible beyond. There are plenty of day trips to visit the stunning surroundings—go hiking, climbing, or just relax by the lakes and visit the region's best hot springs.

SIGHTS

The main sights in Ibarra are its squares and churches. **Iglesia La Merced** stands on the west side of Parque La Merced. Inside is a small religious museum and a famous image of the Virgin of La Merced, worshipped by pilgrims from throughout the province. Two blocks east, the **Cathedral Ibarra,** which underwent a major restoration in 2000, shares the north side of the leafy Parque Pedro Moncayo, while to the west stands the stately **Palacio Municipal.** East of this is the ornate **Iglesia de San Agustín.**

On the north end of town, the drab, modern **Iglesia Santo Domingo** backs the small Plazoleta Boyacá, decorated with a monument

© WWW.TOURIBARRA.GOB.EC

Catedral Ibarra is the pride of the city after a major restoration.

NORTHERN SIERRA

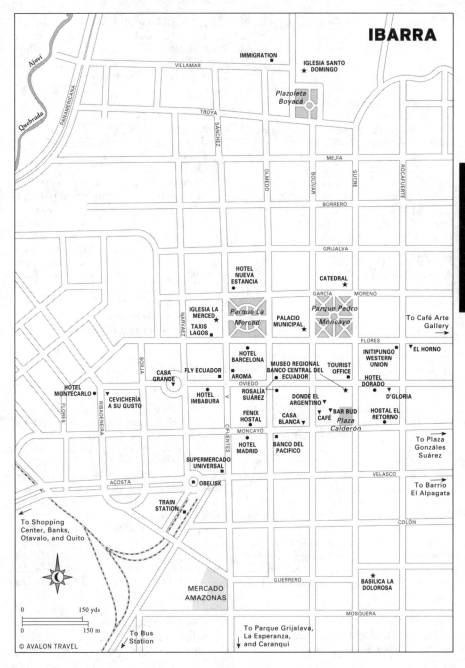

IBARRA

IMMIGRATION

IGLESIA SANTO
★ DOMINGO

*Plazoleta
Boyacá*

PANAMERICANA

Ajavi

Quebrada

VILLAMAR

TROYA

SANCHEZ

MEJÍA

OLMEDO

BOLIVAR

SUCRE

ROCAFUERTE

BORRERO

GRIJALVA

HOTEL
NUEVA
ESTANCIA

CATEDRAL
★

GARCÍA   MORENO

IGLESIA LA
MERCED ★

*Parque La
Merced*

PALACIO
MUNICIPAL
★

*Parque Pedro
Moncayo*

To Café Arte
Gallery ⟶

NARVAEZ

TAXIS
LAGOS

FLORES

▼ EL HORNO

BORJA

CASA
GRANDE
▼

FLY ECUADOR

HOTEL
BARCELONA

AROMA

MUSEO REGIONAL
BANCO CENTRAL DEL
ECUADOR

TOURIST
OFFICE
★

INITIPUNGO
WESTERN
UNION

OVIEDO

HOTEL
DORADO

HOTEL
MONTECARLO ●

CEVICHERÍA
A SU GUSTO
▼

HOTEL
IMBABURA
●

ROSALÍA
SUÁREZ
●

DONDE EL
ARGENTINO ▼

D'GLORIA
●

FLORES

RIBADENEIRA

FENIX
HOSTAL
●

CASA
BLANCA ▼

▼ BAR BUD
CAFÉ

*Plaza
Calderón*

HOSTAL EL
RETORNO
●

MONCAYO

Y

CFUENTES

HOTEL
MADRID
●

BANCO DEL
PACIFICO

To Plaza
Gonzáles
Suárez ⟶

SUPERMERCADO
UNIVERSAL
■

VELASCO

ACOSTA

◎ OBELISK

To Barrio
El Alpagata ⟶

TRAIN
STATION
■

COLÓN

To Shopping
Center, Banks,
Otavalo, and Quito ⟵

MERCADO
AMAZONAS

GUERRERO

★
BASÍLICA LA
DOLOROSA

MOSQUERA

0   150 yds
0   150 m

© AVALON TRAVEL

To Bus
Station

To Parque Grijalava,
La Esperanza,
↓ and Caranqui

celebrating Simón Bolívar's victory at the battle of Ibarra in nearby Caranqui. On the south side of town is the **Basílica La Dolorosa** (Sucre and Mosquera). Built in 1928, this church suffered a collapsed dome in a 1987 earthquake, but was reopened in 1992. A huge ornate wooden altar fills the otherwise plain interior.

Beyond the churches and squares, The **Museo Regional Banco Central del Ecuador** (Sucre and Oviedo, tel. 6/264-4087, 8:30 A.M.–1:30 P.M. and 2:30–4:30 P.M. Mon.–Sat., free) is definitely worth a look. It has an interesting collection of ancient artifacts from the northern highlands as well as historic photography housed in a restored colonial building. Descriptions are in English, and free guides are available.

ENTERTAINMENT AND EVENTS

Ibarra is a sleepy city, but it does have a university population and a few options for after-hours entertainment. On the quiet eastern edge of town is a real find: the **Café Arte** (Salinas 543 at Oviedo, tel. 6/295-0806, 5 P.M.–midnight Mon.–Sat., entrées $3–6), opened by local painter Olmedo Moncayo in 1996. There are art exhibitions, a diverse menu, and live music on weekends, attracting renowned local and international musicians. Another pleasant spot for a drink is **Bar Bud** (Plaza Calderón, tel. 6/264-0034, 4 P.M.–midnight Wed.–Sat., 10 A.M.–4 P.M. Sun.), with good views of the square.

Like elsewhere in the province, the celebration of **Inty Raymi,** which combines with the Roman Catholic **Festival of San Juan,** is held in late June and is one of the biggest parties of the year. The **Fiesta del Virgen del Carmen** is held on July 16.

Neighboring Laguna Yahuarcocha is the focus of the **Fiesta de los Lagos,** celebrated the last weekend of September with car races on a track around the water and an agricultural and industrial fair.

SHOPPING

Musicians will love the handmade guitars, mandolins, and *requintos* (small guitars) of

Marco Carrillo at **Guitarras Carillo** (Mariano Acosta 13–32 at Galindo). Instruments start at $100. The **Mercado Amazonas** sells clothing, electronics, and pretty much everything else, but take care with your belongings in crowded areas.

RECREATION

Do you have the urge to see Ibarra and a big chunk of the northern Sierra from above? If so, call **Fly Ecuador** (Oviedo 913 at Sánchez and Cifuentes, tel. 6/295-3297 or 6/295-1293, www.flyecuador.com.ec) for a tandem paragliding ride from the slopes of Imbabura ($60 pp). The school also rents and sells equipment.

A more conventional way to see the countryside is by **train** (tel. 6/295-0390, www.ferrocarrilesdelecuador.gob.ec). The once-famous route used to run all the way to San Lorenzo, in the mangroves near the Colombian frontier. Nowadays the train only makes the two-hour trip to Salinas (Fri.–Sun., $10 one-way, $15 round-trip). It was reopened in 2011 as part of a project to regenerate the entire nationwide route.

ACCOMMODATIONS
Under $10

Avoid the cluster of run-down centrally located *residenciales* south of the plazas because most are seedy motels. The weathered colonial **Hotel Imbabura** (Oviedo 933 at Narváez, tel. 6/295-0155, www.hostalimbabura-lapileta.com, $7 pp) is a good budget choice, with roomy if basic quarters and shared baths around a bright courtyard as well as friendly, elderly owners who can show you a small archaeological museum at the back.

Hostal El Retorno (Pedro Moncayo 4–32 at Sucre, tel. 6/295-7722, www.hostalelretorno.com, $8 pp) is a very good deal, offering decent guest rooms with TVs and private baths. It's at the mouth of the alley between Sucre and Rocafuerte. **Hostal El Dorado** (Oviedo 541 at Sucre, tel. 6/295-8700, $10 pp) is very well located near the museum and has decent guest rooms for the price.

Other good deals in the budget range

include **Fenix Hostal** (Pedro Moncayo 7-44, tel. 6/295-3993, $8–10 pp) and **Hotel Madrid** (Moncayo, tel. 6/295-5301, $8 pp), directly opposite. If you can bag a view of Parque La Merced, the basic guest rooms at **Hotel Barcelona** (Flores 8-51 at Olmedo, tel. 6/260-0871, $7–9 pp) are adequate.

$10-25

The best mid-range hotel in town, with a prime location on the north side of Parque La Merced, is **(Hotel Nueva Estancia** (García Moreno 7-58, tel. 6/295-1444, $19 s, $31 d), with spacious carpeted guest rooms and a good restaurant downstairs.

$25-50

One of the best hotels in Ibarra is the **(Hotel Montecarlo** (Rivadeneira 5-61 at Oviedo, tel. 6/295-8266, fax 6/295-8182, $27 s, $44 d), with comfortable guest rooms and cable TV. The small pool, hot tub, sauna, and steam room are open on weekends and are also available to nonguests (7:30–9 P.M. Wed.–Fri., 10 A.M.–9 P.M. Sat., 10 A.M.–10 P.M. Sun., $4 pp).

Six kilometers south of Ibarra near the village of Bellavista is the **Hostería Natabuela** (Bellavista, tel. 6/293-2032, tel./fax 6/293-2482, www.hosterianatabuela.com, $36 s, $55 d, breakfast included). Neatly trimmed hedges and flowers line the brick paths between the guest rooms, and there's a pool, sauna, and steam room available on weekends. Guest rooms come with TVs, phones, and private baths.

Several high-quality hotels can be found among the estates and flower farms just south of Ibarra along the Panamericana. Down a cobbled road west of the Panamericana is the **Rancho Carolina** (near Hacienda Chorlaví, tel. 6/293-2444, www.ranchodecarolina.com, $30 s, $60 d), with dark wood railings contrasting with the thick whitewashed walls. The dining room surrounds a pretty covered courtyard with a fountain, and all food is grown on the premises. Fifteen brightly-colored guest rooms decorated with plants and antiques surround

the pool, and there's a horse-drawn carriage available to rent.

$50-75

The magnificent **(Hacienda Chorlaví** (tel. 6/293-2222 or 6/293-2223, fax 6/293-2224, www.haciendachorlavi.com, $57 s, $66 d) sits four kilometers south of Ibarra. It has been owned by the Tobar family for 150 years, since the days when the *hostería* commanded farmlands stretching to the slopes of Imbabura; it was opened to guests in 1970. The name supposedly translates as "nest of love lulled by the waters of the yellow river," but with a pool, a sauna, tennis, squash, and a soccer field to keep you busy, you might not have time left for anything else. On weekends, services are held in the tiny church, and there are performances of folkloric music and dance. Antique art and furniture adorn the 52 guest rooms, some of which have fireplaces. The restaurant serves organic vegetables grown in the gardens. Evening cocktails are served next door at the **Taberna Los Monjes** (no phone, 6 P.M.–midnight Thurs.–Sat.).

FOOD

Ibarra definitely has a sweet tooth and is known for its *arrope de mora* (blackberry syrup) and *nogadas* (nougat candies). Numerous shops selling these and other sweets crowd the southeast corner of Parque La Merced. Of course, the most famous indulgences in Ibarra are the delicious *helados de paila,* a type of sorbet pioneered by Rosalía Suárez in 1896. There are several *heladerías* selling these in town, but the best is the original **(Heladería Rosalía Suárez** (Olmedo and Oviedo, tel. 6/295-8722, $0.50–3), run by Rosalía's grandchildren.

On the quiet eastern edge of town, **(Café Arte** (Salinas 543 at Oviedo, tel. 6/295-0806, 5 P.M.–midnight Mon.–Sat., entrées $3–6) was opened by local painter Olmedo Moncayo in 1996. Browse exhibits of contemporary art, choose from a wide-ranging menu that includes everything from burgers to tacos and filet mignon, and enjoy live music on weekends.

For Italian, **El Horno** (Rocafuerte 6-38 at Flores, no phone, entrées from $3) makes a good

NORTHERN SIERRA

HELADOS DE PAILA

Ibarra's most delicious treats are *helados de paila*, sorbet that rivals anything found in Italy or gourmet restaurants in other parts of the world. The only ingredients are ice (*helado* means "iced"), sugar, and fruit. They are mixed by hand with a large wooden paddle in a *paila* (a large copper pan). Salt sprinkled on the ice under the *paila* keeps the mixture from freezing solid, and the result is a delectable treat, as close to pure frozen fruit as you can get.

The process of making *helados de paila* was begun by Rosalía Suárez in her Ibarra kitchen in 1896 and has been carried on virtually unchanged by her descendants since her death 25 years ago at age 105. In Ibarra, there are two family-run branches of the famous *heladería* (ice cream shop) on the north and south side of Olmedo at Oviedo. Now *helados de paila* are sold all over Ecuador, but Rosalía's are the original and the best.

© WWW.TOURIBARRA.GOB.EC

Helados de paila from Ibarra are famous throughout Ecuador.

pizza in a big clay oven. For Chinese, several *chifas* and small restaurants line Olmedo south of the park. For seafood, there are several *cevicherías* on Oviedo and Rivadeneira. Try **Cevichería A Su Gusto** (no phone, lunch and dinner daily, entrées $5), where they'll whip up a *ceviche* to your taste. For local staples, the **Casa Blanca Restaurant** (Bolívar and Moncayo, no phone, breakfast, lunch, and dinner daily, entrées $3) serves a good *menú del día* ($3) in the open courtyard of an old colonial house; it is also a

good choice for breakfast. **D'Gloria** (Oviedo and Sucre, tel. 6/295-0699, 8:30 A.M.–8 P.M. daily, entrées $3–6) is popular with locals for fruit pies, crepes, and salads. **Donde El Argentino** (Plaza Calderón, tel. 9/945-9004, noon–9 P.M. daily, entrées $5–9) is the best place for barbecued meat.

INFORMATION AND SERVICES

There's a very helpful **municipal tourist office** (Sucre and Oviedo, tel. 6/260-8489, www.touribarra.gob.ec, 8 A.M.–12:30 P.M. and 2–6 P.M. Mon.–Fri.) near Plaza Calderón. The website is very informative.

A **post office** is way to the east on Salinas, one block from the Iglesia San Francisco and the Plaza González Suárez. Keep trudging north for the **immigration office** on Villamar next to the Iglesia Santo Domingo. A good Internet café is **Zonanet** (Moncayo 5-74).

The **Banco del Pacífico** (Olmedo and Moncayo) changes traveler's checks. You can have money wired to you via **Western Union** on Flores and Rocafuerte.

GETTING THERE AND AROUND

Midway between Quito and the Colombian border, Ibarra is a travel hub of the northern Sierra. All buses leave from the new bus terminal south of the *mercado*. **Cooperativa Trans Espejo** runs buses to El Angel at 30 minutes past every hour (1 hour, $1.25), and **Cooperativa Cotacachi** sends buses to Cotacachi every 15 minutes from morning until night (30 minutes, $0.40). **Transportes Valle de Chota** runs one daily bus via Julio Andrade and La Bonita directly to Lago Agrio (8 hours, $9). **Aerotaxi Andina** runs to Quito four times per hour (2.5 hours, $2.50), as well as Esmeraldas (10 hours, $8) and Guayaquil (10 hours, $10). Other companies go to Tulcán (2.5 hours, $2.50), and CITA operates a direct route to Ambato for (5.5 hours, $5) that bypasses Quito—the quickest way to get south. Buses to San Antonio de Ibarra (15 minutes, $0.25) leave regularly from the obelisk.

A taxi is one of the best ways to see the area and costs about $5 per hour or $25 per day. **Taxis Lagos de Ibarra** (Flores 9-24 at Cifuentes, tel. 6/295-5150) can be hired for local tours and run shared services all the way to Otavalo and Quito. A ride to Quito costs $8 and is far quicker than the bus.

SOUTH OF IBARRA
San Antonio de Ibarra

This small town, six kilometers west of Ibarra, is renowned as a major center for woodcarving.

The back streets and main plaza are lined with workshops, often just the artists' empty living rooms, where they hew, plane, and sand blocks of cedar and *naranjillo* wood. Pieces range from artistic to religious and comical; prices range from $1 into the hundreds of dollars.

The main plaza has the largest stores, including one with interesting abstract stone sculptures. The gallery of **Luis Potosí** (tel. 6/293-2056) is the most famous, with a selection of beautiful and expensive carvings.

Buses to San Antonio de Ibarra (15 minutes, $0.25) leave from the obelisk (Sánchez and Cifuentes) in Ibarra. If your bus lets you out on the Panamericana, follow the street uphill to the east to the town's main plaza.

La Esperanza and Imbabura

Many Ibarrans relocated to this pretty town, officially called La Esperanza de Ibarra (Hope of Ibarra), nine kilometers south of the original city, after the 1868 quake. In the hope of avoiding future catastrophes, La Esperanza's new residents dedicated their town to Santa Marianita, the patron saint of earthquakes. At 2,505 meters elevation, La Esperanza sits at the foot of Volcán Imbabura (4,609 meters), making it a good departure point for climbing the volcano or its smaller sibling, **Cubilche** (3,802 meters). The climb up Cubilche takes about four hours from La Esperanza, and you can descend the other side to Lago San Pablo in another three hours, or retrace your steps. Watch the deep, matted grass in the valley between Cubilche and Imbabura on the way down; it can be a hassle to wade through. Climbing Imbabura is a bit more of an undertaking, but it's still possible to reach the summit and get back in one long day with no special equipment. Plan on leaving at or before dawn and taking a solid 10 hours round-trip from La Esperanza. The IGM *San Pablo del Lago* 1:50,000 map covers the mountain, although it's not crucial for the climb.

A **day hike** around the base of Imbabura is another option, best done clockwise starting from La Esperanza. To fully enjoy it, plan on a full day with an early start.

Señora Aida Buitrón has run the rustic, tranquil **Ⓒ Casa Aida** (La Esperanza, tel. 6/266-0221, www.casaaida.com, $7 pp with shared bath) for more than three decades. She'll reminisce about visits from Bob Dylan and Pink Floyd back in the days when famous musicians used to search for magic mushrooms in the fields after rains. Breakfasts cost $2.50, and tasty vegetarian dinners are $4.

Cooperativa La Esperanza buses (30 minutes, $0.50) run from the Parque Germán Grijalva in Ibarra, on Mosquera five blocks south of the obelisk (Sánchez and Cifuentes). Taxis to La Esperanza cost $5.

LAGUNA YAHUARCOCHA

When gazing on the tranquil waters of this beautiful lake, it's difficult to imagine the carnage that gave birth to its name (Blood Lake). In 1495, Inca leader Huayna Capac inflicted the final defeat on the local Cara people. Between 20,000 and 50,000 Cara were slain and their bodies dumped into the lake, turning the waters crimson. The surviving Cara warriors were apparently so respected by the Inca that they were employed as royal bodyguards.

These days Yahuarcocha is far more peaceful, and it is a popular weekend retreat for Ibarrans. The lake is surrounded by mountains and lined by *tortora* reeds, which are woven into *esteras* (mats) and canoes. The wide road encircling the lake is used for annual car races, and on weekends it is lined with vendors selling lake trout. At a few places near the entrance from the highway, you can rent rowboats ($2 per hour).

To get here, head north from Ibarra along the Panamericana to the large sign announcing the lake turnoff to the right. Alternately, you can turn right slightly earlier onto a dirt road that leads up to a hilltop with a beautiful view of Ibarra and the lake. Descend to the lakeside pueblo of **San Miguel de Yahuarcocha**, known locally for its *curanderos* (faith healers) and *brujos* (sorcerers). Buses run from Ibarra to Yahuarcocha every few minutes from the obelisk (Sánchez and Cifuentes) or the market on Guerrero.

Lake Yahuarcocha's tranquil setting hides a bloody past.

NORTHERN SIERRA

Accommodations and Food

Overlooking Yahuarcocha is the **Hotel El Conquistador** (Laguna Yahuarcocha, tel. 6/295-3985, fax 6/264-0780, $24 s, $48 d, breakfast included), with a large restaurant and a discotheque. Guest rooms have TVs and private baths. Next door is the newer, slightly nicer **Hotel Imperio Del Sol** (tel. 6/295-9794 or 6/295-9795, $36 s or $48 d, breakfast included). You'll pass the **Hostería El Prado** (Panamericana near Laguna Yahuarcocha, tel./fax 6/295-9570 or 6/264-3460, $42 s, $61 d, breakfast included) on the Panamericana just before arriving at the entrance to the lake. It's a pleasant country hotel with an indoor pool, a sauna, a steam room, and a restaurant. Ten huge guest rooms have phones, color TVs, and private baths, and laundry service is available.

WEST OF IBARRA
Piñan Lakes Hike

Ibarra is a good starting point for the southeastern portion of the Cotacachi-Cayapas Reserve. Transportes Urcuquí buses from the terminal in Ibarra head west every half hour via Urcuquí to Irunguicho (labeled "Irubincho" on the IGM *Ibarra* 1:250,000 map), four kilometers away. Irunguicho is the departure point for loop hike to the numerous **Lagunas de Piñan** at the base of Yana Urcu de Piñan.

A clear, steep path leaves from Irunguicho to the north-northwest. At Cerro Churuloma, one hour's hike away, you'll find campsites and the last available water until the lakes. Heading west, you'll pass Cerro Hugo (4,010 meters), with beautiful views of Cayambe, Cotopaxi, and Cotacachi, followed by Cerro Albuqui (4,062 meters). Five–six hours from Irunguicho lies Lago Yanacocha, the first of this cluster of tiny *páramo* jewels.

Lago Yanacocha is just east of Yana Urcu and mirrored by Lago Sucapillo to the west. To the south is the larger Lago Burrococha, with a good campsite to the south. To reach it from Yanacocha, climb the ridge to the south, then head west-southwest past some small ponds until you hit a trail heading west. Many other small lakes and ponds dot the landscape. It's

possible to continue from here another 12 kilometers west to the larger and more remote **Laguna Doñoso.**

The hike out winds south, then east, joining with a dirt road. The last two hours of the six-hour walk are on a cobbled road, leading to **Otavalillo** and the Hacienda El Hospital. From there, it's one more hour's hike uphill to Irunguicho, three kilometers north, where you can catch a ride back to Urcuquí or Ibarra. The IGM 1:50,000 *Imantag* map is sufficient, but the 1:25,000 *Cerro Yana Urcu* provides more detail. Take a compass.

To make things far easier, **Piñan Turismo Comunitario** (tel. 6/292-3633, www.pinant-rek.com) can organize guided tours to this region. Accommodations are available at a refuge ($12 pp). Meals are available, and guides and horses can be hired for $20 pp per day.

Chachimbiro Hot Springs

The mineral-water pools at Chachimbiro Hot Springs ($6 pp), 42 kilometers northwest of Ibarra, used to be run by a local foundation but have recently been taken over by the local government. Surrounded by trails and organic gardens, the pools range from cool to scalding (45–55°C) and are used by locals to treat a range of illnesses. There's also a steam bath and a sauna. After the thermal baths at Papallacta and in Baños, these are among the best in Ecuador.

Daily buses leave from the terminal at 7 A.M. and noon, returning at noon and 3 P.M., taking nearly two hours to reach the pools. You can also hire a taxi from Ibarra (1 hour, $15 one-way). Taxi drivers will often wait to take you back. You can spend the night in a cabin (tel. 6/292-3633, www.chachimbiro.com, $25–30 pp, including meals and spa use). The place is often packed on weekends, when the restaurant is open.

Seven kilometers from Chachimbiro and a few hundred meters down the hill from Tumbabiro is the attractive **Hostería Pantavi** (tel. 6/293-4185, www.hosteriapantavi.com, $38 s, $50 d, breakfast included), built on the foundations of the old San Clemente hacienda.

There are attractive guest rooms, mature gardens, and a swimming pool, with plans for a sauna and vapor rooms. The restaurant and bar are filled with artwork.

IBARRA TO THE COAST

Traveling from Ibarra to the beach is considered a 4–5-hour journey, and many buses ply this spectacular route daily. New destinations are opening in the forests along the way.

Siete Cascadas

Fifteen kilometers past Lita, Siete Cascadas offers cabin accommodations (tel. 9/430-7434, $10 pp) or simply a lunch stop with time to hike and explore the seven waterfalls set amid copious vegetation. There's a **police checkpoint** here, where you need to show your passport or ID.

Guallupe

Also known as La Carolina or Limonal, Guallupe is on the new road to the coast from the Chota valley. Many buses stop here for lunch, and there are several small food stands and a couple of pleasant hostels with pools. Consider renting a bike in Ibarra and taking it on the bus or train to Salinas, then riding downhill to Guallupe for an overnight stay, return by bus the next day.

There is also access from here to the **Hacienda Primavera Wilderness Ecolodge** (tel. 6/301-1231, www.haciendaprimavera. com, $83 pp) set deep in the cloud forest at 1,200 meters elevation. The hacienda receives excellent reviews, and rates include full board, horse rides, use of the pool, and comfortable accommodations.

Bospas Fruit Forest Farm

Belgian Piet Sabbe manages the tropical Bospas Fruit Forest Farm (tel. 6/264-8692, www.bospas.org) near Limonal in the Mira Valley, 1.5 hours northwest of Ibarra on the road to San Lorenzo. The farm is an ongoing experiment in sustainable organic farming, and its staff constantly experiments with crop diversification, agroforestry, and permaculture techniques.

Traditional crops such as beans, yucca, and corn are grown among fruit trees that provide shade, timber, water conservation, and soil anchoring, aided by vetiver grass planted in contour lines on the slopes.

Three private guest rooms ($18 pp) in a stone guesthouse surrounded by forest gardens are available for travelers, complete with private baths and porches with hammocks. Dorm beds ($13 pp) are also available. Piet's wife, Olda, is an excellent cook and serves three meals a day. Hiking and horseback rides in the surrounding mountains can be arranged ($12 pp per day), and a four-day tour of the northern highlands' many distinct ecological regions can also be arranged.

Guests are encouraged to learn about sustainable farming techniques, and the farm accepts volunteers, who are asked to contribute $220 per month for room and board or $15 per day for shorter stays (minimum five days).

Cerro Golondrinas

Northwest of Ibarra, Cerro Golondrinas (tel. 6/264-8662, www.fgolondrinas.org) is a small cloud-forest reserve protecting a wide range of habitats, from *páramo* at 4,000 meters to premontane forest below 1,500 meters. Birders stand a good chance of adding to their life lists here: 210 species of birds have been recorded near Cerro Golondrinas peak (3,120 meters), along with condors in the mountains and toucans and parrots at lower elevations. Sloths, monkeys, and coatimundis hide in the lower forests, and foxes and deer inhabit the *páramo*.

You can enter the reserve from the bottom via the village of Guallupe, which is near La Carolina on the road to San Lorenzo, or from the top by way of the town of El Angel. One of the best ways to see the reserve is to go on the four-day trek ($250 pp, $220 pp for groups of 5–8) organized by the **Fundación Golondrinas** (tel. 6/264-8679). This moderately strenuous journey takes you by foot and on horseback from the *páramo* in El Angel down to the cloud forest and Guallupe.

It is possible to do the trek on your own.

Independent travelers can stay in Guallupe in the foundation's **El Tolondro** hostel (tel. 6/264-8679, $18 pp, all meals included). To get here, take the Ibarra–San Lorenzo bus and ask to be dropped off in Guallupe (48 kilometers from Ibarra), then walk 10 minutes uphill, following the signs. During the trek, you can also stay at the foundation's **El Corazón Cloudforest Lodge** ($25 pp, all meals included), at 2,200 meters in the heart of the reserve. It takes four hours to get there (local guides and horses can be arranged at the foundation's office in Guallupe), and it's a bit Spartan, with only four bunk beds, an outhouse, and a fire for cooking—but for the price, the incredible views from the ridge top are a steal.

Also along the trek route, the inhabitants of the village of **Morán** (accessed from El Angel) on the edge of the *páramo* run the **Cabaña de Morán** (tel. 6/264-8679, $10 pp, all meals included, plus $2 pp entrance fee). If you're pressed for time, the foundation also offers two-day visits ($120 pp) to the lower reaches of the reserve from Guallupe.

In addition to managing the reserve, the foundation is deeply involved in local conservation and education. It draws inspiration from its founder, Maria Eliza Manteca Oñate, who won a Rolex Award for Enterprise in 2000 for her efforts in promoting sustainable farming techniques in the Andes. The foundation's main goal is to protect the forest from lumber interests and encroachment by settlers. It administers conservation, environmental education, and agroforestry programs in local communities as well as demonstration farms. The foundation accepts visiting scientists as well as short-term and long-term volunteers. The latter need some experience in horticulture or permaculture techniques and should have a solid grasp of Spanish. Contributions of $280 pp per month are requested for stays of at least one month in exchange for room and board.

IBARRA TO TULCÁN
North of Ibarra, the Panamericana follows the Río Chota upstream and soon splits in the village of Mascarilla, giving you a choice of routes

to reach Tulcán. The older, rougher route heads north through Mira and up into the wilds of El Angel, but it's rarely used these days and the newer, southern route is far better and passes through Chota, Bolívar, and San Gabriel. There's a police checkpoint at the road junction, so have your passport ready. Once you leave the hot, dry Río Chota valley, both routes wind through cloud forest–covered mountains sparkling with lakes, waterfalls, and rivers.

Mascarilla
The friendly inhabitants of this small village, just a short walk from the Panamericana, will be happy to show you their handicrafts projects, which include making beautiful, expressive pottery masks and bowls as well as paper recycling. They have a small store opposite the tiny, clean hostel ($8–10 pp). Accommodations are very limited in town, but homestays can sometimes be arranged on request for $10 per person.

El Angel
By the time your bus finally chugs all the way up to El Angel (pop. 6,000), the town's motto—"Paradise Closer to the Sky"—doesn't seem so far from the truth. At 3,000 meters it definitely feels like you're up on top of something here; the clouds are closer and the air thinner. There's even a street called Río Frío (Cold River). Most travelers come here to visit the Reserva El Angel to the north, even higher in the bright, cold *páramo*.

The rough topiary works in the **Parque Libertad** were begun by José Franco, the father of Tulcán's famous topiary cemetery.

The **Hostería El Angel** (tel. 6/297-7584, $16–20 pp, breakfast included), right at the turnoff, is easily the nicest lodging in town. Eight guest rooms are surrounded by flowers, and facilities include a living room with a fireplace, a cafeteria, laundry service, and hot water. The owners offer tours of the *páramo* on foot, mountain bike, or horseback.

The best of the handful of restaurants in town is the **Asadero Los Faroles** (Parque Libertad, tel. 6/297-7144, breakfast, lunch, and dinner daily, entrées $3).

For information on the reserve, stop by the **El Angel Reserve office** (Salinas 9-32 at Esmeraldas, 2nd Fl., tel. 6/297-7597), inside the small courtyard.

Cooperative Trans Espejo (tel. 6/297-7216) has an office on the Parque Libertad; buses run to and from Quito (4 hours, $4), Ibarra (2 hours, $2), and Tulcán (2 hours, $2). If you miss the last bus of the day, hire a taxi to take you to the Panamericana at Bolívar, where it's easy to flag down a bus passing in either direction.

El Angel Ecological Reserve

High above the town of El Angel is Ecuador's premier *páramo* reserve. Created in 1992, El Angel Ecological Reserve ($10 pp) ranges 3,650–4,770 meters in elevation across some of the most pristine high-elevation country in Ecuador. Throughout the reserve's 15,700 hectares, you'll see the spiky heads of the giant *frailejón* plant, for which El Angel is famous. Locals use it for various curative purposes, including relief of rheumatism—crush a piece of leaf to release the medicinal ingredients, which have a turpentine smell. With similar fuzzy green leaves but without the tall stem is the *orejas de conejo* (rabbit ears). Andean and torrent ducks swim in the streams flowing between lakes stocked with rainbow trout. Hawks and the occasional condor soar on the thermals over the heads of grazing deer.

It is possible to camp here, but be prepared for seriously cold weather. Temperatures in El Angel can drop below freezing, and 150 centimeters of rain per year is not uncommon. Wherever you go in the reserve, be careful with the fragile vegetation—a misplaced footstep can last for months. The best season to visit is during the relatively dry season of May–October, when high winds and intense daylight sun alternate with clouds, drizzle, and nightly chill. The November–April wet season is marked by mud and more precipitation, including snow.

If you want to spend the night in comfort, **Polylepis Lodge** (tel. 6/295-4009, www.polylepislodge.com, $60 pp, meals included) has cottages with fireplaces and private baths. Guided tours are included.

From the town of El Angel, hire a taxi or jeep or hike north through La Libertad into the reserve. This dirt road leads to the crystalline Laguna Crespo, near Cerro El Pelado (4,149 meters). To the west are the Colorado guard post, Cerro Negro (3,674 meters), and Laguna Negra.

An alternate entrance route is along the old road to Tulcán, past the guard post at La Esperanza. Look for a parking area 16 kilometers from El Angel. A trail leads from here to the striking Lagunas Voladero and Potrerillos (45 minutes' hike). The road from Tufiño to Maldonado traverses the northern part of the reserve, skirting Volcán Chiles and the Lagunas Verdes.

For more information on the reserve and how to get there, visit the office in El Angel (Salinas 9-32 at Esmeraldas, 2nd Fl., tel. 6/297-7597).

Bolívar and Gruta La Paz

Several years ago, visiting scientists uncovered a trove of mammoth bones just one kilometer outside the small town of Bolívar. The bones are long gone, but just to the north, one of the most famous icons of Ecuador's northern Sierra sits in a natural cave. The Gruta La Paz (Peace Grotto), also called Rumichaca, contains a chapel dedicated to the Virgen de Nuestra Señora de la Paz dwarfed by a huge natural stone overhang. Stalactites and stalagmites lend the site a Gothic atmosphere amplified by the fluttering bats and dark waters of the Río Apaquí. In addition to the subterranean chapel, attractions include a set of thermal baths (open Wed.–Sun., $1) just outside the cave. There's also an inexpensive guesthouse for pilgrims, who fill the cave on weekends and holidays, especially during Christmas, Holy Week, and the **Fiesta del Virgen de la Paz** on July 8. At other times, you can have the bat-filled cavern almost completely to yourself. Private buses can be hired from Bolívar or San Gabriel, and trucks carrying groups leave from San Gabriel and Tulcán on weekends.

Tulcán and the Colombian Border

Tulcán (pop. 63,000) is the highest provincial capital in the country at 3,000 meters and is considerably colder than Ibarra and Otavalo. You may feel little reason to hang around here on the way to or from Colombia, and at the time of this writing the border crossing north of town is the only safe one between the two countries. While Tulcán isn't the prettiest town in Ecuador, the amazing topiary gardens in the municipal cemetery have to be seen to be believed, and it's worth stopping here briefly just to visit them. Throughout the city, no hedge is left unshaped, both in parks and on military bases. For visitors with more time, the high *páramo* road west through Tufiño and Maldonado is unique in Ecuador.

Approximately six kilometers from the Colombian border, Tulcán has typical border-town hustle and bustle. You can buy anything here, and much of it is less than legal. Note that even though this is deemed the only safe border crossing, the city has its rough edges, so be careful walking around at night. Note also that the areas around Tulcán are not particularly safe, so don't stray from the city center. Wherever you go, make sure you carry your passport, as police checks are very common, and you'll be in trouble without proper ID.

SIGHTS
◖ Tulcán's Municipal Cemetery
Local resident José Franco started the famous topiary works in Tulcán's municipal cemetery decades ago. Today, Franco is buried amid the splendor of his creations in the Escultura en Verde del Campo Santo (Sculpture in Green of the Holy Field), under an epitaph that calls his creation "a cemetery so beautiful, it invites one to die." Monumental cypresses have been trained and trimmed into figures from Roman, Greek, Inca, and Aztec mythology, interspersed with arches, passageways, and intriguing geometric shapes. The cemetery has become such an attraction that vendors sell film and ice cream outside the gates. Needless

to say, exercise discretion if a burial procession is in progress.

ENTERTAINMENT AND EVENTS
There are dance clubs all over town, but they change names and locations regularly, so ask around. Things get busy on weekends, but be careful going out at night. The disco at **Hotel Sara Espindola** (Sucre and Ayacucho, tel. 6/298-6209, 8 P.M.–2 A.M. Fri.–Sat.) is a safe bet.

The **Fiesta Municipal** (Apr. 11) warms things up every year, as does the **Fiesta del Provincilización del Carchi** (Nov. 19).

SHOPPING
Tulcán is like one big shopping mall: It seems that every other door opens into a clothing store. The main **food market** spreads along Boyacá between Bolívar and Sucre, and there's another between Sucre and Olmedo, two blocks west of Rocafuerte. The *mercado central* has the usual clothing and food stalls.

ACCOMMODATIONS
None of Tulcán's hotels are particularly noteworthy. Double-check if and when hot water is available. **Hotel Azteca** (Pasaje San Francisco between Bolívar and Atahualpa, tel. 6/298-0481, $7 pp) is passable for cheap accommodations. The 52 guest rooms have cable TV, and there's a disco downstairs (light sleepers beware). Near the *terminal terrestre,* the **Hotel Los Alpes** (JP Arellano, tel. 6/298-2235, $8 pp) has guest rooms with private baths and TVs. Across Sucre is a better option, **Hotel Internacional Torres del Oro** (Sucre and Rocafuerte, tel. 6/298-0296, $12 pp), with a restaurant and guarded parking.

◖ **Sara Espindola** (Sucre and Ayacucho, tel. 6/298-2464, $25 s, $50 d), just below the central plaza, is the best in town, with a disco, laundry service, and a good restaurant. Its sauna and steam-room spa facilities are

NORTHERN SIERRA

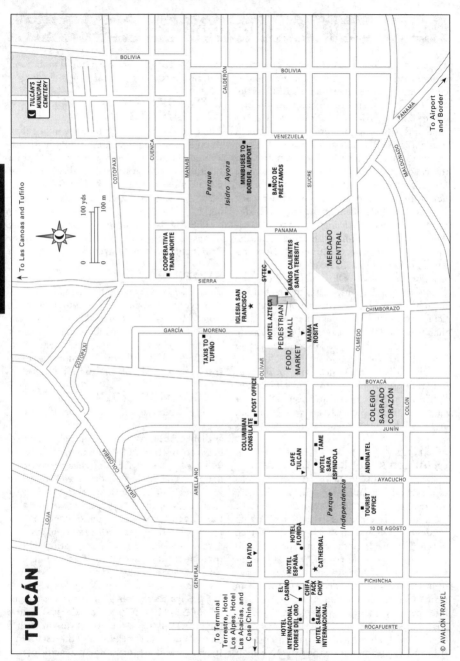

NORTHERN SIERRA

TULCÁN

BOLIVIA

TULCÁN'S MUNICIPAL CEMETERY

CALDERÓN

BOLIVIA

To Airport and Border

PANAMA

CUENCA

COTOPAXI

VENEZUELA

MALDONADO

MANABÍ

Parque Isidro Ayora

MINIBUSES TO BORDER, AIRPORT

BANCO DE PRÉSTAMOS

SUCRE

To Las Canoas and Tufiño

100 yds

100 m

COOPERATIVA TRANS-NORTE

PANAMA

BAÑOS CALIENTES SANTA TERESITA

SYTEC

MERCADO CENTRAL

SIERRA

CHIMBORAZO

IGLESIA SAN FRANCISCO

HOTEL AZTECA

PEDESTRIAN MALL

OLMEDO

GARCÍA

MORENO

MAMA ROSITA

COTOPAXI

TAXIS TO TUFIÑO

FOOD MARKET

BOLÍVAR

BOYACÁ

COLEGIO SAGRADO CORAZON

COLÓN

COLOMBIA

POST OFFICE

JUNÍN

COLUMBIAN CONSULATE

ARELLANO

CAFE TULCÁN

HOTEL TAME SARA ESPINDOLA

ANDINATEL

AYACUCHO

GRAN COLOMBIA

Parque Independencia

TOURIST OFFICE

LOJA

10 DE AGOSTO

EL PATIO

HOTEL FLORIDA

HOTEL ESPAÑA

CATHEDRAL

GENERAL

PICHINCHA

To Terminal Terrestre, Hotel Los Alpes, Hotel Las Acacias, and Casa China

EL CASINO

CHIFA PACK CHOY

HOTEL INTERNACIONAL TORRES DEL ORO

HOTEL SAENZ INTERNACIONAL

ROCAFUERTE

© AVALON TRAVEL

included in the rates but are also open to non-residents ($5 pp).

FOOD

Tulcán's food picks are even fewer than its hotel selection. Several restaurants specializing in Colombian food are scattered throughout town, including **El Patio** (Bolívar between Pichincha and 10 de Agosto, tel. 6/298-4872, 8 A.M.–9 P.M. Mon.–Sat., 8 A.M.–6 P.M. Sun., entrées $3–5), which has a tiled courtyard decorated with old photos and antiques. For Ecuadorian fare, especially fried pork, try **Mama Rosita** (Sucre and Chimborazo, tel. 6/296-1192, 9 A.M.–7 P.M. daily, entrées $2–3). Beneath Hotel Unicornio, **Chifa Pack Choy** (Sucre and Pichincha, tel. 6/298-0638, noon–11 P.M. daily, entrées $3) serves up tasty Chinese.

INFORMATION AND SERVICES

The **tourist information office** (tel. 6/298-5760, 8 A.M.–6 P.M. Mon.–Fri.) is on Cotopaxi. The **post office** is across the street from the food market on Bolívar. Sidewalk money changers along Ayacucho are happy to transform your dollars into Colombian pesos. Rates are better in Tulcán than at the border or in Colombia. The **Banco Pichincha** (Sucre and 10 de Agosto) and the **Banco de Préstamos** (on Parque Ayora) change traveler's checks. The **police station** is at Avenida Manabi and Guatemala (tel. 6/298-0622).

GETTING THERE AND AROUND
Buses

The *terminal terrestre* (bus terminal) is on Bolívar, 1.5 kilometers south of the center of Tulcán—a $1 taxi ride, $0.20 bus ride, or 30-minute walk from the main plaza. Being the only northern border town, Tulcán has buses leaving for just about every major city in the country, including Ibarra (2.5 hours, $2.50), Quito (5 hours, $5), Ambato (8 hours, $6) and even an *ejecutivo* bus to Huaquillas (18 hours, $22) if you want to bypass Ecuador

altogether and go straight to Peru. A new service on **Transportes Putumayo** connects Tulcán directly with Lago Agrio (7 hours, $7) and Coca (9 hours, $9) along the new frontier road through La Bonita, Puerto Libre, and Lumbaquí. One bus per day runs to both destinations.

In town, **Cooperativa Trans-Norte** buses depart hourly to Tufiño (1 hour, $1) in the morning and, when full, in the afternoon. Trans-Norte also sends buses to Chical (4 hours, $4). *Colectivo* taxis on García Moreno and Avellano run to Tufiño when four people fill the seats; for a little extra, they will continue to Agua Hediondas. *Colectivos* also run to the border and the airport from the Parque Isidro Ayora ($0.75) when full.

Air

The **TAME** office (tel. 6/298-0675) next to the Hotel Sara Espindola on Sucre sells tickets to Quito (Mon., Wed., Fri., Sun., $50 one-way) as well as connections for Guayaquil (Mon., Wed., Fri., $110 one-way) and Calí, Colombia ($78 one-way). The airport is two kilometers north of Tulcán on the road to the border; a taxi costs $1.25 each way.

WEST OF TULCÁN

The road west from Tulcán follows the Río San Juan (called the Mayasquer in Colombia), which serves as the international border, much of the way to the ocean. This unspoiled area has been described as even more beautiful than the El Angel Reserve because it's even more remote. Condors circle over kilometers of untouched *páramo* and cloud forest all the way to El Chical, and the road becomes impassable soon after. Note that the border region away from Tulcán is not safe, and it is certainly not recommended to take this route all the way to the coast.

Tufiño

Thermal baths bubbling up from the smoldering core of Volcán Chiles are the main attraction in this town, 18 kilometers from Tulcán. There aren't any places to stay in Tufiño, but you can get a meal in the market or at one of several small shops. A restaurant-disco is open on weekends.

Bring your passport, because visiting the pools means crossing the border: The **Balnearios Aguas Termales** are actually in Colombia, but you are allowed to cross for the day to visit them. Be aware that the security situation in this region has recently deteriorated.

To get to the **Aguas Hediondas** ("stinking waters") pools—the warmest and most scenic—head west from Tufiño on a dirt road for three kilometers, then turn to the right at the large sign and go another eight kilometers into a beautiful, remote valley. Several buses each day connect Tulcán with Tufiño, but only the noon bus travels up this dirt road to the turnoff. A direct bus from Tulcán to the pools leaves at 8 A.M. on Sunday. A truck to the pools costs $10, and the driver will wait for you.

Past Tufiño, the road enters the El Angel Reserve and climbs the lower reaches of Volcán Chiles on the right. The higher the road winds, the more windswept and impressive the *páramo* becomes. You'll pass at least five waterfalls on the way to the town of **Maldonado,** some of them within a short walk of the road.

Volcán Chiles

Climb the summit of Volcán Chiles (4,768 meters) and you can stand with one foot in Colombia and one in Ecuador, because Chiles' peak pokes right through the border. The weather is the main concern in this otherwise straightforward ascent: dress for rain and snow, and be prepared for most mornings to be clouded in. Guides can occasionally be found

in Tufiño. The trailhead is about 20 kilometers (30 minutes' drive) past Tufiño. A private truck to the trailhead from Tufiño costs $3, or you can hop off a bus bound for Maldonado or El Chical. The climb from the road to the peak and back takes about six hours. The IGM *Tufiño and Volcán Chiles* 1:50,000 map is helpful, but it may be hard to buy a copy because of border tensions.

THE COLOMBIAN BORDER

Seven kilometers north of Tulcán, a bridge over the Río Carchi at **Rumichaca** marks the only recommended border crossing with Colombia. It is open around the clock and crawls with moneychangers, but if you need your passport stamped coming in or out, cross between 6 A.M. and 10 P.M. Keep your eyes open if you decide to change money on either side of the border; official Ecuadorian changers should have photo IDs. There's an ATM on the Colombian side, but it does not have U.S. dollars.

Exit formalities from Ecuador are relatively more straightforward, if less orderly, than in Colombia. Direct any questions to the **Ecuadorian immigration office** (open 24 hours) or the **Ministerio de Turismo** office (tel. 6/298-4184, 8:30 A.M.–1 P.M. and 1:30–5 P.M. Mon.–Fri.), both located in the CENAF buildings at the bridge.

Taxis from Tulcán to the border cost $4 one-way, and microbuses ($0.80) leave from the Parque Isidro Ayora when full. On the Colombian side, it's 13 kilometers to Ipiales, and *colectivos* ($1) make the trip regularly. Buses run from Ipiales to Pasto (2 hours, 500 pesos), 90 kilometers farther northeast.

CENTRAL SIERRA

South of Quito, the Central Highlands contain Ecuador's most dramatic Andean scenery. The Panamericana runs down between two parallel mountain chains along the famous "Avenue of the Volcanoes." Eight of Ecuador's 10 highest peaks are found here: towering Chimborazo (6,310 meters), picture-perfect Cotopaxi (5,897 meters), the nine peaks of El Altar (5,319 meters), highly active Sangay (5,230 meters), the twin peaks of Iliniza Sur (5,263 meters) and Iliniza Norte (5,116 meters), tempestuous "Throat of Fire" Tungurahua (5,023 meters), and Carihuairazo (5,018 meters), Chimborazo's little brother. There are so many peaks in this region that climbers are spoiled for choice on where to start. There's plenty for day hikers too, including Ecuador's most visited national park,

Cotopaxi, and its most spectacular lake, the extinct Laguna Quilotoa, whose turquoise waters are a wonder to behold.

In the rolling valleys of patchwork quilt of countryside below the mountains, you'll find a string of colonial cities. Each is tucked into its own river basin, and farmland fills in most of the level space between. Large plantations hark back to the days when forced labor supported farms stretching beyond the horizon. The more remote and spectacular areas, fully stocked with volcanoes, lakes, and rivers, have been set aside as parks or reserves.

Indigenous cultures dominate the Central Sierra. During their reign, the Incas established outposts all along the road to Quito to keep the local populations in line. Today, indigenous pride burns brightly here, and 75

© BEN WESTWOOD

HIGHLIGHTS

◖ Cotopaxi National Park: Ecuador's most popular mainland national park is home to llamas, wild horses, and the Andean condor, and it is dominated by the country's highest and most beautiful volcano (page 127).

◖ Laguna Quilotoa: The luminous turquoise water of this lake in an extinct volcano's caldera is one of Ecuador's most stunning sights, and the Quilotoa Loop around nearby indigenous villages is an unbeatable hike (page 137).

◖ The Waterfall Route from Baños to Puyo: Go cycling, hiking, rafting, and canyoneering to your heart's content in the Pastaza Valley before soaking in the thermal baths of this idyllic spa town nestled below Volcán Tungurahua (page 155).

◖ Chimborazo Fauna Reserve: Drive, hike, or cycle through the lunar landscapes of this reserve, home to reintroduced herds of vicuñas, in the shadow of Ecuador's highest mountain (page 157).

◖ Nariz del Diablo Train Ride: Parts of the rail system are back up and running, and this section through a series of switchbacks through the Devil's Nose below Alausí is still one of the world's most dramatic train rides (page 167).

LOOK FOR ◖ TO FIND RECOMMENDED SIGHTS, ACTIVITIES, DINING, AND LODGING.

percent of Chimborazo Province residents consider themselves of native descent. Dozens of different groups inhabit the highlands, often each in its own town. Small communities in the mountains plant crops at elevations as high as 4,000 meters, supplementing their income through shepherding and crafts. Clothing and customs are the most distinguishing characteristics, from the white-and-black garments of the Salasaca to the white-fringed red ponchos of the Quisapinchas, and there is a bustling market every day of the week where you can pick up bargains on everything from textiles to leather goods and *tagua* carvings. The largest towns in the region—Ambato, Riobamba, and Latacunga—have their own distinct

identities and act as the commercial centers of Tungurahua, Chimborazo, and Cotopaxi Provinces, respectively.

With the regeneration of the Quito–Guayaquil train line, exploring parts of the Central Sierra is easier than ever. The Avenue of the Volcanoes route between Quito and Latacunga is now open, and the dramatic section descending La Nariz del Diablo, south of Riobamba, has recently reopened. By 2013 you may be able to ride all the way from Quito to Riobamba.

Away from the hustle and bustle is arguably Ecuador's best tourist town, Baños, a place so idyllic and relaxing that you may find it hard to leave.

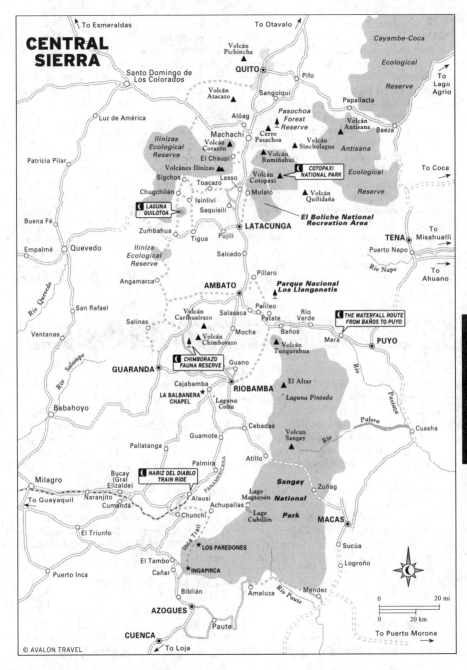

CENTRAL SIERRA

To Esmeraldas

To Otavalo

Santo Domingo de Los Colorados

Luz de América

Patricia Pilar

Volcán Pichincha ▲

QUITO ◉

Pifo

Sangolquí

Papallacta

Cayambe-Coca

Ecological

Reserve

To Lago Agrio

Volcán Atacazo ▲

Alóag

Machachi

Volcán Corazón ▲

El Chaupi

Ilinizas Ecological Reserve

Volcánes Ilinizas ▲▲

Sigchos

Toacazo

Lasso

Pasochoa Forest Reserve

Cerro Pasachoa ▲

Volcán Rumiñahui ▲

Volcán Sincholagua ▲

Volcán Antisana ▲

Baeza

To Coca

Antisana

CEN. **COTOPAXI NATIONAL PARK**

Volcán Cotopaxi ▲

Ecological

Chugchilán

Isinliví

Saquisilí

Mulaló

Volcán Quilindaña ▲

Reserve

Buena Fé

CEN. **LAGUNA QUILOTOA**

El Boliche National Recreation Area

Empalmé

Quevedo

Zumbahua

Tigua

Pujilí

LATACUNGA

TENA ◉

To Misahuallí

Puerto Napo

Río Napo

To Ahuano

Río Quevedo

Iliniza Ecological Reserve

Salcedo

San Rafael

Angamarca

AMBATO ◉

Píllaro

Pelileo

Patate

Río Verde

Parque Nacional Los Llanganatis ▲

CEN. **THE WATERFALL ROUTE FROM BAÑOS TO PUYO**

Ventanas

Salinas

Volcán Carihuairazo ▲

Salasaca

Mocha

Baños

Mera

PUYO ◉

Volcán Chimborazo ▲

Río Pastaza

Río Solampe

CEN. **CHIMBORAZO FAUNA RESERVE**

Guano

Volcán Tungurahua ▲

GUARANDA ◉

Cajabamba

RIOBAMBA ◉

El Altar ▲

Laguna Pintada

Cuasha

Babahoyo

★ **LA BALBANERA CHAPEL**

Laguna Colta

Palora

Guamote

Cebadas

Volcán Sangay ▲

Río

Pallatanga

Palmira

Atillo

Sangay

Zuñag

Milagro

CEN. **NARIZ DEL DIABLO TRAIN RIDE**

Bucay (Gral Elizalde)

Alausí

Lago Magtayán

National

To Guayaquil

Naranjito

Cumandá

Achupallas

Lago Cubillín

Park

MACAS ◉

El Triunfo

Chunchi

Inca Trail

★ **LOS PAREDONES**

Sucúa

Puerto Inca

El Tambo

★ **INGAPIRCA**

Cañar

Logroño

Biblián

Amaluza

Mendez

Río Paute

0   20 mi

AZOGUES ◉

Paute

0   20 km

CUENCA ◉

To Loja

To Puerto Morona

© AVALON TRAVEL

PLANNING YOUR TIME

To see the highlights of the Central Sierra, ideally you need a week, although you could rush through in less time. By far the most popular destination is **Baños,** which doubles as the adventure and spa capital of the region, with adrenaline and relaxation available in equal measure. Don't be surprised if you stay longer than planned. Baños makes a good base for exploring the surrounding hills and for organizing short trips into the Oriente through Puyo. **Cotopaxi,** Ecuador's picture-perfect volcano, is also hugely popular, both as a day trip to the national park and as a climb (but only if you are acclimated and prepared). The turquoise waters of **Laguna Quilotoa** are jaw-droppingly beautiful and can be visited on a day trip or overnight, but it's better to take your time and do at least a portion of the hike along the **Quilotoa Loop.**

The renovated train system is another highlight of this region. A new route has opened recently through the spectacular **Avenue of Volcanoes** between Quito and Latacunga. More famously, south of Riobamba you can travel along the most hair-raising portion along **La Nariz del Diablo** (Devil's Nose), a dramatic set of switchbacks west of Alausí. Note that riding on the roof is no longer allowed. Riobamba is also a good base to organize hikes and climbs up Ecuador's highest mountain, Chimborazo, and its surrounding reserve, home to herds of vicuña.

If you have time to spare, you can explore some of the Central Sierra's characterful colonial haciendas that offer fine accommodations, hiking, and horseback riding. There are also several markets in the region, and shoppers will certainly be kept busy—the indigenous bustle of Saquisilí, Zumbahua, and Salasaca, leather goods in Guano, and in Pelileo enough jeans to clothe Texas.

Machachi and Aloasí

These small towns are the first settlements of note you reach after leaving the urban sprawl of southern Quito. Machachi (elevation 2,950 meters) sits on the Panamericana highway, while Aloasí is just to the west. Now that the train line running south of Quito is open, these towns see a few more visitors on weekends, but most only stay for a brief stopover at the train station.

The setting of the towns, surrounded by mountains, is certainly dramatic: Volcán Atacazo is to the north, Pasochoa to the northeast, Sincholagua to the east, Rumiñahui to the south, the Ilinizas to the southwest, and Corazón to the west. Machachi is a good base for climbing any of these; Aloasí makes a slightly better base for climbing Corazón.

SIGHTS

Machachi's central plaza is surrounded by an ornate painted church, the Teatro Municipal, and a few leather shops selling clothes and shoes. The main market day is Sunday. Machachi's main attraction is the **Güitig factory** (7:30 A.M.–3:30 P.M. Mon.–Fri., $0.50), four kilometers east of town, where Ecuador's most famous mineral water is bottled. There are three crystal-clear mineral pools (two cold, one lukewarm) just past the bottling plant set among gorgeous flower gardens, picnic areas, and sports facilities. Tours of the plant itself are available on weekdays (ask the guards at the entrance). Taxis to the plant cost $2 one-way, or you can just walk east on Pareja out of town, following it as it turns into Ricardo Salvador about halfway to the factory.

ACCOMMODATIONS AND FOOD

In Machachi, a good place to spend the night is the **Hostería Chiguac** (Calle Las Caras, Machachi, tel. 2/231-0396, www.hosteria-chiguac.com, $12 pp, breakfast included), three blocks east of the church plaza. Guest rooms with private baths and hot water have great views of Rumiñahui. Another option in Machachi with more basic guest rooms is **Hotel Estancia Real** (Luis Cordero, Machachi, tel. 2/231-5760, $8 pp).

A more pleasant option is in Aloasí, right next to the train station. **La Estación de Machachi** (La Estación, Aloasí, tel. 2/230-9246, $40 s, $50–60 d) is a renovated 19th-century hacienda with a friendly atmosphere and woodstoves to ward off the high-altitude chill. Choose guest rooms or cabins; breakfast is included if you stay in a cabin, and lunches and dinners (from $10) are available. Get here by taxi from Machachi ($2) or a local bus from the church.

Dining options are few, but the most popular spot is along the Panamericana: **El Café de la Vaca** (Panamericana Km. 23, tel. 2/231-5012, 8 A.M.–5:30 P.M. daily, $3–8) feeds hungry drivers as well as locals.

GETTING THERE AND AROUND

Any bus running south along the Panamericana can drop you at one of the two entrances to Machachi, leaving a two-kilometer walk into town. Buses from Quito run from the southern Quitumbe terminal. Buses back to Quito leave Machachi from two blocks west of the plaza. To travel in more style with a guided tour of the Avenue of the Volcanoes, take the train ($15 round-trip) from Quito to Machachi. It leaves Quito's Chimbacalle station at 8 A.M. Thursday–Sunday, returning in the afternoon.

Taxis can be hired to take you up the rough roads to the bases of nearby mountains; a one-way trip to Cotopaxi costs about $30.

ILINIZA ECOLOGICAL RESERVE

West of the Panamericana are the twin peaks of Iliniza Norte (5,126 meters) and Iliniza Sur

The old Quito-Guayaquil railway runs south of Quito through Machachi and Latacunga.

© FERROCARRILES DE ECUADOR

(5,248 meters), which stand only one kilometer apart. The 149,000-hectare reserve that encloses them was established relatively recently, in 1996. The reserve also includes Cerro Corazón, Laguna Quilotoa, and a significant chunk of cloud forest. Most climbers enter the reserve near Machachi. The entrance fee, charged only for those climbing the Ilinizas, is $5 pp.

Climbing the Ilinizas

These sister peaks are remnants of what used to be one volcano, and they're like night and day for climbers. **Iliniza Sur,** the taller and more difficult of the two, is the sixth-highest peak in Ecuador. Besides El Altar, Iliniza Sur was the only mountain in Ecuador that Edward Whymper couldn't climb, although he tried twice. The Carrel brothers, though, made the 1880 expedition a success by reaching the summit on their own. The first Ecuadorian climber reached the top in 1950. Even though glacial retreat is well under way on Iliniza Sur, it's still a challenging endeavor and a good introduction to Ecuador's more difficult peaks above 5,000 meters. Check with climbing-tour operators in Quito for the latest route information.

Iliniza Norte, Ecuador's eighth-highest peak (5,126 meters), was one of the few in the country to be climbed first by Ecuadorians—in this case, by Nicolás Martínez and Alejandro Villavicencio, accompanied by the Austrian climber Franz Hiti, in 1912. In the dry season, technical equipment and experience are not necessary, making Iliniza Norte accessible part of the year to hardy hikers undaunted by some minor rock climbing. It's commonly used by tour operators as preparation for tackling higher peaks such as Cotopaxi.

The approach to both mountains leads from the Panamericana to a hut on the saddle separating the two peaks. Ten kilometers south of Machachi, take a turnoff that leads seven kilometers southwest to the village of El Chaupi (elevation 3,310 meters). Buses run directly to El Chaupi from Machachi, or take a taxi.

Three kilometers beyond the village is the **Hacienda San José del Chaupi** (tel. 9/973-7985, Quito tel. 2/257-0066, www.hostal.biz/sanjose.html, $10 pp), a working farm that provides a good starting point for climbing any of the peaks in the area. Guest rooms have hot water, kitchens, and fireplaces, with continental breakfast included. Horses are available for rent.

Another good lodging option is **Hostal Llovizna** (tel. 9/969-9068, 14–18 pp), just past the church in El Chaupi. Owner Vladimir Gallo also runs the climbing refuge and can arrange horses to carry luggage.

From El Chaupi, it's a five-hour hike to the **Nuevos Horizontes refuge** (www.ilinizarefuge.com, dorm $10 pp). There's a $5 entrance fee at a checkpoint along the way. At 4,600 meters, only about 500 meters below either peak, this is one of the oldest mountaineering huts in Ecuador and can accommodate about 24 people. It features bunk beds, stoves, and cooking and eating utensils. Water is available from a nearby stream. Bring a sleeping bag and food.

Climbing Volcán Corazón

A short distance west of Machachi across the Panamericana sits this extinct volcano, first climbed in 1738 by Charles Marie de La Condamine while on a break from measuring the planet. At 4,788 meters, Corazón is a challenging day climb, consisting mostly of easy uphill hiking through grassy fields, with some moderate but exposed rock scrambling for the last 500 meters. With a 4WD vehicle, you can get to within two hours of the top, but you'll need permission to go through the private land along the way. Count on about 5–6 hours of hiking from the highway. A taxi from Machachi (about $10) can drop you off partway up the road, usually near the tree farm, cutting the ascent time by 1–2 hours.

Machachi to Latacunga

◖ COTOPAXI NATIONAL PARK

Ecuador's top mainland national park is second only to the Galápagos in the annual number of visitors, and it's easy to see why. Less than two hours south of Quito, 33,400 stunning hectares enclose one of the most beautiful volcanoes in the Americas, along with two other peaks higher than 4,700 meters, and extensive verdant *páramo* where llamas graze and wild horses gallop. Tours of the park vary from gentle hikes and cycle rides to scaling the volcano itself, considered one of Ecuador's best climbs.

Flora and Fauna

The lower elevations on the edges of the park contain wet montane forests at about 3,600–3,800 meters, but the largest section is covered by sub-Andean *páramo* at 4,000–4,500 meters. This is where you'll find most of the park's animals: deer, rabbits, and the endemic marsupial mouse. More elusive are pumas and endangered spectacled bears. There are more than 90 species of birds, including carunculated caracaras, shrike-tyrants, ground-tyrants, great thrushes, rufous-naped brush-finches, Andean gulls, noble snipes, and brown-backed chat-tyrants (related to flycatchers). If you're lucky, you may spot an Andean condor soaring overhead.

Shrubby blueberries and lupines bloom next to Indian paintbrush and members of the daisy family, while the occasional terrestrial bromeliad is pollinated by hummingbirds. You might spot the *urcu rosa,* a small blue mountain rose, hidden among the tough *ugsha* grass. Above 4,500 meters to the snowline at 4,700 meters, plunging temperatures keep the mossy tussocks of the Andean tundra relatively empty.

Access

The two main entrances to the park are south of Machachi along the Panamericana. The first turnoff, 16 kilometers south of Machachi, is also the entrance to El Boliche National Recreation Area. It passes the CLIRSEN satellite tracking station before forking three ways.

Take the right fork and follow the train tracks for 500 meters. From here, it's six kilometers downhill through a forest to a campsite with fireplaces and simple cabins.

The second entrance turnoff is nine kilometers farther south; this is the most popular access point, making it easier to hitch a ride into the park, especially on weekends (although the road washes out occasionally in the rainy season). It joins with the northern access road at the park boundary, where you pay the entrance fee ($10 pp) at the gate, which is open daily.

The road through the park curves in a semicircle north around Volcán Cotopaxi. As it heads northeast, it passes the administrative center at **Campamiento Mariscal Sucre,** 10 kilometers from the gate. A small museum here has an exhibition on the geology, history, flora, and fauna of the park. Shortly beyond the museum, which is usually the first stop on a guided tour, there's a path leading to **Laguna Limpiopungo,** a shallow lake at 3,800 meters elevation whose reeds provide a habitat for several species of birds.

On a small hill 15 kilometers beyond the lake are the oval ruins of **El Salitre,** formerly an Inca *pucara* (fortress), abandoned soon after the arrival of the Spanish.

A trail leads around the lake to the northwest for access to Rumiñahui. Shortly beyond that trail, another jeep track heads nine kilometers south to the **Jose Rivas Refuge,** the best base for climbing expeditions. Note that the hike to the refuge is tougher than you may expect if you're not fully acclimated (which you won't be if you're coming from Quito).

Many of the day tours include mountain biking in the park, which is a great way to cover more distance. You are usually taken up to a refuge for a dramatic downhill ride, which gets the adrenaline pumping without tiring you out.

Climbing Volcán Cotopaxi

Cotopaxi may not be Ecuador's highest

mountain but it's certainly the most photogenic. This perfectly symmetrical cone has been captivating climbers and photographers for years, and many of the local indigenous people, who named it "the neck of the moon" in Kichwa, still worship the volcano as god of the valley. However, Cotopaxi's beauty masks the beast that lies within. While it is probably not the world's highest active volcano (that title most likely belongs to Llullaillaco on the Chilean-Argentine border, which erupted in 1877), there's no denying Cotopaxi's destructive ability.

Cotopaxi's first recorded eruption disrupted a battle between the Spanish and the Inca in 1534, and since then it has erupted on over 10 occasions, destroying Latacunga several times. Eruptions in 1742, 1768, and 1877 were the worst, killing hundreds of people. Cotopaxi registered minor eruptions in 1906 and as recently as the 1940s, but at present activity is limited to steam rising from the crater, only visible to climbers who reach the summit.

HOT LOVE

The Kichwa people of the Sierra have always revered the country's volcanoes, considering them to be people with human personalities and flaws. Long ago, according to legend, the handsome volcano Cotopaxi took a liking to the young, passionate Tungurahua. Tungurahua was no angel, however, and it wasn't long before the object of her affections turned to the taller Chimborazo. Their love child was Guagua Pichincha (*guagua* means "baby" in Kichwa), a badly behaved volcano that went north to live with his grandfather Rucu Pichincha. The last time that Guagua had a tantrum and erupted was in 1999, and soon afterward Tungurahua followed suit; locals believe that this was the mother answering the child. Luckily for climbers, Cotopaxi and Chimborazo have kept quiet about the whole geological drama.

A German and Colombian climbing team first set foot on Cotopaxi's glacier-covered peak in 1872, followed 10 years later by Edward Whymper, who opened the northern route still in use today. The climb is not technically difficult, as the many climbers who scale the ice-covered slopes regularly will attest. Crevasses are usually large and obvious, making the climb mostly an uphill slog. However, less than half of those who attempt the summit actually reach it. You need to be in very good physical condition, be fully acclimated, and have an experienced guide and a certain amount of luck with the conditions. Technical equipment is necessary: ice axes, crampons, ropes, and marker wands.

Although Cotopaxi can be climbed year-round—it sees more clear days than almost any other peak in the Ecuadorian Andes—the best months are December–January. August–September are also good but windy. February–April can be clear and dry as well, while August–December are usually windy and cloudy.

As with any peak over 5,000 meters, acclimation is essential. If you've been staying in Quito at 2,800 meters, this is unlikely to be sufficient acclimation to scale Cotopaxi on a two-day excursion (although you may be lucky). Ideally you should trek and sleep at around 4,000 meters for a couple of days, or even better, do a practice climb of a smaller peak such as Iliniza Norte or Rumiñahui before attempting Cotopaxi.

The road to the refuge heads south from the main park road for nine kilometers to the parking area at 4,600 meters. A half-hour hike up a steep, sandy trail brings you to the José Ribas refuge (4,800 meters), which was built in 1971 by the San Gabriel Climbing Club. The two-story shelter is fully equipped with bunk beds ($20 pp), cooking facilities, running water, and snacks and water for sale as well as lockable storage space for gear. A night's stay is usually included in the price of a guided tour.

To reach the summit, catch a few hours of sleep before waking around midnight to start climbing. It takes 6–10 hours from the refuge, and the route contains smoking fumaroles reeking of sulfur. The views over the other volcanoes on the "avenue" are spectacular, and you should be able to see the lights of Quito in the distance. The descent takes 3–6 hours.

Climbing Volcán Rumiñahui

This peak, 13 kilometers northwest of Cotopaxi, was named after Atahualpa's bravest general, who famously hid the huge Inca ransom after Atahualpa's death and refused to give up its whereabouts when tortured by the Spanish. The history of its name is luckily the most violent aspect of Rumiñahui (4,712 meters), which is heavily eroded and officially dormant but most probably extinct. There are actually three peaks, and the volcano offers a relatively straightforward climb, combining an uphill hike with a bit of scrambling, but because the quality of rock can be poor, a rope and climbing protection are recommended for the more exposed stretches.

The east side of Rumiñahui is reached through Cotopaxi Park along tracks that skirt Laguna Limpiopungo to the north or south. A path toward the central peak is clearly visible along a well-defined ridge. From the lake to the base is about a two-hour hike, and camping along the way is possible. The south peak involves some moderate technical rock climbing (class 5.5). The IGM *Machachi* and *Sincholagua* 1:50,000 maps cover this area.

EL BOLICHE NATIONAL RECREATION AREA

Ecuador's smallest nationally protected area at 1,077 hectares, El Boliche National Recreation Area hugs the southwestern side of Cotopaxi National Park. Boliche is perfect for visitors who are more interested in weekend family picnics and mild hikes than mountaineering, with cabins, camping spots, sports fields, and self-guided trails. The habitat here at 3,500 meters is dominated by pine trees planted through reforestation programs in the 1960s and 1970s. The pines have actually disrupted the local ecosystem and caused problems for Quito's water supply, which draws heavily on this area.

However, the thickly forested trails are very beautiful and make a refreshing change from the grasslands that dominate the rest of the region. Visitors may catch sight of deer, rabbits, and the occasional wolf. Llamas and *guarizos* (offspring of llamas and alpacas) have been released in the park and are reproducing well.

The entrance to El Boliche is the same as the northern turnoff for Cotopaxi off the Panamericana—16 kilometers south of Machachi. Admission ($10 pp) is combined with the entry to Cotopaxi. The train service from Quito to Latacunga passes through Thursday–Sunday.

ACCOMMODATIONS AND FOOD

There are no real towns in this area, just haciendas and hotels; the only venues that serve food are the hotels.

$10-25

Most of the accommodations in the area around Cotopaxi National Park are in the mid- to high-end category. The most economical option is **Cuello de Luna** (El Chasqui, Panamericana S. Km. 44, tel. 3/271-8068 or 9/970-0330, www.cuellodeluna.com, dorm $18 pp, $40 s, $50 d), just two kilometers from the main park entrance. There are spacious cabins or dorms in the loft.

About 25 kilometers south of the main entrance to the park is **Tambopaxi** (Quito office: Diego de Almagro and La Pinta, tel. 2/222-0241, www.tambopaxi.com, dorm $19 pp, $90 s, $110 d), which has comfortable dorms in the main lodge and more expensive private guest rooms in a separate lodge. There are great views of Cotopaxi. Camping costs $6 pp.

$25-50

Near the northern entrance of the park is **Hacienda El Porvenir** (Quito office: Lactea 250 at Chimborazo, tel. 2/204-1520, www.volcanoland.com, $43 s, $50 d), also known as Volcano Land. Straw mats on the walls and fireplaces in the dining room and living rooms supply a comfortable atmosphere, and there are views of Cotopaxi from the large patio. Tours are offered on foot, mountain bike, and horseback into the nearby hills. Camping is available for $4 pp.

A newer option is **Secret Garden Cotopaxi** (Cotopaxi National Park, tel. 9/357-2714, www.secretgardencotopaxi.com, dorm $38 pp, $65 s or d, meals included), sister hotel of the backpacker favorite in Quito. This eco-lodge is set in the foothills of Pasochoa, near the village of Pedregal, overlooking the national park. The rates include three meals, snacks, drinks, and use of mountain bikes. Many guest rooms have their own fireplaces, and transfers are available from the Secret Garden in Quito (depending on the number of people).

$50-75

Located in Lasso about 10 minutes by car south of the main park entrance, **Hostería San Mateo** (Vía Latacunga Km. 55, Lasso, tel. 3/271-9015, fax 3/271-9471, www.hosteriasanmateo.com, $66 s, $72 d) has six beautiful guest rooms with private baths and a cabin for up to four people decorated in Ecuadorian country style. There's a swimming pool and a bar for relaxing after horseback riding and hiking. Owner Francisco Baca's family has a 400-year history in Ecuador, and he maintains interests in cattle and dairy ranching as well as organic vegetable farming.

One of Ecuador's oldest haciendas, dating from 1695, **Hacienda La Ciénega** (Quito office: Cordero, tel. 2/254-9126 or 3/271-9052, www.hosterialacienega.com, $63 s, $88 d, breakfast included) now operates as a hotel. The setting is straight out of the 17th century, when the estate belonged to the Marquis of Maenza and stretched from Quito to Ambato. La Condamine, Von Humboldt, Juan José Flores, and Velasco Ibarra all found shelter here over the centuries.

The square building surrounds a flower-filled courtyard with a fountain, where a set of ornately carved wooden doors open into the small private chapel. Horses graze near flower-filled greenhouses to the rear of the courtyard. A sign on the west side of the Panamericana one kilometer south of Lasso points down a paved lane, where the hacienda gate opens on the left after one kilometer.

Gabriel Espinosa and his friendly family run the comfortable **Hacienda La Alegría** (Alóag, Machachi, tel. 2/246-2319 or 9/980-2526, info@alegriafarm.com, www.hacienda-laalegria.com, from $65 pp, breakfast included) on the old railroad line in the shadow of Volcán Corazón. Horseback riding is the focus here, and they run 1–2-day trips into the hills in every direction. Old equestrian photos and equipment decorate the beautiful old building, which can accommodate 24 guests in newer extensions. Meals include produce from the hacienda's organic farm. Rates range from $65 pp for bed-and-breakfast to $180 pp for full board, including rides and hacienda visits. Transportation from Quito ($45) can be arranged.

$100-200

Immense pumice walls greet visitors at **Hato Verde** (Panamericana Km. 55, Mulaló, tel. 3/271-9348 or 3/271-9902, www.hacienda-hatoverde.com, $134 s, $183 d, breakfast included), with nine cozy guest rooms and a family atmosphere. The house has retained much of the 120-year-old building's character. At night, the fires are lit and the shutters closed; in the mornings, they are opened to display great views of Cotopaxi volcano and the farmlands. Fresh milk and cheese produced on the farm are a feature of the country breakfasts. Hato Verde is just a few hundred meters from the Panamericana, south of Cotopaxi.

Over $200

Opened in 1995, **Hacienda Yanahurco** (Cotopaxi National Park, tel. 2/244-5248, www.haciendayanahurco.com, $225 pp, all meals and tours included) is east of the volcano, and access is normally from the northern entrance road to Cotopaxi National Park. This retreat offers outdoor activities on the lands of an old family hacienda: guided hiking, fishing, bird-watching, and especially horseback-riding excursions on 26,000 private hectares. Seven guest rooms in the ranch-style buildings have fireplaces and private baths. The fishing here is particularly good; brook, rainbow, and brown trout fill the streams. The annual roundup of wild horses in November is a very special three-day weekend event that should be reserved well in advance.

All-inclusive packages include activities, food, and accommodations in the expansive main hacienda, based on a minimum group size of four. Camping is available from $15 pp. The private, locked entrance road is reached by turning east from the main park entrance road at Laguna Limpiopungo.

Hacienda San Agustín de Callo (Lasso, Cotopaxi, tel./fax 3/271-9160, Quito office tel. 2/290-6157, www.incahacienda.com, $278 s, $424 d, three meals and excursions included) owes as much of its history to the Inca as to the Spanish. It was originally built as an Augustinian convent on the site of a ruined Inca outpost. The chapel and dining room both incorporate massive Inca stonework, and Inca remains have been unearthed during restorations. The nearby Cerro de Callo is a perfectly round hill thought to be an Inca burial mound. Trekking, fishing, and cycling excursions are included.

The hacienda sits along the road that parallels the Panamericana north of Mulaló. Take the southern turnoff to Cotopaxi National Park and turn right (south) toward Mulaló instead of continuing straight into the park. You'll pass the Hacienda Los Nevados before reaching the San Agustín turnoff to the west.

Latacunga and Vicinity

Latacunga is the capital of Cotopaxi Province and the closest city to Volcán Cotopaxi, which towers over the valley just 30 kilometers northeast. Since Topa Inca Yupanqui left his regional chiefs to oversee this newly conquered region with the words *Llagtata-cunuai* ("I leave this land in your care"), the residents of Latacunga (pop. 75,000) seem to have remained content for their city's fate to be forever linked to the volcano.

As the land erupted into war between the Spanish and the Incas in 1534, Cotopaxi also began to spit fire, and the conquerors, who had never witnessed a volcanic eruption, fled in terror. The local indigenous people, however, worshipped Cotopaxi as god of the valley, and the regular eruptions didn't prevent the founding of Latacunga on the banks of the Río Cutuchi in the late 1500s. In the past three centuries Cotopaxi has destroyed the city several times in more than 10 eruptions: Those in 1698, 1742, and 1877 were the most destructive, and whether through human folly or dogged determination, the city was rebuilt each time in the exact same location. Cotopaxi continued to rumble away in minor eruptions in the early 1900s and as recently as the 1940s, and it is still considered active, with smoke visible to climbers who reach the crater. Needless to say, nobody bothers much about insurance around here.

Modern-day Latacunga is a charming, friendly city where people go about their business calmly in Cotopaxi's shadow. First impressions are not great on arrival at the bus station in the city's industrial outskirts, but persevere to the center and you'll find well-preserved colonial squares, churches, and cobbled streets. While it takes less than a day to take in Latacunga's sights, the city also makes a good base to explore Cotopaxi and the Quilotoa Loop, and hikes and climbs to both destinations can be organized by a few excellent local operators in town.

SIGHTS
Latacunga's pretty main square, **Parque Vicente León,** is flanked on the south side by an impressive whitewashed **cathedral** with carved wooden doors and the elegant **town hall** on the east side. One block to the east is **Parque Bolívar,** and a couple of blocks north is another impressive church, **Iglesia Santo Domingo,** overlooking Santo Domingo square,

CENTRAL SIERRA

© BEN WESTWOOD

Latacunga's cathedral and Parque Vicente León

which hosts a small market. A few blocks southwest, **Parque La Filantrópica** is guarded by the grand old **Hospital General,** a historic landmark to the south.

For the best views of the town and surrounding valley, head east of town to **Mirador de la Virgen del Calvario.** On clear days you can see Cotopaxi. To get here, go east on Maldonado, climb the steps, and walk to the left, up Oriente, to the statue.

Markets
Plaza Chile, northwest of the center, hosts Latacunga's market, which spills down almost to the river on the busiest days, Tuesday and Sunday. It's not aimed at visitors, but there is a small selection of textiles and hats as well as plenty of snacks and fruit. To the east, the less spectacular daily municipal market borders the Iglesia de la Merced between Valencia and Echeverría.

Museums
Built on the site of an old Jesuit flour mill along

the river, the **Casa de la Cultura** (8 A.M.–noon and 2–6 P.M. Tues.–Fri., 8 A.M.–3 P.M. Sat., $0.50) contains part of the old water mill as well as an impressive ethnographic collection of ceramics, paintings, dolls in indigenous festival costumes, and colonial artifacts.

The flower-filled courtyard of the **Casa de los Marqueses** (8 A.M.–noon and 2–6 P.M. Mon.–Fri., free) has a small exhibition of archaeological artifacts and antique furniture.

ENTERTAINMENT AND EVENTS
Latacunga's **Fiesta de la Santissima Virgen de la Merced** (Sept. 22–24), known familiarly as **Fiesta de La Mama Negra,** is one of the more colorful and outstanding events in Ecuador. It centers on a small black icon of the Virgin carved by an indigenous artisan in the 17th century to protect the city against Volcán Cotopaxi. The streets fill with a colorful cast of characters, dancers, and revelers.

There are two separate festivals of the same name: the religious Mama Negra (Sept. 22–24)

and the secular Mama Negra, on the Saturday before November 11, when Latacunga celebrates its **Independence Day.**

RECREATION AND TOURS

Latacunga has a small selection of climbing and hiking operators, including these recommendations: **Volcán Route** (2 de Mayo and Guayaquil, tel. 3/281-2452, www.volcanroute.com), **Expeditiones Tovar** (Guayaquil and Quito, tel. 3/281-1333, www.tovarexpeditions.com), **Tierra Zero** (Padre Salcedo and Quito, tel. 3/280-4327), and **Tributrek,** which operates out of Hostal Tiana (Vivero and Ordoñez, tel. 3/281-0147, www.tributrek.com). All operators offer climbs of Cotopaxi (day trips from $45 pp, two-day climbs from $160 pp), and tours to Quilotoa (one day from $40 pp, three-day trek of the loop from $130 pp).

ACCOMMODATIONS

Latacunga has a decent selection of accommodations, both budget and mid-range.

LA MAMA NEGRA

Latacunga hosts one of the biggest festivals in the Ecuadorian highlands. It's worth making a beeline for the city to experience this most flamboyant of celebrations, which combines Roman Catholic, indigenous, and African traditions in a heady mix of religion and hedonism.

There are actually two festivals: the religious festival, known as **Santisima Tragedia,** held on September 24, and the more raucous secular **Fiesta de Mama Negra,** usually beginning on the Saturday prior to November 11, Latacunga's Independence Day.

The exact origin of the festival has various versions. The most likely origin of the religious festival is in the 18th century when local residents petitioned the Virgin Mary, patron saint of Cotopaxi, to protect them from the erupting volcano. Even though it didn't really work, because Latacunga was destroyed several times, the annual celebration in honor of *La Virgen de las Mercedes* persisted. The character of La Mama Negra, a blackened man dressed up as a gaudy woman that flies in the face of political correctness, probably originated from the local fascination with African slaves brought to Ecuador by the Spanish conquerors to work in the mines.

During La Mama Negra festivities, the streets are filled with a colorful cast of characters. Verse tellers – more or less public jesters – tell poems and recite comical *loas* (limericks) filled with nuggets of ironic truth. Whip-wielding, colorfully attired *camisonas* (transvestites) share the stage with *huacos* (witches) dressed in masks and white robes, who act out a ritual cleansing by blowing smoke and *aguardiente* on the spectators (including unsuspecting visitors). The celebration culminates in the arrival on horseback of La Mama Negra herself, dressed in an elaborate costume and bearing dolls to represent her children. She sprays the crowd with milk and water, and the drinking continues long into the night and beyond.

Under $10

Latacunga's best hotels are within a block or two of Parque Vicente León. The quiet **Hotel Estanbul** (Quevedo 6-44, between Salcado and Guayaquil, tel. 3/280-0354, $9–11 pp) is a perennial budget traveler's favorite, with decent guest rooms with shared or private baths. Run by a friendly Dutch-Ecuadorian couple, **Hostal Tiana** (Vivero and Ordoñez, tel. 3/281-0147, www.hostaltiana.com, dorm $9 pp, $11–25 pp) has recently changed location but still offers good-quality guest rooms with private or shared baths as well as dorms. The hotel's agency can organize tours.

$10-25

Hotel Cotopaxi (tel. 3/280-1310, $10 pp) and **Hotel Central** (tel. 3/280-2912, $10 pp) occupy the same building overlooking the main square, Parque Vicente León, and both offer comfortable guest rooms with private baths and cable TV. Slightly quieter and more elegant is **Hotel Rosim,** just off the square (Quito and Salcedo, tel. 3/280-2172, www.hotelrosim.com, $13 pp), with firm beds and cable TV.

$25-50

The **Hotel Rodelu** (Quito 1631 and Salcedo, tel. 3/280-0956, fax 3/281-2341, www.rodelu.com.ec, $27 s, $44 d) has swish guest rooms with private baths, TVs, and in-room telephones. The wood paneling, indigenous motifs, and an excellent restaurant make this a top-notch choice. A new mid-range option in town is **Villa de Tacunga** (Sánchez de Orellana and Guayaquil, tel. 3/281-2352, www.villadetacunga.com, $42 s, $61 d) with elegant guest rooms adjacent to a spacious courtyard restaurant.

FOOD

The best-known local specialty is *chugchucara*—a singular fried dish that includes chunks of pork, crispy skins, potatoes, plantains, and fresh and toasted corn—and *allullas* (ah-YU-zhahs), doughy cookies made with cheese and pork fat. If your arteries can take it, the best place to try them are restaurants along the stretch of Ordoñez southeast of the center. The grand pillars and stone decor of **La Mama Negra** (Ordoñez and Rumiñahui, tel. 3/280-5401, 10 A.M.–7 P.M. Tues.–Sun., $6–7) is one of the better establishments.

As in most towns in the Andes, you can always depend on the pizza in Latacunga. One of the best places to try a variety of toppings as well as pasta dishes is **Pizzeria Rodelu** (Quito 1631 and Salcedo, tel. 3/280-0956, 7:30 A.M.–10 P.M. Mon.–Sat., 7:30 A.M.–8 P.M. Sun., $6–9), which also does excellent meat and chicken. **Pizzeria Buon Giorno** (Orellana and Maldonado, tel. 3/280-4924, 1–11 P.M. Mon.–Sat., closed Sun., $4–6) on the main square is another good choice with great lasagna and a wide range of large salads.

For cheap set lunches ($2.50) and range of pricier barbecued chicken and meat specialties, try the cozy **El Copihue Rojo** (Quito and Tarqui, tel. 3/280-1725, noon–3 P.M. and 6–9 P.M. Mon.–Sat., $7–9) behind the cathedral.

For Chinese soups, noodles, fried rice, and sweet and sour dishes, head to **Chifa Miraflores** (Salcedo and 2 de Mayo, tel. 3/280-9079, 10 A.M.–10 P.M. daily, $3–5).

SERVICES

On the main square, Parque Vicente León, the **Banco Pichincha** has an ATM and handles some foreign currency, or try **Banco de Guayaquil** (Maldonado 7-20). The **post office** is at Quevedo and Maldonado. The **hospital** is on Hermanas Páez near 2 de Mayo.

CAPTUR (Sánchez de Orellana and Guayaquil, tel. 3/281-4968, 9 A.M.–6 P.M. Mon.–Fri.) is the local tourist office; maps, brochures, and a little information in Spanish are available.

GETTING THERE AND AROUND

Latacunga's **bus terminal** is right on the Panamericana at the west end of town. Various companies run buses to Quito (1.5 hours, $1.50), Ambato (1 hour, $1), and Saquisilí (20 minutes, $0.50). Transportes Cotopaxi heads to Quevedo (5 hours, $5) via Zumbahua. Transportes Primavera buses go to Salcedo (20 minutes, $0.50), and Transportes Pujilí will take you to Pujilí (15 minutes, $0.25).

To get to Quilotoa and Chugchilán, there is only one direct bus per day (around noon). If you miss it, take the first bus to Zumbahua and take a taxi from there.

Taxis are available for day trips to Zumbahua or Quilotoa and Cotopaxi National Park ($40–50). Taxis around town cost from $1.

SAQUISILÍ

Saquisilí, a 20-minute bus ride northwest of Latacunga, is known for its bustling Thursday market. It's not really aimed at visitors, but it is gaining popularity as a more authentic experience of an indigenous market than Otavalo. On market day, eight plazas in the center of town flood with traders. There's a food market, an animal market, and a textile market to keep you busy as well as all manner of household goods for sale. You can buy Otavalo sweaters, Tigua paintings, herbal remedies, and squealing piglets (if you want to adopt one), and the smells of roasted pork and guinea pig are never far away. The animal market is particularly interesting, with chickens, llamas, alpacas, cows, sheep, and horses being traded.

Most people come just for the morning, but accommodations are available at the **San Carlos Hotel** (Bolívar and Sucre, tel. 3/227-1981, $7 s, $12 d), with private baths and hot water. **Gilocarmelo** (Calle Chimborazo, tel. 3/272-1630, www.hosteriagilocarmelo.com, $15–19 pp, breakfast included), a five-minute walk east of the main northern bus parking area near the cemetery, offers more comfortable guest rooms as well as a sauna, a steam bath, and a swimming pool; hiking and horseback tours are available.

Saquisilí is a few kilometers off the Panamericana, two hours south of Quito. Ask the bus driver to drop you off at the junction and take another bus, or a better option is to catch the regular buses from Latacunga's bus terminal (20 minutes, $0.50).

THE QUILOTOA LOOP

The road northwest of Latacunga loops through a series of remote indigenous villages. The spectacular scenery in this region—in particular the incredible beauty of Lake Quilotoa—makes this a very popular hiking destination. The lake itself can be reached on a day trip, or you can spend anything from a couple of days to the best part of a week hiking through the undulating landscapes.

Transportation around the entire loop is limited to two direct buses per day, and less than half of the 200 kilometers of road are paved, with the remainder made up of rough dirt tracks that are sometimes impassable in the rainy season. While this makes getting around a little complicated, it's also part of the reason why the loop remains refreshingly remote and unspoiled. In addition to the breathtaking scenery, the indigenous communities have held on to their traditions. Along with the villages around Otavalo, this is one of the best regions in the Andes to experience thriving Kichwa culture.

Getting There and Around

There's no escaping that getting around the Quilotoa Loop can be a challenge. There are only two buses daily, often jam-packed with locals and even the occasional animal. If you miss the bus, you can try your luck at hiring a pickup truck to take you to the next town.

Two regular Transportes Iliniza buses travel the entire loop daily, one in each direction. All times listed below are the official times. You must arrive on time or risk missing the bus (and most likely not getting a seat). Bear in mind that the bus is often late. The bus traveling on the most popular route leaves daily at noon from Latacunga's bus terminal, heading clockwise around the loop. It passes Zumbahua at 1:30 P.M. ($1.50), Quilotoa at 2 P.M. ($2), and arrives in Chugchilán at about 3:30 P.M. ($3). The other bus heads counterclockwise around the loop from Latacunga to Chugchilán, leaving from the Latacunga bus terminal at 11:30 A.M. It passes Saquisilí at 11:50 A.M. ($0.50), Sigchos at about 1:30 P.M. ($2), and Chugchilán around 3 P.M. ($3).

Both buses stay overnight in the plaza at Chugchilán, leaving before dawn the next morning as they head in opposite directions back to Latacunga. The counterclockwise bus leaves at the ungodly hour of 4 A.M., passing Quilotoa at 5 A.M., Zumbahua at 5:30 A.M., and reaching Latacunga at 7:30 A.M. In the other direction, the bus leaves Chugchilán even earlier at 3 A.M., passing Sigchos at 4 A.M., Saquisilí at 7 A.M., and arriving in Latacunga at 7:30 A.M.

If you miss the daily bus, all is not lost. Going clockwise from Latacunga, there are hourly buses to Zumbahua (2 hours, $1.50) bound for Quevedo near the coast. From Zumbahua, you can hire a pickup truck ($5 pp, $10 minimum per group) to Quilotoa. Hiring a truck to Chugchilán is more difficult because of the quality of the road, and it costs at least $25 from Quilotoa and $35 from Zumbahua.

Going counterclockwise, there are several buses hourly from Latacunga to Saquisilí (20 minutes, $0.50), and seven buses 9:30 A.M.–6 P.M. to Sigchos (2 hours, $2). Getting to Chugchilán from Sigchos is tricky, but you may be able to hire a pickup truck for about $25.

Pujilí

Some 12 kilometers west of Latacunga, this bustling little market town springs to life on Sundays and Wednesdays when Plaza Sucre, a couple of blocks from the main squares, fills with market stalls. It is not aimed at visitors, but it is pleasant to visit.

Of more interest are the multicolored steps just up from the bus terminal that lead up to the *mirador* (lookout) at **Cerro Sinchaguasín.** It's a steep 15-minute walk to the top, which commands spectacular views of the valley with Cotopaxi in the distance.

Tigua

West of Pujilí, the road climbs higher, offering

stunning views over the valley below. After about 40 kilometers, you reach the village of Tigua (elevation 3,600 meters), a cluster of indigenous communities famed for their artwork. Hundreds of artists in town paint bright depictions of Andean life onto sheep hides. On the main road, one of the best galleries in town is **Galería Tigua-Chimbacucho** (no phone), run by Alfredo Toaquiza, whose father pioneered the art form.

There is not much else to do in Tigua, but if you want to stay, the best place is **La Posada de Tigua** (Hacienda Agricola-Ganadera Tigua-Chimbacucho, Vía Latacunga-Zumbahua Km. 49, tel. 3/281-3682 or 3/280-0454, $30 pp, breakfast and dinner included), a working 19th-century ranch with cozy guest rooms, fresh food, and horseback tours available.

Zumbahua

About 15 kilometers west of Tigua, the town of Zumbahua becomes the weekend hub of the region during its busy **Saturday market,** when indigenous people flock to town with livestock and various wares carried by llama. The town gets surprisingly noisy on Saturday nights, and most travelers just pass through, but you could be stuck if you miss the bus and can't find a pickup truck to take you to Quilotoa. Note that it can be hard to find a room on Friday night.

Of the basic hotels around the main plaza, **Hotel Quilotoa** (Plaza Central, tel. 8/614-0686, $6–7 pp) is a dependable, friendly place with private baths and a rooftop terrace. Tigua painters have a gallery next to the new community **Samana Huasi** (Vía Latacunga-Zumbahua, tel. 3/282-4868, $6), on the main road toward Pujilí.

◖ Laguna Quilotoa

The luminous turquoise water of this lake in an extinct volcano is perhaps the most breathtaking sight in Ecuador. On a clear day, the spectacle of the sky reflected in the mineral-rich waters 400 meters below the rim, with the snow-capped peaks of Ilinizas and Cotopaxi in the distance, is jaw-droppingly beautiful.

CENTRAL SIERRA

© UDY BRILL

Laguna Quilotoa, in an extinct volcano, is one of Ecuador's most spectacular sights.

Laguna Quilotoa was formed about 800 years ago after a massive eruption led to the collapse of the volcano. Locals believe that the lake is bottomless, and geologists estimate its depth at 250 meters.

Now part of the Iliniza Ecological Reserve, the entrance fee is a mere $1 pp to enter the village of Quilotoa (elevation 3,900 meters) and access the lake. Note that the lake is sometimes shrouded in mist (most commonly in the afternoon), so it's best to plan an overnight stop here to avoid disappointment.

The hike around the rim (4–5 hours) is the best way to appreciate the stunning views. The walk down to the lake (under 2 hours round-trip) is also spectacular. Donkeys ($5) are sometimes available to carry you back up, and canoes ($5 pp) can be rented on the lake.

Accommodations can be found along the turnoff from the main road, where a few Tigua artists run humble hostels with fireplaces, wool blankets, and simple home-cooked food. It gets very cold at night here, so bring plenty of warm clothes. Local artist Humberto Latacunga's **Hostal Cabañas Quilotoa** (Vía Quilotoa, tel. 3/281-4625 or 9/212-5962, $8–10 pp, breakfast and dinner included) has simple guest rooms with fireplaces and hot-water showers. Humberto's beautiful paintings and carved wooden masks are for sale in the restaurant. Another option farther up the hill is **Princesa Toa** (tel. 9/455-6944, $8–10 pp, breakfast and dinner included), which offers cheap set lunches ($2.50).

The only mid-range lodging in town is the **Quilotoa Crater Lake Lodge** (tel. 2/252-7835 or 9/794-2123, $40 s or d, breakfast included), which overlooks the lake and boasts panoramic views. Guest rooms are warm and comfortable, and the restaurant is the best in the village.

Chugchilán

One of the most popular trails on the Quilotoa Loop is the five-hour hike to Chugchilán (elevation 3,180 meters), 22 kilometers to the north. The dramatic route skirts cliff edges, passes through the village of Guayama (the only place for refreshments), and descends into the precipitous Río Toachi canyon at Sihui before making the final uphill push to Chugchilán. Maps are available at the Black Sheep Inn in Chugchilán and at Cabañas Quilotoa. It's not advisable to do this hike alone, and it is best to leave no later than 1 P.M. It's possible to do the return trip between Chugchilán and Laguna Quilotoa in one long day, but you would have to start very early. Doing it in the opposite direction, from Chugchilán, involves more uphill hiking, but the advantage is that you can time your trip to catch a bus back from Quilotoa at 2 P.M.

The hike west to Isinliví or Guantualó, which has a traditional Monday market, starts on the road about three kilometers north of Chugchilán. Take the path opposite the road to the cheese factory or the turnoff at Chinaló to reach Itualó, and cross the bridge over the Toachi River.

Chugchilán itself is a poor, remote mountain village, home to about 25 families. There's a women's **knitting cooperative** selling clothing and a small **cheese factory** outside town on the road to Sigchos. There is a small **Sunday market** and a few small shops in the center, good for stocking up on provisions for hiking. The phone service in town is quite unreliable, and your best bet is the **Andinatel** office on the main plaza.

The best budget accommodations in town are found at the homey **Hostal Mama Hilda** (tel. 3/270-8075 or 3/270-8005, $17–21 pp, breakfast and dinner included). Run by the friendly owner, Mama Hilda, the building dates from the 1850s and used to be the town's schoolhouse. There are simple but comfortable guest rooms with shared or private baths, and some have woodstoves to keep warm.

The nearby **Hostal Cloud Forest** (tel. 3/270-8016 or 8/270-8181, www.hostalcloudforest.com, $12–15 pp, breakfast and dinner included) has expanded recently and now has 80 guest rooms. It's another good budget option with guest rooms that have shared or private baths, a popular restaurant, and a living room kept warm by a fireplace. Volunteer placements to teach in the local school are available.

Both hostels offer horseback riding (4–5 hours, $15 pp), and guides to hike from Laguna Quilotoa to Chugchilán cost $15 per group. Transportation can be hired on local trucks to or from Laguna Quilotoa, Zumbahua, or Sigchos ($25–30).

The town's most famous accommodations used to be found at the award-winning **Black Sheep Inn** (tel. 3/270-8077, www.blacksheepinn.com). In 2011, however, the inn, run by founders Michelle Kirby and Andres Hammerman, was converted into a retreat center specializing in hosting group events and is no longer open to visitors. The inn has been a model of ecological sustainability and self-sufficiency for many years, with composting toilets, organic gardens, a greenhouse, and a full recycling program. There's a gym, a yoga studio, a steam room, and a hot tub as well as a solar-powered waterslide and a 100-meter-long zip-line between two eucalyptus trees. Llamas, ducks, dogs, chickens, and, of course, the odd black sheep wander the grounds, which spill down the hillside above the town. For further information on organizing group events, which must be booked well in advance, consult the website.

Sigchos

About 24 kilometers north of Chugchilán, the road undulates down to the little town of Sigchos, which fills up for its Sunday market but is otherwise unremarkable. If you're hiking from Chugchilán, you could opt to stay here at **La Posada** (Galo Atiaga and Las Ilinizas, tel. 3/271-4224, $6 pp), which has small but clean guest rooms and a good restaurant (7 A.M.–9 P.M. daily) downstairs offering set meals ($2) and chicken, meat, and fish entrées ($3–4).

Isinliví

A worthwhile detour from the traditional Quilotoa Loop is 12 kilometers southeast of Sigchos to the village of Isinliví, which boasts a beautiful setting and is home to an Italian-run cooperative of artisans specializing in wood-carving. There are many excellent hiking and mountain-biking routes in the area, including trails to Quilotoa (7 hours' hike), Chugchilán (4 hours), and the colorful Monday market in Guantualó (1 hour).

A good place to stay is **Llullu Llama Hostal** (tel. 3/281-4790, www.llullullama.com, $18–21 pp), run by the same Dutch-Ecuadorian couple that runs Hostal Tiana in Latacunga. The name means "new flame" in Kichwa. Set in a renovated old country house are five private guest rooms, four loft rooms, and a dormitory. Breakfast and dinner are available, along with box lunches on request. You can rent horses with local guides and obtain clear hiking maps with instructions.

Ambato and Vicinity

Most travelers pass through the capital of Tungurahua Province on their way to Riobamba or Baños because Ambato (pop. 180,000, elevation 2,580 meters) is much more a commercial hub than a tourist town. Indeed, Ambateños are among the wealthiest people in the Central Sierra, and everybody seems to own a car, as you'll notice from the disproportionate amount of traffic.

The busy streets do have some interesting attractions that make the city worth a stroll, however, if only for a few hours. The most interesting involve two of Ambato's most famous Juans: Juan Montalvo was one of Ecuador's foremost writers and liberals and has a park named after him with an adjacent museum. Even more impressive is the estate of Juan León Mera, composer of Ecuador's rousing national anthem. It is set on the banks of the river northeast of town.

HISTORY

Ambato has a turbulent history, first shaken by wars and more recently by earthquakes.

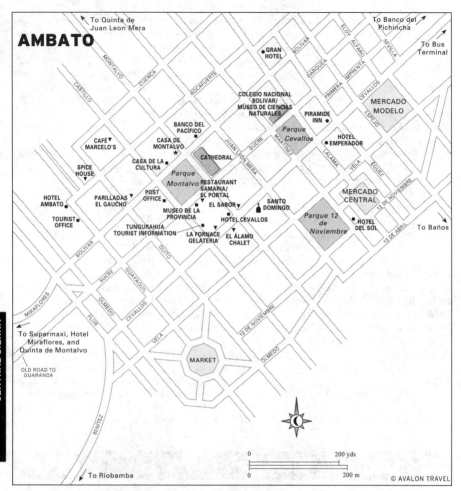

The original inhabitants, the Cashapamba, were conquered by the Cara before being overrun themselves by the Inca, who established a settlement here along the Inca highway to Quito. Atahualpa defeated his half-brother Huáscar near the city before being captured by the Spanish. After the conquest, the city of Ambato was founded in 1535 by Sebastián de Benalcázar, who also founded Quito.

Just as Ambato was beginning to grow, it was hit by a massive earthquake in 1698, which destroyed most of the city. The surviving residents rebuilt the city a few kilometers to the south, and Ambato began to thrive, becoming a gathering place for intellectuals in the 19th century. The three Juans (Juan Montalvo, Juan León Mera, and political essayist Juan Benigno Vela) came to national prominence, drawing writers and luminaries from Quito and Guayaquil, and the city is still known as *cuna de los tres Juanes* (cradle of the three Juans).

Disaster struck again in 1949 when Ambato

was hit by another strong quake, which caused extensive damage. As a result, most of the city's colonial character has disappeared, including the original cathedral, which has been replaced by a huge modern structure.

Today, Ambato is a busy commercial center, producing everything from vehicles and clothing to fruit and flowers, the latter two famously celebrated during Carnival. Many of Ecuador's banks are also based here due to the city's geographically central location.

SIGHTS

Parque Montalvo, graced by a statue of the city's most famous son, Juan Montalvo, is backed by Ambato's brash, modern, white-domed **cathedral,** which was built after the 1949 earthquake. The interior is far more impressive, with huge bronze statues, wood carvings, and wonderful acoustics during mass. On the corner of Montalvo and Bolívar is the **Casa de Montalvo** (tel. 3/282-4248, 9 A.M.–noon and 2–6 P.M. Mon.–Fri., 10 A.M.–1 P.M. Sat., $1), where author Juan Montalvo was born and laid to rest. A noted liberal, he was forced into exile by conservative president Gabriel García Moreno in 1869. The house has a collection of photos, manuscripts, clothing, and a life-size portrait. Juan Montalvo's body is on display in the mausoleum, and while his face is covered by a death mask, his decayed fingers remain rather unnervingly visible. The Montalvo experience is completed by a visit to the writer's summer home, **La Quinta de Montalvo** (8 A.M.–6 P.M. Tues.–Sat., free) in the Ficoa suburb. Head west on Miraflores and across the river onto Avenida Los Guacamayos, or take a taxi ($1).

More impressive and well worth the short trip north over the Río Ambato is the home of Juan León Mera, who sought solace at **La Quinta de Mera** (Av. Rodrigo Pachana Lalama, 9 A.M.–5 P.M. Tues.–Sun., $1) between penning his country's national anthem and *Cumandá,* a novel depicting indigenous life in 19th-century Ecuador. The grand old 19th-century adobe building houses a museum with period

© BEN WESTWOOD

Parque Montalvo

furnishings and artifacts from Mera's family. The house sits amid **Jardín Botanico La Liria,** 13 hectares of well-maintained botanical gardens, including a small gorge with its own microclimate. To get there, take a taxi ($1.50) or walk north on Montalvo to the bridge over the river. From there, take a bus labeled "Atocha" or walk, taking a right on Capulíes. The walk should take about 45 minutes.

If you have more time to kill in the center of Ambato, the **Museo de Ciencias Naturales** (tel. 3/282-7395, 8:30 A.M.–12:30 P.M. and 2:30–6:30 P.M. Mon.–Fri., $2), in the Colegio Nacional Bolívar on Parque Cevallos, is worth a visit for its impressive collection of stuffed birds and mammals. Highlights include some beautiful birds, especially the condors, and a display of historical photographs. The exhibition has a rather grisly ending with a bizarre section on deformed animals, such as six-legged lambs. **Museo de la Provincia** (Sucre, no phone, 9 A.M.–1 P.M. and 2–6 P.M. daily, free), inside the renovated *Casa del Portal* on Parque Montalvo, has a small exhibition of art and photography.

ENTERTAINMENT AND EVENTS

Ambato is renowned for its **Fiesta de la Fruta y de las Flores** during Carnival (Feb. or Mar.), when the whole city is decked out in fruit and flowers. It's one of Ecuador's most lavish annual affairs with huge parades, bullfights, dancing, painting, and theater exhibitions as well as the obligatory beauty contest. Hotels are often full during this time, so book ahead if you plan to spend the night.

Outside Carnival, Ambato's nightlife is surprisingly low-key for such a bustling city. Many young people seem to head for Baños to let their hair down along with the visitors. The new **Mall de los Andes** (Atahualpa and Victor Hugo), south of Ambato on the road to Huachi, contains the cinema Cinemark, with three theaters. In Ambato, **El Portal** (Sucre, tel. 3/242-4507, 8 A.M.–midnight Mon.–Thurs., 8 A.M.–2 A.M. Fri.–Sat.) on Parque Montalvo is a good spot to sip cocktails in cozy surroundings and catch live music on the weekend.

SHOPPING

Ambateños are not only among the richest but also the best-dressed people in the Sierra, and it's no surprise that the city and small towns nearby are great for shopping. In addition to the city's huge markets, Ambato is the leather center of the Central Sierra. Almost every block has its own upscale boutique selling suede and leather clothes, luggage, shoes, and accessories. You can also have clothes custom-made by several private *sastres* (tailors). Almost everything is of high quality, so expect to pay accordingly. For the best deals, take the rural bus ($0.50) from Plaza Rodó to the small village of **Quisapincha,** 10 kilometers to the west, where leather jackets cost $30–50.

Markets

Ambato is famous for having some of the largest markets in the country. The **Mercado Central,** east of Parque 12 de Noviembre, hosts a main market on Monday and smaller ones on Wednesday and Friday. Markets are held daily, but those three days are the largest. The flowers are one of the main attractions, grown in farms throughout the central Sierra and sold in bright, colorful fragrant bunches along a whole row of stalls. Another large market is the **Mercado Modelo,** a few blocks northeast of the Mercado Central. More than half a dozen smaller markets throughout the city specialize in everything from vegetables and fruit to shoes, animals, and tourist goods. For supermarket goods, try the new **Mall de los Andes,** south on the road to Huachi.

ACCOMMODATIONS

Ambato doesn't have a great range of accommodations, which is why most travelers spend the night in Baños or Riobamba. The cheapest of the budget options are clustered around Parque 12 de Noviembre, but many of them are rather seedy. The best of these is probably **Hotel del Sol** (Luis Martínez and 12 de Noviembre, tel. 3/282-5258, $10 s, $18 d). For a bit more comfort, **Gran Hotel** (Rocafuerte and Lalama, tel. 3/282-4235, $15 pp) and **Hotel Piramide** (Mariano Eguez and Cevallos, tel. 3/242-1920, $15 pp) have decent rooms with private baths and TV. **Hotel Cevallos** (Cevallos and Montalvo, tel. 3/242-2009, $18 s, $34 d) has a better location near Parque Montalvo.

One of the best hotels in town is the modern **Hotel Ambato** (Guayaquil and Rocafuerte, tel. 3/242-1793, www.hotelambato.com, $47 s, $68 d, breakfast included), overlooking the river. The hotel has all the amenities: a gift shop, a casino, laundry facilities, Internet access, and room service, and its Restaurante Ficoa is one of the best in the city.

For a more rural experience, head to **Quinta Loren** (Calle Los Taxos and Guaytambos, tel. 3/246-0699, www.quintaloren.com, $30 s, $55 d), surrounded by beautiful gardens and fruit orchards. Guest rooms are elegantly decorated, and there's a top-quality gourmet restaurant.

FOOD

For traditional Ecuadorian food, try the **Alamo Chalet** (Cevallos 6-12 at Montalvo, tel. 3/282-4704, 8 A.M.–10 P.M. daily, entrées $4), with a wide range of *comida típica* and pasta as well as a pleasant setting with art-covered walls. **Parilladas El Gaucho** (Bolívar and Quito, tel. 3/282-8969, noon–11 P.M. Mon.–Sat., noon–4 P.M. Sun., entrées $7–10) is the place for sizzling steaks.

For the best wood-fired-oven pizzas, head to **La Fornace** (Cevallos, tel. 3/282-3244, noon–10 P.M. daily, entrées $4–6).

One of the most highly recommended restaurants in town is 🅒 **Café Marcelo's** (Castillo and Rocafuerte, tel. 3/282-8208, 9 A.M.–10 P.M. daily, entrées $6–10), with fine Ecuadorian cooking, snacks, and great ice cream. Nearby, the **Spice House** (Rocafuerte and Quito, tel. 3/282-4584, 8:30 A.M.–6 P.M. Mon.–Fri., entrées $5–8) serves red meat and chicken in a range of imaginative sauces, including peach, fig, and red wine.

INFORMATION AND SERVICES

Ambato's **tourist information office** (Guayaquil and Rocafuerte, tel. 3/282-1800, 8 A.M.–5 P.M. Mon.–Fri.) is beside the Hotel Ambato, or just off Parque Montalvo, try

Tungurahua Province's **tourist information office** (Castillo, tel. 3/242-6290, 8 A.M.–4:30 P.M. Mon.–Fri.).

Banco del Pacífico (Lalama and Cevallos) handles traveler's checks, and there are ATMs at **Banco del Pichincha** and **Banco de Guayaquil**. The **post office** (Castillo and Bolívar) is on the southwest side of Parque Montalvo.

GETTING THERE AND AROUND

Ambato's **bus station,** two kilometers north of town, can be reached by taxi ($1.50) or local bus from Parque Cevallos. Buses run north to Quito (2.5 hours, $2.50) and Latacunga (1 hour, $1), and south to Riobamba (1.5 hours, $1.50).

Rather annoyingly, it is a bit more complicated to get to Baños. Take a taxi ($1.50) or bus to the Mercado Mayorista (more a busy highway than a market), where buses (45 minutes, $0.80) pass several times per hour.

Most taxis around town charge $1–2.

PÍLLARO AND PARQUE NACIONAL LLANGANATES

Just 20 kilometers northeast of Ambato, San Antonio de Píllaro sits at 2,800 meters elevation amid rich farmland planted with grains, papayas, and oranges. Píllaro's main claim to fame is access to the Llanganates, an area cloaked in mystery and clouds. Legend has it that Atahualpa's gold treasure is hidden in this area, and Píllaro is one of the starting points for many expeditions that have searched for it in vain (or have been kept very quiet).

Sleepy Píllaro comes to life during its outstanding fiestas. Examples of traditional, ornate **Corpus Christi costumes** worn in Píllaro during the June festival are on display in Ambato's Museo de Ciencias Naturales. At New Year and until January 6, *Diabladas* parade the streets dressed exotically in red with exuberant devil masks. Parades and dances for the **Celebration of Apostle Santiago the Elder** (St. James) begins on July 25 and lasts until August 10, Quito's Independence Day, when there are bullfights and a Pamplona-style bull run thunders through Píllaro's narrow streets.

Cheap guest rooms with private baths are available at the basic **Novo Hostal** (Rocafuerte and Sucre, tel. 3/287-4936, $5 pp). **Hotel Chelo's** (Guzman and Montalvo, tel. 3/287-3404, $10 pp) has better guest rooms with hot showers and cable TV.

Treasure hunters and trekkers who are determined to explore the 220,000 hectares of **Llanganates National Park** should bring plenty of waterproof gear as well as supplies of food and water. The weather is notoriously wet and foggy, and facilities are minimal—one reason why General Rumiñahui is rumored to have hidden his treasure here. It is a rugged, unspoiled region, however, filled with mountains, lakes, *páramo,* and impenetrable forest. Your best bet is with a trekking operator in Baños, or you may be able to hire a guide and mules in Píllaro.

SALASACA AND PELILEO

Fourteen kilometers southeast of Ambato, Salasaca is home to the Salasaca people, who stand out as a unique culture in the Ecuadorian highlands. The ancestors of the Salasaca *indígenas* were relocated to Ecuador from Bolivia by the Inca in the 15th century under a policy intended to minimize local uprisings among conquered peoples.

The Salasaca are well-known for their distinctive dress of long black ponchos and white hats. Wearing black has led to the common misconception that they are in perpetual mourning for Atahualpa, but you'll be dismissed if you mention this to the locals.

The Salasaca have thrived in Ecuador and are renowned for their woven tapestries. These cloth decorations usually feature fine weaving and intricate designs of animals, birds, and plants. Weaving is the domain of men, and boys first sit at the looms as early as age 10. You can visit any day, but the craft market is biggest

on Sunday. Weaver **Alonso Pilla** welcomes visitors to his home and workshop, where he weaves tapestries and *fajas,* the traditional Andean belts. He and his family run the cozy little *Hostal Runa Huasi* (Ruta Ambato-Baños, tel. 9/984-0125, $12 pp, breakfast included). Alonso also runs half-day tours of local communities ($10 pp).

About six kilometers from Salasaca toward Baños is Pelileo, the complete opposite in terms of shopping. You'll find little of Ecuador's original culture here, but there are stall after stall of blue jeans, reflecting a national obsession with denim, which most young people wear in preference to indigenous clothing. The range on offer, particularly on weekends, is enormous, so if you need to stock up, this is the best place. To visit Pelileo and Salasaca, hop off any bus running between Ambato and Baños; there are several buses per hour.

PATATE

This quiet town filled with evacuees when the Tungurahua volcano woke up in 1999 and has become a popular spot for volcano-watchers to see the sporadic fireworks that continue to shoot out of the "throat of fire." People also stop in the plaza to sample the traditional *arepas* (the recipe is said to be pre-Inca) with glasses of *chichi de uva,* a local cane spirit macerated with grape juice.

There are a couple of historic haciendas on the edge of town: The 300-year-old **Hacienda Leito** (Vía Baños-Patate Km. 8, tel. 3/285-9329, www.haciendaleito.com, $78 pp, breakfast and dinner included) has spacious guest rooms, a spa, and great views of the volcano. **Hacienda Manteles** (Vía Baños-Patate, tel. 2/223-3484, www.haciendamanteles.com, $105 s, $150 d) has immaculate guest rooms and is well-known for its ecological practices, with an organic garden and 200 hectares of cloud forest. Horseback riding, bird-watching, and zip-lining over the cloud forest are available.

Baños and Vicinity

Locals proudly call Baños (pop. 18,000) *pedacito de cielo* (a little piece of heaven), and this is no exaggeration. Don't be surprised if you end up staying longer than planned. In fact, you may find it very hard to leave. Foreigners and locals alike flock to this tranquil town at an ideal elevation of 1,820 meters in the verdant Andean lowlands to enjoy its springlike climate, abundant spas, and adventure sports. Here you can be as active or as downright lazy and self-indulgent as you like. Hike, cycle, raft, and bungee-jump to your heart's content in the stunning hills of the Pastaza Valley, and then have your muscles pummeled into sweet submission at one of the many spas. Then, of course, there are the relaxing soaks in the volcanic baths that give the town its name. Baños also has an excellent range of accommodations, experienced tour operators, some of the best international restaurants in Ecuador, and busy nightlife on weekends.

Perched between the base of the Tungurahua volcano and the Río Pastaza gorge, Baños enjoys a mild subtropical climate year-round. The Cascada Cabellera de la Virgen (Virgin's Hair Waterfall), visible from anywhere in town, tumbles down the steep hillside and is the site of the town's most popular hot springs. The town is well-known to Ecuadorians and foreign backpackers, but while many of Ecuador's other relaxation spots on the beach have boomed to the point of being spoiled, Baños is only marginally busier than it was a decade ago, which only adds to its charm. This may have something to do with the fact that the town is literally paradise at the gates of hell in the form of the enormous active volcano Tungurahua. After many years of uneasy sleep, Tungurahua, which fittingly means "throat of fire" in Kichwa, erupted suddenly in 1999. The volcano's crater is just 20 kilometers from Baños, but luckily it lies on the opposite side of the mountain to the town; Baños was covered in ash but otherwise remained unscathed. The government took the precaution of ordering a complete evacuation. Residents protested but were forcibly removed by the army. Four months later, about half the city's inhabitants returned, finding Baños still in one piece but many of their homes and businesses emptied by looters. Tungurahua has erupted regularly, in 2006, 2008, and 2010, but Baños continues to escape damage and the tourism industry remains robust, although landslides have affected areas on the edge of town. Tungurahua remains highly active at the time of writing. It is often wreathed in clouds and only visible from the hills above town.

It's not surprising in a devoutly Catholic country that the locals believe that the town's continued survival in the face of volcanic destruction is the work of the Virgin Mary, who, according to legend, appeared on the hill when Tungurahua erupted in 1773 and diverted the lava flow away from the town. Locals also believe that the Virgin blessed the town with holy water containing healing properties, hence the construction of public baths, and the town's full name: Baños de Agua Santa (Holy-water Baths).

SIGHTS
Iglesia de Nuestra Señora de Agua Santa

The center of town is dominated by the enormous church, La Basílica de Nuestra Señora de Agua Santa, erected in the Virgin Mary's honor. The black rock walls of the Dominican church are accented with red trim and twin white-topped towers. Inside, 10 huge paintings around the perimeter of the nave record incidents when the Virgin saved the faithful from various disasters, including Tungurahua's eruptions, car wrecks, and plunges into the river Pastaza.

The statue of the Virgin sits near a holy-water spring to the left of the main body of the church. Upstairs, a **museum** (8 A.M.–4 P.M. daily, $0.50) houses the Virgin's processional clothing, religious relics, and a slightly odd collection of stuffed animals.

CENTRAL SIERRA

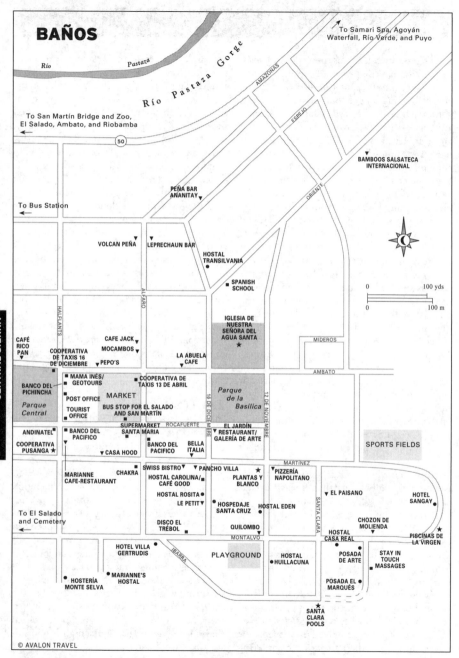

BAÑOS

Río   Pastaza

Río Pastaza Gorge

Río Pastaza Gorge

To Samari Spa, Agoyán
Waterfall, Río Verde, and Puyo

AMAZONAS

ESPEJO

To San Martín Bridge and Zoo,
El Salado, Ambato, and Riobamba

50

BAMBOOS SALSATECA
INTERNACIONAL

ORIENTE

To Bus Station

PEÑA BAR
ANANITAY

VOLCAN PEÑA   LEPRECHAUN BAR

HOSTAL
TRANSILVANIA

SPANISH
SCHOOL

ALFARO

0   100 yds

0   100 m

HALFLANTS

CAFÉ
RICO
PAN

CAFE JACK

MOCAMBOS

COOPERATIVA
DE TAXIS 16
DE DICIEMBRE   PEPO'S

LA ABUELA
CAFE

IGLESIA DE
NUESTRA
SEÑORA DEL
AGUA SANTA

MIDEROS

BANCO DEL
PICHINCHA

Parque
Central

MAMA INÉS/
GEOTOURS

POST OFFICE

TOURIST
OFFICE

COOPERATIVA DE
TAXIS 13 DE ABRIL

MARKET

BUS STOP FOR EL SALADO
AND SAN MARTÍN

Parque
de la
Basílica

AMBATO

16 DE DICIEMBRE

12 DE NOVIEMBRE

ANDINATEL

COOPERATIVA
PUSANGA

BANCO DEL
PACIFICO

CASA HOOD

SUPERMARKET   ROCAFUERTE
SANTA MARIA

BANCO DEL
PACIFICO

BELLA
ITALIA

EL JARDÍN
RESTAURANT/
GALERÍA DE ARTE

SPORTS FIELDS

MARTÍNEZ

MARIANNE
CAFE-RESTAURANT

CHAKRA

SWISS BISTRO   PANCHO VILLA

HOSTAL CAROLINA/
CAFÉ GOOD

HOSTAL ROSITA

LE PETIT

DISCO EL
TRÉBOL

PLANTAS Y
BLANCO

PIZZERÍA
NAPOLITANO

SANTA CLARA

EL PAISANO

HOTEL
SANGAY

To El Salado
and Cemetery

HOSPEDAJE
SANTA CRUZ

QUILOMBO

HOSTAL EDEN

MONTALVO

CHOZON DE
MOLIENDA

HOSTAL
CASA REAL

PISCINAS DE
LA VIRGEN

POSADA
DE ARTE

STAY IN
TOUCH
MASSAGES

IBARRA

HOTEL VILLA
GERTRUDIS

MARIANNE'S
HOSTAL

HOSTERÍA
MONTE SELVA

PLAYGROUND

HOSTAL
HUILLACUNA

POSADA EL
MARQUÉS

SANTA
CLARA
POOLS

© AVALON TRAVEL

Thermal Baths

The thermal springs from which Baños takes its name are recommended for the curative properties of their dissolved minerals. There are a total of four sets of public baths around town, but only two are warm. Many of the better hotels in town also have their own baths, but they don't draw on volcanic waters. The public baths get very busy on weekends and even on weekdays in the afternoons and early evenings. Many locals use the springs as actual baths, so it's best not to submerge your head, and the earlier you get here, the cleaner they are. The brownish-yellow waters don't immediately look appealing, but there's no denying the therapeutic effects of an hour or so soaking in them.

Piscinas de la Virgen (5 A.M.–5 P.M. and 6–10 P.M. daily, $2 pp daytime, $3 pp evening) are the most popular baths in town, with three pools ranging from very cold (18°C) to warm (37°C) and hot (45°C). The location is spectacular, at the foot of the Virgin's Hair waterfall,

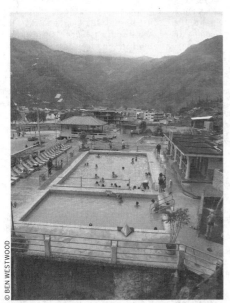

the thermal baths at Piscinas de la Virgen in Baños

with views over the town and valley. Cold spouts make for a bracing but refreshing break from the hot baths, and at the center of the complex you can see where the scalding waters gush from the rocks. Stow your belongings in the locker room. Although thefts are rare, it's best to avoid bringing valuables.

There are two other sets of baths in town, but the waters are cold and they are mainly used by local families as swimming pools. **Santa Clara Pools** (9 A.M.–5 P.M. Sat.–Sun., $1 pp) features a large cold pool, waterslides, a sauna, and a steam room.

On the eastern edge of town, on the far side of the Bascún Creek canyon, **Piscina El Salado** (5 A.M.–5 P.M. daily, $3 pp) is the best alternative to Piscinas de la Virgen, with five pools ranging from lukewarm (16°C) to hot (42°C). Note that the complex has recently been rebuilt after being destroyed by a landslide in 2008. It's still officially in a high-risk area, so it is best avoided when the volcano is active or after heavy rains. Look for a paved road just across the bridge east of Baños on the way to Ambato and Riobamba. Buses from the center of town run to the springs every half hour throughout the day, or else it's a 40-minute walk or 10-minute taxi ride ($1.50). Another route from town is reached by walking west on Martínez.

Volcán Tungurahua

The fate of Baños is inextricably linked to the 5,016-meter volcano that lies just eight kilometers south of town. The fact that the crater lies on the opposite side to the town has saved Baños from destruction, and the volcano supplies the thermal waters that have made it famous. This comparatively young volcano is one of Ecuador's more temperamental, having erupted violently in 1773, 1877, and 1916 before its most recent awakening in 1999. The current level of activity shows no signs of abating, with regular eruptions in the last decade, including an eruption in 2010 when a 10-kilometer-high ash cloud covered this author's backyard in Guayaquil, about 300 kilometers away.

FOOL'S GOLD: THE INCA'S LOST RANSOM

One of the most famous mysteries – and treasure hunts – in the Americas began in 1532 when Inca leader Atahualpa was captured by the Spanish at Cajamarca in Peru. Conquistador Francisco Pizarro threatened to execute him unless he bought his freedom, and with customary confidence, Atahualpa placed his hand on the wall to indicate how he could fill the room with gold and silver to save his own life. Atahualpa's subjects, who revered him as a god, set about collecting the largest ransom ever assembled from all corners of his conquered empire.

Pizarro became fearful of Atahualpa's power, however, and went back on his word, staging a mock trial and sentencing him to death. Just before his execution, Atahualpa converted to Christianity in return for leniency, believing that being burned at the stake would prevent his body reaching the afterlife. He was strangled in July 1533. When this news reached Atahualpa's general, Rumiñahui, he quickly hid the largest part of the ransom, which was being transported from Ecuador. The fortune was estimated at 15,000 kilograms of gold and silver, including an 82-kilogram throne of solid gold. The entire ransom was spirited away almost overnight on the shoulders of porters who were ordered to commit suicide to avoid interrogation. The Spanish began a frantic campaign of torture and killing but failed to find any answers. Even as they were burned alive, Inca nobles taunted the invaders, saying that the treasure would never be found.

Over the years, accounts of the treasure's size, location, and very existence have drifted like clouds over the Andes. The wild, inhospitable Llanganati Mountains soon emerged as the most probable location of the lost riches. Part of the Eastern Cordillera, the range stretches across the Central Sierra from the Río Patate Valley north almost to Volcán Quilindaña, with the highest point at Cerro Hermoso (4,571 meters). Rumiñahui could hardly have found a more forbidding spot in the entire Inca empire, where wind, rain, and fog make it all too easy to get lost. Rumors about the treasure's exact whereabouts included deep caves and the bottom of an icy lake.

Enter a poor Spanish soldier under Pizarro named Valverde, who married an indigenous woman in Latacunga. As unlikely as it seems, he claimed that his wife's father, the chief of Píllaro, the closest town to the Llanganatis, told him where the ransom was hidden. On his deathbed, Valverde dictated a map named the *Derrotero* ("Path") that contained detailed directions through the Llanganati Mountains to

---

Tungurahua's activity has made climbing it complicated. Two Germans first scaled the peak in 1873, but subsequent eruptions changed the mountain's appearance and summit completely. The crater has expanded to more than 400 meters in diameter—five times wider than it was when it began to erupt. Tungurahua used to be considered the easiest snow climb in Ecuador—one of the few in the country where you started out amid tropical vegetation and finished in snow and ice. Until the risk of eruption lessens, however, climbing is highly discouraged. Check with the **South American Explorers** (SAE, Quito clubhouse: Jorge Washington 311 at Plaza, tel./fax 2/222-5228, quitoclub@saexplorers.org, www.saexplorers.org, 9:30 A.M.–5 P.M. Mon.–Fri., 9:30 A.M.–8 P.M. Thurs., 9:30 A.M.–noon Sat.) or locally for the latest volcano update. The best source is the **Ecuadorian Geophysical Institute** (www.igepn.edu.ec), which frequently updates its website.

If you want to get close enough to the volcano to see some plumes of steam or fire, most operators in Baños organize tours to go up, but bear in mind that on most nights you will see very little action.

ENTERTAINMENT AND EVENTS
Nightlife

Baños has very good nightlife for such a small

a lake where the treasure lay, although it also contained some vague, confusing passages. The king of Spain sent the map to the authorities in Latacunga, where various expeditions were organized, but no treasure was found, and many explorers never returned, fueling the rumor that both the area and the treasure it contained were cursed.

The trail went cold until British botanist Richard Spruce came across a copy of the map in the 1850s. He also uncovered a map drawn by Anastasio Guzman, a Spanish botanist and farmer who had lived in Píllaro. Building on the knowledge of many trips into the Llanganatis, Guzman's 1800 map roughly corresponded with Valverde's guide. Seven years later, Guzman walked off a cliff in his sleep. The account of the treasure, along with a copy of the *Derrotero*, appeared as the final chapter in Spruce's *Notes of a Botanist on the Amazon and Andes*, published in 1908.

Spruce's writings inspired Nova Scotian explorer Barth Blake to travel to Ecuador. According to letters written to a friend, Blake did indeed strike gold after an expedition into Llanganati. In one letter he wrote: "There are thousands of gold and silver pieces of Inca and pre-Inca handicraft, the most beautiful goldsmith works you are not able to imagine." He took as much gold as he could, but claimed, "I could not remove it alone, nor could thousands of men." Blake's best friend, who accompanied him on the expedition, died in the mountains, and Blake reportedly journeyed to North America to organize an expedition to remove the rest of the gold, but mysteriously disappeared on the way.

Many treasure hunters in the early 20th century followed Blake and shared similarly mysterious fates, including Scotsman Erskine Loch, who shot himself after a failed expedition, and American Colonel Brooks, who ended up in a mental institution after his wife died of pneumonia in the mountains.

British author Mark Honigsbaum is the most recent writer to investigate the story in his 2004 book *Valverde's Gold*. He concluded:

> My own feeling is that this gold was probably taken out centuries ago. If not, and it's still there, I think it's lost forever, because those mountains are so vast and inaccessible that you're looking for a needle in a haystack.

It remains to be seen whether his words will dampen the gold lust of future treasure hunters.

town. The constant stream of backpackers is joined on weekends by a flood of locals who head for the stretch of Eloy Alfaro north of Ambato, the main street. **Mocambo** (Alfaro, tel. 3/274-0923, 4 P.M.–midnight Sun.–Thurs., 4 P.M.–2 A.M. Fri.–Sat.) has three floors with darts, pool, and music videos and is popular with gringos. Farther up is a long-established rock bar, **Jack Rock Café** (Alfaro, tel. 3/274-1329, 4 P.M.–midnight Sun.–Thurs., 4 P.M.–2 A.M. Fri.–Sat.), which mixes in Latin music on the weekend. Toward the end of the street are the more raucous options. The **Leprechaun Bar** (Alfaro and Oriente, tel. 3/274-1537, 7 P.M.–midnight Sun.–Thurs., 7 P.M.–2 A.M. Fri.–Sat.) has the best of both worlds, with a bar in the back garden with a roaring fire and a dance floor that gets packed later on. Opposite, **Volcán Peña Bar** (Alfaro and Oriente, tel. 3/274-2379, 7 P.M.–midnight Sun.–Thurs., 7 P.M.–2 A.M. Fri.–Sat.) attracts a more local crowd onto its dance floor.

The **Peña Bar Amanitay** (16 de Diciembre and Espejo, tel. 3/274-2396, 9 P.M.–midnight daily) has folkloric music from 9:30 P.M. on weekends. Away from the main drag at the south end of town, **Trebol** (Montalvo and 16 de Diciembre, tel. 3/274-1501, 9 P.M.–2 A.M. Thurs.–Sat., $2) is another very popular disco.

Festivals

Baños's **Canonization Festival** is celebrated

December 15–16 with bands and processions, and the festival of **Nuestra Señor del Agua Santa** brings in crowds of pilgrims in October.

SHOPPING

Baños certainly has a sweet tooth, and the traditional local candy makes a popular gift. The best are *membrillo* (a red gelatinous block of guava) and *milcocha,* chewy sugarcane bars that you can watch being made, swung over wooden pegs.

For indigenous clothing, take your pick from scores of stores on and near the main street, Ambato. Haggling is obligatory. On the **Pasaje Artesanal,** which leads along the side of the market between Ambato and Rocafuerte, there are many stalls selling jewelry and *tagua* carvings.

The **Galería de Arte Huillacuna** (12 de Noviembre and Montalvo, tel. 3/274-0909, 8:30 A.M.–7:30 P.M. daily) displays sculptures, paintings, and drawings by local artists and offers accommodations upstairs.

For handmade guitars, visit **Guitarras Guevara** (Halflants, tel. 3/274-0941), which has instruments ranging $75–300 in price.

RECREATION AND TOURS
Hiking Around Baños

The steep hillside west of town can be scaled by two routes. The most common is to head south on Maldonado and take a path that climbs up to **Bellavista,** where a white cross stands. At night, when the hills fade from view, this illuminated cross seems to float in the middle of the sky above town. The views are spectacular over Baños and the Pastaza Valley stretching down toward the Oriente. The path continues steeply up to the village of Runtún (elevation 2,600 meters), two hours away and with good views of Tungurahua. You can then loop around and head back down to Baños past the statue of **La Virgen del Agua Santa.**

Alternately, head south on Mera, and then head to the right past the cemetery to reach the Virgin statue. The walk up takes about half an hour and provides good views of Tungurahua around the corner. The path continues above the statue all the way to the top of the hillside and Runtún, or a downhill branch can be taken back down to Mera.

More good hikes follow the Pastaza: cross the main road near the bus station and continue over the road bridge at **Puente San Francisco.** A network of trails crisscrosses the hillside facing Baños. The village of **Illuchi,** about a two-hour hike from the river, is a good turning-around point, with views of Baños, Tungurahua, and the river.

The **Puente San Martín** crosses the Pastaza just to the west of town. To reach it, cross the bridge out of Baños, pass the turnoff to Piscina El Salado, and turn right. Near the bridge is the **Cascada Inés María,** a small waterfall, and the **San Martín Zoo** (8 A.M.–5 P.M. daily, $1.50) opened in 1994 as a refuge for sick and injured animals from the Amazon. The zoo has an impressive range of birds and mammals, including monkeys, pumas, and a jaguar, although some of the enclosures are rather small. There is a small **aquarium** (8 A.M.–5 P.M. daily, $1) opposite the zoo that has tropical fish as well as reptiles and birds.

Mountain Biking

A faster and more exhilarating way to enjoy the stunning scenery around Baños is on two wheels. By far the most popular excursion is the downhill route to Puyo. The old road passes along the gorge of the Río Pastaza, offering spectacular views and dropping nearly 1,000 meters through rapidly changing terrain that becomes more and more tropical as you reach Puyo, 61 kilometers to the east. Most people don't make it that far but are content to visit the series of waterfalls, including **Manto de la Novia** and **Pailón del Diablo,** in the first half of the route, and then either cycling or catching a bus back (you can usually stow the bike on the roof). Bikes can be rented at most agencies in Baños for $8 per day including a helmet, a repair kit, and a map, or take a full-day guided tour ($40 pp) to visit the waterfalls, ending in Machay.

Horseback Riding

Horses are another popular way to get into the hills, costing around $16 pp for two hours including a guide, or $60 per day. The most popular route is Nahuazo, at the foot of Tungurahua. Keep in mind that reports of ill or mistreated horses have been on the rise in the last few years. Look for healthy, well-treated animals, and try out the saddle for fit before you head out on your ride. Don't accept blankets instead of saddles.

Rafting and Kayaking

Although it's not as renowned as Tena, the white-water rafting near Baños is good. The most popular routes are along Río Patate, which has sections of Class 3 rapids and short sections of Class 4. A half-day trip costs $30 pp.

Kayaking is also available, but you need to take a course ($60 pp per day) if you're not experienced.

Adventure Sports

There are various other activities to get your adrenaline flowing. Canyoneering in Río Blanco is great fun. Full-day trips cost $30 pp, usually including four waterfalls. Swing jumping (not bungee) is available off the 100-meter-high Puente San Francisco ($20 pp), and tandem paragliding can be done in Pelileo. Renting all-terrain vehicles is another popular craze around Baños, but be careful, particularly on hilly terrain, as accidents have been reported.

Climbing to the summit of Tungurahua is obviously not allowed (and highly dangerous), but there are excursions to the refuge at 3,830 meters. You can do it in one day for $60 pp or overnight for $120 pp.

A range of rainforest trips can be arranged from Baños, and after Quito it's probably the best place to book one. The most common and economical tours go into communities near Puyo, but bear in mind that this is secondary rainforest. For primary rainforest, you need to book a trip that goes through Coca or Lago Agrio, although there are pockets of primary rainforest east of Tena and Misahualli.

Tour Operators

Baños has an enormous number of tour agencies, and it's tough to keep the trustworthy separate from the fly-by-night rip-off artists. The following agencies have been repeatedly recommended, but it's a good idea to check with the **South American Explorers** (SAE, Quito clubhouse: Jorge Washington 311 at Plaza, tel./fax 2/222-5228, quitoclub@saexplorers.org, www.saexplorers.org, 9:30 A.M.–5 P.M. Mon.-Fri., 9:30 A.M.–8 P.M. Thurs., 9:30 A.M.–noon Sat.) for a current list. Almost all agencies offer hiking, cycling, rafting, kayaking, canyoneering, swing-jumping, climbing tours, and rainforest expeditions.

Geotours (Ambato and Halflants, tel./fax 3/274-1344, geotoursbanios@yahoo.es, www.geotoursbanios.com) was the first adventure operator to open in town nearly 20 years ago and is still one of the best. **Córdova Tours** (Maldonado and Espejo, tel. 3/274-0923, ojosvolcan@hotmail.com, www.cordovatours.banios.com) is also dependable for a wide range of tours and rents 4WD vehicles. **Jose and Two Dogs** (Maldonado and Martínez, tel./fax 3/274-0746) is more professional than its name suggests and is recommended for horseback riding and hiking.

Many agencies specialize in tours of the Amazon. **Sebastián Moya Expediciones** (Oriente and Halflants, tel. 3/248-4287, wulopez@hotmail.com) is owned by Shuar guide Sebastián Moya and run under the auspices of the Yawa Jee Shuar Indigenous Foundation, a private nonprofit dedicated to sustainable, low-impact tourism to benefit Shuar communities. **Expediciones Amazonicas** (Oriente between Alfaro and Halflants, tel. 3/274-0506, www.baniosxtreme.com/amazonicas) has received positive reports for its wide range of rainforest trips via Puyo and Lago Agrio as well as adventure tours, rafting, and climbing.

Most feedback on **Rainforestur** (Ambato and Maldonado, tel./fax 3/274-0743, www.rainforestur.com.ec) has been positive. Guides speak English, French, and German and offer tours of the surrounding area and Cuyabeno. **Vasco Tours** (Alfaro and Martínez, tel. 3/274-1017) is run by Flor Vasco and Juan Medina in Quito and has received positive feedback for their tours to Huaorani indigenous communities.

Massage and Spa Therapies

No spa town would be complete without massages, and Baños has plenty of places offering a wide range of spa therapies to soothe those aches and pains. Many of the hotels have an on-site masseuse, but quality is variable. One of the best in town is **Chakra** (Alfaro and Luis Martínez, tel. 3/274-2027, www.chakramassages.com), run by a local, Carmen Sánchez, who specializes in Swedish massage as well as reflexology and beauty treatments. Also recommended are the American-Ecuadorian husband-and-wife team Geoffrey and Edith at **Stay in Touch** (Av. Montalvo, tel. 3/274-0973). A one-hour full-body massage costs $27; spinal manipulations are also available.

ACCOMMODATIONS

Baños has more than 130 hotels, and competition keeps prices down. Most are budget and mid-range hotels and will negotiate their rates for midweek stays. However, be warned that prices usually double on national holidays, and locals are happy to pay these rates, so you'll be hard-pressed to find a room without a reservation. The best hotels are at the south end of town.

Under $10

There are plenty of cheap hotels in town, but avoid the ones toward the northern end, which tend to be run-down. The backpacker institution **Hostal Plantas y Blanco** (Martínez and 12 de Noviembre, tel. 3/274-0044, dorm $5.50–7.50 pp, rooms $8.50–11 pp) continues to offer a great deal and is a good meeting spot for kindred spirits. There's a rooftop terrace, sun loungers, kitchen, Turkish baths ($2.75 pp), free Internet access, and compact but clean guest rooms. The hotel's fresh fruit and

pancakes are one of the best breakfasts in town. **Hostal Transilvania** (16 de Diciembre and Oriente, tel. 3/274-2281, www.hostal-transilvania.com, $7.50 pp, breakfast included) is far more welcoming than its name suggests. This Israeli-owned place is an incredibly good deal with well-maintained guest rooms and a colorful café where big breakfasts are served on petrified-wood tables. It fills up fast.

Hospedaje Santa Cruz (16 de Diciembre and Martínez, tel. 3/274-0648, $9.50 pp) is another good budget option, with two ground-floor patios with fireplaces, games, magazines, a self-service bar, free Internet access, and simple but colorful guest rooms. **Hostal Carolina** (16 de Diciember, tel. 3/274-0592, $7 pp) is another safe bet, with friendly service and simple, well-maintained guest rooms above a vegetarian café. **Hostal Rosita** (16 de Diciembre near Martínez, tel. 3/274-0396, $7 pp) is another good-value budget option with free Internet access and two larger apartments for longer stays.

$10-25

For a few extra dollars, Baños has an excellent selection of mid-range hotels. **Hostal Eden** (12 de Noviembre, tel. 3/274-0616, $10 pp) is a cut above the budget options with decent guest rooms with cable TV facing a pleasant garden courtyard and a cheap restaurant attached. **Hostal Casa Real** (Montalvo y Pasaje Ibarra, tel. 3/274-0215, $12 pp) is a great-value choice close to the waterfall. Guest rooms have murals of wildlife, and the massages in the spa upstairs are very good. For a more artistic experience, stay at **Huillacuna** (12 de Noviembre and Montalvo, tel. 3/274-2909, $15 pp, breakfast included), a beautifully laid-out hotel with guest rooms set around a gallery offering both a feast of art on the walls and a culinary feast at breakfast.

One of the best options in this range is the French-run **Hostal Jardín Marianne** (Montalvo and Halflants, tel. 3/274-1947, $15 pp). These comfortable new guest rooms with balconies in tranquil surroundings are perfect for a relaxing break.

Off Montalvo near the waterfall is the **Posada El Marqués** (tel. 3/274-0053, $23 s,

$35 d), a homey, family-run place with newly upgraded guest rooms in the large main house. Guest rooms are spacious, clean, and quiet, with private baths and hot water.

$25-50

Hostal Posada del Arte (Pasaje Ibarra and Montalvo, tel. 3/274-0083, www.posadadelarte.com, $28–30 s, $52–56 d) is a special place with walls adorned with South American art and plushly decorated guest rooms with chimneys to keep you warm. The restaurant is excellent, with home-brewed ales and a range of international specialties.

The best place to stay in Baños itself is **Hostería Monte Selva** (tel. 3/274-0566, www.monteselvaecuador.com, $38 s, $63 d, $99 suites). These cabins and guest rooms snuggled at the foot of the hillside at the south end of Halflants are set in beautiful gardens with excellent facilities that include a large pool, a sauna, a steam room, and jetted tubs. A range of spa therapies are on offer, and the hotel has an "eco-park" near Puyo where it runs excursions—although you may find it hard to leave the comfort of the hotel.

With a more businesslike atmosphere, the big peach-colored building at the base of the waterfall is **Hotel Sangay** (tel. 3/274-0490, fax 3/274-0056, $24–56 s, $40–70 d). Choose between guest rooms in the main hotel, cabins out back, and executive suites beyond that. Guests can work up a sweat with tennis or squash before crossing the street to the baths. The hotel's spa therapies are highly recommended.

$100-200

On the crest of the hill overlooking Baños sits Swiss-Ecuadorian **Luna Runtún** (tel. 3/274-0882, fax 3/274-0376, www.lunaruntun.com, $154 s or d, breakfast and dinner included). The guest rooms are rustic but underwhelming for the cost; the surroundings, however, are what make this a special place. The hacienda feel is enhanced by flower gardens, fountains, and tiled roofs. Enjoy massage, Reiki, and beauty treatments in the garden spa, which uses plants from the garden and ashes

and stones from the nearby volcano. The highlight is the spectacular view over Baños and the Pastaza Valley from the hot pools and adjacent Café del Cielo. Tungurahua also peeks through the clouds to the south. A taxi to the hotel from Baños costs about $7, and a private shuttle is available.

Samari Spa (tel. 3/274-1855, fax 3/274-1859, www.samarispa.com, $186 s or d, breakfast included) is on the road to the rainforest just one kilometer out of town, so it's quiet and relaxing. The opulent facilities include 37 guest rooms, suites, a covered pool, a sauna, a steam-hydro massage, and spa-therapy and massage rooms. The original volcanic-rock building has been tastefully restored and sits in beautifully landscaped gardens. The acclaimed restaurant offers all meals and caters to conventions or small groups.

FOOD

Like its hotel offerings, Baños has an amazing range of food options for such a small town, with restaurants that rival those in Quito and Cuenca. The best food tends to be international, with plenty of standard Ecuadorian fare also on offer. If you really want to go local, sink your teeth into one of the *cuyes* (guinea pigs) that are roasted in front of the market on Ambato. For those with a sweet tooth, sip sugarcane juice at the stalls near the bus terminal and munch on candy such as *membrillo* (a red gelatinous block of guava) and *milcocha* (chewy sugarcane bars), available from dozens of stalls all over town.

Ecuadorian

La Abuela Café (Ambato and 16 de Diciembre, tel. 3/274-2962, 8 A.M.–11 P.M. daily, entrées $6) is popular for local specialties such as *churrasco* and *llapingacho*. **Café Rico Pan** (Ambato, tel. 3/274-0387, 7 A.M.–8 P.M. Mon.–Thurs., 7 A.M.–noon Sun., entrées $2–4) is one of the best bakeries in town and a good place for breakfast and snacks.

International

One of the best restaurants in town is **Casa Hood** (Martínez and Halflants, tel. 3/274-2668, 4–10 P.M. Wed.–Mon., entrées $4–5), run by American expat and longtime resident Ray Hood. His restaurant is renowned for its healthy, eclectic menu with Asian, Mexican, and Italian entrées plus a wide range of juices, smoothies, teas, and cakes. The funky art and books will keep you busy until your tasty food arrives.

For delicious French cuisine, try the **(Marianne Café-Restaurant** (Halflants between Martínez and Rocafuerte, tel. 3/274-1947, noon–11 P.M. daily, entrées $6–9), a quaint little restaurant snuggled in an interior courtyard. Specialties include beef fondue, steak milanesa, fresh trout, French onion soup, and crepes galore. **Le Petit Restaurant** (16 de Diciembre and Montalvo, tel. 3/274-0936, noon–10 P.M. Tues.–Sun., entrées $6–9), part of Le Petit Alberge hotel, is another good choice for French food. For the best cheese and meat fondues in town, as well as a range of European specialties, head to the friendly **Swiss Bistro** (Martínez and Alfaro, tel. 3/274-2262, noon–11 P.M. daily, entrées $6–10).

For Italian pasta and pizza in all its variations, stop by **La Bella Italia** (Martínez and Alfaro, tel. 3/271-0121, 7 A.M.–9 P.M. daily, entrées $4–8). **Pizzeria Napolitano** (12 de Noviembre and Martínez, tel. 3/274-2341, noon–10 P.M. daily, entrées $4–8) cooks up 11 different kinds of pizza along with meat and seafood dishes.

Pancho Villa (Martínez and 16 de Diciembre, tel. 3/274-2138, 12:30–10 P.M. Mon.–Sat., closed Sun., entrées $6–7) does the best Mexican tacos, fajitas, and enchiladas in town.

The restaurant at **(Hostal Posada del Arte** (Pasaje Ibarra and Montalvo, tel. 3/274-0083, www.posadadelarte.com, 8 A.M.–10 P.M. daily, entrées $5–8) is excellent, with home-brewed ales and a range of international specialties that include Swedish meatballs and beef stroganoff.

For the best grilled meats, try the eccentric, creative surroundings of **Quilombo** (Montalvo and 16 de Diciembre, tel. 3/274-2880, noon–3 P.M. and 6 P.M.–9:30 P.M. daily, entrées $6–10), a friendly Argentine-run place where the menu is written on dice. Barbecued meat, imaginative dishes such as steak in

ginger sauce, and oven-baked pizzas are served under a thatched roof in a spacious garden at **Chozón de Molienda** (Montalvo and Pasaje Ibarra, tel. 3/274-1816, 6:30–11:30 P.M. daily, entrées $5–8).

For vegetarian food, the building housing **El Paisano** (Santa Clara 288 at Martínez, tel. 9/261-0037, 7 A.M.–10 P.M. daily, entrées $3–6) doesn't look very inviting, but the vegetarian fare is cheap and excellent, making good use of fresh ingredients. For more vegetarian options, **El Jardín Restaurant/Galería de Arte** (Rocafuerte and 16 de Diciembre, tel. 3/274-0875, 1–11 P.M. daily, entrées $6–9) has a good selection as well as specialties such as Thai shrimp and steak with pepper and cream, served in a garden overlooking the cathedral. **Café Good** (16 de Diciembre, tel. 3/274-0592, 8 A.M.–10 P.M. daily, entrées $4–7) is another vegetarian option with a mix of local, European, and Asian fare.

INFORMATION AND SERVICES

Head to the **Departamento de Turismo del Municipio** (Halflants and Rocafuerte, tel. 3/274-0483, www.baniosadn.ec, 8 A.M.–12:30 P.M. and 2–5:30 P.M. daily) on the Parque Central for brochures, maps, and directories on Baños's long list of places to stay, places to eat, and things to do.

The **Banco del Pacífico** (Halflants and Rocafuerte) and **Banco del Pichincha** (Ambato and Halflants) both have ATMs and change traveler's checks.

There are dozens of Internet cafés, and many hotels have free Internet access, but **Direct Connect** (Martínez) also provides Internet access. For international phone calls, head to **Andinatel** (Rocafuerte and Halflants).

The **police station** is on Thomas Halflants near Ambato (tel. 3/274-0122), the **hospital** is on Montalvo near Pastaza (tel. 3/274-0443), and the **post office** is on Halflants near Ambato (tel. 3/274-0901).

Spanish Lessons

Outside of Quito and Cuenca, Baños is

probably the most popular place in Ecuador to stay and study Spanish. Most schools offer individual and group instruction, starting at $5 per hour. Recommended is **Baños Spanish Center** (Oriente and Cañar, tel./fax 3/274-0632, tel. 8/704-5072, baniosspanishcenter@hotmail.com, www.spanishcenterschool.com) was the first school to open in Baños and is run by Elizabeth Barrionuevo, who speaks Spanish, English, and German. She has been recommended as an excellent teacher and also offers dancing and cooking lessons.

Other recommended schools include **Ciudad de Baños Languages School** (Ambato and Alfaro, tel. 3/274-0317, www.escueladeidiomas.banios.com), **Mayra's Spanish School** (Efren Reyes and Martínez, tel. 3/274-2850, www.mayraspanishschool.com), and **Raices Spanish School** (16 de Diciembre and Suárez, tel./fax 3/274-1921, www.spanishlessons.org).

GETTING THERE AND AROUND

The central **bus station** is bordered by Reyes and Maldonado, along the main road at the north end of Baños. Buses run to most cities in the Sierra as well as the Oriente, including buses to Quito (3.5 hours, $3.50), Ambato (1 hour, $1), Puyo (2 hours, $2), and Riobamba (2.5 hours, $2.50), which will be cheaper and take only 1.5 hours if the direct road reopens. Local buses to **El Salado** and **San Martín** leave regularly from the bus stop at Alfaro and Martínez, beside the Santa María supermarket.

There are lots of taxis at the bus station and around the main square. Journeys within town cost $1, and to the outskirts $1.50. If you want to reserve a taxi ahead of time, stop by **Cooperativa de Taxis** (Ambato and Halflants) or **Cooperativa de Taxis 13 de Abril** (Rocafuerte and Alfaro).

◖ THE WATERFALL ROUTE FROM BAÑOS TO PUYO

This spectacular 61-kilometer road drops nearly 1,000 meters in elevation along the Pastaza Valley to the edge of the Oriente.

There are nearly a dozen waterfalls along the newly christened Ruta de las Cascadas, which has developed into a major tourist attraction with several *tarabitas* (cable-cars) across the valley as well as a range of adventure sports. There are three ways to see this route: You can hop on a Baños–Puyo bus and stop off at the waterfalls, take a guided tour, or the best option is to hire a bicycle and take in the scenery at your leisure and see how far you get toward Puyo. If you feel too tired to cycle back uphill, you can always take a bus back and stow your bike on top.

The new Baños–Puyo road goes through half a dozen tunnels, only the first of which is open to cyclists. Along the rest of the route cyclists bypass the tunnels and take the old road, enjoying wonderful canyon views along the cliff face.

Leaving Baños, cross the Agoyán hydroelectric dam and the first set of cable car rides to small waterfalls, including the Agoyán.

© BEN WESTWOOD

There are now two waterfalls at Manto de la Novia following a landslide in 2010.

CENTRAL SIERRA

After 40 minutes, you pass one of the most impressive waterfalls on the route, **Manto de la Novia** (Bride's Veil). For a small tip, the *tarabita* staff will watch your bike. Take the hair-raising *tarabita* ($1) 500 meters across the gorge from where you can take a short walk down to a viewing platform or a longer hike (20 minutes) down to the bottom of the gorge to stand at the foot of the waterfall. It's an awe-inspiring sight, but also sobering. In February 2010 a huge landslide here killed five residents and swept away houses, and there are now two waterfalls where for centuries there was only one. You can cross the rickety bridge back across the gorge and walk back up to the main road.

After Manto de Novia, it's 40 minutes farther to Río Verde, 18 kilometers from Baños, an emerging town with several hotels, small restaurants, and shops selling local crafts. More importantly, this is the access point to **El Pailón del Diablo** (Devil's Cauldron), a dramatic waterfall tumbling between vertical walls into a deep depression. Follow the signs to the path leading down into a forested gorge, which offers welcome shade. There is a tiny suspension bridge (maximum capacity: 5 people), and it costs $1 to walk down to a set of three platforms to view the waterfall up close. There is also a path cut into the rocks called Grieta al Cielo (Crevice to Heaven) that you can walk along, crouching, to go inside a cave behind the waterfall.

Most people visit Río Verde for an hour or so, but the stunning setting has led to some good accommodations options. **Miramelindo** (Vía Baños–Puyo Km. 18, tel. 3/249-3004, www.miramelindo.banios.com, $25 pp, breakfast included) has rustic guest rooms beside the river, with an orchid garden, a jetted tub, a sauna, steam baths, and free guided tours to the waterfall. A couple of kilometers farther east on the Baños–Puyo road is **Pequeño Paraíso** (tel. 9/981-9776, www.hostel-banos-pequenoparaiso.com, $17–20 pp, breakfast and dinner included), where comfortable cabins and dorms sit on grounds full of fruit trees with great views over the canyon.

About 2.5 kilometers east of Río Verde is the village of **Machay,** where trails lead up into the hills to a series of small waterfalls. The most impressive, **Manantial del Dorado,** is at the end of the trail, but this is quite a hike—over four hours there and back—and better done on a guided tour.

Most people turn back at this point, but if you keep going along the road, you'll reach **Río Negro,** after which the scenery opens out to reveal views of the widening valley, and the scenery becomes noticeably more tropical. The town of **Mera** is next, after 17 kilometers, and then there's a **police checkpoint** where you will probably be required to show your passport. About seven kilometers farther is the small airport of **Shell,** which runs small charter services to visit remote indigenous communities in the rainforest. About 10 kilometers farther on is **Puyo.**

Ambato to Guaranda

The most common route from the central highlands to the coast is south to Riobamba and southwest via Pallatanga and Bucay. However, the road west of Ambato to Guaranda is far more spectacular and puts the "high" into the word *highway*. West of Ambato, the road climbs over 4,000 meters through misty, rolling *páramo* into Chimborazo Reserve, offering spectacular close-up views of Ecuador's highest mountain before dropping down to Guaranda. This 100-kilometer route is the highest paved road in Ecuador.

The journey takes about two hours by bus. Because the road from Guaranda to Riobamba is almost as thrilling, the ride out and back is a highly recommended detour if you're heading north or south on the Panamericana, even if Guaranda isn't on your list. If you're heading to the coast, you can continue on from Guaranda. Alternately, spend the day (or the night) in Guaranda or nearby Salinas before returning to Ambato or Riobamba.

◀ CHIMBORAZO FAUNA RESERVE

An hour by bus west of Riobamba and Ambato lies the 58,560-hectare Chimborazo Fauna Reserve, which lies within three provinces: Cotopaxi, Tungurahua, and Bolívar. The reserve's main attraction is Ecuador's highest mountain, Chimborazo (6,268 meters), which is also the farthest point from the center of the earth and closest point to the sun. Even though it is some 2,500 meters shorter than Everest when measured from sea level, Chimborazo's peak is actually farther from the center of the earth because of the earth's equatorial bulge. Climbing Chimborazo is no mean feat and requires both serious preparation and luck with the conditions. The craggy peak next to it, Carihuairazo (5,020 meters), is considerably lower but also challenging and is often used as a preparation climb.

For nonclimbers, the reserve has plenty to offer, and it's worth it at the very least to drive through here to gaze on its unworldly landscapes. The western side of Chimborazo, in particular, is made up of dry terrain that recalls the Bolivian high plains. The reserve's *páramo,* farther down, is home to thousands of llamas, vicuñas, and alpacas. Vicuñas had been hunted to extinction in Ecuador but were reintroduced from Chile and Bolivia in the 1980s and now number over 2,500.

The reserve can be entered either near Pogyos on the road between Ambato and Guaranda or on the road from Riobamba to Guaranda near Pulingui San Pablo, from where it is eight kilometers to the refuge. A taxi can be arranged from Riobamba ($35), or you can take a full-day guided tour that includes hikes around the park and between the two refuges ($45 pp) with **Alta Montaña** (Avenida Daniel León Borja 35-17 at Uruguay, Riobamba, tel. 3/294-2215).

Climbing Volcán Chimborazo

Chimborazo, whose name comes from the Kichwa for "snowy place to be crossed,"

Due to the Ecuatorial ridge, Chimborazo is further from the center of the earth than Everest.

© CHRIS O'CONNELL

Alpaca inhabit the high *páramo* of Chimborazo Fauna Reserve.

actually consists of two peaks with five separate summits between them. English climber Edward Whymper along with Italians Jean-Antoine Carrel and Louis Carrel were the first to stand atop Chimborazo in 1880, having ascended via what is known today as the Whymper Route.

If you want to tell people you've been to the real roof of the world, bear in mind that the climb is challenging. Most people take the Normal Route in preference to the more dangerous Whymper Route, and while it's not technically difficult, it still demands knowledge, experience, and above all, enough time to acclimate. The upper slopes are prone to avalanches—a bad one in 1993 killed 10 climbers, and the melting of the mountain's glaciers has led to changes in the route. The ascent takes 7–10 hours, and the descent 3–4 hours. Although Chimborazo can be climbed year-round, the best months are December–January. February–April brings rain and heavy snowfall; by June you can expect high winds, clear sky, and good snow.

Climbing without a guide is strongly discouraged, and it's best to book a tour from Riobamba or Quito. A recommended agency in Riobamba is **Alta Montaña** (Avenida Daniel León Borja 35-17 at Uruguay, tel. 3/294-2215). Two-day ascents of Chimborazo cost $220 pp. Two-day hikes between Chimborazo and Carihuairazo cost $140 pp.

Climbing Volcán Carihuairazo

Sharing the Abraspungo Valley with its big brother, Chimborazo, Carihuairazo (ka-ree-why-RAH-zo) takes its name from the Kichwa for "strong freezing wind." Both the Maxima (5,020 meters) and Mocha (height disputed) peaks are covered with snow and ice, making technique and experience necessary for the ascent. Both summits are part of a large caldera almost two kilometers in diameter, open to the north. Whymper and the Carrels first climbed the Mocha peak in 1880, while Maxima remained unconquered until a Colombian, German, and French expedition reached the summit in 1951.

These days, the Maxima peak is the more commonly climbed, and it makes good practice for tackling Chimborazo. There is a new refuge at 4,600 meters, which is used as base for the climb. Hiring a guide is strongly recommended for climbing and hiking in this area.

SALINAS

This small town, at a chilly 3,550 meters in the hills high above Guaranda, has made a name for itself in recent years with its food cooperatives. The town has become a model for redevelopment and self-sufficiency in South America. It was all made possible by an Italian Salesian monk who came here in 1971. Appalled by the high levels of malnutrition and infant mortality, he set up a cooperative to boost the town's dairy production. A Swiss technician was brought in, and the **Quesera de la Cooperativa Salinas** (Salinas Cooperative Cheese Factory) was born. Their cheeses—everything from mozzarella to gruyère—are sold all over Ecuador under the name El Salinerito, and profits go directly to the local community. Other projects have followed, including an excellent chocolate factory and a wool cooperative just outside town.

You can stop by the factories yourself, but it's better to arrange a guided tour of all three ($6 pp) on the main plaza at the **tourism office** (Plaza Central, tel. 3/239-0022, www.elsalinerito.com, 8 A.M.–1 P.M. and 2–5 P.M. daily). To help the locals further, you can make a purchase when you visit the cooperatives, and with so much delicious cheese and chocolate on offer, you'll likely be very happy to. The tourist office can also advise on hikes around the town. There are mineral-water springs 15 minutes from town, and the old salt mines are a two-hour walk.

Accommodations

There are very few hotels in town. By far the best is at **Hotel Refugio** (Vía Samilagua, tel. 3/239-0022 or 3/221-0044, www.turismosalinas.com, $7–13 pp), which has comfortable guest rooms, a roaring fireplace in the lobby, and good views of town. Choose from shared or private baths. Tours can be organized from the hotel.

Food

For food, if you haven't stuffed your face with cheese and chocolate, try **La Minga** (El Salinerito and Guayamas, tel. 3/239-0042, 7:30 A.M.–10 P.M. daily, entrées $1.50–3), which does filling set lunches and soups.

Getting There

Getting to Salinas can be a challenge. There are four direct buses from Guaranda's Plaza Roja, leaving in the early morning and around noon. If you miss these, the best option is to take a pickup truck from Plaza Roja ($1). If you're coming from Ambato, either go to Guaranda first, or get off at the intersection with the road to Salinas and catch the first passing pickup truck to go the remaining 20 kilometers to Salinas.

GUARANDA

Guaranda (pop. 31,000) proudly calls itself "the Rome of Ecuador," which may seem faintly ridiculous until you learn that the title refers to the seven hills that the town is built around. There's little in the way of Roman grandeur in Guaranda, but the capital of Bolívar Province is an attractive place with a small-town feel. The cobbled streets, stately main square, and hilly surroundings make it an interesting day trip or overnight stop, even though it's no longer on the main route between Quito and Guayaquil. The celebrations around Carnival are particularly raucous, when people flood in from all the neighboring villages to sing, dance, and drink.

Sights

The city's castle-like **cathedral** sits on the edge of **Parque Bolívar,** the town's most attractive square. Overlooking the town, three kilometers to the west, is **El Indio Guarango,** a five-meter statue of a heavily muscled warrior. The views from the small plaza surrounding the statue are worth the hike. A taxi from the center costs about $2.50.

CENTRAL SIERRA

Guaranda's main church on Parque Bolívar

© BEN WESTWOOD

Entertainment and Events

Carnival in Guaranda is one of the most festive and traditional in the highlands—expect plenty of drinking, street dancing, live music, water balloons, and sprayed foam.

Nightlife is low-key the rest of the year, but try **Los 7 Santos** (Convención de 1884 and 10 de Agosto, tel. 3/298-0612, 10 A.M.–midnight Mon.–Sat.), an arty café that is a good place for a drink. The local drink of choice is *pájaro azul,* a blue liquor made with local herbs.

Shopping

The city's two **markets,** held on Saturday and Wednesday, are in the Plaza 15 de Mayo at the north end of town and in the concrete Mercado 10 de Noviembre at the south end.

Accommodations

One of Guaranda's best hotels is **Complejo Turístico La Colina** (Guayaquil and Guaranda, tel. 3/298-1954, $38 s, $65 d, breakfast included) on a hill overlooking town. It has a bar and a restaurant along with a pool and sauna open to the public (8 A.M.–6 P.M. daily, $3 pp).

To reach the hotel, head east on Moreno and take a left up the hill on Guayaquil.

Next to the municipal building in the city center is the **Hotel Cochabamba** (García Moreno and 7 de Mayo, tel. 3/298-1958, fax 3/298-2125, $17 s, $28 d), with comfortable guest rooms and a good restaurant.

Hotel Bolívar (Olmedo and Pichincha, tel. 3/298-0547, $15 s, $25 d) has pleasant guest rooms set around a plant-filled courtyard.

The best budget option in town is **Hostal de las Flores** (Pichincha and Rocafuerte, tel. 3/298-0644, $10 pp), with clean, homey guest rooms in a refurbished old building.

Food

Guaranda certainly doesn't compete with Rome in its culinary offerings, but you can get good pizza here, made with fresh cheese from nearby Salinas. The best place to try it is **Pizzería La Salinerita** (Av. General Enríquez, tel. 3/298-5406, noon–10 P.M. Mon.–Sat., entrées $3–7). On the main square, head to **Pizzeria Buon Giorno** (Sucre and García Moreno, tel. 3/298-3603, 1–9 P.M. Tues.–Sat., entrées $5–10).

The restaurant at **Hotel Cochabamba** (García Moreno and 7 de Mayo, tel. 3/298-1958, 8 A.M.–10 P.M. daily, entrées $3–7) has a good selection of meat and chicken dishes as well as a set lunch ($2.50). Another good choice for local fare is **La Bohemia** (Convención de 1884 and 10 de Agosto, tel. 3/298-4368, 8 A.M.–9 P.M. Mon.–Sat., entrées $6–7), also with a set lunch ($2.50). Or try **La Estancia** (García Moreno, tel. 3/298-3157, noon–10 P.M. Mon.–Sat., entrées $3–5) for chicken, steaks, and pasta.

Getting There and Around

Guaranda's **bus station** is a 20-minute walk east of the city center on Moreno. There are several buses each hour to Ambato (2 hours, $2) and Riobamba (2 hours, $2), plus hourly service to Guayaquil (4.5 hours, $4) and Quito (4.5 hours, $4.50). The narrow road to Riobamba is as dramatic as the route to Ambato and not for the faint-hearted, clinging to the sides of the hills with sheer drop-offs a bit too close for comfort. Taxis around town cost $1.

Riobamba and Vicinity

If you're traveling south from Ambato or Quito, the capital of Chimborazo Province, Riobamba (pop. 180,000, elevation 2,750 meters), is quite a contrast. Its wide, palm-lined avenues and quiet, elegant squares suit its comparatively slow pace of life perfectly. Visitors are mainly drawn to Riobamba to take the train ride south to La Nariz del Diablo or to climb nearby Chimborazo, which towers over the west of the city. However, Riobamba's charms make it a pleasant place to be based for a day or two. People take their time here; a 2–3-hour-long lunch break is the norm, and parts of the city are almost deserted in the early morning and evening. The traffic is also lighter than in Ambato or Cuenca.

The strong indigenous heritage of Riobamba dates back to prehistoric times. Puruhá *indígenas* were the first to settle here at the south end of the Avenue of the Volcanoes. The Inca stay was brief before the Spanish arrived in 1534 to found their first capital near the present-day city of Cajabamba, 17 kilometers to the south. A catastrophic earthquake in 1797 destroyed most of Riobamba, prompting the surviving residents to rebuild in the city's present location. The stones of the original cathedral were transported, and it was painstakingly rebuilt to exactly the same dimensions. The city's pride was further boosted soon afterward in 1830 when Ecuador's first constitution was written and signed here, an event commemorated in the name of the city's main thoroughfare, Primera Constituyente.

The city's mixed indigenous and colonial heritage is best exemplified by its name, which combines the Spanish word for river with the Kichwa word for valley.

SIGHTS
Museums and Galleries
One of South America's foremost religious art museums is housed in the former **Convento de la Concepción** (Argentinos and Larrea, tel. 3/296-5212, 9 A.M.–12:30 P.M. and 3–5:30 P.M. Tues.–Sat., $3) in the Convento de la Concepción church. The museum contains 210 paintings and sculptures, many of them priceless, in 14 rooms. Don't miss the marvelous inlaid *barguesos* (chests of drawers) or the museum's priceless monstrance—a gold- and jewel-encrusted vessel in which the consecrated host was displayed to the faithful during mass. The monstrance was stolen in 2007, but most of it (except the base) was recovered by police and returned in mid-2008. A reconstructed nun's room, complete with wire scourges, gives an idea of Spartan convent life during the colonial period. Free guided tours are available in Spanish.

Parks, Churches, and Monuments
Riobamba's two most beautiful squares are at the south end of town. The **basilica** next

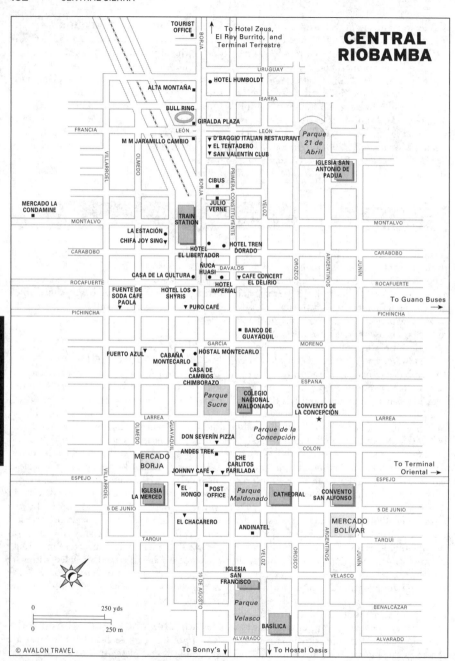

CENTRAL RIOBAMBA

TOURIST OFFICE

To Hotel Zeus, El Rey Burrito, and Terminal Terrestre

BORJA

URUGUAY

HOTEL HUMBOLDT

ALTA MONTAÑA

IBARRA

BULL RING

GIRALDA PLAZA

FRANCIA

LEÓN

LEÓN

Parque 21 de Abril

M M JARAMILLO CAMBIO

▼ D'BAGGIO ITALIAN RESTAURANT
▼ EL TENTADERO
▼ SAN VALENTÍN CLUB

IGLESIA SAN ANTONIO DE PADUA

VILLARROEL

OLMEDO

BORJA

PRIMERA

CONSTITUYENTE

VELOZ

CIBUS

MERCADO LA CONDAMINE

JULIO VERNE

MONTALVO

MONTALVO

TRAIN STATION

LA ESTACIÓN
CHIFA JOY SING ▼

HOTEL TREN DORADO

CARABOBO

HOTEL EL LIBERTADOR

CARABOBO

DAVALOS

CASA DE LA CULTURA ▼

NUCA HUASI

OROZCO

ARGENTINOS

JUNIN

ROCAFUERTE

▼ CAFE CONCERT EL DELIRIO

ROCAFUERTE

HOTEL IMPERIAL

To Guano Buses →

FUENTE DE SODA CAFÉ PAOLA ▼

HOTEL LOS SHYRIS ●

▼ PURO CAFÉ

PICHINCHA

PICHINCHA

■ BANCO DE GUAYAQUIL

GARCÍA

MORENO

PUERTO AZUL ▼

CABAÑA MONTECARLO ▼

▼ HOSTAL MONTECARLO

CASA DE CAMBIOS CHIMBORAZO

ESPAÑA

Parque Sucre

COLEGIO NACIONAL MALDONADO

CONVENTO DE LA CONCEPCIÓN ★

LARREA

LARREA

OLMEDO

GUAYAQUIL

DON SEVERÍN PIZZA ▼

Parque de la Concepción

ANDES TREK ▼

COLÓN

MERCADO BORJA

CHE CARLITOS PARRILLADA

JOHNNY CAFÉ ▼

To Terminal Oriental →

VILLARROEL

ESPEJO

ESPEJO

IGLESIA LA MERCED

▼ EL HONGO

■ POST OFFICE

Parque Maldonado

CATHEDRAL

CONVENTO SAN ALFONSO

5 DE JUNIO

5 DE JUNIO

ARGENTINOS

▼ EL CHACARERO

ANDINATEL ■

MERCADO BOLÍVAR

TARQUI

TARQUI

VELOZ

OROSCO

JUNIN

VELASCO

IGLESIA SAN FRANCISCO

10 DE AGOSTO

Parque Velasco

BENALCAZAR

BASÍLICA

ALVARADO

ALVARADO

0   250 yds

0   250 m

© AVALON TRAVEL

To Bonny's ↓

↓ To Hostal Oasis

© BEN WESTWOOD

Riobamba's cathedral was painstakingly transported and rebuilt in a new location after the 1797 earthquake.

to the **Parque La Libertad** is famous for being the only round church in the country. Riobambeños are particularly proud of this one because local talent was responsible for most of its design and construction during the late 19th century. A few blocks west, the pleasant colonial **Parque Maldonado** has a monument to Pedro Vicente Maldonado under the gaze of the city's **cathedral,** reconstructed here after the 1797 earthquake.

Named after the date Riobamba was founded, the **Parque 21 de Abril** (Argentinos and León) occupies a small hill at the north end of town called La Loma de Quito. It offers a great view of the city and mist-shrouded volcanoes on the horizon, along with an historic mural. On the north side of the park sits the small **Iglesia San Antonio de Padua,** with an impressive wood altar.

ENTERTAINMENT AND EVENTS

The **Founding of Riobamba,** celebrated April 19–21, commemorates the Independence Battle of Tapi in 1821, and coincides with an **agricultural, livestock, and crafts fair** to produce the city's largest annual festival. The **Independence of Riobamba** on November 11 is another big celebration.

The best area for nightlife is along Avenida Borja north of the center. The bar **El Tentadero** (Borja and León, 8 P.M.–midnight Thurs., 8 P.M.–2 A.M. Fri.–Sat., $2) is one of the town's busiest discos, playing a mix of electronic and Latin music.

SHOPPING

Giralda Plaza (Borja and León) is a small *centro comercial* with cafés, shops, and a supermarket.

Arts and Crafts

Several shops on Borja sell *tagua* nut carvings. **Ricardo Tagua** (Borja and León, no phone) is one of the best, as is **The Tagua Shop** (Daniel León Borja 35-17 at Ibarra, tel. 3/294-2215), which shares the office of the Alta Montaña tour company. You can watch the carvings being made at the Tagua Shop, which stocks other crafts as well.

Markets

Saturday is the main market day, with Thursday close behind, when the city floods with traders, and don't be surprised to see herds of cattle passing through town. Crafts and indigenous clothing are sold in **Parque de la Concepción** (Orozco and Larrea), south of the convent. Of particular note are the baskets and mats woven by nearby *indígenas* out of reeds from the Laguna Colta. The produce market in **Plaza Simón Bolívar** also carries pottery and baskets. Also significant are the **Mercado Borja** (across Espejo from the Iglesia La Merced), the **Mercado La Condamine** (five blocks south of the train station), and the **Mercado San Francisco** (bounded by 10 de Agosto, Primera Constituyente, Velasco, and Benalcázar).

RECREATION AND TOURS

Riobamba has several high-quality mountain-guide services to tackle nearby peaks, including Chimborazo and Carihuairazo. All of the organizations and individuals listed here are fully licensed.

Alta Montaña (Daniel León Borja 35-17 at Uruguay, tel./fax 3/294-2215, aventurag@ ch.pro.ec) is the best known and trusted. It offers trips for just about any destination and activity you can imagine, from climbing and hiking the Inca Trail to bird-watching and horseback riding, and Alta Montaña's guides are the best in the business. A four-person trip up Chimborazo costs $220 pp, all-inclusive. Two-day ascents of Carihuairazo cost $175 pp, and two-day hikes between Chimborazo and Carihuairazo cost $140 pp.

Marcelo Puruncajas directs **Andes Trek** (Esmeraldas 21 at Espejo, tel./fax 3/295-1275, www.andes-trek.com). He has climbed since 1958 and speaks English. The shop rents equipment, runs mountain-biking trips and Amazon tours, and has 4WD service available.

Marco Cruz operates **Expediciones Andinas** (tel. 3/236-4278, www.expediciones-andinas.

com), three kilometers toward Guano and across the street from the Albergue Abraspungo. Climbing is its specialty, but llama treks and mountain-biking tours are also available.

The **Julio Verne** travel agency (Calle El Espectador 22-35 at Borja, tel. 3/296-3436, www.julioverne-travel.com) receives regular recommendations for its climbing, trekking, and rainforest trips, and the staff speaks German, Dutch, English, and a little French.

Galo Brito of **Pro Bici** (Primera Constituyente 23-51 at Larrea, tel. 3/294-1880, www.probici.com) guides mountain-biking excursions personalized for each group's ability, from extreme descents of Chimborazo to quiet village tours. Galo, who offers high-quality Cannondale aluminum-frame bikes and a support vehicle, speaks English and a little French and German. Rentals cost $15–25 pp, and one-day tours start at $30 pp.

ACCOMMODATIONS
Under $10

Most of the budget hotels are clustered near the train station. **Hostal Ñuca Huasi** (10 de Agosto and Dávalos, tel. 3/296-6669, $4–6 pp) has basic guest rooms in a shabby but characterful old building. The **Hotel Imperial** (Rocafuerte 22-15 at 10 de Agosto, tel. 3/296-0429, $6 pp) has reasonable guest rooms for the price. The modern **Hotel Los Shyris** (10 de Agosto and Rocafuerte, tel. 3/296-0323, $8–10 pp) is perhaps the best deal in this range with private baths, cable TV, and hot water.

$10-25

With its quiet garden and homey atmosphere at the south end of town, **Hostal Oasis** (Veloz 15-32 at Almagro, tel. 3/296-1210, $12 pp) is one of the best-located hotels in town, with tasteful guest rooms and a flower-filled courtyard. Closer to the station, **Hotel Tren Dorado** (Carabobo 22-35 and 10 de Agosto, tel. 3/296-4890, $11 pp) has well-decorated guest rooms, a restaurant, a TV room, and an early breakfast available at 5:30 A.M. on train days. **Hotel El Libertador** (Borja 29-22, tel. 3/294-7393,

$15 s, $25 d) is excellent value with spacious, tastefully furnished guest rooms in a colonial-style building overlooking the train station. **Hostal Montecarlo** (10 de Agosto 25-41, tel. 3/296-0557, $18 s, $33 d) is one of the most characterful hotels in the center, with a covered courtyard and marble floors.

$25-50

The seven-story **Hotel Zeus** (Borja, tel. 3/296-8036, $25–38 s, $37–50 d), west of the center, has spectacular views, an elegant restaurant, and a spa center. The pricier guest rooms are considerably nicer, with better furnishings and bathtubs.

$50-75

(**Hostería La Andaluza** (tel. 3/294-9370, http://hosteriaandaluza.com, $68 s, $88 d), is a fine converted hacienda 16 kilometers north of Riobamba that commands spectacular views. The hotel boasts 55 guest rooms, two large restaurants, a gym, a sauna, a steam room, a games room, and a playground on the extensive grounds. Tiled roofs and fountains lead back to the workshops, where the *hostería's* famous Andaluza hams are slowly cured in sea salt. Most of the guest rooms have antique furnishings and fireplaces.

$75-100

Set in the Las Abras suburb three kilometers north of Riobamba on the way to Guano, the **Hacienda Abraspungu** (tel. 3/236-4031, www.haciendaaabraspungo.com, $79 s, $109 d, breakfast included) began its career as a pre- and postclimbing lodge before metamorphosing into a country inn in 1994. Everything here rings of mountaineering, from the hotel's name (after the valley between Chimborazo and Carihuairazo) to the black-and-white photos of climbers and mountains on every wall, taken by Marco Cruz of Expediciones Andinas, across the lane. The parking lot is filled with 4WD vehicles, and antique climbing gear hangs from the walls. Each of the 42 guest rooms is named after a different Ecuadorian mountain, and they're all connected by whitewashed hallways trimmed with rough wood beams and decorated with indigenous hats, masks, and old farming tools.

FOOD

Riobamba has a few decent restaurants, but the selection is not as good as nearby Baños. Most restaurants close by 10 P.M., and few are open on Sunday.

One of the best in town is (**Café Concert El Delirio** (Primera Constituyente and Rocafuerte, tel. 3/296-6441, noon–10 P.M. Tues.–Sun., $6–9), in the former home of the great liberator Simón Bolívar and named after one of his famous poems. This snug, classy restaurant around a small courtyard garden is adorned with paintings and has a fireplace to ward off the chill. Another upscale pick is the **Cabaña Montecarlo** (García Moreno 21-40, tel. 3/296-1577, noon–9:30 P.M. Mon.–Sat., lunch only Sun., entrées $5), offering decent Ecuadorian fare and pasta in a chalet atmosphere.

For good Italian food, there are several options. (**Pizzeria D'Baggios** (Borja 33-24, tel. 3/296-1832, noon–10 P.M. Mon.–Sat., $4–8) is unbeatable for sumptuous pizza and calzone handmade in front of you, and **El Chacarero** (5 de Junio 21-46 at 10 de Agosto, tel. 3/296-9292, 3–10:30 P.M. daily, $4–7) also has good pizza and pasta.

The **San Valentine Club** (Av León Borja and Torres, tel. 3/296-3137, 5 P.M.–midnight Tues.–Sat., entrées $3–5) serves Mexican food, pizzas, pies, and fast food in an informal atmosphere.

For the best Mexican burritos and enchiladas, including vegetarian options, try **El Rey del Burrito** (Borja 38-36, tel. 3/295-3230, 11 A.M.–11 P.M. Mon.–Sat., 11 A.M.–4 P.M. Sun., $3–5).

A good place for fresh coffee, sandwiches, and breakfasts is **Puro Café** (Pichincha 12-37, 9:30 A.M.–2 P.M. and 3:30–9:30 P.M. daily, $2–4).

INFORMATION

The **tourist information office** (Borja and Primeras Olympiadas, tel. 3/294-1213,

8 A.M.–noon and 2–6 P.M. Mon.–Fri.) has maps and brochures, and staff can recommend mountain guides and equipment sources in the city. The revamped train station has a new tourist information office (tel. 3/294-7389, 8 A.M.–noon and 2–6 P.M. Mon.–Fri.).

The headquarters for Sangay National Park and Chimborazo National Park is the **Ministerio del Ambiente** (9 de Octubre and Cicrumvalación, tel. 3/296-3779 or 3/261-·0029, 8 A.M.–1 P.M. and 2–5 P.M. Mon.–Fri.), in a small office next to the larger Ministerio de Agricultura y Ganadera building. It provides information on the parks for climbers and hikers. The guard posts at Candelaria and Alao can be contacted from here by radio to check on trail conditions.

SERVICES

ATMs and counter services can be found at **Banco del Pichincha** (García Moreno and Primera Constituyente) and **Banco Guayaquil** (Primera Constituyente). **MM Jaramillo Arteaga** (Borja and León) and **Chimborazo** (beside the Hostal Montecarlo) exchange traveler's checks and handle a reasonable selection of other currencies. The **police station** is on Borja (tel. 3/296-1913). The best hospitals are **Hospital Policlínico** (Olmedo 11-01, tel. 3/296-1705), southeast of downtown, and **Clínica Metropolitana** (Juní 25-28, tel. 3/294-1930). The **post office** is on the corner of Espejo and 10 de Agosto.

GETTING THERE AND AROUND
Bus and Taxi
Riobamba's main **terminal terrestre** (La Prensa and Borja) bus terminal is about two kilometers west of the center. Buses come and go between here and Quito (4 hours, $4), Ambato (1 hour, $1), and Cuenca (6 hours, $6). To reach Baños, everything depends on the current state of Volcán Tungurahua. If the direct road is closed, buses from the main terminal go via Ambato, where you usually have to change. If the road is open, head to the **Terminal Oriente,** 12 blocks north of Primera

Constituyente along Espejo. There are regular buses from here to Baños (1.5 hours, $2) and cities in the Oriente such as Tena (7 hours, $6). Buses to Guano leave from Pichincha and York, nine blocks north of Primera Constituyente.

Taxis around town cost $1–1.50. A **private taxi** to the refuge on Chimborazo (about $40) can hold up to five people.

Train
The train service south from Riobamba is due to open in mid-2012 after extensive renovation work. When the line reopens, you can take the three-hour journey to Alausí and then the 2.5 hour journey along the famously hair-raising Nariz del Diablo (Devil's Nose), a spectacular set of switchbacks carved into the mountainside, before returning to Riobamba the same day.

When the service from Riobamba resumes, trains will leave at 6:30 A.M. Tuesday–Sunday and return at about 5 P.M. Prices are unconfirmed at the time of writing, but fares are likely to be about $30 round-trip.

Until the Riobamba line reopens, you have to take a bus from Riobamba's main terminal to Alausí (2 hours, $1.50). Buses leave every half hour throughout the day starting at 5 A.M. Even when the train line reopens, you may prefer to save a little time and money and get the bus to Alausí for the best part of the ride. Train fare from Alausí to Sibambe past La Nariz del Diablo is $20 pp round-trip.

It's advisable to make reservations in advance (the day before, if possible) at the train station in Riobamba (Av. de los Volcanes, tel. 3/296-7316 or 3/296-1038, www.ferrocarrilesdelecuador.gob.ec). If you are only traveling along the Alausí–Sibambe section, you can still reserve seats in Riobamba and collect the ticket in Alausí. On weekends, the train is usually completely booked, and standing is not allowed.

CAJABAMBA AND VICINITY
About 20 kilometers southwest of Riobamba on the Panamericana is the tiny village of Cajabamba. It is unremarkable nowadays, but this was the original site of Riobamba before

the 1797 earthquake destroyed the city, causing its relocation.

A few kilometers farther south, at the intersection with the road to Bucay and Guayaquil, is **La Balbanera Chapel,** known as the oldest church in Ecuador. When the Spanish first arrived in Ecuador in 1534, one of the first things they built was this church on the shore of the reedy **Laguna Colta.** Since then, it has undergone a complete renovation—by human hands and earthquakes—but stepping inside the meter-thick stone walls still comes close to taking you back centuries.

GUANO AND SANTA TERESITA

Eight kilometers north of Riobamba, artisans in the craft village of **Guano** sell distinctive wool rugs, wall hangings, and leather goods from shops on and around the main square. Abstract and pre-Colombian motifs predominate in the weavings, which are much thicker and more durable than the usual thin tapestries. The prices of leather jackets and shoes are particularly competitive here. Saturday is market day, but the shopping is good any day of the week.

From Guano, it's a 20-minute walk to Santa Teresita and the tepid **Los Elenes thermal baths** (8 A.M.–6 P.M. daily, $1), which at least have great views of Tungurahua and El Altar to the east. Camping is permitted, and there's a small cafeteria.

GUAMOTE

The morning trains come through this small indigenous community on the way to Alausí. Otherwise, the main reason to come to Guamote, 50 kilometers south of Riobamba in a quiet mountain basin, is for market day on Thursday. It is one of the largest in the region and rivals the market in Saquisilí, although it's not really aimed at visitors, with only a smattering of handicrafts. The focal point is the chaotic animal market. You're not likely to buy anything, but it is an interesting experience, if hardly an advertisement for animal rights.

To see the market at its best, spend the night here and get up early. There are a couple of older, cheap hostels close to the train station, the best of which is just up the hill at the Belgian- and Ecuadorian-run **Inti Sisa** (JM Plaza and García Moreno, tel. 3/291-6529, www.intisisa.org, dorm $10 pp, $14.50 pp). This small hostel, with a few private guest rooms and a spacious dormitory, uses its profits to support educational programs in town and in the area, and it accepts volunteers.

ALAUSÍ

Set on the edge of a gorge with a giant statue of patron saint San Pedro dominating the town, Alausí is a fittingly dramatic departure point for the most dramatic train ride in Ecuador—La Nariz del Diablo (Devil's Nose). When train service resumes from Riobamba in mid-2012, the train stops in Alausí in the mid-morning before embarking on its two-hour descent and then returning to Riobamba in the early afternoon. Some people shorten the train ride by boarding here for the best part, making Alausí an alternate overnight stay to Riobamba. It is also the starting point for heading south to Achupallas and hiking the Inca Trail to Ingapirca.

Aside from the train service, Alausí springs to life for market day on Sunday, when indigenous people come down from the nearby *páramo* wearing their best and most colorful clothing. You can get a closer look at the statue of Saint Peter and admire the panoramic views by climbing the Lluglli hill.

The town's festival is celebrated on June 29 with bullfights and colorful parades.

◀ Nariz del Diablo Train Ride

Alausí's **train station,** the goal of most visitors, sits behind the small plaza at the north end of 5 de Junio. The train through the famous Nariz del Diablo (Devil's Nose) to Sibambe (departs 8 A.M., 11 A.M., and 3 P.M. Tues.–Sun., $20 pp) takes 2.5 hours. When train service from Riobamba to Alausí resumes, the train will leave Riobamba at 6:30 A.M., stopping in Alausí three hours later.

Buying tickets in advance is strongly recommended, especially for weekend trips, because standing is not allowed. You can buy a ticket at the train station in Alausí (tel. 3/293-0126, www.ferrocarrilesdelecuador.gob.ec) or make a reservation at the train station in Riobamba (Av. de los Volcanes, tel. 3/296-7316 or 3/296-1038, www.ferrocarrilesdelecuador.gob.ec) and collect the ticket at the train station in Alausí.

The Devil's Nose was one of the most incredible feats of railroad engineering when it was completed in the early 1900s. The train descends through a hair-raising series of switchbacks that are so tight the entire train has to back up momentarily to fit through. Just below the switchbacks, the train stops near Sibambe, turns around, and climbs back through the entire route. For the best views, sit on the right-hand side of the train if you can. Riding on the roof is now prohibited following the deaths of two Japanese visitors in 2007.

If you are coming from Riobamba, the return journey takes all day, but you can shorten it by taking the bus back from Alausí to Riobamba (2 hours, $1.50). Buses from Alausí also run to Quito and Cuenca.

Accommodations and Food

Alausí has a small selection of hotels, which is likely to grow quickly now that the trains runs more frequently. One block from 5 de Junio, **Hotel Europa** (García Moreno 159 and Chile, tel. 3/293-0200, $5–8 pp) is a good budget option with old wooden balconies, simple guest rooms with shared or private baths, and a Chinese restaurant (8 A.M.–10 P.M. daily, $3–4). **Hotel Pan-Americano** (5 de Junio and 9 de Octubre, tel. 3/293-0156, $6–10 pp) also has decent guest rooms with shared or private baths and a restaurant downstairs (8 A.M.–10 P.M. daily, $3–4).

One of the best places in town is **Hostería La Quinta** (Eloy Alfaro 121, tel. 3/293-0247, www.hosteria-la-quinta.com, $36 s, $56 d, breakfast included), with comfortable guest rooms and great views of the train line. It fills up fast, so book in advance.

About three kilometers outside town,

Hostería Pircabamba (Villalva and Pedro de Loza, tel. 3/293-0180, www.pircapamba.com, $20 pp, breakfast included) has traditional whitewashed brick-and-wood guest rooms with views of Alausí and the surrounding valleys. Horseback excursions are available.

Some of the best food in Alausí can be found in the various hotel restaurants, including **Hotel Pan-Americano** and **Hotel Europa.** Inside the train station, **Café La Higuera** (tel. 3/293-1582, 8 A.M.–8 P.M. daily, $2–3) is a good place to grab breakfast before the train ride or a set lunch on the way back. Right next to the station, **El Mesón de Tren** (Ricaurte and Eloy Alfaro, tel. 3/293-0243, 8 A.M.–6 P.M. daily, $3) offers filling local specialties such as roast pork and *llapingacho,* a potato dish.

Information and Services

You can exchange traveler's checks at the **Banco de Guayaquil** (5 de Junio and Ricaurte), on the ground floor of the Municipal Building near the train station. The **post office** (García Moreno and 9 de Octubre) is one block uphill from 5 de Junio, past the Hotel Pan-Americano. A covered **market** spreads along García Moreno between Pedro Loza and Chile, uphill from 5 de Junio.

Buses head to Ambato (3 hours, $3), Cuenca (4 hours, $5), Guayaquil (5 hours, $5), Quito (5 hours, $6), and Riobamba (2 hours, $1.50) from the corner of 9 de Octubre and 5 de Julio. More buses pass on the highway up the hill ($1 by taxi), picking up passengers at the gas station on the Panamericana.

To begin the Inca Trail, occasional trucks bound for Achupallas, where the market is on Saturday, leave from 5 de Junio. There is more transportation available 30 minutes south at the road junction at **La Moya,** just after the river crossing.

SANGAY NATIONAL PARK

The largest park in Ecuador's Central Sierra connects Chimborazo, Tungurahua, and Morona-Santiago Provinces. The park contains two of Ecuador's most active volcanoes, Tungurahua and Sangay, as well as the extinct

El Altar, which may have been the country's highest peak before it collapsed spectacularly in the 15th century.

Created in 1979, the park initially protected 270,000 hectares. UNESCO declared it a World Heritage Site four years later, and in 1992 the Ecuadorian government more than doubled the size of the park to over 500,000 hectares.

In 1993, Sangay was placed on UNESCO's List of World Heritage in Danger primarily because of problems caused by the construction of a road bisecting the park from Guamote to Macas. Most of the park's backcountry, though, is still pristine and hard to reach, and the park contains some of the wildest terrain in the Central Highlands.

The park's elevation ranges 900–5,319 meters (the top of El Altar) and contains nine different terrains, from lowland rainforest to alpine tundra. There is staggering diversity of flora and fauna. Most of the larger animals are concentrated in the park's lower southern side, including anteaters, jaguars, monkeys, bears, and most of Sangay's estimated 230 species of birds, including the Andean condor. The higher regions protect one of the last sizable refuges of the Andean tapir near Volcán Sangay. The highly endangered *pudú* deer can also be found in the park. This nocturnal deer is one of the world's smallest, weighing just 10 kilograms and standing just 40 centimeters tall.

Two indigenous groups currently live in Sangay Park: the Canelos (lowland) Kichwa to the north, and the Shuar near Macas.

There are many gateways to Sangay. From the west, you can enter the park through Alao, via Chambo, Guayllabamba, Pungala, Licto, or Atillo, and farther southeast via Cebadas. Hiring a private truck or taxi is surest way to make the journey to Alao, southeast of Riobamba. Entrance to the park costs $10.

There are daily Transportes Riobamba buses from Riobamba's Terminal Oriente that take the road to Macas. From Guamote, before Cebadas, a road connects to the Atillo road. Farther south past Palmira is another road to the guard post near the Lagunas Ozogoche.

There is an excellent hiking trail between Atillo and Ozogoche Lakes.

For further information on Sangay National Park, visit www.parquesangay.org.ec.

Volcán El Altar

While Sangay to the south and Tungurahua to the north continue to spew out lava and ash on a regular basis, El Altar (5,315 meters) is long since extinct, but it went out in spectacular style, according to geologists. The jagged remains of El Altar's crater bear witness to what must have been an incredible cataclysm as one of the highest mountains in the world blew apart in an ancient explosion, leaving a C-shaped crater over three kilometers in diameter open to the west. Also known as Capac Urcu (Grand Mountain), El Altar is merely a shell of its former self, but it's still the fifth-highest mountain in Ecuador and probably the most technical climb. El Altar can still do damage, though, despite being extinct: In 2000 part of a glacier fell into a lake, killing several locals.

El Altar has no less than nine separate summits, each with religious names. Counterclockwise from south to north, they are Obispo, "the bishop," El Altar's highest (5,315 meters); Monjas Grande (5,160 meters) and Chico (5,080 meters), "the big and little nuns"; Tabernáculo, "the tabernacle," three peaks of which Sur (5,100 meters) is the highest; Los Frailes, "the friars," a quartet topped by Grande (5,180 meters); and finally, Canónigo (5,260 meters), "the canon." None of these peaks were climbed before 1963, when an Italian team led by Marino Tremonti first stood atop El Obispo. All have been climbed since then, but many new routes remain open.

With one of the longest approaches in the country, El Altar is thought by many to be Ecuador's finest climb. It takes 2–3 days to undertake, so it requires careful planning and a good guide. For a more easygoing experience, hikers can enjoy the trek to the base, one of the most impressive mountain spectacles in Ecuador, with jagged snowy peaks cupping a volcanic lake. The IGM *Cerros Negros* and *Laguna Pintada* 1:25,000 maps cover the area.

CENTRAL SIERRA

The easiest route to El Altar is taking a bus from Riobamba toward Baños and getting off at Penipe. This road has frequently been closed in recent years due to Volcán Tungurahua's activity, so inquire locally about the current situation. From Penipe, make your way southeast to the village of Candelaria (elevation 3,100 meters). There are occasional direct buses from Riobamba to Candelaria. Two kilometers past the center of Candelaria (don't blink) is the left-hand turnoff for the ranger station, where you register and pay the park entrance fee ($10). About one kilometer up the track is the **Hacienda El Releche** (tel. 3/296-0848 or 3/296-0848, http://haciendareleche.com, $12 pp), which has surprisingly comfortable accommodations with shared hot-water showers, kitchen facilities, and a great fireplace for drying sodden clothes. Horses can also be rented for the trek to the base.

After 4–5 hours of moderate uphill hiking, the Collanes Plain and El Altar itself come into view. During rainy periods, the plain becomes a sodden bog, but in clear weather the view competes for best in the country. The best time to do this hike is December–March, as there is wetter, foggier weather from April onward. To make your life easier, arrange a guided tour with an operator in Riobamba or Baños.

Volcán Sangay

Sangay (5,230 meters) has been erupting continuously since the 1930s and is one of the world's most active volcanoes. Its name derives from the Kichwa word for "frighten," but the danger doesn't stop adrenaline junkies from climbing it. Don't embark on this climb lightly, though—it's dangerous. Two members of a British expedition were killed in 1976, and the volcano has been sending out columns of ash regularly in the past few years, most recently in 2009. Most guides won't even make the ascent themselves, instead choosing to point out the way and wait for you at the bottom. Take rubber boots and wear a helmet, because the hike to the base can be muddy, and the volcano regularly blows out lava-rock bombs. Finally, leave for the peak attempt early in the morning and ascend and descend quickly to minimize your time on the slopes. The best months to make the climb are October–February, the driest time in the area. July–August are sodden, making the hike to the base more of a two-day slog. Several IGM maps will make your life easier: the *Sangay* and *Laguna Tinguichaca* 1:50,000 maps, and the 1:25,000 *N IV-F3c Río Culbreillas* and *N V-B1*. Check the latest geological situation with the Ecuadorian Geophysical Institute (www.igepn.edu.ec).

SOUTHERN SIERRA

Heading south of Riobamba, the towering mountains of the Central Highlands are replaced by undulating green hills. Everything is mellower down here—the climate warms up little by little as you move south, and the people are well known for their sweet temperaments and singsong accents.

This region's relative isolation from the rest of the country has helped the people to hold on to their traditions. The population is noticeably sparser, with fewer towns and villages between the main cities. Loja and Cuenca are far more conservative at heart than commercial Guayaquil and cosmopolitan Quito, and the indigenous heritage thrives in the cultures of the Cañari and Saraguro Indians. Furthermore, this is the region where the legacy of the brief Inca conquest of Ecuador is most visible. There are ruins in and around Cuenca and at Ingapirca, and there is even a lesser-known Inca Trail.

There are few peaks over 4,000 meters in the provinces of Cañar, Azuay, and Loja, and the landscape receives less visitor attention than the snowy peaks farther north. Deeper into the hills, however, it becomes more rugged and isolated, particularly in the two largest national parks, Cajas and Podocarpus, within touching distance of Cuenca and Loja, respectively.

East of Loja is one of Ecuador's remotest regions in the forbidding Cordillera del Condor. This is the inaccessible area that was the center of a long-running border dispute with Peru, only settled in 1998.

HIGHLIGHTS

◖ Ingapirca Ruins: The Inca empire's only remaining sun temple is the centerpiece of Ecuador's most impressive set of pre-Columbian ruins (page 174).

◖ Catedral Nueva: Cuenca's historic center is dominated by the massive twin-towered facade and sky-blue domes of the new cathedral, a UNESCO World Heritage Site (page 179).

◖ El Cajas National Park: Only an hour from Cuenca, hike through rugged and chilly moorland, past jagged rocks and hundreds of lakes (page 191).

◖ Podocarpus National Park: Ecuador's southernmost national park near Loja drops dramatically from Andean *páramo* to tropical rainforest and boasts some 600 bird species (page 205).

◖ Vilcabamba: The famous "Valley of Longevity" may or may not help you live longer, but its balmy climate, beautiful hikes, and spas are the perfect repose for weary travelers (page 207).

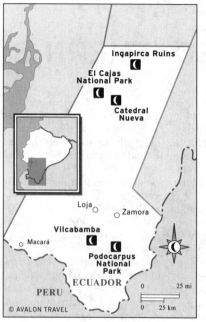

LOOK FOR ◖ TO FIND RECOMMENDED SIGHTS, ACTIVITIES, DINING, AND LODGING.

PLANNING YOUR TIME

You need the best part of a week to see the highlights of the southern Sierra. **Cuenca's** historic center and museums take up a day or two, but it's worth spending longer in this most pleasant of Ecuadorian cities. A day trip to the misty lakes and rugged, cold hills of **El Cajas National Park** offers excellent hiking, and the ruins at **Ingapirca** will fill another day. More serious hikers can consider staying overnight in Cajas or doing the three-day hike along Ecuador's lesser-known **Inca Trail** south from Achupallas to Ingapirca.

Farther south is the fascinating city of **Loja,** famed for its musicians and, more recently, its ecological practices. An hour to the south is

the small town of **Vilcabamba,** knowm as the "valley of longevity" and made famous by its healthy, elderly inhabitants. It's a relaxing place to stay for a few days with hiking and horseback riding as well as plenty of massage to ease aching limbs. Those with more time on their hands can explore **Podocarpus National Park,** one of the least visited parks in the Sierra, where the terrain drops down from rugged moors to dense forests on the edge of the Amazon rainforest.

If you're heading to or from Peru, the crossing via **Macará** southwest of Loja is far more pleasant than coastal Huaquillas, and there is an even quieter border post at **Zumba.**

Getting around the southern Sierra takes a bit longer than in the rest of the mountains.

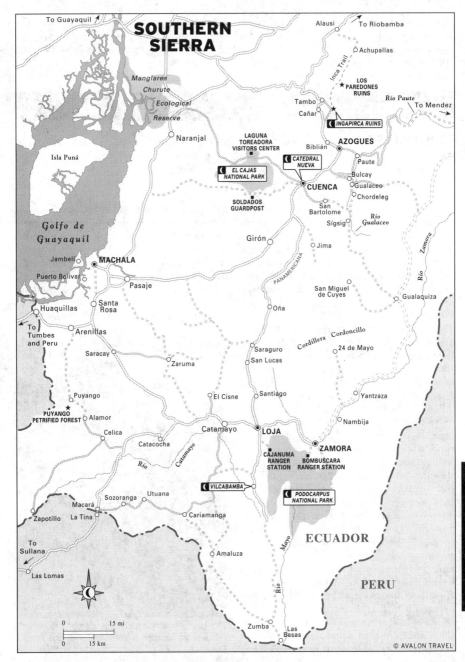

SOUTHERN SIERRA

Distances between the main destinations are a bit longer: Cuenca is six hours by bus from Riobamba and a long 10-hour ride from Quito (although only 4.5 hours from Guayaquil).

Loja is four hours farther south of Cuenca. You might consider flying to either city from Quito or Guayaquil; there are daily flights ($60–80 one-way).

Ingapirca and Vicinity

█ INGAPIRCA RUINS

The sight of the Inca empire's only remaining sun temple standing proudly on a hill at 3,200 meters elevation with panoramic views over the surrounding countryside is highly impressive. Ingapirca, which means " Inca stone wall," is easily Ecuador's best set of pre-Columbian ruins and well worth a day trip from Cuenca or a 10-kilometer detour off the Panamericana. However, comparisons with Machu Picchu will fall well short, and if you're traveling up from Peru, you may find the ruins rather modest.

History

The Cañari lived here long before the Incas arrived, erecting a Temple of the Moon, the foundations of which are still visible today. The Incas, led by Huayna Capac, arrived at the end of the 15th century and defeated the Cañari after a long, drawn-out battle. Interestingly, following their victory, the Inca had enough respect for the Cañari to build a community together, and constructed their own Temple of the Sun to complement the original temple. As well as employing their astonishing stonework, the Inca also built a complex underground irrigation network. Ingapirca was almost certainly used for ritual sacrifices because female skeletons have been unearthed on a site that was probably a convent for maidens.

Ingapirca's position overlooking the surrounding valley was of key strategic importance, but the city's growth was short-lived because the Spanish arrived before it was even completed. Ingapirca was ransacked and much of the stonework taken by the Spanish to build churches in Cuenca and beyond. The site lay abandoned until the Ecuadorian government began a restoration process in the mid-20th

century, and the site was opened to the public in 1966. It is now run by a group of local Cañari *indígenas.*

The Site

Much of the site is little more than stone foundations, and it takes imagination and a guided tour to bring it to life. The famous rounded Temple of the Sun is well-preserved, however, and forms an impressive centerpiece to the complex. Surrounding it are five hectares of low stone walls and grassy slopes. The small **Pilaloma** complex on the south side marks the original Cañari settlement, next to a pointy-roofed

The Ingapirca ruins are the site of the only remaining Temple of the Sun from the Inca Empire.

THE INCA TRAIL TO INGAPIRCA

It may not be as famous or impressive as the trail in Peru, but keen hikers can make the most of the beautiful hilltop views in the countryside between Alausí and Cuenca on this three-day trail.

Keep in mind that you'll be hiking at higher than 3,000 meters elevation the whole way, and that the trail follows a river, so it can get muddy – make sure you are acclimated, take it slow, and bring waterproof boots. The entire trail is not well marked, so maps are a good idea. The IGM *Alausí, Juncal,* and *Cañar* 1:50,000 maps cover the area and should put the trip within range of even weekend hikers – with a compass. Take plenty of food, water, and camping equipment, as facilities are thin on the ground. Alternately, book a guided trek with tour companies in Quito or Cuenca.

The start of the trail is at Achupallas. From Alausí, take any bus south for about 10 kilometers, then tackle a steep climb or hitch a ride to Achupallas. Alternately, a taxi from Alausí direct to Achupallas costs $7.

Leave Achupallas to the south past the elementary school, cross the Río Azuay, and reach the west bank of the Río Candrul after passing through a natural hole in the rock. From here, the trail heads clearly south between Cerro Mapahuña and Cerro Pucará.

There's a good campsite on the south side of Laguna Tres Cruces at 4,200 meters elevation, 14 kilometers and 6-7 hours from Achupallas.

Day 2 takes you southwest along Cuchilla Tres Cruces, which commands great views of the Quebrada Espíndola valley. This is the highest point along the hike (4,400 meters). Río Sansahuín and Río Espíndola join the Candrul near here. Descend into the valley to the left of the final peak, Quillo Loma. There are remains of an Inca road and foundations of an Inca bridge. There is also a trail to Laguna Culebrillas, and more ruins at Paredones. Although it would be possible to push to Ingapirca in one long second day, most hikers choose to spend the night among the graffitied ruins of Los Paredones (Big Walls), east of Laguna Culebrillas and 10 kilometers from Laguna Tres Cruces.

On day 3, head southwest from Paredones on the seven-meter-wide Inca road. After the village of San José, turn right to El Rodeo, then follow the road up to Ingapirca. It takes nearly five hours in total.

Note that there have been reports of thefts at campsites along the route. It's best not to take any valuables along the route. You can also avoid this problem by hiring locals with mules to carry your luggage.

replica of an Inca house and round depressions called *colcas* that were used to store food.

A fragment of Inca road called the **Ingañan** leads past bodegas used for food storage to an exterior plaza known as **La Condamine,** named after the French scientist's visit in 1748. These were the nobles' living quarters, including the *acllahuasi*—dwellings of ceremonial virgins where skeletons have been found.

The highlight of the complex is the **Temple of the Sun,** also known as El Castillo (The Castle). The mind-boggling stonework that is the hallmark of Inca construction can be appreciated in this two-story structure, hand-carved so precisely that mortar was unnecessary. Steps lead up to a trapezoidal doorway (four-sided, with two parallel sides) and a rectangular platform. It's entertaining to stand in the sentry posts of the temple and hear your whispers reverberate around the walls. Take a few moments to appreciate the view from here—the temple's location is as mesmerizing as its construction.

To the right of the temple there are ruins of the more sinister side of Inca culture: A V-shaped rock was supposedly used for human and animal sacrifices. Next to it is a larger stone with 28 holes that was thought to be used as a lunar calendar; the holes caught rainwater that told the date by reflecting the moon's light differently throughout the month.

Just outside the complex is a small **museum**

SOUTHERN SIERRA

(included in the entrance fee), which houses a collection of Cañari and Inca ceramics, sculptures, tools, traditional dress, and a skeleton found at the site. An **artisanal shop** next door sells regional crafts; a café and public toilets are across the way.

Guides are available on-site (included in the entrance fee), but note that few speak much English. The guide is important to provide information to enable you to get the most out of your visit. Ask around for a guide who speaks more English (and give a tip) or alternately book a tour from Cuenca.

Visiting Ingapirca

The ruins are open 8 A.M.–6 P.M. daily. Entrance costs $6 and includes a free tour; tips, as always, are appreciated.

From Cuenca, Trans-Cañar buses run direct from the main *terminal terrestre* at 9 A.M. and 1 P.M. daily (two hours, $2.50), returning at 1 P.M. and 4 P.M. On weekends, buses return at 1 P.M. only. Most tour companies in Cuenca offer organized excursions (from $45 pp).

If you're traveling from the north along the Panamericana, get off the bus at Cañar, or better, El Tambo. There are buses every half hour between the two towns, you can take a taxi (from $5), or it's a three-hour hike.

Most people just come for the day, but there are some accommodations nearby. About one kilometer before arriving at the ruins, in the village of Ingapirca, the family-run **Residencial Inti Huasi** (Vía a Ingapirca, tel. 7/221-5171, $6 pp) has clean but basic guest rooms with hot water and private baths, and a popular restaurant serves Ecuadorian fare from $3. Bring warm clothes as nights are cold here.

For a more upmarket stay, the refurbished **Posada Ingapirca** (tel. 7/221-5116 or 7/283-1120, www.grupo-santaana.net, $52 s, $73 d, breakfast included) has 22 comfortable, rustic guest rooms with private baths and hot water. Set in a restored farm building overlooking the ruins, adorned with indigenous art, lodging here is a delightful step back in time. Even if you don't stay, it's worth coming for lunch to warm up by the fireplace and take in the views in more comfort.

Cañar

Most visitors go straight to Ingapirca and return to Cuenca, but there is enough time to stop off at this town for a closer look at the home of the local Cañari *indígenas*. Although they were defeated by the Inca, their culture has survived, and you can see them in this town dressed in brightly colored ponchos and white felt bowlers. They are well-known for their double-sided weavings, which are sold in town. The best time to visit is market day on Sunday morning.

Accommodations in Cañar are limited and rather run-down. **Residencial Monica** (Plaza Central, tel. 7/223-5486, $5–8 pp) has guest rooms with shared or private baths and hot water.

Buses leave every 20 minutes from the east side of town ($1, ask for directions) to the village of Ingapirca (not the ruins), taking almost an hour. Transportes Cañar has departures every 15 minutes to Cuenca (2 hours, $1.50) from its office on 24 de Mayo, a few blocks east of the plaza. For buses direct to the Ingapirca ruins, it's best to walk to the Panamericana or go via El Tambo.

Cuenca and Vicinity

Ecuador's third city is arguably its most beautiful, and with only 331,000 inhabitants, it's far smaller than Quito and Guayaquil, retaining a more intimate atmosphere. The city is comparatively safe, the climate pleasantly cool, and the locals with their singsong accents are very welcoming. There are plenty of kindred spirits too because Cuenca has become very popular both with travelers and retired folk looking for a quiet, scenic city to study or simply relax.

Cuenca (elevation 2,530 meters), capital of Azuay Province, is known as the "Athens of Ecuador" because of its architectural beauty. The center was declared a UNESCO World Heritage site in 1996, and walking around the stately squares, churches, and colonial houses is a delightful experience. Devout Catholicism dominates the city, both architecturally and culturally; consider the city's municipal motto: *Primero Díos, Después Vos* (First God, Then You). The city is not without its Bohemian streak, however: There are seven universities here with a large student population, and Cuenca was also the first regular meeting place for poets in Latin America.

Cuenca also has a proud sporting tradition. The city is home to Jefferson Pérez, who became Ecuador's first and only Olympic medalist in 1996 by taking the gold in speed walking. At age 22, he was also the youngest-ever Olympic walking champion. A devout Catholic, he chose not to bask in his fame but celebrated his Olympic win by embarking on a 450-kilometer pilgrimage from Quito to Cuenca. He went on to become a three-time world champion, set the world record for the 20-kilometer walk, and retired after winning the silver medal in Beijing in 2008. Cuencanos—and all Ecuadorians—are fiercely proud of Jefferson Pérez, and locals will often be seen practicing speed walking in the city's parks. Luis Chocho, Pérez's first trainer, has a city academy that has trained generations of champion speed-walkers. Cycling and jogging are also very popular in Cuenca; on a recent visit, I met a diminutive, middle-aged taxi driver who was enthusing about beating a "Dutch giant" half his age in a half-marathon.

HISTORY

Cuenca began as a Cañari settlement called Guapondelig, meaning "valley of flowers." The Incas arrived in the 15th century and overcame fierce resistance from the Cañari before transforming the site into the palatial city Tomebamba. It was a favorite residence of Huayna Capac, the ruling hub of the northern reaches of the Inca Empire, and its grounds and buildings, suitably fit for a king, were said to rival Cuzco itself.

In the civil war that followed the sudden death of the ruling Inca, his son Atahualpa was briefly imprisoned by his half brother with the help of the local Cañari *indígenas*. After a narrow escape, Atahualpa defeated his brother and razed the city in revenge, putting its entire population to death.

After Atahualpa's death and the completion of the Spanish conquest, lieutenant Gil Ramírez Dávalos refounded the city of Santa Ana de los Cuatro Ríos de Cuenca (*cuenca* means "river basin") in 1557 on the ruins of Tomebamba, using much of the original Inca stonework to construct churches. Alongside Quito and Guayaquil, it served as a capital of one of the three provinces that made up the territory of Ecuador. Growth over the following centuries was slow because of Cuenca's isolation from the northern Sierra. The 1739 French expedition to measure the size of the earth at the Equator provided the most excitement in years, before a local economic boom in the 19th century, as Cuenca became a major exporter of Panama hats, quinine, and other goods.

It wasn't until the mid-20th century that decent roads connecting Cuenca to the rest of the country were completed, transforming it from a sleepy market center into a modern city. The economic crisis in 2000 hit Cuenca hard, however, and thousands of residents

SOUTHERN SIERRA

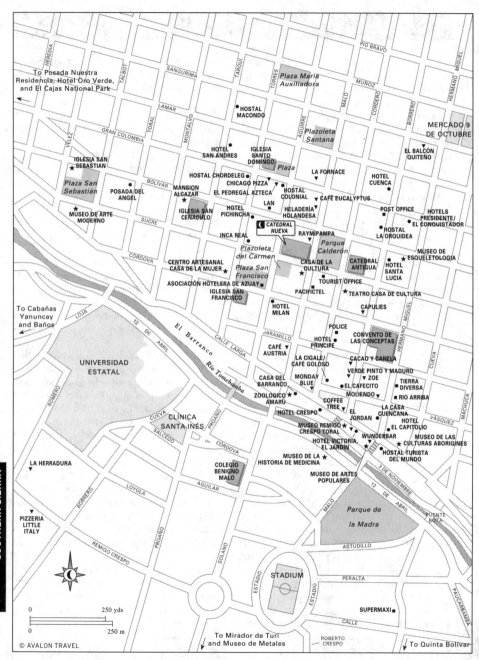

To Posada Nuestra Residencia, Hotel Oro Verde, and El Cajas National Park

To Cabañas Yanuncay and Baños

MERCADO 9 DE OCTUBRE

Plaza Maria Auxiliadora

Plazoleta Santana

EL BALCÓN QUITEÑO

HOSTAL MACONDO

IGLESIA SAN SEBASTIAN

HOTEL SAN ANDRES

IGLESIA SANTO DOMINGO

Plaza

LA FORNACE

HOTEL CUENCA

Plaza San Sebastián

POSADA DEL ANGEL

HOSTAL CHORDELEG

CHICAGO PIZZA

EL PEDREGAL AZTECA

HOSTAL COLONIAL

CAFÉ EUCALYPTUS

HOTELS PRESIDENTE/ EL CONQUISTADOR

MUSEO DE ARTE MODERNO

MANSION ALCAZAR

IGLESIA SAN CENÁCULO

HOTEL PICHINCHA

LAN

HELADERÍA HOLANDESA

POST OFFICE

CATEDRAL NUEVA

HOSTAL LA ORQUIDEA

MUSEO DE ESQUELETOLOGÍA

INCA REAL

RAYMIPAMPA

Parque Calderón

CENTRO ARTESANAL CASA DE LA MUJER

Plazoleta del Carmen

CASA DE LA CULTURA

CATEDRAL ANTIGUA

HOTEL SANTA LUCIA

Plaza San Francisco

ASOCIACIÓN HOTELERA DE AZUAY

IGLESIA SAN FRANCISCO

TOURIST OFFICE

PACIFICTEL

TEATRO CASA DE CULTURA

HOTEL MILAN

CAPULIES

POLICE

CONVENTO DE LAS CONCEPTAS

CAFÉ AUSTRIA

HOTEL PRINCIPE

UNIVERSIDAD ESTATAL

El Barranco

Río Tomebamba

LA CIGALE/ CAFÉ GOLOSO

CACAO Y CANELA

VERDE PINTO Y MADURO

ZOE

TIERRA DIVERSA

CASA DEL BARRANCO

MONDAY BLUE

EL CAFECITO

MOLIENDO

RIO ARRIBA

ZOOLÓGICO AMARÚ

COFFEE TREE

EL JORDAN

LA CASA CUENCANA

HOTEL EL CAPITOLIO

HOTEL CRESPO

MUSEO REMIGO CRESPO TORAL

WUNDERBAR

MUSEO DE LAS CULTURAS ABORIGINES

CLÍNICA SANTA INÉS

HOTEL VICTORIA/ EL JARDÍN

HOSTAL TURISTA DEL MUNDO

LA HERRADURA

MUSEO DE LA HISTORIA DE MEDICINA

COLEGIO BENIGNO MALO

MUSEO DE ARTES POPULARES

PIZZERIA LITTLE ITALY

Parque de la Madra

STADIUM

SUPERMAXI

To Mirador de Turi and Museo de Metales

To Quinta Bolívar

0   250 yds

0   250 m

© AVALON TRAVEL

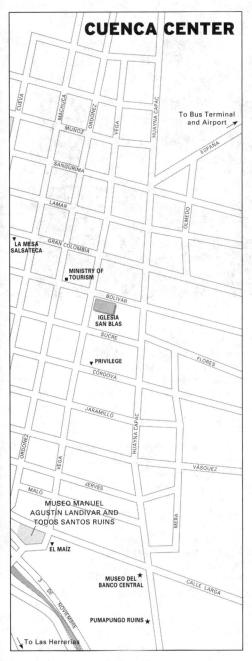

CUENCA CENTER

emigrated. Some have returned, using their savings from the United States and Spain to build dream homes, while many others remain abroad. Ironically, as many locals have left, North American and European seniors have arrived, drawn to Cuenca as a retirement destination. However, the city is large enough not to become dominated by the burgeoning expat community, and Cuenca retains its colonial character, preserved further by its status as a UNESCO World Heritage Site.

ORIENTATION

Four rivers feed the fertile Tomebamba Valley that cradles Cuenca. The Ríos Tomebamba and Yanuncay flow down from El Cajas National Park to the west, joining with the Ríos Tarqui and Machángara to form the Río Cuenca on their way east to the rainforest. The Tomebamba divides the city center into two sections: to the north, the historical center has changed little since colonial times, whereas gleaming glass buildings and modern suburbs, less frequented by visitors, are found to the south.

Central Cuenca is relatively safe to walk around until 10 P.M. or so, although it's wise to be careful in the market areas, particularly Mercado 9 de Octubre. Later on, it's advisable to take a taxi.

SIGHTS

Cuenca's wealth of religious architecture makes it easy to believe the local saying that the city has a church for every Sunday of the year (the tourist office claims that there are indeed 52). The churches of San Sebastián to the west and San Blas to the east once marked the city's boundaries. Note that many museums and attractions (as well as most restaurants) are closed on Sunday, the best day to take a day trip outside the city.

◖ Catedral Nueva and Parque Calderon

Palm and pine trees fill charming Parque Calderón, Cuenca's central park. On its west side is the immense twin-towered facade of

SOUTHERN SIERRA

Cuenca's Catedral Nueva is one of the most spectacular cathedrals in South America.

one of Ecuador's architectural wonders—the Catedral de la Inmaculada Concepción, usually called simply the Catedral Nueva (New Cathedral). Begun in 1880 by an ambitious local bishop who decided the old cathedral wasn't big enough, it was originally planned as South America's largest church, with room for 10,000 worshippers. Work stopped in 1908 because of "architectural miscalculations," leaving the square twin towers unfinished. Quite how it would have looked if the bishop's ambitions had been realized defies imagination, but the pink travertine facade is still a stunning sight. For an even better view, walk around to the north side of the park to see the twin blue domes, covered with tiles imported from central Europe.

Inside, the Catedral Nueva is even more awe-inspiring, with a stunning gold-leaf altar, pink marble pillars, and stained glass windows from Belgium and Germany. Services fill the nave with voices chanting prayers in Latin and Spanish. Even if you're feeling burned-out on churches, this one is not to be missed.

On the opposite side of the park, the Catedral El Sagrario, better known as **Catedral Antigua** (Old Cathedral), is the city's oldest building, begun in 1557 with stones from the ruins of the Inca palace of Pumapungo. The steeple was used by La Condamine's group as one of the fixed points in measurements of the shape of the earth, inspiring a Spanish scientist visiting in 1804 to comment that this spire was more famous than the Egyptian pyramids. In a recent renovation, original 16th-century frescoes were discovered on the walls. Religious services were held here until the construction of the Catedral Nueva. Today it is often used for concerts.

Plazoleta del Carmen, Plaza San Francisco, and Iglesia Santo Domingo

West of Parque Calderon, next to the Cathedral, flower vendors in new kiosks fill this tiny square plaza, also called the Plaza de las Flores, with colors and scents every day. The twin spires of the **Iglesia El Carmen de** la **Asunción,** founded in 1682, rise behind a small fountain with stones carved in Spanish baroque style framing the main entrance. A handful of nuns inhabit the **Monasterio del Carmen.** A painted refectory includes colonial masterworks by Caspicara (Manuel Chili) and Miguel de Santiago.

One block to the south is a clothes market on Plaza San Francisco, overlooked by the peach-and-white church of the same name, reconstructed in the early 20th century. It contains a lavish baroque altarpiece, which is intricately carved and covered with gold leaf.

Three blocks to the north, on Gran Colombia and Padre Aguirre, the Virgen del Rosario is the most precious icon in the **Iglesia Santo Domingo** (Colombia between Torres and Aguirre). Gold and jewels donated by Cuenca's wealthiest women encrust the Virgin's crown.

Plaza San Sebastián and Museo de Arte Moderno

At the western edge of the colonial center, the 17th-century **Iglesia San Sebastián** occupies the north side of this park. Facing it is the Museo de Arte Moderno (Sucre 15-27 at Coronel Talbot, tel. 7/283-1027, 8:30 A.M.–1 P.M. and 3–6:30 P.M. Mon.–Fri., 9 A.M.–1 P.M. Sat.–Sun., free), which has an interesting history. The building began as a *Casa de Temperancia* (House of Temperance). In the late 19th century, the story goes, a local bishop returning home one night came across a drunken man laid out in the street. When he turned out to be a priest, the bishop decided that Cuenca's drunks needed a place to sleep it off, and he began the Casa de Temperancia in 1876. Cells used to house the inebriated were later used for criminals when the building became a jail. After passing through various incarnations as a home for beggars, children, and the insane, the stately old structure was barely saved from destruction by the famous Ecuadorian painter Luis Crespo Ordóñez and was inaugurated as a museum in 1981. The setup is excellent, with lots of white space (notice the thick colonial walls) and long,

flower-filled courtyards setting off intricate modern sculptures and paintings.

Museo and Convento de las Conceptas

Cuenca's richest religious art collection is housed in the museum of the Convento de las Conceptas (Hermano Miguel 6-33 at Jaramillo, tel. 7/283-0625, 9 A.M.–5:30 P.M. Mon.–Fri., 10 A.M.–1 P.M. Sat.–Sun., $2.50), which occupies the block bounded by Córdova, Jaramillo, Borrero, and Hermano Miguel; the entrance is on Miguel. In the late 17th century, one Doña Ordóñez dedicated one of the finest houses in the city to serve as the convent on the condition that her three daughters would be accepted. The doors were shut in 1682, leaving a holiday on December 8 as one of the few times the Conceptor nuns are allowed to glimpse the outside world. Twenty-two rooms of sculpture and painting include many treasures from the Sangurima school of colonial art, along with crucifixes dating back to the 17th century.

Along Calle Large and Río Tomebamba

A stroll along Calle Larga takes visitors past five museums as well as hotels housed in restored colonial buildings, restaurants, and many new nightspots. Beginning at the west end is the **Museo del Sombrero** (Larga 10-41 at Torres, tel. 7/283-1569, 9 A.M.–6 P.M. Mon.–Fri., 9:30 A.M.–5 P.M. Sat., 9:30 A.M.–1:30 P.M. Sun., free), where the process of making and finishing Panama hats is explained. Huge old machines used to form the hats are on display, as well as good descriptions of the different stages of production. It's a good place to shop, although more expensive than in the surrounding villages such as Chordeleg and Sígsig. Standard hats cost $15, *finos* cost from $50, and *superfinos* from $200.

One block to the west is the **Zoologico Amarú** (Benigno Malo 4-64 at Larga, tel. 7/282-6337, 9 A.M.–1 P.M. and 3–6 P.M. Mon.–Fri., 10 A.M.–5 P.M. Sat.–Sun., $2). Ogle at Ecuador's multitudinous snakes, including

© BEN WESTWOOD

This La Tolita statue is just one of 5,000 archaeological pieces at Museo de las Culturas Aborigines.

the feared fer-de-lance, as well as other reptiles, amphibians, and fish, including piranha.

Two blocks farther down is the restored home of a 19th-century intellectual, **Museo Remigio Crespo Toral** (Larga 7-27 at Borrero, tel. 7/283-3208, 9 A.M.–1 P.M. and 3–6 P.M. Mon.–Fri., 9 A.M.–1 P.M. Sat.–Sun., free). This wooden building overlooking the Río Tomebamba contains a sparse but high-quality collection of religious sculptures, paintings, archaeological relics, and *artesanías*.

Most impressive of all the museums along Calle Larga is the extraordinary private collection of a local historian, Dr. Juan Cordero, on display at the **Museo de las Culturas Aborigines** (Larga 5-24 at Cueva, tel. 7/283-9181, 8:30 A.M.–6:30 P.M. Mon.–Fri., 9 A.M.–1 P.M. Sat., $2). Some 5,000 pre-Columbian pieces, second only to the collection in Museo Banco Central in Quito, span every Ecuadorian culture from 13,000 B.C. up to the Spanish conquest. Highlights include La Tolita statues of breastfeeding women, coca-chewing

Guangalo figurines complete with bulging cheeks, Panzaleo pots made with tubes that act as built-in straws, and a macabre gold-toothed skull. Optional guides speak English, Spanish, and French and are recommended as they provide detail on the intricacies of this fascinating collection.

Walking east, you'll pass the **Puente Roto,** the broken remains of a bridge that once crossed the river, used as a viewpoint. A little farther is the **Museo Manuel Agustín Landívar** (Larga and Vega, tel. 7/282-1177, 8 A.M.–1 P.M. and 3–6 P.M. Mon.–Fri., $1). In 1970, workers clearing a small park between Calle Larga and Avenida Todos Santos unearthed a confusing jumble of rocks. Careful digging revealed layers of cultures: large, crude blocks of Cañari origin, finer Inca stonework with characteristic trapezoidal niches, and a Spanish watermill using both of the previous styles as a foundation. The entrance to the ruins is through the museum. Guides are available in English, Spanish, and Mandarin.

At the bottom of the La Escalinata stairway (a continuation of Hermano Miguel) along the river is the **Museo de Artes Populares** (Hermano Miguel 3-23 at Larga, tel. 7/282-9451, 9:30 A.M.–1 P.M. and 2–6 P.M. Mon.–Fri., 10 A.M.–1 P.M. Sat., free), with a collection of folk art and clothing that includes colorful masks and a crafts shop run by the Interamerican Center for the Development of Popular Arts (CIDAP).

Cross the river and walk across 12 de Abril to the right to the macabre **Museo de la Historia de la Medicina** (12 de Abril, no phone, 9 A.M.–5:30 P.M. Mon.–Fri., $1). This old military hospital houses a bizarre collection of medical history, from ledger books and bedpans to an X-ray machine that would make Dr. Frankenstein proud. Most unsettling are the saws and harnesses used for amputations and corpses in glass cases.

Museo del Banco Central

A 15-minute walk east of the center is the city's top museum and one of the best in Ecuador. The glass edifice of the Banco Central doesn't look like much from the outside, but spread over three floors it houses the best archaeological collection in the southern Sierra, the **Museo del Banco Central** (Larga and Huayna Capac, tel. 7/283-1255, ext. 502, 9 A.M.–6 P.M. Mon.–Fri., 9 A.M.–1 P.M. Sat., $3 adults, $1.50 children). As well as pre-Columbian pottery, the museum also includes a large collection of colonial art and an excellent ethnographic exhibition of Ecuador's indigenous cultures, with animated dioramas, recreated dwellings, and a display of five *tsantsas* (shrunken heads).

The entrance fee includes access to the **Pumapungo ruins** at the back. Pumapungo was once Huayna Capac's palace-away-from-home and reputed to be one of the grandest in the Inca empire. It soon fell into ruin after the Spanish conquest, and many Pumapungo stones found their way into the foundations and walls of buildings in Cuenca's colonial center. German archaeologist Max Uhle rediscovered the ruins in 1922. Along with a temple to Viracocha, the Inca creator-god, Uhle uncovered the skeleton of a man in a specially widened section of wall, evidence of the pre-Columbian custom of burying a man alive in the foundation of a new wall to give it strength. Shattered jars, widespread scorching, and rooms filled with ash gave silent witness to Pumapungo's violent end.

Nowadays, the ruins on view to visitors are little more than row upon row of walls and foundations, but it's still an interesting site, and the hillside setting overlooking the river is impressive. Below the ruins are landscaped gardens and a bird rescue center with parrots, hawks, and a black-chested eagle.

Architecture and Green Space

The round portico of the **Banco del Azuay** (Bolívar and Borrero) features Doric columns supporting a cupola of rose-colored travertine, which forms the elegant entrance to another space for visiting art exhibits. The same material decorates the imposing three-story facade of the **Palacio de Justicia** on the southeast corner of Parque Calderón, originally built for use as the University of Cuenca.

The district of Las Herrerías, with its ancient houses, is across the bridge at the southern end of Huayna Capac, below the Pumapungo ruins. Cuencanos come here to buy the traditional ornate crosses that adorn the roofs of finished homes; the wrought iron–working shops make a great variety of other useful items too. Nearby is an exuberant sculpture of the god Vulcan breaking free of the ground.

The grassy slopes of the Río Tomebamba, known as **El Barranco,** make an afternoon meander down 3 de Noviembre one of the more enjoyable urban walks in the country. Colonial houses and modern apartments spill down from Larga almost to the riverbank, where generations of indigenous women have laid out their washing to dry.

West of the city at La Quinta Balzay on the grounds of University of Cuenca, you can find the excellent *Orquidario* (tel. 7/284-2893, 8 A.M.–noon and 2 P.M.–6 P.M. Mon.–Fri., $1 pp), a beautiful orchid garden of some 400 species that's well worth a taxi ride (about $2–3).

Mirador de Turi

For the best views of Cuenca, head four kilometers south of the center along Avenida Solano up to the Mirador de Turi, a lookout with spectacular views over the city and the peaks of El Cajas in the distance. Look closely and you can pick out the blue domes of Cuenca's new cathedral. Processions from Cuenca on Good Friday lead to the small white Iglesia de Turi. Buses leave from 12 de Abril and Solano ($0.25), or a taxi costs about $3. Climb the stairs farther up to **Reina del Cisne** (tel. 7/403-8973), which sells a wide range of artisanal wares.

ENTERTAINMENT AND EVENTS
Nightlife

Nightlife is not nearly as raucous in Cuenca as in Quito or Guayaquil, which is not a bad thing. During the week many places close early, and it's very quiet after dark. On Friday–Saturday evenings, though, the bars and discos along Calle Larga get quite busy with a predominantly young crowd.

Cuenca's local papers, *Tiempo* and *El Mercurio,* list what's showing at Cuenca's movie theaters—at least those still surviving since the opening of the six-screen **Multicines** in the Millenium Plaza (Peralta and Merchán), and another set at Mall del Rio beside the Rio Tarqui. The **Teatro Casa de la Cultura** (Cordero 7–42 at Córdova, tel. 7/282-2446), not to be confused with the Casa de la Cultura on Sucre and Aguirre, occasionally hosts movies and houses the popular Cinema Café.

Along Calle Larga, there are plenty of bars; it's a case of wandering down and seeing which one looks appealing. Look out for **Monday Blue** (Calle Larga and Cordero, tel. 7/282-3182, 4:30 P.M.–midnight Mon.–Sat., entrées $3–5). This funky little bar has walls covered in art and eclectic beer memorabilia, and serves cheap Mexican and Italian food. Farther down, the **Coffee Tree** (Larga 7-92 at Borrero, tel. 8/722-5225, http://coffeetree. com.ec) is a good place to sit outside and watch the evening get going. Head down the steps of La Escalinata (south from Miguel) to reach **Wunderbar** (Hermano Miguel 3-43 at Larga, tel. 7/283-1274, 8 A.M.–1 A.M. Mon.–Sat.), a small, cave-like place with German beers and occasional live music.

One block up, **El Cafecito** (Honorato Vásquez 7-36 at Borrero, tel. 7/283-2337, www. cafecito.net, 7 A.M.–midnight daily) is a good spot for a quiet drink. It's popular with backpackers and features music on the weekends. Just along the road, **Café Goloso** (Honorato Vásquez and Cordero, tel. 7/283-5308, 7 A.M.– midnight daily) has a wide range of cheap drinks during happy hour (5–8 P.M. daily).

For salsa dancing, head to the small *salsateca* **La Mesa** (Gran Colombia 3-55 at Ordóñez, tel. 7/283-3300, 9 P.M.–2 A.M. Wed.–Sat.). It's particularly good on Wednesday evenings. **Zoe's** (Borrero and Jaramillo, tel. 7/284-1005, 5 P.M.–midnight Mon.–Thurs., 5 P.M.–2 A.M. Fri.–Sat.) is a bar-restaurant with a busy dance floor on weekends pumping out electronica. Across the street, the well-named **Verde, Pintón and Maduro** (Borrero and Honorato Vásquez, tel. 7/282-4871, 5 P.M.–midnight

Mon.–Thurs., 5 P.M.–2 A.M. Fri.–Sat.) has a wider range of music.

For great food and drink and a friendly atmosphere, head to the American-run **(Café Eucalyptus** (Gran Colombia 9-41 at Malo, tel. 7/284-9157, www.cafeeucalyptus.com, 5 P.M.–midnight Mon.–Thurs., 5 P.M.–2 A.M. Fri.–Sat.). This Cuenca institution draws a more mature crowd that soaks up a Bohemian vibe, drinks from a wide-ranging international menu, and enjoys live music on weekends.

Festivals

Cuenca's main festivals include **Corpus Christi** (usually in June), nine weeks after Easter, which often coincides with an indigenous celebration, Inti Raymi. There are regular fireworks displays in Parque Calderón, paper balloons rise into the air, and the park resembles an open-air candy festival. The **Foundation of Cuenca,** April 10–13, is another big event, and celebrations for Cuenca's **Independence** on November 3 are combined with All Saints' Day (Nov. 1) and All Souls' Day (Nov. 2) for a three-day festival of theater, art, and dancing.

Cuenca's **Christmas festival** is one of the most famous in the country. The Pase del Niño Viajero—said to be the best holiday parade in Ecuador—begins on the morning of Christmas Eve. *Indígenas* from surrounding villages throng the streets. Symbols of prosperity, including strings of banknotes, poultry, and bottles of alcohol, are both carried and worn in the hope of arranging for even more of the same over the next year. The procession winds from the Iglesia San Sebastián to the cathedral, and the festivities don't stop until the next day.

Epiphany (Jan. 6) is also celebrated with parades and revelry.

SHOPPING

Cuenca and its surrounding villages offer great shopping opportunities—everything from finely wrought jewelry to handmade ceramics, indigenous textiles, antiques, and religious icons.

The most famous product made locally is

the Panama hat. Even though these hats originate from Montecristi on the coast, Cuenca is Ecuador's production and export center. Some of Ecuador's finer hats are made in the southern Sierra by families who have woven the *toquilla* straw for generations. **Homero Ortega Padre e Hijos** (Dávalos 3–86, tel. 7/280-9000, www.homeroortega.com) exports sombreros around the world from a shop behind the *terminal terrestre*. Nearby on the same street, the German-Ecuadorian K. Dorfzaun (Dávalos, no phone, www.kdorfzaun.com) is another renowned manufacturer. In town, the most convenient place is **Rafael Paredes and Hijos** (Larga 10-41, tel. 7/283-1569) at the Museo del Sombrero, although prices tend to be higher. One of the oldest and most renowned hatmakers in Cuenca is octogenarian Alberto Pulla, who also has a shop (Tarqui and Córdova, tel. 7/282-9399).

For ceramics, **Eduardo Vega** has a private workshop and gallery (Vía a Turi 201, tel. 7/288-1407, www.eduardovega.com) in the gardens of his house 60 meters below the Turi lookout. In town, visit **Artesa** (Gran Colombia and Cordero, tel. 7/284-2647, www.artesa.com.ec), one of Ecuador's top ceramics manufacturers.

For jewelry, it's better to go to Chordeleg, but there are several *joyerías* (jewelry shops) in Cuenca, concentrated on Cordero near Colombia, along Colombia between Aguirre and Cordero, and in the Plazoleta Santana at the corner of Mariscal Lamar and Malo.

Many antiques stores surround Las Conceptas along Córdova. The **Centro Artesanal Casa de la Mujer** (General Torres, across from the Plaza San Francisco Market) is a mall with more than 100 vendors selling just about every type of *artesanía* imaginable, from baskets and balsa sculptures to Panama hats and paintings. Here you will find **Mama Kinoa,** the indigenous organization that runs a restaurant with traditional foods, and **Cushihuari,** part of an organization promoting community tourism and cultural exchange programs.

Markets

Cuenca's main market day is Thursday, with

© BEN WESTWOOD

The Panama hat is one of Cuenca's prime exports.

smaller markets on Saturday and minimal vending the rest of the week. The **Mercado 9 de Octubre** sees the most goods changing hands, including crafts, clothes, and *cuyes* (guinea pigs), but be careful when shopping here. The flower and plant market in the **Plazoleta del Carmen** is one of the most photogenic in the southern Sierra.

Otavalo textiles and everyday goods are sold in the **Plaza de San Francisco** and the **Plaza Rotary,** and a local market fills the small plaza fronting **Las Conceptas.** Panama hat weavers sell directly to wholesalers in the **Plaza María Auxiliadora.**

On Sunday, head out of Cuenca to the surrounding villages of Gualaceo, Chordeleg, and Sígsig for the best bargains.

RECREATION AND TOURS

Cuenca does not have nearly as many tour operators as Quito, partly because many of the surrounding attractions can easily be visited independently. The local hiking and climbing specialists are the not-for-profit **Club de Andinismo Sangay** (Gran Colombia 7-39 at Cordero, tel./fax 7/282-9958, www.clubsangay.com). They have information on climbing courses and hikes into El Cajas National Park and organize very cheap group hikes (under $10 pp), usually on Sunday.

Expediciones Apullacta (Gran Colombia 11-02 at General Torres, Suite 111, tel. 7/283-7815, www.apullacta.com) runs day trips to El Cajas ($40 pp), Ingapirca ($45 pp), and surrounding artisanal villages ($45 pp) that include English- or Spanish-speaking guides and lunch.

Terra Diversa (Hermano Miguel 5-42 at Vásquez, tel. 7/282-3782) is run by two experienced guides, Juan Heredia and José Saltos, and offers a wide selection of tours from Cuenca. The staff speaks English, and their information center is open daily.

Hualambari Tours (Borrero 9-67 at Colombia, tel./fax 7/283-0371) has day trips to El Cajas, Ingapirca, and nearby villages. Guides speak English, Spanish, German, French, and Italian.

Cuenca is very easy to explore independently, but if you want a whistle-stop bus tour (2 hours, $5 pp), they are run by **Vanservice** (tel. 7/281-6409, www.vanservice.com.ec, 9 A.M.–3 P.M. Tues.–Sat.) from Plaza San Sebastián.

ACCOMMODATIONS

Cuenca has a vast range of accommodations, mostly of a high standard. While budget accommodations are more limited, in the mid-range and high end there are dozens of appealing options in restored colonial buildings

ANDEAN GENETIC ADAPTATIONS

Ever wondered why you're left breathless by the high altitude while locals in Ecuador seem to take it in stride? It's not all about acclimation, according to research from the University of British Columbia. Studies in Peru have shown that indigenous people living at high elevations have larger lungs and hearts – up to one-fifth bigger than normal. Their hearts are therefore able to pump two quarts more blood through their bodies than lowlanders.

The research also showed that highland people's muscles operate differently. When you and I push our muscles to the point of anaerobic metabolism (relying on stored-up energy, rather than oxygen from the outside air), they produce lactic acid that eventually builds up and causes cramps. Tests on local indigenous people have proved that muscles accumulate *less* lactate byproducts. It is not clear exactly why, but scientists theorize that it may be due to the highlanders' preference for carbohydrates (grains, potatoes, and rice) rather than fats as body fuel. Their muscles act the same, however, when they're brought down to sea level, suggesting an actual genetic adaptation.

Researchers hope to use this information to help people survive the temporary lack of oxygen caused by strokes and heart attacks.

with courtyards or gardens for $20 pp upward, most including breakfast.

Under $10

Cuenca has relatively few hotels catering to travelers on a tight budget, and many of the cheapest venues in the center double as seedy motels, so avoid these. The best area for decent budget hotels is around Calle Larga and Hermano Miguel. One of the cheapest deals in town can be found at **Hostal Turista del Mundo** (tel. 7/282-9125, $6–10 pp), where the guest rooms have shared or private baths. There's also a TV room, a shared kitchen, and great views of the river. Nearby, **La Casa Cuencana** (Hermano Miguel 4-36, tel. 7/282-6009, $7–8 pp) has great-value guest rooms with terra-cotta walls adorned with artwork, a friendly family atmosphere, and a rooftop terrace. Opposite, **Hotel El Capitolio** (Hermano Miguel 4-19, tel. 7/282-4446, $8 pp) is an equally good budget option offering basic guest rooms with shared baths in a quiet setting.

A block in from Calle Larga, **El Cafécito** (Vásquez 7-36 at Cordero, tel. 7/283-2337, www.cafecito.net, dorm $7 pp, $15 s, $25 d) is a friendly little café with a twin in Quito. Choose from dorm beds or simple guest rooms with private baths. Just down the road, a new hotel of comparable quality and prices has opened: **Hostal La Cigale** (Vásquez and Cordero, tel. 7/283-5308, dorm $8 pp, $15 s, $22 d) has simple guest rooms, and the attached **The Café Goloso** is a popular place for drinks in the early evening.

North of the center, **Hotel Pichincha** (Torres 8-82 at Bolívar, tel. 7/282-3868, $6.50–7.50 pp) is a well-run hotel popular with budget travelers for its cheap guest rooms with shared baths and a shared kitchen.

$10-25

Most of the hotels along the river are quite pricey, but **Casa del Barranco** (Larga 8-41 at Cordero, tel. 7/283-9763, www.casadelbarranco.com, $20 s, $31 d) bucks the trend. This historic house has paintings by local artists and breakfast served in the café overlooking the river. Guest rooms have private baths and TVs.

The colonial **Hostal Macondo** (Tarqui 11-64 at Mariscal Lamar, tel. 7/284-0697, www.hostalmacondo.com, $19–25 s, $28–35 d, breakfast included) has a comfortable lounge area, kitchen facilities, and good guest rooms around a pretty garden. The hostel has the same owners as Expediciones Apullacta, where you can book a wide range of tours.

The warm guest rooms at the **Hostal La Orquidea** (Borrero 9-31 at Bolívar, tel. 7/282-4511, fax 7/283-5844, $15 s, $24 d) are great value. Each has a TV and a phone, and there's a good restaurant.

For a more historic ambience, the endearingly weathered 18th-century **Hostal Colonial** (Gran Colombia 10-13 at Aguirre, tel. 7/284-1644, $18 s, $34 d) has cozy guest rooms around a pleasant courtyard restaurant. Farther up the street, the colonial **Hostal Chordeleg** (Colombia and Torres, tel. 7/282-4611, fax 7/282-2536, $25 s, $40 d) is a little smarter with correspondingly higher rates.

$25-50

Hotel Principe (Jaramillo and Cordero, tel. 7/284-7287, www.hotelprincipecuenca.com, $31 s, $46 d) is actually a replica colonial house, but it certainly is convincing. Comfortable guest rooms are set around a compact courtyard, and the restaurant is adorned with local artwork. **Hotel Cuenca** (Borrero and Gran Colombia, tel. 7/283-3711, $30 s, $46 d) has 30 good-quality guest rooms and a restaurant, El Carbon, specializing in barbecue. **Hotel San Andres** (Gran Colombia 11-66, tel. 7/284-1497, www.hotelsansanandres.net, $42 s, $63 d) is another attractive colonial building with well-appointed guest rooms, a courtyard, and a small garden at the back. Orange and blue is an unusual choice of colors, but **Posada del Angel** (Bolívar 14-11 at Estevez de Toral, tel. 7/284-0695, $40 s, $57 d) still manages to look elegant, with charming guest rooms around an enclosed courtyard.

$50-75

Hotel Inca Real (General Torres and Sucre, tel. 7/282-3636, www.hotelincareal.com.ec, $51 s, $67 d, buffet breakfast included) has smallish rooms in a restored 19th-century house. **Casa de Aguila** (Sucre and Montalvo, tel. 7/283-6498, www.hotelcasadelaguila.com, $67 s, $79 d, breakfast included), which means "eagle house," is a beautifully restored colonial building dating from 1802 with warm peach-colored walls and elegantly furnished guest rooms.

Beautiful guest rooms with wall-to-wall windows overlooking the Río Tomebamba are available at one of the top hotels in town, **Hotel Victoria** (Larga 6-93 at Borrero, tel. 7/282-7401, santaana@etapaonline.net.ec, $71 s, $91 d). Most of the spacious, elegantly furnished guest rooms have views of the extensive gardens and river. This renovated building also houses gourmet restaurant El Jardín downstairs.

$75-100

Farther along to the west, **Hotel Crespo** (Larga 7-93 at Cordero, tel. 7/284-2571, $89 s, $113 d, breakfast included) is a good choice, with guest rooms that have views over the river.

$100-200

A pair of recently renovated colonial mansions have been converted into two of the best city hotels in the country. The **Hotel Santa Lucía** (Borrero 8-44 at Sucre, tel. 7/282-8000, www.santaluciahotel.com, $108 s, $133 d) was built by Azuay's first provincial governor in 1859, and it also houses an attractive café in the front and an Italian restaurant on the central patio. The **Hotel Oro Verde** (Lasso, tel. 7/409-0000, www.oroverdehotels.com, $110 s, $134 d, airport transfers included) is three kilometers west of the city center on the way to El Cajas along the Río Tomebamba. Along with a Swiss restaurant considered one of the best in the city, there's a bar, a deli, an outdoor pool, a gym, and a sauna.

The **Mansion Alcazar** (Bolívar 12-55 at Tarqui, tel. 7/282-3918, $122 s, $202 d) is one of the most stylish hotels in Ecuador, with a 19th-century ambience glittering with crystal chandeliers and locally crafted art and furniture. The hotel features 14 uniquely decorated guest rooms and suites, a gourmet restaurant called Casa de Alonso, a bar, a library, and extensive gardens.

FOOD

Cuenca has a great selection of restaurants, the best in Ecuador outside Quito, with many excellent local and international eateries. The city also has a sweet tooth, and it's worth browsing the stores for local specialties such as *membrillo* (a red block of gelatinous fruit) to munch on as you're wandering around.

Cafés and Sweets

El Cafecito (Vásquez 7-36 at Cordero, tel. 7/283-2337, www.cafecito.net, entrées $3) is very popular, partly because the hamburgers, pasta, and Mexican entrées are so cheap. Another very popular place is **Cacao and Canela** (Jaramillo and Borrero, tel. 7/282-0945, 4 P.M.–midnight Mon.–Sat., $2–3). This snug café serves a huge selection of chocolate drinks with flavors ranging from almond and mozzarella to rum. The cakes and pastries are a perfect accompaniment.

Local

The best place in the center to enjoy Ecuadorian food is **Raymipampa** (Benigno Malo 859, tel. 7/283-4159, 8:30 A.M.–11 P.M. daily, entrées $4–6) under the colonnaded arches of the New Cathedral on the west side of Parque Calderón. It gets very busy with visitors and locals alike wolfing down seafood, meat and chicken specialties as well as sweet and savory crepes. Along Calle Larga, another authentic place with a quieter atmosphere is a yellow house called **El Maiz** (Larga 1-279 at Vega, tel. 7/284-0224, 11 A.M.–9 P.M. Mon.–Sat., entrées $5–6), serving goat stew, trout, and a variety of creative dishes using quinoa. Another good local restaurant doing all the meat, chicken, and fish staples well is **Los Capulies** (Córdoba and Borrero, tel. 7/284-5887, 9 A.M.–4 P.M. and 6–11 P.M. Mon.–Sat., entrées $4–6), in a pleasant courtyard setting.

International

◖ El Jardín (Larga 693 at Borrero, tel. 7/282-7401, lunch and dinner daily, entrées $8–20), in the Hotel Victoria, is one of the best restaurants in town. There are wonderful views over the river along with international cuisine prepared from scratch—everything from *ceviche* and langoustine to beef bourguignonne—which means the service is accordingly very slow.

◖ El Pedregal Azteca (Colombia 10-33, tel. 7/282-3652, lunch and dinner Mon.–Sat., entrées $5–10) is one of the best Mexican restaurants this side of Yucatán. Try specialties such as *mole poblano* (chicken with chocolate, chilies, and almonds).

Now German-run, **Café Austria** (Malo and Jaramillo, tel. 7/284-0899, 9 A.M.–11 P.M. daily, entrées $6–8) offers specialties like roulade and goulash plus great coffee and cakes. Note that this is one of the best options on Sunday, when most places are closed.

For Middle Eastern, head to **El Jordan** (Larga 6-111 at Borrero, tel. 7/285-0517, lunch and dinner Mon.–Sat., entrées $6–9), which serves well-presented moussaka, falafels, and the like in a beautiful setting overlooking the river with Moorish and French decor.

For the best curry in town, head to new favorite **◖ Taj Mahal** (Larga and Benigno Malo, no phone, lunch and dinner daily, entrées $3–5). Run by a cheerful Pakistani, this brightly colored place serves great *jalfrezi* and *biryani* as well as traditional yogurt, and it doubles as a kebab restaurant. There are often highly entertaining Bollywood movies on the big screen.

For tasty Colombian *arepas* and filling lunches, head to **Moliendo** (Honorato Vásquez 6–24, tel. 7/282-8710, 9 A.M.–9 P.M. Mon.–Sat., entrées $2–4).

New York Pizza (Tarqui and Mariscal Lamar, tel. 7/284-2792, 11 A.M.–10 P.M. daily, entrées $2–10) is one of the best options for Italian slices (from $2.50) and family-size pizzas ($10–15). Everything else on the menu, from ravioli to *churrasco,* is under $6.

Supermarkets

To stock up for yourself, there's a **Supermaxi** (De las Amíricas) just north of Ordóñez Lazo, west of the center. You can also go to the new malls, Millenium Plaza or Mall del Río.

INFORMATION AND SERVICES
Visitor Information

There's a well-staffed **Itur office** (Sucre between Cordero and Malo, tel. 7/285-0521, 8 A.M.–8 P.M. Mon.–Fri., 8:30 A.M.–1:30 P.M. Sat.) on Parque Calderón in the municipal offices, where you can also pick up a free copy of the useful *Agenda Conmemorativa,* published every month and packed with information, cultural events, exhibitions, concerts, and photos. There are also offices in the bus terminal and the airport.

The **Ministerio de Turismo** (Bolívar and Tomas Ordóñez, tel. 7/282-2058, 9 A.M.–5 P.M. Mon.–Fri.) has an office with maps and brochures. For information on Azuay Province, the **Camara de Turismo del Azuay** (Larga and Huayna Capac, 9 A.M.–5 P.M. Mon.–Fri., tel. 7/284-5657) has a new office near the Museo del Banco Central.

Money Exchange and Communications

Most *casas de cambio* are found east of Parque Calderón. **Vaz Cambios** (Gran Colombia 7-98 at Cordero, tel. 7/283-3434) has a branch with

CONSULATES IN CUENCA

- **Brazil:** Ramírez Dávalos 1434 at Turuhuaico, tel. 7/408-9054

- **Chile:** Paseo 3 de Noviembre 2406 at Escalinata, tel. 7/284-0061

- **France:** Gran Colombia 661, Ed. Gran Colombia, tel. 7/283-4644

- **Germany:** Bolívar 9-18 at Malo, tel. 7/282-2783

Western Union money-transfer service available. **Delgado Travel** (Gran Colombia and Mariano Cueva, tel. 7/283-3673) is another dependable option.

If you'd rather deal with a bank, the **Banco del Pacífico** (Malo 975 at Gran Colombia) makes cash advances on credit cards. Most banks also have **ATMs** for up to $500 daily in cash withdrawals.

Cuenca's **post office** (Borrero and Gran Colombia) is in the center of town.

Language Schools

Cuenca is a very popular city to study Spanish for extended periods, which explains the many high-quality language schools in town. The **Centro de Estudios Interamericanos** (Cordero and Jaramillo, tel. 7/283-9003, www.cedei.org) offers Spanish classes ($6 per hour) as well as courses in Kichwa, colonial Latin American history, and Andean literature. It can also arrange positions teaching English.

Nexus Lenguas y Culturas (3 de Noviembre 2-47 at Jacarandá, tel. 7/283-4677) offers Spanish classes ($5 per hour) and has positions teaching English locally. The **Centro Cultural Ecuatoriano-Norteamericano Abraham Lincoln** (Borrero 5-18 at Vásquez, tel. 7/284-1737, tel./fax 7/282-3898, www.cena.org.ec) is recommended ($7 per hour). It can also arrange homestays with local families.

The **Si Centro** (Borrero and Sucre, tel. 7/282-0429) language school comes recommended as well. **Fundación Amauta** (Miguel and Córdova, tel. 7/284-6206) is highly recommended by the tourist office, as it also works with local communities and development.

Health Care

The 24-hour **Clínica Santa Inés** (Córdova 2-67 at Agustín Cueva, tel. 7/281-7888) is just across the river from the center and employs a few English-speaking doctors. **Clínica Hospital Monte Sinai** (Miguel Cordero 6-111 at Solano, tel. 7/288-5595) is another highly regarded hospital in the city.

GETTING THERE AND AROUND
Buses

Cuenca's *terminal terrestre* is probably the most orderly and pleasant bus terminal in the country. It is two blocks northeast of the traffic circle at España and Huayna Capac. Several companies run luxury bus services to Guayaquil (4 hours, $8), which recently increased in price, and Macas (7 hours, $8.50). Panamericana (España 5-24) has an office just beyond the bus station and sends luxury buses to Quito (10 hours, $12) daily at 10 P.M. Buses to Loja (4.5 hours, $7.50) travel via Saraguro, and Transportes Cañar has direct buses to Ingapirca ($2.50) at 9 A.M. and 1 P.M. daily. Jahuay has more regular buses to Tambo ($1.80), where you change for Ingapirca. For El Cajas National Park (45 minutes, $2), take a Guayaquil bus and ask the driver to let you off at the entrance.

For Gualaceo, Chordeleg, and Sigig, buses run every hour. Buses to other small towns and villages around Cuenca leave from Terminal Sur, close to the Feria Libre outdoor market on Avenida de las Américas. Local city buses cost $0.25.

Taxis and Car Rental

The minimum taxi fare in Cuenca is $1.25, which will get you to most places in town (taxis don't have meters). The bus station and airport are each a $2 ride from the city center. Reputable, prebookable companies include **Ejecutivo** (tel. 7/280-9605) and **Andino** (tel. 7/282-3893). For car rental, try **Localiza** (tel. 7/408-4631) at the airport or bus terminal.

Air

Planes leave from Cuenca's Mariscal Lamar airport, two kilometers northeast of the town center on Avenida España. It's a 10-minute walk from the *terminal terrestre* or a short hop by taxi or local bus.

TAME has offices in town (Astudillo 2-22, tel. 7/288-9581 or 7/410-3104) and at the airport (tel. 7/286-6400) and flies to Quito (Mon.–Sat., $85 one-way) and Guayaquil

CUENCA AIRLINE OFFICES

- **Aerogal:** España 1114, tel. 7/286-1041 or 7/281-5250, www.aerogal.com.ec

- **Air Cuenca:** tel. 7/408-4410 or 7/408-3381, www.postges-ec.com

- **Avianca:** Córdova 8-40 at Luis Cordero, tel. 7/245-5563, www.avianca.com

- **Copa:** Lamar 989 at Aguirre, tel. 7/284-2970, www.copaair.com

- **LAN:** Bolívar 9-18 at Malo, tel. 7/282-2783, www.lan.com

- **Lufthansa:** Bolívar 9-18 at Malo, tel. 7/282-2783, www.lufthansa.com

- **TACA:** Sucre 7-70 at Cordero, tel. 7/283-7360, www.taca.com

- **TAME:** Astudillo 2-22 at España, tel. 7/410-3104, www.tame.com.ec

(Mon.–Sat., $70 one-way). For similar prices, **Icaro, Aerogal,** and **Air Cuenca** also regularly fly to Quito and Guayaquil.

BAÑOS

Don't confuse this tiny town eight kilometers southwest of Cuenca with its larger namesake in Tungurahua Province. It's not as impressive as a spa resort but nevertheless offers the best opportunity for a relaxing few hours to ease those limbs after days of hikes and sightseeing.

While the benefit of the mineral content of the waters is debatable, there are several commercial warm baths. The most attractive is at **Hostería Durán** (tel. 7/289-2485, www.hosteriaduran.com, $58 s, $85 d, baths only $5.50) which has two warm pool heated to 38°C. This full resort boasts tennis courts, a gym, waterslides, and plush guest rooms with all the amenities. The *hostería* **Rodas** (tel. 7/289-2161, www.hosteriarodas.com, $50 s, $70 d, baths

$2) has a less appealing outdoor pool, but inside the small hot pool is the hottest in town. A third set of baths is found at **Agapantos** (tel. 7/289-2493, www.agapantos.com, $2.25), which has two warm pools.

Take a taxi from Cuenca ($4–5), or catch a local bus at the intersection of 12 de Abril and Solano, south of the river, which then passes the Plaza San Francisco on Córdova. Buses run from Cuenca to the top of the hill, where a baby-blue church with tiled domes is worth a look. Hostería Durán is a short distance below, surrounded by a billiards hall, discos, and restaurants.

◖ EL CAJAS NATIONAL PARK

If you're longing for fresh air and rugged landscapes after a few days' sightseeing in the city, this huge national park on Cuenca's doorstep is the best place to go. It's only an hour from the city by bus, so it is easily visited on a day trip. With dramatic open rolling land and jagged rocks, Cajas feels almost like the Scottish Highlands. Among the park's 28,000 hectares there are more than 200 lakes here and a variety of trails, ranging from a gentle hour-long stroll to two-day hikes. It's also an excellent place for trout fishing, and even though it's popular among locals, the park is big enough to find solitude.

Most of El Cajas lies above 3,000 meters elevation, with *páramo* covering most of the rugged terrain. Frost and ice above 4,000 meters try their best to deter the thriving of hardy vegetation, such as the tiny quinoa tree, which clings to life higher than any other tree in the world. The park straddles the continental divide, so rivers rush both east to the Amazon and west to the Pacific Ocean. El Cajas is the continental divide's most westerly point in South America.

Visitors stand a good chance of seeing the wild llamas that were reintroduced to the park in the late 1990s. The park's other animal inhabitants, such as spectacled bears, pumas, and oncillas, are more elusive. A long bird list includes hummingbirds, toucans, and Andean condors.

SOUTHERN SIERRA

© BEN WESTWOOD

Cerro San Luis rises above Laguna Toreadora at the entrance to El Cajas National Park.

Archaeology

Fragments of Inca roads throughout the reserve link numerous *tambos*—ruins of way stations along the royal highway, which ran through here all the way to the coast. Traces of the roads connect Laguna Luspa to Laguna Mamamag, and Laguna Ingacocha to Laguna Ingacarretero. The area near Molleturo Hill has the highest concentration of ruins in El Cajas, where great views of Chimborazo and El Altar give evidence of the Inca skill at picking sites that were both scenic and easily defended. Other ruins can be found near Laguna Toreadora and Laguna Atugyacu.

Visiting the Park

The main route to El Cajas from Cuenca is along the main road down to Guayaquil, which climbs to 4,000 meters before dropping down dramatically to sea level in just 1.5 hours. Just 34 kilometers from Cuenca is the main entrance to the park at the Laguna Toreadora **visitors center** (6 A.M.–5 P.M. daily, park entry $2 pp).

Buses heading to Guayaquil every hour from Cuenca's main *terminal terrestre* take about 45 minutes to reach Laguna Toreadora ($2). There are also buses run by Occidental leaving from their bus terminal (Mariscal Lamar and Miguel Heredia). To return, simply flag down a bus on the main road outside the entrance.

Ask to be dropped at the *refugio* (tel. 7/237-0126), where you can pay the recently reduced entrance fee ($2 pp), which includes a free map and an information sheet. You can stay overnight here, but there is only capacity for six people, so advanced booking is advisable. There are kitchen facilities and electricity but no hot water.

You'll certainly work up an appetite hiking here, and the restaurant just up the hill from the refuge serves great meals, including delicious *locro de papas* (potato soup, $2), trout ($4), and a three-course set lunch ($7.50).

El Cajas is full of hiking trails; eight are clearly marked, ranging from three hours to two full days. Note that groups numbering eight or more must be accompanied by a

© BEN WESTWOOD

Llamas were reintroduced into the high plains of El Cajas in the late 1990s.

guide. Around Laguna Toreadora is the most popular short hike, the trail to Laguna Totoras and Laguna Patoquinuas takes about six hours, and climbing Cerro San Luis, the highest point in the park at 4,200 meters, takes about four hours. Another popular day hike is the trail from the Tres Cruces hill, four kilometers west of the information center, up over the continental divide (4,103 meters) and past Laguna Larga, Laguna Tagllacocha, and Laguna Luspa.

Overnight hikes include a trek to the Inca ruins by Lago Osohuayco and the hike from Miguir to the southern park guard post at Soldados. Be warned that trails have a tendency to peter out, and the weather can turn on you in a minute. Whatever time of year, the high elevation means it gets cold. Night temperatures can drop below freezing, and deaths from exposure have occurred here. Even during the day it's cold, although it heats up considerably when the sun breaks through. The solution is to bring plenty of layers—ideally a thick sweater or jacket as well as waterproof clothing. Also

bring maps, a compass, and waterproof boots. Consider fishing gear and a compass if you plan to wander far afield. Four IGM 1:50,000 maps cover the area: *Cuenca, Chaucha, San Felipe de Molleturo,* and *Chiquintad,* although the map included in the entrance fee is usually good enough.

The August–January dry season is the best time to visit, promising the most sun and regular but short rain showers. The rainy season, February–July, has the highest average temperature but more precipitation. The entire park is at 3,000–4,000 meters elevation, and high elevations make acclimation essential—hike high and sleep low. If you're not adjusted to Cuenca's elevation (2,500 meters), you'll find hiking in Cajas very difficult. If traveling up from Guayaquil, you should ideally take a day or two to adjust before coming to El Cajas.

Tour companies in Cuenca organize excursions to El Cajas (from $40 pp). Try **Expediciones Apullacta** (Gran Colombia 11-02 at General Torres, Suite 111, tel. 7/283-7815, www.apullacta.com). Overnight tours

SOUTHERN SIERRA

(from $150 pp) include a guide, food, transportation, and camping gear.

EAST OF CUENCA

The hills above Cuenca to the east contain several villages renowned for their crafts, especially jewelry and hats. Sunday is market day and easily the most interesting day to visit, but plenty of stores open throughout the week. There are several buses per hour from Cuenca running regularly to Gualaceo ($0.60), Chordeleg ($0.75), and Sígsig ($1.25), so it's quite easy to visit all three on a day trip. The trip can also be done as a loop by returning through the hillside village of San Bartolomé, where generations of craftspeople have made guitars by hand, then crossing over the *páramo* to El Valle and Cuenca. Alternately, if you have the extra cash, most Cuenca tour operators offer guided trips ($45 pp) to the villages on weekends.

Gualaceo

On the banks of the Río Gualaceo, 34 kilometers from Cuenca, this small town hosts the largest indigenous market in the area every Sunday. Three separate markets—fruits and vegetables, crafts and clothes, and produce and household goods—blend effectively into one. Visitors come for the fine woven and embroidered textiles, such as the *macana* shawls with macramé fringe, and for the impressive surrounding scenery that has earned Gualaceo the nickname "the garden of Azuay." Gualaceo's **Peach Festival** in early March features exhibitions of flowers and crafts. The center of town itself is not quite as picturesque as the name suggests, however, and shopping aside, Chordeleg and Sígsig are actually prettier.

Most visitors just pass through, but if you decide to stay, the budget **Residencial Gualaceo** (Gran Colombia, tel. 7/225-5006, $6 s, $10 d), a few blocks northwest of the main plaza, has adequate guest rooms. Inexpensive **Restaurant Don Q** (Gran Colombia and 9 de Octubre, no phone, lunch daily), on the northwest corner of the main plaza, does the usual staples well and is popular with locals.

Buses for Gualaceo leave every 15 minutes from Cuenca's *terminal terrestre* (45 minutes, $0.60). Gualaceo's bus station is on the east side of Roldos between Cordero and Reyes, southeast of the main market plaza.

Chordeleg and South

Just five kilometers south of Gualaceo, a pleasant two-hour walk if you're feeling energetic, this small village has specialized in jewelry for centuries, turning silver and gold from nearby mines into finely wrought rings, bracelets, necklaces, and earrings. On the main square and dotted around town are scores of *joyerías* (jewelry shops), and it's also a good place to shop for clothing, including Panama hats. It gets very busy on Sunday, with a wider range but slightly higher prices. A small **Museo Comunidad** (23 de Enero 4-21, tel. 7/222-3095, 8 A.M.–5 P.M. Tues.–Sun., free) on the main plaza has displays on the history and techniques of making jewelry and other local crafts such as ceramics, hat weaving, and textiles.

Grab a bite to eat on the main square at **El Yugo** (Plaza Central Chordeleg, no phone, breakfast, lunch, and dinner daily, $2–4), which does good lunches.

Sígsig

Some 26 kilometers by bus south of Chordeleg (20 minutes, $0.25), this pretty town hosts a smaller Sunday market but is known more for the Panama hat factory just outside town, **ATMA** (Associación de Toquilleras María Auxiliadora, tel. 7/226-6377). It's worth making the trip out here for the best-quality hats. *Superfinos* sell for $50–80, less than half the price of many stores in Cuenca, and even the cheapest standard hats are of better quality in Sígsig. It's not that easy to find the factory on foot, so it's better to take a taxi from the center ($1).

Sígsig has an attractive main square and is surrounded by impressive scenery, good for hiking, and there are some archaeological sites: 10 kilometers south of town are the famous precolonial caves of Chobshi, and nearby are the Inca ruins at Shabalula. Other impressive areas

8 A.M.–6 P.M. daily, $1.25), which commemorates a treaty signed in 1829 between Gran Colombia and Peru shortly before the emergence of the Ecuadorian nation.

About 5 kilometers out of town is **El Chorro,** a long waterfall tumbling down a cliff surrounded by lush vegetation. It's a two-hour hike, but the scenery is well worth it. There's a refuge right next to the waterfall, **El Chorro de Girón** (tel. 7/227-5783, $5 pp) that offers guest rooms and camping as well as a restaurant, although it's mainly open on weekends and is often closed during the week.

Jima

This village, about 20 kilometers southeast of Cuenca, has a small amount of community-based tourism thanks to U.S. Peace Corps volunteers who helped to set up the nonprofit **Fundación Turística Jima** a few years ago. The town has some very good day hikes and is the starting point for a 3–4-day trek through San Miguel de Cuyes and La Florida to the edge of the rainforest. Guides can be hired through the foundation, and hikes (about $60 per group per day) include lodging and food. Contact Nancy Uyaguari at **Fundación Turística Jima** (Amazona, tel. 7/241-8278, caritas2011@gmail.com) for further information on tourism and volunteering.

There are very limited accommodations in town, but **Hotel Jima** (Benigno Torres, tel. 7/241-8003, $6–10 pp) has guest rooms with shared and private baths and provides meals. In town, **El Pucón** (Amazona, tel. 7/241-8278, lunch and dinner daily, entrées $2–3) restaurant is a good place to eat.

The biggest event in town is the rowdy **Festival de la Chicha de Jora,** held on the first Saturday in October, which includes a contest to judge the best *chicha* (a bitter alcoholic drink made from maize), along with dancing and presumably lots of drinking.

Transportes Jima buses leave Cuenca (2 hours, $2) every couple of hours 8:30 A.M.–5 P.M., boarding opposite the Feria Libre outdoor market on Avenida de las Américas.

Traditional indigenous cultures thrive in the villages around Cuenca.

© BEN WESTWOOD

nearby include the mountain of Fasayñan, the hills of Huallil, the lakes of Ayllon, the shore of the Río Santa Bárbara, and the lake at San Sebastián. For longer hikes, the Chaquiñan walking road southeast to Gualaquiza in the Amazon lowlands takes 2–3 days.

The surrounding attractions mean that staying in Sígsig makes more sense than in the other towns. There is a decent mid-range hotel opposite the bus station, **Fasayñan Hotel** (tel. 7/226-7021 or 8/673-8366, $12.50 pp, breakfast included), which has guest rooms with private baths and a restaurant downstairs.

SOUTH TO LOJA
Girón and El Chorro

The Panamericana highway splits 15 kilometers south of Cuenca. The western branch makes its way downhill to Machala, reaching Girón after 27 kilometers. This is a spot relatively untouched by tourism. The town itself has a pretty central square with a museum, **Museo Casa de los Tratados** (Bolívar and Andrés Córdova, tel. 7/227-5061,

SOUTHERN SIERRA

Saraguro

The eastern branch of the Panamericana climbs over the Tinajilla Pass (3,527 meters) before reaching this village, which is home to the famous Saraguro *indígenas*. Walk down the hill from the highway to the main square, handsome church, and indigenous artisanal shops. The town is busiest during the **Sunday-morning market,** when most of the Saraguros from surrounding villages flood the town. Ask directions to the home workshop of **Manuel Encarnación Quishpe,** who weaves dozens of different kinds of textiles.

There is good **hiking** in the area, and suggested hikes nearby include the Hizzikaka (Sinincapa) Caves, the Virgen Kaka Waterfall, Puglla Mountain, and the Washapamba Cloud Forest. Local guides are available to lead the 3–4-day hike to the rainforest as well as several other routes. Local tourism association **Operadora de Turismo Saraurku** (10 de Marzo, tel. 7/220-0331 or 8/594-7476, www. turismosaraguro.com) has an office on the main plaza and can arrange family homestays ($27 pp), including three meals, and also three-

© BEN WESTWOOD

THE SARAGUROS

The indigenous Saraguros, whose name means "corn germination" in Kichwa, are a unique indigenous culture in Ecuador, originating from Lake Titicaca on the border of southern Peru and Bolivia. They were brought here in the 16th century by the Inca *mitma* system (a policy of relocating colonies), and over 30,000 thrive in the town of Saraguro and nearby mountain villages of Oñacapa, Lagunas, Quisuginchir, and Tuncarta.

The Saraguros are known for their distinctive dress, which is most commonly black. Men wear black pants, leather belts decorated with silver, sleeveless shirts known as *cushma*, and a poncho. Women wear long, black pleated skirts, embroidered blouses, black wool shawls, and elegant beaded necklaces. Both sexes wear wide-brimmed hats, usually black or white, and wear their hair in a single braid running down their backs.

The predominance of black has led to a common misconception that the Saraguros are in perpetual mourning for the death of Inca leader Atahualpa, but you'll be dismissed if you mention this locally. In fact, Saraguro also wear dark blue and other colors.

The financially successful Saraguros began as crafts makers, but they've since moved on to herding cattle as far as the Amazonian province of Zamora-Chinchipe in search of grazing land. Nowadays, crafts and farming remain common professions, but education has increased markedly in the community in

The Saraguros were moved by the Inca from Bolivia to Ecuador.

the past 30 years, and many Saraguros are now doctors, lawyers, and teachers. Some of the younger generation cast off their official dress, and many have migrated to other parts of Ecuador and even Italy and Spain, but local community groups are working hard to preserve their unique heritage.

For further information on the Saraguros, visit www.saraguro.org.

day tours to Amazon communities ($250 pp). Horseback riding and cycling is also available. For further information on community tourism, contact **Fundación Jatari** (Loja and Guayaquil, tel. 7/220-0071, www.jatari.org), which was constructing a Saraguro community museum at the time of this writing.

Most travelers visit for a couple of hours, but if you want to stay, there are a few simple hotels in town. The best in the center is **Samana Wasi** (10 de Marzo and Panamericana, tel. 7/220-0315, $10 pp). On the outskirts of town toward the peak is the best place to stay in the whole area: The adobe and wood **☾ Hostal Achik Wasi** (near Saraguro, tel. 7/220-0058,

$15 pp, breakfast included) has clean, comfortable guest rooms, hot showers, and balconies with great views over the town.

Outside the hotels, **Mama Cuchara** (Parque Central, no phone, breakfast, lunch, and dinner daily, $2–3) is the best place to eat in town. True to its name (Mother Spoon), it serves up traditional meals washed down with *horchata,* a refreshing pink drink made with 19 herbs and flowers. Profits go to a local women's association.

Buses to Loja (1.5 hours) and Cuenca (3 hours) pass every half hour and stop in front of the bus companies' offices on Calle Azuay; some also loop through the plaza before leaving.

Loja and Vicinity

Most travelers pass through Loja (pop. 187,000) on their way to Vilcabamba, Cuenca, or Peru, but in doing so they miss one of the most interesting cities in Ecuador. In everything from ecology and health food to music and education, Loja is one of Ecuador's most culturally advanced cities.

Paradoxically, Loja is also one of the oldest cities in the country, founded in 1546. A short-lived gold boom was followed by Ecuador's first hydroelectric project, opened west of the city in 1897. Through the 20th century, buoyed by pioneers such as Bernardo Valdivieso and feminist doctor Matilde Hidalgo, Loja developed as a center of education and boasts one of Ecuador's best universities, Universidad Técnica Particular de Loja, as well as technical colleges and a leading music conservatory.

In 2001, Loja won Best in Community Involvement Criteria in the International Awards for Livable Communities, and it is certainly one of Ecuador's cleanest cities: There are no beggars on the streets, many old buildings have been attractively painted, and the town has a highly organized recycling program that is a model for the rest of the country. Loja still has some work to do with its traffic

system, however; too many cars clog up the narrow streets in the center during the week.

The city also has a strong musical heritage and thriving local music scene. Local musicians play every weekend, there are a huge number of music shops, and even the taxi drivers seem proud of their music collections.

At an elevation of 2,100 meters, Loja is warmer than the other cities in the Sierra and is used by visitors mainly as a gateway for accessing the Peruvian border, the southern Amazon, the Podocarpus Reserve, and Vilcabamba. Linger for a day or so because the town has much to offer, and its vibrant local heritage contrasts strongly with the increasingly internationalized Vilcabamba.

SIGHTS
City Center
Río Zamora and Río Malacatus bracket the city center, intersecting just north of it. North of the center, the replica castle **Portón de la Ciudad** (City Gate) is impressive, particularly when lit up at night. It contains a small art gallery and café. Four blocks farther south along Bolívar you can walk a historical route through the center that takes in three elegant plazas and four churches. The first is Iglesia

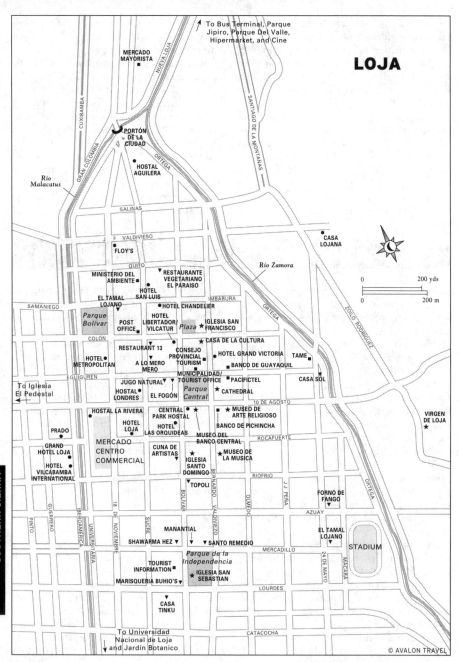

To Bus Terminal, Parque
Jipiro, Parque Del Valle,
Hipermarket, and Cine

MERCADO
MAYORISTA

LOJA

NUEVA LOJA

CUXIBAMBA

GRAN COLOMBIA

SANTIAGO DE LA MONTAÑAS

PORTÓN
DE LA
CIUDAD

ORTEGA

HOSTAL
AGUILERA

Río
Malacatus

SALINAS

J F VALDIVIESO

CASA
LOJANA

FLOY'S

QUITO

Río Zamora

MINISTERIO DEL
AMBIENTE

RESTAURANTE
VEGETARIANO
EL PARAISO

ORTEGA

0   200 yds
0   200 m

EL TAMAL
LOJANO

HOTEL
SAN LUIS

IMBABURA

SAMANIEGO

HOTEL CHANDELIER

Parque
Bolívar

POST
OFFICE

HOTEL
LIBERTADOR/
VILCATUR

Plaza

IGLESIA SAN
FRANCISCO

ZOILO RODRIGUEZ

COLÓN

CASA DE LA CULTURA

RESTAURANT 13

CONSEJO
PROVINCIAL
TOURISM

HOTEL GRAND VICTORIA

TAME

HOTEL
METROPOLITAN

A LO MERO
MERO

BANCO DE GUAYAQUIL

EGUIGUREN

MUNICIPALIDAD/
TOURIST OFFICE

PACIFICTEL

CASA SOL

To Iglesia
El Pedestal

JUGO NATURAL

Parque
Central

HOSTAL
LONDRES

EL FOGÓN

CATHEDRAL

10 DE AGOSTO

VIRGEN
DE LOJA

HOSTAL LA RIVERA

CENTRAL
PARK HOSTAL

MUSEO DE
ARTE RELIGIOSO

PRADO

HOTEL
LOJA

HOTEL
LAS ORQUIDEAS

BANCO DE PICHINCHA

GRAND
HOTEL LOJA

MERCADO
CENTRO
COMMERCIAL

CUNA DE
ARTISTAS

MUSEO DEL
BANCO CENTRAL

ROCAFUERTE

HOTEL
VILCABAMBA
INTERNATIONAL

MUSEO DE
LA MUSICA

IGLESIA
SANTO
DOMINGO

RIOFRIO

GUERRERO

BERGAMERICA

UNIVERSITARIA

18 DE NOVIEMBRE

TOPOLI

BOLIVAR

VALDIVIEZO

BERNARDO

OLMEDO

J J PEÑA

FORNO DE
FANGO

AZUAY

PINTO

SUCRE

MANANTIAL

24 DE MAYO

EL TAMAL
LOJANO

ORTEGA

MACARA

STADIUM

SHAWARMA HEZ

SANTO REMEDIO

MERCADILLO

Parque de la
Independencia

TOURIST
INFORMATION

IGLESIA SAN
SEBASTIAN

MARISQUERIA BUHIO'S

LOURDES

CASA
TINKU

To Universidad
Nacional de Loja
and Jardín Botanico

CATACOCHA

© AVALON TRAVEL

San Francisco, and one block to the south is **Parque Central.** In the center of the park, a statue of Loja's great educator Bernardo Valdivieso stands proudly. On the east side towers the city's white **cathedral,** trimmed with yellow and gold. The ornate interior with its coffered ceiling is very impressive, and the cathedral hosts the *Virgen del Cisne* icon from late August to the beginning of November. On the north end is the Municipal Building, tourist information center, and a small museum (no phone, 9 A.M.–1 P.M. and 2–5 P.M. Mon.–Fri., free) dedicated to feminist and medical pioneer Dr. Matilde Hidalgo. On the south end is the **Museo del Banco Central** (tel. 7/257-3004, 9 A.M.–1 P.M. and 2–5 P.M. Mon.–Fri., free), which has small exhibits of pre-Columbian ceramics, modern art, and historic black-and-white photography.

Four blocks farther south is Loja's most beautiful square, **Parque de la Independencia** (also known as Plaza San Sebastián), which competes with any of the plazas in Cuenca or Quito

Locals gathered at Parque de la Independencia in 1820 to mark Ecuador's birth as a nation.

in terms of beauty. It was here that Lojanos gathered on November 18, 1820, to declare independence from Spain, and the struggles with the Spanish are depicted on etchings at the base of the towering clock tower, which is particularly impressive when lit up at night. All the surrounding colonial buildings have been restored with brightly painted walls, shutters, and balconies, and the pretty blue-and-white Iglesia San Sebastián sits at the south end.

One block south of the plaza, **Calle Lourdes** is one of the city's most attractive colonial streets and has recently been restored. Stroll along, stop for a coffee, browse the artisanal wares, and stop by the renowned Casa Tinku on weekend evenings for live music.

Loja has a few other small museums. **Museo de Arte Religioso** (10 de Agosto 12-78 at Bernardo, tel. 7/256-1109, 9 A.M.–noon and 2–5 P.M. Mon.–Fri., $1), in the Monastery of the Madres Conceptas, has a small collection of religious art. More impressive is the **Museo de la Música** (Bernardo between Riofrio and Rocafuerte, tel. 7/256-1342, 8:30 A.M.–12:30 P.M. and 3–7 P.M. Mon.–Fri., $0.25) on the patio of Colegio Bernardo Valdivieso. Housed around a pretty courtyard, this museum documents the city's proud musical heritage from the 19th century to the present day.

Loja's best views are from the *Virgen del Loja* statue, east and uphill on Rocafuerte, and the **Iglesia El Pedestal,** also called the Balcón de Loja (Loja Balcony), west of the city center on 10 de Agosto.

Outside the Center

For fresh air and a family atmosphere, head a few kilometers north of the center to **Parque Jipiro.** Fluctuating somewhere between beauty and tackiness, this park is quite an achievement. There are scores of replicas of famous world landmarks, including Moscow's Saint Basil's Cathedral, a Japanese pagoda, an Asian temple, and a mosque. Most of the buildings have family attractions built into them, including slides, videos, and a planetarium, and there's also a small avian zoo with ostriches as

A WOMAN'S PLACE

Matilde Hidalgo de Procel (1889-1974) is arguably the most important woman in Ecuador's history and a key figure in the feminist movement in all of South America. She is famous for many firsts – the first woman to graduate from a high school in Ecuador, the first woman to vote in an election in South America, and the first woman to hold elected office in her country. She constantly challenged Ecuador's male-dominated society and made great strides in both politics and medicine.

Matilde was born in Loja in 1889. After her father died, her mother had to work as a seamstress to maintain Matilde and her five siblings. Matilde went to elementary school at the Immaculate Conception of the Sisters of Charity. On graduating from sixth grade, the highest level available to girls at the time, Matilde was determined to study further, and with her mother's support applied successfully to the secular high school, Colegio Bernardo Valdivieso, despite widespread local opposition.

Matilde shrugged off abuse from local people – the local priest forced her to sit outside the church to listen to mass – and graduated with honors from high school. She continued her studies at the University of Cuenca, where she obtained a doctorate in medicine in 1923,

becoming the first Ecuadorian woman to receive this title. Two years later, Matilde married lawyer Fernando Procel, and the couple had two children.

During the presidency of José Luis Tamayo, Dr. Hidalgo announced her intention to vote in the next presidential elections, daring the authorities to deny her this right. The issue was put under ministerial consultation, which eventually ruled in her favor. In 1924 Dr. Matilde Hidalgo became the first woman in Latin America to exercise her constitutional right to vote in an election. Many countries soon followed suit and allowed women to vote.

She didn't stop there, though, and entered politics, becoming the first elected councilwoman of Machala, and in 1941 she became the first woman candidate and the first elected woman public administrator in Loja, the city that was once horrified by her ambitions.

She was equally successful as a doctor and founded the Ecuadorian Red Cross. She was also a poet: The best-known of her poems is titled *El Deber de la Mujer* (The Duty of Woman).

Dr. Matilde Hidalgo was awarded the National Order of Merit in 1971 and died three years later in Guayaquil. There is a small museum dedicated to her on the north side of Loja's Parque Central.

well as a pond for boating. To get here, take a taxi ($1.25) or a bus north from Universitaria.

South of the center spreads the campus of the respected **Universidad Nacional de Loja**. Across the highway from the campus is the 90-hectare **Parque Universitario La Argelia** (8 A.M.–6 P.M. daily, $1), which has trails up through the forest and impressive views over Loja and the surrounding valley. Across the road is the **Jardín Botánico Reinaldo Espinosa** (tel. 7/264-2764, 9 A.M.–4 P.M. Mon.–Fri., $1), which has more than 200 species of orchids. Both attractions can be rather hard to find, and the entrances are farther along than the signs lead you to believe. Take a taxi from central Loja ($2), or southbound

buses marked "Argelia Capuli" pass the garden and the park.

ENTERTAINMENT AND EVENTS
Nightlife

For such a musical city, Loja is surprisingly quiet at night. There are only a handful of venues in the center, and live music is mainly restricted to Friday and Saturday nights. You can catch live bands at **Casa Tinku** (Lourdes and Bolívar, tel. 9/575-3999, 8 P.M.–2 A.M. Fri.–Sat.) or at **Santo Remedio** (Mercadillo, tel. 8/473-8910, 5 P.M.–midnight Tues.–Wed., 5 P.M.–2 A.M. Fri.–Sat.) on the north end of Plaza de la Independencia. Both venues double as discos and pump out electronic music till the early hours. For a more relaxed, Bohemian atmosphere, stop by the aptly named **Cuna de Artistas** (Artists Cradle) (Bolívar and Riofrio, no phone, noon–midnight Mon.–Thurs., noon–2 A.M. Fri.–Sat.). This courtyard café is where Loja's hip, creative community hangs out. There is rarely scheduled music, but instead, anyone can get up and play on the open-mike stage (including this author). The music is accompanied by snacks and a variety of cocktails and hot toddies—try the local specialty *guayusa caliente.*

Festivals
The biggest event in Loja's calendar is the arrival of the **Virgen del Cisne** in early September, accompanied by huge processions and fairs in Parque Del Valle and Parque Jipiro. Loja's **Independence** is celebrated on November 18, and the **Feast of San Sebastián** (Dec. 8) coincides with the festival commemorating the **Foundation of Loja.**

SHOPPING
You don't really come to Loja to shop, and there isn't a wide range of indigenous wares in town, although try Calle Lourdes for a few artisanal products. More impressive is the huge **Mercado Centro Comercial** (10 de Agosto and 18 de Noviembre), one of the biggest indoor markets in Ecuador, with everything from clothing and electronics to fruit and meat. It's a good place to spot visiting Saraguro *indígenas.* For a completely modern shopping experience, head north of Portón de La Ciudad to **La Valle** mall, which has cinemas, food courts, and clothing stores.

RECREATION AND TOURS
Vilcatur (Colón 14-30 at Bolívar, tel./fax 7/257-1443 or 7/258-8014, tours@vilcatur.com) operates out of the Hotel Libertador, offering a two-day tour ($80 pp, 2-person minimum) to the petrified forest at Bosque Petrificado de Puyango as well as bird-watching in Podocarpus ($35 pp). Tours also go to Saraguro, El Cisne, and other destinations nearby.
    Exploraves Birdwatchers (Lourdes 14-80 at Sucre, tel./fax 7/258-2434, www.exploraves.com) is the leading birding tour operator in the area, with tours to Podocarpus and other destinations led by local expert Pablo Andrade. **Sisacuna Tours** (Valdivieso and Mercadillo, tel. 7/257-0334) is another recommended operator, with a wide range of hiking, climbing, and horseback tours in southern Ecuador.

ACCOMMODATIONS
Under $10
Lodging is a little more expensive in Loja than in Vilcabamba due to its status as a commercial center, but look hard enough and there are some budget options. **Hostal Londres** (Sucre 07-51, tel. 7/256-1936, $5 pp) is a dependable, friendly place with small, basic guest rooms and shared baths. **Hotel Loja** (Rocafuerte 15-27 at Sucre, tel. 7/257-0241, $5–8 pp) has similar offerings. Another budget choice is **Hostal San Luis** (Sucre 04-62 at Quito, tel. 7/257-0370, $8 pp).

$10-25
Hotel Las Orquideas (Bolívar and 10 de Agosto, tel. 7/258-7008, $10 s, $18 d) is probably the pick of the budget options with clean, neat guest rooms with TVs and private baths. **Hotel Metropolitan** (18 de Noviembre 06-31, tel. 7/257-0007, $12 s, $24 d) is a decent enough choice with wooden-floored guest rooms, cable TV, and private baths. Its obsession with pink walls and red bedspreads aside, **Central Park Hostal** (10 de Agosto and Bolívar, tel. 7/256-1103, $17 s, $33 d) is the best deal in this range, ideally located right on the Parque Central. North of the center, next to Portón de la Ciudad, **Hostal Aguilera** (Sucre 108 at Emiliano Ortega, tel. 7/258-4660, $22 s, $31 d) has well-equipped guest rooms and a restaurant attached.

$25-50
The sleek, businesslike **Floy's Hotel** (18 de Noviembre and Quito, tel. 7/257-3821, $25 s, $40 d, breakfast included) is an immaculate option in this range with brand-new guest rooms.

Across the river to the west is a trio of mid-range hotels. **The Prado** (Rocafuerte and Iberoamérica, tel. 7/258-9290, www.hotel-prado.com.ec, $30 s, $40 d, breakfast included) is probably the best value. **Hotel Vilcabamba Internacional** (Iberoamérica and Rocafuerte, tel. 7/257-3393, $29 s, $39 d) has guest rooms of comparable quality, along with its own La Bastilla Restaurant. **Grand Hotel Loja** (Rocafuerte and Manuel Agustín Aguirre, tel. 7/258-6600, www.grandhotelloja.com, $36 s, $54 d), farther along the road, has a sauna, a steam room, and a buffet breakfast.

$50-75

North of the center, **(Hotel Libertador** (Colón 14-30 at Bolívar, tel. 7/256-0779, $50 s, $61 d) offers a more elegant, charming setting with spacious guest rooms, a sauna, a steam room, a jetted tub, and a pool. **Casa Lojana** (Paris 0008 at Zoila Rodriguez, tel. 7/258-5984, $73 s, $98 d, breakfast included), run partly by tourism students of the local university, has elegant guest rooms.

$100-200

Grand Victoria Boutique Hotel (Bernardo 6-50 at Eguiguren, tel. 7/258-3500, www.grandvictoriabh.com, $110 s, $134 d, buffet breakfast included) provides the most upscale accommodations in Loja. Rates include use of the spa and pool. The elegant restaurant is open to nonguests for lunch and dinner ($6–12) and offers reasonably priced, well-presented meals.

FOOD
Local

There are plenty of places to try the local specialties—tamales (corn dough steamed with chicken, meat, or cheese), *quimbolitos* (sweet steamed pudding with raisins) and the pick of the bunch, *humitas* (steamed sweet corn with cheese). They're good for breakfast, snacks, or light lunches. **El Tamal Lojano** (18 de Noviembre, tel. 7/258-2977, breakfast, lunch, and dinner daily, $1–2), with another branch on 24 de Mayo, is one of the best

places to sample them. Another popular local place, **Manantial** (Bolívar and Mercadillo, no phone, breakfast, lunch, and dinner daily, $2) with a wide-ranging menu, is packed at lunchtime for the cheap set lunch. East of the center, a charming café, **Casa Sol** (24 de Mayo, tel. 7/258-8597, breakfast, lunch, and dinner daily, $1–2), serves local dishes that include *repe,* traditional Loja plantain soup, on a colonial terrace.

The pick of the cafés in the center is **(El Jugo Natural** (Eguiguren and Bolívar, tel. 7/257-5256, 7 A.M.–8 P.M. daily, $1–3), which offers a huge eclectic range of imaginative fruit and vegetable juices plus vegetarian specialties, fresh bread, and ice cream. Another good choice for veggies is **Restaurant Vegetariano El Paraíso** (Sucre and Imbabura, tel. 7/257-6977, breakfast, lunch, and dinner daily, $2.50), with a cheap set lunch.

For grilled meat and chicken, head to **Fogón Grill** (Eguiguren and Bolívar, tel. 7/258-4474, noon–8 P.M. daily, entrées $4.50–6). For seafood, **Marisquería Buhío** (Lourdes and Bolívar, no phone, lunch and dinner daily, entrées $2–5) serves up fried fish, *ceviche, cazuela,* and a good-value set lunch ($2). There's another branch at Eguiguren and Bolívar.

International

Loja has some very good restaurants serving international food. For Mexican, try to squeeze in the extremely popular **A Lo Mero Mero** (Sucre 6-22 at Colón, no phone, 9:30 A.M.–9 P.M. Mon.–Sat., entrées $2–3), which serves tacos, enchiladas and all the classic dishes at very low prices.

For fast food, the corner café **Topoli** (Riofrio and Bolívar, tel. 7/258-8315, breakfast, lunch, and dinner daily, entrées $2–5) features tasty breakfasts and yogurt in the morning and burgers, hot dogs, and pizza later on.

For Middle Eastern, head to **(Shawarma Hez** (Bolívar and Mercadillo, tel. 7/256-2757, 3 P.M.–midnight Mon.–Sat., entrées $2–4), an exquisitely decorated restaurant with walls covered in Arabic hangings and artwork. The menu contains a wide range of kebabs, and seating on sofas and floor cushions completes an authentic experience.

Many other international restaurants have moved east of the center along 24 de Mayo. You'll find the best pizza and pasta in town at **Forno di Fango** (24 de Mayo and Azuay, tel. 7/258-2905, www.fornodifango.com.ec, lunch and dinner daily, entrées $3–7), which serves up cannelloni, lasagna, fettuccine, and a dozen varieties of pizza. Small portions of most dishes are available.

Most of the fancier options are attached to upscale hotels, such as **La Castellana** (Colón 14-30 at Bolívar, tel. 7/256-0779, lunch and dinner daily, entrées $5–10) in the Hotel Libertador, **Los Zarzas** (Rocafuerte and Manuel Agustín Aguirre, tel. 7/258-6600, www.grandhotelloja.com, lunch and dinner daily, entrées $5–10) at Grand Hotel Loja, and **Restaurant Victoria** (Bernardo 6-50 at Eguiguren, tel. 7/258-3500, www.grandvictoriabh.com, lunch and dinner daily, entrées from $10) at Grand Victoria Boutique Hotel.

INFORMATION AND SERVICES

The **tourist information center** (Parque Central, tel. 7/258-1251, 8 A.M.–1 P.M. and 2–6:30 P.M. Mon.–Fri., 9 A.M.–1 P.M. Sat.) in the Municipal Building stocks maps and information on activities in the region.

Banco de Guayaquil, on Eguiguren just east of Parque Central, will change traveler's checks, or on Parque Central try **Banco Bolívariano** or **Banco de Pichincha.** There are also several moneychangers on 10 de Agosto, including **La Moneda** and **Compraventa.**

Loja's **post office** is at Colón 15-09 at Sucre. Information on entering Peru to the south can be found at the **Peruvian Consulate** (Rodriguez 03-05 at Carrión, tel. 7/257-9068).

The city's main hospital is *Isidro Ayora* (Iberoamérica and Juan José Samaniego, tel. 7/257-0540).

If you're thinking of visiting Podocarpus National Park, check in with the **Ministerio del Ambiente** (Sucre between Quito and Imbabura, 3rd Fl., tel. 7/257-1534 or 7/258-5421, 8 A.M.–12:30 P.M. and 1–4:30 P.M. Mon.–Fri.).

The **Fundación Arco Iris** (Ciprés 12-202 at Acacias, Sector la Pradera, tel. 7/258-8680, www.arcoiris.org.ec) administers the San Francisco Cloud Forest adjoining Podocarpus National Park and can provide information on the park as well.

GETTING THERE AND AROUND

Loja's *terminal terrestre* is clean, modern, and organized. It's a 10-minute bus ride or a 20-minute walk north of the city center on Cuxibamba. A taxi costs $1–1.50. Local buses run north on Universitaria and back down Iberoamérica and Aguirre every few minutes.

Vilcabamba Turis buses leave for Vilcabamba every half hour from the terminal (75 minutes, $1). For a faster service, **Taxi Ruta** crams four people into one car (45 minutes, $1.50), leaving from Iberoamérica and Chile, 500 meters south of the city center. Local buses heading south on Iberoamérica pass nearby.

Several companies offer luxury overnight buses for Quito (11–12 hours, $20). Normal buses to Quito are $14. There are hourly buses with **Viajeros Internacional** to Cuenca (4 hours, $7.50). **Nambija** runs buses to Zamora (1.5 hours, $2.50) and overnight to Guayaquil (8 hours, $9).

To cross to Peru, **Transportes Loja Internacional** and **Nambija** go via Macará (6 hours, $6) seven times per day. You can also buy tickets direct to Piura in Peru (9 hours, $10) and hop off the bus to do the immigration formalities. **Nambija** and **Sur Oriente** run buses via the more remote crossing south of Zumba (6 hours, $7.50).

Flights to Quito (from $80 one-way) with **TAME** (24 de Mayo and Ortega, tel. 7/257-0248) leave from the La Toma airport in nearby Catamayo. To Guayaquil (from $75 one-way), there are two flights per day with **SAEREO** (tel. 800/723-736, www.saereo.com). To get to the airport, there are buses every half hour from the *terminal terrestre* to Catamayo (40 minutes, $1), and from there, take a taxi ($1). A taxi direct from Loja to the airport costs $15–20.

EAST OF LOJA

If you want to take the road least traveled to the Ecuadorian Amazon, you'll find it east of Loja via the town of Zamora. You are unlikely to see any other visitors, which can be appealing, although bear in mind that it can be harder to arrange tours, especially if you're traveling alone. The bus ride from Loja is particularly scenic, dropping down from 2,500 meters elevation through wooded valleys and past waterfalls to 970 meters at Zamora.

Zamora

Ecuador is full of dramatic descents from the Andean plains, and the contrast is striking between Loja's rolling countryside and the tropical forest that surrounds Zamora. At under 1,000 meters elevation, you'll be discarding that woolen sweater pretty quickly in a subtropical climate that averages a comfortable 21°C.

Zamora, 65 kilometers east of Loja, is one of the remotest towns in Ecuador. It was founded by the Spanish in 1550, but endured constant raids and was controlled for periods by indigenous people from both the Sierra (Saraguro) and the Oriente (Shuar). It became the capital of the new province of Zamora-Chinchipe in 1953 and has experienced something of a gold boom in recent years with lucrative mining in the surrounding area. The town has two nicknames—City of Birds and Waterfalls as well as Mining Capital of Ecuador, and there is an uneasy relationship between the two. The town mixes unsightly concrete slabs with an elegant plaza, but it is surrounded by stunning hilly scenery. Zamora is no more than passable as a destination in itself, but the town is improving with a new bus station and a new *malecón* walkway along the river. The main reason to come here is to head into the Oriente, but tourist facilities are decidedly limited, and light-skinned foreigners often draw open-mouthed stares from locals.

The town's other claim to fame is the **El Reloj Gigante** (Giant Clock) located at the southeast end of town. Certainly the largest clock in the country and claiming ambitiously to be the largest in the world, it is set on 150 square meters of slope. The minute hand alone is nearly 15 meters long.

At the north end of town, the main plaza and **Cathedral** are pleasant enough. North on Tamayo, the **Tzanka Ecological Refuge** (tel. 7/260-5692, 8 A.M.–6 P.M. daily, $2) has a small zoo with Amazonian animals, including sloths, monkeys, and parrots, along with an orchid garden and a small museum. The refuge also offers a small restaurant and guest rooms for rent ($15 pp, breakfast included) as well as rainforest tours. North of this is the *malecón,* which makes for a pleasant stroll along the river.

Zamora has limited lodging options, and tourism is undeveloped. In town, one of the best options is **Hotel Betania** (Francisco de Orellana and Diego de Vaca, tel. 7/260-7030, $10 pp) with guest rooms that have private baths and cable TV. Another decent option is the **Orillas de Zamora** (Diego de Vaca and Alonso de Mercadillo, tel. 7/260-5565, $12 s, $21 d), with well-maintained guest rooms, some overlooking the river.

Hotel Gimyfa (Diego de Vaca, tel. 7/260-5024, $10 s or d), one block east of the plaza, has guest rooms with TVs, private baths, and hot water. Probably the best in the center is **Hotel Samuria** (24 de Mayo and Diego de Vaca, tel. 7/260-7801, $16 pp), with quiet, modern guest rooms and a restaurant attached.

About three kilometers east of town are far more natural surroundings at the Belgian-run **C Copalinga** (tel. 9/347-7013, www.copalinga.com, $14–33 pp). There are 14 cabins with surrounding trails offering excellent bird-watching. Reserve in advance. A taxi from town costs $2.50.

Eating options are similarly limited in Zamora. The best place for local meat and fish as well as local specialties like frog's legs is **La Choza** (Sevilla de Oro, tel. 7/260-5504, 7 A.M.–8 P.M. daily, entrées $3). For fast food (burgers, sandwiches, hot dogs, ice cream), try **King Ice** (Diego de Vaca and Tamayo, tel. 7/260-5378, 8 A.M.–midnight daily, entrées $3–5). **Agape** (Sevilla de Oro and 24 de Mayo, no phone, 10 A.M.–9 P.M. Mon.–Sat., entrées $3–5) is a slightly more upscale place serving meat, fish, and sometimes frog's legs.

The **post office** (Sevilla de Oro) sits a few doors east of the plaza. For information on Podocarpus, stop by the **Ministerio del Ambiente** office (tel. 7/260-6606, 8 A.M.–12:30 P.M. and 1:30–4:30 P.M. Mon.–Fri.), across from the cemetery a short distance out of town on the road to Loja. There's a **tourist office** (Plaza Central, tel. 7/260-5996, 8 A.M.–12:30 P.M. and 2–5 P.M. Mon.–Fri.) with maps and local information on the third floor of the municipal building on the main plaza.

For tours, **BioAventura** (Tamayo and Mosquera, tel. 7/260-7063 or 9/381-4472, www.bioaventurazamora.blogspot.com) is the best tour operator in town, offering cycling, adventure sports, trekking in Podocarpus, and stays in Shuar communities. Note that departures depend on numbers, so you may find it difficult if you're not traveling with plenty of companions.

The **bus terminal** (Amazonas) is a few blocks east of the plaza, across from the **market.** Buses and *rancheros* head out to various small towns, and buses run to Gualaquiza (5 hours, $5) and hourly to Loja (1.5 hours, $2.40).

◖ PODOCARPUS NATIONAL PARK

Ecuador's southernmost national park encompasses dramatically diverse terrain—from high-elevation *páramo* down to tropical rainforest across a vast 1,460-square-kilometer expanse. Its relatively remote location leaves the park out of reach for most foreign visitors, who don't make it this far south, but they are missing large tracts of virgin forest sheltering an astonishing array of species, and some of the most spectacular scenery lies within easy access of Loja and Vilcabamba. Although poaching, illegal colonizing, and especially mining have

taken their toll, large sections of the park remain untouched, and the bird-watching here is particularly good, with more than 600 bird species.

Natural History

Podocarpus, named after the evergreen tree that is Ecuador's only endemic conifer, was established in December 1982. The park stretches across two very different regions. Beginning in the province of Loja, the *zona alta* (high Andes section) makes up the largest area, rising to 3,773 meters elevation in the Nudo de Sabanilla mountain range. The *zona baja* (lower section) in Zamora-Chinchipe Province to the east stretches down to 1,000 meters elevation on the edge of the Amazon rainforest.

Most of Podocarpus lies at 2,000–3,000 meters elevation and consists of hillsides covered with moist cloud forest and waterfalls. The park contains an incredible 136 lakes that feed over a dozen rivers in the two provinces.

More than 40 percent of the park's thousands of plant species are endemic. Sadly, many of the Podocarpus conifers have been cut down for their high-quality wood, but some remain, growing up to 40 meters tall. The cascarilla tree (*Cinchona succirubra*), once the world's only source of quinine to fight malaria, is common on the western slopes. Other common plants include orchids, bromeliads, palms, tree ferns, and wild *naranjilla*.

Although you will be very lucky to see them, many animals live in Podocarpus. Species include spectacled bears, mountain tapirs, ocelots, pumas, and deer. The park is also a bird-watcher's paradise; among the 600 recorded species are 61 species of hummingbirds, 81 different tanagers, the endangered bearded guan, the Neblina metaltail, and the Andean toucan. The main entrance at Cajanuma is renowned as an excellent spot for bird-watching.

Fundación Jocotoco (Quito office: Los Shyris N37-146 at El Comercio, tel. 2/227-2013, www.fjocotoco.org), which is very active in southern Ecuador, took its name from the call of a new species of antpitta that was discovered on the park boundaries in 1998—its call sounds like a cross between an owl's hoot and a dog's bark. International funding has allowed the foundation to purchase tracts of land adjacent to the park to protect the second-largest known antpitta in the world.

Visiting Podocarpus

The park **entrance fee** has been reduced to $2 pp, paid at either entrance. The cabins ($3 pp) inside the park are preferable to camping, due to the unpredictable high-altitude weather.

Podocarpus has two main gateways. The most commonly used is in the *zona alta*. Head 14 kilometers south of Loja (or north from Vilcabamba) to the turnoff for the **Cajanuma ranger station.** Buses to Vilcabamba can drop you off here, but it's another nine kilometers uphill. You can also take a taxi directly from Vilcabamba ($15). At the entrance is the **refugio,** opened in 1995 with the help of the Nature Conservancy, the World Wildlife Fund, and the U.S. Peace Corps. It has space and facilities for up to 20 people. Book your spot with the Ministerio del Ambiente in Loja beforehand.

Grab a map and hit one of the many marked *senderos* (trails) that wind off into the woods, ranging from the half-hour, 400-meter loop Sendero Oso de Anteojos (Spectacled Bear Trail) to the two-day hike to Lagunas del Compadre. The Sendero al Mirador takes 3–4 hours to reach a lookout point at 3,050 meters elevation.

The **San Francisco Cloud Forest,** administered by the Fundación Arco Iris and the Ministerio del Ambiente, is west of Loja on the road to Zamora. Here you can hike the Sendero los Romerillos (4 hours round-trip) to a grove of ancient Podocarpus trees and stay in a simple but comfortable **lodge** ($8–10 pp) with hot showers and kitchen facilities. Reserve in advance in Loja with Arco Iris (Ciprés 12-202 at Acacias, Sector la Pradera, tel. 7/258-8680, www.arcoiris.org.ec).

Reach the *zona baja* via Zamora. This is the less visited section of the park, with lower-elevation, more tropical landscapes.

Six kilometers south of the city (walk or take a taxi), down the west side of the Río Bombuscara, is the **Bombuscara ranger station.** After a dip in the river, try one of the numerous short trails, and keep your eyes open—maybe you'll see a gray tinamou, coppery-chested jacamar, Ecuadorian piedtail hummingbird, one of a whole spectrum of tanagers (paradise, orange-eared, blue-necked, bay-headed, green-and-gold, and spotted), or a white-breasted parakeet (*Pyrrhura albipectus*). The Sendero Higuerones is the longest trail (3–4 hours round-trip). There are basic cabins available ($3 pp).

For most of the park, October–December are the driest months overall, while February–April sees the most rain. Temperatures vary from 12°C average in the high Andes to 18°C in the rainforest. Raingear is a must. The west side of Podocarpus is covered by the IGM *Río Sabanilla* and *Vilcabamba* 1:50,000 maps (or the *Gonzanamá* 1:100,000 map), and the east side falls within the *Zamora* and *Cordillera de Tzunantza* 1:50,000 maps. Tour companies in Loja, Zamora, and Vilcabamba offer trips.

CATAMAYO AND EL CISNE

Catamayo, 31 kilometers west of Loja, is the site of the city's **La Toma Airport.** There daily flights to Quito with TAME and to Guayaquil with SAEREO.

Just north of Catamayo is **El Cisne,** the site of Ecuador's biggest pilgrimage. The icon of the **Virgen del Cisne** (Virgin of the Swan) was first venerated by Spanish knights in the Middle Ages and brought over to Ecuador in 1594. She is credited with countless miracles and is one of the most venerated images in the Ecuadorian Andes. The Virgin's **Santuario** is kept in the town of Cisne, and a five-day festival starting on August 15 draws thousands of pilgrims from around Ecuador and northern Peru bearing the image on their shoulders on the road to Loja. Don't attempt to take a bus along this route during the pilgrimage, because the whole route is blocked. The Virgin arrives in Loja on August 20, where it stays until November 1, when the procession is repeated in reverse. There is a smaller festival on May 30.

November–August you can see the virgin's image in the church in Cisne. Take a bus from Loja's terminal to Catamayo (40 minutes, $1).

VILCABAMBA

This small town, nestled at 1,500 meters elevation in undulating Andean foothills, is Ecuador's southernmost backpacker hub and an ideal stop between Ecuador and Peru. Visitors are drawn here by the town's idyllic climate, relaxing ambience, and excellent hiking.

Vilcabamba first came to the attention of the rest of the world in 1955 when *Reader's Digest* published an article documenting a remarkable healthy elderly population in the area. Rumors abounded that the locals all lived to age 120, but further investigation showed this to be somewhat exaggerated. However, there was no denying the relative health of the town's seniors, raised in an agricultural community and drinking the natural mineral water that

SOUTHERN SIERRA

© AVALON TRAVEL

FOREVER YOUNG: VILCABAMBA'S CLAIM TO FAME

Ever since *Reader's Digest* brought the longevity of Vilcabamba residents to the world's attention in 1955, this small town in the Andean foothills has had a reputation as the Valley of Eternal Youth.

The original article focused not just on the age of the residents but on the lack of common illnesses such as heart disease and osteoporosis. Worldwide interest led to further studies, and in 1971 a survey found 819 townspeople older than 100 – a little over 1 percent of the population. In comparison, the United States at the time had only one per 330,000. These figures aroused considerable excitement, but seven years later the numbers were discredited when an anthropological research team from universities in Wisconsin and California concluded that nobody in Vilcabamba was older than 96.

Anecdotal evidence also pointed to a certain amount of fabrication of the truth. Visiting in 1970, a Harvard University researcher was introduced to Miguel Carpio as the oldest person in the village, aged 121. Four years later, the same scientist returned and was introduced once again to Carpio – then said to be 132. It seemed likely therefore that many residents had been lying about their ages in order to gain attention and status (age is particularly revered in Latin America).

This setback did not mean that Vilcabamba's healthy reputation was unfounded, however. Whether the elderly residents were 90 or 120, nobody could deny that they seemed very healthy and active. Scientists have long lists of theories of how people older than 100 pull it off. All agree that clean water and air are two fundamental building blocks. Next comes lots of physical activity – well into old age – to increase cardiovascular fitness. All of these factors were present in Vilcabamba in the 1970s – horses were used instead of cars, and water high in beneficial minerals came rushing out of the nearby hills. The residents worked mainly in agriculture and did physical work well into old age.

Diet is also crucial. Rural folks in towns such as Vilcabamba eat a diet primarily based on rice and vegetables with smaller amounts of protein than is eaten in the developed world. Rearing animals costs time and money, so slaughtering one is not undertaken lightly. According to scientists, a low-fat diet may head off atherosclerosis (fatty buildup in the arteries). It's also thought that high levels of magnesium in Vilcabamba's water may help break up saturated fats and prevent arteriosclerosis.

However, it's not all about physical health; psychological health is important too. In an old-fashioned society where divorce was stigmatized, many Vilcabambans stayed married for life with all the companionship and support that came with that status. In a small community, there was a stronger sense of belonging and a wider support network of extended family and neighbors all contributing to a more contented life.

Genetics may also play a part. Perhaps Vilcabambans simply have strong genes and, because the community had lived in relative isolation for many years, the good genes continued to breed together.

Ironically, though, Vilcabamba's fame for long life may well have caused residents' health to decline in recent years. While it's still a relatively quiet town, the arrival of international tourism and foreign investors has led to more cars and therefore dirtier air, more processed and fatty food, and more sedentary jobs that don't involve physical labor. Correspondingly, you'll be lucky to come across more elderly residents in Vilcabamba than in any other town in Ecuador. The younger generation, who eat burgers, smoke, and spend time sitting in cars and at computers, may have no greater chance of living longer than their counterparts in North America.

The good news is that, according to recent testing, Vilcabamba's water remains as pure as ever, and the town's mineral water industry continues to thrive. A Texas-based company has even marketed a "Vilcabamba formula" multivitamin modeled on the mineral content of the local water. There is, it seems, something in the water in Vilcabamba.

flows out of the surrounding hills. Scientists have tested the water, and it has even won international competitions, resulting in a growing industry; there are three drinking-water plants in town.

By the 1980s, hippies had started to arrive, attracted not only by the organic existence but also by the hallucinogenic San Pedro cactus, which grows locally and has long been prized by indigenous shamans.

As word spread of the newly christened "Valley of Longevity" or "Valley of Eternal Youth," so did property prices as wealthy foreigners bought up land, and an expat community quickly grew. These days, Vilcabamba no longer offers a step back in time—cars have replaced horses; Internet cafés, restaurants, and hotels have sprung up; and young Ecuadorians and middle-aged foreigners buying up property have increasingly replaced the original inhabitants. Don't come here expecting to see octogenarians jogging down the street—the town's famous elderly population has mainly passed on, while the remaining few spend most of their time at home, tired of being asked how old they are.

Vilcabamba is far from spoiled, however; its relative remoteness means that it is unlikely ever to be overrun with visitors, and it remains one of Ecuador's most pleasant tourist towns. The expats know they are on to a good thing—it's still a great place to relax, whether for a couple of days or decades of retirement.

As for hallucinogen-seeking hippies, the town has far fewer these days, but you may well bump into the odd glazed-eyed traveler. An Austrian expat named Felicia offers shamanic ceremonies, but bear in mind that while many police turn a blind eye, preparing and imbibing the hallucinogenic San Pedro cactus remains illegal.

Entertainment and Events

Nightlife is low-key in Vilcabamba, but a new nightclub **Sonic** (next to the bus terminal, no phone, 8 P.M.–2 A.M. Fri.–Sat., $1) pumps out electronic music on weekends. Otherwise, grab a couple of beers at **El Punto** (corner of Diego Vaca de Vega and Sucre, no phone, 8 A.M.–midnight daily) overlooking the main square. For a quieter drink and a wider range of alcohol choices in a rustic setting, head east of town to **Shanta's** (Diego Vaca de Vega, tel. 8/562-7802, 1:30–9:30 P.M. daily). The more adventurous can try the snake juice ($2), made from pickled coral snake, sugar cane, and *aguardiente.*

In late February, Vilcabamba's annual **festival** brings visitors from throughout southern Ecuador for a long weekend of music, dancing, horseback riding competitions, and general revelry.

Recreation and Tours

There's not a huge amount to do in the town of Vilcabamba itself. Once you've taken in the ornate main square and pampered yourself in the spas at some of the hotels, it's time to get out the hiking boots to appreciate the stunning scenery that surrounds the town.

The most spectacular hike is up to the jagged **Cerro Mandango** peak that looms 500 meters above the town. Walk south along Avenida Eterna Juventud to find the trail entrance and pay the entrance fee ($1.50), which includes a bottle of water. It's a steep 45-minute climb through forest and cow pastures to the first peak, from which there are breathtaking views over Podocarpus National Park. You can either retrace your steps or continue the longer, rather unnerving trek across the very narrow ridgeline to the second peak before looping around and descending slowly toward town. The longer walk is about four hours. Note that there are occasional robberies on the trail, so avoid taking valuables, and preferably don't walk it alone. The hike should be avoided altogether on windy, wet days, and the long route is not advisable at all in the rainy season.

Easier trails can be found at the east edge of town at the **Rumi Wilco Nature Reserve** (www.rumiwilco.com). It's an idyllic spot just 10 minutes from town. Give a donation ($2) and make your way along half a dozen short trails through 40 hectares of protected forest that lead up from the river Chamba to a ridge

© BEN WESTWOOD

Cerro Mandango, viewed here from Madre Tierra, is one of the most dramatic hikes from Vilcabamba.

overlooking the valley. Rumi Wilco is run by former Galápagos guide **Orlando Falco,** who lives on-site with his family and is a fountain of knowledge about local ecology.

There are several other hikes around town, and many of the hotels as well as the tourist office can provide maps and directions. Popular trails include the **Agua de Hierro Springs** and viewpoints on the eastern side of the valley. To get into the forest, head to the **Cabañas Río Yambala** (Charlie's Cabañas), where you can climb to viewpoints, swimming holes, and waterfalls on your way to Las Palmas Reserve and Podocarpus National Park.

Horseback riding is another popular activity. For short rides, most operators in town charge $30 pp for a day trip. Longer two-day ($80 pp) and three-day ($120 pp) trips combine riding and hiking in Podocarpus National Park, with overnight stays in refuges. There are several operators in town, but the longest operating is **Caballos Gavilán** (Sucre between Vega and Agua de Hierro, tel. 9/016-1759, gavilanhorse@yahoo.com), run by New Zealand expat

Gavin Moore, who guides and cooks for you on 2–3-day treks to his cloud forest cabin situated at 2,500 meters elevation. Next door, Swiss-run **Monta Tour** (Sucre, tel. 8/914-4812) offers a similar itinerary, as does **Apaches Tour** (Sucre, tel. 7/264-0415), on the northwest edge of the main square, whose tours stay at Solomaco refuge.

Accommodations

One of the highlights of Vilcabamba is the excellent accommodations—there is a wide range for such a small town, and competition keeps prices reasonable. Most mid-range hotels include breakfast.

IN TOWN

The cheapest rooms in Vilcabamba are at the **Hotel Valle Sagrado** (Fernando de la Vega, tel. 7/264-0386, $5–7 pp) just off the main plaza. Guest rooms are basic but decent. Far better is the homey **Hostal Las Margaritas** (Sucre and Jaramillo, tel. 7/264-0051, $10 pp), two blocks south of the main plaza. This large white family house has comfortable guest rooms upstairs that are excellent value for the price.

In the mid-range, the best choice is the French-run 【 **Le Rendez-Vous** (Diego Vaca de Vega 06-43, www.rendezvousecuador. com, $11–16 s, $18–26 d, breakfast included). Spotless guest rooms with hammocks and showers with very hot water are set around attractive gardens. Breakfast includes delicious homemade bread.

Just off the main plaza is the brightly colored **Jardín Escondido** (Sucre, tel. 7/264-0281, www.jardin-escondido.com, $15 s, $25 d). Guest rooms are simple but well-kept, and as the name (Hidden Garden) suggests, it has a secluded atmosphere. The small pool has seen better days, but the Mexican restaurant attached is the best in town.

OUTSIDE TOWN
Vilcabamba's best lodgings are found outside town, although many are still within walking distance. Heading north, great value can be found at **Paraíso** (Av. Eterna Juventud, tel. 7/264-0266, $11–15 s, $22–30 d, breakfast included), which has comfortable guest rooms with firm beds, cable TV, and private baths. There is a beautiful pool area with a sauna and an adjacent steam bath, which is also available to nonguests ($2).

Farther out of town on the road to Loja, **Hostería Vilcabamba** (Vía Vilcabamba–Loja, tel. 7/264-0271, fax 7/264-0273, $34 s, $50 d) is a step up in quality and price, where guest rooms in large bungalows are set amid extensive leafy gardens. Guests can sun themselves on the pool terrace, be pampered in the spa, or simply enjoy great views of the valley. The *hostería* has a bar, a small café, a sizeable pool, a sauna, and a steam bath.

For the best spa treatments in town and one of Ecuador's premier spa hotels, head farther north to the award-winning 【 **Hostería Madre Tierra** (tel./fax 7/264-0087, www.vilcabambamadretierra.com, $14–42 s, $25–60 d, breakfast included). Under new management, this exquisitely laid-out *hostería* has immaculate guest rooms, many with spectacular views

of the valley, and the spa is unrivalled, with a wide range of massages, mud baths, herbal wraps, and even colonic irrigation. Treatments range $12–60 and are available to nonguests with advance reservations. The fresh, wholesome breakfast is another highlight. A taxi from town costs $1.

At the other end of town, about two kilometers south on the road to Yangana, is the 【 **Hostería Izhcayluma** (tel. 7/302-5162 or 7/264-0095, www.izhcayluma.com, dorm $10 pp, $16–25 s, $26–38 d, buffet breakfast included), owned by a pair of German brothers. With trademark efficiency, they've created an excellent complex on a hill with spectacular views (the hotel's name means "between two hills" in Inca). There's a pool area, spa treatments, a choice of cabins and guest rooms, baths decorated with stones from the local river, a great restaurant, and a lively bar. The owners have mapped out several trails around Vilcabamba for keen hikers.

If you want to get as far away from the backpacker crowds as possible, the best place to do it is **Cabañas Río Yambala** (tel. 9/106-2762, www.vilcabamba-hotel.com, $10–15 pp), also known as Charlie's Cabañas. Deep in the countryside five kilometers east of town are four cabins in a beautiful riverside setting. Monthly stays cost from $300. Run by American owner Charlie, who's been in Vilcabamba for 30 years, this is a favorite retreat for budget travelers seeking splendid isolation to the accompaniment of rushing water. The owner also arranges hikes and horseback rides to a cloud forest refuge in the foothills of Podocarpus National Park. They've set up a marked trail system nearby and run guided day trips on horseback. It's a one-hour uphill slog from town, or take a taxi for $3.

While other hoteliers pay lip service to ecology, for a truly natural experience on the edge of town, head to **Rumi Wilco Ecolodge** (no phone, www.rumiwilco.com, $7–13 pp, camping $3.50 pp), run by Argentine scientists Alicia and Orlando Falco, who worked for many years as guides in the Galápagos and the Amazon. Just a 10-minute walk from town, you'll find yourself in a thickly forested 40-hectare nature reserve offering complete seclusion. There is a choice of four adobe and four bamboo cabins on the edge of the Río Chambo. The lodge has its own freshwater system that has been tested as safe to drink (a rarity in Ecuador). There are cooking facilities and a bonfire area next to the river. A network of short trails leads around the reserve, the longest of which commands sweeping views over the valley.

Food

Many of the best restaurants are attached to hotels, but there is also a cluster of good options in the center. Just below the plaza is **Vilcabamba Natural Yogurt** (Bolívar, no phone, 8 A.M.–10 P.M. daily, entrées $2–3), offering the best value in town with delicious crepes, burgers, breakfasts, homemade yogurt, and juices. At the northeast corner of the plaza, **La Terraza** (Bolívar and Diego Vaca de Vega, tel. 9/166-7995, 8 A.M.–10 P.M. daily, entrées $5–7) is a popular restaurant, serving Mexican fajitas, Thai noodles, pasta, and pizza as well as a great-value two-course lunch ($2.50).

The restaurant **El Punto** (Sucre and Diego Vaca de Vega, no phone, 8 A.M.–10 P.M. daily, entrées $4–5), on the northeast corner of the plaza, has changed to Swiss management and is swiftly becoming a hub in the evenings, serving up hot and cold drinks as well as pizza and local fare. **Shanta's** (Diego Vaca de Vega, tel. 8/562-7802, 1:30–9:30 P.M. daily, entrées $4–6), east of town, also serves cheap pizza and pasta.

The best Mexican in town is found at **Jardín Escondido** (Sucre, tel. 7/264-0281, 8 A.M.–8 P.M. daily, entrées $4–6), just north of the plaza. Fajitas, quesadillas, and burritos are all done exceptionally well, and there are also good pasta and curry dishes. Try the delicious mole (chicken cooked with chocolate, chilies, and almonds).

For mouthwatering German and Hungarian specialties such as Bavarian Stroganoff and goulash as well as real German beer, head up to **Izchcayluma** (tel. 7/264-0095, www.izchcayluma.com, 8 A.M.–10 P.M. daily, entrées $5–7), two kilometers south of town.

For organic specialties, including a wide range of fruit and vegetable juices ($2–3), imaginative salads, Mexican specialties, soups, pasta, and pizza, try **Sambuca** (Bolívar, tel. 8/947-5082, www.vilcabambasambuca.com, 8 A.M.–10 P.M. daily, entrées $4–7), on the east side of the main plaza.

Information and Services

The **tourist office** (Bolívar and Diego Vaca de Vega, tel. 7/264-0890, www.vilcabamba.org, 8 A.M.–1 P.M. and 3–6 P.M. daily) on the main plaza is helpful and stocks maps and information. The website is also a good source of information. The **post office** (Agua de Hierro and Bolívar) shares the **police** building one block north of the plaza.

There's one new ATM (Bolívar and Diego Vaca de Vega) in town on the northeast corner of the main square. Bear in mind that, according to locals, it frequently runs out of money on weekends.

In such a relaxing atmosphere, especially after some hiking, a massage is just the ticket. Most of the best massages can be found at hotels such as Madre Tierra and Izchcayluma, but for slightly cheaper yet still excellent service, visit Karina at **Massage Beauty Care** (Bolívar, tel. 7/264-0359 or 8/122-3456), next to Natural Yogurt, who offers full-body massage ($15) and exfoliations ($10).

Getting There and Around

Two bus companies go to Loja (75 minutes, $1): **Sur Oriente** and the slightly faster **Vilcabamba Turis** leave every half hour from the bus terminal (Jaramillo and Eterna Juventud). For a faster service, **Taxi Ruta** crams four people into one car to Loja (45 minutes, $1.50). To go to Peru, there are buses passing through Vilcabamba to Zumba. If you want to cross via Macará to Piura, take a bus directly from Loja.

Crossing into Peru

The busiest and most frantic route into Peru is via the coastal town of Huaquillas, but for a more scenic route, more and more travelers are crossing in the highlands south of Vilcabamba. There are two main crossing points, via Zumba or Macará. Going via Zumba is more time-consuming and involves several transfers. It is a very beautiful route, however, and more convenient for reaching the ruins of Chachapoyas in Peru. Traveling via Macará is more direct, with buses running from Loja to Piura in Peru, stopping only briefly at the border. Note that if you're heading to Lima, crossings via Macará or Huaquillas are far better.

MACARÁ

Back in 1995, Macará (pop. 15,000) was the scene of a gun battle in Ecuador's long-running border dispute with Peru. Thankfully, since the border agreement in 1998, this is a safe crossing. Because fewer visitors come this far out, the border crossing at Macará is simpler and therefore preferable to Huaquillas to the north. The mountain scenery here is also more impressive.

Accommodations

Most travelers simply pass through Macará, and it is becoming increasingly common to take a direct bus from Loja to Piura, stopping briefly in Macará to do the border paperwork. If you need to stay overnight, however, **Hostal El Conquistador** (Bolívar, tel. 7/269-4057, $10 pp) has rooms with air-conditioning and private baths. The **Hotel Espiga de Oro** (Ante and 10 de Agosto, tel. 7/269-4405, $8–10 pp), between the plaza and the market, is also good.

Food

Grab seafood and local fare at **Restaurant D'Marco's** (Calderón and Veintimilla, tel. 7/269-5111, lunch and dinner daily, entrées $5) or **El Buen Sabor Macareño** (Manuel Rengel

and Bolívar, tel. 7/269-4193, lunch and dinner daily, entrées $3–4).

Getting There

If you're traveling north, **Cooperativa Loja** and **Sur Oriente** both send buses to Loja (6 hours, $6).

Crossing the Border

The Panamericana rolls southwest from the center of town for 2.5 kilometers to a bridge at the Peruvian border. Taxis and trucks make the trip to *la frontera* often, or you can walk it in less than an hour. Get your exit stamp at the Ecuadorian immigration office (open 24 hours), then cross the bridge into La Tina, Peru, and get the entry stamp in the Peruvian immigration office (open 24 hours) in the building on the right. *Colectivos* run from the Peruvian side to Suyo (20 minutes), Sullana (2 hours), and Piura (40 minutes farther). If you're on a direct bus between Piura and Loja, simply get off the bus to complete the documentation and resume your journey.

ZUMBA

Crossing into Peru south of **Zumba,** 235 kilometers south of Vilcabamba, is more complicated but allows you to take a shortcut to the **Chachapoyas ruins** on the Peruvian side. There are about eight buses per day from Loja's bus terminal (6 hours, $7.50) traveling via Vilcabamba. Take the early bus with Sur Oriente (formerly Cariamanga) to cross the frontier the same day. It leaves Loja at 5:30 A.M. and passes Vilcabamba at about 6:15 A.M.; it arrives in Zumba at 1 P.M., where you can have lunch before the *ranchero* bus to La Balsa leaves at 2:30 P.M. Alternately, take one of the four night buses that leave Loja 9:30 P.M.–midnight, and cross in the morning. All the buses originate in Loja, so you have to flag them down on the road in front of the Vilcabamba bus station.

The Ecuadorian immigration office is not

far from the bridge, but you may have to search around for officials. Do not cross without getting the correct entry and exit stamps. Taxis on the Peruvian side wait to take you to the town of San Ignacio, where you can change money. There are a couple of hotels in San Ignacio, Peru—**Hostal La Posada** is basic and **Gran Hotel** is a good mid-range choice. Chachapoyas is seven hours farther south of San Ignacio.

THE ORIENTE

The Oriente is the huge area of rainforest east of the Andes that makes up nearly half the country's geographical area, although only 5 percent of Ecuador's population lives here, and few of the other 95 percent have much interest in visiting, opting for beaches, spas, and mountain lakes over bug-infested rainforest treks. For intrepid explorers, though, the idea of being up the Amazon, ideally with a paddle, is irresistible. If this is your first visit to South America, you would be missing an unforgettable experience by not venturing into the continent's breathtaking Amazon landscapes, teeming with wildlife such as playful pink dolphins and parakeets along with less-than-playful alligators and anacondas. Canoe rides through seemingly endless tributaries, bird-watching at the top of the 50-meter-high forest canopy,

adrenaline-pumping night walks to tarantula holes, and a blowgun shooting class with indigenous people are but a few of the experiences that await you in this land where time seems to have stood still.

The wild landscapes and indigenous people of the rainforest lay undisturbed for centuries until 1542, when a certain Spaniard, Francisco de Orellana, embarked on his ambitious, ill-fated journey in search of the gold of Eldorado. Many explorers and missionaries followed in later years, only to come back empty-handed or else end up as shrunken heads.

The Spanish quest for gold was replaced in the 20th century by the quest for the black gold of petroleum. Since its discovery in the 1960s, more and more people have been drawn to rapidly growing rainforest towns such as Coca and

© BEN WESTWOOD

THE ORIENTE

HIGHLIGHTS

《 Papallacta Hot Springs: Break up the long bus ride from Quito to the Oriente by stopping for a soak at the best hot springs in the country (page 221).

《 Cuyabeno Wildlife Reserve: The flooded rainforests and countless tributaries of Río Aguarico contain amazing aquatic wildlife, including pink dolphins, black and white caimans, and giant otters (page 227).

《 Yasuní National Park: In 10,000 square kilometers of the most biodiverse terrain on the planet, watching flocks of parakeets and parrots drinking at clay licks is just one of the countless highlights. (page 233).

《 Tena: Ecuador's white-water rafting capital is also the Oriente's most pleasant town and a good base to organize community tours and rainforest hikes (page 239).

《 Kapawi Ecolodge: Reachable only by float plane, Kapawi is Ecuador's most remote – and luxurious – Amazon experience (page 255).

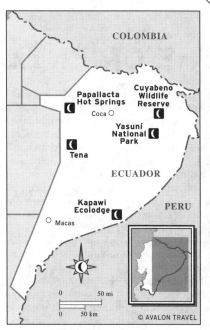

LOOK FOR 《 TO FIND RECOMMENDED SIGHTS, ACTIVITIES, DINING, AND LODGING.

Lago Agrio. Enormous environmental damage has been done, and lawsuits by affected indigenous communities are still ongoing. At present, battle lines are being drawn between oil companies, who want to exploit untapped oil fields, and ecologists and local indigenous groups, who want the rainforest to be left in peace.

While head-shrinking practices are thankfully a thing of the past, many indigenous people have hung on to their traditions and continue to live in large reservations in remote sections of the rainforest, attempting to withstand outside pressures to drill on their land. Throughout the region, Kichwa words on maps show the influence of the Lowland Kichwa, who inhabit the foothills and forests in western

Napo and northern Pastaza Provinces. Also in the north are pockets of Siona-Secoya and Cofán. The Huaorani have a huge reserve in central Napo Province and spill over into Yasuní National Park. To the south, the Shuar and Achuar continue to live in isolation, although their ancestral lands were divided by the decades-long border dispute with Peru, which ended in 1998. Tours deep into indigenous territory can be organized with time and effort, as can cheaper, more easygoing excursions to communities closer to the main towns.

The rivers are the highways in the Oriente, and once you reach the literal end of the road, the only way to travel is on the waters of the Ríos Coca and Aguarico, which run into the

THE ORIENTE

Pasto

Túquerres

Laguna
La Cocha

El Chical

Ipiales

TULCÁN

COLOMBIA

Cotacachi-
Cayapas
Ecological
Reserve

Apuela

Lago
Cuicocha

Chota

IBARRA

Picudo

Río Guamués

Río San Miguel

LAGO AGRIO
(NUEVA LOJA)

Tigre
Playa

Puerto El Carmen

Río

Otavalo

Equator

Cayambe-Coca
Ecological
Reserve

Río Coca

Lagunas de
Cuyabeno

Putumayo

Río
Lagartococha

QUITO

Volcán Reventador

Río Quijos

San Rafael Falls

*Sumaco-Napo
Galeras
National
Park*

La Joya de
los Sachas

Shushufindi

Tarapoa

Río Aguarico

Pañacocha
Protected Forest

Pañacocha

Río Napo

**CUYABENO
WILDLIFE RESERVE**

Lago
Imuya

Papallacta

**PAPALLACTA
HOT SPRINGS**

Baeza

Volcán Antisana

Antisana
Ecological
Reserve

Volcán
Sumaco

Río
Payamino

**COCA (PUERTO
FRANCISCO DE
ORELLANA)**

NAPO
WILDLIFE
CENTER

Loreto

YACHANA LODGE

**YASUNÍ
NATIONAL PARK**

LATACUNGA

Archidona

TENA

Río

Bataburo
(Tiguiño)

*Huaorani
Reserve*

Nuevo
Rocafuerte

Puerto Napo

Misahualli

AMBATO

Río
Tiguiño

BATABURO
LODGE

Río

SEE "LOWER
RÍO NAPO" MAP

Baños

PUYO

SEE "TENA AND UPPER
RÍO NAPO" MAP

Río

Cononaco

RIOBAMBA

Curaray

ECUADOR

MACAS

Río Paute

Sucúa

Río Upano

Río
Pastaza

**KAPAWI
ECOLODGE**

Méndez

Morona

Santiago

Río Zamora

CUEVA DE
LOS TAYOS

PERU

Gualaquiza

Río Santiago

0   30 mi

0   30 km

© AVALON TRAVEL

INDIGENOUS ORGANIZATIONS

- **Abya Yala Fund for Indigenous Self-Development in South & Meso America** (P.O. Box 28386, Oakland, CA 94604, U.S. tel. 510/763-6553, U.S. fax 510/763-6588, abyayala@earthlink.net, http://ayf.nativeweb.org): seeks to support indigenous peoples in economic, social, and cultural ways, including with the publication of a journal on Indian rights.

- **Confederation of Indigenous Nationalities of Ecuador (CONAIE)** (Granados 2553 at 6 de Diciembre, Quito, tel. 2/245-2335, conaie@ecuanex.net.ec, http://conaie.nativeweb.org): Formed in 1986, the largest indigenous organization in Ecuador serves as a political mouthpiece for its members, focusing on ecology, land rights, education, and indigenous culture.

- **Confederation of Indigenous Nationalities of the Ecuadorian Amazon (CONFENIAE)** (6 de Diciembre 159 at Pazmino, Suite 408, Quito, tel. 3/288-5134, www.ecuanex.net.ec/confeniae): The Shuar, Achuar, Huaorani, Siona-Secoya, Cofán, Zaparo, and Lowland Quechua groups banded together in 1980 to defend and legalize their historical territories in the Ecuadorian Amazon. Their umbrella organization seeks to promote the social, political, and economic development of indigenous communities.

- **Federación de la Comunidad Union Nativos de la Amazonia Ecuatoriana (FCUNAE)** (Camilo de Torrano, Coca, tel. 6/288-1033, www.fcunae.nativeweb.org):

This Coca-based federation offers tours to Kichwa and Cofán communities.

- **Federación Interprovincial de Centros Shuar** (Av. Domingo Comín 1738 at Victorino Abarca, Sucúa, tel. 7/274-0108, www.ficsh.org.ec): Shuar federation conducting political meetings throughout Ecuador.

- **Fundación para Desarrollo Comunitario Indígena de Pastaza (FUNDECOIPA)** (Bosque Protector Arútam, Vía Puyo-Macas Km. 48, Casilla 16-01-788, Puyo, www.fundecoipa.com): organizing tours and volunteering opportunities to communities in the southern Oriente, including Shuar communities.

- **Fundación Sobrevivencia Cofán** (tel. 2/247-4763, kimreyanna@gmail.com, www.cofan.org): offers tours to Cofán communities.

- **Fundación Vihoma** (tel. 9/107-7578, www.secoyas.com): offers tours to Secoya communities.

- **RICANCIE** (Agusto Rueda, Tena, tel. 6/288-8479, ricancie@hotmail.com, www.ricancie.nativeweb.org): This network of 10 Kichwa communities offers stays along the upper Río Napo.

- **Scientific Institute of Indigenous Cultures (ICCI)** (Calle Gaspar de Carvajal N26-27 at Luis Mosquera Narváez, Quito, tel. 2/320-3696, icci@ecuanex.net.ec, http://icci.nativeweb.org): a private, nonprofit institution that works toward the organization and preservation of different indigenous groups.

larger Río Coca, flowing all the way to Peru, where it joins the Amazon.

PLANNING YOUR TIME

Where you visit and for how long depends on what type of experience you want in the Oriente. If you're looking to stay in the middle of primary rainforest, the northern town of **Coca** is the best hub to reach areas in and

around **Limoncocha Reserve** and **Yasuní National Park. Lago Agrio,** farther north, offers access to **Cuyabeno Reserve.** Both areas offer the most spectacular pristine rainforest, and staying at the cluster of excellent lodges, such as the **Napo Wildlife Center,** is an unforgettable experience.

Unfortunately, reaching such beauty necessitates traveling via the unsightly oil towns of

Lago Agrio and Coca. Both can be reached from Quito by a long bus ride (over 8 hours) or a half-hour flight (from $65 one-way). The advantage of flying is that you have breakfast in Quito, spend as little time as possible in Coca and Lago Agrio, and reach your rainforest lodge by early afternoon. Traveling by bus, on the other hand, although arduous, has its advantages too. The roads have improved markedly in recent years, and on the way there are some excellent stops, including **Papallacta Hot Springs,** which rank as the best in the country, the spectacular **San Rafael Falls,** and white-water rafting around **Baeza.** For the best of both worlds, consider flying into the rainforest and taking a bus back at the end of your tour when you have fewer time constraints.

Farther south, on the upper reaches of the Río Napo, the area around **Tena** and **Misahualli** is very popular with travelers. Lodges here tend to be cheaper and offer a different experience. The landscape is mainly made up of secondary rainforest with more human settlements and agriculture. The local Kichwa villages are a key attraction of tours here, but downstream from Misahualli you can reach pockets of primary rainforest. Rainforest tours aside, Tena is also Ecuador's white-water rafting center, with plenty of Class 3 and Class 4 rapids close to town. Tena is also more easily accessible, five hours by bus from both Quito and Baños.

Puyo, southwest of Tena, is the most easily accessible rainforest town, with some interesting parks, walks, and wildlife centers dotted around its fringes. It is very much a "rainforest-lite" experience if you want a brief introduction to the region, usually accessed from Baños, which is just 1.5 hours away by bus. Puyo also has plenty of indigenous communities close to town that can be visited on tours.

The southern Oriente is the least visited area and offers a glimpse of how the entire Amazon basin used to be. There is very little oil or industrial exploration in this region, and tourism has been equally slow to develop due to a lack of infrastructure. This is part of the region's charm, and the small town of Macas,

along with Tena, is the most appealing town in the Oriente. While arranging last-minute tours can be tricky, rewarding stays in indigenous communities such as Shuar villages can be organized here. Macas is four hours from Puyo, five hours from Riobamba, and seven hours from Cuenca. Far off to the east, close to the Peruvian border, one of the best rainforest retreats in Ecuador is **Kapawi Ecolodge,** accessed only by charter plane.

Most rainforest tours run 4–6 days. If you're going deeper into the rainforest, a tour of less than four days is not recommended because you spend the better part of two days traveling. For lighter experiences, two-day tours from Puyo and Tena can give you a brief but rewarding glimpse of rainforest life.

Note that the rewards of the rainforests come at a cost to comfort. If you want luxury travel, the Oriente is probably not for you. The bus rides are long if you can't afford a flight, the weather is often very hot and humid, it rains a lot (it's not called rainforest for nothing) and there are mosquitoes and stinging insects to be dealt with. But it would be a great shame to come to Ecuador and not experience the wonders of the Amazon basin, and you'll be hard-pressed to find a country in the world with cheaper, easier access to pristine rainforests still inhabited by traditional indigenous people.

What to Take

Make sure that you pack well for a rainforest trip, as shopping opportunities are few in the Oriente. Annual rainfall averages 300 centimeters, so bring plenty of wet-weather gear: a rain poncho, waterproof clothing, and boots. Daily highs average 30°C, so expect to sweat a lot and bring plenty of light pants and shirts. Long pants and long sleeves are preferable, despite the heat, for reducing insect bites. Bring swimwear, a hat and sunglasses, plenty of insect repellant (the most effective brands contain DEET), after-bite cream, and don't forget the sunblock (it's not raining all the time). A day pack is essential (ideally waterproof); bring a camera and, if possible, a pair of binoculars.

A torch is essential for night walks and for waking at night (when there is often no electricity and it's pitch dark). A first-aid kit is advisable, although guides and lodges are obligated to stock basic medical supplies.

Regarding malaria, Ecuador's rainforest is officially in a malaria zone, but it's extremely rare, and most visitors here don't bother with antimalarial medications. I have yet to meet a single traveler or local person who has caught the disease in Ecuador, but if you want to be cautious, Malarone is the most recommended medication. Avoid Lariam (mefloquine) completely due to its dangerous side effects.

Quito to Baeza

The road east of Quito to Baeza was built in the early 1970s to provide access to the oil towns of Lago Agrio and Coca as well as the all-important oil pipeline. Countless oil tankers, supply trucks, and buses follow the pipeline as it snakes up out of the rainforest. Recent road improvements have made the long journey a little shorter and more comfortable, but traffic to the Oriente has correspondingly increased where industry and the population are expanding quickly.

The road climbs up the Eastern Cordillera outside Quito, and the air grows cold and thin as you reach 4,100 meters. After nearly two hours, the road reaches Papallacta, the site of Ecuador's best thermal baths. An entrance to the Cayambe-Coca Ecological Reserve is across from a statue of the Virgin, and trails lead off into the *páramo*. If the weather is clear, there are magnificent views of the Volcán Antisana to the south. From Papallacta it's all downhill, with the roadside vegetation turning to cloud forest fed by the Amazon mists from below. The road forks at Baeza, heading south to Tena and north to Lago Agrio. Coca can be reached on either route, but the southern route is more popular.

PAPALLACTA
Lake District
Shortly after the road to Baeza crests the Eastern Cordillera, about 60 kilometers from Quito, it approaches the Papallacta lake district on the northern (left) side. This gorgeous stretch of country, filling the southern tip of the Cayambe-Coca Ecological Reserve, offers plenty of hiking possibilities among moody glacial lakes and crumbling hills that evoke the craggy countryside of Scotland. It's only a few hours from Quito, and any bus heading toward Tena or Lago Agrio can drop you along the way. Be ready for wet, boggy conditions, particularly June–August. The best time to hike here is October–February. Note that it's easy to get lost, so take a compass and a map. The IGM *Papallacta, Laguna de Mica,* and *Sincholagua* 1:50,000 maps cover the area.

At the crest of Papallacta Pass, the statue of the Virgin on the south side of the road marks the start of a great day hike among the lakes. Head up the dirt road opposite the Virgin toward the antenna-topped hill to the north, stop at the new guard-post house. Pay the $2 entry fee and head up to the "360 hill," which has a panoramic view of the surrounding *páramo*. Horses ($6 per hour) can also be rented. From here, hike downhill to the northeast toward the southern end of Laguna Parcacha, then southeast from there toward the park guard station south of Laguna Loreto. A dirt road heads south to the Papallacta hot springs.

The rest of the Lake District spreads north from Papallacta, with multiday hikes connecting bordering towns like Pifo and Oyacachi. Laguna Papallacta, the largest lake in the area, lies to the south of hot springs on the Río Papallacta.

Longer hikes in the area, including into the Reserva Ecológica Cayambe-Coca, can be arranged with Fundación Ecológica Rumicocha, which has an office in Papallacta (General

Quisquis, tel. 6/232-0637, www.rumicocha.
org.ec). Guides cost from $15 per day.

C Papallacta Hot Springs

Whether you're on the way to the rainforest,
on a hiking trip, or simply want a day trip out
of Quito, don't miss the chance to soak your
limbs in the best set of thermal baths in the
country. Nestled in a steep Andean valley at
a bracing 3,225 meters elevation, the springs
attract crowds of Quiteños on weekends but it
is relatively quiet during the week. A sign on
the left-hand side of the road to Baeza, a few
kilometers past the Laguna Papallacta, points
up a dirt track. It's a 20-minute walk from the
highway, so if you're laden with luggage, take
a taxi ($2).

At the top of the road, you'll reach the
Termas de Papallacta (Quito tel. 2/256-
8989 or Papallacta tel. 6/232-0040, www.
termaspapallacta.com). The public section
(6 A.M.–9 P.M. daily, $7 pp) is pleasantly land-
scaped and surrounded by facilities, including
changing rooms, bag storage, towel and locker
rental, and a pricey café-restaurant. The baths
range from paddling-pool to swimming-pool
size, and from ice-cold to scalding hot. There
are horseback trips available on weekends. The
private spa next door (8 A.M.–7 P.M. daily, $18
pp) offers spa pools with water jets and bubble
jets. The center also offers massages, a sauna,
and other spa treatments.

The Fundación Terra operates an information center on the hill to the right of the
baths called the **Exploratorio** ($2), which in-
troduces visitors to the ecology of the section
of the Papallacta River canyon between the
baths and the border of the Cayambe-Coca
Reserve. Three short walking trails have been
developed: You can hike the one-kilometer trail
on your own, but the two- and four-kilometer
trails require a guide.

Accommodations
Papallacta has a few lodging offerings, ranging
from budget to luxury. Most hotels have restaurants attached. In town there are a couple
of options at the cheap end of the scale. **La**

Choza de Don Wilson (Quisquis, tel. 6/232-
0627, $15 s, $30 d) is the best of these, with an
enclosed hot pool, good views over the valley,
and a popular restaurant serving a set menu
($4). **Hotel Coturpa** (Quisquis, tel. 6/232-
0640, $17 s, $30 d, breakfast included) is adequate, but the thermal pools are only filled
for tour groups.

On the way to the baths, **Hostería Pampa
de Papallacta** (tel. 6/232-0624, $35 s, $55
d, breakfast included) has been recently refurbished and offers more comfortable guest
rooms and its own hot pools. **Hostal Antisana**
(tel. 6/232-0626, $17 s, $34 d) is closer to the
baths, but more basic with rather cold guest
rooms.

For the best accommodations in town, reserve one of the 36 smart guest rooms or 12
thatched adobe cabins at the **Hotel Termas
de Papallacta** (Quito office: Foch E7-38 at
Reina Victoria, tel. 2/256-8989, Papallacta tel.
6/232-0040, www.termaspapallacta.com, $135
s or d, 6-person cabins $192). Prices include
access to the hotel's private baths, and there is
a choice of three restaurants (entrées $6–12).
The hotel also operates a 250-hectare ranch on
the Papallacta River for birding and hiking excursions into the cloud forest.

Getting There and Around
Papallacta has several buses every hour from
Quito's Quitumbe station (2 hours, $2.50).
Take any bus heading to Tena, Lago Agrio, or
Coca and ask the driver to let you off either at
the junction to the baths or in town. To continue into the Oriente, simply wait on the main
highway in town and flag down a bus. To get
to the baths from town, take a taxi ($2) if you
don't want to do the 20-minute walk.

ANTISANA ECOLOGICAL RESERVE
Since 1993 the Antisana Ecological Reserve
($5) has protected a large chunk of the
Ecuadorian Andes between the provinces of
Pichincha and Napo. An elevation range of
more than 4,500 meters, all the way to the top
of the Volcán Antisana (5,704 meters), encloses

two distinct ecosystems. Temperatures in the lower humid cloud forest (1,200–3,800 meters) can reach 25°C, while nights in the high *páramo* (3,800–4,700 meters) often drop well below freezing.

The reserve's upper reaches are home to more than 50 bird species. One of the most significant condor populations in the country soar in the high thin air. Other rare species, such as the carunculated caracara and black-faced ibis, stick closer to the ground. Tapirs, spectacled bears, pumas, and dwarf *pudú* deer hide in the lower forests. Such species richness partly comes from proximity to the Cayambe-Coca Ecological Reserve and Sumaco-Napo Galeras National Park: Animals can migrate among Antisana's 1,200 square kilometers and the other reserves relatively easily, and conservation efforts often carry over area boundaries.

The Antisana Reserve protects one of the most important watersheds in the country, which provides the majority of Quito's water supply. The glaciers of Antisana Volcano feed the Río Quijos to the west and trout-filled Laguna Micacocha in the direction of Sincholagua. Hunting, overgrazing, and encroachment by settlers are all-too-common threats, along with timber extraction in the eastern reaches.

Antisana is a comparatively infrequently visited national park. The easiest access point is via the village of Pintag, 30 kilometers southeast of Quito.

Climbing Volcán Antisana

Ecuador's fourth-highest peak looms southeast of Quito in a remote cloudy area seldom visible even from afar. Four peaks surround an ice-filled crater that was active into the 18th century. Edward Whymper, Jean-Antoine Carrel, and Louis Carrel first climbed the highest peak in 1880, leaving the other three (all close to 5,500 meters) for later adventurers. Its remote location, bad weather, and lack of huts make Antisana a difficult climb.

The route begins 6–7 kilometers east of Sangolquí on the road to Pifo, passing through the village of **Pintag** (five kilometers) and

Hacienda Pimantura (12–13 kilometers) as it heads southeast toward the mountain. The IGM *Pintag* 1:100,000 map covers the area.

BAEZA

After the ride down from Papallacta, this small mountain town is a convenient spot to break up the long bus journey from Quito to the Oriente. Founded in the 16th century as a mission settlement on the eastern slope of the Andes, the town itself has little in the way of sights, but its location amid hills close to three forested reserves makes it a good base for hikers.

The road from Quito splits just west of town. The left fork follows the oil pipeline and the Río Quijos northeast toward Lago Agrio, then south to Coca. The right fork heads through the middle of Baeza to Tena. The colonial part of Baeza comes first, consisting of a few streets sloping up steeply toward the church. A newer section of town is farther along across the Río Machángara.

Recreation

A few great hiking trails take full advantage of Baeza's lofty views. To follow the **Camino de la Antena** (Antenna Trail), head up through the old part of town to the right of the church. You'll pass a cemetery on your way to a fork in the trail just across the Río Machángara. The right-hand fork continues along the river for quite a ways, and the left fork climbs up to a set of antennas overlooking the area. A farther branch continues along the mountaintop over town, with great views of the entire Quijos Valley on clear days. Expect to take 3–4 hours to reach the antennas, more if the trail is muddy from recent rain. Whichever path you pick, the **birding** in the pastures and cloud forest is bound to be great: Dusky *pihas,* grass-green tanagers, Andean guans, and black-billed mountain toucans may all make an appearance. The **Granary Trail** connects the old and new villages, beginning by the road below Bar-Restaurant Gina (signed). It runs south past a small waterfall and through the forested hillside to the south end of the new village. It tends to be a little muddy at times, so good boots are advisable.

Accommodations and Food

Baeza's accommodations offerings are rather scant and limited to basic budget accommodations because most travelers pass through. In the colonial part of town, try **Gina's** (Baeza Colonial, tel. 6/232-0471, $8 pp), above the restaurant called Gina's, one of the best places in town to eat.

In the new town, try **Hostal Bambu's** (Nueva Andalucía, tel. 6/232-0219, $8 pp) or **Hotel Samay** (Nueva Andalucía, tel. 6/232-0170, $6–10 pp), both of which have hot water. For restaurants, try **Gina's** (Baeza Colonial, tel. 6/232-0471, 7 A.M.–9 P.M. daily, entrées $3–4) or **El Viejo** (Nueva Andalucía, tel. 6/232-0442, 7 A.M.–9 P.M. daily, entrées $5)

which both offer a wide range of fish, meat, and vegetarian dishes.

Information and Services

A tiny **police** station sits in the old section of town, along with a small military base. For information on hiking in the area, stop by the **Centro de Comunicación Ambiental** (Ramírez Dávilos and Rey Felipe II, tel. 6/232-0605) in the old town.

Getting There

Any bus between Quito and cities in the northern Oriente passes through Baeza, making it easy to hop on or off in town. Buses to and from Coca and Lago Agrio pass by "La Y" (pronounced "La Yay"), the highway intersection just west of town, whereas those to Tena go right through town. Buses to Quito (3 hours, $3) stop below the market in new Baeza.

Northern Oriente

Leaving Baeza, you can take the road northeast toward Lago Agrio or south to Tena and Coca. Whichever route you choose, it's a dramatic descent from the Andes into rainforest that becomes denser and denser as the elevation drops into the Quijos Valley. The farther east you travel, the greater the concentration of primary rainforest. In the north, the area east of Lago Agrio is dominated by Río Aguarico, which flows through the Cuyabeno Reserve, and farther south Río Coca flows past Yasuní National Park all the way to the Peruvian border at Nuevo Rocafuerte.

To get to unforgettable swaths of primary rainforest means going through the forgettable oil towns of Lago Agrio or Coca. Neither make for pleasant stays, and if you fly in, you'll avoid spending much time in them. Traveling by bus from Quito, however, usually necessitates an overnight stay.

Tena, Misahualli, and Puyo offer a different experience—mainly secondary rainforest, although there are pockets of primary forest

east of Misahualli that can be reached by boat. These towns also offer interesting encounters with local indigenous communities, but if you want unspoiled rainforest, head farther east.

SAN RAFAEL FALLS

If you take the long bus ride to Lago Agrio, the saving grace is passing the highest waterfall in Ecuador, which roars 145 meters over a rock shelf into the Río Quijos. It is 66 kilometers (1.5 hours) from Baeza, and it's easy to miss the stop, so be sure to inform the driver. Follow the dirt road downhill over the small Río Reventador and past a guard post, where foreigners are supposed to pay a rather hefty $10 entrance fee. If you're lucky, the entrance may be deserted.

There are two trails to the falls—the first offers a view opposite the falls and takes 1.5 hours round-trip. The second, more difficult trail offers a more spectacular view from above the falls and takes 2.5 hours. The trail can be slippery and difficult, even dangerous in places,

THE AMAZON'S FIERCE CREATURES

Tell most Ecuadorians that you're heading into the rainforest, and they'll look at you with a mixture of fright, awe, and pity. This is mainly due to the reputation of the Amazon as home to countless species of fierce creatures that bite, sting, and even swallow you whole. But how dangerous are the many weird and wonderful creatures of the Ecuadorian rainforest? Here's a profile of the most famous and infamous, and how to survive them:

Caimans: There are two species of these reptiles, white and black. The white caiman, also known as spectacled or common caiman, is the most docile and considered harmless to humans, although they may bite if provoked. They grow up to two meters long and feed on insects, crustaceans, and small fish. The black caiman is far bigger, between three and four meters, although some grow up to six meters long. They are one of the largest alligators in the world, similar to the American alligator, and have been hunted to near extinction. They do not seek out humans but may attack if a human enters their territory. Locals are usually aware of where black caimans live, and it is not safe to swim in these areas. They usually sleep during the day and can be spotted more easily on night canoe excursions (they don't tend to attack boats).

Candirú catfish: Also known as the toothpick fish, this creature is every man's worst nightmare. These parasitic fish can grow to around 15 centimeters and usually target bigger fish, feeding on the host's blood. They are translucent and very hard to spot. More worryingly, they are attracted by the smell of urine. An infamous incident occurred in Brazil in 1997 when a *candirú* swam up a man's urethra after he waded into the river naked and urinated (the fish was removed in surgery, and the man made a full recovery). Wear a tight pair of swimming trunks and avoid urinating, and you should be fine.

Conga ants: They are also known as bullet ants and nicknamed by locals "24-hour ants" because of their potent bite, the effects of which last for an entire day. These ants are the largest in the rainforest, growing up to three centimeters, and their bite is far stronger than a wasp. Pain and swelling can sometimes be accompanied by a fever and allergic reaction, whereupon medical attention should be sought. The ants most commonly bite if the nest is disturbed, and most guides are aware of nest locations. The ants have their uses, though: Local indigenous people hunt and cook them, and also use the venom to treat rheumatism.

Frogs: Poison dart frogs are so named because some indigenous people in Central and South America have used their venom for hunting. Most species are brightly colored and very small, usually 2-6 centimeters. They are mostly diurnal and can be seen during the day in moist areas. They secrete toxins through their skin to deter predators, and the toxin attacks the nerves, leading to potential heart failure. The most poisonous species contains enough poison to kill a dozen humans. Staying safe is easy: don't touch them.

Jaguars: This is the third-largest cat in the world, after the tiger and lion, and the only

---

so consider asking for a guide at the entrance. Bromeliads and *Cecropia* trees decorate the forest alongside giant ferns with fronds as big as horses. Birders, keep your eyes peeled: Guiana cock-of-the-rocks are frequently seen here.

If you're not in a hurry, consider spending the night. Near the entrance, the **Hostería Reventador** (Vía a la Cascada de San Rafael, tel. 6/281-8221 or 9/498-9098, www.hosteriaelreventador.com, $12 pp) has basic guest rooms, a pool, and a restaurant. The owner can be hired as a guide, and for a small tip you can leave your luggage here while you visit the falls if you want to catch the bus after visiting.

VOLCÁN REVENTADOR

The "exploder" is one of the most active volcanoes in Ecuador, and it justified its name by erupting suddenly in 2002, shooting 200 million tonnes of ash and rock 17 kilometers

panther species found in the Americas, along with its cousin, the black panther. Worshipped by the local indigenous population, it is sadly endangered, and you will be extraordinarily lucky to see one in Ecuador outside a zoo. They are easily startled and will usually be long gone before a group approaches. Adults grow to 1.5–1.8 meters long and weigh up to 135 kilograms. The jaguar is a carnivore and feeds on caimans, deer, capybaras (giant rodents), and tapirs as well as smaller rodents and birds. Unlike lions and tigers, jaguars rarely attack humans, although a fatal attack occurred in Guyana in 2009.

Piranha fish: The most famous fish in the Amazon is the subject of many myths, the most common being that groups can strip a cow to the bone in seconds. The truth is that piranha, which grow up to 25 centimeters long, are omnivorous and many are vegetarian, feeding on the riverbeds. However, red-bellied piranhas are meat-eaters and are the most aggressive, with razor-sharp teeth. They feed mainly on small fish but will also attack larger fish and small mammals. They only tend to attack humans if they smell blood or in self-defense (if you step on one, for example), and the famous feeding frenzies happen in rare cases of a shortage of food. Local people routinely fish for piranhas, and it's a common part of a rainforest tour; the flesh is tasty, albeit with a lot of bones. Don't go swimming in rainforest rivers and lakes if you have cuts or wounds.

Snakes: The Amazon rainforest contains a huge variety of snakes. The most famous is, of course, the anaconda, which has received a very bad reputation as a result of a very bad Hollywood movie a few years back. Anacondas are aquatic snakes and can grow up to five meters long. They are constrictors and squeeze the life out of their prey, feeding mainly on fish, rodents, and occasionally small caimans. Attacks have been reported on larger mammals such as dogs, but attacks on humans are extremely rare.

One of the most dangerous snakes in Ecuador is the fer-de-lance (spearhead), known ominously as the "X" locally. Its bite can be fatal, but an antidote is available at hospitals. A bite from the coral snake, however, has no known cure at present. Luckily for us, most snakes are far more scared of us than we are of them and will be long gone when they hear humans approaching. The danger lies in surprising one dozing in the foliage, so stick to the trails.

Spiders: Tarantulas are one of the most infamous residents of the Amazon, and again, a Hollywood movie has a lot to answer for. Deaths from any spider bite are rare worldwide, and tarantula bites are almost unheard of because they have comparatively low toxicity. Bites are reported to be no more painful than a wasp sting, although some species can cause prolonged pain and swelling. Tarantulas are also comparatively docile and will often sit unconcerned a few steps away from humans. One of the most dangerous spiders in Ecuador is the banana spider or Brazilian wandering spider. It is not a tarantula, and has a potentially fatal bite, although an antidote is available.

into the sky. The ash cloud covered three provinces and closed Quito airport. The entire south rim of the old three-kilometer crater is missing, opening a view of a new, smaller volcanic cone in the middle, surrounded by sulfur-encrusted rocks. Reventador continued to rumble into 2004, and in July 2008 it began another cycle of activity. It stands at a height of 3,562 meters, but geologists estimate that it was one of Ecuador's highest peaks before regular eruptions since 1541 cut it down to its present size.

Since the first ascent by a scientific expedition in 1931, Reventador hasn't been climbed often because of its muddy approach and constant volcanic activity. Because the 2–4-day trek to the top crosses everything from pastures to lava-covered wasteland, hiring a guide is essential. The climb is further complicated by the fact that eruptions have changed the terrain significantly from that recorded on the IGM *Volcán El Reventador* 1:50,000 map. The approach is sodden, and the peak is often clouded over, so climbers should bring machetes, rubber boots, waterproof tents and rope, compasses, and maps.

The trail begins shortly past the entrance to San Rafael Falls. There's a refuge at 2,300 meters, about 4–5 hours from the road, with bunk beds. It takes 7–8 hours to reach the summit from the refuge, and another five hours or so to descend.

Do not attempt this climb alone, and check on current volcanic activity beforehand at the Instituto Geofísico website (www.igepn.edu. ec).

CASCALES

This quiet little agricultural village, just 40 minutes from Lago Agrio, offers a pleasant alternative to overnight stays in the noisy oil town. If you choose to travel by day to see the spectacular scenery, you can make stops at Papallacta and San Rafael and overnight in the basic rooms of **Paraíso Dorado** (Vía a Lago Agrio, tel. 9/471-5191, $7 pp), or overnight here at the end of a rainforest trip before continuing to Quito. Several short rainforest walks are offered by Paraíso Dorado's owners.

LAGO AGRIO

The capital of Sucumbíos Province, Lago Agrio (pop. 55,000) was carved from the rainforest in 1972 as a field headquarters for Texaco's explorations in the Oriente. Settlers from the southern Oriente named it Nueva Loja, still its official name, while the oil workers nicknamed it Lago Agrio, the Spanish translation of Sour Lake, Texas, Texaco's original headquarters in the early 20th century. Whatever you call it, Lago Agrio is certainly more sour than sweet. It's an oil town through and through, and evidence of the pollution that the industry wrought on the surrounding rainforest is still visible. Environmental degradation is not the worst of Lago's problems, however: The town's proximity to the Colombian border, just 25 kilometers to the north, has made it an unstable

SPEAKING COFÁN

- *kasete* – good morning
- *kuse kuse* – good evening
- *meenga'kay* – How are you?
- *hayo* – yes
- *may'en* – no
- *chietzafpopoem* – thank you
- *chieegaychu* – good-bye
- *vatoova* – caiman
- *cornsipeendo* – harpy eagle
- *taysy* – jaguar
- *na'en* – river
- *coovy* – tapir
- *tsa'coer* – water

place and a haven for drug traffickers, guerrillas, and paramilitaries. In an infamous incident in 2008, the Colombian army crossed two kilometers into Ecuadorian territory just north of town to bomb a FARC guerrilla camp, killing leader Raúl Reyes and several Ecuadorians. The border situation remains very volatile; do not attempt to cross into Colombia from here.

Although visitors have not been targeted in town, consider avoiding spending a night in Lago Agrio. Either fly in the early morning or stay overnight in one of the towns on the way from Quito and get up early enough to meet your tour group to head to Cuyabeno. If you stay in the town, stay in the center, and don't stray from the main street.

Accommodations and Food

The popular **Hotel D'Mario** (Av. Quito, tel. 6/283-0456, www.hoteldmario.com, $15 s, $27 d) has guest rooms with cable TV, air-conditioning, and private baths along with a pool and free Internet. **Hotel Gran Colombia**

(Av. Quito, tel. 6/283-1032, $22 s, $28 d) also has decent guest rooms with air-conditioning and cable TV. The nicest place in town is **La Cascada** (Av. Quito and Amazonas, tel. 6/283-2229, $30 s, $52 d), with a pool and a spa. All guest rooms come with private baths, cable TV, minibars, and air-conditioning.

You are safer eating in your hotel on Avenida Quito than wandering around town. **Restaurant D'Mario** (Av. Quito, tel. 3/283-0172, 7 A.M.–10 P.M. daily, entrées $4–6) does a decent pizza and is often packed with gringos. **Restaurant Gran Colombia** (Av. Quito, tel. 3/283-1032, 7 A.M.–10 P.M. daily, entrées $4–6) does staples such as *chuleta* and *ceviche* and also has good ice cream.

Information and Services

There are several banks in the center. **Banco de Guayaquil** (Quito and 12 de Febrero) changes traveler's checks, and **Banco de Pichincha** (12 de Febrero) has an ATM. The best clinic for medical attention is **Clínica González** (Quito and 12 de Febrero, tel. 6/283-0728). The **police station** is at Avenida Quito and Manabi (tel. 6/283-0101).

Getting There and Around

The *terminal terrestre* bus terminal is two kilometers north of Lago Agrio. There are hourly departures to Quito (8 hours, $8) and a 7 P.M. overnight bus to Guayaquil (14 hours, $15). There are also overnight buses to Tena, Puyo, Ambato, Riobamba, and Cuenca. **Transportes Putumayo** has service to Tulcán for those heading to Colombia and also runs buses to Coca (3 hours, $3), or take a *ranchero* to Coca from Avenida Amazonas in town.

TAME (9 de Octubre and Orellana, tel. 6/283-0113) flies to Quito (Mon.–Sat., from $67 one-way). Flights depart Quito at 9 A.M., returning from Lago Agrio at 10 A.M. There is an extra flight on Friday afternoon. Book a few days in advance if possible. **VIPSA** (tel. 6/283-0333, www.vipec.com) has an office at the airport and also runs daily flights to Quito. Local buses run to the airport, or take a taxi ($3–4).

Taxis around town cost $1–2.

◖ CUYABENO WILDLIFE RESERVE

Most of the eastern half of Sucumbíos Province falls within the beautiful Cuyabeno Wildlife Reserve ($20) of unique flooded rainforest that spreads out over more than 6,000 square kilometers east of Lago Agrio all the way to the Peruvian border. The Río Aguarico, which translates as "rich water," carves its way through the reserve, and countless tributaries offer unforgettable canoe rides to hidden lagoons. There is astonishing biodiversity of plants, trees, mammals, and, in particular, aquatic wildlife: pink freshwater dolphins, white and black caimans, and giant otters can be observed here. In the west, terra firma forests stay dry most of the year, while seasonally flooded areas of low-water marshes border permanently flooded forests to the east.

More than 200 species of trees per hectare have been recorded here, including many species of palm, guava, and native trees like the *zapote silvestre* (forest apple), *uva de arbol* (tree grape), and *cerezo de tierra* (ground cherry). Birders won't be disappointed because Cuyabeno contains at least one-third of all the bird species in the entire Amazon basin (500 recorded species at last count). Raucous blue-and-yellow macaws fly overhead, and the ringed kingfisher, the largest of five kingfisher species in the reserve, is often startled from its riverside perch by passing canoes. Mammal species include the fisher bat, which snatches fish from lakes and rivers, and *saki* monkeys with long furry tails.

Unfortunately, exploitation of the black riches underneath Cuyabeno have done huge damage to the western part of the reserve. There were at least six recorded oil spills in the region in the 1980s, and legal action against oil companies is ongoing. The Ecuadorian government expanded the size of the reserve in 1991 in an effort to compensate indigenous people and protect even more of the Río Cuyabeno's watershed from colonization. The eastern section is only reachable on a day-long motorboat ride, a remoteness that will hopefully help to protect it.

Swing on a vine at the Cuyabeno Wildlife Reserve.

© BEN WESTWOOD

The Siona-Secoya people inhabit the upper reaches of the Río Aguarico near the Río Cuyabeno. Groups of Lowland Kichwa are occasionally encountered downstream, along with a small enclave of Cofán at Zábalo. Two Shuar communities have recently moved into the far eastern part of the reserve.

Visiting Cuyabeno

The only way to experience the reserve is by going on a tour or staying at a permanent lodge. Access is via the road southeast from Lago Agrio, where groups board motorboats at Dureno or Chiritza to be whisked downriver.

The range of lodges in Cuyabeno is more limited than those near Coca and Tena. One of the best-known is **Cuyabeno Lodge,** near the refuge's Laguna Grande, run by **Neotropic Turis** (Pinto E4-338 at Amazonas, Quito, tel. 2/252-1212, fax 2/255-4902, www.neotropic-turis.com). These comfortable bungalows are built with natural materials and have private baths. Some of Ecuador's finest naturalist guides lead hikes and canoe trips into the forest

in conjunction with indigenous Siona people; expeditions of four days ($350 pp) and five days ($430 pp) don't include transportation from Quito or the $20 reserve entrance fee.

Tapir Lodge, run by **Nomadtrek** (Juan León Mera and Wilson, Quito, tel. 2/290-2670, www.tapirlodge.com, $580–725 pp) is the other good quality lodge in Cuyabeno.

Dracaena (Joaquín Pinto and Amazonas, Quito, tel. 2/254-6590, www.amazondracaena.com) runs two basic lodges in the area that are more camps than actual lodges. Tours to the **Nicky Lodge** cost $170–200 pp. The lodge has an observation tower, and there are Secoya and Kichwa communities close by. Four-day ($240 pp) and five-day ($280 pp) stays at **Dracaena Camp Site** include tours to the local Siona communities. **Jamu Lodge** (Calama and Reina Victoria, Quito, tel. 2/222-0614) is another, cheaper option, with four-day ($245 pp) and five-day ($285 pp) stays.

For extended visits with the Cofán people, contact Randy Borman at *Fundación Sobrevivencia Cofán* (tel. 2/247-4763, kimreyanna@gmail.com, www.cofan.org). Trips range 4–10 days (from $100 pp per day) with accommodations in the Cofán community of Zabalo in the Cuyabeno wildlife reserve. A minimum group size of four is required.

COCA

People flock to Coca (pop. 45,000) for vastly different reasons: Visitors come through on a quest to see the green riches of pristine rainforest, while workers and entrepreneurs come in search of the oil riches lying deep underneath. Coca has developed since the 1980s into Ecuador's key oil town and at the same time remains the best hub to reach primary rainforest. Tourism and oil do not mix easily, though, and while the infrastructure provided by industry improves access to rainforest lodges, conflicts are inevitable. At the time of this writing, the Coca region is entering a critical period with the impending decision of whether or not to drill for oil in Yasuní National Park.

Officially named Puerto Francisco de Orellana, Coca was declared the capital of the new province of Orellana, which split off from Napo in 1998. The population is growing faster here than almost anywhere else in Ecuador. It's the closest sizable city to undisturbed rainforest in Ecuador—Yasuní National Park is just downstream—but there's little to keep you here for long. While it isn't as dangerous as Lago Agrio, if you're flying in, there's no need to stay in Coca. Coming by bus usually necessitates an overnight stop.

Recreation and Tours

Coca serves as the gateway to Ecuador's upper Amazon, offering relatively easy access to the rainforest down the lower Napo River. These days, however, booking a rainforest tour locally is not easy because of a dearth of local operators. You may find something locally, but tours are better booked in Quito, Tena, or Baños. Most of the best lodges either have online booking or offices in Quito. Tours of 4–5 days are most popular; less than that and you'll spend more time traveling than actually being in the rainforest.

If you want to pick up a tour locally, recommended operators include **Wildlife Amazon,** with an office in Hotel San Fermín (Quito and Bolívar, tel. 6/288-0802, www.wildlifeamazon. com) which offers tours to Yasuní, Limoncocha Reserve, and Pañacocha Lodge. You can pick up last-minute deals to **Yarina Lodge** at Hotel Oasis (Camilo de Torrano, tel. 6/288-0206). Other recommended local guides include Luis Duarte at **La Casa de Maito** (tel. 6/288-2309, luisemerald@gmail.com), Sandro Ramos (tel. 9/702-4893, sandroidalio@hotmail.com), and Jhon Andi Palomeque (tel. 6/288-1441, jhon_junjla@yahoo.com).

Evenings in Coca can get quite raucous with oil workers living it up. There are several cafés, bars, and food kiosks along the *malecón*. **The Emerald Forest Blues Bar** (Quito and Espejo, tel. 6/288-2280, noon–midnight Sun.–Thurs., noon–2 A.M. Fri.–Sat.) is a popular drinking spot both for lunch and late in the evening. The disco **El Bunker** downstairs at Hostería La Misión (Camilo de Torrano, tel. 6/288-0260, 9 P.M.–midnight Sun.–Thurs., 9 P.M.–2 A.M. Fri.–Sat.) is a good nightlife option, especially on weekends. Be careful walking around late at night.

Accommodations

Budget options are limited in Coca, but there are enough decent hotels to find a place to spend one night. The best of the cheapies is probably **Hotel Oasis** (Camilo de Torrano, tel. 6/288-0206, $9–13 s, $12–18 d), which has rooms with fans or air-conditioning. Guest rooms don't face the river, but the pleasant terrace does. You can book tours to Yarina Lodge.

The best mid-range option in town is **Hotel La Misión** (Camilo de Torrano, tel. 6/288-0260, $26 s, $38 d), overlooking the river. Guest rooms have private baths, hot water, TVs, and air-conditioning. There's a restaurant, a pool with a waterslide, and a disco on weekends. Toucans, parrots, and the occasional monkey perch next to the pool.

In the center of town, the **Hotel El Auca** (Napo between Rocafuerte and Moreno, tel. 6/280-0127 or 6/288-0600, $28–38 s, $44–54 d) is one of the top hotels in Coca and a popular meeting place for four tour groups. Wooden cabins fill an inner courtyard with hammocks, flowers, and rainforest birds. Cabins have private baths, fans, TVs, and hot water. The hotel features a restaurant with a patio overlooking the street plus newer, more expensive guest rooms with air-conditioning in the main building.

Food

For cheap but delicious fish, head to **La Casa de Maito** (Espejo, tel. 6/288-0285, 7 A.M.–6 P.M. daily, entrées $4–6). Most of Coca's best restaurants are in its hotels. **Dayuma** at Hostería La Misión (Camilo de Torrano, tel. 6/288-0260, 7 A.M.–10 P.M. daily, entrées $6–12) serves fish, meat, and salads on the riverside terrace. **El Auca** (Napo between Rocafuerte and Moreno, tel. 6/280-0127, 7 A.M.–10 P.M. daily, entrées $8–11) has a large and varied menu that includes *camarones al ajillo* (shrimp in garlic sauce) and *chuleta Hawaiana* (Hawaiian pork chops) as well as vegetarian options.

Information and Services

The **tourist information office** (Transporte Fluviales Orellana Bldg., Chimborazo, tel. 6/288-0532, www.orellanaturistica.gob.ec, 8 A.M.–noon and 1:30–6 P.M. Mon.–Fri.) is on the riverside and has maps and brochures. The best health clinic is **Clínica Sinai** (Napo and Moreno). The **police station** is on Vicente Rocafuerte near Napo.

Getting There and Around

Coca's *terminal terrestre* bus terminal is eight blocks north of the river, off Napo. Take a taxi from town ($1), or there are regular public buses. The major long-distance bus companies have private terminals closer to the center, however. The road that connects Coca to the road between Baeza and Tena, heading through Loreto and south of Sumaco-Napo Galeras National Park, is the shortest route to Quito.

Buses to Tena (5 hours, $7) leave hourly from the *terminal terrestre*. **Transportes Baños** (tel. 6/288-0182) sends the most comfortable buses to Tena twice a day from its office (Napo and Bolívar). It also offers services to Quito (9 hours, $10), Baños (7 hours, $9), and Guayaquil (13 hours, $15). **Transportes Loja** (Amazonas and Cuenca) and **Transportes Esmeraldas** (Bolívar and 6 de Diciembre) also run buses to Quito.

TAME (tel. 6/288-1078), **VIPSA** (tel. 6/288-1747), and **Icaro** (tel. 6/288-0546) fly to Quito ($65 one-way) every day of the week.

Boats with Cooperativas de Transporte Fluvial Orellana (at the docks on Chimborazo, tel. 6/283-2184) down the Río Napo leave at 7 A.M. on Sunday, Tuesday, Thursday, and Friday heading as far as Nuevo Rocafuerte on the Peruvian border (10 hours, $15).

Lower Río Napo

Río Napo is Ecuador's largest river, born in the foothills of Cotopaxi, flowing 1,000 kilometers through the lowland wilderness into Peru and Brazil, where it joins the Amazon to finally empty into the Atlantic Ocean. The river sees quite a lot of traffic these days—don't be surprised to see huge trucks being taken across the river on barges—and even though it has lost much of its original wildness, there are countless streams that lead into virgin rainforest where the trappings of modern culture are refreshingly absent.

East of Coca, as industrial development fades from view, towns become fewer and smaller, and half a dozen decent lodges take advantage of the wide river's easy access. Booking in advance is the best way to tour the area, including Yasuní National Park, which, like all of Ecuador's rainforest reserves, should only be visited in the company of a qualified guide.

A boat is the only way to reach most jungle lodges from Coca.

YARINA LODGE

Opened in 1998 on 470 hectares of primary rainforest, Yarina Lodge is still professionally run by the original owners. Despite the reserve's location just one hour downriver from Coca, the wildlife viewing is quite good, and caimans are particularly common. Native guides take you to visit local homes, pan for gold, and climb the 40-meter-tall observation tower. Four-day ($360) and five-day ($450) tours can be reserved through the **Yuturi Travel Agency** (Amazonas N24-236 at Colón, Quito, tel. 2/250-4037 or 2/250-3225, www.yarinalodge.com).

LIMONCOCHA AND POMPEYA

The **Limoncocha Biological Reserve** was created in 1985 to protect 28,000 hectares of rainforest surrounding Lake Limoncocha and a five-kilometer stretch of the Río Napo. It is reachable 33 kilometers downstream from Coca via the village of Pompeya.

Once considered one of the premier birding spots in the country, Limoncocha boasted more than 400 species sighted within 12 square kilometers of the lake. The area has seen its share of turmoil, however: For decades, oil companies have blasted and drilled almost directly on the shores of the lake. In 1982 the Ecuadorian government ordered the Summer Institute of Linguistics (SIL), the largest missionary-linguistic organization in the world, out of its Ecuadorian headquarters in Limoncocha. Because the SIL provided many services that the small town otherwise lacked, the group's abrupt departure left Limoncocha's fate in jeopardy. In 1991, six years after the creation of the reserve, Metropolitan Touring decided that local habitats were too heavily impacted by oil drilling and discontinued their operation in the rainforest.

Things have recovered somewhat after local communities lobbied the oil companies to build a road bypassing the village and to alter their blasting methods. Bird populations have begun to rebound, and now the lake echoes with screeches and caws more often than with the roar of dynamite. Lake Yanacocha to the east is rumored to contain a population of particularly large anacondas.

Besides its birds, the oxbow lake is known for an important ceramics find nearby. Pieces from the Napo Phase (circa A.D. 1190–1480) reflect a great aesthetic change in indigenous

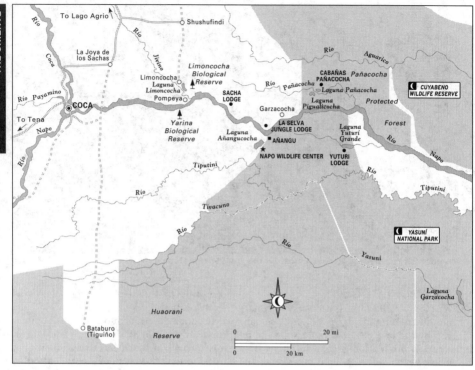

pottery. Archaeologists have deduced from the works' decoration that the ancient inhabitants practiced secondary burial, a practice in which bodies were buried, then exhumed after a few months and reinterred in large ceramic containers sculpted especially for the ritual.

If you are staying here, it's also worth visiting Pompeya on Sunday to experience an indigenous rainforest market in which indigenous Napo people trade food and clothing.

Also on the lake is the Kichwa village of **Limoncocha,** where locals have formed an ecotourism cooperative that provides Kichwa lessons, guided tours, and accommodations for visitors. It's possible to stay in town and explore the area for about $40 pp per day, including lodging in cabins, food, and guides. Two small shops sell supplies, and canoes can be rented.

To get here from Coca, take one of the frequent buses or *rancheros* to Shushufindi (2 hours, $2), then catch another bus to Limoncocha. One leaves in the early morning, another near noon, and a third late in the afternoon (1.5 hours, $1.25). The Hotel El Auca in Coca is a good source of information about Limoncocha because one of its guides is from the area. Trips can also be booked through the German-run **Hostal Limoncocha** (tel. 6/288-7583, http://limoncocha.tripod.com) in Tena. Tours cost from $45 pp per day.

A short ride downriver is the Capuchin mission and archaeological museum at **Pompeya,** on a small island near the north bank of the Napo. Keep going to the **Isla de los Monos** (Monkey Island), where a few different species of primates roam wild; with a good guide, sightings are nearly guaranteed. These two sights are often combined with a visit to Limoncocha and can easily be visited independently from the town.

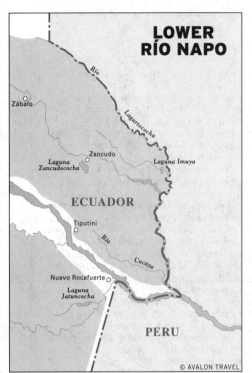

☾ YASUNÍ NATIONAL PARK

Yasuní National Park ($20) is one of Ecuador's last great wildernesses and the country's largest mainland national park. The 9,620-square-kilometer terrain ranges from upland tropical forest to seasonally flooded forest, marshes, swamps, lakes, and rivers. Untouched by the last ice age, this park is one of the world's most biodiverse areas, with 500 species of birds, including harpy eagles; 130 species of amphibians; 100,000 species of insects; and more than 60 percent of Ecuador's mammals, including jaguars, pumas, giant otters, tapirs, and monkeys.

UNESCO declared Yasuní a biosphere reserve in 1979, but sadly this didn't prevent oil exploration. The construction of a road, Vía Maxus, and drilling on the boundaries of the park has done damage. The future of the park depends enormously on the government's

Yasuní-ITT project, which aims to secure payment for Ecuador to leave an estimated 900 million barrels of oil unexploited underneath the park. But with or without permission, oil companies continue to flout environmental regulations in the area.

There is a small number of indigenous people living within the park boundaries, but the biggest ethnic group from this area, the Huaorani, have their own reserve to the south.

Despite the problems, large sections of the park remain unscathed. Yasuní still offers some of the best opportunities in Ecuador to experience pristine rainforest, and most tours coming through Coca will include a visit to the park. In addition to rainforest hikes, one of the highlights of a visit to the park are the **clay parrot licks,** where hundreds of birds flock to drink on a daily basis in one of nature's most awe-inspiring spectacles.

RECREATION
River Boat Trips

For a completely different rainforest experience, with comfortable air-conditioned cabins, consider opting for one of the cruise boats that move up and down the Río Napo, selecting the most interesting sights for day visits.

The **Manatee** (Gaspar de Villarroel and 6 de Diciembre, Quito, tel. 2/244-8985, www.manateeamazonexplorer.com), taking its name from the aquatic mammal also known as the sea cow, offers four-day ($650 pp) and five-day ($870 pp).

The Misión hotel in Coca operates the **Flotel La Misión** (tel. 6/288-0260, www.flotelamision.com). The boat makes four-day ($793 pp) and five-day ($910 pp) trips as well as a seven-night trip to Iquitos, Peru (from $1,832 pp).

ACCOMMODATIONS
Sacha Lodge

The Swiss-owned Sacha Lodge offers first-class accommodations and service only 2.5 hours downstream from Coca and is one of the best and most popular lodges in the area. The lodge owns 2,000 hectares of the more than 7,000 hectares of mostly primary rainforest

GREEN VERSUS BLACK

Ever since oil was discovered under the Ecuadorian rainforest in the 1960s, the petroleum industry has been on a collision course with environmentalists and local indigenous communities. In the 1970s Texaco was granted permission to drill around Lago Agrio, which was named after the corporation's original headquarters, Sour Lake, in Texas. When oil prices plummeted in the 1980s, pressure increased on the Ecuadorian government to increase extraction in the Oriente. Despite protests from local indigenous people, the government asserted that the oil reserves beneath their lands belonged to the state.

Even when done properly, extracting oil causes serious damage. Deforestation occurs to create air strips for helicopters and light aircraft as well as for the construction of roads, and during drilling, waste products contaminate rivers and lakes. However, seriously negligent practices led to worse environmental degradation in Ecuador. The pipeline out of the rainforest was poorly constructed and caused 64 million liters of oil to leak. Deliberate dumping of oil in pits has been far worse, amounting to billions of liters, according to environmentalists.

Large areas near Lago Agrio and Coca became environmental disaster areas, forcing many indigenous people to abandon their communities, in particular the Cofán, Siona, and Secoya in the north. Others were bought off with bribes, but by far the worst affected were those who stayed. Harvard University researchers found a huge rise in cancer rates and birth defects in areas affected by oil activity due to the contaminated water supply.

Texaco, now Chevron, was one of the major players in partnership with the state-owned company Petroecuador, extracting over 3 billion liters of oil between 1964 and 1992. In 1993, a $6 billion lawsuit was filed on behalf of 30,000 indigenous Ecuadorians in the United States, accusing Texaco of intentionally dumping 68 million liters of crude oil into the rainforest, an incredible 30 times more oil than was spilled in the *Exxon Valdez* disaster in Alaska in 1989. Two years later, Texaco embarked on a $40 million cleanup program, blasted as woefully inadequate by the plaintiffs but, to their shock, accepted as sufficient by the Ecuadorian government at the time. Chevron has since blamed Petroecuador for any existing pollution because the state-owned company has controlled oil extraction in the area since 1992.

After a decade of legal wrangling, the case was moved to Ecuadorian courts, and the amount demanded increased to $27 billion. Following allegations of corruption and judicial bias by Chevron, in 2011 the court in Lago Agrio ordered Chevron to pay $9 billion in compensation, one of the largest environmental damage awards ever. This could be a hollow victory because Chevron, condemning the judgment as illegitimate, can go through three stages of appeal, which could take years. Additionally, the plaintiffs would have to fight Chevron in U.S. courts to receive payment, as the company has no assets in Ecuador.

While the legal wrangling continues, the water supply in large sections of the rainforest remains dangerously polluted and investment is badly needed to clean it up. Although the foreign multinational oil companies have left, the state-owned company is desperate for government go-ahead to drill underneath Yasuní National Park. The battle between green and black is far from over.

For further information, visit the **Amazon Defense Coalition** (www.texacotoxico.org) as well as **Chevron** (www.chevron.com/Ecuador) for the company's side of the story.

TO DRILL OR NOT TO DRILL: THE YASUNÍ-ITT PROJECT

In 2007, President Rafael Correa's government launched one of its most ambitious and innovative projects, the Yasuní-ITT initiative. The central idea is that Ecuador, as a comparatively poor country, should be paid about $3.6 billion over 13 years by developed nations as compensation for not exploiting the estimated 900 million barrels of oil in the Ishpingo, Tambococha, and Tiputini (ITT) fields underneath Yasuní National Park. Correa and his government argue that, due to oil's importance as Ecuador's top export (and source of one-third of his government's revenues), the nation deserves to be rewarded for protecting a unique biosphere and thus helping efforts to curb global warming by saving 407 million tonnes in carbon emissions.

Although the project initially received very favorable response from international media and governments, getting firm investment commitments amid the ongoing global economic downturn has proved very difficult. So far, a mere $100,000 has been donated by Chile. One issue has been President Correa's reluctance to accept conditions on how the money is spent.

With Ecuador's oil supplies dwindling and public expenditure increasing, there is increasing financial pressure to drill. The project is currently at a crucial stage, and Correa has threatened to exploit Yasuní if funds are not secured, even though constitutional experts claim that this would be illegal. Drilling is already happening along the park's borders.

For further information on the current situation, visit www.yasuni-itt.gov.ec or www.sosyasuni.org.

---

that surround the small complex on the shore of Laguna El Pilche. Ten cabins with private baths and gas-heated hot water are connected by thatched walkways to the dining hall, where gourmet meals are served.

A 43-meter viewing tower built around a kapok tree affords guests the occasional view of Volcán Sumaco to the west along with views of up to 200 bird species that have been spotted from the tower. Birders will love the 270-meter canopy walkway and the salt lick just downriver near Añangu, where squawking flocks of parrots, parakeets, and macaws squabble over the mineral-rich soil on the riverbank.

All nature-viewing excursions from the lodge are accompanied by two guides—one local and one English-speaking biologist—for every 4–7 people. Four-day ($729 pp) and five-day ($920 pp) tours don't include airfare from Quito, but members of South American Explorers (SAE) get a 15 percent discount. Sacha is very popular, so book well in advance. For reservations, contact the office in Quito (Julio Zaldumbide 397 at Valladolid, Quito, tel. 2/250-9115, www.sachalodge.com).

Napo Wildlife Center

One of the newest Amazon lodges in the country, opened in 2003, the Napo Wildlife Center is also one of the best. The lodge sits on Añangu Lake inside Yasuní National Park. It is run by local Kichwa Indians, who insure that visitors have an outstanding wildlife and cultural experience while having as little impact as possible. After a two-hour motor canoe ride down the Napo from Coca, guests switch over to dugout canoes and are paddled two more hours upstream to the lake. Ten comfortable, thatched-roof bungalows each have private baths and mosquito nets, and a five-story observation tower overlooks the dining room and lounge.

Excursions include climbing the 36-meter canopy observation tower, visiting local indigenous communities, hiking through the forest, and spending time at two of the most easily accessible clay licks in the country, where dozens of parrots and parakeets converge (the best months are December–January). More than 560 species of birds have been recorded nearby. Four-day ($760 pp) and five-day ($950

THE ORIENTE

© BEN WESTWOOD

Dozens of parrots descending from the trees to drink at the clay licks are an awe-inspiring sight.

pp) tours are possible to the center, which is very popular, so advanced booking is essential. For reservations, contact the Quito office (Río Yaupi N31-90 at Mariana de Jesús, Quito, tel. 2/600-5893 or 2/600-5819, www.napowildlifecenter.com).

La Selva Jungle Lodge

La Selva Jungle Lodge was one of the first in this area and has been offering tours since 1984. The main lodge and 16 cabins overlook the Laguna Garzacocha, which is reported to be safe for bathing, even though piranhas, white caimans, and the odd anaconda live in it.

Residents of two local indigenous communities are employed at the lodge. English-speaking and local guides lead hikes and canoe rides, both day and night, as well as excursions to Yasuní National Park across the river. Highlights include the lodge's 30-meter canopy tower, with excellent views of birds in the early morning; the nearby butterfly farm, which exports species worldwide; and a spot for fishing

for piranha in the lake (and have it served up for dinner, if you're lucky).

The food at La Selva is renowned as the best among Ecuador's rainforest lodges, featuring a combination of international and Ecuadorian cuisine, including local river fish and a special Amazon pizza.

Four-day ($717 pp) and five-day ($852 pp) tours don't include airfare to and from Coca, but last-minute discounts are sometimes offered. Make reservations in Quito (San Salvador E7-85 at Carrión, Quito, tel. 2/255-0995, www.laselvarainforestlodge.com).

Sani Lodge

This fairly new lodge is located on 37,000 hectares of Kichwa-owned communal lands, three hours downstream from Coca. The staff at Sani are proud of their preservation work within the community. The aim is to become a model of ecological, community-based tourism development while training the local people and maintaining international standards of service. Facilities are more basic than at some of the other nearby lodges, but the opportunities to view black caimans at night are particularly good. Four-day ($627 pp) and five-day ($814 pp) tours can be reserved through the office in Quito (San Ignacio and 6 de Diciembre, Quito, tel. 2/254-3492, www.sanilodge.com).

Amazon Dolphin Lodge

The organization that used to run Yuturi Lodge has replaced it with new accommodations on Lake Pañacocha in the 56,000-hectare Lake Pañacocha Reserve. Amazon Dolphin Lodge is one of the newest and remotest lodges in the region, five hours downstream from Coca. With more than 500 species of birds in the surrounding forest, including orange-cheeked parrots, black-crowned tityras, collared puffbirds, and paradise tanagers, bird-watchers are guaranteed to add to their life lists during a visit. There are also many species of monkeys, otters, as well as pink Amazon dolphins that can be seen in the lake. Four-day ($600 pp) and five-day ($750 pp) stays can be reserved through the **Yuturi Conservation Group** (Amazonas N24-236 at Colón, Quito, tel. 2/250-4037 or 2/250-3225, www.amazondolphinlodge.com).

Yachana Lodge

The Yachana Foundation was opened by American Douglas McMeekin in 1995 to protect the communities and forests in the Oriente region. Located three hours by boat upstream from Coca, Yachana aims to educate visitors while providing a source of funds for local community development. Perched near the village of Mondaña, the lodge oversees 280 hectares of land stretching 30 kilometers in either direction, including primary and secondary rainforest and agricultural land.

Yachana bills itself as "a place for learning," giving guests the opportunity to do things such as becoming a beekeeper for a day (bee suit included). Canoe excursions and 15 kilometers of trails allow you to enjoy the rainforest on your own or under the direction of local guides before returning to the rustic but comfortable accommodations for the night. Yachana isn't a place to see animals in the virgin forest, but if you'd like to meet local people and know that part of your fee goes toward supporting the local health care center, then Yachana is for you. The lodge has won several awards, including *Condé Nast Traveler*'s Ecotourism Award in 2004 and the National Geographic Award in 2008.

Four-day ($630 pp) and five-day ($840 pp) visits can be reserved through the office in Quito (Reina Victoria N21-226 and Vicente Ramón, Quito, tel. 2/252-3777, www.yachana.com).

South to Tena and Vicinity

Ecuador's central Amazon is busier and more populated, with its accessibility from Quito and Baños attracting more tourism traffic. The drawback is that this area mainly consists of secondary rainforest with ever-expanding population areas, roads, and agriculture. The benefits are that tours can easily be arranged last-minute on location, however, and the region offers easy access to indigenous communities as well as adrenaline-filled activities such as white-water rafting. If you want to get to primary rainforest, it is possible to reach more pristine areas east along the river from Misahualli.

BAEZA TO TENA
Cabañas San Isidro

American Mitch Lysinger and his wife Carmen have welcomed visitors to their cattle farm in the Cosanga Valley since the 1970s. The Cabañas (Quito office: tel. 2/290-6769, www.cabanasanisidro.com, $72 s, $104 d) are very eco-minded: one-quarter of the income earned from tourism goes toward buying more land for conservation and, together with partners, they now own more than 1,000 hectares of forest. Eleven cabins with private baths and hot showers surround a main farmhouse enclosing the dining area, a bar, and a sitting room. An observation tower overlooks the surrounding cloud forest, where numerous trails lead off to archaeological sites, streams, and waterfalls. A biology station has been opened nearby. San Isidro sits a few kilometers up the road above Cosanga. Reservations are essential.

Sumaco-Napo Galeras National Park and Volcán Sumaco

Volcán Sumaco juts from the rainforest east of Baeza, anchoring one of Ecuador's newest national parks. Created in 1994, Sumaco-Napo Galeras National Park ($5 pp) covers more than 200,000 hectares of lowland and high-elevation rainforest, where countless tributaries of the Ríos Napo and Coca begin. A small island section of the park encloses the Cordillera Galeras, south of the road between Narupa and Coca.

Cloud forests on the slopes of the volcano are unique because of their geographical isolation. Many unique species have evolved as a result, including 28 species of bats and 13 types of rodents. Pumas, jaguars, and oncillas leave their prints in the mud, and river otters occasionally doze on riverbanks.

Up to 400 centimeters of rain per year is the norm, and temperatures can range 10–25°C. The dry season runs November–February.

The few people who venture into Sumaco-Napo Galeras are usually intent on scaling the park's namesake volcano. The 3,900-meter **Volcán Sumaco** was first climbed in 1865. It's a long, difficult approach requiring at least three days of hiking and hacking before the final steep ascent.

Sumaco is called "potentially active" because, although there aren't any recent records of eruptions, its conical shape indicates activity within the last few centuries. Odds are low that it will erupt when you're on it, but the smart money says it isn't dead yet. October–December offer the driest conditions and clearest views from the summit. Look for the IGM *Volcán Sumaco* 1:50,000 map to check out the ascent.

Take the road east from Narupa to Coca to begin the ascent. Ask for guides in the Kichwa settlement of Wawa Sumaco; the guard post and visitor's center is just a few hundred meters from the main road, up the entry to Pacto Sumaco. Guides cost around $38 pp per day, which includes food and accommodations in refuges.

For further information, call the park's office in Tena (tel. 6/288-8497, www.sumaco. org). Three basic refuges ($3 pp) within the park are poorly maintained but dry.

Wildsumaco Lodge

Nearly seven kilometers from Wawa Sumaco, this Swedish- and American-run lodge (office: tel. 2/244-6175, lodge: tel. 6/301-8343, www.wildsumaco.com, $120 pp) offers superb bird-watching, great views over the forest, and extensive forest trails. There are 10 comfortable double cabins and a dining area with a fireplace, plus a spotters' deck at canopy level, where birders can locate such special finds as the yellow-throated spadebill, gray-tailed *piha,* military macaw, coppery-chested jacamar, Napo sabrewing, chestnut-crowned gnateater, and more than 370 other species. Rates include all meals, transportation from Narupa or Coca, and a local guide; specialized bird guides are available. Information about the lodge's foundation, which accepts volunteers, can be found at www.riopucunofoundation.org.

Archidona and the Jumandy Caves

Some 10 kilometers north of Tena, the small town of Archidona sits quietly away from the tourist crowds. The town has a rather curious striped brown-and-white church and a pleasant square, but the main reason to come here is to visit the caves, four kilometers north of town on the Baeza–Tena road.

Las Cavernas de Jumandy are the largest caves in the region, set in an eight-hectare tourist complex (9 A.M.–5 P.M. daily, $2 pp). A slow river flows out of a large, dark opening in the hillside, filling a pool equipped with waterslides and surrounded by playgrounds and sports fields. There's also a restaurant and a bar.

The main cave is named after a warrior chief who supposedly hid here before leading an uprising against the Spanish in 1578. The beginning section is heavily trafficked, illuminated, and riddled with graffiti, but the entire complex extends for kilometers underground, and guides can lead you much farther. Three hundred meters in, you have to swim across a small lake, and that's just the beginning. The complex also has a hotel (tel. 6/288-9185, $10 pp) with private guest rooms with hot water.

☾ TENA

Wherever you're traveling from—Puyo, Coca, or Baeza—reaching Tena (pop. 27,000, elevation 500 meters) is likely to be a pleasant surprise. While many of Ecuador's rainforest towns are unsightly, to say the least, Tena is a tranquil, orderly town with an attractive location on the confluence of the Ríos Tena and Pano. Forest sprouts from its edges while rivers and their tributaries gush down to the Amazon basin to the east.

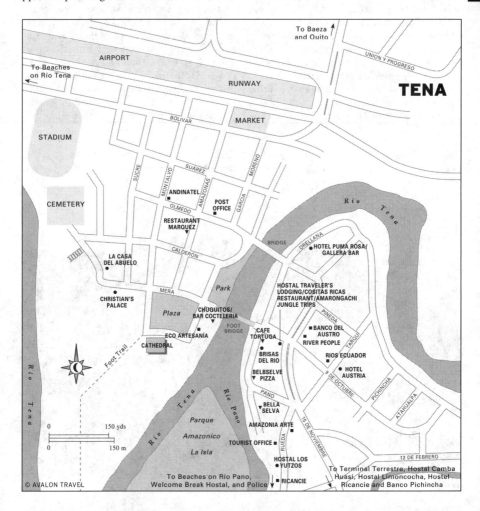

© AVALON TRAVEL

The capital of Napo Province as well as a gateway to the rainforest, Tena is a great place to base yourself for a few days, either to book a rainforest tour or to go racing down the rapids on rafts or kayaks; Tena is Ecuador's undisputed water-sports capital.

Tena is one of the Oriente's oldest towns, founded in the 16th century as a missionary and trading outpost, about as far into the forest as the Spanish were willing to settle. Unlike Lago Agrio and Coca, which developed quickly on the back of the recent oil boom, Tena has developed at a sustainable rate and retained its strong identity—the indigenous monument in the main square is just one example. Walking along the riverside promenade is a relaxing experience, and tourism amenities are also of a higher standard and wider range than in other rainforest towns, with plenty of good hotels, restaurants, and tour operators.

Sights

The town's Parque Central is a pleasant place to sit and take in the surroundings, including the indigenous monument at the center and the Cathedral on the west side, from where you can often hear services resonate through the town in the early mornings. The *malecón* on either side of the river is also ideal for a stroll to take in the views.

At the south end of town, where the Pano River joins the Tena, a small island has been converted into a rainforest-style park, **Parque Amazonico La Isla** (8:30 A.M.–6 P.M. daily, $1 pp). Gravel paths wander through 22 forested hectares past enclosures with native animals, including a jaguarundi, a tapir, and several monkeys, one of whom is notoriously bad-tempered. There is a canopy view from the *mirador,* and an ornamental and medicinal plant garden. Note that in 2010 the bridge to La Isla was washed away after heavy rains, and until the bridge is rebuilt, visitors need to pass by the tourist office to arrange a short canoe ride across the river.

Entertainment and Events

Discoteca Gallera (Orellana, tel. 6/287-0311,

© BEN WESTWOOD

Tena's riverside location makes it the Oriente's prettiest town.

8:30 P.M.–2 A.M. Fri.–Sat., $2 pp) at the Hotel Puma Rosa is one of the city's largest and most popular discos. For a quieter evening overlooking the river, try **Bar Cocteleria** below Chuquitos restaurant (García Moreno, tel. 6/288-7630, 5 P.M.–late daily). Tena celebrates its **founding** on November 15.

Shopping

You'll find Tena's best selection of souvenirs, particularly woven bags and jewelry, at **Eco Artesania** (no phone) on the main plaza. **Amazonia Arte** (15 de Noviembre, no phone) is another good store for handmade jewelry and various artisanal crafts.

Recreation and Tours

Operating out of the Hostal Traveller's Lodging, **Amarongachi Jungle Trips** (15 de Noviembre and 9 de Octubre, tel./fax 6/288-6372, www.amarongachi.com) offers recommended tours within a relatively short distance of town, including a four-day trip ($160 pp) visiting Lowland Kichwa communities and viewing wildlife from the Cabañas Shangri-La atop a 150-meter riverside cliff. Amarongachi also offers rafting, canyoneering, and rainforest treks.

RICANCIE (Agusto Rueda, tel. 6/288-8479, ricancie@hotmail.com, www.ricancie.nativeweb.org) is a network of 10 Kichwa communities along the upper Río Napo that offers hiking, canoeing, and explanations of traditional lifestyles and medicine during well-run 2–7-day programs (from $30 pp per day). You can pick the minds of local experts about medicinal plants and forest life, visit a shaman, learn to make pottery, play traditional music, or participate in a *minga* (communal work event). Some of the guides speak a little English, but you'll get more out of the experience if you or someone in your group knows some Spanish, or if you ask for a translator.

Tena has developed into Ecuador's watersports capital, and there is excellent **whitewater rafting** and **kayaking** nearby. Day trips ($55–70 pp) and two-day trips (from $130 pp) are available and include overnight camping.

The most famous stretches of river are along the Jondachi and Jatunyacu (both Class 3), and the wilder Misahuallí and Hollín (Class 4). Be sure to book with one of the reputable operators in town, ideally accredited by AGAR. Recommended operators include British-run **River People** (15 de Noviembre and 9 de Octubre, tel. 6/288-8384, www.riverpeoplerafting.com) and **Ríos Ecuador** (Tarqui, tel. 6/288-6727, or Quito tel. 2/290-4054, www.riosecuador.com).

Accommodations

One of the best budget options is **A Welcome Break** (Agusto Rueda and 12 de Febrero, tel. 6/288-6301, $6–10 pp) in a quiet location just south of the center. Guests can use the kitchen, and there's a good restaurant attached.

More centrally located is **Hostal Traveller's Lodging** (15 de Noviembre and 9 de Octubre, tel. 6/288-6372, $7–13 pp), a backpacker favorite offering good value. Guest rooms downstairs have cold-water showers, fans, and TVs, while more comfortable guest rooms upstairs have hot water and air-conditioning, and some have river views. Cositas Ricas Restaurant and Amarongachi Jungle Trips operate out of the same building, and you can book tours to the stunning rainforest lodge, Cabañas Shangri-La.

Directly on the *malecón* is **Hostal Brisa del Rio** (Orellana, tel. 6/288-6444, $8–13 pp), a friendly place with good-value guest rooms with a choice of shared or private baths.

On the hill out of town, catching the breeze and enjoying the quiet is the efficient German-run **Hostal Limoncocha** (tel. 6/288-7583, http://limoncocha.tripod.com, $6–8 s, $15 d). Guest rooms have private baths and fans, and a small terrace is available for sitting and watching the sunset. The lodge can arrange rainforest tours to Limoncocha Reserve as well as rafting and kayaking tours.

In the mid-range, a good choice is **Hotel Christian's Palace** (Mera and Sucre, tel. 6/288-6047, $25 s, $44 d), with comfortable guest rooms and a pool, a sauna, and a gym at the back. Guest rooms at the **Hotel Puma**

Rosa (Orellana, tel. 6/287-0311, $15 s, $25 d) are centered around a plant-filled courtyard. Guest rooms have private baths, hot water, and cable TV, and the on-site disco creates a party atmosphere on weekends. For a more intimate family atmosphere, head to **La Casa del Abuelo** (Mera, tel. 6/288-6318, $17 s, $24 d) for quiet guest rooms with wood furnishings. The guest rooms upstairs are better. Prices are the same at the sister hotel **Establo de Tomas** (tel. 6/288-6318, $17 s, $24 d) on the edge of the rainforest outside town.

Perhaps the most attractive lodging in Tena can be found at the **(Hostal Los Yutzos** (Agusto Rueda and 15 de Noviembre, tel. 6/288-6717, www.uchutican.com/yutzos, $24–36 s, $40–48 d, breakfast included). Overlooking the Río Pano and Parque La Isla, guest rooms are set among leafy gardens and well equipped with private baths, cable TV, hot water, and refrigerators.

Food

Tena has a decent number of good, inexpensive eateries. One of the best in terms of location is **Café Tortuga** (Orellana, tel. 9/529-5419, 7:30 A.M.–9 P.M. daily, entrées $2–4), which overlooks the river and serves a huge range of cheap fare, including pancakes, salads, burgers, and pasta. The **Cositas Ricas Restaurant** (15 de Noviembre and 9 de Octubre, tel. 6/288-6372, 7:30 A.M.–9:30 P.M. daily, entrées $4–6, set lunch $2.75) in the Hostal Traveller's Lodging serves generous breakfasts and cheap meals, including pizza, vegetarian items, chicken, fish, and meat.

(Chuquitos (García Moreno, tel. 6/288-7630, 7:30 A.M.–9:30 P.M. daily, entrées $6–7), a local favorite below the plaza, has a great riverside location and serves large portions of seafood, meat, and Chinese items. The tilapia is particularly good.

For Italian food, **Pizza Bella Selva** (Orellana and Pano, tel. 6/288-7964, 10 A.M.–midnight daily, entrées $2–14) serves up great pizza and pasta.

Fine dining is hard to come by in the Oriente, but **(Marquis Grille** (Amazonas, tel. 6/288-6513, noon–3 P.M. and 6–11 P.M. daily, entrées $8–20) is the best restaurant for kilometers. With attentive service, walls adorned with rainforest scenery, a couple of resident sloths, and a wide range of fine cuisine, including filet mignon and paella, this is the best place in town by far.

Information and Services

The staff at Tena's **tourist office** (Agusto Rueda, tel. 6/288-8046, 7:30 A.M.–12:30 P.M. and 2–5 P.M. Mon.–Fri.), near Hostal Los Yutzos, are friendly and helpful. They offer a free map and city brochure and can direct you to the best tour operators in town.

Travelers can change money at **Banco del Austro** (15 de Noviembre, between the bridges). The local **police station** (Agusto Rueda and Segundo Baquero) is at the south end of town, and the **post office** (Olmedo near Amazonas) is northwest of the footbridge. The **hospital** (tel. 6/288-6305) is south of town on the road to Puerto Napo.

Getting There and Around

The **terminal terrestre** bus terminal sits about one kilometer south of the footbridge on 15 de Noviembre. Local buses labeled "Terminal" run down 15 de Noviembre. Buses run to Quito (5 hours, $6), Baeza (3 hours, $3), Puyo (2.5 hours, $2.50), Baños (4 hours, $4), Coca (4.5 hours, $7), and Lago Agrio (7 hours, $8). Buses to Misahualli (40 minutes, $0.80) pass the bus stop on 15 de Noviembre in front of the terminal more or less hourly. Buses to Archidona and the Jumandy Caves leave often from the corner of Bolívar and Amazonas. Taxis to the terminal and to most destinations around town cost $1.

MISAHUALLI

Misahualli, still officially known as Puerto Napo, clings to its past status as the main port on the upper Río Napo, but there's no escaping that this small town, seven kilometers south of Tena, has seen better days. Most of the tourist traffic has switched to Tena or flies in through Coca, and fewer visitors come through Misahualli. There's still something appealing

© BEN WESTWOOD

Capuchin monkeys in Misahualli are infamous for making mischief.

about this sleepy backwater, however, and taking a boat downriver from here is a cheaper way to reach pockets of primary rainforest.

The town itself has a small main square on the banks of the Río Misahualli. There's a small selection of accommodations, restaurants, and a couple of tour operators. Just beyond the square, there are regular services downstream from the docks to indigenous communities, the butterfly garden, and a couple of lodges. The footbridge over the Napo makes it possible to walk over to the southern bank of the river and down to Jatun Sacha for a visit to the reserve.

The most famous—and notorious—residents of Misahualli are the monkeys. This troop of more than 20 capuchin monkeys takes over the square most days, especially in the early morning and early evening, and are well-known for making mischief—from swiping a soda to opening bags and making off with belongings. The monkeys can become aggressive if provoked, and it's no joke if they take something of value because you're unlikely to get it back without a fight (and possibly a rabies shot).

Recreation and Tours

One of the best excursions from Misahualli is **El Camino a Las Cascadas,** a waterfall hike that starts seven kilometers west of town on the road to Puerto Napo where a bridge crosses the Río Latas. Follow the river upstream on a muddy path past smaller falls to the big one with a swimming hole at the base.

Roughly four kilometers out of town on the road to Tena is a **butterfly farm** (8 A.M.–1 P.M. and 3–5 P.M. daily, $2.50), opened by Pepe Tapia González of Ecoselva. The large mesh enclosure has 15 species of *mariposas,* with more on the way as appropriate food and cocoon plants are added. Take a bus headed to Tena, or a taxi ($2.50).

You can organize rainforest tours out of Misahualli, but visitor numbers are quite low here, making it harder to put a group together. It's easier to join a group in Tena, and some tours arranged in Tena start in Misahualli.

Ecoselva (tel. 6/289-0019, ecoselva@yahoo. es), below Hostal Shaw on the main square, is an excellent agency run by the friendly and highly regarded English-speaking biologist Pepe Tapia González. Tours lasting 1–10 days ($35–50 pp per day) are available.

Expediciones Douglas Clark (tel. 6/289-0085, douglasclarkeexpediciones@yahoo. com), another good choice, has been run by Ecuadorian Douglas Clark for more than two decades. Operating out of his Hotel Marena Internacional, Douglas runs tours ($35–50 pp per day) to his Cabañas Sinchi Runa, south of Misahualli at the confluence of the Ríos Arajuno and Puni, as well as to Pañacocha and the Río Yasuní.

Teodoro Rivadeneyra, President of Napo Guides Association, runs **Teorumi** (tel. 6/289-0313, teorumi@yahoo.com, www.teorumi. com) just off the main plaza. He speaks fluent English and offers a wide selection of tours ($40–60 pp), including one to the Shiripuno community.

Accommodations and Food
The least expensive hotels and restaurants crowd the plaza. Run by Ecoselva, **Hostal Shaw** (Plaza de Misahualli, tel. 6/289-0019, $8 pp) has simple guest rooms with fans and private baths. Downstairs, the café offers a wide selection of meals. Just off the plaza, rainforest guide Douglas Clark's **Hostal Clarke's** (Juana Arteaga and José Antonio Santander, tel. 6/289-0085, $12 pp) has the best budget rooms in town and a large swimming pool.

The main plaza has plenty of standard eateries. The pick of the bunch is probably **Doña Gloria** (Plaza de Misahualli, tel. 6/289-0100, breakfast, lunch, and dinner daily, entrées $5–6, set lunch $2.75) which serves a wide range of chicken, meat, and river fish.

About 100 meters up the road toward Puerto Napo, you'll pass the **Albergue Español** (Av. Principal, tel. 6/289-0127, www.alberguesspanol.com, $12 pp, breakfast included), which has good guest rooms, some with views of the Río Napo ($8 pp). The hotel owns the 1,000-hectare Jaguar Reserve. Two-night tours

cost $130 pp, or take a day trip. Five hundred meters farther brings you to the hotel **France Amazonia** (Av. Principal, tel. 6/289-0009, www.france-amazonia.com, $24 s, $36 d, breakfast included), which has comfortable guest rooms and a pool.

If you keep going and take a right at the fork in the road (the road straight ahead goes to Puerto Napo), in just over two kilometers you'll reach **El Jardín Alemán** (Tomás Bermur 22 at Urrutia, tel. 2/224-7878 or 6/289-0122, www.eljardinaleman.com, $84 pp). A main lodge with satellite TV, a restaurant, a bar, and laundry facilities sits on 125 hectares of primary and secondary rainforest on the west bank of the Río Misahualli. Suites and double rooms are equipped with fans, terraces, and private baths. There is a good restaurant, a sun terrace, and an outdoor jetted tub. A wide range of tours include horseback riding into the forest, rafting on the river, or panning for gold.

The 🦜 **Misahualli Jungle Lodge** (Quito office: Enrique Iturralde and Av. de la Prensa, tel. 2/224-9651 or 6/289-0063, www.misahuallirainforest.com, $57 pp, breakfast included) occupies a tranquil clearing in a 145-hectare preserve across the Río Misahualli from town. Guests are free to wander along well-marked trails into the forest, chat, read, and relax in front of the satellite TV in the central building, or do laps in the pool. Drop-ins are welcome, and it's worth making an afternoon visit from Misahualli. A regular canoe service ($0.50) runs until 9 P.M.

Getting There and Around
Buses from Tena (40 minutes, $0.80) circle the plaza before heading back out of town roughly every hour. The rocky sandbar at the confluence of Ríos Napo and Misahualli is usually occupied by **motor canoes** waiting to depart to lodges and villages downriver. Prices are fixed, but ask in town beforehand to avoid being overcharged. Boat services run to Coca when there are enough passengers. Most places in town are within walking distance, but ask around for taxis farther afield, which can

usually be arranged from one of the tour operator's offices.

UPPER RÍO NAPO

From Puerto Napo to Coca, the river is the main artery of life, bringing water and nutrients to the forest, supplies to the colonists, and visitors to the lodges. This stretch is narrower and wilder than the river below Coca, twisting around islands as it rises and falls abruptly in response to rainfall and drought.

Oil prospecting brought the first wave of settlers to the area decades ago when towns like Misahualli consisted of little more than a crossroads and a general store. Recent roads

east from Puerto Napo have opened the region even more to colonization, agriculture, and cattle ranching.

Today, almost all of the rainforest along the first 50 or so kilometers of the river has been disturbed in some way, except for small protected areas around the lodges and Jatun Sacha. The rainforest becomes more pristine farther downriver and away from the banks of the upper stretch.

Jatun Sacha Biological Station

Ecuador's premier tropical field research station was begun in 1985 by an Ecuadorian and two North Americans, who gained title to 140

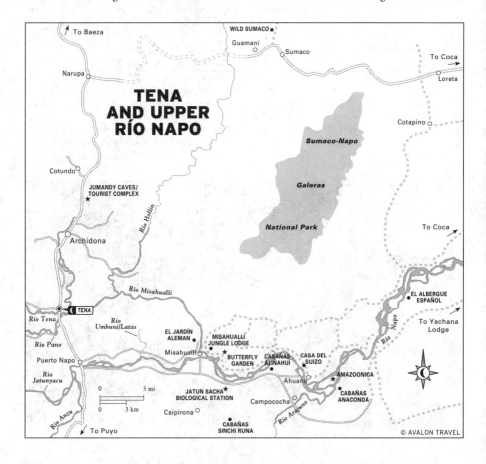

hectares of forest along the upper Río Napo. With the help of various foreign organizations and charities, the nonprofit **Fundación Jatun Sacha** (Pasaje Eugenio de Santillán N34-28 and Maurián, Urb. Rumipamba, Quito, tel. 2/243-2240, www.jatunsacha.org) was created in 1989 to manage the field station and promote conservation of and education about the rainforest to Ecuadorians and foreigners alike.

Now Jatun Sacha is one of the most prestigious tropical research stations in South America, welcoming scientists and visitors to its 2,500 hectares of protected rainforest. The name means "big forest" in Kichwa, and indeed 80 percent of Jatun Sacha's holdings are undisturbed primary rainforest, forming a transitional zone between the lower slopes of the Andes and the true Amazon lowlands farther east.

Facilities for visiting scientists and students consist of bunk beds in raised wooden cabins, along with a main building with a dining hall, kitchen, bathrooms, electricity, and a modest library. Well-maintained trails lead to the river and a 30-meter canopy observation tower.

Volunteer positions are available in education, station maintenance, and conservation, as well as at the station's Amazon Plant Conservation Center, an experimental medicinal garden completed in 1993. A fee of $312 pp for two weeks, payable in advance, covers meals and lodging.

Jatun Sacha is 22 kilometers east of the bridge over the river at Puerto Napo; it is marked by a sign on the right-hand side of the road. Buses from Tena headed for the villages of Campococha or Ahuano pass the entrance to the station (look for the "Centinela de Tena" bus in Tena's main terminal). Overnight stays cost $30 pp, including three meals; guides cost $30 per group, and day entrance costs $6 pp, including a map. A taxi from Misahualli costs $5.

Cabañas Aliñahui and Butterfly Lodge

This former cattle ranch evolved into an ecologically minded lodge in the mid-1990s and was run by Jatun Sacha until 2005. There are eight comfortable cabins set in 100 hectares of forest. Three lookout towers command fabulous views of the surrounding rainforest and distant ice-capped volcanoes, which gave the

© BEN WESTWOOD

Predators are deterred by owl butterflies' distinctive wings.

cabins their Kichwa name, "beautiful view." Rainwater fills the toilets and sinks, solar power provides the electricity, and septic tanks take care of waste. The food is simple and wholesome, and an evening drink at the bar goes well with the muted roar of the forest.

A wide range of activities starts with visits to Jatun Sacha, a few hours by foot along the side of the river. Aliñahui is also known as the Butterfly Lodge due to the 750 species of butterflies found along self-guided trails that wind through the forest. More than 100 species of orchids have also been found nearby. Excursions to indigenous communities and caves by canoe or on horseback can be arranged.

Three-day (from $165 pp) and five-day ($240 pp) tours are possible, and you can visit Aliñahui on your own ($50 pp per day, meals included). Reservations and information are handled through the Aliñahui office in Quito (Inglaterra 1373 at Amazonas, tel. 2/227-4510, www.ecuadoramazonlodge.com).

To reach the cabins, take the road east from Puerto Napo along the south bank of the Río Napo. After 25 kilometers, a turnoff heads north 1.5 kilometers to the bridge over the river. Five or so buses per day leave Tena heading to Santa Rosa or Ahuano, or take a public canoe from Misahualli.

CASA DEL SUIZO

For a pampered rainforest experience, stay at the Casa del Suizo. Owned by an Ecuadorian-Swiss partnership that also owns Sacha Lodge east of Coca, this elegant lodge offers 20 guest rooms and 30 cabins on the Río Napo's north bank near Ahuano. With superb buffet-style food, a pool, and a bar, you could almost forget you're in the rainforest.

The immediate area isn't as pristine as it once was, and it is not great for wildlife viewing, so cultural tours are more the focus. Visits to a local Kichwa village are one possible activity, as are rainforest hikes and views from the *mirador* (balcony) topping the three-story main building are wonderful. The lodge is also relatively easy to reach, making it the perfect place for those who want to see the forest without

much effort or discomfort. Lodging ($94 pp per night) includes food and guides. Three-day tours ($455 pp) include transfers from Quito. Make reservations through the office in Quito (Julio Zaldumbide 397 at Valladolid, tel. 2/256-6090, www.casadelsuizo.com).

Cabañas Albergue Español

One of the oldest lodges in the Ecuadorian Amazon is just under two hours downriver from Misahualli. Set on 1,000 hectares of primary forest, this historic place, once known as Jaguar Lodge, has been in business since 1969. It is now owned by the same owners as El Albergue Español. Ten cabins blend wooden beams and clean white walls, and each has a private bath with hot water.

Thanks to the hotel's relative isolation, primary rainforest nearby can be explored on foot and by canoe. Rainforest treks and visits to Kichwa villages with local guides are all included in the surprisingly reasonably priced visits of two nights ($130 pp) or four nights ($220 pp). Transportation isn't included unless there are at least four in the group, so factor in another $90 per group for the trip by private canoe. Reserve through El Albergue Español (tel. 6/289-0127 or 6/289-0004, www.alber-gueespanol.com).

PUYO

If you're arriving from Tena or Baños, at first glance Puyo (pop. 37,000) will fail to impress. The capital of Pastaza Province is a busy, congested town with a center filled with concrete buildings and too much traffic. Look farther, however, to the edges of town, and Puyo has parks, wildlife sanctuaries, and indigenous communities, and it serves as a gateway to "rainforest-lite" tours from nearby Baños.

The nearby military airfield at Shell also keeps Puyo busy with missionaries, oil companies, local indigenous people, and visitors all passing through on their way to the rainforest.

The climate here also reminds you that you're in the rainforest: the town's name means "cloudy" in a local language, and wet weather is the norm, although at 950 meters above sea level, it's cooler here than in the northern rainforest towns.

Sights

There's very little to see in the center of Puyo, but it's worth stopping by the **Museo Etnoarqueológico** (Atahualpa and 9 de Octubre, tel. 3/288-5605, 8 A.M.–4 P.M. daily, free), which has a small exhibition of indigenous dwellings.

The most interesting sights are on the edge of town. Walking north from the center along Calle Loja for about 500 meters brings you to a rickety bridge across the river, and beyond it is the **Pedagogical Ethnobotanical OMAERE Park** (tel. 3/288-7656 or 3/288-9582, www.fundacionomaere.org, 9 A.M.–5 P.M. Tues.–Sun., $3 pp, minimum group price $5), a small botanical reserve with some 1,000 species of Amazonian plants used by indigenous people. Five of the 15.6 hectares are primary rainforest, and a team of indigenous guides are on hand to lead you through the forest past indigenous dwellings. It's an educational experience and a welcome glimpse of the rainforest if you're not traveling deeper into the Oriente. Past the park, there is a new walkway built by the local government running along the river for a couple of kilometers, emerging on the main road to Tena.

On the other side of town on the road to Macas is **El Jardín Botánico Las Orquideas** (tel. 3/288-4855, 8:30 A.M.–4 P.M. Mon.–Sat., 8:30 A.M.–noon Sun., $5), with 300 orchid species and endangered rainforest plants. Look for the bus to "Los Angeles," and ask to be dropped off at Las Orquideas, about a 10-minute ride. A taxi costs $2–3.

Farther along the road to Macas is the rescue center **Paseo de los Monos** (tel. 9/474-0070, 8 A.M.–5 P.M. daily, $2), where confiscated and maltreated monkeys are cared for and allowed to roam free on a privately owned reserve. The bus to Arajuno goes right by the entrance (look for the sign). A taxi from Puyo costs about $5.

Another popular day trip is to **Fundación**

Hola Vida (8 A.M.–5 P.M. daily, $1.50), with trails through 225 hectares of secondary rainforest and a beautiful waterfall, 27 kilometers south of Puyo. A taxi from Puyo costs $10 each way.

Recreation and Tours

Most travelers book rainforest tours from Quito or Baños, but Puyo has plenty of reputable operators with options ranging from short community tours close to town to visits to far-flung communities such as the Huaorani, only reachable by light aircraft from the Shell airport, 10 kilometers west of town.

Run by the Sarayaku community, **Papangu Tours** (27 de Febrero and Sucre, tel. 3/288-7684, www.sarayaku.com) has been recommended for tours to Kichwa and Shuar communities near Puyo. Tours include a three-day visit to a Shuar community ($65 pp per day, 3-person minimum), four hours from Puyo by car and on foot. Four-day tours to Sarayaku ($508 pp) involve a return flight from Shell. Trips can be tailored to the group's interests, but English-speaking guides cost an extra $40 pp per day for a minimum of four people.

Diego Escobar, a local environmentalist, runs **Madre Selva** (Ceslao Marín 668, tel. 3/289-0449, www.madreselvaecuador.com), which offers 1–4-day tours (from $35 pp per day). English-speaking, licensed guides are available. **Selva Vida** (Ceslao Marín and Atahualpa, tel. 3/288-9729, www.selvavida-travel.com) offers a range of tours ($30–40 pp per day) close to Puyo. Four-day tours to Huaorani communities ($800 pp) include round-trip airfare. **Amazonía** (Atahualpa and 9 de Octubre, tel. 3/288-3219) offers a similar range of tours.

Accommodations

If you came to Puyo, you want to experience forest, not concrete, so it's best to avoid the hotels in the center. If you must, one of the best budget hotels in town is the **Hotel Araucano** (Ceslao Marín and 27 de Febrero, tel. 3/288-5686, $8 pp, breakfast included), with cozy but basic guest rooms with private baths and hot water. You can add a TV for $2 more.

By far the best place to stay in the center is **Hostería Turingia** (Ceslao Marín and Orellana, tel. 3/288-5180, $25 s, $40 d), one of the oldest hotels in town, dating from 1955. It features alpine-style cabins surrounded by flowers, with a pool, a bar, a patio, and "Sneaky" the boa constrictor.

You're far better off heading north of the center for the pick of Puyo's lodging options. **Posada Real** (4 de Enero and 9 de Octubre, tel. 3/288-5887, $25 pp, breakfast included) is a beautiful mustard-colored colonial house with plush guest rooms. **Las Palmas** (20 de Julio and 4 de Enero, tel. 3/288-4832, $12 pp, breakfast included), an attractive yellow colonial-style building with parrots in the back gardens, is more economical.

Walking north of town on Calle Loja, **El Pigual** (Tungurahua, tel. 3/288-7972, www.elpigualecuador.com, $62 s, $102 d, breakfast included) is one of the fanciest places in town, with a pool, a sauna, a steam bath, and a volleyball court.

Cross the bridge, and just before reaching OMAERE Park, there are a couple of *hosterías*.

The best is **℄ El Jardín** (Obrero, tel. 3/288-7770, $33 pp, breakfast included), with comfortable modern guest rooms in a rustic wooden building overlooking charming gardens where parrots and parakeets chatter. The restaurant is one of the best in the area.

Food

The best food in Puyo is found at **℄ El Jardín** (Obrero, tel. 3/288-7770, noon–4 P.M. and 6–10 P.M. Mon.–Sat., noon–4 P.M. Sun., entrées $7–12), north of town by the river. The specialties of award-winning chef Sofia include *pollo ishpingo* (chicken in cinnamon), pork in plum sauce, and trout in ginger.

In town, there are dozens of *comedores* and cheap restaurants lining Atahualpa, as well as 24 de Mayo between 27 de Febrero and 9 de Octubre. For the best of traditional rainforest fare, try **El Fogón** (Atahualpa and 27 de Febrero, tel. 8/494-8156, noon–3 P.M. and 6–9 P.M. daily, entrées $3–6), formerly El Toro Asado. Specialties include filet mignon and, for the more adventurous, *guanta,* an Amazonian rodent.

© BEN WESTWOOD

parrots at El Jardín near Puyo

For more refined (and expensive) fare, stop by the restaurant at the **Hostería Turingia** (Ceslao Marín and Orellana, tel. 3/288-5180, 8 A.M.–9 P.M. daily, entrées $5–10). For an authentic Neapolitan pizza or Italian dinner, head to **O'Sole Mio** (Pichincha and Guaranda, tel. 3/288-4768, 6–10 P.M. Wed.–Sun., entrées $5–7).

Information and Services

Banco de Pichincha (10 de Agosto) and **Banco del Austro** (Atahualpa) both have ATMS. The **Ministerío de Turismo** (Atahualpa and Marín, tel. 3/288-3681) offers a slim selection of maps of the area, or visit the **Itur** office (Orellana and 9 de Octubre, tel. 3/288-5122, ext. 111, 8 A.M.–4 P.M. Mon.–Fri.) next to the market.

There's a **police station** (9 de Octubre, tel. 3/288-5102) one block north of the main plaza. The **hospital** (tel. 3/288-3873) is also on 9 de Octubre, and the **post office** is at 27 de Febrero and Atahualpa.

For the best artisanal wares, head to **AMWAE** (Atahualpa and Villamil, tel. 3/288-8908), where traditional Huaorani products, including jewelry, hammocks, and even blowguns, are sold.

Further information about Huaorani communities can be obtained from the political body ONHAE (tel. 3/288-6148).

Getting There and Around

The main **bus terminal** is south of the town center and can be reached by buses marked "Terminal," running down 9 de Octubre every 15 minutes. Direct lines go to most major cities in the highlands and on the coast, including Baños (1.5 hours, $2), Tena (2.5 hours, $3), Macas (4 hours, $5), Ambato (3 hours, $3), Ríobamba (4 hours, $4), Quito (5 hours, $5), and Guayaquil (8 hours, $9).

A taxi trip within the city limits, including out to the bus station, costs about $1, and $2–4 for attractions on the edge of town.

Southern Oriente

South of Puyo is the road less traveled, and Morona-Santiago is one of Ecuador's remotest provinces. The capital, Macas, is the only significant town in this region and one of the least visited rainforest towns, although there are more tours available to local communities than in the past. Improvements to the road from Puyo may also lead to Macas gaining a gradual increase in tourism traffic, but for now it remains refreshingly remote. Far to the east, where the Río Pastaza reaches the Peruvian border, Kapawi Eco-Lodge, one of the best in Ecuador, sits in splendid isolation. The region south of Macas was the focus of fighting between Ecuador and Peru in the 1980s and is even more remote.

MACAS AND VICINITY

Macas (pop. 23,000) sees the least tourism traffic of all the main rainforest towns, which may suit you. If you're coming from Cuenca or even Riobamba, Macas is the closest rainforest

town, and both roads promise a spectacular descent from the Andes to the Oriente through Sangay National Park.

The capital of Morona-Santiago Province is perhaps the most pleasant rainforest town, along with Tena. Macas has a beautiful setting, a mild climate at over 1,000 meters elevation, along with friendly inhabitants, and it is surprisingly clean. To the east, the Río Upano meanders through a wide valley separating the Cordillera de Cutucú from the Andes, which loom to the west beyond the airport and the small Río Surumbaino. It's worth a walk to the quiet, residential south end of Macas for a view of the hills and the river.

The serene landscape belies a troubled past, though. The original settlement was destroyed at the turn of the 17th century in a Shuar uprising, then rebuilt, only to endure repeated attacks through the 19th century. A foot trail to Riobamba was the only link to the outside

SPEAKING ACHUAR

- *wiña jai* – good morning/afternoon/ evening
- *ja ai* – yes
- *atsa* – no
- *yaitiam* – What is your name?
- *wiyait jai...* – My name is...
- *wetai* – Let's go
- *yumi* – water
- *yurumak* – food
- *maketai* – thank you
- *wea jai* – good-bye

Arqueológico Municipal (Mon.–Fri., free). The exhibition of Shuar culture includes blow-pipes, funeral urns, and headdresses made of animal heads.

For the best views of the surrounding mountains to the west and rainforest to the east, head five blocks north along Don Bosco adjacent to the river to the lookout at **Parque Recreacional.** Volcán Sangay, Ecuador's seventh-highest mountain at 5,230 meters, can be seen on clear days 40 kilometers to the northwest.

Entertainment

Macas is not overflowing with night-time action, but for after-dinner drinks and live music on weekends, head to **Café Bar La Maravilla** (Soasti and Sucre, tel. 7/270-0158, 4 P.M.–midnight Mon.–Sat., entrées $3–6). The main disco in town is **Acuario** (Sucre, tel. 7/270-1601, 9 P.M.–2 A.M. Thurs.–Sat.).

Visiting Shuar Villages

Macas is a good starting point to explore the southern Oriente and to arrange stays in Shuar villages. Note that while the days of shrinking the heads of intruders have long since passed, to visit indigenous territories you must go on an organized tour. If you aren't traveling in a group, also note that rainforest tours are less frequent from Macas than from other towns, so patience and flexibility are required.

Remote Shuar communities are situated mainly to the east of the town. The closest community is at **Buena Esperanza,** a two-hour drive and one-hour hike to the northeast, where you can try killing pieces of fruit with a blowpipe as well as hiking in the rainforest and riding canoes. Another accessible village is **Kunkup,** a two-hour bus ride and one-hour hike to the north.

Deeper in the rainforest, involving a one-hour bus ride and a three-hour hike, is **Macuma,** set in primary rainforest, where you can learn about hunting and fishing techniques and go on rainforest hikes to waterfalls.

One of the more remote, accessible Shuar villages is **Yaupi,** reachable on a 35-minute

world until well into the 1800s, and that trail is now essentially the route of the new road.

Macas was the nearest major town to the border fighting with Peru, which erupted most recently in 1995 before a peace treaty three years later finally laid the issue to rest.

The town's proud indigenous heritage is still strong, and local Shuar leaders have recently come into conflict with the national government. Macas was the scene of persistent demonstrations from 2009 through 2011 against plans to increase mining exploitation and gain control of the local water supply.

Sights

The modern **cathedral** on the **Parque Central** was finished in 1992 and boasts stained-glass windows worthy of a much larger temple. The hallowed image of La Purísima de Macas commemorates a vision of the Virgin that appeared to a local family in 1595, when the town was called Sevilla del Oro. From the main square, there are good views across the town to the hills beyond. Two blocks to the west is La Casa de Cultura, which contains the **Museo**

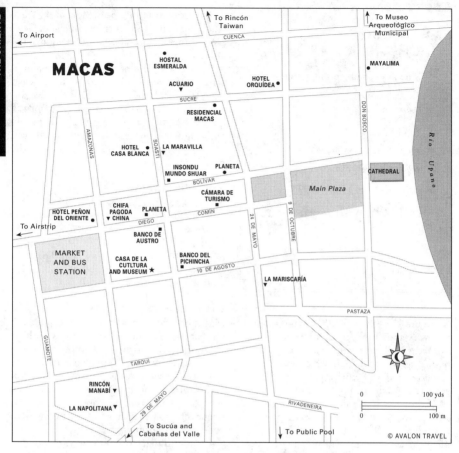

MACAS

To Airport

To Rincón
Taiwan

To Museo
Arqueológico
Municipal

CUENCA

HOSTAL
ESMERALDA

MAYALIMA

ACUARIO

HOTEL
ORQUÍDEA

SUCRE

RESIDENCIAL
MACAS

DON BOSCO

Río Upano

HOTEL
CASA BLANCA

SOASTI

LA MARAVILLA

INSONDU
MUNDO SHUAR

PLANETA

CÁMARA DE
TURISMO

CATHEDRAL

Main Plaza

BOLÍVAR

To Airstrip

HOTEL PEÑON
DEL ORIENTE

CHIFA
PAGODA
CHINA

PLANETA

COMÍN

AMAZONAS

DIEGO

BANCO DE
AUSTRO

24 DE MAYO

9 DE OCTUBRE

MARKET
AND BUS
STATION

CASA DE LA
CULTURA
AND MUSEUM ★

BANCO DEL
PICHINCHA

10 DE AGOSTO

LA MARISCARÍA

PASTAZA

GUAMOTE

TAROUI

RINCÓN
MANABÍ

RIVADENEIRA

0   100 yds

LA NAPOLITANA

28 DE MAYO

To Sucúa and
Cabañas del Valle

To Public Pool

0   100 m

© AVALON TRAVEL

flight from Macas or a seven-hour bus ride followed by a canoe ride. Lodging is usually with Shuar families living on the shores of Lake Kumpak, with night and day hikes in the rainforest.

Recommended local tour operators include **Planeta** (Comín and Soasti, tel. 7/270-1328, planeta_ms@hotmail.com) and **Insondu Mundo Shuar** (Bolívar and Soasti, tel. 7/270-2533, www.mundoshuar.com). Both run trips to the nearby Shuar communities and to Yaupi, where you can stay with an indigenous family (from $50 pp per day, transportation and guide included).

Recreation

As well as rainforest trips and community tours, there is rafting and tubing on nearby rivers, plus occasional tours to Parque Nacional Sangay. Rafting trips on the Río Upano are mostly seasonal (Nov.–Mar.) and require at least four people. Make arrangements in advance with **Yacu Amu** (Foch 746 at Amazonas, Quito, tel. 2/290-4054, www.yacuamu.com).

To reach the eastern slopes of **Sangay National Park,** head to the town of General Proaño, just north of Macas, where guides are available for hire. From here, a 90-minute bus

HEADHUNTERS:
SHRINKING THE MYTHS OF THE SHUAR

The Shuar are a subgroup of the Jivaro, who have lived for centuries in the rainforests of modern-day Ecuador and Peru. They were largely undisturbed by the Inca, but after the conquest, the Spanish quest for gold led to attempts at colonization. The Spanish started to impose new laws, including taxation, which deeply angered the Jivaro, renowned for their fierce combative nature. In 1599 a group of Jivaro warriors attacked the Spanish outpost of Logrono, killing thousands of settlers. The Spanish governor was allegedly killed by having molten gold poured down his throat until his bowels burst – a particularly gruesome attempt at poetic justice. Spanish colonization attempts, quite understandably, diminished after this incident, and the Jivaro acquired their reputation as the most brutal of South American tribes. They continued to fight among themselves, with constant clashes between the Shuar and neighboring Achuar.

The tradition of head-shrinking was very common; the Shuar believed that the souls of their enemies would take revenge after death, so they employed a special ceremony to sew shut the eyes and mouth of the victim to trap the soul inside. The head was then shrunk, and warriors carried the *tsantsa* as a trophy.

Things began to change in the latter 19th century when several brave Roman Catholic missionaries successfully contacted the Shuar. In 1935 the Ecuadorian government created a huge Shuar Reserve in the southern Oriente, but the discovery of oil in the 1970s led to further clashes with indigenous people resisting pressure to drill. These problems are ongoing today, and recent demonstrations erupted in violence in Macas in 2010.

The Shuar have many unique customs and beliefs. They use blowguns for hunting and often fish with their hands. They do not believe in natural death, believing instead that invisible darts or *tsentsaks* can be shot at victims using the help of a shaman to cause illness or even death.

While there is no evidence that the Shuar practice head-shrinking any more, they have found more useful ways to employ their warrior skills, with many joining the Ecuadorian army, famously outwitting the Peruvians in the 1995 Cenepa War. The highest honor is to be a warrior, and evidence of their fighting spirit is clear from their language. One common greeting – *pyngarek huma* – translates as "Are you tranquil?"

ride (twice a day, three days a week) can drop you at the trailheads near the village of 9 de Octubre. Plan on a minimum of 3–4 days for any excursion. Note that it's easier to access the national park from the highlands.

Accommodations

Macas has somewhat limited hotel offerings, but the range is improving slowly. Budget travelers should check out the **Residencial Macas** (Sucre and 24 de Mayo, tel. 7/270-0254, $12 s, $15 d), which has simple guest rooms with private baths and cable TV. **Hotel Orquidea** (Sucre and 9 de Octubre, tel. 7/270-0970, $11 pp) is another good budget option. One of the best in town is **Hostal Casa Blanca** (Soasti and Sucre, tel. 7/270-0195, $15 s, $25 d,

breakfast included), with decent guest rooms, a café, a small garden, and a swimming pool.

Food

Many of the best eateries in town are near the bus terminal. The **Chifa Pagoda China** (Amazonas and Comín, tel. 7/270-0280, 11 A.M.–10:30 P.M. daily, $4–6) is a very good Chinese restaurant, serving generous, tasty portions of *chaulafans* and *tallarines*. **Rincon Manabita** (Amazonas and Tarqui, tel. 7/270-2340, noon–10:30 P.M. daily, entrées $3–5) is popular for seafood. For the best Italian, try **La Napolitana** (Amazonas and Tarqui, tel. 7/270-0486, 8 A.M.–11 P.M. daily, entrées $3–9), which serves pizza, pasta, and barbecue as well as great fish, including tilapia and trout.

For a more creative atmosphere and some after-dinner drinks, head to **Café Bar La Maravilla** (Soasti and Sucre, tel. 7/270-0158, 4 P.M.–midnight Mon.–Sat., entrées $3–6). Adorned with indigenous artifacts, there's a variety of meat dishes, snacks, imaginative cocktails and juices, and live music on weekends.

Information and Services

The **Cámara de Turismo** (Comín, tel. 7/270-1606, www.macas.gov.ec, 8 A.M.–noon Mon.–Sat.) has brochures and advice on tours. **Banco de Austro** (Comín and Soasti) and **Banco del Pichincha** (10 de Agosto and Soasti) both have ATMs. The **post office** is on 9 de Octubre. There is a small **police station** in the bus terminal.

Getting There

The **bus terminal** is in the center of town. Buses run to Quito (8 hours, $8), Puyo (3 hours, $4), Riobamba (5 hours, $5), Cuenca (7 hours, $8), and Guayaquil (10 hours, $10).

TAME (tel. 7/270-1978) flies to Quito (Sun.–Fri., $77 pp one-way), and **SAEREO** (tel. 800/723-736, www.saereo.com) flies to Guayaquil (daily, $70 pp one-way).

SOUTH FROM MACAS

Twenty-three kilometers south of Macas is the village of **Sucúa,** the center of the Shuar Federation. Vendors sell traditional crafts, and visits to Shuar villages can be arranged through the office of the Shuar Federation (Domingo Comín 17-38, tel. 7/274-0108, www.ficsh.org.ec), three blocks south of the park.

A few meager hotels and restaurants cluster near the central plaza—try the **Hotel Romanza** (Olson and Carvajal, tel. 7/274-0943, $11 pp, breakfast included). **Tisho's Pizza** (Pastor Bernal and Sanguirama, tel. 7/274-0943, 11 A.M.–11 P.M. daily, entrées $3–5) is a good spot for Italian food.

Buses leave Sucúa for Macas every half hour from dawn to dusk (1 hour, $1).

The road southward follows the Río Upano, passing close to the town of **Méndez,** an attractive and peaceful town with a circular main plaza near the juncture of the Ríos Paute and Zapote. The road splits at Méndez. A side road heads south along the Río Namangoza, then east along the Río Santiago to the remote outpost of **Morona.** The road to Cuenca through Amaluza heads west from here, but it is not always passable in the rainy season, so inquire locally if the buses are going through.

Sixty-four kilometers before Morona is the settlement of **Santiago,** on the shore of the Río Santiago, where canoes and guides can be hired to visit **La Cueva de los Tayos** (Cave of the Oilbirds). These strange nocturnal birds use echolocation—like the clicks of bats and dolphins, except audible to humans—to find fruit by night and locate their nests deep within the earth. The high oil content of the birds' abdominal fat, a side effect of the oily palm fruits they eat, led *indígenas* and early settlers to boil the poor creatures down into an effective lamp fuel. Because it is 85 meters deep and black as night, you should venture into the cave only with a guide. Tour companies in Macas, including **Planeta** (Comín and Soasti, Macas, tel. 7/270-1328, planeta_ms@hotmail.com), can organize visits.

After 43 kilometers, the main road southwest from Méndez reaches **Limón** (official name: General Leónidas Plaza Gutiérrez), where you can find modest but comfortable rooms with shared bathrooms at the **Hotel Dreamhouse** (Quito and Bolívar, tel. 7/277-0166, $10 pp).

A spectacular road climbs west from the town to higher than 4,000 meters before descending to Gualaceo and Cuenca. At **Gualaquiza,** 80 kilometers farther south, you can stay at the modern, multilevel **Hotel Internacional** (Cuenca and Moreno, tel. 7/278-0637, $11 pp) with clean but small rooms. For nourishing sandwiches, breakfasts, and snacks, head to **Canela y Café** (Pezantez, tel. 7/278-0201, 9 A.M.–11 P.M. daily). From Gualaquiza's small bus terminal, south of the center, buses run to Loja (6 hours, $6), Zamora (4 hours, $4), and Cuenca (7 hours, $7).

SANGAY NATIONAL PARK

West of Macas, the enormous Sangay National Park protects 5,000 square kilometers of richly diverse landscapes, from the fiery peak of Volcán Tungurahua through *páramo* grasslands and Andean foothills to the edge of the Amazon basin. The lowland section of the park can be accessed from Macas, but tours are few and far between. It's heavy going and easy to get lost, so don't venture in without a compass and an IGM map. There is a park office in Macas (Juan de la Cruz and Guamote, tel. 7/270-2368, www.parquesangay.org.ec), south of the bus station, where guides can be organized. The closest access point is the town of General Proaño, just north of Macas, where guides can also be hired. From there, a 90-minute bus ride (twice a day, three days a week) can drop you at the trailheads near the village of 9 de Octubre. Plan on a minimum of 3–4 days for any excursion. Note that it is easier to access the national park from the highlands.

C KAPAWI ECOLODGE

Set in pristine primary rainforest deep in a remote corner of the southern Oriente, Kapawi Ecolodge combines the most comfortable accommodations and service available in the Ecuadorian rainforest with the highest principles of ecotourism.

The lodge was begun in 1993 on the Río Pastaza within a stone's throw of the Peruvian border in the heart of the 8,000-square-kilometer Ecuadorian Achuar territory. After securing permission from OINAE, the indigenous group's political organization, in 1996 the lodge was able to provide local communities with jobs and ongoing economic support in the form of rent paid for the land. Most of the employees who work for the lodge are Achuar, and Kapawi passed into Achuar management in 2008. The lodge has won several international ecotourism awards.

The lodge itself was built entirely with native materials and methods—incredibly, not a single metal nail was used in the construction. Walkways link bungalows that can accommodate 50 people, who may find it easy to forget they're more than 100 kilometers from the nearest city of any size and a 10-day hike from the nearest road. The lodge is as eco-friendly as possible: One of the largest private solar projects in South America powers the lights, all the trash is recycled, and even the soap is biodegradable.

Two main buildings house a small library, a boutique, a meeting room, and a dining hall, which specializes in exotic rainforest fruit and local delicacies. Activities begin after an early breakfast. Silent electric motors power dugout canoes that take you down narrow black-water streams, where long-nosed bats and Amazon kingfishers launch from waterside branches. Flocks of blue-and-yellow macaws claim sandbars in the wide Río Pastaza, and this is the only place in the country where you might spot an Orinoco goose.

Hikes ranging from easy to difficult are led by indigenous and biologist guides. Electric-blue morpho butterflies dance down forest trails, while troops of squirrel monkeys make huge leaps from branch to bending branch along the river. Indigenous guides demonstrate how forest dwellers knock on buttress roots to signal over long distances, and point out countless plants put to good use by the Achuar.

One of the highlights is a visit to an Achuar settlement. After a traditional greeting by your guide and a brief chat with the owner, your group will be served *nijiamanch,* a sour beverage made from chewed-up yucca fermented with human saliva. At least pretend to drink—to refuse would be considered an insult. A tour of the small *chakra,* where various medicinal plants are cultivated, follows.

Four-day ($799 pp) and five-day ($999 pp) visits to Kapawi include accommodations, meals, and excursions (supplementary charges for singles apply). Not included is the round-trip flight from Shell ($306); private van transportation from Quito to Shell ($60), if required; and a $20 contribution to the local Achuar community. Reservations can be made through the Quito office (Foch E7-38 at Reina Victoria, tel. 2/600-9333, fax 2/600-9334, www.kapawi.com), or in the United States, contact Canodros (U.S. tel. 800/613-6026, www.canodros.com).

NORTH AND CENTRAL COASTS AND LOWLANDS

The north and central coast of Ecuador is the road less traveled. While it does not have the "wow" factor of Caribbean or Brazilian beaches, this is the most scenic part of the coast. If you make your way through the un-inviting larger towns, you'll be rewarded with stays in isolated fishing villages with beautiful beaches, some of which are developing into backpacker hubs.

Esmeraldas Province gets nearly 300 centimeters of rain per year, and the northern coast is considerably wetter than the south. While this causes problems with flooding in the rainy season, it also makes the region more beautiful, with verdant vegetation backing the beaches. The tropical dry forests of Manabí Province turn into rainforest farther north and inland, and despite deforestation, much of it can be explored on day trips and overnight stays from the beach resorts. The best area for this by far is Machalilla National Park in Manabí. On the shore, in addition to long sandy stretches there are interesting tours to areas of mangroves that have escaped the clutches of shrimp farming. On the beaches, the region has several excellent surf spots—notably Canoa and Mompiche.

The coast has cultural attractions as well as natural beauty. Ecuador's oldest advanced culture, the Valdivia, can be traced back to 3500 B.C. in the south of Manabí, along with the Manteña-Huancavilca culture, which flourished until the Spanish conquest. Manabí is dotted with museums and archaeological sites from Salango and Agua Blanca to Montecristi and Bahía de Caráquez farther north. Esmeraldas is home of the vibrant Afro-Ecuadorian culture,

HIGHLIGHTS

◖ **Playa de Oro:** Learn how to be a hunter-gatherer, listen for the grunts of wildcats, and try your hand at gold-panning at this community deep in primary rainforest in Esmeraldas (page 264).

◖ **Mompiche:** Rough it with the surfers or enjoy the lap of luxury at Ecuador's newest top-class hotel in this emerging resort, surrounded by stunning scenery (page 270).

◖ **Canoa:** This small surf town is developing quickly but is still a quieter alternative to raucous Montañita (page 273).

◖ **Río Muchacho Organic Farm:** Learn how to make bread out of yucca and jewelry out of seeds, and then go horseback riding and hiking in the forest and swimming under waterfalls in this slice of ecological Eden (page 275).

◖ **Bahía de Caráquez:** This self-styled "eco-city" is the coast's most attractive and cleanest urban area and boasts a dramatic location on a narrow peninsula (page 276).

◖ **Machalilla National Park:** Protected coastal forest, archaeological relics, pristine beaches, unrivalled whale-watching, and the birdlife of Isla de la Plata, "the poor man's Galápagos," are all reasons to visit (page 288).

LOOK FOR ◖ TO FIND RECOMMENDED SIGHTS, ACTIVITIES, DINING, AND LODGING.

people descended from escaped slaves who landed here in the 16th century. They lived isolated for many years and have preserved many traditions of music and dance.

Mosquitoes are a problem on the northern coast, so carry plenty of repellant and consider bringing your own mosquito net. The sun is very strong, so sunblock, a hat, and sunglasses are obligatory. More importantly, the northern coast is sadly one of Ecuador's worst regions for crime. Muggings are common, particularly in Atacames. Don't walk alone on the beach at night, and single women should take particular care. Note that the areas north toward the Colombian border, including San Lorenzo, are notoriously lawless and should be avoided completely. Pickpockets and theft on public

transportation and from hotel rooms is also common, so keep your wits about you.

PLANNING YOUR TIME

Getting around this part of the country usually involves lengthy bus rides, unless you have the budget to fly from Quito to Manta or Esmeraldas ($60–70 one-way). From Quito, most buses go through **Santo Domingo de los Colorados,** and it's easy to reach most resort towns in 6–8 hours. There are daily direct buses to the resort towns, which should be booked in advance and are preferable to making several changes and risking being stuck in a run-down town. From Latacunga, travel via **Quevedo,** and from Guayaquil via **Jipijapa** and **Portoviejo.** The roads here, as in most of

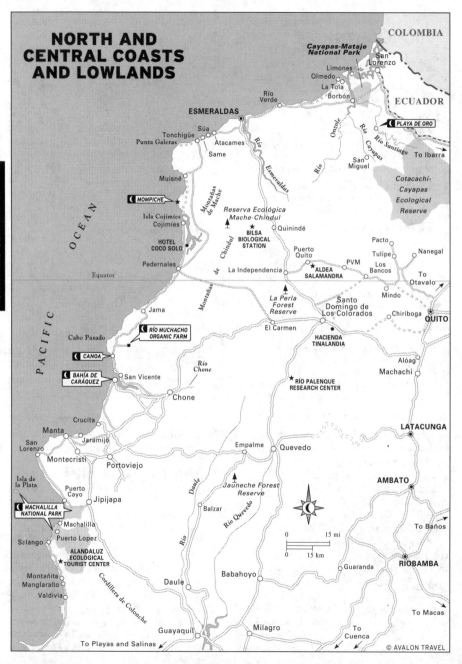

NORTH AND CENTRAL COASTS AND LOWLANDS

COLOMBIA

ECUADOR

Cayapas-Mataje National Park

San Lorenzo

Limones
Olmedo
La Tola
Borbón

Río Verde

ESMERALDAS

PLAYA DE ORO

Súa
Tonchigüe
Punta Galeras
Atacames
Same

Río Esmeraldas

Ontole

Río Santiago

Río Cayapas

San Miguel

To Ibarra

Muisné

Montañas de Mache

Reserva Ecológica Mache-Chindul

Cotacachi-Cayapas Ecological Reserve

MOMPICHE

Isla Cojímies
Cojímies

BILSA BIOLOGICAL STATION

Quinindé

Pacto
Tulipe
Los Bancos
Nanegal

HOTEL COCO SOLO

Puerto Quito

PVM

OCEAN

Montañas de Chindul

La Independencia

ALDEA SALAMANDRA

To Otavalo

Pedernales

Equator

Mindo

La Perla Forest Reserve

Santo Domingo de Los Colorados

Chiriboga

QUITO

Jama

Montañas

El Carmen

HACIENDA TINALANDIA

Cabo Pasado

RÍO MUCHACHO ORGANIC FARM

Alóag
Machachi

CANOA

BAHÍA DE CARÁQUEZ

San Vicente

Río Chone

Chone

RÍO PALENQUE RESEARCH CENTER

PACIFIC

Crucita

Manta

Jaramijó

San Lorenzo

Montecristi

Portoviejo

Empalme

Quevedo

LATACUNGA

Isla de la Plata

Puerto Cayo

Jipijapa

Jauneche Forest Reserve

AMBATO

MACHALILLA NATIONAL PARK

Machalilla

Balzar

Río Daule

To Baños

Puerto Lopez

Salango

ALANDALUZ ECOLOGICAL TOURIST CENTER

Río Quevedo

RIOBAMBA

Montañita
Manglaralto

Guaranda

Valdivia

Cordillera de Colonche

Daule

Babahoyo

Río Daule

0   15 mi

0   15 km

To Macas

Guayaquil

Milagro

To Cuenca

To Playas and Salinas

© AVALON TRAVEL

Ecuador, have improved markedly in the past three years, with a big government investment paying big rewards. Move off the main highway, however, and potholes and dirt roads are still all too common.

There are two high seasons—Christmas–Easter, when the weather is warmer but also wetter, and June–September, which is cooler but coincides with both the vacation period for schools in the mountains and the peak period for whale-watching. Prices vary widely and can rise 30–100 percent in high season. If you show up in a busy resort town at vacation time without a reservation, you may have serious trouble finding a decent room.

You can see the best of the north coast in 5–7 days, although you may end up staying longer if you love the surf and sand. There's little reason to stop at the biggest cities of Santo Domingo, Portoviejo, Esmeraldas, and even Manta—they serve as gateways to more pleasant destinations. The main resort in Esmeraldas Province is **Atacames,** great if you want to party, but be careful. There is better lodging and quieter beaches around **Tonchigüe, Same,** and **Súa. Mompiche** is developing both as a surfing destination and as a luxury resort due to the multimillion-dollar De Cameron resort outside town.

In Manabí Province, **Bahía de Caráquez** is arguably the region's best, cleanest "eco-city," having undergone an impressive transformation in recent years. Around Bahía, there are some interesting islands, mangroves, and the green beacon **Río Muchacho Organic Farm.** The surfing center **Canoa** is just to the north and is one of the region's most pleasant beach resorts. The other tourism hub is **Puerto López,** the best base to explore **Machalilla National Park**'s tropical dry forest, protected beaches, and **Isla de la Plata,** "the poor man's Galápagos." There are plenty of alternatives to Puerto López as a base, with the southern villages of **Puerto Rico** and **Ayampe** beginning to develop.

Western Lowlands

West of Quito, the landscape changes dramatically, dropping from the Andes through cloud forests to the agricultural plains of Ecuador's breadbasket. Whether it's green gold (bananas) or brown gold (cacao beans), the huge plantations in this region provide employment to many and riches to few—something the current President Rafael Correa is trying to change. From an ecological point of view, the costs of Ecuador's agricultural boom have been high, with more than 95 percent of the lowland forests cleared to make way for farmland in the 20th century. There are limited attractions for visitors in this region, and most travelers pass straight through, but look hard enough and there are a few small forest reserves that are worth visiting.

THE ROAD TO SANTO DOMINGO

If you are heading to the coast from Quito, one of the highlights is the hair-raising 2,000-meter descent through lush cloud forest to Santo Domingo de los Colorados. Leaving Quito, the road climbs through *páramo* (Andean grassland) with views of two volcanoes—Atacazo (4,463 meters) and Corazón (4,790 meters)—before the steep drop into the Río Toachi valley. It's preferable to do this route early in the morning because the scenery is more spectacular before the mist descends, and this also avoids an overnight stop in Santo Domingo.

SANTO DOMINGO AND VICINITY

Ecuador's fourth-largest city, Santo Domingo de Los Colorados (pop. 300,000), is far from being its fourth most appealing. This rapidly expanding city is an important agricultural and trading center as well as a transportation hub, but it's hardly a tourism center. It is only three hours west of Quito by bus, but at an elevation of 625 meters, the difference in climate is huge, and you'll be sweltering in no time at midday. Once you've wandered around the busy market in the center, there's little else to do in the city itself. If you're traveling between Quito and the coast, it may be tempting to stop here, but unless you're stuck, staying the night only makes sense for those going on nearby excursions, notably to visit the Tsáchila. These indigenous people gave the town its name ("Santo Domingo of the Colored Ones") because of their use of red achiote hair paste.

Entertainment and Events

Santo Domingo's **Canonization Anniversary** festival takes place on July 3, when the town floods with visitors attending fairs and agricultural festivals. For nightlife, head east of the center on the far end of Avenida Quito, where there are plenty of bars as well as the city's most happening disco, **Salsoteca Jungle** (Av. Quito, no phone, 9 P.M.–2 A.M. Thurs.–Sat.).

Tours

Turismo Zaracay (29 de Mayo and Cocaniguas, tel. 2/275-0546, turismo_zaracay@hotmail.com) offers one-day tours ($25 pp) to visit **Tsáchila** communities seven kilometers south of Santo Domingo as well as overnight stays ($45 pp, meals included) with a Tsáchila family. The agency offers various other trips—a one-day rafting tour on the Río Toachi ($50 pp) includes lunch, a guide, and transportation.

Accommodations

Santo Domingo's status as commercial center means that hotels fill up quickly with businesspeople. The cheapest hotels are in the market area, but it's not particularly safe at night. If you end up stuck here, the best budget options are along the noisy main street, 29 de Mayo. **Hotel El Colorado** (29 de Mayo, tel. 2/275-0266, $8 s, $16 d) is a basic, cheap option. **Diana Real** (29 de Mayo and Loja, tel. 2/275-1380, $18 s, $24 d) has larger, better guest rooms, and **Hotel del Pacifico** (29 de Mayo, tel. 2/275-2806, $25 s, $39 d) is a good mid-range option. Some guest rooms have

air-conditioning. **Gran Hotel Santo Domingo** (Río Toachi and Galápagos, tel. 2/276-7950, $50 s, $72 d) is a pricier mid-range choice.

For a far more upscale experience at higher prices, an alternative place to stay is east of the center on the far end of Avenida Quito, where there is a string of restaurants and bars. **Hotel La Siesta** (Av. Quito 12-26 at Pallatanga, tel. 2/275-1013, $15 s, $25 d), has decent guest rooms. Farther along is the more upmarket **Hotel de Toachi** (Av. Quito, tel. 2/275-4688, $35 s, $60 d, breakfast included). Guest rooms have air-conditioning, cable TV, and there's a pool. The best of the bunch is the **Hotel Zaracay** (Av. Quito, tel. 2/275-0316, www.hotelzaracay.com, $58 s, $85 d, breakfast included), just past Hotel de Toachi, built in a country-estate style with thatched roofs, landscaped gardens, tennis courts, and a small pool. Guest rooms have phones, TVs, and air-conditioning. Advance reservations are advised.

Food

There are plenty of basic restaurants along 29 de Mayo serving set lunches and dinners. For something a bit better, head to **La Tonga** inside Gran Hotel Santo Domingo (Río Toachi and Galápagos, tel. 2/276-7950, 7 A.M.–10:30 P.M. daily, entrées $5), which has vegetarian, international, and local specialties, including *caldo de gallina* (chicken broth) and filet mignon.

In the bar-restaurant area east of the center on Avenida Quito, one good option is **Restaurante Timoneiro** (Av. Quito 115, tel. 2/275-1642, entrées $3–5), serving chicken soup and filling set meals.

Services

The **post office** (Tsáchilas and Río Baba) is a few blocks north of the plaza on the right.

Getting There and Around

Santo Domingo's **bus terminal** is two kilometers north of the center, and for many travelers, it is their only experience of the city. To get to the center, buses run to and from the bus terminal regularly, passing north on Tsáchilas and returning west down 29 de Mayo.

From Santo Domingo, there are several buses per hour to Quito (3 hours, $3), Guayaquil (5 hours, $6), Esmeraldas (3.5 hours, $4), Bahía de Caráquez (6 hours, $6), and Manta (7 hours, $7). There are also several buses direct to Machala (8 hours, $8). For destinations in the highlands, there are buses to Ambato (4 hours, $4), Riobamba (5 hours, $5), and Baños (5 hours, $5). Transportes Kennedy has several direct buses per day to Mindo (4 hours, $4), more convenient than going via Quito.

Hacienda Tinalandia

Hacienda Tinalandia is named after the Russian woman who started this reserve some 50 years ago. Nowadays it is run by her children and is still considered one of the best birding spots in the country, with more than 350 species identified. Bird-watchers will be delighted by species such as the rufous-tailed hummingbird, pale-legged *hornero,* and rusty margin flycatcher flitting through 80 hectares of protected rainforest along the Río Toachi. Another 240 hectares are protected next to the reserve. There are several hiking trails as well as rafting and horseback trips available. Temperatures average 22°C, and May–September are the driest months.

You can visit Tinalandia on a day trip for $10. It's not a cheap place to stay, but the views are remarkable. Rates can include all meals ($123 s, $212 d) or only the guest rooms ($86 s, $117 d). Make reservations and arrange guides and transportation through the hacienda's office in Quito (Av. Del Parque, Calle 3, Lote 98, #43-78, 2nd Fl., Urb. El Bosque, tel./fax 2/244-9028 or 9/946-7741, www.tinalandia. com). To get here, either take a bus to Santo Domingo and take a taxi, or ask the bus driver to drop you—the entrance is 500 meters from the highway. The Hacienda can also arrange private transfers for advanced bookings.

SANTO DOMINGO TO GUAYAQUIL
Río Palenque Science Center

This reserve and research center contains 100 hectares of lowland forest but is becoming a threatened pocket of conservation surrounded by African palm and banana plantations. Nevertheless, it's still a biodiversity hot spot, with 360 bird species and an incredible 1,200 species of plants at last count. Birding highlights include the rufous-fronted wood quail and the southern nightingale wren.

Facilities are geared more toward researchers than casual visitors. The small field station has a kitchen, generator electricity by day, and private baths with cold showers. Guests pay $5 to visit for the day, and guest rooms ($35 s, $60 d) and dorms ($13 pp) are available.

The reserve is about 40 kilometers southwest of Santo Domingo, shortly past the village of Patricia Pilar, and 1.5 kilometers down a side road. For information, contact the Centro Científico Río Palenque (tel. 9/974-5790) or the Wong Foundation in Guayaquil (tel. 4/220-8670, www.fundacionwong.org).

Quevedo

Resting on the banks of the wide, brown Río Quevedo, the muggy, bustling settlement of Quevedo is known as the "Chinatown of Ecuador" for its large Asian population. Most travelers just pass through, stopping off for a meal at one of the many *chifas* before continuing to Guayaquil, Santo Domingo, or Latacunga. There is little to do in Quevedo beyond sampling the food, reputed to be the best Chinese cuisine in Ecuador, and it's best to stay close to the main street, 7 de Octubre.

ACCOMMODATIONS AND FOOD

The **Hotel Ejecutivo International** (Calle 4a 214 at 7 de Octubre, tel. 5/275-1780 or 5/275-1781, fax 5/275-0596, $13 s, $20 d) is a good value, with air-conditioning, TVs, and a very good restaurant. Another budget option is **Hotel Casablanca** (Decima 416 near 7 de Octubre, tel. 5/275-4144, $10–14 s, $16–20 d). For more comfort, an Olympic-size pool, and a disco, stay at the **Hotel Olímpico** (Calle 19 117 at Roldos, Ciudadela San José, tel. 5/275-0455 or 5/275-0965, $56 s, $69 d, breakfast included) on the south end of town.

Quevedo's *chifas* are dependable and cheap.

Chifa Pekín (7 de Octubre and Calle 3, lunch and dinner daily, $3–6) and **Café Fenix** (12 de Octubre, tel. 5/276-1460, 9 A.M.–9 P.M. daily, entrées $3–6) are recommended.

GETTING THERE AND AROUND

Like most cities in the western lowlands, Quevedo is a crossroads between the Sierra and the coast. The new bus terminal is off Avenida Walter Andrades, a $1 taxi ride from the city center. Transportes Macuchi runs buses to Quito (4–5 hours, $5), and Transportes Sucre goes to Santo Domingo (1.5 hours, $2) and Guayaquil (3 hours, $4). Transportes Cotopaxi plies the dramatic route to Latacunga (5 hours, $5) and Portoviejo (4 hours, $5).

SANTO DOMINGO TO ESMERALDAS

La Perla Forest Reserve

West Virginian Suzanne Sheppard came to Ecuador in 1949 to start a farm with her husband. After discovering the sad depletion of Ecuador's coastal forests, they established this 250-hectare reserve. Since Suzanne died, her children take care of this reserve (Mon.–Sat., $5 pp), 41 kilometers north of Santo Domingo. It has minimal facilities, but guided visits are available by prior appointment. Camping is also possible. For information, contact the Bosque Protector La Perla office (tel. 9/914-4604).

Bilsa Biological Station

Fundación Jatun Sacha opened this 3,300-hectare field station in 1994, in the middle of what became the **Reserva Ecológica Mache-Chindul** two years later. Over 80 percent of the station is primary rainforest and protects one of the largest areas of the Chocó rainforest in Ecuador, while the rest of the reserve remains vulnerable to illegal logging.

The ecosystem is isolated from the Andes but rugged enough to trap dense fog that supports cloud-forest flora and fauna usually restricted to higher, wetter elevations. There are some 305 recorded species of birds as well as howler monkeys and a small population of wildcats. More than 20,000 plant seedlings are cared for in Bilsa's Center for the Conservation of Western Forest Plants, and 20 new plant species have been identified here.

There are four rustic cabins ($30 pp per day, meals included) available for researchers, students, and natural-history tour groups. Individual visitors should contact the foundation in advance for permission to enter ($5 pp). Volunteers contribute $302 pp for two weeks to offset lodging and meals.

Getting to Bilsa is not easy. The best bet is to hitch a ride from the nearest town, Quinindé, to the village of Herrera, 25 kilometers from the reserve. In the wet season (Jan.–May), you may only get as far as the intersection known as La Y (accommodations are available at the La Laguna de Cube Cabins, just north of La Y, for $10 pp). From here it's a 3–4-hour walk. During the rest of the year, it may be easier to reach the reserve.

For more information, contact the **Fundación Jatun Sacha** (Pasaje Eugenio de Santillán N34-28 at Maurián, Urb. Rumipamba, Quito, tel./fax 2/243-2240, www.jatunsacha.org), which has four other reserves in mainland Ecuador and one in the Galápagos.

North Coast

Esmeraldas Province, on the north coast, is rather like the country's Wild West. Cut off from the rest of Ecuador for many years, the region still retains its own cultural identity, and the Afro-Ecuadorians that dominate the province are boisterous, outgoing, and welcoming. However, with the Wild West comes lawlessness, and statistics show that this is one of Ecuador's most dangerous regions. You are better off bypassing the city of Esmeraldas and avoiding the region north to the Colombian border, where drug smuggling, gangs, and illegal immigration are rife. Instead, head southwest of Esmeraldas, where there are both busy resorts and isolated fishing villages that make for a more relaxing beach break.

Note that due to the wetter climate, malaria and yellow fever are endemic (though rare) in Esmeraldas, so consider taking antimalarial medicine in the rainy season, and get a yellow fever vaccination.

ESMERALDAS AND VICINITY

Esmeraldas was named by the Spanish after they arrived to find the local natives bedecked in emeralds. And while the green landscapes of the province make it worthy of its name, these days the capital city, Esmeraldas, is far from a jewel.

Esmeraldas started out as a fishing port before a short-lived rubber boom led to its expansion into Ecuador's biggest northern port. The oil boom in the late 1970s led to the opening of the country's largest oil refinery, the terminus for the 503-kilometer Trans-Ecuadorian Pipeline. Despite the presence of this major employer, poverty levels remain high, along with high crime rates. Travelers used to come through here on the way to the beach, but the town's tourism industry is very depressed these days. Furthermore, the secure, clean new bus terminal south of town offers good connections to Atacames and other resorts, meaning that bypassing the city of Esmeraldas is easy.

SHIPWRECKED: THE ORIGIN OF THE AFRO-ECUADORIANS

How the Afro-Ecuadorians came to Esmeraldas is a fascinating legend. Soon after the conquest, the Spanish began bringing slaves to South America. In 1553, one ship, en route from Panama to Peru, ran aground off the Ecuadorian coast. The 23 slaves on board rebelled and escaped into the forests of modern-day Esmeraldas. Despite clashes with local indigenous people, the region became a safe haven for escaped slaves due to its remote location, and the population grew rapidly. By the end of the 16th century, the community had declared themselves to be a republic of *zambos* (curly-haired people), and they lived autonomously for most of the colonial era. In the 19th century, the communities were finally permitted by a liberal government to buy the land they had inhabited for years.

Nowadays, Afro-Ecuadorians number over 1 million and make up approximately 8 percent of the total population of Ecuador. The majority still live in Esmeraldas province, with other sizeable populations in the Chota valley of Imbabura as well as in Quito and Guayaquil. The biggest successes of Afro-Ecuadorians have come on the football field, with Afro-Ecuadorian players dominating the World Cup squads in 2002 and 2006. Two Afro-Ecuadorians have also won the Miss Ecuador competition – Monica Chala in 1996 and Lady Mina in 2010. However, racism remains deeply ingrained in Ecuador, and most Afro-Ecuadorians remain poor and underemployed. The country has a long way to go before Afro-Ecuadorians can look forward to equal opportunities.

If you do decide to linger, the city has an impressive cathedral just north of the center, and a lush central park with a statue of liberal hero Luis Vargas Torres. The park is overlooked by a concrete church, **Santuario Nuestra Señora de la Merced,** which features an impressive interior.

Accommodations and Food

The center of town has plenty of cheap, basic hotels, but the quality is poor. **El Trebol** (Cañizares, tel. 6/272-8031, $15 s, $29 d) has passable guest rooms with cable TV. You are better off staying in the northern seaside suburb of Las Palmas, where the **Hotel Cayapas** (Kennedy and Valdez, tel. 6/272-1318, $33 s, $45 d) is probably the best option. Guest rooms have TVs and air-conditioning. Breakfast is served in the open-air **La Tolita** restaurant (tel. 6/272-1318, breakfast, lunch, and dinner daily, entrées $5–10), which has an extensive menu of pasta, seafood, and meat. For Chinese noodles, fried rice, and soups, try **Chifa Asiatica** (Cañizares between Bolívar and Sucre, tel. 6/272-6888, lunch and dinner daily, entrées $3–5) in the center. In Las Palmas, there are plenty of seafood restaurants along the beach and thumping discos on weekends, but be careful at night.

Information and Services

The main **hospital** is at the north end of town (Libertad, tel. 6/271-0012). The **police station** (Bolívar and Cañizares) is two blocks south of the main plaza.

Getting There and Around

The best thing about Esmeraldas is its new bus terminal, about five kilometers south of the city. It's secure and clean, with regular connections to the beach resorts, so staying in the city is unnecessary. La Costeñita runs several buses per hour to Atacames (45 minutes, $0.80), continuing on to Súa and Same (1 hour, $1). There are also regular buses to Muisne (2 hours, $2). Buses to Mompiche are less frequent, with one bus every 2–3 hours (2.5 hours, $3). Note that many buses from Quito to Muisne and Atacames bypass Esmeraldas entirely.

Transportes Esmeraldas has numerous buses, both regular and luxury service, to Quito (6 hours, $7), Guayaquil (9 hours, $9), and Manta (9 hours, $8). Panamericana runs the best luxury buses to Quito and to Guayaquil at 11 P.M. Cita Express has buses to Ambato (7 hours, $7) and Santo Domingo.

TAME (tel. 6/272-6863) has two daily flights to Quito ($60 one-way) and one daily flight to Guayaquil ($90 one-way). You can also fly to Guayaquil by connecting in Quito. **General Rivadeneira Airport** is 15 kilometers northeast of the city. You can take a taxi from the airport to Esmeraldas (30 minutes, $8) or direct to Atacames (1.5 hours, $20).

ESMERALDAS TO THE COLOMBIAN BORDER

Ecuador's northernmost coastline dissolves into a tangle of mangroves as it nears Colombia. Almost 75 percent of the population in the farthest towns has immigrated—often illegally—from Colombia. North of Esmeraldas is the small fishing village of Río Verde. Twenty-two kilometers past Río Verde, the road divides, left to **La Tola** and **Olmedo,** and right inland to **Borbón.** Farther north is the border town of San Lorenzo. Note that this is a very dangerous area due to guerrilla activity and drug-trafficking spilling over the Colombian border, and at the time of writing the British Foreign Office advises against all travel to San Lorenzo. Many of the surrounding towns are also dangerous, so make inquiries locally before venturing into this region. The main reason to come here is to visit the impressive **Reserva Ecológico Manglares Cayapas-Mataje.** The islands and canals of this 51,300-hectare reserve support five species of mangrove, and it is renowned for its birdlife. Another fascinating reserve in the area is the massive **Cotacachi-Cayapas** Ecological Reserve, which stretches up into the Andes, but it is best visited from Otavalo or Ibarra.

◖ PLAYA DE ORO

Although there is no "golden beach" at Playa de Oro, it is an impressive highlight of northern

FRICTION ON THE FRONTIER

The 600-kilometer border between Ecuador and Colombia has been extremely volatile for many years. The long-running armed conflict between left-wing rebels and the Colombian government has all too often spilled into Ecuador, with guerrillas, paramilitaries, and cocaine producers fleeing south.

The U.S. Southern Command, charged with helping to end the Colombian drug trade, expanded an air and naval base near Manta in 1999, costing $80 million. The base supported hundreds of personnel, and several P-3 surveillance aircraft began flying antidrug missions over Colombia. It led to a economic boom for Manta, but many Ecuadorians resented being drawn into Colombia's drug war.

The 10-year lease was up for renewal in 2009, and left-wing president Rafael Correa refused to renew it, fulfilling a long-standing election promise. This decision was met with disappointment and anger by the U.S. military, but they swiftly moved to operate instead out of seven Colombian bases.

A year earlier, tensions between Colombia and Ecuador reached an all-time low point when the Colombian army attacked a campsite inside Ecuadorian territory, north of Lago Agrio, and killed Raúl Reyes, one of guerrilla group FARC's top leaders. Diplomatic relations were broken off, and there was much saber-rattling. The Colombian government accused Correa's government of having links to FARC, a claim Correa stridently denied.

With the departure of Colombian President Álvaro Uribe in August 2010, however, relations have improved markedly. The following month, FARC received the "most crushing blow in its history," according to Colombian president Juan Manuel Santos, when its top military strategist, Jorge Briceño Suárez was killed in an air raid. The Colombian government has since claimed further victories against FARC, but the troubles along the border with Ecuador are far from over.

Ecuador. This remote community was named for the abundance of gold found in the Río Santiago soon after the conquest. There's little gold left these days—the main attractions are the hunter-gatherer community that lives here and the surrounding 10,000 hectares of primary rainforest adjacent to the Cotacachi-Cayapas Ecological Reserve. Outside the Oriente, this is probably the farthest you can get from modern civilization in Ecuador, and a visit to this tight-knit community is an ideal way to combine a rainforest experience with the chance to support a unique, fragile culture. Playa de Oro is one of the few protected areas of the biologically rich Chocó that used to stretch uninterrupted all the way to Panama. It's also the only reserve in the world that protects small wildcats.

The community's ancestors were brought here as slaves by the Spanish to pan for gold in the 16th century. One day, according to local legend, they decided to build a wooden cannon, blasted their master into oblivion, and lived for years as an autonomous community. The British plundered most of the gold in the 19th and early 20th centuries, and the community lived as hunter-gatherers. In 1992 the U.S. charity Earthways provided funding to build a lodge and soon reached an agreement with the villagers to establish an ecotourism project in return for designation of the territory as a reserve for wildcats, giving birth to **Playa de Oro Reserva de Tigrillos.** The community has withstood pressures from mining companies, many of which have been working illegally in areas downriver. All fees from visits go directly to the community, and the residents of Playa de Oro run every aspect of their community, with a voting age of 14.

There are several excellent trails, ranging 1–4 hours, into the forest past a succession of waterfalls. Bird-watchers can spot up to 330 species, and with luck, larger animals such as deer, sloths, anteaters, and monkeys can

The lodge at Playa de Oro offers an intimate experience with a remote, close-knit community.

occasionally be seen. The six species of wildcats—jaguars, pumas, ocelots, margays, oncillas, and jaguarundis—are usually elusive, but their tracks are frequently visible, and you can sometimes hear the grunting of ocelots close to the lodge at night. To go farther into the rainforest, you can rent a boat with a guide for a small fee. It's refreshing to take a dip in the river at the end of a long hike.

In the village of Playa de Oro, there are plenty of activities to get involved in with the locals—from fishing to gold panning (there are small deposits remaining). There are also wooden carvings and drums for sale, which help to supplement the local income.

Visiting Playa del Oro requires advance arrangements, ideally with two weeks' notice. Do not turn up unannounced at Selva Alegre hoping to hitch a ride, because the boat transfer must also be prearranged. The cost of the two-hour boat ride ($50 one-way, $100 round-trip) is shared among the group. The lodge ($50 pp per night) includes all meals, guides, and activities, except additional boat trips. There is

also a $10 reserve entrance fee. There is no electricity, hot water, phones, or Internet—a small price to pay for a few days of complete isolation—but there are toilets and cold showers in the lodge. You can also choose to stay in the village, but the lodge is recommended.

It takes six hours by private vehicle to get to **Selva Alegre** from Quito via Otavalo, and another two hours by boat to the reserve. In Otavalo, Ramiro Buitrón, owner of the **Hostel Amanecer del Valle** (Roca and Quiroga, Otavalo, tel. 6/292-0990 or 9/960-6918, www.hostalvalledelamanecer.com), operates private transfers to Selva Alegre in a van ($100); split among the passengers, depending on group size, it can cost as little as $15–20 pp. The alternative is to take a bus to **Borbón** ($8). There is a 9 P.M. bus from Quito arriving at Borbón at 5 A.M., and then a bus to Selva Alegre at 7 A.M. You can also get an early bus from Esmeraldas to Borbón and transfer there. You must travel in the morning because the boat only makes the trip to Playa de Oro until 3 P.M. Note that Borbón has a reputation for crime, so be alert; the private transfer from Otavalo is certainly the preferable option. For reservations and further information, visit www.touchthejungle.org or contact Tracy Wilson (tracy@touchthejungle.org) or Ramiro Buitrón at Hostel Amanecer del Valle (Roca and Quiroga, Otavalo, tel. 6/292-0990 or 9/960-6918, www.hostalvalledelamanecer.com).

WEST OF ESMERALDAS

This stretch of coastline, which comprises the resorts of **Atacames, Súa, Same,** and **Tonchigüe,** is the most popular in northern Ecuador, attracting thousands of visitors, especially from Quito. It is six hours from the capital for speeding locals and more easily reachable than the southern resorts.

Atacames

Atacames is the northern coast's busiest, brashest beach resort. It's one of the most popular in Ecuador for locals, and if you want a raucous all-night party on the beach, this is the place to be. Foreign visitors, however, are increasingly going elsewhere in search of more relaxing destinations.

First impressions of the town are not great, as all buses stop off in the rather dirty, uninspiring center, inland of the Río Atacames. Either walk over the footbridge or hop on a three-wheeled *mototaxi* ($0.50) to reach a wide beach and the *malecón,* which bustles with beach bars, restaurants, and hotels. The booming sound of *reggaetón* from the beach bars is constant, even early in the morning, regardless of whether they're full or empty.

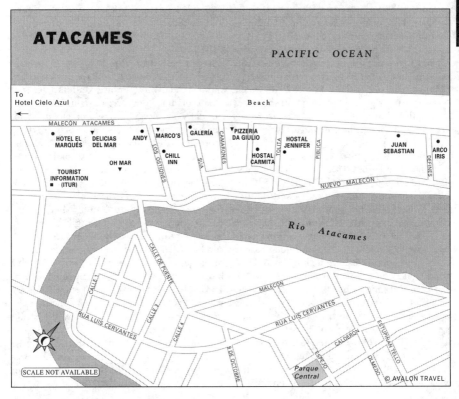

Crime has increased significantly in Atacames in recent years, with thefts and assaults becoming more common, even during the day. Single travelers and female travelers should be particularly careful. Don't take valuables to the beach, never walk on the beach at night, and take a *mototaxi* to your hotel after dark, even if it's only a few blocks from the main drag. When swimming, be careful of the strong undertow.

ACCOMMODATIONS

Atacames has a large number of accommodations for a modest-sized resort, but in high season you'll be surprised how quickly the decent places fill up. While the resort is losing popularity with foreigners, it remains as popular as ever with locals. In high season (Dec.–Apr. and July–Aug.) and on national holidays, reserving ahead is essential.

The cheapest place on the *malecón* is the family-run **Galería** (Malecón, tel. 6/273-1149, $10 s, $15 d), but the guest rooms are very basic. Upstairs, the restaurant does good pizza and pasta dishes. A better budget option is **Andy** (Malecón, tel. 6/276-0221, $15 s, $20 d), which has surprisingly good guest rooms for the price. Two quieter options just off the *malecón* are **Hostal Jennifer** (Malecón and La Tolita, tel. 6/273-1055, www.hostaljennifer.com, $8 s, $15 d) which has peach-colored guest rooms with fans, and **Hostal Carmita** (Las Taguas and Malecón, tel. 6/273-1784, $10 s, $20 d), which is a good value with air-conditioning and cable TV. A new option in town is the friendly Swiss-owned **Hostal Chill Inn** (Los Ostiones, tel. 6/276-0477, www.chillinnecuador.com, $14 s, $20 d). The four guest rooms are a very good value, and the kitchen and TV room makes for a homey atmosphere.

In the mid-range, **Hostal Milamar** (Malecón and La Tolita, tel. 6/273-1363, $25 s, $36 d) is a dependable option on the *malecón* (the back guest rooms are quieter), but it's better to head a few blocks out of the center. German-owned **Cielo Azul** (21 de Noviembre, tel. 6/273-1813, $24 s, $45 d), a couple of blocks south of the *malecón* (walk a block inland), is one of the

better mid-range hotels in town, with comfortable hammocks on balconies and a pool leading directly onto the beach. At the far north end of the *malecón* is **Arco Iris** (Malecón, tel. 6/273-1069, $32 d). You'll feel as if you've stepped into the Oriente, lazing on a hammock tucked away in verdant gardens, although the rustic cabins are getting a little tired. A couple of blocks south is the impressive complex of **Hotel Juan Sebastián** (Malecón, tel. 6/273-1049, www.hoteljuansebastian.com, $40 s, $60 d, breakfast included). The chalet guest rooms are nothing special, but the large pool at the center, lighted at night, makes it worth the extra dough. The best hotel in town is 🌑 **Hotel El Marqués** (Malecón, tel. 6/276-0182, $48 s, $73 d, breakfast included). Set back from the beach, this towering glass structure stands above anything else in Atacames, with spacious top-quality guest rooms, a gym, and a pool.

FOOD

There are cheap seafood stalls selling fresh *ceviche* at the south end of the *malecón*. For more standard restaurants, **Delicias del Mar** (Malecón, no phone, breakfast, lunch, and dinner daily, entrées $3) offers a great-value two-course set meal ($3) all day. For something more intimate, head to 🌑 **Marco's** (Malecón, tel. 6/276-0126, 8 A.M.–10 P.M. daily, entrées $4–7), where a delightful old lady serves up large portions of sumptuous seafood such as *encocado* and *cazuela* in an elegant setting. For pizza, **Pizzeria da Giulio** (Malecón, tel. 6/273-1603, 5:30 P.M.–midnight Tues.–Fri., 11 A.M.–midnight Sat.–Sun., entrées $4–7) is run by a friendly Sardinian who prides himself on large, freshly made pizzas. For seafood, a block inland is **Oh Mar** (Principal, tel. 6/273-1637, 11 A.M.–10 P.M. daily, entrées $6–9), which serves up a feast that includes *ceviche, encocado,* and breaded shrimp as well as steaks and pork chops.

After dinner, Atacames's nightlife is always loud. In high season the town is heaving with partygoers who head for the beach bars, while in low season patrons will beckon you into empty bars. They all serve a similar array of freshly made fruit cocktails. **Caida del Sol** (tel. 6/273-1202) is one of the most popular beach bars.

INFORMATION AND SERVICES

There is a well-stocked **iTur office** on the corner of the main street heading out of the *malecón*. There's an **ATM** next to Hotel Le Castell toward the north end of the *malecón,* and **Banco del Pichincha** (Luis Cervantes) on the main street in the center. The **police station** (Avenida Las Acacias) is over the bridge.

GETTING THERE AND AROUND

Atacames has no bus terminal, so pick up a bus inland on the dusty main street, Luis Cervantes. For Súa, Same, and Muisne, there are several **Trans La Costeñita** and **Trans Pacífico** buses every hour. For Mompiche, 3–4 direct buses per day leave Esmeraldas, or catch a bus heading to Pedernales to drop you off nearby. For Quito (7 hours, $7) and Guayaquil (7–8 hours, $9) use **Trans Esmeraldas, Aerotaxi,** or **Trans Occidentales,** all of which have offices across the footbridge. Bear in mind that on weekends and during national holidays, you must reserve in advance, as demand is high.

Súa

If you prefer the sounds of the sea to the thump of *reggaetón,* head southwest to the quieter resorts. The first is Súa, a small fishing village in a peaceful crescent-shaped bay. The town's name has an interesting history, and the cliffs west of town hold a legend reminiscent of *Romeo and Juliet.* Long ago, a Spanish captain fell in love with a local princess named Súa. She received incorrect news that he had died in battle and threw herself off the cliff. The captain returned, and upon discovering Súa's fate, took the same plunge. Their ghosts still haunt the rocks, according to locals.

Súa is rather undeveloped as a resort, and that's the attraction—it's a world away from nearby Atacames, with a fishing-village atmosphere and a small selection of hotels and restaurants. There are whale-watching tours

in season (June–Sept.), which are cheaper but not as spectacular as tours from Puerto López farther south.

Perched on a hill overlooking the beach on the north side of town, **Hotel Chagra Ramos** (Malecón, tel. 6/273-1006 or 2/244-3822, $8 pp) is one of the best places to stay, with decent cabins with balconies. **Las Buganvillas Hotel** (Malecón, tel. 6/273-1008, $8–10 pp), farther down the *malecón,* also has comfortable guest rooms set facing a pretty courtyard with a small swimming pool. There is a cluster of good seafood restaurants along the *malecón.* Try **Kike's** (Malecón, no phone, 9 A.M.–6 P.M. daily, entrées $4–5).

Same

Same (pronounced SAH-meh) has an impressive three-kilometer-long beach and is the northern coast's most popular luxury resort. You'll have trouble locating the village—it's really a string of hotels, most of which cater to wealthier visitors. They fill up fast, and prices rise by up to 50 percent in high season. The biggest and most fashionable with rich Ecuadorians is **Casa Blanca** (Playa de Casa Blanca, tel. 6/273-3159, $80 s or d, breakfast included), a huge condominium and hotel complex with apartments, several restaurants, a spa, and a golf course designed by Jack Nicklaus. For those on a tighter budget, there are a few mid-range options. For a more informal vibe, try the terra-cotta **Casa de Amigos** (Ruta del Sol, tel. 6/247-0102, $25–30 pp, www.casadeamigosecuador.com), which has comfortable guest rooms and good Mexican food. **Cabanas Isla del Sol** (Playa de Same, tel. 6/273-3470, www.cabanasisladelsol.com, $34–56 s or d) has well-equipped beachfront cabins. **El Acantilado** (Playa de Same, tel. 6/273-3466, $25 s, $50 d) boasts wonderful sea views from its rustic cabins. One of the cheaper options in Same is the family-run **La Terraza** (Playa de Same, tel. 6/247-0320, $12–15 pp), which has comfy four-person guest rooms with private baths and hammocks on the front porch with a view of the ocean.

For food, outside the hotels, head to

German- and Chilean-run **Seaflower Restaurant** (one block from Same beach, tel. 6/247-0369, noon–4 P.M. and 6–9 P.M. daily, entrées $9–12), renowned as one of the best restaurants in the area, with delicious seafood dishes.

Tonchigüe

West of Same, the coastal road splits at **Tonchigüe.** The west branch leads to the lighthouse at **Punta Galera,** and the southern road goes to Muisne. Several Trans Costañita buses per day run from Esmeraldas to Punta Galera, or you can take a bus to Muisne, get off at the junction, and hitch a ride the rest of the way.

Halfway to the lighthouse, the Canadian-run ◖ **Playa Escondida** (tel. 6/273-3106 or 6/273-3122, www.playaescondida.com. ec, $12–18 pp, camping $5 pp) is true to its name (Hidden Beach). This secluded ecological getaway on 34 hectares of semitropical forest against a cliff-backed beach is a truly special place and worth the effort to find it. Choose from rustic cabins or camping, and the restaurant serves a wide range of seafood, meat, and vegetarian dishes.

Muisne

Years ago, the whisperings were that Muisne was the idyllic beach many backpackers dream of stumbling on. Nowadays, though, it's mostly a depressing place. Granted, the long stretch of beach on the west side of the island remains stunningly beautiful and largely unspoiled, but the rest of the island is poverty-stricken and has crime problems; foreign visitors are going elsewhere. The island had serious problems with flooding in the rainy season in 2010, and there's no running water. Locals complain that the previous mayor ran off with most of their money, and they are left scratching a living from fishing and a flagging tourism industry. Note that thefts and assaults have been reported here, so be careful, and single women should not come here alone.

Buses to Muisne arrive at a jetty called **El Relleno,** where frequent launches ($0.20) go across; pay for a personal taxi ($1) if there aren't enough passengers. On arrival in the muddy, dirty town of Muisne, you may wonder what on earth you're doing here, but take a *mototaxi* ($0.50) the two kilometers to the other side of the island and you'll be rewarded with a long white-sand beach.

Accommodations are limited on the beach. The best option is probably **Hostal Las Olas** (tel. 5/248-0782, $10 s, $15 d), which has decent guest rooms on the beachfront. Farther down the beach to the left is **Playa Paraíso** (tel. 5/248-0192, $10 s, $15 d, cabins $25), which has remodeled cabins and guest rooms. **Hotel Calade** (no phone, $8s, $15 d) is one of the cheapest and most basic.

For food, there are a couple of restaurants serving seafood fare, with **Las Palmeiras** (no phone, lunch and dinner daily, entrées $2–4) the local favorite. In high season, a couple of bars open next to the beach.

There are a few tours available on Muisne, mainly to Isla Bonita and the mangroves (about $25 pp, cheaper for larger groups). Inquire locally or contact **Fundecol** (tel. 5/248-0519, www.fundecol.org), which has a small office in the town.

Transcosteñita buses to Muisne leave regularly from Esmeraldas (2.5 hours, $2), stopping at Atacames, Súa, and Same (1 hour, $1) along the way. Trans Esmeraldas runs direct buses to and from Quito (9 hours, $8) and Guayaquil (10 hours, $7).

◖ Mompiche

This modest fishing village is developing rapidly in two contrasting ways—ideal surfing conditions, a beautiful beach, and a few decent hostels are helping to create a small backpackers' hub (think Canoa five years ago), while the completion of the multimillion-dollar Royal Decameron Hotel eight kilometers south of town has become the in place for the wealthy of Quito and Guayaquil.

Mompiche seems to have developed into a microcosm of Ecuadorian society: The extravagant hotel on the hill caters to the upper classes, while the villagers below scratch out a living and wonder when they will finally get

© VICENTE MUÑOZ

Fishing is still the primary livelihood in villages like Mompiche.

the water supply the hotel and the government promised them. There's no doubt, however, that the new hotel has also had benefits for the town, with improved electric, telephone, TV, and Internet connections along with jobs for some of the locals, but the feeling of two different worlds living side by side prevails.

RECREATION

Mompiche's setting is certainly impressive, with thickly forested hills dropping down to a wide beach backed by palm trees. To the north, the wide bay stretches for kilometers up to Punta Galera, and beyond that the mangroves around Muisne are visible in the distance. At the time of this writing, a small *malecón* walkway is being constructed. In the town itself, there's not a lot to do beyond surfing and sunbathing. For experienced surfers, Mompiche offers one of the biggest left point breaks in South America and attracts surfers from around the world in the high season (Dec.–Apr.). On good days, the surf can become the stuff of dreams. Inland, the scenery

is equally dramatic in the forests that border the **Mache Chindul Reserve.** These can be explored on tours from **Hotel Gabeal** (tel. 9/969-6543). Horseback riding costs $10 per hour, and hiking and snorkeling tours to Isla Jupiter cost $15 pp.

ACCOMMODATIONS

Accommodations are limited in Mompiche, although they are slowly developing. The town gets booked up in high season. The two hotels in the center, right on the *malecón*— **Hostal Oga** (Malecón, no phone, $6–10 pp) and **Hostal Tu Regreso** (Malecón, no phone, $6–10 pp)—offer very basic guest rooms and decidedly surly service, but they fill up very fast due to the low rates. For a much better experience, turn right and walk a couple of blocks to reach ◖ **Hotel Gabeal** (tel. 9/969-6543, $10–25 pp), the best option in town, with two impressive tall wooden buildings. The cheaper guest rooms are in the building overlooking the sea, and the pricier guest rooms in the building farther back are more spacious, with hot water and air-conditioning. Camping is available (from $4 pp). The friendly owners operate a range of tours.

Just before the Gabeal, you'll find another good option, the Argentine-owned **La Facha** (tel. 8/873-4271, $7–10 pp), with decent guest rooms along with pizza and barbecue in the small restaurant. Five minutes' walk inland leads to one of the few modern budget hotels in town, **Hotel San Marena** (tel. 9/191-6115, $10 pp), which has large guest rooms and TVs.

In a land where most things takes a bit longer than expected, the speed at which the multimillion-dollar ◖ **Royal Decameron Mompiche** (reservations: Guayaquil tel. 4/602-5602 or Quito tel. 2/604-6969, www.decameron.com, $79 s, $158 d) has been completed is astonishing. Whether luxury travel is your thing or not, it's difficult not to be impressed with the scale of this resort. Perched on a headland eight kilometers above Mompiche, the hotel opened in December 2009 and is very popular at present with wealthy Ecuadorians, keen to tell their friends they've stayed at one of the grandest high-class resorts in the country. There are six swimming pools, four restaurants, a disco, a private beach, and boat launches to a beach club on La Isla Portete. Guest rooms are immaculate, and the service attentive. The only problem is the poor road and the lack of transportation (aside from airport transfers). All inclusive packages are available.

FOOD

Mompiche has some good seafood shacks offering *ceviche, encocado,* lobster, and fried fish for $4–7. The most popular is **La Langosta,** one block south of the center. **El Sol de Oro** is the best option on the *malecón,* or head to **La Facha** (tel. 8/873-4271, lunch and dinner daily, entrées $5), near the Hotel Gabeal, for pizza, seafood, and occasionally barbecue. There are also a few juice stalls around the center offering great fruit shakes.

GETTING THERE

Getting to Mompiche is the biggest hassle. There are a few buses daily from Esmeraldas via Atacames (3 hours, $3), but it's often a long wait. If you miss the direct bus, take a bus to Muisne and change at El Salto, and then take any bus heading south and ask to be dropped off at the entrance to Mompiche. From there, you can hitch a ride, or it's a tough 40-minute hike up a dusty, bumpy road. From Canoa, take a bus to Pedernales, another to Chamanga, and then a bus heading north to Esmeraldas, and ask to be dropped off.

Central Coast

An hour south of Mompiche by bus is the run-down transportation hub of San José de Chamanga. From here, the new road leads south into Manabí, the largest and probably most interesting province on Ecuador's coast. The far north of the province has little of appeal, and most visitors pass straight through here on the way to Canoa, a developing beach resort for surfers and backpackers. Just to the south is **Bahía de Caráquez,** renowned as an "eco-city" and the coast's most beautiful town. This is a good base for visiting ecological highlights such as the mangroves, **Isla Corazón,** and **Río Muchacho Organic Farm.**

To the south is the busy port **Manta,** and close by **Montecristi,** the birthplace of the wrongly named Panama hats. South of this is the most beautiful stretch of coastline and the only protected area, **Machalilla National Park.** The tourism hub is **Puerto López,** convenient for exploring the dry forests and pristine beaches of the mainland park as well as the birdlife of **Isla de la Plata.** The whale-watching here is fantastic June–September.

PEDERNALES

If you're traveling between Manabí and Esmeraldas, you'll probably come through this unattractive transportation hub. The town is a shrimp and agricultural center with a small beach, but it's really not worth stopping here unless you're stuck. By bus, Canoa ($4) is three hours to the south, and Bahía de Caráquez half an hour farther. To get to Mompiche and Atacames, take a bus to **Chamanga** (1.5 hours) and take another bus north to Esmeraldas. There are regular buses to Santo Domingo (3 hours, $4) and Quito (6 hours, $6). If you must stay, there are a few passable hotels in town—**Hotel Arenas** (Av. Plaza Acosta and Robles, tel. 5/268-1170, $12–14 pp) and **Hotel América** (García Moreno, tel. 5/268-1174, $10 s, $16 d) both have decent guest rooms. For more comfort, stay at the beachfront **Royal Hotel** (García Moreno and Malecón, tel. 5/269-1218 or 9/711-5474, $20 s, $40 d), which has better guest rooms with air-conditioning as well as a pool.

◖ CANOA

Canoa is rapidly turning into the resort of choice for backpackers and surfers who want a more chill alternative to crowded Montañita. Canoa's central location means it's farther from Quito than Atacames and farther from Guayaquil than Montañita, and therefore quieter. At present, Canoa is probably the most pleasant backpacking hub on the entire coast, along with Puerto López, but with the new bridge in nearby Bahía it's expanding fast, so only time will tell if that will remain the case.

Canoa is one of the few coastal towns that actually benefitted from the 1997–1998 El Niño climate pattern, which expanded the beach. It is a dramatic setting with waves crashing on long stretches of sand overlooked by cliffs and caves to the north. These caves are inhabited by bats and can be explored. The surf is consistently good here, and waves commonly reach around two meters.

Entertainment and Events

There are several surfing contests in the high season (Nov.–Apr.), the biggest of which is in November. Nightlife in Canoa is very seasonal. In low season and during the week, it's very

© PETER STROMBERG

Canoa has developed into one of Ecuador's most pleasant beach resorts.

quiet, but on high-season weekends it can get very busy, with partying spilling onto the beach and the main street. Several restaurants double as good bars for a drink, including **Surf Shak** (Malecón, tel. 9/033-6870, 8 A.M.–11 P.M. Wed.–Mon.) on the beachfront. For dancing on weekends, head to **Coco Bar** (Javier Santos and 30 de Noviembre, tel. 9/957-4189, 6 P.M.–midnight Mon.–Thurs., 6 P.M.–2 A.M. Fri.–Sat.) on the main street, one block in from the beach.

Accommodations

Canoa has plenty of accommodations, but things fill up fast in high season, when prices rise between 25 and 50 percent. To the right of the main junction with the seafront is the firm backpacker favorite **Hotel Bambu** (Malecón, tel. 8/926-5225 or 9/926-3365, www.hotelbambuecuador.com, dorm $8 pp, $10–22 s, $15–22 d). It has a wide range of options, from camping ($3.50 pp) to dorms and guest rooms ranging from quite basic to mid-range comfort with sea views. The restaurant-bar is a good place to hang out, with happy hour daily, and the crepes are particularly popular. Along the beach to the left, there is a string of mainly budget hotels. American-owned **Coco Loco** (Malecón, tel. 9/243-6508, www.cocoloco.com, dorm $6 pp, $13 s, $15–21 d) is a popular option with simple but clean guest rooms, shared or private baths, and a laid-back outdoor lounge area. Next door, **La Vista** (Malecón, tel. 8/647-0222, $16 s, $24 d) is a step up, with higher-quality guest rooms but rather sketchy service. Farther along is **Posada Olmito** (Malecón, tel. 9/553-3341, $7–10 pp), an endearing Dutch-owned place with basic guest rooms in an intricately constructed wooden building with coconut trees and statues in the garden.

Two blocks inland from Hotel Bambu is a very popular hotel, **Pais Libre** (Filomeno Hernández and San Andrés, tel. 5/261-6387, www.hotelpaislibre.com, dorm $6 pp, rooms $7–10 pp), run by friendly local surfer Fabio Coello. Guest rooms are well kept, and the hotel is decorated with artwork. There's a disco-bar next door as well as a small pool set in leafy gardens. Some guest rooms have air-conditioning. Inland, next to the soccer pitch, Spanish-owned **Amalur** (San Andrés, tel. 8/303-5039, www.amalurcanoa.com, $10 pp) is one of the best deals in town, with brand-new colorful guest rooms. If your budget stretches farther, one of the best places to stay is **Hotel Canoa's Wonderland** (Malecón, tel. 5/261-6363, www.hotelcanoaswonderland.com.ec, low season $35 s, $50 d, high season $55 s, $90 d), at the far south end of the *malecón*. The hotel has its own generator, so the water and electricity problems that plague the rest of town are not an issue. Guest rooms are very comfortable with hot water, private balconies, and air-conditioning, and there's a pleasant terrace with a pool.

Food

The most renowned of the many seafood restaurants in Canoa is **Cevichería Saboreame** (Malecón, tel. 9/225-5319, lunch and dinner daily, entrées $3–4), which serves up a great selection of soups and entrées. The *encocado* is delicious. If you're missing American food, head to the friendly hub of Canoa's social scene, **⟨ Surf Shak** (Malecón, tel. 9/033-6870, 8 A.M.–11 P.M. Wed.–Mon., entrées $3–6). They serve big breakfasts, fresh coffee, pizzas, and burgers, and Pete, the owner, is full of useful travel advice. Happy hour is popular in the early evening. Next door, a new international restaurant was under construction at the time of writing; **Nirvana** aims to serve an eclectic menu, and there will be a sports bar, **El Caracol**, downstairs.

A block inland from Coco Loco near the soccer pitch is **⟨ Café Flor** (Bahía de Caráquez, tel. 8/546-2568, 9 A.M.–3 P.M. and 6–9:30 P.M. Mon.–Sat., entrées $5–10), which has vegetarian specials and the best pizza and Mexican food in town. Homemade ale is available in high season. Nearby is a delightful little Spanish restaurant, **Amalur** (San Andrés, tel. 8/303-5039, breakfast, lunch, and dinner daily, entrées $5–6), serving tapas and specialties such as meatballs, grilled pork, and octopus.

Information and Services

A small **tourist information office** (Av 3 de Noviembre and Javier Santos, tel. 5/261-6384 or 9/147-9849), one block inland, is well stocked with leaflets and maps and offers tours to Río Muchacho Organic Farm, an eco-city tour of Bahía de Caráquez, and tours of Isla Corazón and the mangroves. **Surf Shak** (tel. 8/101-1471, www.canoathrills.com, pete@canoathrills.com), on the beachfront to the left, is the best place to organize surf lessons (from $15 pp) and rentals. They also offer kayaking trips ($20 pp) to the caves north of town, paragliding, and tours inland to the tropical dry forest at **Bosque Seco Lalo.**

Note that there is no bank in Canoa, so you need to take a bus to San Vicente (30 minutes) for an ATM, or go to the banks in Bahía de Caráquez. There are several phone centers and an Internet café on the main street.

Getting There

Buses between San Vicente and Pedernales ($0.40) come through every half hour. Reina del Camino operates an early morning and late night bus to Quito (6 hours, $8). If you miss the direct bus from Quito, take a bus either to Pedernales or Bahía de Caráquez and change. From Guayaquil, travel via Bahía de Caráquez and either take the boat across to San Vicente ($0.30) and take a bus from there, or take a direct bus across the new bridge.

◖ RÍO MUCHACHO ORGANIC FARM

For more than 20 years, Río Muchacho, 17 kilometers north of Canoa, has been a beacon of good ecological practice in a country where commercial and environmental concerns all too often come into conflict. The fact that the farm exists at all is due to the power of nature. This region had been the victim of coffee farmers' slash-and-burn practices in the mid-20th century and was reduced to useless scrubland until 10 months of torrential rain during the

© NICOLA MEARS

The Río Muchacho Organic Farm is a model of sustainable development.

1982–1983 El Niño climate pattern led to a complete regeneration of the ecosystem. In 1989, local Dario Proaño and New Zealander Nicola Mears opened the Ecuadorian coast's first organic farm. The project quickly became a great success, and the farm currently supports 92 Montubio families, all living from a combination of sustainable farming, tourism, and handicrafts. All toilets are composted, there are solar panels for electricity, and there's no trash allowed anywhere on the farm. There's also a local primary school with its own tailor-made environmentally-focused curriculum.

Visitors can learn all about the farm's practices and get involved in production on organized tours. The one-day itinerary (from $30 pp) tours the farm, the school, and the crops and includes hiking through the forest to see a 130-year-old strangler fig tree. Guests then learn how to make jewelry out of *tagua* seeds and make their own chocolate. The two-day and three-day (from $115 pp) tours include horseback riding into the rainforest to hear the howler monkeys, swimming under waterfalls, and classes on how to make yucca bread, roast coffee, and catch freshwater shrimp before eating a well-earned organic dinner of everything that has been harvested. Rates include accommodations in rustic eco-cabins. Contact Río Muchacho's office in Canoa (3 de Noviembre and Javier Santos, tel. 5/261-6384, www.rio-muchacho.com) or Guacamayo Tours in Bahía de Caráquez (Bolívar 902 at Arenas, tel. 5/269-1412).

Ⓒ BAHÍA DE CARÁQUEZ

If you thought Ecuador's coastal cities were lacking beauty, come to Bahía de Caráquez (pop. 29,000). This relatively small city is clean, quiet, and boasts a dramatic location—bright white apartments perched elegantly on a sandy peninsula jutting out of the mouth of the Río Chone into the Pacific. As recently as the late 19th century this was Ecuador's biggest port, but the eroding sand banks moved that distinction to Guayaquil and Manta. What Bahía lost in commercial terms it gained in aesthetics, and these

days it's easily the most pleasant coastal city to spend a few days in. The streets are clean thanks to a comprehensive recycling program, many residents shun cars in favor of bicycles, including the taxi drivers, and the parks are well tended—if only every city in the country would follow Bahía's lead. The longest bridge in Ecuador, over the Chone estuary, was opened in November 2010, improving access to Bahía and nearby Canoa.

Bahía, as it is called by locals, received relatively few visitors until the 1990s, when President Sixto Durán Ballén bought property here, and it seemed every government minister and wealthy Quiteño followed, squeezing white apartment blocks onto Bahía's narrow tongue of land. Most of these apartments lie dormant outside the January–April high season, which adds to the air of tranquility.

It hasn't always been tranquil in Bahía, however. The 1997–1998 El Niño climate pattern caused widespread landslides and washed away nearby roads. Just as the city was trying to recover, an earthquake measuring magnitude 7.2 leveled large areas of the city, mainly the rickety houses on the outskirts. Bahía was without electricity or water for months, and over 2,000 people were made homeless. After two such devastating events, the city has not just done a remarkable job of recovering, it has re-invented itself in far better shape. A group of residents led by Dario Proaño, who runs Río Muchacho Organic Farm, secured support to convert Bahía into the "eco-city" that it is today. The eco-drive continues, and city has recently banned all plastic bags and replaced them with biodegradable ones.

Entertainment and Events

Bahía has a couple of noteworthy events—the parade of the **Virgen de La Merced** (Sept. 24) and the city's **canonization** celebration (Nov. 3), with parades, dancing, and a gastronomy festival. Nightlife here is low-key—there's only one disco in town, **Dabei** (Malecón, 8 P.M.–2 A.M. Fri.–Sat., $5) on the north side of the *malecón* in the Yacht Club. Alternately, head to nearby Canoa on weekends.

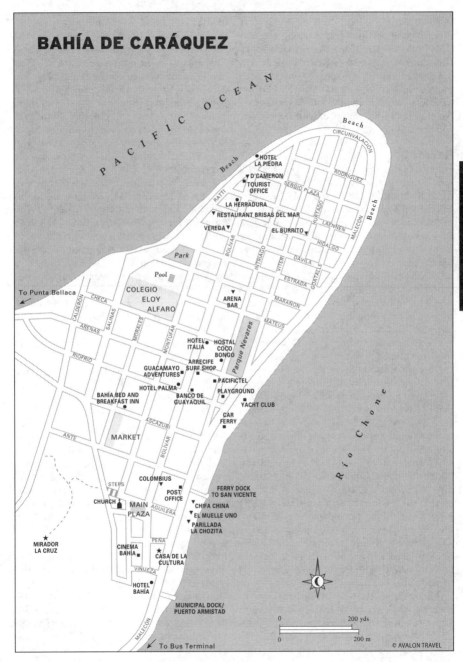

BAHÍA DE CARÁQUEZ

PACIFIC OCEAN

Beach

CIRCUNVALACIÓN

HOTEL LA PIEDRA

D'CAMERON

TOURIST OFFICE

RODRIGUEZ

SERGIO PLAZA

HURTADO

LAENNEN

MALECÓN

Beach

LA HERRADURA

RESTAURANT BRISAS DEL MAR

VEREDA

EL BURRITO

HIDALGO

RATTI

BOLÍVAR

ANTRIAGO

VITERI

DÁVILA

GOATALE

Park

ESTRADA

Pool

MARAÑON

To Punta Bellaca

COLEGIO ELOY ALFARO

ARENA BAR

MATEUS

CHECA

CALDERÓN

SALINAS

ARENAS

MORATES

MONTÚFAR

Parque Nevares

RIOFRIO

HOTEL ITALIA

HOSTAL COCO BONGO

GUACAMAYO ADVENTURES

ARRECIFE SURF SHOP

HOTEL PALMA

PACIFICTEL

PLAYGROUND

BAHÍA BED AND BREAKFAST INN

BANCO DE GUAYAQUIL

YACHT CLUB

CAR FERRY

ANTE

ASCAZUBI

MARKET

BOLÍVAR

Río Chone

STEPS

COLOMBIUS

POST OFFICE

FERRY DOCK TO SAN VICENTE

CHURCH

MAIN PLAZA

AGUILERA

CHIFA CHINA

EL MUELLE UNO

PARILLADA LA CHOZITA

MIRADOR LA CRUZ

PEÑA

CINEMA BAHÍA

CASA DE LA CULTURA

VINUEZA

HOTEL BAHÍA

MUNICIPAL DOCK/ PUERTO ARMISTAD

MALECÓN

To Bus Terminal

0   200 yds

0   200 m

© AVALON TRAVEL

Shopping

Find **artisanal handicrafts** along the *malecón* near the Yacht Club. **Guacamayo Tours** (Bolívar 902 at Arenas, tel. 5/269-1412) sells beautiful handmade paper, envelopes with pressed flowers, as well as T-shirts and other handicrafts. The city **market** (Morales and Ante) offers a wide variety of fruit, vegetables, and seafood.

Recreation

For a coastal resort, Bahía actually has quite a small beach on the south side of the peninsula. The tide comes right in, and the beach gets crowded in high season, but it is beautiful, especially in the early morning. Note that it's not advisable to swim on the north side because the Chone estuary is not clean. If you want a better beach experience, head to nearby Canoa.

The dramatic setting of Bahía is best appreciated from afar. The most convenient spot to take in the spectacular views is at the south end of town via the short hike up to the imposing **Mirador La Cruz.** Another good view is on the boat trip across the bay to San Vicente (the route to Canoa).

Colegio Miguel Valverde (Mejia), three blocks south of the market, has one of Bahía's most-loved residents, a giant Galápagos tortoise named Miguelito, who lives in the grounds and can be visited daily. He has a seemingly insatiable appetite for bananas, so bring a bunch along to feed him, but watch your fingers.

The city's museum, **Museo Banco Central** (Malecón and Peña, tel. 5/269-0361, 10 A.M.–5 P.M. Wed.–Sat.) is one of the best on the coast and well worth a visit. Highlights include tools from Ecuador's oldest civilization, Las Vegas, dating from 8800 B.C., as well as gold pectorals, figurines, ceramics, and a life-size model of a Manteño balsa raft. There is also an interesting history of the famously misnamed Panama hat.

There are several good tour operators in the city, the best of which is **Guacamayo Tours** (Bolívar 902 at Arenas, tel./fax 5/269-1412, www.guacamayotours.com). Run by New Zealander Nicola Mears, the agency can set you up on all the best excursions in the area. There is an eco-city tour that includes the sights listed above plus a visit to Ecopapel to learn how paper is recycled by hand. Excursions go to the fascinating Río Muchacho Organic Farm (from $30 pp, depending on group size).

Another popular excursion is to **Isla Corazón** (from $25 pp), which includes canoeing through impressive mangrove tunnels and hikes on the island, which is home to one of the largest frigate bird colonies in South America. Watching the males inflate their chests to the size of a basketball to attract mates is entrancing. This tour can also be arranged with **Ceibos Tours** (Bolívar and Checa, tel. 5/269-0801, www.ceibostours.com).

A more unusual excursion is to the **Chirije archaeological site,** 15 kilometers south of the city. It can only be reached at low tide by driving along the beach, which adds to the adventure. Experts believe this was once an important port to the Bahía culture (500 B.C.–A.D. 500). Only small sections have been excavated, with artifacts on display in the small on-site museum. Tours (from $30 pp) can be arranged through **Bahía Dolphin Tours** (tel. 5/269-0257, www.chirije.com, www.bahiadolphintours.com), which owns the site, or you can book through Ceibos or Guacamayo.

Accommodations

The view of Bahía from afar could well mislead you into thinking that the city is full of top-end hotels, but the high-rise blocks are mainly apartments rented out in the busy season. The city's lodging options are limited. It gets booked up quickly in high season, but low season is a better bet, and the climate is more comfortable for exploring the surrounding attractions. The cheapest deal in town is the **Bahía Bed and Breakfast Inn** (Ascazubi 316 at Morales, tel. 5/269-0146, $5–8 pp) which has basic guest rooms with shared or private baths, fans, and cable TV in the lounge. The **Hotel Palma** (Bolívar 918 at Riofrio, tel. 5/269-0467, $8 pp) is another basic option, with the unusual feature of showers inside the bedrooms. A better location but decidedly drab guest rooms are found at **Hotel Bahía** (Malecón and Vinueza, tel. 5/269-0602, $10 s, $16 d), at the south end of the *malecón*. If you're lucky enough to get a bay view, it's not a bad deal. A slightly better option in town is **Hotel Italia** (Bolívar and Checa, tel. 5/269-1137, $16 s, $25 d), which has clean, simple guest rooms with private baths. By far the best budget option, though, is (**Hostal Coco Bongo** (Intriagi and Arenas, tel. 8/544-0978, www.coco-bongohostal.com, dorm $6 pp, $15 s, $20-25 d), run by a friendly Aussie named Susie. Overlooking the park, this converted house has guest rooms with hot water, private baths, Wi-Fi, and cable TV. It's a good place to hang out, and the breakfasts are top-notch.

At the higher end, there are a few top-quality hotels near the beach. (**La Herradura** (Hidalgo and Bolívar, tel. 5/269-0446, www.laherradurahotel.com, low season $30 s, $40 d, high season $60 s, $80 d) is head and shoulders above anything in the city in terms of style. The nooks and crannies are filled with eclectic decor, including wagon wheels, saddles, and statues. Colonial art adorns the walls, and the sweet fragrance of *palo santo* fills the air. The hotel's excellent restaurant faces the ocean and offers a range of delicious main dishes ($6-10). Guest rooms have TVs, private baths, air-conditioning, and hot water. A more expensive option suitable for families is **Hotel La Piedra** (Malecón and Bolívar, tel. 5/269-0780, www.hotellapiedra.com, $67 s, $85 d). The hotel has a pool, a gourmet restaurant, a games room, and a bar. The private beach comes in handy in high season. Sea views cost extra.

Food
Outside the higher-end hotels, the best food in town can be found along the passenger ferry wharf on the Chone estuary. There is a string of good-value restaurants offering seafood and barbecue platters. (**El Muelle Uno** (Malecón Santos, tel. 8/989-8927, lunch and dinner Mon.–Sat., entrées $4–8) is one of the most popular of a string of restaurants offering a wide range of *ceviche*, fried fish, and huge, gut-busting barbecue platters. The pleasant view over the bay is the perfect accompaniment to the meal. Farther down, **Puerto Amistad** (Malecón Santos, tel. 5/269-3112, lunch and dinner Mon.–Sat., entrées $5–10), run by an American sailor, offers quesadillas and crepes as well as meat and fish.

In the center of town, the **Arena Bar** (Marañon and Bolívar, tel. 5/269-2024, lunch and dinner Mon.–Sat., entrées $5) is the best place for pizza and pasta, while **Colombius** (Bolívar and Ante, tel. 5/269-0537, lunch and dinner Mon.–Sat., entrées $3) has great salads, seafood, and cheap lunches. Near the beach, **D'Cameron** (Bolívar, tel. 8/662-3805, 9 A.M.–6 P.M. daily, entrées $5) is a dependable option to eat seafood in the open air.

Information and Services
The **tourist information office** (tel. 5/269-1044 or 5/269-0372, 8:30 A.M.–1 P.M. and 2–5 P.M. Mon.–Fri.) is on the corner of Bolívar and Malecón. The local **post office** is opposite the Malecón on Aguilera.

Getting There and Around
Bahía is an easy and pleasant city to walk around, but for weary legs and a little fun, try a *tricyclo* ride ($0.50). Drivers also offer a town tour ($2). Buses to destinations throughout the country leave from the new bus station south of town ($1.50 by taxi, or take a bus heading down the *malecón*). Coactur runs frequent buses to Manta (3 hours, $3) and Guayaquil (6 hours, $6). Reina del Camino runs three buses per day to Quito (8 hours, $9), Esmeraldas (8 hours, $8), Santo Domingo (4 hours, $4), and Guayaquil. To get to Canoa, take a ferry across the bay to San Vicente and get a bus from there, although with the completion of the new bridge, direct bus services will begin from the bus terminal.

The 10-minute **passenger ferry** (about 6 A.M.–11 P.M. daily, $0.30 pp) to San Vicente leaves from the dock at Malecón and Aguilera when full (usually every few minutes).

MANTA AND VICINITY

While Bahía has improved markedly in recent years and has become a model of development, the big-sister city that stole Bahía's status as Ecuador's second port is sadly going downhill. Manta (pop. 225,000) has never been a major tourism draw for foreigners, but the U.S. military base that arrived in 1999 led to increased security and a developing expat population. All this has changed in the last two years, though; President Rafael Correa kept his electoral campaign promise to refuse to renew the military base's lease, and the U.S. soldiers left. With their departure, Manta has become more dangerous, with a marked increase in organized crime, and the expat community has all but dried up. The city is not without its attractions, however; it has good beaches, thriving nightlife, and delicious seafood. The people, as in most of Manabí, are very friendly, and Manta is a useful connection point with regular bus services to most major cities around the country. The city also has an airport if you prefer to shun the long bus ride and fly to the coast.

A major port since pre-Inca times, Manta was officially established by the Spanish in 1565 as a supply point between Panama and Peru. Today, Manta is second only to Guayaquil in the volume of imports and exports, and the city has become the center of the Ecuadorian tuna industry. The arrival of the U.S. military in 1999 brought an economic boom, and the city developed quickly, with a string of high-rise hotels and shopping malls as well as bars and restaurants along Avenida Flavio Reyes, a few blocks inland from the *malecón*. Manta has also become a stop for cruise ships heading south to Chile or north to the Caribbean, but the recent deterioration in security has left the tourism industry struggling for business.

Recreation

The best beach is **Playa Murciélago,** which translates rather oddly as "Bat Beach," in the northwest of town. The *malecón* is pleasant and lined with seafood restaurants, although currents are strong, so take care swimming here.

There's another beach at **Tarqui** to the east, but it is a run-down, seedy area and dangerous at night. Apart from beaches, you can catch a bit of local culture at **Museo del Banco Central** (Malecón, tel. 5/262-6998, 10 A.M.–5 P.M. daily, $1), which has exhibits on Manteño culture and modern art. It's less impressive than the museum in Bahía.

The **Yacht Club** (near the dock at Calle 15) has boats that can be chartered for deep-sea fishing for very high rates. Several tour companies offer snorkeling at the base of the headland and out at Isla de la Plata; try **Metropolitan Touring** (Av. 4, tel. 5/261-3366) or **Delgado Travel** (Av. 6 between Calle 12 and Calle 13, tel. 5/262-2813, www.ecuadorpacificosur. com).

Entertainment and Events

The **Feria Agropecuaria** (Sept. 8–9) is a popular agricultural fair, followed by an **International Theater Festival** in late September and **Manta Day** (Nov. 4).

For nightlife, head to Avenida Flavio Reyes, where there are plenty of bars and discos. **Dream Bar** (Flavio Reyes and Calle 19, tel. 8/254-2647, 8 P.M.–midnight Mon.–Thurs., 8 P.M.–2 A.M. Fri.–Sat.) is currently popular, and **Conga** (Av. 23 and Flavio Reyes, 8 P.M.–midnight Mon.–Thurs., 8 P.M.–2 A.M. Fri.–Sat.) is a popular disco pumping out Latin beats until the early hours.

Accommodations

If you're on a tight budget, you may consider giving Manta a miss. The cheap hotels are nearly all in the unpleasant area near Tarqui beach. This is a dangerous area at night, so be careful, take taxis, and don't wander around after dark. **Hotel Panorama Inn** (Calle 103 and Av. 105, tel. 5/261-1552, $7 pp) has very basic guest rooms. There's a better hotel across the street, also called **Hotel Panorama** (tel. 5/261-1552, $25 s, $35 d), with air-conditioning and a pool. **Hotel Old Navy** (Calle 104 and Malecón, tel. 5/262-5295, $12 pp) is a relatively well-kept budget option with colorful guest rooms. For a more upmarket experience

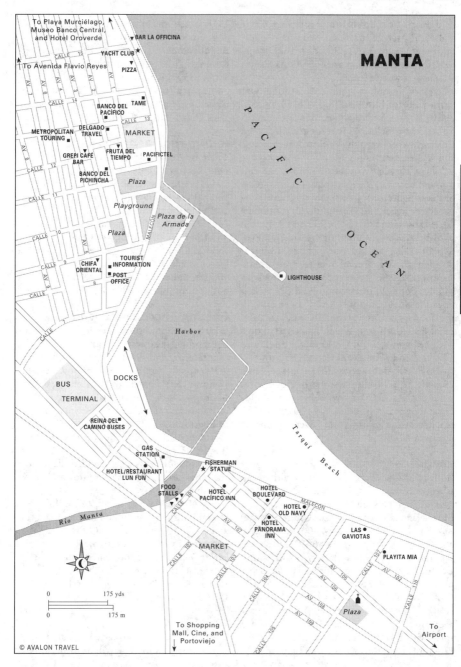

MANTA

To Playa Murciélago,
Museo Banco Central,
and Hotel Oroverde

▼ BAR LA OFFICINA

CALLE 15

YACHT CLUB ★

To Avenida Flavio Reyes

PIZZA ▼

AV 7   AV 6   AV 5   AV 3   AV

CALLE 14

BANCO DEL   ■ TAME
PACÍFICO

■ DELGADO   CALLE 13
METROPOLITAN TRAVEL
TOURING ■   MARKET

AV 8

CALLE 12

GREPI CAFÉ   FRUTA DEL   PACIFICTEL ●
■ BAR   ● TIEMPO
BANCO DEL
PICHINCHA   *Plaza*

CALLE 11

Playground

CALLE 10

MALECÓN

Plaza   Plaza de la
                 Armada

CALLE 9

AV 9

CHIFA ▼   TOURIST
ORIENTAL   ■ INFORMATION
           ■ POST
CALLE   OFFICE
8

CALLE 7

CALLE 5   ■ LIGHTHOUSE

Harbor

DOCKS

BUS
TERMINAL

REINA DEL ■
CAMINO BUSES

GAS
STATION
■

FISHERMAN
★ STATUE

HOTEL/RESTAURANT
LUN FUN

FOOD
STALLS ▼   HOTEL ●   HOTEL ●
▼   PACÍFICO INN BOULEVARD
                              HOTEL ●
Río Manta   OLD NAVY

HOTEL ●
PANORAMA   LAS ●
INN   GAVIOTAS

MARKET   PLAYITA MIA ●

CALLE 101   AV 102   CALLE 104   CALLE 105   AV 106   AV 108   AV 103   CALLE 107   AV 102   CALLE 110

0   175 yds

0   175 m

Plaza

To Shopping
Mall, Cine, and
Portoviejo

To
Airport

© AVALON TRAVEL

Tarquí Beach

P A C I F I C

O C E A N

NORTH AND CENTRAL COASTS

in Tarqui, **Las Gaviotas** (Malecón 109 at Calle 106, tel. 5/262-0140, www.hotelgaviotasmanta.com, $33 s, $50 d, breakfast included) has a bar and cafeteria with a casino attached as well as a pool.

West of Tarqui, in front of the fishing-boat harbor, **Hotel Lun Fun** (Calle 2, tel. 5/262-2966, lunfunhotel@yahoo.com, $40 s, $55 d, breakfast included) is recommended. The Chinese owners keep the place immaculate and run the popular restaurant.

There are plenty of mostly mid-range and top-end hotels in the more pleasant area south of Playa Murcielago. Perfectly positioned between the beach and the nightlife is the homey ◖ **Hostal Manakin** (Calle 20 and Av. 12, tel. 5/262-0413, www.hostelmanakin.net, $35 s, $45 d). With just 10 comfortable, well-appointed guest rooms, it retains an intimate atmosphere missing in many other hotels in Manta. For even more comfort, the next step up is the **Hotel Balandra** (Av. 7 and Calle 20, tel. 5/262-0316, www.hotelbalandramanta.com, $86 s, $100 d) which has guest rooms with sea views, a gym, a sauna, a pool, and a playground. The swankiest place in town is the high-rise **Oro Verde** (Malecón and Calle 23, tel. 5/262-9200, www.oroverdemanta.com, $159 s, $170 d), which has spacious guest rooms, a large pool, a gym, a spa, a kid's playground, a casino, and several gourmet restaurants.

Food

Both of Manta's beaches are lined with cheap seafood restaurants, but bear in mind that Tarqui Beach is not very safe at night, so Murcielago is a better bet. For Chinese, **Hotel Lun Fun** (Calle 2, tel. 5/262-2966, noon–3 P.M. and 6–10 P.M. daily, entrées $6–12) has a great reputation for noodles, fried rice, and soups. East of Playa Murcielago, for Italian pizza and pasta, **Pizzeria Topi** (Malecón, tel. 5/262-1180, lunch and dinner daily, entrées $5–9) is popular. Otherwise, it's best to head to the area around Avenida Flavio Reyes, which is lined with good restaurants and bars. **Marisco Flipper** (Flavio Reyes and Calle 20, tel. 8/499-

1535, lunch and dinner daily, entrées $4–5) is good for seafood soup and grilled fish. **Beachcomber** (Corner of Calle 20 and Flavio Reyes, tel. 5/262-5463, lunch and dinner daily, entrées $3–7) is renowned for grilled meat. For burgers, try **Trosky Burguer** (Flavio Reyes and Calle 18, tel. 8/729-4571, 6 P.M.–midnight Tues.–Sun., entrées $2–5).

Information and Services

There is a **tourist information office** (Pasaje Egas between Calles 10 and 11, tel. 5/262-2944, 9 A.M.–5 P.M. Mon.–Fri.) in town, and another on the Playa Murcielago *malecón*.

Banco Pichincha (Av. 2 between Calles 11 and 12) changes foreign currency on the second floor, and the **Banco del Pacífico** (Av. 2 and Calle 13) will change traveler's checks. The local hospital, **Clínica Manta** (tel. 5/292-1566), and the **police station** (tel. 5/292-0900) are both on Avenida 4 de Noviembre.

Getting There and Around

Like the area that surrounds it, Manta's main bus terminal, just west of Tarqui, is in dire need of a facelift, and don't hang round here longer than you have to. Buses run to Guayaquil (4 hours, $5), Esmeraldas (9 hours, $8), and Quito (8 hours, $8). Other buses travel north to Bahía de Caráquez (3 hours, $3) and south to Puerto López (2 hours, $2).

To avoid the bus station, **Panamericana** (Calle 12 and Av. 4, tel. 5/262-5898) and **Flota Imbabura** (Malecón and Calle 8) both run comfortable buses to Quito and Santo Domingo ($10).

TAME (Calle 13, tel. 5/262-2006) sells tickets on the *malecón* just north of the theater park. Flights leave for Quito (daily, $68 one-way) from Eloy Alfaro airport, five kilometers northeast of the center of town. **Icaro** (Malecón and Calle 23, tel. 5/262-7327) also flies to Quito ($58 one-way) and Guayaquil ($67 one-way).

Crucita

Crucita is a small fishing town that is developing into a tourist destination because of

THE PANAMA MISNOMER: MONTECRISTI HATS

© CHRIS O'CONNELL

Panama hats actually originate from Montecristi.

It's a source of much frustration to Ecuadorians that they supplied one of the world's finest and most famous hats, only for another country to get the credit. This straw hat, known locally as *sombrero de paja toquilla*, should in fact be called a Montecristi hat, but history conspired to attribute it wrongly to Panama.

The origin of the mistake dates back to the early 19th century when Spanish entrepreneurs recognized the quality of the hats and began exporting them via Panama. After independence, the trade continued to grow rapidly. When construction of the Panama Canal began in 1904, exiled Ecuadorian president Eloy Alfaro, whose father had exported the hats for many years, noticed the needs of thousands of workers toiling in the hot sun, and he ordered 220,000 hats to be sent from Ecuador. U.S. president Theodore Roosevelt heard about the popularity of the hat and was photographed wearing one while visiting the canal construction in 1906. The photo of the president was published worldwide with the caption "The president and his Panama hat," and the misnomer was born.

The production of the hats continues unabated. The time and effort required to make one is astonishing. The *toquilla* palms that grow around Montecristi are harvested for their shoots, which are beaten on the ground, the leaves removed, and then tied into bundles, boiled, and dried for three days. The finished straw is then woven into hats by hatmakers on the coast, but production is greatest around Cuenca in the southern highlands.

There are four classes of hats, depending on the tightness of the weave, from standard to high-quality *superfino*. After weaving, the hats are bleached white, banded, and ready to sell. A standard hat sells for $10-20, while the high-quality *superfino* versions fetch $100-500. It may seem like a lot to pay for a hat, but not when you consider the talent and artistry that goes into making it.

its beach and great conditions for paragliding. Visitors come from around the globe to paraglide, and several competitions are held annually. Paragliding lessons are available at **Hotel Voladores** (Nueva Loja and Principal, tel. 5/234-0200, $8 pp) on the south end of the beach. The hotel has guest rooms with private baths and fans. Hang gliding is also popular.

Montecristi

Montecristi is famous both as the birthplace of the famously misnamed Panama hats and also as the birthplace of Ecuador's liberal president and revolutionary hero, Eloy Alfaro. The town was founded soon after the conquest in 1536 by settlers from Manta fleeing repeated pirate attacks. Montecristi's profile was raised considerably in 2008 when President Rafael Correa chose to base the temporary National Assembly here to draft a new constitution. The assembly building, high above the town, is now mainly used as a conference center, but it also houses an interesting museum, **Centro Cívico Ciudad Alfaro** (9 A.M.–1 P.M. and 2:30–6 P.M. daily, tel. 5/231-1210, www.ciuadadalfaro.gob.ec, free), documenting the life of Eloy Alfaro, who was President of Ecuador twice (1899–1901 and 1906–1911). His key achievements included the construction of the Guayaquil–Quito railroad and a range of liberal legislation, including separating the church from the state, introducing a state education system, and allowing women to work. He was assassinated by angry conservatives in Quito in 1912. The mausoleum where Alfaro's ashes rest, in front of the museum, is even more impressive, with a copper sculpture surrounded by replica Manteño chairs and overlooked by the faces of dozens of fellow revolutionaries. To get to the museum, it's best to take a taxi ($1) from the center of town.

In the town itself, there is a pleasant main square and a small **Museo Arqueológico** (9 de Julio and Manta, no phone, 9 A.M.–6 P.M. Mon.–Sat., donation) on the main street. The hats are the other main draw of Montecristi. Alfaro's father was one of several merchants that helped to make the local straw hats famous. Shops selling hats and other woven

goods line the main street, 9 de Julio. One of the best places to purchase high-quality *superfino* hats is the home of **José Chávez Franco** (Rocafuerte 386, tel. 5/231-0343, 7 A.M.–7 P.M. daily).

Montecristi is between Portoviejo and Manta, roughly 30 minutes from both by bus (under $1).

Portoviejo

Portoviejo (pop. 228,000) is the capital of Manabí Province, and after Manta is the largest city in the province. It's also officially the hottest city in Ecuador. Statistics aside, there is little of appeal in this dusty, busy commercial center. Portoviejo is an important transportation hub with a large bus terminal, so you may have to pass through. If you are stuck, the **Parque Eloy Alfaro** and modern **cathedral** are pleasant enough, and **Hotel New York** (Olmedo and Francisco de Moreira, tel. 5/263-2395, $22 s, $35 d), right on the plaza, has decent guest rooms with TVs and air-conditioning. Regular buses run to Manta (45 minutes, $1); Jipijapa (45 minutes, $1.40), where you can change to get to Puerto López; Bahía de Caráquez (2 hours, $2); Guayaquil (4 hours, $4); and Quito (8 hours, $9).

Picoazá and Ciudad de los Cerros

West of Portoviejo, the small town of Picoazá has recently been the scene of intense archaeological interest after the discovery of two hilltop settlements, Cerro de Hojas and Cerro Jaboncilla, thought to be key cities of the ancient Manteño culture. Some 3,500 hectares are now protected by the government, and a small area of Ciudad de los Cerros (tel. 5/231-2210 ext. 110, 9 A.M.–5 P.M. daily, free) was opened to visitors in late 2010. There is an interpretative center and trails through the ruins, which include a pyramid structure, walls, artificial hills, and agricultural terraces. Guides are available for hire. To get to Ciudad de los Cerros, you can take a bus to Picoazá and walk four kilometers; it's better to take a taxi from the Portoviejo bus terminal to the Ceibos-Amazonas neighborhood of Picoazá (about $5).

© CIUDAD ALFARO

The interpretative center at Ciudad de los Cerros recreates a scene from the Manteño culture.

Jipijapa

The name Jipijapa (pronounced "hippy-happa") is the best thing about the town, and perhaps it's worth stopping just to say you've been here. It's not much of a town, though, and you won't find any happy hippies here. There are, however, plenty of Panama hats and decent coffee because the town is in the middle of a fertile region of coffee plantations. Like Portoviejo, it's mainly used by travelers to change buses. The bus terminal on the edge of town has regular services to Puerto López, Manta, and Portoviejo, all taking around one hour and costing $1–2.

PUERTO LÓPEZ

Puerto López boasts one of the most attractive locations on the coast, set in a wide bay surrounded by the green hills of Ecuador's largest protected coastal forest. The town itself could do with a face-lift, but the dusty *malecón* has a certain beaten-down charm about it, and the fishermen heading out to dozens of boats dotting the bay give the town a vibrant feel in the morning. It is quieter than other coastal resorts, and it is the best base to explore **Machalilla National Park,** take a boat trip to **Isla del Plata,** and book whale-watching tours. Note that the town gets very busy on weekends during the June–September whale-watching season, so booking accommodations in advance is advisable.

Recreation and Tours

Humpback whales breed in the waters off the coast June–September. You can often see these marine giants from the beach, but it's far better to take a tour for a close-up view. There are several reputable tour operators in town that offer whale-watching. The rest of the year, the most popular tours are to Isla de la Plata and land tours to the forests and beaches of the other parts of Machalilla National Park. Boat trips ($35–40 pp) include a guide and a light lunch but not the park entrance fee. Recommended companies include **Bosque Marino** (tel. 9/707-1120, www.bosquemarino.com) and **Exploramar**

HUMPBACK WHALES

Puerto López's biggest attraction is the arrival of humpback whales June–September. Humpback whales are famous for being the most acrobatic of large whales. They like to breach out of the water regularly, often twirling on their way down. There are various theories as to why they do this– it may be part of the mating ritual or just playful behavior. The whales also frequently pop their heads above water to survey the surroundings and slap their tails against the water, often in rough seas, possibly as a warning to other whales. As well as being acrobats, humpbacks are also the noisiest and most talented singers. The males sing long, varied songs in a wide range of frequencies, most commonly in the mating season.

Humpback whales travel up to 5,000 kilometers during the arctic winter to mate, when up to 20 males surround the females to compete. The gestation period last about 12 months, so the mothers return the next year to give birth in warm waters because the newborns have insufficient fat reserves to survive in cold waters. The adults grow to 16 meters long and weigh over 40 tonnes. They can dive for up to 30 minutes before returning to the surface to breathe through two blowholes. They usually swim at speeds under 5-15 kilometers per hour but can reach 25 kilometers per hour in short bursts.

Sadly, humpback whales are an endangered species – the global population, once around 1 million, is now estimated to be less than 50,000. The invention of the harpoon in the late 19th century was instrumental in this decline, and illegal whaling remains a serious problem worldwide. For further information, contact the **World Wildlife Fund** (www.wwf.org) or the **Whales and Dolphin Conservation Society** (www.wdcs.org).

Diving (tel. 5/256-3905, www.exploradiving.com), which also offers diving trips and PADI certification. Also try **Perfil Turístico** (Malecón and Lascano, tel. 5/230-0147) at the Hotel Pacífico or **Naturis** (General Córdova and Juan Montalvo, tel. 5/230-0218, www.machalillatours.com), which specializes in community tourism and offers a wide range of multiple-activity trips, including kayaking, fishing, and snorkeling ($25 pp) as well as tours to San Sebastián. Spanish courses are also available.

Entertainment and Events

The town hosts a festival dedicated to the arrival of the humpback whales, **World of Whales,** at the start of the season in late June, featuring street parties and parades.

Nightlife is very quiet in Puerto López, and bars open and close sporadically during high season. There are a few bamboo beach bars to choose from and an occasional disco, **Taurus** (no phone, 7 P.M.–2 A.M. Fri.–Sat.) on the northern end of the *malecón.*

Accommodations

Puerto López has plenty of decent budget and mid-range accommodations, but book ahead in the whale-watching season as the best fill up fast and prices rise by about 50 percent. At the budget end, there are a cluster of cheap, basic wooden cabins a block or so from the beach. One of the most popular is the laid-back **Sol Inn** (Juan Montalvo and Eloy Alfaro, tel. 5/230-0248, dorm $6 pp, $10–12 s, $14–16 d). Another popular choice at the north end of town is **Hostal Itapoa** (Malecón, tel. 9/314-5894, $10 pp), a friendly Brazilian-run place with cabins and guest rooms set in a small garden just off the *malecón.*

The hotels on the *malecón* tend to cost $20–30 for a double room. One of the newest and the best value in this price range is **Hostería Nantu** (Malecón, tel. 9/781-4636, $20 s, $30 d), which has firm beds, hot water, a small pool, and a games room. Other good mid-range choices include **Hostal Isla los Islotes** (Malecón and General Córdoba, tel. 5/230-0108, $15 s, $20 d) and **Hotel Ruta del**

Sol (Malecón and Mariscal Sucre, tel. 5/230-0236, www.puertolopez.net, $15 s, $30 d), which has well-equipped guest rooms with air-conditioning and cable TV. For something a little different, try the boutique style of **Hotel Piedra del Mar** (General Córdoba and Malecón, tel. 5/230-0227, www.piedradelmar. com, $25 s, $50 d). The colonial-style courtyard, pebble-dashed walls, and small pool mark this as one of the best options in the center. An upmarket option on the *malecón* is **Hotel Pacifico** (Malecón and Lascano, tel. 5/262-6250, $20–35 s, $30–56 d), which has two classes of guest rooms. The cheaper ones at the back are nothing special, but the better guest rooms with ocean views, air-conditioning, balconies, and hammocks are good, if a bit over-priced. The hotel's best feature is its swimming pool set in lush gardens.

The best-known lodging in town is still the ℂ **Hostería Mandala** (Malecón, tel. 5/230-0181, www.hosteriamandala.info, $22 s, $45 d). The individual cabins are set among dense tropical gardens filled with exotic flowers and trees. The German and Italian owners have painstakingly decorated each cabin with unique designs. There's also an excellent restaurant serving homemade bread and ice cream, plus a music room and a library upstairs. If you want to get farther away from it all, right at the north end of the *malecón* is **Hostería Oceanic** (Malecón, tel. 9/621-1065, www.hosteriaoceanic.com, $48 s or d). This is a quiet area surrounded by hills and a deserted stretch of beach. Immaculate newly furnished cabins are set around a swimming pool with a miniature waterfall. There are doubles and several cabins for larger groups.

Food

Puerto López is not overflowing with varied dinner options, but as you would expect in a fishing port, there is plenty of good seafood at the restaurants along the *malecón*. ℂ **Carmita's** (Malecón, tel. 5/230-0149, 8 A.M.–9 P.M. daily, entrées $4–5) is probably the best of these, with a wide selection of dishes served in a polished setting. Farther up,

Espuma del Mar (Malecón, tel. 5/230-0187, 8 A.M.–9 P.M. daily, entrées $4–5) is another dependable option and good for breakfast as well if you ignore the rather tacky decor. For a more informal atmosphere and some creative seafood dishes, try **Spondylus** (Malecón, no phone, lunch and dinner daily, entrées $4–5), but avoid the oyster that gave the restaurant its name because it's endangered. One of the best places to eat and socialize is ℂ **The Whale Café** (Malecón, no phone, 8 A.M.–9 P.M. daily, entrées $6–9), at the south end of the *malecón*, popular for its vegetarian dishes, pancakes, homemade bread, and pizzas. The Thai noodles are particularly delicious, and the American owners are very helpful with travel advice.

A block inland is the **Patacón Pisa'o** (General Córdoba, tel. 9/127-4206, 5 P.M.–midnight Mon.–Sat., entrées $3), which serves Colombian specialties such as *arepas*. Stray too far from the *malecón* and Puerto López's dusty, potholed edges become apparent, but it's worth checking out **Bellitalia** (Montalvo, tel. 5/230-0361, 6–11 P.M. Mon.–Sat., entrées $6) for the town's best Italian food in a candlelit setting.

Information and Services

Just north of the market, the local **iTur office** and **Machalilla National Park headquarters** (Machalilla and Atahualpa, tel. 5/230-0102, turismo@puertolopez.gov.ec, daily) have plenty of leaflets, maps, and attentive service. You can pay the park entrance fee here, through any of the agencies on the *malecón*, or at the park entrances. Exchange money and traveler's checks at the **Banco Pichincha** (Córdova and Machalilla), which also has the only ATM in town. The **post office** is on the *malecón* south of Córdova.

Getting There and Around

All buses to and from Puerto López stop on the main road next to the market, a five-minute walk to the waterfront, or you can take a *tricyclo* taxi ($0.50), or pay a little more for a *mototaxi* to hotels outside the center. Buses from Puerto López run regularly along the coast road south to La Libertad (3 hours, $3) and north to Manta (2 hours, $2.50), as well as north to Jipijapa (1.5 hours, $1.50), which is the best hub to change buses for Guayaquil and destinations inland. **Reina del Camino** (tel. 5/230-0207) offers comfortable, secure buses directly to and from Avenida Patria in Quito (10 hours, $12) at 8 A.M. and 8 P.M.

◖ MACHALILLA NATIONAL PARK

Ecuador's only coastal national park, set up in 1979, preserves what's left of the country's tropical dry forest that once stretched all the way to Panama. Only about 1 percent of the original forest remains in Ecuador, and the park contains most of it—about 60,000 hectares. In contrast to the somewhat barren backdrops

in other coastal areas, this is the most beautiful stretch of Ecuador's coast, with densely forested hills, crowned by *Opuntia* candelabra cacti and *palo santo* trees, sloping down to pristine peaceful beaches. Off the coast, the islands of Salango and La Plata make great day trips, the latter famous for its birdlife, including frigates, boobies, and waved albatross. Of course, the biggest wildlife attraction is the singing, somersaulting population of humpback whales that visit June–September.

There are several prices for park entrance, which can be bought in Puerto López at the park office (Machalilla and Atahualpa, tel. 5/230-0102, turismo@puertolopez.gov.ec, daily), including a full ticket covering the mainland and Isla de la Plata ($20), Isla de la Plata only ($15), and the mainland only ($12).

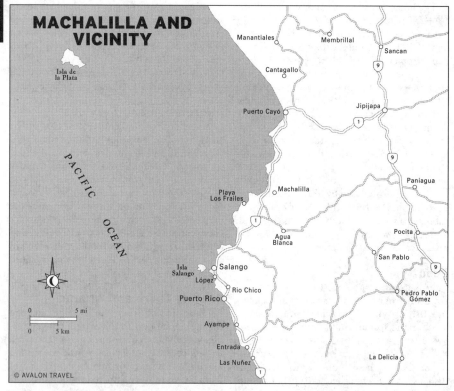

MACHALILLA AND VICINITY

Isla de la Plata

Manantiales   Membrillal   Sancan

Cantagallo

9

Puerto Cayó   Jipijapa

1

9

PACIFIC OCEAN

Paniagua

Playa Los Frailes   Machalilla

1

Agua Blanca   Pocita

San Pablo

Isla Salango   Salango   9

López

Rio Chico   Pedro Pablo Gómez

Puerto Rico

Ayampe

0   5 mi
0   5 km

Entrada

Las Nuñez   La Delicia

1

© AVALON TRAVEL

Isla de la Plata

The moniker "the poor man's Galápagos" is a little unfair to this small island 37 kilometers northwest of Puerto López. Any comparison with the famous archipelago is bound to come up short, but Isla de la Plata is well worth a day trip, which can be combined with whale-watching in the summer months. The island's name (Silver Island) arose from a legend that English sea captain Francis Drake buried treasure here after an assault on a Spanish galleon at the end of the 16th century. These days, the main treasures are the wildlife. Boats land at Drake Bay, and there are two circular paths through the hills, commanding sweeping views of the interior down to the cliff-tops on the opposite side. The shortest and most popular walk, Sendero Machete, takes about three hours. Highlights include blue-footed and masked boobies, which peer curiously at you as you pass within a few meters of them. There are also frigate birds, red-footed boobies, and waved albatross, most commonly on view April–October. The island has a small colony of sea lions, but it's rare to see them. Note that there is very little shade, so bring sunscreen and a hat. The day trip usually finishes with swimming and snorkeling among tropical fish in the bay.

Agua Blanca and San Sebastián

The most accessible point to explore the park's dry forest is Agua Blanca, a village inhabited by some 300 indigenous people and an important archaeological site of the Manteño culture that lived here A.D. 800–1500. Many of the most interesting artifacts have been moved to the museum in Salango, but there is an interesting collection of sculptures, funeral urns, and slightly bizarrely, pickled snakes. A guided tour of Agua Blanca ($5) includes the museum and a two-hour forest walk that includes the Manteño ruins. The forest is filled with towering *ceibos, barbasco,* and fragrant *palo santo* trees, whose wood is burned as incense and doubles as mosquito repellent. There are spectacular views up to San Sebastián from lookout points, and the tour ends with a refreshing but pungent dip in

a natural sulfur pool, considered sacred by local indigenous people.

Farther inland, the landscape rises to 800 meters, where dry forest becomes cloud forest in San Sebastián. This virgin forest can be explored on a four-hour, 20-kilometer hike or horseback ride ($15 pp) with a mandatory guide ($20 per group) hired in Agua Blanca or Puerto López. It can be done in a day, but you can also camp overnight or stay with local villagers. The forest boasts many species of orchids as well as howler monkeys, anteaters, and more than 350 species of birds.

GETTING THERE

To get to Agua Blanca and San Sebastián, you can take a bus north from Puerto López and then walk the dusty five-kilometer trail up a dirt track, or better, hire a *mototaxi* ($5 one-way, $10 round-trip). Alternately, take a guided tour from Puerto López.

Playa los Frailes

Pristine waters, a perfect crescent-shaped beach, a backdrop of terra-cotta cliffs and lush forested hills—Los Frailes is rightly regarded as one of Ecuador's most spectacular beaches. It is a special place, and if you come early enough, you may have it to yourself. Swimming and sunbathing can be accompanied by a three-kilometer walk to the black-sand cove of La Playita and Playa La Tortuguita, which offers good snorkeling.

Los Frailes is 10 kilometers north of Puerto López. There are guided tours, but it's easy to visit on your own. Taking a bus to the entrance necessitates an unpleasant 40-minute hike up the road. Alternately, take a taxi from Puerto López and arrange a collection time ($5 one-way, $10 round-trip). It's possible to combine Agua Blanca and Los Frailes in one day. Note that if you only plan to visit the beach, you still have to pay the $12 national park entrance fee.

SALANGO

South of Puerto López, the road winds through a succession of small fishing villages, the largest of which is Salango. While it's not much of a destination in itself, it's worth stopping at this small town to see the archaeological museum, **Museo Arqueológico de Salango** (www.salango.com.ec, 9 A.M.–5 P.M. daily, $1.50) with a well-presented exhibition of pottery and sculptures from ancient Valdivia and Manteña cultures as well as an investigative center. At the time of writing the museum is being expanded, with interactive exhibitions planned; check the website for updated information.

There's not much else to do around town, but as an interesting excursion, hire a fishing boat to Isla Salango, two kilometers offshore, to see the seabirds.

Accommodations

Salango doesn't have many good accommodations, but a couple of kilometers south of town, **Hostería Piqueros Patas Azules** (tel. 4/278-0279, www.hosteriapiqueros.com, $35 s, $51 d) has brightly colored cabins that sleep 2–5 people. It also has a small private museum ($1), but the main attraction is the stretch of deserted beach on your doorstep.

Food

If you stop for lunch, there are a couple of very good seafood restaurants: **Restaurante Delfin Magico** (Frente al Parque, tel. 4/278-0291, lunch and dinner daily, entrées $4–6) and **El Pelicano** (Principal, tel. 4/278-0295, lunch and dinner daily, entrées $4–6). The fish or shrimp cooked in peanut sauce is a particular specialty.

PUERTO RICO AND VICINITY

Blink and you may miss Puerto Rico—it's more a collection of houses than an actual town. However, the get-away-from-it-all vibe makes it an attractive alternate base to busier Puerto López, and two of the most attractive *hosterías* in the region are found in this area.

Accommodations

Hostería Alándaluz (Ruta del Sol Km. 12, Vía Puerto López, tel. 4/278-0690 or 4/278-0686, Quito office tel. 2/244-0790, www.alandaluzhosteria.com, $24–63 s, $31–84 d) has made a name for itself as one of the few ecologically friendly lodges along the Ruta del Sol. It has a

Puerto Rico is a quieter alternative to Puerto Lopez.

© LA BARQUITA

full recycling program, composting toilets, and an organic garden providing much of the fresh food in the restaurant. The extensive gardens, charming wooden cabins, and private beach make this an idyllic location, and the open-air restaurant is a particular highlight, if a little expensive. The *hostería* also organizes snorkeling, horseback, and cycling tours as well as excursions to Machalilla and the hotel's own wildlife sanctuary on the Río Ayampe. It all seems too good to be true, and it may well be: Alándaluz seems to have become a victim of its own success recently, and it feels rather impersonal, with uniformed staff and a largely absent owner. There are also questions as to whether all of the food is organic. It remains extremely popular, though, and booking in advance is essential. There are six classes of accommodations, and you can camp with your own tent ($7 pp).

The main draw of ❰ **Hostería La Barquita** (Ruta del Sol Km. 15, Vía Puerto López, tel. 4/278-0051, www.hosterialabarquita.com, dorm $20 pp, $33 s, $55 d), near Puerto Rico, is the boat-shaped main building that provides its name (Little Boat). It is a more intimate, friendlier alternative to the nearby Alándaluz. The Swiss owners are very hands-on and full of travel advice for guests. There is a new swimming pool plus a tree-house and an adventure playground frequented by the owners' children. The boat theme is reprised in the cabins, with porthole mirrors, rounded doors, and natural stone locks. New suites with air-conditioning and cable TV are also available. Even if you don't stay here, it's worth stopping to eat in the unique setting of the boat, with open-air seating, sumptuous seafood, and views of the ocean.

AYAMPE

South of Las Tunas, the small town of Ayampe, where the Río Ayampe empties into the sea, is slowly emerging as a surfing destination, and there are a few good places to stay. The most popular with budget travelers is **Cabañas La Tortuga** (Playa de Ayampe, tel. 4/278-0613, www.latortuga.com.ec, $18 s, $30–48 d), which is the only beachfront accommodations. The thatch-roofed cabins are comfortable, and there are a good restaurant, a bar, a games room, and a private beach. There are also well-equipped tents with bunk beds and shared baths, plus camping available ($10 pp). The hotel offers a range of kayaking, horseback, and island tours. A cheaper option nearby is **Cabañas La Iguana** (Ayampe, tel. 4/278-0605, $8 pp), run by a friendly local musician and offering cheap basic cabins.

GUAYAQUIL AND THE SOUTHERN COAST

While Quito is Ecuador's capital and cultural center, the largest city is actually Guayaquil. As the economic center, it used to have little to offer visitors, and the heat and smog were reasons enough to stay away, but the city is doing its best to leave behind its bad reputation, and after major redevelopment, Guayaquil is definitely worth a visit. The long waterfront walkway *malecón,* in particular, is spectacular and leads up to the regenerated artistic district of Las Peñas, whose bars and cafés beckon visitors to linger. The steps lead up to a lighthouse with sweeping views over the city. In the suburbs, the Parque Histórico merits a visit for its entertaining depictions of rural life and a wildlife section created out of natural mangroves. While Guayaquil swelters during the day, it's even hotter at night, and the nightlife here is famously raucous.

Northwest of Guayaquil, the rest of the region is mainly about beaches. Locals and visitors flock here in the thousands to soak up the sun, and there are resorts to suit all tastes: Playas is the choice of simple folk, Salinas is a wannabe Miami Beach for the higher classes, and Montañita is a hippie and surfing mecca where you can dance till dawn and almost forget which country you're in.

South of Guayaquil is the area most frequently bypassed by visitors, where shrimp farms and banana plantations dominate the landscape. However, there are some beautiful spots, in particular the mangroves of Churute and the beach on Jambelí island. A couple of hours' climb into the hills is the well-preserved colonial mining town of Zaruma, with a beautiful center surrounded by spectacular scenery. Closer to the border is the

© CAROLINA WESTWOOD

HIGHLIGHTS

◖ **Montañita:** Surf and sunbathe by day and party by night in the coast's biggest backpacker hub (page 295).

◖ **Malecón 2000:** Guayaquil's regenerated waterfront contains museums, monuments, malls, and gardens stretching three kilometers up to the colorful artistic district of Las Peñas, which boasts sweeping views over the city (page 307).

◖ **Parque de las Iguanas (Parque Bolívar):** New York has urban squirrels, and Guayaquil has urban iguanas. Watch them laze in the sun and occasionally fall out of trees in the shadow of Guayaquil's towering cathedral (page 311).

◖ **Manglares Churute Ecological Reserve:** Rare shorebirds nest among the mangroves in this gigantic reserve south of Guayaquil (page 323).

◖ **Zaruma:** Relax in this dramatic hilltop town, which has colonial architecture, a fascinating gold-mining history, breathtaking views, and a darn good cup of coffee (page 327).

LOOK FOR ◖ TO FIND RECOMMENDED SIGHTS, ACTIVITIES, DINING, AND LODGING.

Bosque Petrificado de Puyango, the largest fossilized forest of its kind outside Arizona.

PLANNING YOUR TIME

The coast of Ecuador is warm year-round, but peak season is actually the rainy season, January–April. Perhaps the best time to visit the beaches is at the end of the rains in May–June. July–October, the weather cools down, and the overcast skies and empty beaches of the off-season can be refreshing or depressing, depending on your point of view. Conversely, inland in Guayaquil, the cool season is the only time when you can sightsee in relative comfort, although hot days are still frequent.

Whatever time of year, be sure to bring sunblock, good sunglasses, and a hat, as the sun can be vicious. Note also that the currents are very strong on the Ecuadorian coast, and people drown here every year, so take care when swimming.

Guayaquil is worth a day or two for its waterfront, city center, Parque Histórico, and great nightlife. Northwest of Guayaquil, spend a day or two in either **Playas, Salinas,** or backpacker favorite **Montañita.** From here you can head farther north to even more beautiful beaches in Manabí Province.

South of Guayaquil, the mangroves of **Churute** are worth a day trip, as is **Jambelí island.** Close to the border with Peru, visiting the petrified forest at **Bosque Petrificado de Puyango** takes a day, while the pretty town of **Zaruma** may tempt you to stay a few days to explore the surroundings and enjoy the relaxing atmosphere.

GUAYAQUIL

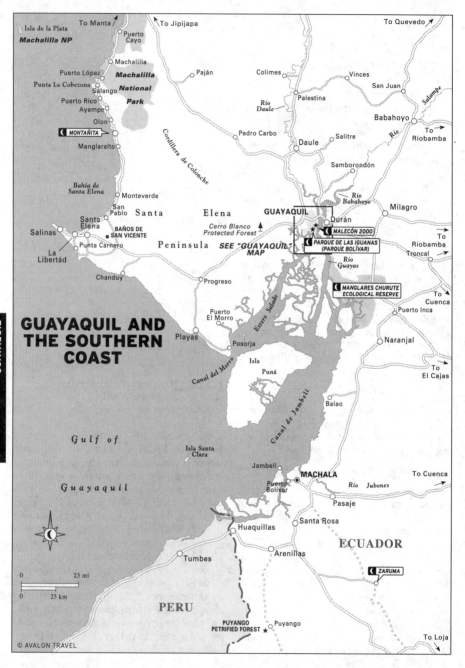

GUAYAQUIL

To Manta
To Jipijapa
To Quevedo

Isla de la Plata
Machalilla NP
Puerto Cayo
Machalilla
Puerto López
Punta La Cobezona
Salango
Puerto Rico
Ayampe
Olon
Manglaralto

Paján
Colimes
Vinces
San Juan

Machalilla National Park

Río Daule
Palestina
Babahoyo
To Riobamba

Pedro Carbo
Daule
Salitre

(MONTAÑITA

Cordillera de Colonche

Samborondón

Bahía de Santa Elena
Monteverde

Santa   Elena

Río Babahoyo

GUAYAQUIL
Durán
Milagro

San Pablo
Santa Elena
Cerro Blanco Protected Forest
(MALECÓN 2000

Salinas
BAÑOS DE SAN VICENTE
Punta Carnero

Peninsula   *SEE "GUAYAQUIL" MAP*

(PARQUE DE LAS IGUANAS (PARQUE BOLÍVAR)

To Riobamba
Troncal

La Libertád

Río Guayas

Chanduy
Progreso

(MANGLARES CHURUTE ECOLOGICAL RESERVE

To Cuenca
Puerto Inca

GUAYAQUIL AND THE SOUTHERN COAST

Puerto El Morro
Playas
Posorja

Naranjal

To El Cajas

Isla Puná

Canal del Morro

Balao

Gulf of

Canal de Jambelí

Guayaquil

Isla Santa Clara

Jambelí
MACHALA
To Cuenca

Puerto Bolívar
Río Jubones
Pasaje

Huaquillas
Santa Rosa

ECUADOR

Tumbes
Arenillas

(ZARUMA

0   25 mi
0   25 km

PERU

PUYANGO PETRIFIED FOREST ★ Puyango

To Loja

© AVALON TRAVEL

Santa Elena Province

Ecuador's newest province, stretching south of Salinas and north of Montañita, split off from Guayas in 2008. On weekends, locals head in droves to long stretches of beaches to get their fill of sun, sea, sand, and shellfish. If you're looking for a relaxing getaway, timing is everything. On peak-season weekends between Christmas and Easter and on national holidays, it gets very crowded in the bigger resorts, so you should either seek out a smaller resort or head farther north. Off-season and midweek, you may well have the beach to yourself. If sunbathing bores you, there is very good surfing in Montañita. If your budget stretches farther, try a deep-sea fishing excursion.

◖ MONTAÑITA AND VICINITY

Montañita is Ecuador's version of a hippie haven, and it's a little pocket of heaven if you like being surrounded by bare-chested, long-haired surfers and their tanned girlfriends. Like other backpacker hubs, you'll probably either love it or hate it, but the infectious energy of the place is undeniable.

Montañita has long been a surfing mecca, with year-round rideable breaks reaching 2–3 meters on good days. It's not the best place for beginners, but you can learn here, and there are plenty of experienced teachers. Conditions are best January–May, and seasoned surfers along with thousands of visitors flock to the international competition around Carnival (usually Feb.) every year.

If you're looking for long stretches of sand, however, you may be disappointed. The beach at high tide is practically nonexistent thanks to the 1997 currents of the El Niño climate pattern, and the remaining beach gets crowded. The town's popularity shows no signs of waning, though, and everybody in town makes a

© BRIAN STEFANELLI

The beach in Montañita was damaged by El Niño in 1998, but it remains one of the best surfing spots on South America's Pacific Coast.

GUAYAQUIL

living from tourism by running hotels, restaurants, Internet cafés, surf shops, or simply hawking their wares in the street. The north end of town toward the point is much quieter and also better for surfing, but beware of rough seas and riptides, particularly June–August. One aspect of the town that has improved is the newly paved road, so the annual mud-fest is a thing of the past, in the center at least. Note that in high season, you need to be careful at night. Don't walk along the beach alone, and female travelers should be particularly vigilant, as assaults have been reported.

Entertainment and Events

There are several surfing competitions in high season, the biggest of which takes place around Carnival (usually mid–late Feb.). It is televised and attracts surfers from around the world. Montañita has a pulsating nightlife on weekends, particularly in high season. The center of the nightlife scene is the restaurant, bar, and disco at **Hola Ola** (Guido Chiriboga and 10 de Agosto, tel. 9/457-5216, www.holaolacafe.com, 8 A.M.–midnight Sun.–Thurs., 8 A.M.–2 A.M. Fri.–Sat.), or the **Cañagrill** (Guido Chiriboga and Costanera a la Playa, tel. 4/206-0086, 8 P.M.–2 A.M. Thurs.–Sat., cover $5 Sat.), a disco that attracts well-known DJs on weekends.

Accommodations

Montañita has a huge number of accommodations options for such a small town, most of them packed into the increasingly crowded center. In peak season it fills up fast, so advanced bookings are advisable, although many cheaper hotels don't take them. Prices also rise by up to 50 percent over the off-season. In the off-season you can negotiate discounts, especially for longer stays. Where you stay depends on how much sleep you want to get: The center gets very noisy throughout the night, particularly on weekends, while north of the center toward the point is quieter with a wider choice of mid-range accommodations.

In the center of town, you are spoiled for budget accommodations choices. Guest rooms

are generally quite basic, but it's easy to secure a room for $10 pp or less. Standing out from the crowd with its thatched roof and brightly colored guest rooms is the well-known **Tikilimbo Hostel** (Guido Chiriboga, tel. 9/954-0607, $10–15 pp). The bamboo beds, large lounge area, and popular international restaurant make this one of the town's focal points. Cheaper options on the same street include **Hostal Casa Blanca** (Guido Chiriboga, tel. 4/277-7931, $8–12 pp) with decent beds, hot water, and hammocks on the balconies. Next door is **Hotel Montañita** (Guido Chiriboga, tel. 4/290-1269, $10–12 pp) and **Cabañas Tsunami** (Guido Chiriboga, tel. 9/714-7344, $8–12 pp), which doubles as a surf shop.

At the north end of Guido Chiriboga, **Hostal Pakaloro** (Costanera, tel. 4/206-0092, $9–12 pp) has newly refurbished guest rooms with private baths and cable TV. Next door, **Montezuma** (Costanera, tel. 8/618-7899, $10 pp) has similar offerings. The best option in the center is the new **◖ Abad Lounge** (Costanera, tel. 4/230-7707, $10–18 pp) on the same street and right on the beach. Many of the brand-new, well-equipped guest rooms have sea views and balconies.

One of the cheapest places in town is just to the right of the junction with the beach: **Centro del Mundo** (Malecón, tel. 9/728-2831, dorm $4 pp, rooms $7 pp) offers strictly no-frills lodging in a three-story beachfront building. Another option right on the beach is **Mochica Sumpa** (Rocafuerte and Malecón, tel. 9/938-7483, $10–15 pp), which has basic guest rooms on either side of the junction with the beach.

For a more comfortable stay in the center, **Charos** (Malecón, tel. 4/206-0044, $20–25 s, $30–45 d) has modern guest rooms with air-conditioning set around a garden terrace and pool. Two blocks inland from the center, **Swisspoint Montañita** (Vía Principal, tel. 4/206-0083, www.swisspointmontanita.com, $25–35 s, $36–56 d) is a charming thatched guesthouse run by a Swiss family, offering bright airy guest rooms and a pleasant porch area.

The rest of the mid-range options are north of town toward the point. **Paradise South** (Playa de Montañita, tel. 4/290-1185 or 9/787-8925, $12–15 s, $25–30 d) has guest rooms in thatched cottages set around a large lawn just off the beach. Farther up is one of the best options, **⟨ Casa del Sol** (Playa de Montañita, tel. 9/248-8581, www.casadelsolsurfcamp.com, $20–50 s, $40–80 d, breakfast included). Run by a Californian surfer, it has developed into a hub for those that love the waves. The guest rooms are well-equipped with air-conditioning and private baths, many with sea views (which cost extra), and the reggae bar and restaurant are great hangouts far from the crowds. Surfing classes and tours are available.

If you want the lap of luxury in Montañita, which is an odd juxtaposition, stay at the high-class **Baja Montañita** (Playa de Montañita, tel. 4/256-8840, www.bajamontanita.com.ec, $91 s or d, buffet breakfast included). Luxury cabins, guest rooms, and suites are all well equipped, and there's a large swimming pool, a gourmet restaurant, and spa treatments.

Food

The center is full of good cafés and restaurants, although bear in mind that in busy periods, service is notoriously slow, so bring a book and patience. Most of the restaurants are close to the main street, Guido Chiriboga, running parallel to the beach one block inland.

The town's social scene increasingly revolves around the Israeli-run **⟨ Hola Ola** (Guido Chiriboga and 10 de Agosto, tel. 9/457-5216, www.holaolacafe.com, 8 A.M.–midnight Sun.–Thurs., 8 A.M.–2 A.M. Fri.–Sat., entrées $5–10). This is a great place for big breakfasts, fresh coffee, and a wide range of meat, seafood, pizza, and snacks. There's also a huge choice of fruit juices and cocktails, and there are parties and live entertainment most weekends. Another good choice for breakfast is **Karukera** (Guido Chiriboga, tel. 9/338-2175, breakfast, lunch, and dinner daily, entrées $4–8), which specializes in crepes and also has Caribbean dishes. For the best range of international cuisine, including Asian, Italian, and Mexican as well as vegetarian specialties, head to the long-standing favorite **⟨ Tikilimbo** (Chiriboga, tel. 9/954-0607, breakfast, lunch, and dinner daily, entrées $6–9).

Information and Services

There is no tourist office in town, but local tour operator **Carpe Diem** (Vicente Rocafuerte and Chiriboga, tel. 9/133-1171), on the main street leading to the beach, can help you out. It's also worth checking out www.infomontanita.com on the Web. There are countless surf shops in town that offer lessons and tours. **Sweet Surf** (Guido Chiriboga, tel. 9/312-2559, www.sweetsurfecuador.com), run by a friendly Swedish-Ecuadorian couple, is recommended. There are two ATMs in town, one in the center near Hotel Montañita and one two blocks north. There are many Internet cafés in the center, charging $1.50 per hour.

Getting There and Around

Three Executive CLP buses run from Guayaquil (3.5 hours, $5) at 5 A.M., 1 P.M., and 5 P.M. daily. If you're headed up or down the coast, there are several buses per hour south to and from Santa Elena (1 hour, $1.50) and north to and from Puerto López (1 hour, $1.50). There are also buses to Manta (3 hours). From Quito, either fly to Guayaquil and head up the coast, or take a bus to Manta or Puerto López (11 hours, $12) and transfer. Getting around Montañita is easy; everywhere is within walking distance.

Robberies have been reported on the outskirts of town, however, so don't walk alone at night.

Olón and San José

Montañita is not for everyone, and you may prefer to stay away from the crowds in a nearby resort. To the north, on the other side of the headland, is the small resort of **Olón,** which has a fine beach and slightly calmer seas for swimming. There are plenty of little seafood shacks along the beach, and the town has a few good hotels, the most interesting of which is **Quimbita** (Principal, tel. 4/278-0204 or

9/496-4706, www.quimbita.com, $10 pp), a charming, colorful place with a permanent art exhibition by the owner.

North of Olón is an even quieter resort, **San José,** which has a couple of excellent accommodations options. **(Cuna Luna** (Ruta de Spondylus, tel. 4/278-0735, www.cunaluna. com, $15–30 pp, breakfast included) is as relaxing as its name (Cradle Moon). This tranquil retreat was conceived as a community tourism project employing local people. The breezy thatched cabins all have sea views, balconies, hammocks, and private baths, and it's a TV-free zone. The restaurant serves a variety of mouthwatering Middle Eastern and seafood dishes such as prawns in coconut and passion fruit.

For a unique experience, head up into the hills above San José to **Samai Lodge** (tel. 4/278-0167, www.sacred-journey.com, $27 s, $45 d), where owners Ed and Tania Tuttle have created a healing, meditation, and yoga retreat. It's an idyllic location with views of the dense forest down to the coast 100 meters below. There's a spa, a vegetarian restaurant, and regular workshops on shamanism as well as shamanic tours around Ecuador.

Manglaralto and Dos Mangas

The quiet fishing village of **Manglaralto** has a few good hotels. **Hostal Manglaralto** (Constitución, tel. 4/290-1369, $10 pp) offers comfortable guest rooms, some with a sea view, but **Kamala Hostería** (Playa Manglaralto, tel. 9/942-3754, www.kamalaweb.com, dorm $15 pp, $30 d) is by far the most interesting option. Individual cabins are set around a small swimming pool in front of the beach, and there's a bar, a restaurant, and a dive school. Dorm beds are available. At the southern end of town, another friendly place that is popular with backpackers is **Tagua Lodge** (Calle 10 de Agosto y Flavio Alfaro, tel. 9/942-6819, www.tagua-lodge.com, $10 pp), which has simple accommodations with private baths and hot water as well as a decent restaurant-bar (breakfast, lunch, and dinner Fri.–Sun., entrées $5) that serves pizza, pasta, vegetarian specialties, pancakes, and salad on weekends.

A popular excursion near Montañita is to **Dos Mangas,** a community of 950 people living from crafts and agriculture. You can combine a visit to the village with a hike into the tropical dry forest of the Cordillera de Chongón. There are two paths through the forest leading to waterfalls and natural pools. The park entrance fee is $1. Trucks ($0.25) from the main coastal road head to Dos Mangas every hour, and you can hire guides and horses. Alternately, book a tour to Dos Mangas in Montañita.

Ayangue

Sheltered bays are hard to locate on the Ruta del Sol, with too many exposed resorts with strong currents, but the petite fishing village of Ayangue is a notable exception. Here the sea is calm and so warm in peak season it's like taking a bath. Ayangue is a well-kept secret because it's a couple of kilometers from the main highway and requires a wait for an occasional bus or friendly local to get here. It's worth the effort, though, for the sheltered swimming on a beach dotted with seafood restaurants.

There are a couple of decent hotels if you choose to stay the night. **Hotel Sol y Mar** (tel. 4/291-6014, $8–15 pp), one block inland from the beach, has simple guest rooms with TVs and private baths as well as pricier guest rooms with air-conditioning and balconies. To treat yourself, head up to the top of the hills south of town: **Cumbres de Ayangue** (tel. 4/291-6040, www.cumbresdeayangue.com, from $85) has one of the most spectacular locations on the coast, perched on cliffs with hair-raising panoramic views over the coves and the bay. The setting of the swimming pool is particularly impressive, with sheer drops on either side. Guest rooms are overpriced, but if you're short on cash, take a taxi from Ayangue and just stop for lunch in the restaurant to admire the view.

SALINAS AND VICINITY

At first, Salinas seems like a tourism enigma: It is one of Ecuador's biggest resorts and is hugely popular with Guayacos, but still, foreign visitors tend to give it a miss. Salinas has the feel of a wannabe Miami Beach, and perhaps that explains why it appeals to wealthy locals who buy up the high-rise apartments, but leaves foreigners unmoved. There's very little that is authentically Ecuadorian about Salinas—it's overpriced, and in high season, overcrowded. The resort does have a very pleasant waterfront, however, a good beach with calm seas (a rarity in this region), as well as great seafood restaurants. Its sister bay, Chipipe, to the south, is also worth visiting for its long, slightly quieter beach. On high-season weekends, Salinas is a real party town if you want to mix it up with rich kids, but be aware that local gangs are savvy to this, and robberies on the beach have been reported at night.

Entertainment

Nightlife in Salinas is heavily seasonal. The wealthy of Guayaquil decamp here between Christmas and Easter to party, and weekends get very busy. **Ocean** (9 P.M.–2 A.M. Fri.–Sat.) is a favorite on the *malecón*. **Flintstone's Rockabar** (Gallo and Cuadra, 8 P.M.–2 A.M. Fri.–Sat.) attracts a more eclectic crowd with its pool tables and funky decor, and **Nassau** (Tercera, 8 P.M.–2 A.M. Fri.–Sat., cover $20 pp) is more exclusive.

Recreation and Tours

Sunbathing and swimming fill most visitors' vacations here, but there is more action out to sea. The ocean floor drops steeply to 3,000 meters just 40 kilometers off the shore of Salinas. Deep-sea fishing excursions can be booked at **Pesca Tours** (Hotel Barceló, Malecón, tel. 4/244-3365 or 4/277-2391, fishing@pescatours.com.ec). Day charters start at $500, not including food, so get a large group together. To take a tour and see the shorebirds that gather at lagoons about five kilometers southwest of town, look for Ben Haase at the **Oystercatcher Bar** (General Enríquez Gallo between Calle 47 and Calle 50, tel. 4/277-8329), who offers a morning trip ($40) for up to 10 people.

Salinas has plenty of water sports—from pedal boats to waterskiing, all of which can be arranged on the beach. There are better places to surf, but for a gentle introduction, surfing equipment and classes are available along the *malecón* at **Tropical Surf Shop** and **Surf and Sport Surf Shop**.

Accommodations

There's no escaping the fact that Salinas is not cheap, and there are very few options for those on a tight budget. In high season, prices rise by 30–50 percent, and the small beach is jam-packed. Most of the cheaper accommodations are away from the *malecón* along less attractive streets. Prices quoted are for low season.

For cheap, basic, but clean guest rooms, try one of the three branches of **Hotel Oro del Mar** (Calle 23 and General Enríquez Gallo, tel. 4/277-1334; Calle 18 and Av. 2, tel. 4/277-1389; Av. 12 and Calle 38, tel. 4/278-6057, $15 pp). Guest rooms have private baths and TVs; air-conditioning costs extra. **Hotel Yulee** (Eloy Alfaro and Mercedes Molina, Chipipe, tel. 4/277-2028, $8–15 pp) is another budget option, housed in a colonial-style building behind the high rises. The cheaper guest rooms have fans and shared baths, and larger guest rooms have private baths and air-conditioning. **Hostal Las Olas** (Las Palmeras 252, tel. 4/277-2501 or 4/277-2526, $15 pp) is another good option with clean air-conditioned guest rooms. The best budget option on the *malecón* is the colorful, friendly **Cocos** (tel. 4/277-4349, www.cocos-hostal.com., $20 pp), which has comfortable guest rooms with air-conditioning. There is an attractive restaurant, a games room, and a terrace. It is popular, so book ahead.

In the mid-range, **Hotel Francisco** (Gallo and Calle 20, tel. 4/277-3544 or 4/277-4106, $37 s, $50 d) and its better-located sister **Francisco II** (Malecón, tel. 4/277-4133, $37 s, $50 d) have tastefully furnished guest rooms, a pool, and a pleasant bar area. High-rise glitz is swapped for leafy rainforest vibes at **Hostería Ecológica El Faro** (Malecón, tel. 4/293-0680, www.hosteriaelfaroecolodge.com, from $90, breakfast included). This colorful new eco-lodge at the northern end of the *malecón* has gardens filled with pines, palms,

GUAYAQUIL

and exotic flowers as well as birds, squirrels, tortoises, parrots, and monkeys. The spacious guest rooms are decorated with local artwork and pine furniture, and the restaurant serves high-quality seafood.

Salinas has plenty of high-rise luxury hotels for those with money to burn. **Barcelo Colón** (Malecón between Calle 38 and Calle 40, tel. 4/277-1610, www.barcelocolonmiramar.com, from $164) is the snazziest, where the who's who of Ecuador spend the night. There's a pool, a spa, a jetted tub, a gym, tennis courts, and three restaurants.

Food

One of the highlights of Salinas is the food. The wealthy locals that frequent the resort expect good-quality restaurants, and there are plenty of them, mainly along the *malecón*. Prices are slightly higher than elsewhere, but there are plenty of places to eat for $5–8. **Oh Mar** (Malecón, tel. 4/277-2826, lunch and dinner daily, $5–8) is a good option with a wide-ranging menu including *cazuela, ceviche,* and breaded shrimp. For a break from seafood, **La Bella Italia** (Malecón, tel. 4/277-1361, lunch and dinner daily, $4–7) prepares great pizza and pasta. The pick of the restaurants on the *malecón,* with a rustic ambience and an eclectic international menu, is **Amazon** (tel. 4/227-3671, lunch and dinner daily, entrées $6–10). One of the best for seafood is actually inland, walking south toward Chipipe: **Ostra Nostra** (Eloy Alfaro and Las Almendras, tel. 4/277-4028, lunch and dinner daily, entrées $4–7), specializing in oysters, is popular with locals and always busy.

The cheapest seafood is found at the informal stalls at **Cevichelandia** (Calle 17 and General Enríquez Gallo), but the bowls of seafood sit there for hours, so sanitation can certainly be a problem.

Information and Services

The **tourist information office** (General Enríquez Gallo and Calle 30, tel. 9/623-6725) is open sporadically, mainly in high season. **Banco del Pacífico** (Av. 3 between Calle 18

and Calle 19) is the best place to change traveler's checks and some foreign currencies. There are several ATMs along the *malecón*. For incoming boaters, the **Capitanía del Puerto** is on the *malecón* at Calle 30, and the **post office** is at Avenida 2 and Calle 17.

Getting There and Around

There are several buses per hour to and from Guayaquil's main terminal (2.5 hours, $3.50) with CLP or Liberpesa. Transesmeraldes (www.transesmeraldas.com) runs night buses to and from Quito (11 hours, $11). To get to other destinations in the region, head to Salinas's ugly sister town La Libertad, 20 minutes away. This is the transportation hub for the Santa Elena Peninsula, with regular buses north to Montañita, Puerto López, and Manta. To get to La Libertad, take a bus from Avenida 7 ($0.35) or a taxi ($3).

Baños de San Vicente

Thermal baths are hard to find along Ecuador's coast, so if the beach doesn't relax you enough, visit the small complex of thermal baths at Baños de San Vicente (Vía Guayaquil–Santa Elena, tel. 4/253-5100, 7:30 A.M.–6 P.M. daily, $2 pp). The turnoff is a few kilometers along the road between Santa Elena and Guayaquil, so take a bus from Santa Elena or La Libertad ($0.50), then take the shuttle service to the complex ($2). There's a pool, a sauna, and a therapeutic mud pit. Half-hour massages ($4) and steam baths ($3) are available. On-site lodging is at the **Hotel Florida** (tel. 4/253-5100, $20 pp, meals included).

Museo Los Amantes de Sumpa

One kilometer west of Santa Elena, the small Museo Los Amantes de Sumpa (Vía Libertad–Salinas, tel. 4/294-1020, www.museoamantesdesumpa.com, 10 A.M.–5 P.M. Tues.–Sat., 11 A.M.–3 P.M. Sun., $1 pp) is well worth visiting. Two hundred sets of skeletons were unearthed in a local cemetery in the 1970s, including the "Lovers of Sumpa," the well-preserved bones of a man and woman in an 8,000-year-old embrace. The museum has displays on five pre-Hispanic coastal cultures, and other highlights include a full-size traditional *campesino* house and a Manteño balsa sailboat. Buses heading east of La Libertad or west of Santa Elena can drop you off nearby, or take a taxi.

PLAYAS AND VICINITY

The closest beach resort to Guayaquil is General Villamil, better known by the rather unoriginal name Playas (Beaches). This resort has none of the pretensions of Salinas, attracting lower- and middle-class Guayacos rather than the wealthy, and that's part of its appeal. The surrounding barren scrubland makes a rather charmless backdrop, but Playas has a new *malecón,* some new hotels, and a pleasant main square, and it seems to be doing its best to move up in the world. There are countless seafood shacks dishing out sumptuous lunches, and the beach is very long—walking down it, you can always find a quieter spot, or take a *mototaxi* ($0.50–1) out of town. However, take particular care with the strong currents; people do drown here. The resort's proximity to Guayaquil means you can visit as a day trip, but there are some good hotels if you choose to stay. Prices are more reasonable here than in Salinas, but like all south coast resorts, it is heavily seasonal—jam-packed on weekends and vacations from Christmas to Easter, when prices rise, and very quiet the rest of the year.

Recreation and Entertainment

Most people come to Playas to lie on the beach, drink a few beers, and fill up on seafood lunches. On high-season weekends, half the population of Guayas seems to flood here.

The strong currents mean that Playas is a good spot for surfing, and while most foreigners head north to Montañita and Canoa, Playas offers a closer option to Guayaquil. Surfing facilities are limited, but make inquiries at the local surf club run by Juan Gutiérrez at his restaurant **Jalisco** (Paquisha and Av. 7), one block from the beach.

Nightlife in Playas is heavily seasonal, but there are a few places open year-round.

D'Alex (Jaime Roldós and Av. 8, no phone, 8 P.M.–2 A.M. Fri.–Sat.), facing the Banco Pichincha near the main plaza, plays mainly salsa. On the *malecón,* a block east of the center, **Oh Sole Mio** (Malecón, no phone, 8 P.M.–2 A.M. Fri.–Sat.) has live Latin music under a giant thatched roof.

Accommodations

Accommodations in Playas are underwhelming, but there are a few well-priced hotels on the waterfront if you choose to stay. Note that they fill up fast in high season. In the budget category, the blue-and-white **Hotel Playas** (Malecón and Jambelí, tel. 4/276-0611, $10 pp) has decent guest rooms with fans, TVs, and cold-water showers; air-conditioning costs extra. Farther along to the east, **Hostal Cattan** (Jambelí and 3 de Noviembre, tel. 4/276-0179, $10 pp) has more basic guest rooms.

In the mid-range, shun the glitzy-looking hotels on the main street and head to **Hotel Dorado** (Malecón, tel. 4/276-0402, $15 s, $25 d) for comfortable guest rooms with air-conditioning, hot water, and cable TV.

The area west of town is dotted with numerous *hosterías,* mainly in the mid-range. **Los Patios** (Vía Playas–Posorja Km. 1.5, tel. 4/276-1115, $20 s, $35 d) has an ideal location with a small pool area leading directly onto the beach. The restaurant is popular, but the guest rooms are a little basic for the price. About one kilometer farther along, the Swiss-run **Hostería Bellavista** (tel. 4/276-0600, $47 s, $70 d) is a step up in quality, with more comfortable guest rooms with cable TV and air-conditioning. There are also two pools, a squash court, and a sauna.

Food

A highlight of Playas is eating a plate of fresh seafood, and you are spoiled for choice, even in low season. Most people simply choose whichever beach-hut café looks appealing, and they all serve pretty much the same fare—fish and shrimp fried, grilled, steamed, or breaded as well as hot soups and cold *ceviche.* For a wide-ranging menu in a more conventional setting,

GUAYAQUIL

try either **La Cabaña Típica** (Malecón, tel. 4/276-0464, lunch and dinner daily, entrées $4–6) or **Restaurant Jalisco** (Paquisha and Av. 7, no phone, lunch and dinner daily, entrées $3–5) back in town. A few blocks inland is the town's best restaurant, **Los Ajos** (Av. Jaime Roldos and Calle 8, no phone, lunch and dinner daily, entrées $8–12), which serves well-prepared seafood and meat dishes.

Playas is also well-known for its empanadas, tasty pastries filled with cheese, ham, chicken, or meat. They are rather greasy but still delicious, and the long-running **Empanadas de Playas** (Roldos, in front of Parque Infantil, tel. 9/137-7855, 3–11 P.M. Mon.–Fri., 10 A.M.–11 P.M. Sat.–Sun., $0.80–$1.50) at the east end of Malecón is the best place to try them.

Information and Services

The **post office** is on Garay near the bus office, and the **Cabañas Telefonias** (Garay near Guayaquil) are available for phone calls. There are a few Internet cafés in the center of town. ATMs at **Banco de Guayaquil** (Guayaquil and Paquisha) and **Banco de Pichincha** are on the main plaza.

Getting There and Around

Frequent buses to **Guayaquil** (1.5 hours, $2) leave with **Transportes Posorja** (near the church and the main plaza) or the faster **Transportes Villamil** (Guayaquil and Paquisha). The easiest way to travel between Playas and Santa Elena or Salinas is to take a Guayaquil-bound bus and transfer at Progreso.

Posorja and Isla de Puná

The road down to the southern tip of the peninsula at Punta Arenas is known as the Data highway, because it passes through two towns: Data de Villamil and Data de Posorja. Posorja

is the gateway for reaching Isla de Puná across the Canal del Morro. This large island has an area of over 900 square kilometers and has an interesting history; it was once ruled by Tumpis Indians who fought bravely against the Spanish conquistadores. Tourism is in its infancy but may develop in the next few years. There are regular boat trips ($25 for 2–10 people) on weekends from the docks at the far west end of Posorja (tel. 9/421-5306 for bookings and information). Highlights are the dolphins in the Morro channel, birdlife that includes pelicans and occasional frigates and boobies in the **Farallones** islets, as well as deserted beaches. Camping is possible in the small village of **Bellavista** on the island.

Puerto El Morro

This small town a few kilometers east of Playas has become popular because of its marine life, especially dolphins. It's an enjoyable day trip from Guayaquil and can easily be combined with a dip in Playas to cool off afterward. Take a boat trip across the estuary through mangroves and past schools of dolphins. The shorter route (1.5 hours, $5) takes in the mangroves, dolphins, and some fishing, while the longer route (3 hours, $8) includes a longer boat trip and a walk on the **Isla de los Pájaros**, which has large populations of frigate birds, pelicans, and blue-footed boobies. Both can be arranged with a community tourism project, **Ecoclub Los Delfines de Puerto el Morro** (tel. 4/252-9496, puertoelmorro@ yahoo.com, www.puertoelmorro.blogspot.com). Alternately, book group tours ($40 pp) in Guayaquil through **Ecua Andino Planet** (Escobedo 835 at Junín, Suite 205, tel. 4/600-2636, www.ecua-andino.com). To get there yourself, take a bus from Guayaquil's main terminal to Playas (1.5 hours) and then transfer for Puerto El Morro (30 minutes).

Guayaquil and Vicinity

Ecuador's largest city has finally begun to stand up as a tourist destination and bury its bad reputation. *Dirty* and *dangerous* were two words that used to sum up Guayaquil (pop. 2.3 million), and there was little to offer visitors in the 1990s. This has changed in recent years, however, and while it can hardly rival Quito in terms of beauty, there is now plenty to keep you busy for a couple of days. If you're arriving from the mountains, there's quite a contrast between Quito's cool, colonial charms and Guayaquil hot, humid vivacity—it feels like a different country.

Guayaquil sits on the west side of the Río Guayas, formed by the Ríos Daule and Babahoyo (the latter charmingly translates as

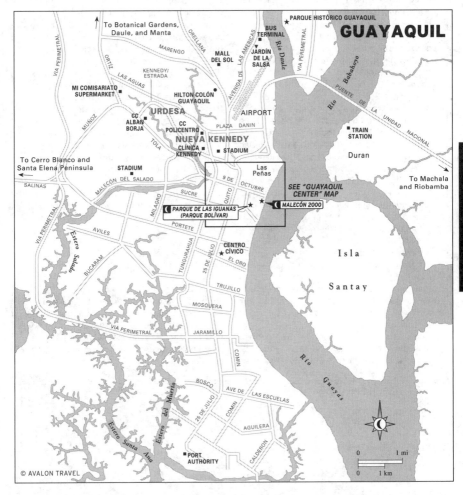

GUAYAQUIL

A TALE OF TWO CITIES: QUITO AND GUAYAQUIL

If these two cities were sisters, Quito might be the conservative Goody Two-shoes, wrapped in a woolen sweater, staying in with a good book while her sexy sister Guayaquil goes out in a miniskirt and designer shoes to catch up on the latest gossip and tear it up on the dance floor.

Ecuador's history has long been a tale of two cities, and like jealous siblings, the rivalry ranges from friendly banter to deep resentment, and it goes back a long time. In precolonial times, the two centers were populated by different ethnic groups who had little contact due to the distance and forbidding terrain separating the cities. The Inca conquered Quito in the late 15th century, but Guayaquil was never under Inca control.

After the Spanish conquest, the Audiencia de Quito was set up, and the Andean city began to assert control over Ecuador's political and economic affairs, even though Guayaquil grew as the agricultural and trading center. This led to resentment on the coast, and the old adage sprang up that "Guayaquil makes the money, but Quito spends it." Quiteños, on the other hand, began to view Guayacos as uncultured, loud-mouthed merchants who regularly had to be saved from plundering pirates.

Independence did little to unite the cities, and Ecuador was barely held together as liberalism on the coast clashed with conservatism in the mountains. The cacao boom, followed by the banana boom, reinforced the Guayaco idea that they make all the money. The growth of the flower industry in Quito, however, as well as the oil boom in the Amazon have helped to spread the wealth around.

In politics, regionalism has always been milked by presidential candidates, and since the return of democracy in 1979, it has often come down to a race between a Guayaquil candidate and a Quito candidate. Guayaquil has had its fair share of presidents: ill-fated leftwinger Jaime Roldós Aguilera, hard-line León Febres Cordero, and "El Loco"(Crazy Man) Abdalá Bucaram, while Quito has produced the liberal Rodrigo Borja Cevallos, conservative Sixto Durán Ballén, and more recently Jamil Mahuad, who presided over the country's worst economic crisis in a generation in 2000. Billionaire banana mogul Álvaro Noboa from Guayaquil has tried three times to become president and each time has fallen at the final hurdle; it seems he can never secure the support of the Andean voters, embodying much of what they dislike about wealthy *costeños* (coast dwellers). The current incumbent, Rafael Correa, somewhat bucks the regionalist trend – he's from Guayaquil but does his best to cultivate support in the mountains by wearing indigenous shirts and criticizing Guayacos' worship of the Miami lifestyle. His popularity is markedly lower in Guayaquil as a result.

On a social level, Ecuadorians' regionalist attitudes can be lighthearted but get increasingly touchy, especially after a few drinks. Many *costeños* consider *serranos* (mountain people) to be conservative, uptight, hypocritical, and two-faced. They also delight in impersonating Quiteños singsong accent and strong pronunciation of the letter *s*. *Serranos*, on the other hand, call *costeños* *"monos"* (monkeys) and consider them rude, uncultured, immoral gossips.

One of the few times when this regionalism scarcely matters is when the nation stops to watch its beloved football team. Then every Ecuadorian, no matter where they're from, unites behind the yellow shirt of the Tricolores.

"dribble hole"). The Guayas empties into the Gulf of Guayaquil, leading to the Pacific, 50 kilometers to the southwest. The city's riverside position led to its emergence as Ecuador's commercial center, with more than half the country's companies based here, and Guayaquil is now the biggest port on South America's Pacific coast. Most of the city is only a few meters above sea level, so flooding is common in the rainy season.

Guayaquil has undergone quite a transformation in the past decade and has won a United Nations award for redevelopment. The city's new promotional line, "Pearl of the Pacific," may be a typical example of the local tendency to exaggerate, but there's no denying Guayaquil's newfound beauty and confidence as a destination. Arriving at the new airport or bus terminal is far more pleasant than it used to be, the public transportation system includes the new Metrovía trolleybus modeled on Quito's system, and most importantly, the city center is safer with policed pedestrianized zones. The tourism centerpiece is the *malecón*, a three-kilometer promenade along the river Guayas up to the colorful artistic district of Las Peñas. Here you can climb the stairs to the lighthouse at the top and gaze out over an impressive panorama of the city and surrounding countryside. At the bottom of the hill is the city's latest project, Puerto Santa Ana, lined with restaurants, cafés, luxury apartments, and a marina under construction.

Most Galápagos tours now come through Guayaquil, boosting its tourism industry; the city's abundance of top-class hotels and conference facilities suit high-end visitors and businesspeople alike. Be aware, however, that the heat and pollution can certainly affect your sightseeing experience. It's best to start early or wait until late afternoon, avoiding the fierce midday sun. Weekends are quieter and better for sightseeing, when the city center empties out.

HISTORY

Guayaquil was founded by the Spanish conquistador Francisco de Orellana on July 25,

1537, a date celebrated fervently by locals every year. Its position close to the Pacific and fertile agricultural surroundings quickly made the city one of the most important ports in the Spanish empire. Unfortunately, Guayaquil's riches also made the city vulnerable to pirate attacks; the bloodiest incident was in April 1687, when English and French pirates under the command of George d'Hout attacked the city and took local women hostage as concubines. More than 70 citizens were killed, and the women were finally released after a ransom was paid.

As the city's economic status grew, so did its population and corresponding problems with disease. Regular flooding and a lack of sanitary facilities led to outbreaks of typhoid, dysentery, and yellow fever.

On October 9, 1820, Guayaquil became the first city in Ecuador to declare its independence from Spain, nearly two years before the rest of the country, a source of much pride for the locals. The partnership between the country's two largest cities was always uneasy, with Guayaquil's liberal-minded merchants often clashing with Quito's conservatives.

Guayaquil's rapid growth was threatened when 70 percent of the city was destroyed by a huge fire on October 5, 1896. Reconstruction was quick but careless, and it explains the lack of colonial architecture in the center. Guayaquil recovered and continued to grow as a commercial center, but the wealth was kept by a small super-rich class while the vast majority of the city remained very poor.

Although sanitation improved markedly in the 20th century, the city continues to suffer from high levels of poverty, especially among the thousands of immigrants who have set up ramshackle homes on the outskirts of the city. Most recently, successive mayors León Febres Cordero and Jaime Nebot have brought huge improvements to public transportation and the water system as well as increased tourism facilities. Most of the changes have been concentrated in the center of the city, however, with the outlying barrios as poor as ever. Current president Rafael Correa has seized on this to

GUAYAQUIL

MONKEY SAY, MONKEY DO

Guayacos have been nicknamed *monos* (monkeys) by their fellow Ecuadorians for years, and although some find it mildly offensive, local citizens mostly shrug and accept it as a joke. There are various versions of the origin of the phrase – some people say that it's because the city's people copy everything their neighbors do and buy; others say it's a reference to Guayacos' demonstrative, chatty nature, but the most interesting theory comes from a colonial legend.

In the 17th century, Spanish King Carlos II was known as "El Hechizado" (The Hexed One) because of his mental and physical disabilities. He had a fascination for animals and asked his subjects to bring him some of the most unusual exotic creatures from the Americas to entertain him. He was particularly interested in monkeys, and so a request was sent to scores of haciendas around Guayaquil. Some 30 species of monkeys were assembled in the city center, and a committee chose two to be sent to Spain.

The king was delighted with the monkeys and spent hours playing with them, even feeding them himself. One day, though, the king was suffering with his nerves and went to the chapel to seek solace. One of the monkeys escaped from its cage and followed him without being seen. As the king was praying, the monkey jumped on the altar and caused a commotion, jumping and screaming. The king was terrified and cried out: "I have seen the devil!" Although his guards tried to explain that the monkey had simply escaped, the king was extremely upset and took to his bed with a fever.

News of this ridiculous incident spread through the court, and whenever visitors arrived in Madrid from Guayaquil, the joke would be made: "Be careful, sirs, here comes a monkey from Guayaquil to cause us more terror." The luckless king died aged just 35 in 1700, but the joke lived on and soon spread to Ecuador, where the *mono* nickname became widely used.

cement his claim to be the real champion of Guayaquil's poor, with low-cost housing projects and support for *micro-empresas* (small businesses).

ORIENTATION

Most of Guayaquil's tourist attractions are concentrated in the center, about five kilometers south of the bus station and airport. The center is a mix of gleaming high-rises and drab concrete slabs, punctuated by pockets of colonial architecture and a couple of elegant parks. Traffic congestion is a factor during the day, so you should walk to most attractions. Because of the heat, though, it's best to start early or wait until late afternoon to do sightseeing. The best places to escape the city's sprawl are the *malecón* and the artistic district of **Las Peñas.**

North of the center, there are several residential neighborhoods that include La Garzota, Sauces, and Alborada, with **Kennedy** and **Urdesa** most interesting for visitors because

of their restaurants, nightclubs, and shopping malls, but few hotels. East of the airport, cross the impressive Puente de la Unidad Nacional over the Ríos Daule and Babahoyo to the swanky neighborhoods of **Entre Ríos** and **La Puntilla.** This is Guayaquil's version of Beverly Hills, where the wealthy live in gated communities with swimming pools, tennis courts, and palm trees. It is a world away from the city and worth a visit mainly because of the **Parque Histórico,** one of the city's best attractions. Across a second bridge is **Durán,** mainly a poor area chiefly known for its large festival in October, but also the starting point for the regenerated railroad, which should run all the way to Quito by 2014.

CLIMATE

If Guayaquil had a beach, the city's average temperature of 28–32°C year-round might be ideal, but unfortunately there isn't one. There's no escaping the fact that this city is very hot and

THE GENERALS MEET

The two greatest leaders in Latin America's independence struggle met just once – in Guayaquil in 1822. Today, the largest statue on Guayaquil's riverfront commemorates the meeting.

Simón Bolívar and José de San Martín, both brilliant generals, had communicated but had never met face-to-face. Bolívar, a Venezuelan, operated in the north, while San Martín, an Argentine, fought in the south. San Martín requested the meeting because of his concerns over the fate of Guayaquil, which at the time could have been annexed by either Peru or Colombia. Bolívar was focused on his great idea of forming Gran Colombia, leading to a united South America.

The strong-willed Bolívar was determined to take charge and rushed from Quito to Guayaquil before San Martín, who traveled from Peru. When San Martín arrived, Bolívar welcomed him warmly to "Gran Colombian soil," and at a banquet that night raised a toast to "the two greatest men in South America." What was discussed at the meeting is unclear, but it seems that Bolívar got his way because San Martín left the same day, resigned his position soon afterward, and sailed to Europe. He remains a national hero in Argentina. Bolívar then took over the task of liberating Peru and set up his beloved Gran Colombia, which encompassed Ecuador, Colombia, Venezuela, and Panama. The new nation was doomed to fail, and after a brief stint as dictator, Bolívar resigned his position as president in 1830 and died of tuberculosis soon afterward.

humid, often unbearably so. January–April are the hottest months, with an average of 12–15 days of rain and high humidity levels. It is dry June–December, with overcast, slightly cooler days, but sightseeing at midday in Guayaquil is rarely comfortable. Many of the wealthier Guayacos are addicted to air-conditioning, and when you start to overheat after an hour of strolling around, the delicious cool air of a mall or hotel lobby is very enticing.

SAFETY CONSIDERATIONS

Poverty levels are high in Guayaquil, and crime is a serious issue. Muggings and carjackings (known as *secuestros express*) are common, although mainly rich Ecuadorians are targeted. Take taxis at night, never take unmarked cabs, and consider using a prebooked service (ask at your hotel for a recommended company). Avoid aimless wandering at any time of day—go directly from place to place, and stay on the main streets in the center.

SIGHTS
◖ Malecón 2000
Guayaquil's waterfront is the pride of the city

and symbol of its redevelopment. In the late 1990s, Mayor León Febres Cordero launched Malecón 2000 (7 A.M. to midnight daily), a hugely ambitious project to completely overhaul the run-down area along the river Guayas. Current mayor Jaime Nebot has continued the work, and the result is an astonishing achievement that has won a United Nations award.

This three-kilometer promenade is by far the biggest attraction in the city, with historic monuments, modern sculptures, museums, botanical gardens, fountains, bridges, children's play areas, shopping outlets, and restaurants. The cool breezes off the river and the watchful eye of security guards make Malecón 2000 the most relaxing place to spend time in Guayaquil.

The best starting point is **La Plaza Cívica** at the end of 9 de Octubre. A highlight is **La Rotonda,** a statue depicting a famous meeting of South America's two most prominent liberators, José de San Martín and Simón Bolívar. This semicircular statue is Malecón's most important historical monument and is particularly striking when lit up at night. For light entertainment, stand with a partner at opposite

GUAYAQUIL

sides of the semicircle and whisper into the pillars to hear your voices carry.

Walk south of *La Rotonda* past towers dedicated to the four elements. You'll reach the Guayaquil Yacht Club (free), where there is an attractive three-masted sailboat docked several months of the year. Farther south is the 23-meter **Moorish Clock Tower.** This is the latest incarnation, built in 1931, of a clock tower that dates back to the 18th century. Just down from the clock tower is the **Henry Morgan** (afternoon–evening Sun.–Thurs., late-night trips Fri.–Sat., $5), a replica of the famous Welsh pirate's 17th-century ship. A one-hour trip is a great way to see Guayaquil from the river. South of this is a rather bland **shopping mall,** selling mainly modern items rather than artisanal wares, but you may enjoy the opportunity to escape the heat. On the other side is an outdoor food court with cheap restaurants serving fast food and seafood specialties. Farther south is the quietest part of Malecón 2000, at **Plaza Olmedo,** with its contemplative monument of José Joaquín de Olmedo (1780–1847), the first mayor of Guayaquil. Beyond that is **La Plaza de la Integraciín** and a small **artisans market.** You can cross the road and enter the **Bahía** black market, but be careful as it can be a dangerous area.

North of La Rotonda is a large children's playground and exercise area leading to a beautiful set of **botanical gardens** with more than 300 species of trees and other plants. This is one of the highlights of Malecón 2000, and it's worth getting lost in the greenery and forgetting you're in the middle of the city. Above the gardens are 32 transparent panels with the names of more than 48,000 citizens who contributed to the Malecón 2000 project.

North of the botanical gardens is the **Museo Guayaquil en La Historia** (tel. 4/256-3078, 10 a.m.–6:30 p.m. daily, $2.50), which tells a fascinating history of the city from prehistoric times to the present in 14 dioramas. It's one of the few museums in Guayaquil where everything is in English, so it's worth a visit. Above the museum is one of South America's only **IMAX** cinemas, with a 180-degree screen.

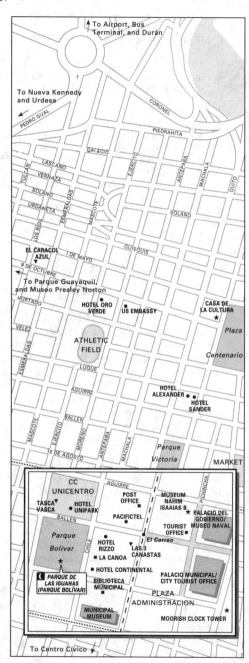

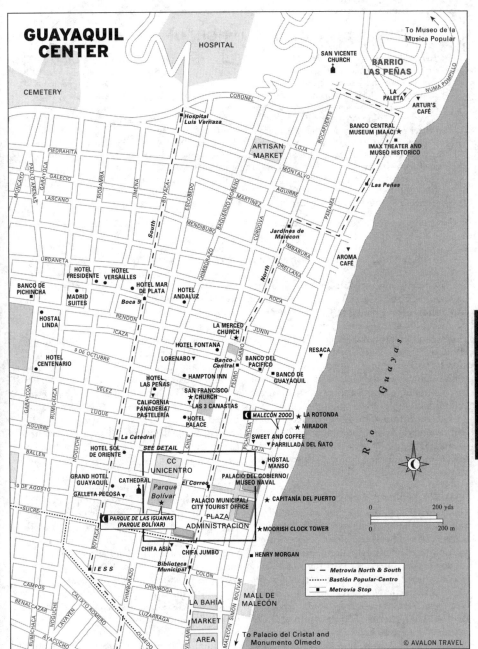

GUAYAQUIL CENTER

GUAYAQUIL

CEMETERY

HOSPITAL

To Museo de la
Musica Popular

SAN VICENTE
CHURCH

BARRIO
LAS PEÑAS

LA
PALETA

ARTUR'S
CAFÉ

NUMA POMPILLO

CORONEL

Hospital
Luis Vernaza

BANCO CENTRAL
MUSEUM (MAAC) ★

IMAX THEATER AND
MUSEO HISTORICO

ARTISAN
MARKET

LOJA

MONTALVO

AGUIRRE

Las Peñas

PIEDRAHITA

MOCAYO
GARAYCOA
GALECIO
PAVESI / PULLO OTERO
RIOBAMBA
ESCOBEDO
BAQUERIZO MORENO
MARTINEZ
CORDOVA
PANAMA

LASCANO
JIMENA
BOYACA

MENDIBURO

Jardines de
Malecon

IMBABURA

AROMA
CAFÉ

URDANETA

South

North

ORELLANA

ROCA

HOTEL
PRESIDENTE

HOTEL
VERSAILLES

BANCO DE
PICHINCHA

MADRID
SUITES

HOTEL MAR
DE PLATA

Boca 9

HOTEL
ANDALUZ

HOSTAL
LINDA

RENDON

LA MERCED
CHURCH ★

JUNIN

ICAZA

HOTEL FONTANA

9 DE OCTUBRE

LORENABO ▼

Banco
Central ■

BANCO DEL
PACIFICO

RESACA

HOTEL
CENTENARIO

HAMPTON INN

BANCO DE
GUAYAQUIL

VELEZ

HOTEL
LAS PEÑAS

GARAYCOA
RUMICHACA

PEDRO CARBO

LUQUE

SAN FRANCISCO ★
CHURCH

CALIFORNIA
PANADERIA/
PASTELERIA

LAS 3 CANASTAS

AGUIRRE

HOTEL
PALACE

MALECÓN 2000 ★ LA ROTONDA

★ MIRADOR

BALLEN

La Catedral ■

HOTEL SOL
DE ORIENTE

SEE DETAIL

CHILE

PICHINCHA

LOJA

SWEET AND COFFEE ▼
▼ PARRILLADA DEL ÑATO

NOGUCHE

CC
UNICENTRO

HOSTAL
MANSO

GRAND HOTEL
GUAYAQUIL

CATHEDRAL

Parque
Bolívar

El Correo

PALACIO DEL GOBIERNO/
MUSEO NAVAL

10 DE AGOSTO

GALLETA PECOSA ▼

PALACIO MUNICIPAL/
CITY TOURIST OFFICE

★ CAPITANÍA DEL PUERTO

SUCRE

PARQUE DE LAS IGUANAS
(PARQUE BOLÍVAR)

PLAZA
ADMINISTRACIÓN

★ Moorish Clock Tower

BOYACA

CHIFA ASIA

CHIFA JUMBO

■ HENRY MORGAN

IESS

Biblioteca
Municipal

COLON

CAMPOS

CHIMBORAZO

CHIRIBOGA

BENALCAZAR
NOGUCHE
CALIXTO ROMERO
LAVAYEN

RUMICHACA
AYACUCHO

LA BAHÍA

MARKET

AREA

LUZARRAGA

OLMEDO

MALECON SIMON BOLIVAR
VILLAMIL

MALL DE
MALECÓN

To Palacio del Cristal and
Monumento Olmedo

Rio Guayas

— Metrovía North & South
..... Bastión Popular-Centro
■ Metrovía Stop

0   200 yds
0   200 m

© AVALON TRAVEL

WHAT'S IN A NAME? THE ORIGIN OF *GUAYAQUIL*

Many visitors have never even heard of Guayaquil before they come to Ecuador, and the city's unusual name may have something to do with this. It's also far from the easiest name to pronounce (gwhy-ya-KEEL). The origin of the name has several versions. The favored story of locals, which has been passed down through the generations, is that the city was run by an Indian chief called Guayas and his wife, Quil. When the Spanish invaded, Guayas refused to surrender and chose to fight to the death, killing his wife rather than giving her up to the strapping Spaniards (it's unclear whether Quil had any say in this decision).

A rather less exciting theory, preferred by local historians, is that *Guayaquil* derived from the indigenous words *hua illa Quilca*, meaning "beautiful green land of the river Quilca," in reverence to the fertile surroundings that remain the agricultural heartland of Ecuador's coast.

In 1547, after the conquest, the name given to the city was quite a mouthful: "Very Noble and Very Loyal City of Santiago of Guayaquil." Suffice to say, the "very noble and very loyal" part was dropped in 1820 when the locals finally kicked the Spanish out.

It's an interesting but rather disorienting experience.

The north end of Malecón 2000 culminates in the Banco Central's impressive **Museo Antropológico y de Arte Contemporáneo** (MAAC, Malecón and Loja, tel. 4/230-9383, www.malecon2000.com/museo.htm, 10 A.M.–6 P.M. Tues.–Sat., 10 A.M.–4 P.M. Sun., $1.50, free Sun.), which has an exhibition on ancient history, a huge collection of pre-Columbian ceramics, and a modern art exhibition.

Further information about Malecón 2000 can be obtained from the Fundación Malecón office (Sargento Vargas 116 at Olmedo, tel. 4/252-4530 or 4/252-4211, www.malecon2000.com).

Las Peñas and Cerro Santa Ana

The north end of Malecón 2000 connects conveniently with the colorful artistic district of **Las Peñas.** This is the oldest neighborhood in Guayaquil and has the largest concentration of colonial architecture. Like the waterfront, this area used to be run-down and dangerous but has been completely regenerated in recent years, with freshly painted colonial balconies and security guards. The main draw is the climb up 444 steps past cafés and art galleries. You may work up a sweat, so come early in the morning, or even better, in the early evening, and then stay for a drink in the many alluring bars. At the top is an open-air museum, **Museo El Fortín del Santa Ana** (free), which has original cannons and replicas of Spanish galleons. There is also a small chapel and lighthouse, which can be climbed for fabulous views over the city, Guayas estuary, and Santay Island to the east.

As well as climbing the hill, you can also walk around to the right of the steps along the cobbled street called **Numa Pompilio Llona,** named after the Guayaco who wrote Ecuador's rousing national anthem. There are several art galleries and the city's most interesting bar, La Paleta.

Puerto Santa Ana

At the northern end of Numa Pompilio Llona, the old district blends into the ultramodern Puerto Santa Ana, the city's latest grand project. Here, shops, cafés, and luxury apartments line the riverside, and a large marina is currently under construction. There are three museums at the entrance to the riverside walkway. The museum on the ground floor, currently under construction, is dedicated to *fútbol* (soccer) and specifically to Guayaquil's two major teams, Barcelona and Emelec. Upstairs, the second floor is divided into two museums.

On the left is **Museo de la Música Popular Guayaquileña Julio Jaramillo** (tel. 9/553-1966, 10 A.M.–1 P.M. and 2–5 P.M. Wed.–Sat., free), dedicated to Guayaquil's most famous musician. The museum tells the story of the development of the city's music scene in the early 20th century with original gramophones and instruments, and there is a biography of Jaramillo and his broken-hearted songs of love and loss. Julio Jaramillo died of liver cirrhosis at 42, so it's fitting that next door is a museum dedicated to the history of brewing, **Museo Pilsener** (tel. 9/553-196610, A.M.–1 P.M. and 2–5 P.M. Wed.–Sat., free). The country's first and enduringly popular pilsner was actually launched by a Czech immigrant, Francisco Bolek, in 1913.

◖ Parque de las Iguanas (Parque Bolívar)

Guayaquil's city center has a dearth of colonial architecture, but the area around the **cathedral** is the most attractive part. The original cathedral was destroyed by fire and rebuilt in 1936. This huge white neo-Gothic structure towers over the west side of Parque Bolívar, better known as Parque de las Iguanas. The centerpiece of the park is an imposing monument of South American liberator Simón Bolívar on horseback, but even Bolívar can't compete with the sight of dozens of urban iguanas descending from the tall trees to laze around on the grass. Visitors and locals alike flock here to watch these tame lizards, but don't let their lethargy fool you, as they can run very fast if startled. There's also a fish pond filled with turtles and a red squirrel, which seems to interest many locals more than the iguanas.

Museo Municipal

One block southwest of the Parque de las Iguanas is the Museo Municipal (tel. 4/259-9500, Sucre and Chile, 9 A.M.–5 P.M. Tues.–Sat., free). This is one of the oldest museums in Ecuador and probably the best in the city. The Pre-Hispanic room has fossils, including the tooth of a mastodon dating back 10,000 years, plus sculptures from Ecuador's oldest civilization, the Valdivia, and a huge Manteña funeral urn. In the colonial section, there is a model of colonial Guayaquil and original cannons and muskets. Don't miss the room of portraits of Ecuadorian presidents upstairs,

GUAYAQUIL

© CAROLINA WESTWOOD

Iguanas in Parque Bolívar descend from the trees and laze on the grass to the delight of visitors.

nicknamed "the room of thieves" by many locals. There are five shrunken heads on display in a closed room upstairs, which can only be viewed on guided tours. Free English tours are recommended because all the exhibitions are in Spanish.

Plaza de la Administración and Vicinity

A few blocks east of Parque de las Iguanas toward the *malecón* is a pleasant pedestrianized zone around **Plaza de la Administraciín**, dominated by the grand buildings of the local government and a monument to Mariscal Sucre. Most impressive is the Renaissance-style **Palacio Municipal,** whose Corinthian columns support an arched interior passage covered by a glass ceiling. To the north is **Museo Nahim Isaias** (Pichincha and Clemente Ballén, tel. 4/232-4182, 10 A.M.–5 P.M. Mon.–Fri., 10 A.M.–2:30 P.M. Sat., $1.50), which houses a well-presented collection of colonial paintings, sculptures, and artifacts.

9 de Octubre and Plaza Centenario

Avenida 9 de Octubre carves its way through central Guayaquil from the Malecón del Salado past Parque Centenario to Malecón 2000. It's an impressive walk, although the traffic and heat can have an impact on the experience. The highlight along 9 de Octubre is **Plaza San Francisco,** three blocks from the *malecón* and dominated by the Iglesia San Francisco. Here you can relax by the large fountain and statue of Pedro Carbo.

Central Guayaquil's largest square lies in the middle of 9 de Octubre between the two *malecóns*. The focal point is the **Monument to the Heroes of Independence,** with four statues representing heroism, justice, patriotism, and history. On the west side is the **Casa de la Cultura** (tel. 4/230-0500), with an impressive collection of art and archaeology. Farther west toward Malecón del Salado is **Museo Presley Norton** (9 de Octubre and Carchi, tel. 4/229-3423, 10 A.M.–6 P.M. Mon.–Sat., free). This new museum houses a small exhibition on "Life and customs of the settlers of ancient Ecuador" and is named after a pioneering Ecuadorian archaeologist who died in 1993.

Malecón del Salado and Vicinity

A junior version of Malecón 2000 at the opposite end of 9 de Octubre, Malecón del Salado is named after the tributary of the river Guayas that it straddles. Citizens bathed here in the late 19th century, but it's too dirty nowadays. The pleasant walkway that undulates up and down bridges makes for a pleasant stroll, however, and if you work up an appetite, there is a cluster of good seafood restaurants at the end. It's a 20-minute walk straight up 9 de Octubre from Malecón 2000, or take a taxi ($2).

General Cemetery

Guayaquil's General Cemetery (Julian Coronel and Machala), at the north end of the city center, is one of the most impressive in South America. The contrast is stark between the lavish, decorated mausoleums on the east side and the wooden crosses on the west side where poorer residents have buried their dead illegally. One of the grandest tombs is that of former president Victor Emilio Estrada, who made a pact with the devil, according to legend, and whose spirit haunts the cemetery. Supernatural dangers aside, the cemetery is not very safe. Robberies have been reported, so never come alone or at night, and don't wander far from the central area.

Parque Histórico

Across the bridge in the wealthy district of Entre Ríos, the eight-hectare Parque Histórico (Entre Ríos, tel. 4/283-3807, www.parquehistorico.com, 9 A.M.–4:30 P.M. Wed.–Sun., $3 Wed.–Sat., $4.50 Sun.) is definitely worth the trip out of town. The park is divided into three zones: The wildlife zone was created out of the natural mangroves of the Río Daule and provides a snapshot of the Ecuadorian rainforest with 50 species, including deer, wildcats, tapirs, monkeys, sloths, ocelots, tortoises, parrots, toucans, and caimans. The traditions

© CHRIS O'CONNELL

Some of Guayaquil's lost colonial buildings are rebuilt at the Parque Histórico.

zone depicts rural life in reconstructed haciendas and has boisterous music and comedy shows on weekends. In the urban architecture zone, some of Guayaquil's lost colonial buildings have been reproduced, and **Café 1900** is the ideal place to have a coffee and gaze over the river.

There are buses to Entre Ríos from the terminal, or get a taxi from downtown ($4–5). After visiting the park, it's worth walking up to the several malls, such as Riocentro and Village Plaza, if you fancy shopping with Guayaquil's wealthy classes. This is the city's richest area, nicknamed "Little Miami."

ENTERTAINMENT AND EVENTS
Nightlife

Guayaquil's nightlife rivals Quito's, and the locals, of course, will tell you that it beats the capital hands down. Like Quito, bars are usually empty before 9 P.M., and the night gets going toward midnight on weekends. It can be a bit expensive, with cover charges ranging $5–20 in the upmarket joints. The in places change regularly, so for the latest information, visit www.farras.com or www.guayaquilcaliente.com.

The breezy, Bohemian atmosphere of Las Peñas makes it the most pleasant area to visit at night, with countless bars, cafés, and restaurants. It's also far safer than alternative nightspots in the city, with regular police patrols. At the bottom of the steps, one of the city's best bars to catch live music is **Diva Nicotina** (Escalinata, tel. 9/909-9208, 7 P.M.–midnight Mon.–Thurs., 7 P.M.–2 A.M. Fri.–Sat., cover $5 on live music nights). Many of the city's best musicians play here—everything from Latin rock to jazz and Cuban habanera. The bar is stocked with a huge range of liquor, and there are Cuban cigars if you want to puff away while you listen. Next door, **El Galeon de Artur's** (Escalinata, tel. 4/231-1073, 6 P.M.–midnight Mon.–Thurs., 6 P.M.–2 A.M. Fri.–Sat.) has DJs and live music on weekends. Farther up the steps, there are plenty of endearing little bars serving beer, cocktails, and tapas, some commanding great views over the river.

JULIO JARAMILLO: THE NIGHTINGALE OF AMERICA

If you hear a melancholy song accompanied by an acoustic guitar while you're wandering around Guayaquil, chances are it's Julio Jaramillo, Ecuador's most famous 20th-century musician. Known as the *ruiseñor* (nightingale) of America, Julio Jaramillo was born in Guayaquil on October 1, 1935. He learned to play the guitar and sing from an early age and developed an emotional singing style that captivated his audience. He was versatile and sang in many styles – from traditional Ecuadorian *pasillo* to more popular styles such as bolero, waltz, and tango. His first success came in 1956 with a version of "Nuestro Juramento" (Our Oath). He continued to be Ecuador's biggest music stars for the next 20 years, and his fame spread throughout Latin America, especially to Venezuela, Colombia, and Mexico. He recorded an incredible 4,000 songs in total, and when he wasn't performing he spent much of his time womanizing – he fathered at least 40 children – and drinking. It was this vice that finished him off, when he succumbed to liver cirrhosis in 1978 aged just 42. His death was mourned by a crowd of 200,000, and several fans attempted suicide. Today his music is loved by generations of Ecuadorians, and his birthday has been declared national *pasillo* day to celebrate his signature genre. For further information, visit www.museojuliojaramillo.com.

Hidden away from the main drag of Las Peñas, around the corner to the right and up cobbled Numa Pompilio Llona, is one of Guayaquil's most interesting bars, **◖ La Paleta** (Numa Pompilio Llona 174, tel. 4/232-0930, 8 A.M.–2 A.M. Tues.–Sat., $10 minimum). The city's creative crowd comes here to enjoy the eclectic, colorful decor, low ceilings, cozy nooks and crannies, and wide-ranging menu of cocktails and tapas. It epitomizes the arty atmosphere of the district, and if you're not in Guayaquil for long, this is one place you shouldn't miss.

In the center, the main nightlife area is the **Zona Rosa** (Pink Zone) between downtown and Las Peñas. It runs along Rocafuerte and Panama between Roca and Montalvo. Take a taxi there and back, and don't wander away from the main drag. The in places change regularly, but one of the most popular new bars for live rock and Latin music is **Ojos de Perro Azul** (Panama and Padre Aguirre, tel. 9/473-4475, 8 P.M.–midnight Wed.–Thurs., 8 P.M.–2 A.M. Fri.–Sat.), which translates intriguingly as "blue dog's eyes." **Bar Santo Remedio** (Imbabura and Panama, tel. 4/230-0686, 8 P.M.–midnight Mon.–Thurs., 8 P.M.–2 A.M. Fri.–Sat.) is another popular new bar, while **El Colonial** (Rocafuerte 623, tel. 4/230-1156, 4 P.M.–midnight Mon.–Thurs., 4 P.M.–2 A.M. Fri.–Sat.) nearby is a more traditional Peñas bar with local dishes and live music on weekends. **Vulcano** (Rocafuerte and Aguirre, tel. 4/230-0948, 10 P.M.–2 A.M. Fri.–Sat.) is the city's main gay and lesbian bar.

Zona Rosa has plenty of raucous discos, mainly pumping out a mix of techno and *reggaetón*. Note that most places charge $10 cover on weekends. Popular places at present include **Cali Salsoteca** (Panama and Martínez, tel. 4/230-9914, 8 P.M.–2 A.M. Thurs.–Sat.), **Kaos** (Padre Aguirre and Panama, tel. 4/256-2257, 8 P.M.–2 A.M. Thurs.–Sat.), and **Zouk** (Panama and Imbabura, tel. 4/230-8065, www.discotecazouk.com, 8 P.M.–2 A.M. Thurs.–Sat.).

As an alternative to the city center, the northern district of **Urdesa** ($3 by taxi) has thriving nightlife, with restaurants and bars lining the main street, Victor Emilio Estrada. **Manantial** (Estrada and Las Monjas, tel. 4/288-4288, 9:30 A.M.–midnight Mon.–Thurs., 9:30 A.M.–2 A.M. Fri.–Sat.) is a Guayaquil institution, an informal bar-restaurant that is nearly always busy. Here you can fill up on Ecuadorian staples accompanied by pitchers of beer. Afterward, head farther down the street to **Chappus** (Estrada and Las Monjas, tel. 4/288-1181, 7 P.M.–midnight Mon.–Thurs., 7 P.M.–2 A.M. Fri.–Sat., cover $10 Fri.–Sat.). This rustic, wooden bar has been entertaining for years. Either have a quiet drink upstairs or shake it on the dance floor downstairs later on. It gets very busy on weekends (when men pay a cover charge) but you are guaranteed a fun, raucous evening.

Other alternatives north of the center include **Fizz** (Francisco Orellana and Cornejo, Kennedy, tel. 4/268-4263, 9 P.M.–2 A.M. Thurs.–Sat.) and the famous **El Jardín de Salsa** (Las Américas, tel. 4/239-6083, 8 P.M.–2 A.M. Thurs.–Sat.), near the airport, which has one of the biggest dance floors in Ecuador.

Cinema and Theaters

Listings for movies and theater performances appear in *El Telegrafo* and *El Universo,* Guayaquil's two major newspapers. There are two movie theaters in the center—**Supercines** (9 de Octubre and Rumichaca, tel. 4/252-2054), and the 180-degree screen of the **IMAX** (tel. 4/256-3069, www.imaxmalecon2000.com) at the north end of Malecón 2000. Otherwise, hit the malls—the best options are **Cinemark** in Mall del Sol (tel. 4/269-2015, www.cinemark.com.ec) or **Supercines** (at San Marino, tel. 4/208-3268, www.supercines.com).

The best theatrical performances are at the **Teatro Centro de Arte** (Vía a la Costa Km. 4.5, tel. 4/200-3699, www.teatrocentrodearte.org) north of the center (take a taxi). **Centro Cultural Sarao** (Ciudadela Kennedy, tel. 4/229-5118) also has dance and theater performances on Friday–Saturday.

Festivals

The biggest parties in Guayaquil take place at New Year, when the city is filled with fireworks and burning effigies of *El Año Viejo,* which could be anyone from the President to Bart Simpson. **Carnival** is also big, punctuated by balloons filled with water (or other liquids,

if you're unlucky), although many residents choose to escape the heat and head for the beach or the mountains. **Bolívar's Birthday** (July 24–25) is combined with the **Foundation of Guayaquil** for one of the city's largest celebrations and the **Independence of Guayaquil** is celebrated October 9–12. In early October, **Durán,** the rather run-down town across the river, springs to life with a large music festival, *La Feria de Durán,* attracting 300,000 people to Latin pop concerts.

SHOPPING

Shopping in Guayaquil is split into two very different experiences—lower-priced openair markets in the center or higher-priced air-conditioned malls. **La Bahía,** opposite Malecón 2000 north of Olmedo, is the city's black market. You can find everything here—shoes, clothing, electronics, and, unfortunately, most of the city's stolen cell phones. It's all semilegal with a faint air of danger, so take care and don't go with much money or valuables.

For a much better shopping experience, go to the **Mercado Artesanal** (artisans market, Loja between Moreno and Córdova, 9:30 A.M.–6:30 P.M. daily), a few blocks inland from the north end of Malecón. If you've already been to Otavalo or similar markets in the mountains, this will come up short, and it's a bit more expensive. Nevertheless, more than 250 stores offer a wide selection of indigenous clothing, Panama hats, bags, leather goods, handicrafts, and ornaments. Foreigners are usually given inflated prices, so haggle away and aim for about 70 percent of the original price. There is a smaller market offering similar goods at the south end of Malecón 2000.

The most relaxed shopping experience is in Las Peñas, where you'll find dozens of alluring little stores selling artisanal wares, paintings, and sculptures.

For a more Americanized shopping experience, hit the malls, of which there are plenty in Guayaquil. Guayacos love malls, and the wealthier classes seem to model their lifestyles on Miami. In the city center, the most convenient

GUAYAQUIL

mall is **Unicentro,** on the north side of Parque de las Iguanas. To the north, Kennedy has two large malls—**Policentro** and **San Marino.** The best-value mall for shopping, with prices to rival the black market, is the new mall inside the new bus terminal. However, all these malls pale into insignificance when compared with **Mall del Sol.** This gigantic mall is the largest in Ecuador and has more than 150 stores, a large food court, and a 10-screen cinema. While the food court is cheap, most of the stores are overpriced, so it's best as a place to hang out. If you are tired of the city center, it's worth heading here for an afternoon, and it's air-conditioned, of course, so you can cool off. Mall del Sol is between Kennedy and the airport, six kilometers from downtown (taxi from downtown $3–4).

Bookstores are not nearly as easy to find in Guayaquil as in Quito. The best stores are **Mr Books** (Mall del Sol, tel. 4/208-2578) or **Librimundi** (San Marino mall, tel. 4/208-3202).

RECREATION AND TOURS

Guayaquil has quite a few travel agencies, but not nearly as many as Quito. For Galápagos and rainforest trips, prices are similar to Quito, although last-minute bargains can be harder to come by.

Canodros (Urb. Santa Leonor, Solar 10, tel. 4/228-5711, fax 4/228-7651, U.S. tel. 800/613-6026, www.canodros.com) has Galápagos cruises aboard the *Galápagos Explorer II* and also arranges rainforest visits to Kapawi Ecolodge in the southern Oriente. **Centro Viajero** (Baquerizo Moreno 1119 at 9 de Octubre, 8th Fl., Suite 805, tel. 4/230-1283) offers a range of Galápagos cruises. **Chasquitur** (Acacias 605 at Las Monjas, tel. 4/288-8988, fax 4/238-8987, chasquitur@ yahoo.com) is one of the best operators for tours around Guayaquil, including Manglares Churute Ecological Reserve. Whale-watching tours are available July–September, and dolphin-watching is possible in the mangroves year-round. **Ecua Andino Planet** (Escobedo 835 at Junín, P2, Suite 205, tel. 4/600-2636, www.ecua-andino.com) offers a wide range of

tours throughout the country but specializes in the coast. Tours to Puerto El Morro and Machalilla can be booked here. **Galasam** (9 de Octubre 424 at Córdova, Ed. Gran Pasaje, tel. 4/230-4488, fax 4/231-1485, www.gala-sam.com.ec) is well known for cheap tours to the Galápagos, but quality is variable. **Metropolitan Touring** (Calle 11 NE 103 at Av. 1 NE, Atarazana, tel./fax 4/228-4666) is one of Ecuador's largest tour operators and the first Galápagos operator, running cruises since way back in the 1960s. They focus on higher-end tours but have a huge range of options for the Galápagos, the coast, the Sierra, and the Oriente. The sales office is in the Hilton Colón in Kennedy.

Half-day tours ($20 pp) of the Botanical Gardens and the Parque Histórico Guayaquil can be booked through the **Hotel Sol de Oriente.** A small fleet of roofless double-decker "Guayaquil Visión" **tourist buses** make the rounds of the *malecón,* Las Peñas, and the major parks and plazas. Ninety-minute tours (Sat.–Sun. and holidays, $5 pp) leave every two hours from the Plaza Calderón at the south end of Malecón 2000. You can buy tickets onboard at the three *malecón* stops.

ACCOMMODATIONS

For such a large city, Guayaquil is sadly lacking in good budget and mid-range accommodations. Many of the cheap hotels in the center double as seedy motels for locals to meet lovers in secret, while the top-end hotels charge very high rates. However, the city has a few good mid-range hotels—mainly near Parque de las Iguanas and Parque Centenario. The center gets noisy, so ask for a back room or a higher floor.

$10-25

If you want to stay in the center on a tight budget without having to suffer dark, seedy guest rooms, your best bet is **Hotel Mar de Plata** (Junín 718 at Boyacá, tel. 4/231-0580, $10 s, $20 d, air-conditioning $5 extra). The guest rooms are simple but clean with private baths and cable TV, and the hotel is very convenient for sightseeing. Another budget choice with basic guest rooms is **Hotel Sander** (Luque 1101 at Moncayo, tel. 4/232-0030 or 4/232-0944, $13 s, $15 d). A more colorful option is **Hostal Suites Madrid** (Quisquis 305 at Rumichaca, tel. 4/230-7804, $15 s, $25 d) with bright airy guest rooms, patterned bedspreads, background music, a feast of artwork covering the walls, and friendly service.

Decent budget accommodations outside the center are hard to find, but North American–run **Dreamkapture Inn** (Juan Sixto Bernal, Manzana 2, Villa 21, tel. 4/224-2909, www.dreamkapture.com, dorm $10 pp, $16–20 s, $23–30 d, breakfast included) is worth finding. It is a few kilometers north of the center in the Alborada neighborhood, but it is secure, well maintained, and a good value. There is a small waterfall and a pool, hammocks to relax in, and a small travel agency under American management.

$25-50

Guayaquil has an increasing number of good mid-range accommodations in the center. The elegant Spanish-style **(Hotel Andaluz** (Junín 842 at Baquerizo Moreno, tel. 4/230-5796 or 4/231-1057, www.hotelandaluz-ec.com, $25 s, $40 d) is perhaps the best mid-range deal downtown. Well-appointed guest rooms with hot water, air-conditioning, and a splash of Ecuadorian art are complemented by a pleasant living room area with leather sofas and a TV, plus a garden terrace on the roof. Not as aesthetically pleasing as the Andaluz but perfectly located right on Parque de las Iguanas is **Hotel Rizzo** (Clemente Ballén and Chile, tel. 4/232-5210, $30 s, $40 d). The guest rooms are compact but decent, some have small balconies, and others overlook the park. Downstairs is a good café, Jambelí, that serves set menus for breakfast, lunch, and dinner.

Another good mid-range option with an ideal location right on Parque Centenario is **Hostal Linda** (Lorenzo de Garaicoa 809, tel. 4/256-2495, $25 s, $40 d), which overlooks Parque Centenario. Guest rooms are plushly decorated with new furniture and marble

floors. Note that guest rooms with one double bed are surprisingly the same price as singles ($25). **Hotel Versailles** (Quisquis 100 at Ximena, tel. 4/230-8773, www.hotelversailles.com.ec, $25 s or d, breakfast included), while not as grand as its name, is good value for two. Guest rooms have hot water, air-conditioning, and cable TV.

Boutique hotels are hard to find in Guayaquil, but **(Hostal Manso** (Malecón 1406 at Aguirre, tel. 4/252-6644, www.manso.ec, $25–90) has carved itself out a little niche. You could easily miss its small front door tucked into a large block opposite the *malecón*, but inside is a welcoming slice of Arabia with warm maroon decor, floor cushions, and hammocks in the bar. The guest rooms are individually colored and designed. The best have private baths and air-conditioning, and the cheapest do not. There's a big price difference between the cheapest and most expensive, but don't expect luxury; the atmosphere and original designs are the main draw. There are regular theater and music performances in the lounge.

If you want a home away from home, head outside the center to the **Tangara Guest House** (Sáenz and O'Leary, Ciudadela Bolivariana, Bloque F, Casa 1, tel. 4/228-4445 or 4/228-2828, $45 s, $55 d, breakfast and airport transfers included). This friendly family-run place has six welcoming guest rooms with private baths, a fully-equipped kitchen, and a living room. It is between the airport and the bus station. Another option even farther out is **Iguanazu Hostal** (Ciudadela la Cogra, Km. 3.5, Villa 2, tel. 4/220-1143 or 9/986-7968, www.iguanazuhostel.com, dorm $15 pp, $45 s, $55 d). It's hard to find, but its hilltop location offers a different lodging experience to the rest of Guayaquil. With friendly management, eight charming wooden-floored guest rooms, a lush lawn, a pool, a living room, and great views of the city, it's worth seeking out.

$50-75

The sleek **Sol de Oriente** (Aguirre 603 at Escobedo, tel. 4/232-5500, www.hotelsol-oriente.com, $52 s, $92 d, buffet breakfast included) brings a slice of Asia to Guayaquil, although it mainly caters to businesspeople. The guest rooms are well equipped, with cable TV and Wi-Fi, while downstairs are four restaurants, including the respected Great Wall, a breakfast buffet, and a karaoke bar. You can try to forget your vocal performance with a spell in the spa.

Hotel Las Peñas (Escobedo 1215 between 9 de Octubre and Vélez, tel. 4/232-3355, www.hlpgye ec, $54 s, $ 61 d) is more modern than the name would suggest. It's centrally located and has 30 immaculate guest rooms. There's also a private shuttle service and a great café downstairs. The peach and pink balconies of **Hotel La Fontana** (P. Icaza 404 at Córdova, tel. 4/230-3967 or 4/230-7230, hlafontana@ ecutel.net, $50 s, $60 d) are a breath of fresh air to the otherwise mundane chain hotels in downtown's commercial district. Guest rooms have air-conditioning, private baths with hot water, cable TV, and telephones.

$75-100

A slickly run, modern, but not cheap hotel is the renovated **Hotel Palace** (Chile 214–216 at Luque, tel. 4/232-1080, www.hotelpalaceguayaquil.com. ec, $97 s, $109 d), with immaculate guest rooms, a gym, a popular restaurant, and a deli.

Close to the cathedral, **Grand Hotel Guayaquil** (Boyacá 1600 at 10 de Agosto, tel. 4/232-9690, U.S. tel. 800/989-0025, www. grandhotelguayaquil.com, $97 s, $110 d, suites $122) doesn't look all that impressive from the outside, but inside are 180 luxury guest rooms with cable TV, a sports complex, a landscaped pool, a spa, a sauna, a rooftop sundeck, and two restaurants.

$100-200

Guests at the elegant ◖ **Unipark Hotel** (Ballén 406 at Chile, tel. 4/232-7100, fax 4/232-8352, U.S. tel. 800/447-7462, unipark@oroverde-hotels.com, $140 s or d) can amuse themselves in the attached shopping mall, which features a casino and a video arcade. The Unipark has El Parque French restaurant, the Unicafe, and the upstairs Unibar, which specializes in sushi

and has great views of Parque de las Iguanas. There's also a gym with a hot tub and a sauna. Reception is on the second floor.

◖ **Hotel Oro Verde** (9 de Octubre and Moreno, tel. 4/232-7999, fax 4/232-9350, www.oroverdehotels.com, $160 s, $170 d, buffet breakfast and airport transfers included) is easily the top hotel in the center of Guayaquil, boasting 192 guest rooms and 62 suites with air-conditioning, satellite TV, and video players. There's also a deli, a casino, three gourmet restaurants, a piano bar, and a fitness center.

Outside the center, the **Hilton Colón Guayaquil** (Orellana, Ciudadela Kennedy Norte, tel. 4/268-9000, fax 4/268-9149, U.S. reservations 800/445-8667, from $185) is the best luxury option and is five minutes from the airport. The 274 guest rooms and 20 suites have climate control, noise-insulated windows, cable TV, and phones. Downstairs there's a casino, a gym, a pool, five restaurants, and a 24-hour café.

FOOD

Rather like its hotels, Guayaquil's has a glut of cheap, rock-bottom places and a big jump up to the expensive gourmet restaurants. Many of the best restaurants are in wealthier areas of the suburbs, and the geography of the city makes it difficult to browse. The center has its fair share of top-quality restaurants, mainly attached to hotels, and is also full of cheap places offering $2–3 *almuerzos* (set lunches), but quality is variable. There are plenty of food stalls to grab a decent lunch on the south end of Malecón 2000. In the evening, Las Peñas is the most pleasant place to browse eateries, while the Urdesa neighborhood's main avenue, Victor Emilio Estrada, is lined with good restaurants. While it's far from an authentic Ecuadorian experience, a safe and comfortable option is to head for the large, varied food courts in malls such as Mall del Sol and San Marino north of the center.

Asian

Sucre and Chile is Guayaquil's *chifa* corner,

with plenty of restaurants offering passable Chinese entrées for $3–5. **Chifa Jumbo** (Sucre 309 at Pedro Carbo, tel. 4/232-9593, lunch and dinner daily, entrées $3–4) is a good budget option, while **Gran Chifa** (Eloy Alfaro 411, tel. 4/241-0270, lunch and dinner daily, entrées $5–7) is a bit pricier with better ambience.

For Japanese cuisine, most of the best places are in Urdesa. **Tsuji** (Estrada 813 at Guayacanes, tel. 4/288-1183, lunch Mon.–Sun., dinner Mon.–Sat., entrées $15) is the classiest establishment, while **Isao** (Bálsamos 102 at Estrada, tel. 4/288-9963, lunch and dinner daily, entrées $8–12) and **Matsuri** (Estrada and Las Monjas, tel. 4/288-5550, lunch and dinner daily, entrées $8–12) are more informal and a bit cheaper.

Bakeries and Snacks

The **Pepa de Oro** (Boyacá 1600 at 10 de Agosto, tel. 4/232-9690, 24 hours daily) coffee shop and cafeteria in the Grand Hotel Guayaquil serves a wide range of juices and empanadas. The **Galleta Pecosa** (10 de Agosto and Boyacá, tel. 4/251-8636, 9 A.M.–8 P.M. Mon.–Sat., 9 A.M.–5 P.M. Sun., $1–3) is a delightful, colorful little bakery with a wide range of cookies and cakes. **California Panadería/Pastelería** (Escobedo and Vélez, tel. 4/264-1441, breakfast, lunch, and dinner daily, $1–3) and **La Española** (Junín and Boyacá, tel. 4/230-2694, 8 A.M.–7:30 P.M. Mon.–Sat., 8 A.M.–3 P.M. Sun., $1–3) are also excellent bakeries. For a slice of beach chic, head to **⟨ Frutabar** (Malecón and Martínez, tel. 4/230-0743, www.frutabar.com, 8 A.M.–midnight daily, entrées $4–6) where a huge selection of *batidos* (fruit shakes) and imaginative burgers are served on misshapen tables, with surfboards and tropical murals brightening the place up.

Ecuadorian

For a budget meal in a comfortable, colorful setting, you can't beat **Las 3 Canastas** (Vélez and Chile, no phone, breakfast, lunch, and dinner daily, entrées $3–4), with big portions of chicken, fish, pork, and meat dishes as well as empanadas and snacks washed down by a huge variety of juices and shakes. There's a small sister café at Pedro Carbo and Clemente Ballén. On the *malecón* itself, **⟨ Aroma Café** (Jardínes Botánicos, Malecón, tel. 9/953-7458, lunch and dinner daily, entrées $5–8) serves a wide range of meat, chicken, and fish dishes in the cool, shaded atmosphere of the botanical gardens. In Las Peñas, head to **Arthur's** (Numa Pompilio Llona 127, tel. 4/231-2230, dinner Mon.–Sat., closed Sun., entrées $6–10). The local specialties, such as breaded sea bass and chicken stew, are a little expensive, but the view over the river and the city is worth it, and there's live music some weekends.

Lo Nuestro (Estrada 903 at Higueras, Urdesa, tel. 4/238-6398, noon–11 P.M. daily, entrées $6–15) offers mid-priced Ecuadorian and Italian fare in Urdesa. **La Canoa** (Chile between 10 de Agosto and Ballén, tel. 4/232-9270, breakfast, lunch, and dinner daily, entrées $8–10) at the Hotel Continental offers pricey but good Ecuadorian dishes such as goat or chicken stew.

Seafood

Most of the restaurants listed above do good seafood dishes, but for a gourmet experience, try **El Caracol Azul** (9 de Octubre 1918 at Los Ríos, tel. 4/228-0461, http://elcaracolazul.ec, lunch and dinner Mon.–Sat., entrées $10–20). Try salmon in tarragon or shrimp in coconut. If you want to eat like a true Guayaco, head to a *casa del cangrejo* (crab house), where hungry patrons attack crustaceans with mallets and suck out the meat in a slurp-fest. The **Red Crab** (Estrada and Laureles, Urdesa, tel. 4/288-7632, www.redcrab.com.ec, lunch and dinner daily, entrées $5–10) is a high-class place with crab, shrimp, and lobster cooked every way imaginable. There's a sister branch on Vía Samborondón.

Steak Houses

The huge **⟨ La Parillada del Ñato** (Estrada 1219 at Laureles, Urdesa, tel. 4/288-3330, lunch and dinner daily, $4–12) is famous for its mammoth portions and is always packed. There are platters of barbecue for meat eaters, and vegetarians can get a good pizza. There's another branch at Luque and Pichincha downtown.

Other International

For a healthy, inexpensive vegetarian meal, try **Lorenabo** (P. Icaza and Córdova, no phone, lunch and dinner Mon.–Sat., entrées $2–3, set lunch $2). The wide range of meat-free Asian, Italian, and local specialties are very economical.

For Italian, the best gourmet place for a splurge is **Trattoria de Enrico** (Bálsamos 504 at Ébanos, Urdesa, tel. 4/238-7079, lunch and dinner daily, entrées $10–15), an award-winning restaurant with low ceilings, dim lighting, and top-class dishes. For cheap, tasty pizzas cooked in a clay oven, try **El Hornero** (Estrada 906, Urdesa, tel. 4/238-4788, lunch and dinner daily, entrées $4–10).

For Spanish tapas and paella, **La Tasca Vasca** (Ballén and Chimborazo, tel. 4/253-4599, lunch and dinner Mon.–Sat., entrées $7–12) is a beautifully laid out restaurant on Parque de las Iguanas with a cozy ambience and waiters in traditional dress.

Recommended but pricey restaurants attached to hotels include **Restaurant 1822** at the Grand Hotel Guayaquil (Boyacá 1600 at 10 de Agosto, tel. 4/232-9690, breakfast, lunch, and dinner daily, entrées $10–20), and the Oro Verde's trio of gourmet restaurants **El Patio, Le Gourmet,** and Swiss-style **Le Fondue** (9 de Octubre and García Moreno, tel. 4/232-7999, breakfast, lunch, and dinner daily, entrées $10–20).

INFORMATION AND SERVICES
Money

Head to Pichincha and Icaza near the *malecón* to find the **Banco del Guayaquil** and the **Banco Pichincha,** both of which have ATMs and offer credit-card cash advances. **Banco de Pacifico** (Icaza and Pichincha) has an ATM nearby. **Cambiosa** (9 de Octubre 113 at Malecón) changes traveler's checks for a high commission, although it's better than at the airport. You can also change money at **Casa de Cambio Delgado** (9 de Octubre between Chimborazo and Chile).

American Express (9 de Octubre 1900 at Esmeraldas, 2nd Fl., tel. 4/239-4984) and **MasterCard** (Ed. San Francisco, Córdova and 9 de Octubre, tel. 4/256-1730) both have offices in the center. There's a 24-hour **Western Union** (Guillermo Pareja Rolando 56, tel. 800/937-837) in the Edificio de Bronce in the Alborada neighborhood as well as a branch in the Centro Comercial Malecón.

Communications

The **post office** is in the building bounded by Ballén, Aguirre, Pedro Carbo, and Chile. **Internet cafés** are everywhere, especially in malls like Unicentro, along Estrada in Urdesa, and along 9 de Octubre downtown.

Health

The biggest problems you are likely to encounter are stomach-related, although dengue fever is present in the rainy season. If you are seriously ill or injured, go to the **Clínica Kennedy** (San Jorge between Calle 9a and Calle 10a, Nueva Kennedy, tel. 4/228-6963), the best hospital in Guayaquil, renowned for its specialists and emergency services. There are also branches in Alborada and on Vía Samborondón. Note that ambulances are slow, so it's best to head straight to the hospital by taxi.

Other Services

The **immigration office** (Avenida Benjamin Rosales, tel. 4/229-7004 or 4/229-7197) opposite the bus terminal can give extensions on visas and answer other border-related questions. The **Ministry of Tourism** (Orellana, Ciudadela Kennedy, across from the World Trade Center, 9 a.m.–5 p.m. Mon.–Fri.) is staffed by helpful English-speaking employees. There's also an office at the airport with friendly staff. The **city tourist office** (Ballén and Pichincha, tel. 4/252-4100, www.guayaquil.gov.ec, 9 a.m.–5 p.m. Mon.–Fri.), opposite

GUAYAQUIL CONSULATES AND EMBASSIES

Most Guayaquil consulates and embassies are open 9 A.M.–noon or 1 P.M. Monday–Friday.

- **Australia:** Rocafuerte 520, 2nd Fl., tel. 4/601-7529

- **Austria:** Circunvalación Sur 718, tel./fax 4/238-4886

- **Belgium:** José Antonio Campos and García Avilés, tel. 4/281-0505 or 4/281-0508

- **Brazil:** Juan Tanca Marengo Km. 1.5, tel. 4/227-7065

- **Canada:** Joaquin Orrantia and Juan Tanca Marengo, tel. 4/215-8333

- **Chile:** 9 de Octubre 100 and Malecón, Ed. Banco Previsora, 23rd Fl., Suite 3, tel. 4/256-2995 or 4/256-4619

- **Colombia:** Orellana, Ed. World Trade Center, Torre B, 11th Fl., tel. 4/263-0674

- **Finland:** Francisco Orellana and V. H. Sicouret, tel. 4/268-2771

- **France:** José Mascote and Hurtado, tel./fax 4/232-8442

- **Germany:** Las Monjas and Arosemena, Km. 2.5, Ed. Berlin, tel. 4/220-6867 or 4/220-6868

- **Israel:** 9 de Octubre 729 and Boyacá, 4th Fl., tel. 4/253-4503

- **Italy:** P. Icaza and Baquerizo Moreno, tel. 4/256-8358

- **Japan:** Vía a Daule Km. 11.5, tel. 4/210-0600

- **Netherlands:** Av. 9 de Octubre 731, 5th Fl., between García Avilés and Boyacá, tel. 4/232-2709

- **Norway:** Malecón del Salado 106 and Todos los Santos, tel. 4/238-9610

- **Panama:** Miguel Herradura Alcívar, Manzana 208, Villa 28, at Juan Rolando Coello, Kennedy Norte, tel./fax 4/228-5984

- **Peru:** Orellana, Ed. Porta, 14th Fl., tel. 4/228-0114

- **Spain:** Tungurahua and Vélez, tel. 4/601-7460

- **Sweden:** Vía a Daule Km. 6.5, tel. 4/225-4111, fax 4/229-5000

- **Switzerland:** Juan Tanca Marengo Km. 1.8 at Castillo, Ed. Conauto, 5th Fl., tel. 4/268-1900, ext. 034

- **United Kingdom:** Córdova 623 at Solano, tel. 4/256-0400, ext. 318 or ext. 336

- **United States:** 9 de Octubre 1571 at García Moreno, tel. 4/232-3570

- **Venezuela:** Chile 329 at Aguirre, 2nd Fl., tel. 4/232-6600 or 4/232-6566

the Palacio Municipal, stocks more general information about the city and area. There's also a small tourist information center in a train car north of La Rotonda on the *malecón*.

For maps, stop by the **Instituto Geográfico Militar** (IGM, Av. Quito 402 at Solano, tel. 4/239-3351).

GETTING THERE AND AROUND
Land
Taxi drivers in Guayaquil are notorious for driving badly and overcharging foreigners. Few of them use meters, so negotiate the price in advance. It's worth asking at your hotel for the approximate price and then telling the driver, rather than waiting for them to give you an inflated price. As a guide, short journeys around downtown should be about $2, and trips from downtown to the airport, Urdesa, and other northern districts $3–4. Never take unmarked cabs, and if possible, ask your hotel to call you a taxi from a reputable company. Reliable firms include **Movisat** (tel. 4/259-3333),

Fastline (tel. 4/282-3333), and **Solservice** (tel. 4/287-1195).

The poor traffic situation downtown means that **local buses** ($0.25) are not really worth it for short distances. Even then, buses are slow and often jam-packed, and pickpockets can be a problem. Bus number 52 goes from the *malecón* to Urdesa, number 2 goes to the airport, and number 13 goes to the northern malls.

The **Metrovía** service ($0.25) is cleaner and faster. It's a good way to get to and from the main bus terminal if you don't want to take a taxi. Crossing to the Metrovía terminal from the bus terminal is by no means easy, however—you usually need to run across six lanes of traffic. The line runs south from Hospital Luis Vernaza to La Catedral, the most convenient stop for the downtown sights, and then farther south. It returns north from Biblioteca Municipal to Las Peñas and north to the terminal. Note that pickpockets are also a problem on Metrovía, so don't carry valuables, and be vigilant.

Guayaquil's new **bus terminal** is just north of the airport and a huge improvement over the previous dingy terminal. It's clean, efficient, and doubles as a shopping mall with some of the best prices in the city. Buy your ticket at one of the 80 windows and head up the escalator to the gate to catch your bus. There are departures for just about every city in the country. The most popular trips:

- **Atacames** (9 hours, $9): two buses daily, one night bus, Transesmeraldas or Occidentales
- **Bahía de Caráquez** (7 hours, $5): hourly, Reina del Camino
- **Baños** (6–7 hours, $7): three direct buses daily, Transportes Baños or Flota Pelileo
- **Canoa** (7 hours, $8): two buses daily, Reina del Camino
- **Cuenca** (4 hours, $8): every 30 minutes, Ejecutivo San Luis, Express Sucre, or Supertaxis Cuenca
- **Loja** (9 hours, $12): eight buses daily, Coop Loja
- **Manta** (3 hours, $5): hourly, Reina del Camino

- **Puerto López** (4 hours, $4): eight buses daily via Jipijapa, Reina del Camino
- **Quito** (9 hours, $9): hourly, Panamericana or Flota Imbabura
- **Riobamba** (4–5 hours, $4): hourly, Ecuador Ejecutivo and Chimborazo
- **Salinas** (2 hours, $3.50): CLP and Liberpesa

There are also direct buses to **Piura** (10 hours, $12–15) in Peru via **Huaquillas** and **Tumbes** with CIFA (tel. 4/213-0379).

Renting a car in Guayaquil is expensive, starting at around $50 per day before insurance, tax, or gasoline. It's also not recommended, as the standard of driving is atrocious, and the excess charges are alarmingly high. If you really must, major companies at the airport include: **Avis** (tel. 4/216-9092), **Budget** (tel. 4/228-8510), **Expo** (tel. 4/216-9088), **Localiza** (tel. 800/562-254), **Rentauto** (tel. 4/390-4520), and **Seretur** (tel. 4/216-9184). Three of these companies have main offices in the city: **Avis** (CC Olímpico, Av. Kennedy and Las Américas, tel. 4/228-5498, fax 4/228-5519), **Budget** (Las Américas 900 at Andrade, tel. 4/228-4559), and **Localiza** (Francisco Boloña 713, tel. 4/239-5236).

Air

Guayaquil's award-winning new **José J. Olmedo International Airport** (Las Américas, tel. 4/216-9000, www.tagsa.aero) is five kilometers north of the city center. It's Ecuador's only international airport besides Quito's and has flights to a wide range of North American, South American, and some European destinations. The international departure tax is $28 pp, payable in cash.

Five airlines operate domestic flights. Note that the Quito route is particularly competitive, and you can save a lot with promotions and advance online booking. Fares are sometimes as low as $40 one-way, but last-minute they usually rise to $55–70.

National airline **TAME** (tel. 800/500-800 or 4/256-0778, www.tame.com.ec) has the widest range of services. TAME flies to Quito ($60

GUAYAQUIL AIRLINE NUMBERS

- **Air Canada:** tel. 800/010-135 or 4/245-3009
- **Air France/KLM:** tel. 4/216-9068 or 4/216-9050
- **American Airlines:** tel. 4/259-8800
- **Avianca:** tel. 800/003-434
- **Continental:** tel. 800/222-333
- **Copa:** tel. 4/230-3211
- **Delta:** tel. 800/101-060
- **EMETEBE:** tel. 4/229-2492
- **Iberia:** tel. 4/232-9558
- **LAN:** tel. 800/101-075 or 4/259-8500
- **Lufthansa:** tel. 4/259-8060
- **Santa Bárbara:** tel. 4/216-9108 or 4/216-9109
- **TACA/Lacsa:** tel. 800/008-222, reservations 4/232-1007
- **TAME:** tel. 4/231-6492 or 4/231-6507

one-way) 10–12 times daily, to Cuenca ($66 one-way) three times daily, and to Esmeraldas ($100 one-way) once daily. For Lago Agrio, Macas, and Tulcán (from $120 one-way), connect via Quito. For the Galápagos, flights to Baltra ($312–355 round-trip) are three times daily, and to San Cristóbal ($312–355 round-trip), four times a week. Note that only Galápagos residents can buy one-way tickets.

LAN (tel. 800/101-075 or 4/259-8500, www.lan.com) is sometimes cheaper, offering daily flights to Quito ($61 one-way), Cuenca ($43 one-way), and Baltra ($327 round-trip).

Aerogal (tel. 4/268-7566) flies to Quito and Cuenca ($66 one-way) daily, to Baltra ($337 round-trip) daily, and to San Cristóbal ($337 round-trip) several times a week.

Icaro (tel. 800/883-567 or 4/390-5060) offers some of the cheapest flights to Quito ($50 one-way) daily.

New airline **Saereo** (tel. 7/293-4104, www.saereo.com) flies to the southern cities of Machala ($61 one-way) once per week and Loja ($80 one-way) twice per week.

NEAR GUAYAQUIL
Cerro Blanco Protected Forest

If a few days in Guayaquil leaves you craving fresh air and green spaces, this is the nearest place to get it. Cerro Blanco (tel. 4/287-4947 or 4/287-4946, www.bosquecerroblanco.com, 8 A.M.–4 P.M. daily, $4 pp, camping $3 pp) protects 6,000 hectares of tropical dry forest in the Chongón-Colonche hills. The biggest draw is the birdlife, with nearly 200 species that include the endangered great green macaw, symbol of the reserve and known locally as the "*papagayo* of Guayaquil." Other highlights include many species of butterflies, giant *ceibos* trees, and the low roar of howler monkeys from the treetops later on. There are four trails, and only the shortest, to the butterfly garden, can be done independently; the longer, more impressive trails require a guide ($10–15). There is a small camping area with restroom facilities. Just one kilometer west of Cerro Blanco's entrance is the village of **Puerto Hondo,** whose mangrove swamps can be toured on a motorized canoe (tel. 9/140-0186, 9 A.M.–4 P.M. Sat.–Sun., by reservation only Mon.–Fri., $7).

Cerro Blanco and Puerto Hondo are about 15 kilometers west of Guayaquil. Take any bus toward Salinas from the terminal and ask the driver to drop you off. It's a short walk from the highway to the information center.

◖ Manglares Churute Ecological Reserve

Manglares Churute (tel. 9/276-3653 or 4/229-3131, 8 A.M.–6 P.M. daily, $10 pp), 45 kilometers south of Guayaquil, protects 50,000 hectares of mangroves from shrimp farming. The reserve is home to a wealth of diversity due to its varied landscapes, from tangled mangroves rising 700 meters to hilly forest. The

GUAYAQUIL

surrounding salt flats provide shelter for a wide range of shorebirds, such as laughing gulls, roseate spoonbills, ospreys, herons, egrets, and ibis. Hikes into the dry tropical forest are rewarded with the sights of a beautiful waterfall and, with luck, the sight and sound of mantled howler monkeys.

At the park's **information center,** you can view videos and arrange for maps and guides for hikes into the reserve. Four short trails lead downhill to the mangroves and up to the peaks of the Cerros El Mirador and Masvale. Guides ($5) are required, and they speak only Spanish. Boats to explore the mangroves ($60 per day), with room for up to 12 people, can be hired. There are a few basic cabins ($5 pp) near the information center, or camping is available ($3 pp).

The road between Guayaquil and Machala passes the entrance to the reserve on the west side. Not all drivers know it, so make sure yours knows exactly where you want to go, or you may get dropped off in the middle of nowhere. Alternately, you can book a tour of Manglares Churute in Guayaquil through **Chasquitur** (Acacias 605 at Las Monjas, Guayaquil, tel. 4/288-8988, fax 4/238-8987, chasquitur@ yahoo.com).

Zoo El Pantanal

The small Zoo El Pantanal (tel. 4/226-7047, zooelpantanal@hotmail.com, 9 A.M.–5 P.M. daily, $3 pp) was originally an animal rehabilitation center, and it has a collection of at least 60 species, many of which are endangered, including monkeys, crocodiles, tortoises, and big cats. The zoo is located 23 kilometers north of Guayaquil on the road to Daule.

El Oro Province

Most travelers speed through the province of El Oro between Guayaquil and the Peruvian border without stopping. This province was given its name (Gold) due to the plentiful amounts of this precious metal found in the mines inland. Once the treasures were plundered by foreign merchants, the province turned to "brown gold" (cacao) and then "green gold" (bananas). Driving through the province, you'd be forgiven for thinking that it is one enormous banana plantation, and in fact, nearly half of Ecuador's bananas are grown here. **Machala** is the capital of El Oro and is a pleasant enough city, though lacking in visitor attractions. Of more interest is the beach on the nearby island of **Jambelí,** but the highlight of the province is found in the undulating green hills inland from the plantations. It's worth seeking out the beautifully preserved hilltop colonial town of **Zaruma,** especially if you're heading across to Loja and Vilcabamba from the Peruvian border.

Machala and Vicinity

Machala (pop. 228,000), the capital city of El Oro Province, proclaims itself to be the "banana capital of the world," and it's easy to see why when you travel through vast areas of plantations to get here. More than 1 million tonnes of the fruit is exported every year through Puerto Bolívar, seven kilometers to the west, and if you live in North America, chances are one has ended up in your fruit bowl.

After its founding in 1758, Machala enjoyed a cacao boom in the early 20th century that turned it into one of the richest cities on the coast. Bananas began to take over as the main export by the 1950s, and shrimp farming emerged as another key industry in the 1980s. The agricultural riches have helped to make Machala one of the more agreeable cities on the coast, and while it has a lack of visitor attractions, it's a good place to stop overnight, and certainly preferable to Huaquillas. Machala offers easy access to the beaches of Jambelí, and it's the closest large city to the Puyango petrified forest and the easiest transfer point to reach the Ecuadorian highlands via Loja or Cuenca.

ORIENTATION

Machala's streets are oriented diagonally, running northeast–southwest and northwest–southeast. The main road, 25 de Junio, runs along the northeast side of the **Parque Central** and the city's **cathedral,** the most attractive part of the city. One block southwest is **La Casa de Cultura** (Bolívar between 9 de Mayo and Juan Montalvo, tel. 7/293-0711, 9 A.M.–5 A.M. Mon.–Fri., free), which houses a small museum with dozens of pieces of the petrified forest from Puyango. It's worth visiting if you can't make it to the forest itself. About five blocks southeast on Olmedo is the **Parque Colón,** and **Parque de los Héroes** is five blocks northwest of the Parque Central. If you want to escape the heat, head 3.5 kilometers south of town to the huge **El Paseo mall** ($2 by taxi), slap-bang in the middle of the banana plantations. It has department stores, a food court, and a cinema.

ENTERTAINMENT AND EVENTS

Machala's biggest event is the **World Banana Fair,** which takes place the third week in September. The highlight is the election of the Banana Queen. For nightlife, Machala has some bars and discos located in the **Zona Rosa** along Colón, six blocks southwest of 25 de Junio. There are some crime problems in the Zona Rosa, so it is advisable to take a taxi at night.

ACCOMMODATIONS

Many travelers crossing the Peruvian border prefer to spend the night here rather than in Huaquillas, and Machala is a more pleasant place. As a business city, it's hard to find rock-bottom hotel rates, but there are plenty of decent rooms for $30 d. **Hostal Madrid** (Av. 25 de Junio and Guayas, tel. 7/292-2995, $18 s, $30 d) has the best location, just off the main square, and is a very good value with well-presented guest rooms, warm colors, air-conditioning, and cable TV. Most of the other reasonably priced hotels are south of the center. One of the best is **Hotel Bolívar** (Bolívar and Colón, tel. 7/293-0727, $18 s, $28 d). Nearby, **Hostal**

Saloah (Colón and Rocafuerte, tel. 7/293-4344, $18 s, $28 d) has smaller guest rooms for the same price. A slightly cheaper option is **Hotel Ecuatoriano** (Colón and 25 de Junio, tel. 7/293-0197, $15 s, $23 d, air-conditioning $3 pp extra). For a better class of guest room and a pleasant pool and patio area, try **Rizzo Hotel** (Guayas, tel. 7/293-3651, $25 s, $40 d), southwest of the main square. **Grand Hotel Americano** (Tarqui and 25 de Junio, tel. 7/296-6400, $33 s, $48 d) is a more stylish option with a plush reception area and modern guest rooms.

Luxury travelers should book the immaculate guest rooms at ◖ **Hotel Oro Verde** (Circunvalación Norte and Calle Vehicular V7, tel. 7/293-3140, fax 7/293-3150, www.oroverdehotels.com, $132 s, $145 d, breakfast included), surrounded by tropical gardens in the Unioro suburb 10 minutes out of town. Gourmands can sample Oro Mar restaurant as well as a café and gourmet deli.

FOOD

Just north of the main plaza on 25 de Junio are a string of cheap restaurants, including **Asadero Don Pancho** (25 de Junio, no phone, lunch and dinner daily, $2.50) offering barbecued chicken. For Chinese, **Restaurante Gran Chifa** (tel. 7/251-6549, lunch and dinner daily, entrées $4–6) has very good food. North of the plaza, **Chesco Pizzeria** (Guayas 1050, tel. 7/293-6418, 11 A.M.–11 P.M. daily, from $4) has good pizzas. For a more upscale meal, try **Mesón Hispano** (Las Palmeras and Sucre, tel. 7/293-6769, 11 A.M.–midnight Mon.–Sat., entrées $5–12).

The best seafood is along the docks of **Puerto Bolívar,** west of town. There is a string of restaurants here, the best of which is probably **Waikiki** (tel. 7/292-9810, lunch and dinner daily, entrées $5). It's a five-minute cab ride ($3) or a 10-minute bus ride ($0.25) from Machala's Parque Central.

INFORMATION AND SERVICES

Exchange traveler's checks at **Delgado Travel** (9 de Mayo near the plaza, tel. 7/293-1850).

There's a **Banco del Pacífico** (Rocafuerte and Junín), **Banco de Pichincha** (Rocafuerte and Guayas), and half a dozen other banks along the Parque Central. Machala's **post office** is at Bolívar 733 at Montalvo.

For immigration matters, stop by the **Peruvian Consulate** (Manzana 14, Villa 11, Urb. Unioro, tel. 7/293-7040) in the Unioro neighborhood.

The **city tourist office** (9 de Mayo and 25 de Junio, tel. 7/293-2106, 8 A.M.–12:30 P.M. and 1:30–5 P.M. Mon.–Fri.) is on the southeast corner of the main plaza, or try the **El Oro Province tourist office** (Guayas and Pichincha, 2nd Fl., tel. 7/296-0055), which has more information.

For tours to Puyango petrified forest ($20–25 pp) and elsewhere in El Oro, contact **Cristy Viajes** (Juan Montalvo and Pichincha, tel. 7/293-4351) or **Doristour** (Buenavista 606 at Rocafuerte, tel. 7/293-3208). You may need to get a group together to visit Puyango because tours don't depart frequently.

GETTING THERE AND AROUND

It seems incredible that a city the size of Machala has no central bus terminal, but it doesn't. Various *cooperativa* offices are dotted around the center, concentrated in the area bounded by Junín, Sucre, Colón, and Bolívar. **CIFA** (Bolívar and Guayas) buses leave every 20 minutes throughout the day for Huaquillas (75 minutes, $2). **Cooperativa TAC** (Colón 1819 between Rocafuerte and Bolívar) sends buses hourly throughout the day to Zaruma (3 hours, $3). For buses to Guayaquil (3.5 hours, $4), visit **Ecuatoriano Pullman** (25 de Junio and Colón). CIFA also goes to Guayaquil from 25 de Junio 627 at Tarqui. **Panamericana** (Colón and Bolívar) runs buses to Quito (11 hours, $10), and **Transportes Loja** (Tarqui 1813 at Rocafuerte) heads to Loja (6 hours, $6). For Cuenca (4.5 hours, $5) use *Transportes Pullman Sucre y Azuay* (Sucre between Junín and Tarquí).

Several taxi companies line Guayas between Pichincha and Manuel Serrano, including

Coop de Turismo Guayas (tel. 7/293-4382) and **Coturcip** (tel. 7/296-0849). Both run an efficient hourly service to Guayaquil ($10 pp). Pay in advance, and they collect you from the hotel.

Machala's airport is about one kilometer southwest of the center along Montalvo ($1 by taxi). **TAME** (Montalvo between Pichincha and Bolívar, tel. 7/293-0139, www.tame.com. ec) offers two flights daily to Quito (from $86 one-way), and **Saereo** (tel. 7/293-4104, www. saereo.com) flies 30-seater planes to Guayaquil (from $61 one-way).

NEAR MACHALA
Jambelí Island

If you're coming through Machala, you could do worse than to visit this island beach resort on the northern tip of the Archipiélago de Jambelí. One of the few beaches south of Guayaquil, it's a good option for those craving a bit of sun and sea after long bus rides. In high season, it's packed with locals seeking a weekend escape from the city, and in low season and midweek it's often very quiet. Canoes shuttle visitors across the bay and through a channel flanked by mangroves. There are chances to see rufous-necked wood rails or yellow-crowned night herons. In the island's tiny village, on the north side of the island, you'll find a few seafood restaurants and a growing number of accommodations. Most of the amenities are very basic, which is part of the island's charm.

The tides can be quite strong here, and you may be surprised to see the beach covered with sacks, a makeshift attempt to protect the sand and Malecón from the sea.

Most people come here for a day trip, but you can stay overnight. Turn right at the beach to find most of the offerings. **Toa Toa** (tel. 8/493-5696, $5 pp) has battered wooden cabins, rather surprisingly equipped with TVs and private baths, plus a pleasant garden area with games and a bar. For more comfort, **Hospedaje Son de Mar** (tel. 9/386-5257, $25 s or d) has well-equipped modern cabins. Farther up the beach are the best options: **Las Iguanas** (tel.

9/340-8616, $25 d) has colorful guest rooms and a family atmosphere. **Las Tórtolas** (tel. 9/929-7926, www.lastortolasjambeli.com, $40 s or d) is the most comfortable place, with guest rooms in new beachfront bungalows. For food, there are a cluster of seafood restaurants along the beach.

To get to Jambelí, take a taxi ($2.50) or bus from Machala's main plaza to Puerto Bolívar. About 10 canoes ($2.40 round-trip) leave daily from the pier (once every 1.5 hours, on average, but more often in high season). Fishermen will take you on a tour of the mangroves or snorkeling at nearby Isla de Amor ($25).

Note that at the time of this writing, Jambelí had been seriously affected by flooding. The island is particularly vulnerable due to strong currents and an exposed beach, so it's important to check locally on the situation before visiting.

Bosque Petrificado de Puyango

The largest petrified forest in South America and second only to those in Arizona, Bosque Petrificado de Puyango (tel. 7/296-0055, www. bosquepuyango.ec, 9 A.M.–5 P.M. daily, $5 pp) is hidden far off the beaten track in the Río Puyango Valley, just seven kilometers from the Peruvian border. Puyango sits at 360 meters elevation and extends over 2,658 hectares. Many millennia of history are locked away in its rocks: Experts believe that about 100 million years ago, volcanic eruptions covered the forest in ash. Later floods caused the minerals from the ash to seep into the trees, and they hardened into underwater rocks. As the land was later reclaimed from the sea, the forest rose again into what we see today.

Trunks of the petrified *Araucaria* trees are up to 15 meters long and two meters in diameter. If you look closely, there are fossilized plants and ferns trapped in the surrounding rocks. You can even see aquatic creatures such as ammonites, sea turtles, fish, and snails, evidence that this area used to be under the Pacific Ocean some 65 million years ago.

Aside from the petrified trees, the tropical dry forest also has plenty of living creatures—130 species of birds, including parakeets, as well as armadillos and iguanas. There are several walking trails, or hire a guide for a richer experience.

The biggest challenge is getting to Puyango. If you've just arrived in Ecuador at Huaquillas, consider coming here first and then moving onto Loja or back up to Machala. Transportes Loja buses make the trip twice a day from Machala (2.5 hours, $3). Otherwise take a CIFA bus to Arenillas, where a dirt road runs south through Palmales and La Victoria before reaching the village of Puyango 50 kilometers later. There is an interpretative center with a museum in the village, where you can pay the entrance fee. It's an hour's walk to the reserve, or you can hire a pickup truck. There's nowhere to stay in the village, so set out early. The nearest accommodations are in the village of Alamor to the south.

◖ Zaruma

Zaruma is the type of place that puts a travel writer in a tricky situation—a wonderful destination that remains largely undiscovered by foreign visitors. Would it be better to keep it a secret or to tell people to seek out this hidden nugget? I've decided on the latter course because, while Zaruma's beauty cannot be contained, its remote location means it's unlikely to be spoiled by floods of visitors.

Locals have known about Zaruma's charms for years—steep, winding streets, colonial balconies, and a dramatic hilltop location with sweeping views over the valleys. The town, which sits at an elevation of 1,200 meters with an ideally warm climate, also has an interesting history. The discovery of gold here led Spanish King Felipe II to establish Zaruma as a mining base. The gold boom lasted for many years, and Zaruma was the first capital of El Oro province in 1882. In the early 20th century, however, British and American companies plundered the last of the gold, and Zaruma began to decline as an economic center. There are still mines in the surrounding area, and the town's main mine only closed in 2004, to be reopened as a tourist attraction.

Zaruma's ornate main square harks back to the colonial era.

ORIENTATION

Zaruma has a lot of winding streets for such a small town, but you can't really get lost because you just keep climbing until you reach the ornate **Plaza de Independencia** overlooked by the main church, **Santuario de la Virgen del Carmen.** Just off the north side of the square is the small **Museo Municipal** (no phone, 9 A.M.–4 P.M. Wed.–Sun., free), which has a small archaeological collection of pottery and tools as well as more modern items such as a **trapiche** for grinding sugarcane. The other main attraction in town is the disused gold mine, which is now a museum, **Mina Turística El Sexmo** (no phone, 9 A.M.–4 P.M. daily, free). The story goes that a miner found a 1.4-kilogram chunk of gold here and sent it back to Spain as a gift for King Felipe II. The king was so pleased that he decided to reduce taxes from one-fifth to one-sixth of income, giving the mine its name (The Sixth). The mine continued operating until 2004. Visitors can explore a 500-meter-long tunnel, and hats and boots are provided. There's also a short documentary in Spanish about the history of the mine.

Once you've seen the center and the mine, there's not much else to do in the town itself except go hiking to take in the spectacular views. There are several hills, but the best is a half-hour walk north of town to **Cerro El Calvario.** Start from Calle San Francisco past the blue-and-yellow church, the route is signposted from there. It's a steep climb but well worth it for the view from the top, where there is a large statue of the Crucifixion.

ACCOMMODATIONS

Zaruma has limited hotel options, but they are mostly of a good standard. By far the best is **(Hotel Roland** (Alonso de Mercadillo, tel. 7/297-2703, $22 s, $33 d), a friendly family-run place with a swimming pool and great views of the valley. Watch as staff winch your luggage on a pulley down to the chalet rooms below. The only drawback of the hotel is that you have to walk up a steep hill on the busy main road to town. In the center, the best-located hotel is **Romeria Hostal** (Plaza Independencia, tel. 7/297-2618, $11 s, $22 d), with decent guest rooms and a view of the main square from the balcony; the café below is also popular. Other hotel options include the great-value **Hotel Blacio** (El Sexmo and Sucre, tel. 7/297-2045, $10 s, $20 d), down the hill. A little farther up on Sucre, more basic options include **Cerro de Oro** (Sucre, tel. 7/297-2505, $10 pp) and the better-value **Aguila Dorada** (Sucre, tel. 7/297-2755, $8 pp).

FOOD

Breakfast in Zaruma is by far the best meal. Most places in town serve the traditional specialties—*tigrillos* (mashed plantains with cheese and egg) and delicious *humitas* (a whole ear of mashed corn steamed in its leaves, served with cheese). The town claims to produce the best coffee in Ecuador, and it certainly is aromatic. You can pick up a bag in many stores and in the market just off San Francisco. Wrap it up well, though, or your luggage will smell of coffee.

The best restaurant in town is (**200 Millas** (Honorato Márquez, tel. 7/297-2600, breakfast, lunch, and dinner daily, entrées $4–7), down the hill from the center. Coffee and an *humita* is just $0.75, and there's a wide variety of *tigrillos* ($2–3) with or without meat as well as Ecuadorian chicken, pork, and fish staples. Next door, **Saborcito Zarumeño** (Honorato Márquez, no phone, lunch and dinner daily, $2–3) serves cheap set meals and barbecued chicken. Farther up is **Frupizza** (Honorato Márquez, no phone, lunch and dinner daily, entrées $9–15), which, as the name suggests, serves pizza and fruit juices, but it's not cheap. After dinner, there is very little in the way of nightlife, although you could try **Charro's Bar** (Sucre and San Francisco, tel. 9/391-0689, 7 p.m.–midnight Wed.–Thurs., 7 p.m.–2 a.m. Fri.–Sat.) or **Tangobar** (Plaza Independencia, no phone, noon–midnight Mon.–Sat.) on the main square, which serves a range of the local alcohols.

INFORMATION AND SERVICES

On the left side of the main square is a **tourist office** (Plaza Independencia, tel. 7/297-3533, 9 a.m.–4 p.m. Mon.–Fri., www.vivazaruma.com and www.visitezaruma.com), which has helpful staff who can provide maps and information on the attractions in and around town. There is one tour operator in town, **Oro Adventure** (tel. 7/297-2761), which has a small office on the main square. Tito Castillo (tel. 7/297-2761 or 9/309-4707) and Fernando Pinera (tel. 8/636-4625) are the registered guides in town and can offer a range of tours (from $60 pp): The most popular takes in several waterfalls ranging 60–100 meters in height as well as an unusual volcanic rock formation at Cerro de Arcos.

A highlight of the region around Zaruma is the 1,600-hectare **Reserva Buenaventura** ($15). A new bird species, the El Oro parakeet, was discovered in this cloud-forest reserve, home to 300 species of birds, including 24 species of hummingbirds, along with an abundance of orchids. There are also monkeys and elusive wildcats. Guides can be hired to take you on the numerous trails. The entrance is located nine kilometers from the town of Piñas, half an hour down the main road from Zaruma. Take a Machala bus and ask the driver to drop you off.

GETTING THERE AND AROUND

Zaruma is well connected to major cities in Ecuador despite its remote location. There are two bus companies in town, Trans Piñas and TAC, both of which have offices on Honorato Márquez on the way up to the center. Both companies run hourly buses to Machala (2 hours, $3), passing through Piñas; two daily buses to Quito (13 hours, $12); and several buses daily direct to Guayaquil (5 hours, $6.50), Cuenca (6 hours, $7), and Loja (4 hours, $5).

Getting around town is easy, and you can walk to most places. There are taxis that will take you around the main attractions and some outside town ($5–10). Taxis in town cost $1.

Huaquillas

Ecuador's largest southern border town sits

across the Río Zarumilla from Aguas Verde in Peru. This is the easiest and busiest place to cross between Ecuador and Peru, but it's not the most pleasant. Used as a busy trading town, Huaquillas floods with traders looking to strike a good deal, legally or otherwise. It's not a town you want to hang around for long, and luckily there is sufficient transportation to shuttle you south to Peru or north to Machala and Guayaquil.

A cautious attitude should also be adopted when changing money. Coming from Peru, it's best to get rid of Peruvian money before crossing into Ecuador and avoid the dodgy moneychangers in Huaquillas. If you arrive in Ecuador without any U.S. dollars, there's an ATM at the **Banco de Machala** (De la República) near the main plaza.

If you are stuck here late at night, then **Hotel Vanessa** (1 de Mayo 323 at Hualtaco, tel. 7/299-6263, $16 s, $24 d) offers decent guest rooms with private baths and air-conditioning. **The Grand Hotel Hernancor** (1 de Mayo, tel. 7/299-5467, $16 s, $24 d) next door is better quality and more modern. For food, **La Habana** (Cordovez and Santa Rosa, tel. 7/299-5077, lunch and dinner daily, set meal $2) and **Restaurant Picantería** (no phone, lunch and dinner daily, set meal $2) next door are both good options for cheap set menus. **Smir** (no phone, lunch and dinner daily, entrées $4) across the street is slightly better quality with a wide-ranging menu of seafood, meat, and chicken.

To cross the border, get your exit stamp at the Ecuadorian immigration office, inconveniently located four kilometers north of town. Then take a bus or taxi to the bridge, which must be crossed on foot. In Aguas Verdes, complete the entrance formalities in the Peruvian immigration office a few kilometers beyond the bridge; taxis waiting to take you farther into Peru will stop here.

Panamericana (Teniente Cordovez and 10 de Agosto) runs half a dozen direct buses per day to Quito (13 hours, $14–20). **CIFA** (Santa Rosa and Machala) has frequent direct buses to Machala (75 minutes, $2) and Guayaquil (4.5 hours, $5) as well as five buses per day direct between Guayaquil and Tumbes, Sullana, and Piura in Peru via Huaquillas (9 hours, $9). This service is recommended because the staff guide you through the border-crossing process, and there is transportation waiting on the other side of the border.

If you have the option, the smaller border towns of **Macará** and **Zumba,** southwest of Loja, are quieter places to enter and leave Peru.

THE GALÁPAGOS ISLANDS

"Amazing," "breathtaking," "incredible"—how often do tour operators and guidebooks use these words to entice us to book a vacation? And how often does the sight actually take your breath away or defy belief? The Galápagos, however, is one place on earth that lives up to and surpasses expectations, and for which there are insufficient superlatives. It's unquestionably the best place in the world for wildlife watching, both on land and in the water, not least because in this archipelago, the wildlife watches you as much as you watch them.

If you imagine Eden to be a place where creatures live and play together in perfect harmony, then the Galápagos is as close as you can get. It is not uncommon to see sea lions and iguanas sunbathing side by side on the beach while penguins, stingrays, and turtles swim together offshore. There's no fear because there's no need for it in an archipelago with few natural predators. The only timid species seem to be the fish, the food supply for so many. Every other species on the islands is at worst unconcerned by your presence—nonchalant marine turtles, sunbathing iguanas, and plodding giant tortoises—and at best they seem intent on communicating. Try a staring contest with a blue-footed booby and, my personal favorite, an impromptu game of peekaboo with sea lion pups, who delight in swimming with humans.

The Galápagos is also heaven for bird-watchers. Here you don't need to get up at dawn and wait with binoculars for a glimpse of birdlife in the trees. Instead, the birds proudly display themselves—from the male frigates inflating

HIGHLIGHTS

◖ **Charles Darwin Research Station:** Come face-to-face with the giant tortoises that gave the islands their name, including Lonesome George, and learn how scientists are rearing hundreds to be released into the wild (page 368).

◖ **Seymour Norte:** This small island is the best place to see large colonies of blue-footed boobies and frigate birds (page 370).

◖ **Isla Lobos and Kicker Rock (León Dormido):** This site offers the best views of sharks. Snorkel through a narrow channel with white-tipped sharks or scuba dive with hammerheads (page 375).

◖ **Bartolomé Island:** Climb 114 meters up a wooden staircase to enjoy the most photographed sight in the Galápagos, a partially eroded lava formation flanked by two crescent beaches, with the black lava trails of Santiago in the distance (page 377).

◖ **Sierra Negra and the Highlands:** Get out your walking boots and hike past the second-largest volcanic crater in the world before descending into the pungent sulfur mines (page 381).

◖ **Corona del Diablo:** This half-submerged volcanic cone off the coast of Floreana is one of the best snorkeling spots, with marine turtles, sharks, rays, and sea lions. Nearby Enderby and Champion Islands are equally scenic (page 386).

◖ **Punta Suárez:** The biggest breeding site of waved albatross in the world, on the western tip of Española, is one of the top wildlife-viewing sites in the Galápagos Islands (page 387).

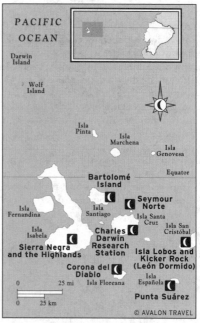

LOOK FOR ◖ TO FIND RECOMMENDED SIGHTS, ACTIVITIES, DINING, AND LODGING.

their red chests to the size of a basketball to the boobies gazing at you as you shuffle past them on the paths, so close you could pat them on the head, to the albatross' circular clacking dance and pelicans dive-bombing the oceans and gulping down lunch.

It's hard to know which way to turn, and you may wish that we humans had evolved with eyes in the backs of our heads. You'll struggle to find disappointed visitors to the Galápagos.

The truth is that a visit to these islands does change you, just like it changed the great Charles Darwin, who was inspired to formulate his monumental theory of evolution after visiting. The Galápagos are both a glimpse of what life was like before human beings started throwing their clumsy weight around, and also a timely reminder that we continue to seek out perfection and do our best to mess it up. Evidence on the Galápagos of human folly is everywhere—the number of endemic species either hunted or driven to near extinction by introduced species is alarming, but equally, the painstaking efforts of conservationists and scientists to restore the balance of the archipelago's

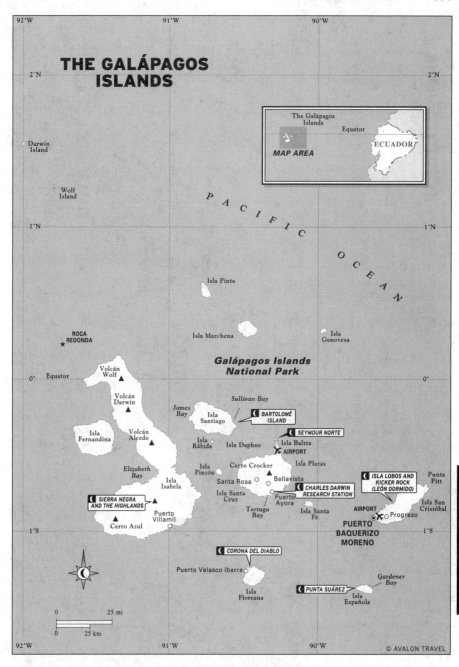

THE GALÁPAGOS
ISLANDS

The Galápagos
Islands

Equator

MAP AREA

ECUADOR

P A C I F I C   O C E A N

Darwin
Island

Wolf
Island

Isla Pinta

ROCA
REDONDA

Isla Marchena

Isla
Genovesa

**Galápagos Islands
National Park**

Volcán
Wolf

Equator

Volcán
Darwin

Sullivan Bay

James
Bay

Isla
Santiago

**BARTOLOMÉ
ISLAND**

Isla
Fernandina

Volcán
Alcedo

Isla
Rábida

Isla Daphne

SEYMOUR NORTE

Isla Baltra
AIRPORT

Isla Plazas

Elizabeth
Bay

Isla
Pinzón

Cerro Crocker

Isla
Isabela

Santa Rosa

Bellavista

**SIERRA NEGRA
AND THE HIGHLANDS**

Isla Santa
Cruz

Puerto
Ayora

**CHARLES DARWIN
RESEARCH STATION**

**ISLA LOBOS AND
KICKER ROCK
(LEÓN DORMIDO)**

Punta
Pitt

Puerto
Villamil

Tortuga
Bay

Isla Santa
Fé

AIRPORT

Isla San
Cristóbal

Cerro Azul

Progreso

**PUERTO
BAQUERIZO
MORENO**

CORONA DEL DIABLO

Puerto Velasco Ibarra

Isla
Floreana

PUNTA SUÁREZ

Isla
Española

Gardener
Bay

0   25 mi

0   25 km

© AVALON TRAVEL

THE GALÁPAGOS ISLANDS

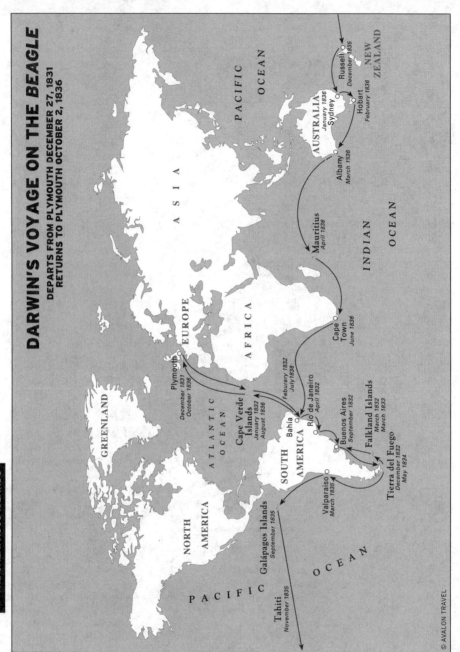

DARWIN'S VOYAGE ON THE BEAGLE

DEPARTS FROM PLYMOUTH DECEMBER 27, 1831
RETURNS TO PLYMOUTH OCTOBER 2, 1836

PACIFIC OCEAN

ASIA

NEW ZEALAND

Russell
December 1835

AUSTRALIA

Sydney
January 1836

Hobart
February 1836

Albany
March 1836

Mauritius
April 1836

INDIAN OCEAN

EUROPE

AFRICA

Cape Town
June 1836

Plymouth
December 1831
October 1836

Cape Verde
Islands
January 1832
August 1836

Feburary 1832
July 1836

Rio de Janeiro
April 1832

Bahia

Buenos Aires
September 1832

Falkland Islands
March 1832
March 1833

SOUTH
AMERICA

Tierra del Fuego
December 1832
May 1834

Valparaíso
March 1835

GREENLAND

ATLANTIC
OCEAN

NORTH
AMERICA

Galápagos Islands
September 1835

Tahiti
November 1835

PACIFIC OCEAN

© AVALON TRAVEL

ecosystem are inspiring. You will likely return from the Galápagos slightly different—filled with a sense of wonder and with a clearer view of the fragile beauty of nature.

HISTORY

The Galápagos Islands' isolation and inhospitable volcanic terrain have been their greatest assets for much of their history, saving them from colonization and degradation until relatively recently. With the South American coast 970 kilometers to the east and nothing but blue Pacific Ocean all the way to French Polynesia, over 5,000 kilometers to the west, the Galápagos really were hidden jewels for centuries.

Early Visitors

It's not clear who the first visitors to the islands were, but it's probable that they were sailors blown off course or hapless fishermen blown out to sea. Most of them were likely unimpressed by the lack of freshwater on the islands. Whether the Incas ever made it here is disputed; in 1572 the Spanish chronicler Pedro Sarmiento de Gamboa claimed that Topa Inca Yupanqui had visited the archipelago, but there is little evidence for this, and many experts consider it a far-fetched legend, especially since the Incas weren't seafaring people.

The discovery of the islands by Europeans was officially made in 1535, when the ship of Tomás de Berlanga, Bishop of Panama, was pushed off course by the Panama Current on its way to Peru. The crew didn't stay long, but the bishop wrote to King Charles V of Spain enthusing about the giant tortoises with shells shaped like riding saddles (called *galápagos* in Spanish), and the name stuck. In 1570 the islands appeared on a world map with the label *Insulae de los Galopegos*. The islands were given their pseudonym Las Islas Encantadas (The Enchanted Islands) by Spanish conquistador Diego de Rivadeneira, who believed the islands to be enchanted, moving with the ocean's currents (it made a better story than his navigation being a little off).

Pirates and Whalers

During the 17th century, the Galápagos were used as a base for Dutch, French, and English pirates, most famously Sir Francis Drake, to mount raids on coastal ports and treasure-filled Spanish galleons. The pirate William Ambrose Cowley made the first working map of the Galápagos, naming islands after British royalty and aristocracy. Floreana and Santiago Islands were originally called Charles and James, respectively, after British monarchs, and Isabela was once called Albemarle after a duke.

Given pirates' propensity to plunder, it's no surprise that they were the first humans to cause damage to the islands' ecosystem. The pirates realized the value of taking a giant tortoise on long voyages to provide fresh meat. Whalers also took thousands of them and stowed them in the ships' holds, where they endured a slow death over the course of a year without food or water. This was the beginning of the drastic reduction in the giant tortoise population, which stood at over 250,000 before humans arrived. Fur seals were another target, sold for their pelts, and by the early 19th century it became clear that the Galápagos were far more valuable than had previously been thought. On February 12, 1832, the newly independent Ecuador fought off halfhearted claims by the United States and Britain to claim the islands officially.

Darwin's Visit

Just three years after Ecuador claimed the archipelago, a young British scientist named Charles Darwin, then aged just 26, visited aboard the HMS *Beagle*. Darwin collected crucial evidence, particularly from the many species of finches, that helped formulate his world-changing theory of evolution published in *On the Origin of Species* in 1859.

These so-called "enchanted islands" became anything but through the rest of the 19th century, when most of the residents were convicts. In an echo of the British policy of sending convicts to Australia, Ecuador commuted the death penalty to a life sentence toiling on the islands, enduring cruel treatment and scratching meager existences such as making dye from lichen. There were colonies on Floreana, San

CHARLES DARWIN AND THE GALÁPAGOS

The world's most famous naturalist changed human beings' view of life on earth forever with his monumental theory of evolution in 1859, and in doing so he also made the Galápagos famous.

Charles Robert Darwin was born in Shropshire, England, in 1809 to an upper middle-class British family. His father was a doctor and determined that his son would follow him into the profession, but Charles had other ideas, collecting specimens and studying botany in his spare time. He neglected his medical studies in Edinburgh in favor of his fascination for nature, and when his father transferred him to Cambridge to study theology, Darwin developed his interest in philosophical works on creation and adaptation.

Soon after graduating, Darwin was thrilled to be given the post of unpaid naturalist onboard HMS *Beagle*, a small sailing vessel that left Plymouth, England, on December 27, 1831. The *Beagle* landed twice on the coast of Africa before crossing the Atlantic and beginning a two-year exploration of South America's eastern coast. Darwin explored the forests of Brazil and the high plains of Uruguay before the *Beagle* rounded Cape Horn in 1834 and headed up the western coast of Chile and Peru.

Darwin arrived in the Galápagos in September 1835 and spent five weeks here, visiting San Cristóbal, Floreana, Santiago, and Isabela. The evidence of evolution was everywhere – the different shapes of finch beaks, iguanas that had learned to swim, and cormorants that no longer needed to fly. The governor of the archipelago remarked to Darwin that he could identify which island a giant tortoise was from by the shape of its shell, and Darwin was particularly struck by the variation in mockingbirds caught on different islands. But far from having a eureka moment, Darwin took samples of species from as many islands as he could and took copious notes, which he analyzed for years afterward.

Even though he was a naturalist, he didn't take to all of the species he encountered, being particularly scathing of the marine iguanas, calling them "most disgusting clumsy lizards."

© BEN WESTWOOD

According to philosopher Daniel Dennett, Charles Darwin had "the single best idea anyone has ever had."

Darwin was also similar in his behavior to other sailors, and wrote of his experience of enjoying giant tortoise meat ("The breast plate roasted with the meat on it is very good") and the less enjoyable taste of iguana meat ("These lizards, when cooked, yield a white meat, which is liked by those whose stomachs soar above all prejudices.").

Darwin returned to England in October 1836, his visit to the Galápagos having changed him fundamentally. He had embarked on the *Beagle* voyage as a firm believer in the biblical story of creation and the idea that God created perfect, immutable creatures. But the evidence of so many variations of subspecies on the islands was undeniable – why else did one finch have a slightly longer beak on an island where its primary food source were insects living in crevices while another finch had a short, stronger beak better for cracking nuts? The only logical explanation was that the finches had adapted to their environment. Darwin was a meticulous man, and it took him more than 20 years to finally publish his findings. A key reason for the delay was Darwin's concern over the impact of his theory on Victorian England's highly evangelical society. In the end, the threat of someone else publishing the theory first finally spurred Darwin to act. A fellow naturalist, Alfred Russel Wallace – younger and less conventional than Darwin – was about to publish a similar theory, in 1858. When Darwin's friends discovered this, they arranged for Darwin and Wallace to read a joint paper to the Linnaean Society of London, formally presenting evolution to the public for the first time. To this day, Wallace is credited as the codiscoverer of natural selection.

On November 24, 1859, Darwin published *On the Origin of Species,* and the world would never be quite the same. The book's central idea, while revolutionary for the Victorians, was extremely simple – that species change over time in order to adapt to the challenges presented in their habitats. One of the biggest inspirations for the idea was the beak shapes of Galápagos finches. This idea became the cornerstone of the process of natural selection. To explain the process, Darwin proposed a mechanism called **descent with modification.** He based it on observations of animals and plants in captivity, which produced many more offspring than their environmental "niche" could possibly support. Only the ones best suited to their environment survived to reproduce.

As many more individuals of each species are born than can possibly survive; and as, consequently, there is a frequently recurring struggle for existence, it follows that any being, if it vary however slightly in any manner profitable to itself, under the complex and sometimes varying conditions of life, will have a better chance of surviving, and thus be naturally selected. From the strong principle of inheritance,

any selected variety will tend to propagate its new and modified form.

The process could even work in "reverse," leading to the loss of adaptations that were suddenly no longer beneficial. On an island with no predators, and hence no need to fly to safety, wings might eventually just get in the way. Birds that could somehow forgo growing them would be able to swim after fish more efficiently and have more energy left over for other things – such as reproduction – than their fellows; thus the cormorant became flightless. The theory applied not just to physical attributes but also to behavior. Birds surrounded by predators would naturally be timid, while birds on the Galápagos, with no natural predators, were uncommonly docile.

Darwin was the first to admit that his theory still needed development, and that he was not the first to suggest this concept, having drawn on the work of a long list of scientists, including Jean-Baptiste Lamarck, Charles Lyell, Thomas Robert Malthus, and Darwin's own grandfather, Erasmus. But his modesty did nothing to quell the uproar that it caused in Victorian society, just as he had feared it would. Churches were particularly unhappy at Darwin's implication that God's work was not perfect but had to be changed over time. Darwin, who had recently been bereaved by the death of his infant son from scarlet fever, was suffering from illness that kept him away from public events and out of the storm. He remained a committed Christian and fervently disagreed that his theory was at odds with belief in God.

With the support of friends and scientific colleagues, however, Darwin's theory gradually became accepted toward the end of his life, and nowadays it is scientific fact. Darwin continued his work into old age, publishing several more books and living out the remainder of his days with his wife and 10 children in Downe House in Kent. He died on April 19, 1882, aged 73. He was given a state funeral, a rare honor outside the royal family, and buried in Westminster Abbey next to Sir Isaac Newton.

Cristóbal, and Isabela, the latter functioning until 1959.

The Early 20th Century

As the world plunged into World War I, the Galápagos were used by the U.S. Navy to protect the entrance to the new Panama Canal, completed in 1914. After the war, the first permanent settlers (apart from convicts) began to arrive, among them the German Wittmer family, whose story on the islands is a ripping yarn of murder and intrigue. During World War II, the U.S. Air Force set up an airport on Baltra to monitor Japanese activity in the South Pacific, and then donated the airport to Ecuador after the war.

Conservation and Tourism: Friends or Foes?

Conservation efforts increased in the mid-20th century, and after some islands had been designated wildlife sanctuaries in the 1930s, the whole archipelago became a national park in 1959. The Charles Darwin Research Center opened in Puerto Ayora in 1964, followed four years later by the Galápagos National Park Service. This was the start of an effort to study and conserve the islands' unique natural heritage, but it also coincided with an increase in tourism. An Ecuadorian company, Metropolitan Touring, began operating exclusive tours in the 1960s, and it remains the largest operator in the islands. Scheduled flights began in the early 1970s, and tourism grew rapidly.

As word spread of fortunes to be made from fishing and tourism, immigration to the islands from the mainland gathered pace and led to increasing friction between conservationists, who wanted a minimal human population, and immigrants, who wanted to make a decent living. The archipelago was among the first 12 regions in the world to receive a UNESCO designation in 1978. In 1986 the Galápagos Marine Resources Reserve was created to protect the waters around the islands. Reserve officials then banned unrestricted fishing in the local waters, sparking angry protests that culminated in a group of machete-wielding fishermen seizing the Darwin Center and threatening the life of tortoise Lonesome George. The Ecuadorian government backtracked and reopened the waters around the archipelago to limited commercial fishing in 1995.

By the late 1990s, the effect of introduced species had become painfully apparent to conservationists, and the Ecuadorian government finally responded by passing laws in 1998 aimed at conserving the islands' biodiversity while encouraging sustainable development. An eradication and quarantine program was set up, restrictions on illegal fishing were expanded, and the percentage of tourist revenue going to the park itself increased. UNESCO designated 133,000 square kilometers of marine reserve around the islands as a World Heritage Site in 2001, a move that aimed to further protect the marine life. That same year, an ecological disaster was narrowly averted when the oil tanker *Jessica* ran aground on San Cristóbal, but favorable winds took most of the spilled fuel away from the islands.

The 21st Century: Galápagos in Danger

Passing laws is all well and good, but if the rules are not respected or enforced effectively, they become useless. Even with tighter regulations, the environmental situation deteriorated after 2001. Lucrative illegal fishing of shark fins and sea cucumbers spiraled out of control, and the local population rose quickly, with locals breeding almost as quickly as the goats they'd introduced. Visitors played a significant role in the problem as well—a tourism boom saw visitor numbers triple in 15 years to reach 160,000 annually in 2007. That same year, the islands were placed on the UNESCO **List of World Heritage in Danger.** This widely publicized move seemed to focus minds locally, and Rafael Correa's government introduced a series of emergency measures to improve the situation. Thousands of illegal immigrants were deported back to the mainland, and getting permission to live on the Galápagos is now far more difficult than it used to be. To tackle illegal fishing, satellite technology has been introduced by the Ecuadorian navy, and fishermen have been given assistance to set up lucrative sportfishing tours, where they catch a handful of fish daily as opposed to boatloads. Tourist arrivals have been restricted and in 2009 fell for the first time, to 145,000. There are also ambitious plans to convert the islands to 100 percent renewable energy by 2017—San Cristóbal already receives more than half its energy from this scheme. The invasive species have proved to be the biggest challenge. Isabela, Floreana, and Santiago have seen goat extermination programs with over 250,000 culled, but other harmful invasive species have proved very difficult to remove, in particular fruit flies, fire ants, and rats.

After all this action, the Ecuadorian government successfully lobbied to have the islands removed from the UNESCO endangered list in July 2010, a decision welcomed by the travel industry but heavily criticized by scientists and conservationists, who claimed it was premature to judge that the islands are out of danger. One comforting fact for environmentalists is that despite the tourism boom, the 70 visitor sites that they frequent represent only 0.01 percent of the archipelago's total land mass, with the rest of the archipelago out of bounds.

If you're interested in helping the Galápagos solve its environmental problems, tax-deductible donations for research, conservation, and environmental education can be sent to the **Charles Darwin Foundation** (407 N. Washington St., Suite 105, Falls Church, VA 22046, U.S. tel. 703/538-6833, darwin@galapagos.org, www.darwinfoundation.org) or the **Galápagos Conservation Trust** (5 Derby St., London, UK W1Y 7AD, UK tel. 20/7629-5049, www.gct.org).

Visiting the Islands

PLANNING YOUR TIME

There are basically two ways to see the Galápagos: on a cruise or on a land-based tour.

Cruises have historically been the most popular, and advantages include the opportunity to travel farther, cover more sites, and spend more time without worrying about getting back to port at dusk. There are also many sites only accessible to cruise tours, and there is less environmental impact than staying on land and the associated pollution from hotels. The drawbacks are that you are on a boat with the same group for several days with a fixed schedule, which doesn't suit everyone. Seasickness is also a factor, even on the most luxurious boats. With the wide choice of classes available, it's important to remember that, by and large, you get what you pay for. You could save a few hundred dollars by opting for the cheapest boat, but you'll end up with a guide with less knowledge, far less comfort and, probably, worse seasickness.

Most cruises are 5–8 days. There are also four-day itineraries, but when you consider that half a day at the beginning and end is spent traveling, a minimum of five days is recommended, and eight days is preferable. In five days, the most common cruise itineraries start at Santa Cruz, taking in Puerto Ayora, the highlands, Seymour Norte, and Plazas, then heading either north or south. Northern tours usually include Bartolomé, Santiago, and Genovesa, while southern itineraries usually take in Santa Fé, San Cristóbal, Floreana, and Española. There is also a slightly more expensive western itinerary that includes Isabela and Fernandina. Eight-day tours usually combine two of these three routes (north and west, north and south, or west and south). It's not possible to see all of the above islands in eight days, and while cruises for longer than eight days do exist, they are rare and are mostly dedicated dive trips. These tours are the only ones that reach the most remote islands of Darwin, Wolf, and Marchena.

THE GALÁPAGOS ISLANDS

ISLAND NAMES

Most of the islands in the Galápagos have a Spanish name and an English name, and some even have three names. This is the legacy of both English and Spanish interest in the islands, whose ownership was not settled until Ecuador claimed them in 1832. Where possible, the Spanish name is used in this book, although some of the smaller islands have a lone English name. All are listed here alphabetically, followed by any variations. All names are official, except Floreana and Santiago, whose official names follow in boldface.

- Baltra (South Seymour)
- Bartolomé (Bartholomew)
- Beagle
- Cowley
- Darwin (Culpepper)
- Enderby
- Española (Hood)
- Fernandina (Narborough)
- Floreana (Santa María; Charles)
- Genovesa (Tower)
- Isabela (Albemarle)
- Marchena (Bindloe)
- Pinta (Abingdon)
- Pinzón (Duncan)
- Plazas
- Rábida (Jervis)
- San Cristóbal (Chatham)
- Santa Cruz (Indefatigable)
- Santa Fé (Barrington)
- Santiago (San Salvador; James)
- Seymour Norte (North Seymour)
- Sin Nombre (Nameless)
- Tortuga (Brattle)
- Wolf (Wenman)

Land-based tours are becoming increasingly popular, particularly for those not suited to spending a long time on a boat. Many operators organize short tours based on one island, or you can do an island-hopping tour. However, with the wide availability of day tours in Puerto Ayora and regular ferries between the three most populous islands (San Cristóbal, Santa Cruz, and Isabela), increasing numbers of budget travelers are shunning tours and doing it themselves, and saving a lot of money. Bear in mind, though, that doing it this way restricts you to day tours close to the main islands, and islands such as Genovesa, Española, and Fernandina become off-limits.

Whatever you decide to do, it's important that you don't get preoccupied with a checklist. Eight days (or even five days) in the Galápagos is an incredible experience to be savored, so don't ruin your enjoyment of it by becoming obsessed with seeing it all.

WHEN TO GO

Although the Galápagos is a year-round destination, the best conditions are December–April. The seas are calmer, the weather mostly sunny and hot, and rain on the larger islands leads to an explosion of greenery. This coincides with the busiest tourist period at Christmas, Carnival (usually in Feb.), and Easter. June–October the weather is cooler, so it's more comfortable on land, but the landscapes are more barren and the sea becomes rougher, so seasickness is more of a problem. The waters can be surprisingly cold for swimming and snorkeling, but on the positive side, the cooler temperatures usually bring higher numbers of marine life to watch. The islands have brief low seasons in May–June and September–October, either side of the July–August high season. These are the best times to secure last-minute availability. The ongoing global economic downturn has affected the islands, however, and cut-price deals can be found year-round if you look hard enough and are flexible.

Note that the time in the Galápagos is one hour earlier than in mainland Ecuador.

WHAT TO BRING

A trip to the Galápagos requires plenty of preparation. While summer clothes are clearly first in the suitcase, there are plenty more items you need to pack. Bring a light jacket or sweater for chilly mornings and cool evenings, plus a rain jacket for visiting the damp highlands. Along with flip-flops, good walking shoes should be packed for negotiating rough lava trails. Most importantly, bring a hat, sunglasses, and plenty of sunblock to protect you from the fierce equatorial sun, which is doubly strong at sea. A refillable water bottle is very useful and also reduces the islands' problem with plastic. Seasickness is a common problem on the Galápagos, both on cruises and particularly on the fast ferries among the islands, so bring seasickness pills. Bring a day pack to take on excursions, and don't forget your swimming gear. You can bring your own snorkel, if you prefer, although tours usually provide them.

Last but not least, bring a decent camera. The Galápagos is hard to beat for photography, so if you were going to consider upgrading, do it before you visit. Also consider investing in a telephoto lens, bring UV and polarizing filters, and bring a decent bag to protect your equipment from water. Bring far more film or digital memory than you'll think you'll need, and expect to take several hundred photos.

SAFETY AND ANNOYANCES

In general the Galápagos is a very safe destination, but visitors do occasionally get into trouble or fall ill. If you're elderly or have heart or blood-pressure problems, you need to pace yourself. You may be surprised at how tiring a trip to the islands can be—eight days packed with hikes, swimming, and snorkeling is a very full schedule. Don't be embarrassed to opt out of a tour if you're not feeling up to it, and always notify the guide of any health issues.

The most common problems are stomach-related or seasickness. For the former, you should carry rehydration packets, and if it's more serious, the guide should be able to get antibiotics. Bactrim Forte is a good local brand to take if you have a food-related illness. For seasickness, eat lightly, drink plenty of fluids, sit in the center of the boat, or take a nap. Local brand Mareol can also help, but bear in mind that it can make you drowsy.

An unexpected annoyance in the Galápagos for women travelers is the unwanted attention of male guides or crew members. Remember that the Galápagos are part of Ecuador, and many local men are notoriously flirtatious and macho. This certainly doesn't apply to all guides, but you may be unlucky enough to have your guide hit on you. If you're traveling alone, you should make clear politely but firmly that you're not interested—perhaps inventing a muscle-bound fiancé and transferring a ring to the appropriate finger may help.

Note that smoking is prohibited on any of the uninhabited islands and at all the visitors sites on the inhabited islands. Most boats have nonsmoking policies as well.

GETTING THERE

Flights to the Galápagos are usually bought separately, although agents can arrange them for you. **TAME** (Quito tel. 2/397-7100, Guayaquil tel. 4/231-0305), **Aerogal** (Quito tel. 2/294-2800, Guayaquil tel. 4/231-0346), and **LAN** (tel. 800/101-075, www.lan.com) all offer round-trip flights to San Cristóbal and Baltra. Prices for foreigners are usually about $350 round-trip from Guayaquil and $400 round-trip from Quito, although there are occasionally promotional fares. *Censo* holders (foreigners with residency status) pay less: about $260–300 round-trip, and for local Galápagos residents it's less than $150 round-trip. Check-in is at least 90 minutes before departure. The flight takes about three hours from Quito, and you're allowed to bring one main piece of luggage up to 20 kilograms. All flights originate in Quito and stop in Guayaquil for at least one hour, where passengers usually disembark while the plane is refueled. Tour operators should reconfirm your flights for you both ways, but if you booked independently, you should do this yourself. Independent travelers must also make sure they fly to the correct island at the correct time to begin the tour; do this *before* booking the tour.

The **National Park entrance fee** is $100 pp for foreigners, and a measly $6 for Ecuadorians. It's payable in cash only on arrival in the Galápagos airport. The new **migratory control card** costs $10 for both Ecuadorians and visitors. Be sure to keep both the receipt for the park fee and the control card—if you lose them, you may be required to pay again.

If you're arriving in the Galápagos on an organized tour, you don't need to worry about transfers because you'll be met at the airport by guides who will direct you to the transfers to your hotel or yacht. For independent travelers, it depends which island you arrive on. San Cristóbal is very easy because the airport is very close to the main port, Baquerizo Moreno. You can walk, but most people take a taxi ($2). For Santa Cruz, it's more complicated: Flights arrive on the tiny island of Baltra, just north of Santa Cruz. Reaching the main port of Puerto Ayora is a three-stage process. First, take a free 10-minute bus ride to the south, followed by a 10-minute ferry crossing ($0.50), and then you can either wait for a bus ($2.50) or take a taxi directly to the port (45 minutes, $15). The entire journey from the airport takes over an hour, although you'll likely be too excited to complain. To return to the airport from Puerto Ayora, take a taxi to the bus terminal north of town, but note that the last bus usually leaves at 9:30 A.M., after which a taxi or private transfer is the only option.

CRUISES

There are five classes of tour boats—economy, tourist, tourist superior, first, and luxury—and trips range 4–8 days, with occasional special charters of 11 and 15 days. When you consider that you spend half of the first and last day traveling, four-day tours are not recommended unless you're really strapped for cash or time—five days should be the minimum. Whatever length of tour you opt for, there's no escaping that it's not cheap. Prices range from less than $750 pp for a five-day economy-class trip to $5,000 for eight days on a luxury-class vessel. Note that arrival and departure days are counted as tour days. Prices include food, accommodations, transfers to and from your boat, trained guides, and all your shore visits. Airfare and insurance are paid separately, and you'll need to factor in tips for the crew plus the cost of alcohol and soft drinks on board.

Itineraries are strictly controlled by the National Park Service to regulate the impact of visitors on delicate sites. Every cruise has a tight schedule, and the feeling of being herded around doesn't suit everyone, but console yourself that cruises have far less impact on the environment than land-based tours, plus you get to see far more.

Note that cabin supplements for singles are usually very high. It doesn't hurt to ask, but you're far better off sharing a cabin.

Economy Boats

Prices for boats in the economy class range $1,000–1,250 pp per week, but there are frequent last-minute deals because older visitors booking from abroad tend to avoid the most basic boats. You may be lucky and have a good experience, but note that every aspect of the service on these small boats, carrying 8–16 passengers, will be basic: Class 1 guides have a low level of training and knowledge and often a poor level of English; cabins are tiny and more prone to rocking, so seasickness is worse; and the food will likely be uninspiring. Economy boats also have smaller engines and can't cover as much distance as the bigger boats.

While this level of boat suits some budget travelers, they are losing popularity to land-based tours. You should also consider that this

GALÁPAGOS TOUR OPERATORS

IN QUITO

- **Andando Tours:** Mariana de Jesús E7-113 at Pradera, tel. 2/323-7330, www.andando-tours.com

- **Etnotur:** Cordero 1313 at Juan León Mera, tel. 2/256-4565

- **Enchanted Expeditions:** De las Alondras N45-102 and De los Lirios, tel. 2/334-0525, fax 2/334-0123, www.galapagosenchant-edexpeditions.com

- **Galápagos Tours:** Amazonas 2331 at Veintimilla, tel. 2/254-6028, www.galapagos-tours.net

- **Galasam:** Amazonas 1354 at Cordero, tel. 2/250-7079, www.galasam.com.ec

- **Guide2Galápagos:** Amazonas N24-196 at Cordero, tel./fax 2/250-8937, www.guide-2galapagos.com

- **Kem Pery Tours:** Pinto 539 at Amazonas, tel. 2/222-6583, www.kempery.com

- **Metropolitan Touring:** De los Palmeras N45-74 at Las Orquideas, tel. 2/298-8200, www.metropolitan-touring.com

- **Ninfa Tour:** Amazonas N24-66 at Pinto, tel. 2/222-3124

- **Nuevo Mundo Expeditions:** Av Coruña N26-207 at Orellana, tel. 2/250-9431, www.nuevomundotravel.com

- **Parir:** General Baquedano near Juan León Mera, tel. 2/222-0892

- **Scuba Iguana:** Amazonas 1004 at Wilson, tel. 2/290-6666, www.scubaiguana.com

- **Safari Ecuador:** Foch E4-132 and Cordero, tel. 2/255-2505, fax 2/222-0426, www.safari.com.ec

- **Via Natura:** Republica del Salvador E9-10 at Shyris, Ed. Onix, 10th Fl., tel. 2/246-9846 or 2/246-9847, www.vianatura.com

IN GUAYAQUIL

- **Centro Viajero:** Baquerizo Moreno 1119 at 9 de Octubre, tel. 4/230-1283

- **Ecoventura:** Central 300, Miraflores, tel. 4/220-7177, www.ecoventura.com

- **Dreamkapture Travel:** Benjamin Carrión and Francisco de Orellana, 12th Fl., Alborada, tel. 4/224-2909, www.dreamkapture.com

- **Galápagos Sub-Aqua:** Orellana 211 at Panama, tel. 4/230-5514

- **Galasam:** 9 de Octubre 424, tel. 4/230-4488, www.galasam.com.ec

- **Metropolitan Touring:** Calle 11A NE103, Atarazana, tel. 4/228-6565, www.metropolitan-touring.com

- **Ninfa Tour:** Córdova 646 at Urdaneta, tel. 4/230-0182

IN THE GALÁPAGOS

- **Galapatur:** Rodríguez Lara and Genovesa, Puerto Ayora, tel. 5/252-6088

- **Galápagos Deep:** Indefatigable and Matazarno, Puerto Ayora, tel. 5/252-7045, www.galapagosdeep.com

- **Galápagos Voyages:** Av. Charles Darwin and Colono, Puerto Ayora, tel. 5/252-6833

- **Metropolitan Touring:** Finch Bay Hotel, Puerto Ayora, tel. 5/252-6297, www.metropolitan-touring.com

- **Moonrise Travel:** Av. Charles Darwin, Puerto Ayora, tel. 5/252-6348

- **Scuba Iguana:** Av. Charles Darwin, Puerto Ayora, tel. 5/252-6497

- **We are the Champions Tours:** Av. Charles Darwin, Puerto Ayora, tel. 5/252-6951, www.wearethechampionstours.com

is probably a once-in-a-lifetime experience, so paying a bit more for better service is advisable.

Moderately Priced Boats

Tourist-class and tourist superior–class boats are the most common cruise choice in the islands. These medium-size sailboats or motorboats hold 10–16 passengers. Everything is better quality than on the economy boats—better cabins (though they are still small), more varied food, and class 2 guides with a higher level of knowledge and better English. These boats also have bigger engines, so they are faster and often cover longer distances, including remote islands such as Genovesa. While the service is not as good as on first-class boats, overall these boats offer the best deal and attract a mixed range of clients—backpackers, Ecuadorians, and older foreign visitors.

Costs range $1,300–1,550 pp per week for tourist class and $1,600–1,950 pp per week for tourist superior class.

First-Class Boats

This is probably the best cruise experience you can get on the islands—these boats are far more comfortable but still have small capacity (mainly 16–26 passengers) to retain an intimate group atmosphere. They can also cover longer distances, and most include a visit to the fascinating western islands of Isabela and Fernandina. Cabins are more comfortable, with beds rather than bunks, and the decor makes the interior a delightful place to spend time, as opposed to many cheaper boats, where you want to escape the interior any chance you get. These are also much sturdier yachts, so seasickness is less of a problem. Guides have to be class 3, so they must hold a degree in natural sciences (usually biology or geology) and speak nearly fluent English. Prices range $2,000–3,800 pp per week.

Luxury Tours

While the largest cruise ships are thankfully a thing of the past on the Galápagos, there is still demand, mainly from older visitors, for a luxury tour with standards comparable to top-class hotels on the mainland.

Most of these ships have capacity for more than 40 passengers, and the biggest, such as the *Galápagos Explorer II,* cater to 100. The food is gourmet standard, the guides are the best in the archipelago, and there are many facilities onboard to keep you busy at the end of the day's tours—spas, massages, gyms, jetted tubs, swimming pools, even karaoke bars, although some people would pay money to avoid the latter. Tours and meals are announced by loudspeaker.

The biggest benefit of these larger boats, like the first-class yachts, is that they are faster and so can reach the outlying islands. Best of all, rolling is minimized, so you're far less likely to get seasick, although it's still possible.

The biggest drawback is the feeling of being herded around in a large group. It's more difficult to have an intimate experience of the wildlife when dozens of other passengers are chatting and clicking their cameras. Due to the size of the group, there is very little flexibility in the tours, and schedules are set in stone. Luxury-class tours start at $3,800 pp per week and climb to over $5,000 pp.

Guides

While the boat you travel on is very important, a good or bad guide can make or break your trip. There's no escaping the fact that, in most cases, you get what you pay for. The good news is that all Galápagos guides are trained and licensed by the National Park Service, and they have all received further training in recent years as part of the government's actions to confront the islands' environmental problems. Guides are qualified in one of three classes, in ascending order of quality: Class 1, usually on economy boats or handling land-based tours, have the lowest level of knowledge and English; class 2, on tourist and tourist superior class boats, are more knowledgeable and often very good; and class 3 guides, on first-class and luxury boats, are the real experts and must have studied natural sciences at university. All guides should speak at least two languages, but class 1 guides often speak little besides Spanish. Every guide has to pass rigorous examinations every three years and complete a training course on the islands every six years to keep his or her certification. When booking a tour, ask about your guide's specific qualifications and what languages he or she speaks.

Booking and Payment

Booking a tour to the Galápagos can be done anywhere from thousands of kilometers away at home in your own country to an agency in Puerto Ayora the night before the cruise leaves. In general, the farther away you are from the islands, the more it costs. You can save over 50 percent of the total price by booking your tour in Ecuador and even more if it's last-minute. Even greater savings can be made booking last-minute in the Galápagos. However, bear in mind that it's very much a question of luck to get what you want last-minute, particularly if you have a specific itinerary in mind.

To book a cruise from abroad, a deposit of at least $200 pp (via wire transfer or Western Union) is required. Ecuador does not permit the use of credit cards for any payments by Internet or telephone, so these can't be used without the owner, the card, and the owner's passport being present in Ecuador. This is to combat credit-card fraud. Even so, only a handful of boats accept credit cards for payment in person, and these still require partial payment in cash or traveler's checks. You can pay for your flights with credit cards, however.

Many travel agencies in Quito and Guayaquil advertize tours, so shopping around is a good idea. The more time you browse, the more likely you are to find a good deal, so it pays to be patient. The best deals come when agencies are desperate to fill the last few spaces on a tour, and you can save between 25 and 50 percent. Note that the best last-minute deals are on the better classes of boats. **South American Explorers** (SAE, Jorge Washington 311 at Plaza, Quito, tel./fax 2/222-5228, quitoclub@saexplorers.org, www.saexplorers.org, 9:30 A.M.–5 P.M. Mon.–Fri., 9:30 A.M.–8 P.M. Thurs., 9:30 A.M.–noon Sat.) in Quito is a good source for up-to-date information on recommended boats. Deposits range 10–50

percent, depending on the boat and the tour operator. You are normally required to have paid in full 30 days before departure, unless it's a last-minute deal.

The biggest savings can be made by flying to Puerto Ayora, checking into a cheap hotel, and browsing the agencies on the waterfront for last-minute deals. It's not unheard of get a cruise for as little as 30 percent of the original price, and a 50 percent discount is common. It's all a question of luck, and it is far less likely in high season (December–April and July–August). If you are doing it this way, consider avoiding the cruises that frequent sites on or close to Santa Cruz, because many of these you can do yourself on day trips.

Ensure you get an itinerary and all the details of what you are paying for printed out. Some travelers find that they pay for what they thought was a superior boat only to wind up with an economy vessel. Direct all complaints concerning tours, before or after, to the Capitanía del Puerto (port captain) if you booked in the islands, and to the agency directly if you booked in Quito or outside the country.

Life on Board
DAILY ROUTINE

When you arrive on your boat, unless you're in first-class or luxury, your first reaction may be: "They didn't say the cabin was *that* small." But bear in mind that your room is really just for sleeping—you'll have far too much to look at outside on deck and at the visitor sites.

You'll meet the rest of the tour group, and your guide will introduce himself or herself and the rest of the crew before going through the tour schedule. Guides will also explain the park rules that you must follow.

Most days have an early start (breakfast at 7 A.M. or earlier) to give you the maximum time at the island sites (and also to get there before the day tours). Most boats tend to travel overnight to save time, and it's one of the joys of the cruise to wake up in a new place. The morning visits usually take 2–3 hours, including the *panga* ride to shore. Your guide will direct the group along the path or down the beach, explaining what you're seeing and filling in relevant natural history details as you go. Be understanding if your guide seems overly concerned about keeping the group together and making everyone stick to the trail. You need to remember that some visitors unwittingly cause damage, and the tour group is the guide's responsibility. Just because you've paid a lot of money doesn't mean you can do what you want. The same sentiment applies when your guides insist that you wear a life-jacket during *panga* rides; they face fines and jail time if they're caught with passengers not wearing them.

Back on board, you'll find your cabin clean and lunch ready. The midday meal is casual—a buffet on cruise ships and fixed menus on smaller vessels. You may find yourself surprisingly hungry after all that hiking and snorkeling, but don't overeat, as you may get lethargic and even seasick if the boat is traveling after lunch. Lots of water and fruit is important to keep your energy and hydration levels up. Your guide will announce the departure time for the afternoon excursion; there's usually an hour's break.

Afternoon visits are similar to the morning, although it's considerably hotter, so take a hat and plenty of sunblock. Late afternoon is famously the best time for photography. Don't miss the incomparable opportunities to snorkel—for many people this is the highlight of the trip. Where else in the world can you swim with sea lions, turtles, stingrays, and sharks? Wetsuits are handy, especially in the cold season, but are not necessary in the warm season; wearing just a swimsuit, most people can last about half an hour in the water before getting chilly.

There's usually some time before dinner to freshen up and enjoy a drink while watching the sunset (just after 6 P.M. year-round). Dinner is the most important meal of the day, and this is your chance to fill up. Formality and quality of food depends on the class of the cruise. After dinner, your guide will review what you saw during the day and preview the next day's schedule.

The higher-class vessels often have after-dinner entertainment. Otherwise, it's a case of swapping tales with your fellow passengers. Alcohol is available, but try not to overdo it—you don't want the next morning's tour ruined by a hangover and interrupted sleep. Bear in mind that drinks are comparatively pricey and not included in the cost of the tour. You may be surprised to be nodding off by 9 P.M., but there's no shame in it. Get plenty of rest because, after all, you didn't come to the Galápagos for the nightlife.

TIPPING

It's customary to tip at the end of the cruise. Remember that, although your tour is expensive, in a country as unequal as Ecuador, the big bucks don't filter down to the lowest level; the crew as well as the guide will very much appreciate your tip. Obviously use your own judgment on how much to give, and your tip should reflect the level of service. Between 5 and 10 percent of the price of the cruise is considered normal. Tip the guide separately, and use the tip box for the rest of the crew.

LAND-BASED TOURS

Sleeping and eating on a boat is not for everybody, and if you are particularly prone to seasickness, consider a land-based itinerary. These are becoming increasingly common, both on organized tours and for independent travelers. Most commonly you will be based in Santa Cruz, but itineraries that take in San Cristóbal and/or Isabela are also popular. Five-day tours start at about $600 pp, but savings can be had last-minute. If you want to do it yourself, you can usually find accommodations in the ports for as little as $20 pp per night. As well as seeing sites on Santa Cruz, San Cristóbal, and Isabela, day tours run regularly from Santa Cruz to Bartolomé, Seymour Norte, or Plazas (each costing a hefty $125 pp), while cheaper tours run to Floreana and Santa Fé ($75 pp). The other islands are out of bounds to day tours. Doing it this way, you could easily spend less than $500 in five days, not including the flights. Note however that there may be no escaping seasickness even on land-based tours, because you will spend plenty of time on boats shuttling to and from the port, and they are generally smaller boats that roll around more.

DIVING IN THE GALÁPAGOS

With such an astonishing array of marine life, it's no surprise that the Galápagos rank among the world's best dive destinations. The New York Zoological Society's Oceanographic Expedition sent divers to the islands for the first time in 1925, and they've been returning ever since. In 1998 the protection of the land sites was extended to a marine zone 74 kilometers offshore, and there are now some 60 dive sites around the archipelago, many of them closed to nondivers.

If you're dreaming of getting your PADI certification and heading straight here, however, be advised that diving in the Galápagos is not for beginners. Local dive schools offer PADI training, but it's overpriced and far from the best place to learn. You are better off not only learning elsewhere but getting a few dives under your belt first. Currents are strong and visibility is often poor, ranging 10–25 meters (half that of the Caribbean). Many dives are in unsheltered water, making holding onto coral not only permitted but essential. It is not ideal for the health of the coral, but it is certainly important for your health. There have been diving accidents here—some people get so excited by what they are seeing that they lose track of time and distance. Luckily, there is a decompression chamber in Puerto Ayora.

For those with sufficient experience, the diving is world-class. Schools of fish stretch out into what seems like eternity, and you're almost guaranteed close encounters with a variety of sharks—small white-tipped reef sharks, larger Galápagos sharks, the dramatically shaped hammerheads, and off the more remote western islands, enormous whale sharks. Add to this extended periods following manta rays, marine iguanas, and the surprisingly fast penguins, then diving in the Red Sea or the Caribbean will pale in comparison.

Recent changes in the laws mean that every boat in the Galápagos must be either a non-diving cruise boat or a dedicated dive boat, so divers are now forced to choose between live-aboard charters, which are very expensive, or a land-based tour with day trips to dive sites. The latter option is becoming more popular because it's far cheaper, but note that you will be restricted to sites within easy reach of Santa Cruz and San Cristóbal. Popular sites include Academy Bay, Santa Fé, Gordon Rocks, Daphne Minor, Mosquera Islet, Seymour, and Cousins.

However, the most spectacular diving can only be experienced on a live-aboard around Darwin and Wolf. These islands are a full day's sail north of the main island group. Schools of hundreds of hammerheads can be seen off Wolf, and gigantic whale sharks cruise slowly by June–November. Bottlenose dolphins are common at Darwin's Arch.

The best diving is during the hot season (December–May), with water temperatures 20–25°C, making a three-millimeter wetsuit adequate. Temperatures drop to 15°C in the cold season, when a six-millimeter wetsuit with hood, booties, and gloves becomes necessary. It's best to bring all your own equipment as renting it locally is expensive and can cause problems because many itineraries go straight to the boat. Bring a mask, dive alert whistle, and sausage or scuba tuba. Boats supply tanks, air, and weights.

Because most visitors depart by plane, you must leave a day free at the end of your dive trip to avoid possible decompression problems (most dive tours spend the last day on Santa Cruz).

Live-aboard options are very limited and are usually booked months in advance. At present, the two best companies are **Ecoventurer** (U.S. tel. 800/633-7972, Guayaquil tel. 4/283-9390, www.ecoventurer.com), operating the MY *Galápagos Sky,* and **Aggressor** (U.S. tel. 800/348-2628, www.aggressor.com), operating the *Galápagos Aggressor I* and *II.* Prices start around $3,800 pp, rising to $4,700 pp for a week.

Dive Agencies

Most large Galápagos tour agencies can book dive trips aboard the small number of equipped boats. A PADI Open Water certificate is essential, and some companies ask for a minimum number of dives, although this depends on the difficulty of the site.

Galápagos Sub-Aqua (Guayaquil tel. 4/230-5514 or 4/230-5507, Puerto Ayora tel. 5/252-6350 or 5/252-6633, www.galapagos-sub-aqua.com) is the longest-operating dive center on the islands, with 20 years of experience and a good safety record. Eight-day live-aboard trips ($3,500–4,500 pp) are offered, and they also have an office in Puerto Ayora, where they offer day dives ($200 pp). Last-minute discounts are available.

Other recommended operators on Avenida Darwin in Puerto Ayora include **Scuba Iguana** (tel. 5/252-6497, www.scubaiguana.com), run by dive master Matías Espinosa, who was featured in the *Galápagos* IMAX movie. Daily dive prices start at $200 pp for two dives in Academy Bay and more for other destinations. Last-minute discounts are available. They also book live-aboard trips. **Nauti Diving** (tel. 5/252-7004, www.nautidiving.com) and **Galápagos Deep** (Indefatigable and Matazarno, tel. 5/252-7045, www.galapagosdeep.com) run day trips.

The Natural World

The landscapes of the Galápagos are as diverse and otherworldly as the wildlife that inhabit them: lush highland forests, pristine white-sand beaches, steaming volcanic peaks, and blackened lava trails strewn with cacti. The 13 volcanic islands and 16 tiny islets that lie scattered over 60,000 square kilometers in the eastern Pacific Ocean form 8,000 square kilometers of land, including 1,350 kilometers of coastline. The islands are actually the tips of underwater volcanoes, which are younger and higher to the west. Isabela, the largest island of the group at 4,275 square kilometers, has six volcanic peaks, and one of these, Cerro Azul, is the highest point on the islands at 1,689 meters.

Some 97 percent of the land mass is in the national park and uninhabited, and only the remaining 3 percent is inhabited. The latest estimated population of the archipelago is 27,000, of whom 7,000 are temporary. The biggest population area is Puerto Ayora on Santa Cruz, followed by the capital Puerto Baquerizo Moreno on San Cristóbal, then Puerto Villamil on Isabela and tiny Puerto Velasco Ibarra on Floreana.

VOLCANIC ORIGINS

The Galápagos archipelago sits directly over a hot spot in the Pacific crust plate, where underlying magma bulges closer to the surface than usual. Millions of years ago, molten rock began to rise through the crust, cooling in the sea and forming mountains that eventually rose above the surface. New volcanoes quickly formed to take the place of older ones and were slowly eroded by the sea and weather, resulting in a rough chain of islands trailing off southeast toward the mainland. Many volcanoes came and went over millions of years; Española, the oldest island in the archipelago, is nearly 3.5 million years old. Fernandina, by comparison, is less than 1 million years old, a mere infant in geological terms. Geologists have found an island forming west of Fernandina, although it will be many thousands of years before it forms, so don't expect it to be included on your itinerary just yet.

Evidence of the islands' volcanic heritage is everywhere. There are many lava flows that have hardened into rocky trails, the most accessible being in Sullivan Bay on Santiago. In the highlands on Santa Cruz you can find collapsed calderas and lava tunnels, while Isabela offers the best close-up view of an active volcano, with trails leading past the second-largest crater in the world at Sierra Negra and into its pungent sulfur mines. Nearby Cerro Azul erupted in May 2008. Fernandina also has

© BEN WESTWOOD

The Sierra Negra volcano on Isabela Island has the second largest crater in the world.

trails through lava fields and experienced the most recent eruption at La Cumbre in April 2009.

THE SEA

The islands' unique ecosystem has been created by the interaction of several ocean currents. The most famous and most powerful is the Humboldt Current that brings cold water from the south along the coast of Chile and Peru. The warmer Panama Current flows down from Central America, every few years bringing the devastatingly warm El Niño current (the most recent was in 1998). A third current is the Equatorial Counter Current (also called the Cromwell Current), which flows deep below the surface and upon encountering the islands is deflected upward, bringing cool water, which is vital to the archipelago's ecosystem. Algae thrive on the nutrients, and fish and marine invertebrates feed on the algae; whales, dolphins, sea lions, and birds eat these fish. The unusually cool waters found around the Galápagos ensure the survival of many species usually found only in colder waters, in particular the Galápagos penguins.

CLIMATE

These currents determine the archipelago's subtropical climate. While there is no variation in hours of sunlight, due to the fact that the islands are right on the equator, the temperature, cloud cover, and rainfall vary considerably throughout the year.

The hot or **rainy season** begins in December when the Panama Current warms the nearby waters to 26°C, and runs until May. Daily showers bring 6–10 centimeters of precipitation per month, with more rain falling in the highlands of the larger islands. As on the coast of Ecuador, the rainy season is also the warmest period, with hot, sunny days punctuated by intermittent showers. The average temperature climbs into the 30s, and the seas are comfortably warm for swimming; February–March are the warmest and sunniest months.

The June–November **dry season** arrives with the colder (20°C) waters from the

THE GALÁPAGOS ISLANDS

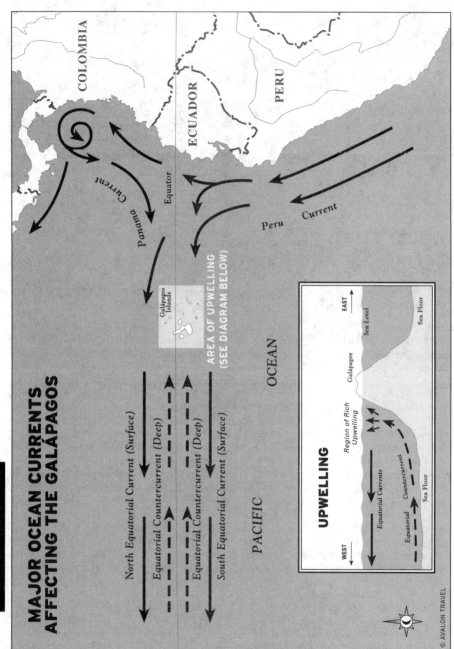

MAJOR OCEAN CURRENTS AFFECTING THE GALÁPAGOS

COLOMBIA

ECUADOR

PERU

Equator

Panama Current

Peru Current

Galápagos Islands

AREA OF UPWELLING (SEE DIAGRAM BELOW)

North Equatorial Current (Surface)

Equatorial Countercurrent (Deep)

Equatorial Countercurrent (Deep)

South Equatorial Current (Surface)

PACIFIC   OCEAN

UPWELLING

EAST

WEST

Sea Level

Sea Floor

Sea Floor

Galápagos

Region of Rich Upwelling

Equatorial Currents

Equatorial Countercurrent

© AVALON TRAVEL

Humboldt Current, and average temperatures drop to less than 27°C. There is very little rain, but you often find *garúa,* a type of misty drizzle in the highlands. Days are generally overcast, the seas colder and rougher, and the landscapes lose their greenery August–November, to be replenished again in the next rainy season. It's surprising how different the climate seems when climbing 500 meters into the highlands—it's often quite hot and sunny on the beaches and drizzling and chilly up in the hills, so it's a good idea to bring a rain jacket and a sweater when heading up. On the larger islands of Fernandina, Isabela, Santa Cruz, and San Cristóbal there is a distinctive type of cloud forest with mosses, lichens, and grasslands.

El Niño

It seems ironic that such a destructive climatic phenomenon should be named after the Christ child. The "devil's current" might be more appropriate, but its arrival around Christmastime gave it its name. The phenomenon brings a surge of warm water down from the north, forcing the Humboldt Current south for up to 18 months. Ocean temperatures rise, clouds gather, and 6–10 centimeters more rain falls per month. For humans, the main problems are flooding and crop loss, but for the wildlife of the Galápagos it is even more devastating. El Niño patterns struck in 1982–1983 and again in 1997–1998, and the warmer sea temperatures killed algae and fish, the main food sources for much of the wildlife. Populations of marine iguanas, sea lions, waved albatross, penguins, and boobies fell sharply, and many have still not recovered. If past history is any guide, the extreme version of El Niño strikes roughly every 15 years, so the next one may be coming soon.

FLORA AND FAUNA

The volcanic landscapes and ocean currents of the Galápagos are fascinating, but it's the creatures inhabiting them that make them truly unique. It seems incredible that a set of rocky islands, parched in the equatorial sun and covered with blackened lava, could be teeming with so much life. Indeed, it's precisely because the landscapes are inhospitable that so many creatures have been forced to adapt and, in doing so, provided living proof for Darwin's theory of evolution. The Galápagos islands are home to 5,000 species, and 1,900 are endemic: one-third of the plants, almost half the birds, half the fish and insects, and 90 percent of the reptiles have all adapted so well to life in the archipelago that they hardly resemble their original mainland ancestors at all.

However, the Galápagos ecosystem is as delicate as it is unique. In an ecological Eden with few natural predators, the arrival of one particular predator—human beings—has upset the balance considerably. Only time will tell if the balance can be restored.

Colonization

One thousand kilometers is a very long way to swim or fly, never mind crawl, so how on earth did the wildlife of the Galápagos come to be here? It seems likely that the strengths of the ocean currents brought mammals such as sea lions to the archipelago, and they flourished in islands surrounded by waters teeming with marine life. Birds may have been blown off course, but more likely migratory birds came here and knew they were on to a good thing with an endless supply of fish and so returned year after year. Insects and plant seeds could also have been carried from the South American continent by high winds, whereas other seeds were probably excreted by birds or arrived stuck to their feet.

Explaining how terrestrial reptiles and rodents arrived is trickier. The most common theory is that they drifted on rafts of vegetation that still wash down Ecuador's ocean-bound rivers. Any animals or plants that happened to be aboard, provided they could survive the journey, stood a slim chance of riding the currents all the way to the Galápagos. With their ability to slow their own metabolism, reptiles are particularly suited for such a long, difficult journey, while larger mammals would have died quickly, which explains the lack of mammals on the islands.

INTRODUCED SPECIES

While humans have long posed a threat to the fragile ecosystem of the Galápagos, the animals and plants that they have brought with them have caused the most serious problems. There are believed to be nearly 1,000 introduced species in the archipelago. The vast majority are plants and insects, but larger creatures that have been introduced include 12 species of mammals, six species of birds, and four species of reptiles.

INTRODUCED ANIMALS

Most of the introduced mammals were brought over as domestic animals – either livestock, beasts of burden, or pets – before escaping into the wild. They all cause damage in their own way. **Donkeys** eat through cactus-tree trunks to get at the juicy pulp, killing the plant in the process. Scattered **horses** and **cattle** roam the highlands, trampling on tortoise eggs, and feral **pigs** are the worst enemy of giant tortoises, gobbling up as many turtle eggs as they can find and sometimes killing hatchlings.

Wild **dogs** are even more bloodthirsty. While pigs kill only for food, wild dogs have been responsible for senseless attacks on iguanas, sea lions, seals, and birds, particularly on Santa Cruz. **Cats** adapt very easily to the wild and are the biggest threat to small birds and chicks on many islands.

While these large animals have wreaked havoc, they are at least relatively easy to spot. **Rats,** on the other hand, have been on the Galápagos even longer, arriving on whaling ships. As any city sanitation worker will tell you, they are extremely difficult to control. Black rats and Norwegian rats are the most common

species. They spread disease to other species and are as much a danger as pigs are to giant tortoises, eating the hatchlings.

Of all the introduced animals, the most damage has arguably been done by **goats.** They eat their way through pretty much anything, demolishing island vegetation and causing both erosion and food shortages for endemic species. They also reproduce at an astonishing rate – three goats left on Pinta in the late 1950s had produced more than 40,000 descendants by 1970. Luckily, goats are also very easy to eliminate, and hundreds of thousands have been culled in recent years. At present, only San Cristóbal, Southern Isabela, and Santa Cruz have remnant goat populations.

Amphibians were the only one of the five classes of vertebrates that had not colonized the Galápagos – until 1998, that is, when a small species of **tree frog** was first captured on Isabela and Santa Cruz. Scientists think the frogs arrived in cargo ships and were able to establish sustainable breeding populations during the particularly wet 1997-1998 El Niño climate pattern.

INTRODUCED PLANTS

The growing human population has brought enormous numbers of plants to the archipelago – more than 500 species is the latest estimate, and most of these have arrived in the past few decades. As any gardener can confirm, unwanted plants can strangle the life out of the endemic species, stealing sun, water, and nutrients. The main problem are fruits – vines such as **passion fruit** and **blackberry** grow quickly into impenetrable thickets,

REPTILES

The Galápagos islands were named after the giant reptiles that inhabit them, and this is one of the only places on earth where reptiles rule the land with no natural predators. The archipelago thus gives us a glimpse of what life might have been like millions of years ago when dinosaurs ruled the planet.

More than 90 percent of the reptile species

in the Galápagos are endemic. In addition to the reptiles described below, the Galápagos harbors five endemic species of **geckos** and three species of **Galápagos snakes.**

Giant Tortoises

Of the 20 species of endemic reptiles, these slow giants are the most famous. They also gave the islands their name—*galápago* is an

and trees such as **guava** and **red quinine** take over entire hillsides. Weeds and flowers have spread from gardens to formerly arid zones on the major islands. Of all the plants, guava trees are perhaps the worst threat, and recent estimates show that they cover 50,000 hectares in the Galápagos.

SOLUTIONS

In the past decade, efforts to eliminate invasive species have been stepped up, but it is no easy task. To prevent the situation from getting worse, the SICGAL organization checks all luggage and packages entering the islands or moving between islands for organic materials of any kind. It may seem unnecessary to do this with foreign visitors, but even a piece of fruit could introduce fruit flies to the islands. The more rigorous checks and penalties for violations have discouraged the locals from importing nonnative species and have led to confiscation of animals, plants, and seeds. Frustratingly, pets are still allowed, but they must be registered and neutered.

In terms of eliminating the species that are already on the islands, the best solution for larger animals is hunting, although with populations in the hundreds of thousands, it's costly and time-consuming. The alternatives are traps, which can ensnare other species, or poisoning, which is risky to the ecosystem. Hunting has reaped rewards, though – in 2002 a four-year campaign succeeded in ridding Santiago Island of 25,000 feral pigs. Even more impressive has been the elimination of goats from Santiago, Isabela, and Floreana – over 250,000 were culled by 2006, and the campaign is ongoing to re-move them from San Cristóbal and Santa Cruz. How the hunters achieved this monumental task was highly impressive. Goats were caught and fitted with radio tracking collars, and their horns painted bright colors. When they were released and rejoined the herds, hunters shot them from helicopters, leaving them to rot. There have been many other smaller-scale victories, but certain species, particularly rats, fire ants, and fruit trees, are proving far more difficult to control.

Regarding endangered species, progress is being made. Giant tortoise populations are being boosted by breeding centers on Santa Cruz, Floreana, San Cristóbal, and Isabela. In 2010 tortoises were reintroduced successfully to the remote island of Pinta, Lonesome George's original home. On Floreana, the population of dark-rumped petrels, which had been hunted to near extinction by dogs, cats, rats, and pigs, has recovered after a concerted effort to eliminate their predators. The endemic Floreana mockingbird is also being reintroduced to the island after its population had been confined to Champion Island. Progress is also being made to combat the tiniest of invasive pests – fire ants. These highly aggressive ants invade birds' nests and also iguana and tortoise eggs. On the remote island of Marchena, insecticide has been trialed successfully to eliminate them, and the program will be extended to other islands.

While the conservationists are winning battles, redressing the balance of the archipelago's ecosystem is a long, hard war, and it will take many years to undo the damage that invasive species have caused.

old Spanish word for a saddle similar in shape to the tortoise shell. They are only found on the Galápagos and, in smaller numbers, on a few islands in the Indian Ocean. They are not fully grown until age 100, reaching 1.5 meters in length and weighing up to 250 kilograms. Many live to the age of 160, although their maximum age is unknown.

The shell of a giant tortoise reveals which island its owner originates from. Saddle-shaped shells evolved on low, arid islands where tortoises needed to lift their heads high to eat tall vegetation, while semicircular domed shells come from higher, lush islands where vegetation grows closer to the ground.

The only time tortoises make any noise is during mating season, when their unearthly groans echo long distances as males joust for

354 THE GALÁPAGOS ISLANDS

dominance. When her eggs are ready to hatch, the female digs a nest for as long as five hours. The eggs are buried under 15 centimeters of earth and kept warm before they hatch in the spring.

The tortoises' famous slow, languid movement is what allows them to live so long, and perhaps we should all take a cue from them and slow down a little. With minimal movement, their metabolism slows significantly, allowing them to survive with very little food and water during the dry season. When the rains come, they come alive, eating, drinking, mating, wallowing in pools of water, and sleeping contentedly in large groups.

The most famous resident is **Lonesome George**, thought to be the last of the Pinta island tortoises and the living embodiment of the tragic recent history of his species. Of the original 14 subspecies, 11 remain and 3 species (Santa Fé, Floreana, and Fernandina) have been hunted into extinction. Indeed, the giant tortoise population has plummeted from some 250,000 before humans arrived to just 20,000 today. Sailors used to be the tortoises' main enemy, but today, the danger comes from introduced species. Pigs dig up nests, cats eat hatchlings, and goats and cattle eat the vegetation and cut off the tortoises' food supply. It's not all bad news, however, because there is a comprehensive rearing program to release tortoises back into the wild, most recently on Pinta island. Charles Darwin Station on Santa Cruz is the most famous place to see these amazing creatures, although breeding centers on Isabela and San Cristóbal are actually bigger and more impressive to visit, and there's also a center on Floreana.

Sea Turtles

The eastern **Pacific green turtle,** known rather confusingly in Spanish as the *tortuga negra* (black turtle), is the most common species in the archipelago, relying on the beaches to lay their eggs. They are rarely seen in large numbers, preferring to swim alone, in couples, or next to their young. The mating season is November–January, after which the females swim ashore to lay eggs on the beaches. The females are actually bigger than the males and can grow to 1.2 meters long. The best-known nesting sites are Tortuga Bay on Santa Cruz, Bartolomé, and Gardner Bay on Española.

Also present in the islands but rarely seen are the **Pacific leatherback** and the **Indo-Pacific hawksbill** turtles.

Marine Iguanas

The only seafaring lizards in the world, **Galápagos marine iguanas** are living proof of evolution. Scientists estimate that this species adapted over 2–3 million years from their land iguana cousins in order to find food underwater in the shape of nutritious coastal seaweed. A flattened snout allows them to press themselves against the rocks to feed, a flattened tail propels them more effectively underwater, long claws grab the rocks firmly, and salt-eliminating glands in the nostrils cleanse the sea salt from their bodies. They feed for an hour a day, always at low tide, and can stay underwater for more than an hour by lowering their heart rate by half.

The seaweed they feed on is true to its name—it's a weed that spreads incredibly quickly throughout the coastline of the islands and supports more than 200,000 marine iguanas on the Galápagos. Males measure about one meter in length and weigh up to 20 kilograms. They are mostly black, with red and green tinges on their backs becoming particularly prominent during the mating season.

After feeding, regulating its body heat fills much of the rest of the marine iguana's day. After a long dive, they must warm up, but not too quickly and not to more than 45°C. To do so, iguanas face the sun, exposing as little surface area as possible, and raise their bodies off the ground to allow air to circulate underneath; they often look like they're striking a yoga pose. On cold days and at night, iguanas congregate into huge piles to conserve heat.

Like much of the wildlife on the archipelago, iguanas were affected by El Niño seasons in the 1980s and 1990s when abnormally warm waters killed the shallow-growing seaweed. The

© BEN WESTWOOD

Marine iguanas have evolved from their land cousins to eat algae below the water.

marine iguanas were not strong enough to dive deeper, and thousands perished. Numbers have slowly recovered, but who knows if they will evolve further over time to become better divers?

Land Iguanas

There are seven subspecies of land iguana in the Galápagos. How they arrived on the island is the cause of much debate—possibly floating on vegetation from the South American coast—but they almost certainly came after their marine cousins, when there was enough vegetation on the islands to survive on land. They live in dry areas and eat berries, flowers, fruits, and cactus pads, ingesting most of their water from food. Newborns are one of the few terrestrial creatures that have a predator to fear—the Galápagos hawk. They are also prey for many introduced species until they are big enough to defend themselves. As a result, the land iguana species on Santiago and Baltra are extinct, while those on other islands are endangered. A captive-breeding program at the Darwin Center is working to boost the population.

Males can weigh up to 13 kilograms and live more than 50 years. They are famous for their head nodding, a territorial threat to other males that can also be employed against humans if they get too close. Note that male iguanas can whip their tails up if startled, so take care approaching them. The Galápagos species are distinctively more yellow than greener mainland iguanas, particularly the subspecies on Santa Fé. There are also hybrids born from mating with marine iguanas. The best places to see land iguanas are on Santa Cruz, Seymour Norte, Plaza Sur, and Santa Fé.

Lava Lizards

Though hardly as impressive as their larger relatives, the seven species of lava lizard are certainly faster—and they have to be to avoid being gobbled up by birds or snakes. You'll see them scurrying over sand and rocks all over the islands. They have various other evasion techniques—changing color to camouflage

© BEN WESTWOOD

Lava lizards change color and even lose their tails to evade predators.

themselves and leaving a breakaway tail in predators' mouths while they make a getaway and grow a new one. They feed on insects, plants, and occasionally each other. The males can often be seen doing a type of push-up as a show of strength, and their Spanish name, *lagartija,* has become a common slang term for this type of exercise.

MAMMALS

In contrast to the abundance of plants, insects, fish, and lizards, the Galápagos have only six types of mammals—sea lions, fur seals, whales, and dolphins, all of whom must have swum to the archipelago. Then there are bats who flew over, and most impressive of all, rice rats who could only have arrived floating on rafts of vegetation.

Sea Lions

A close encounter with sea lions is for many people the highlight of a Galápagos trip. While other creatures show a mild disdain for humans, the sea lions are very communicative,

and the pups are particularly playful in the water, which makes for an incredible snorkeling experience. They seem to delight in playing impromptu games of peekaboo and demonstrate their acrobatic skills underwater. After a hard day's fishing and playing, the sea lions sprawl over beaches and rocks, snoozing to replenish their oxygen supplies. Walking among a colony is another highlight of any trip.

The sea lion population has declined considerably in recent years due to a lack of fish after the 1998 El Niño, but there are still more than 25,000 in the archipelago. Outside their colonies, they are often found dozing on boats and docks.

However, they are called "lions" for a reason (or "wolves" in Spanish—*lobos marinos*). The mature males can reach 2.5 meters in length, considerably bigger than the females, and they are more than a little scary. Males mate with 10–15 females and can be very territorial, so be advised that although most of their posturing is harmless, sea lions occasionally attack—it's the principal cause of animal injury to visitors in the

© DR LOUISE WESTWOOD

Sea lions are often found on jetties.

Galápagos. Steer well clear of patrolling males, especially when snorkeling. Their behavior is understandable, though—with such an uneven ratio of cows to bulls, many bulls are left fending for themselves and plotting their next move, and territorial battles are common. More importantly, sea lions are one of the largest Galápagos residents that have to fear predators, in the shape of sharks and killer whales, so they patrol the shores to protect their beach harems.

The best places to snorkel with sea lions are at various sites on Floreana's north shore and San Cristóbal at La Isla de los Lobos. The best places to walk among a colony are on Plaza Sur, and on San Cristóbal, La Lobería and other nearby beaches.

Fur Seals

Smaller than sea lions, with a thick, furry coat, the Galápagos fur seals are also harder to see because they prefer shaded areas and cooler waters. We are lucky that these endearing animals with their bear-like snouts and small external ears exist at all after they were hunted to the

brink of extinction in the 19th century. The warm, two-layered pelt was in high demand in Europe and the United States, leading to slaughter on a mass scale.

Seal populations recovered slowly through the 20th century but have suffered at the hands of nature as well as humans. The warm currents of El Niño were particularly devastating, killing their supply of fish. Indeed, although they are endemic to the islands, many seals have now migrated to the coast of Peru. There are still estimated to be over 20,000 fur seals inhabiting the northern and western islands of Pinta, Marchena, Santiago, Isabela, and Fernandina.

Whales and Dolphins

The mammals that pop in and out of the water are far easier to see than the several cetaceans (completely aquatic mammals) that live in the waters around the archipelago. There are many species of whales, but it is rare to see them. The massive blue whale is an occasional visitor, but you're more likely to see humpback whales breaching—the best spots are west of Isabela and Fernandina. The killer whales or orcas are the most feared, preying on sea lions and fur seals. Far more commonly seen are schools of dolphins surfing the bow waves of cruise boats and leaping in unison.

Bats and Rats

Two endemic species of bats made the long crossing from the South American mainland—probably by accident—to settle in the Galápagos. Two species of rice rats are left from an original seven that must have arrived floating on vegetation. The rest have been driven to extinction by the larger Norwegian black rat that was introduced by visiting ships and is now a major threat to native species.

SEABIRDS

Surrounded by water rich in fish, it's no surprise that the Galápagos archipelago is teeming with birdlife. Only a small minority—five of the 19 species—are endemic: the Galápagos penguin, flightless cormorant, waved albatross, lava gull,

THE GALÁPAGOS ISLANDS

and swallow-tailed gull. The rest of the species, including the boobies and frigates that get a lot of visitor attention, are found elsewhere in Ecuador and the South American coast.

Boobies

The Spanish sailors who first discovered the Galápagos were very unimpressed by a bird that would simply peer at them curiously instead of fleeing, and so they called these birds *bobos* ("stupid"), and the name stuck. *Amigos* would have been nicer and more appropriate to these amenable birds, who are completely unfazed by humans walking near them on island trails. The insult to their intelligence is particularly unfair because boobies are no chumps—they are astonishingly adept at catching fish, dive-bombing the waters from as high as 25 meters before popping up to the surface and gulping down the luckless prey. The shock of the impact with the sea is diffused by air sacs in the boobies' skulls.

If you're lucky enough to see their mating ritual, it's hilarious: The male marches around, kicking his feet up high, then raises his beak skyward, whistles, and opens his wings as if to say, "How can you resist my bright blue feet?" The bluer the better, in the view of the female, who responds with a honk if she likes what she sees.

Blue-footed boobies are the most commonly seen booby species because they nest on the ground, and the best places to see them are Seymour Norte, Punta Pitt on San Cristóbal, Española, and Genovesa. There are actually far more **red-footed boobies** in the archipelago, but these smaller birds tend to feed farther out to sea and are mainly found on the more remote islands, particularly Genovesa, which hosts the world's largest colony. The **masked boobies** are the biggest and nest on cliff edges because they find it difficult to take off from level ground. They take their name from the black eye mask that contrasts with their bright white plumage.

Frigate Birds

If you're a frigate bird, size clearly matters.

These scavengers are most famous for the bright red chest pouches that males inflate to the size of a basketball to attract females in the mating season. Once inflated, the male spends the entire day that way, calling and flapping his wings at passing females, hoping to attract one to the nest he has built for her. It's particularly romantic because, once the female chooses the best-chested male, they mate for life.

Mating aside, though, frigates are actually the bad guys of the archipelago because they are scavengers who live mainly by stealing food from other birds. They have a wide wingspan that can reach over two meters, but they can't swim, so dive-bombing the sea would result in them sinking like a stone. Instead, they harass other birds, particularly boobies, into coughing up their hard-earned meal in an unpleasant show of avian bullying; they sometimes even steal fish right out of a chick's mouth. They have also learned that humans are a good source of food and are often seen following fishing boats in the hope of scavenging scraps.

Despite their bullying reputation, the sight of the inflated pouches is one of the highlights of bird-watching on the archipelago. The best places to see frigates are Seymour Norte, Punta Pitt, and Española.

Waved Albatross

If you don't go to Española, you probably won't see the largest seabird in the archipelago—it's as simple as that. Nearly the entire world population of the waved albatross nests on this island April–November before migrating to Peru. Because of their 2.5-meter wingspan, it is quite a sight to see them taking off and landing. Española gets so busy in mating season that landing areas, most famously Punta Suárez, are nicknamed "albatross airports." Once they're out of the skies, though, these graceful fliers become surprisingly awkward; they often fall over after landing and then waddle around clumsily. It's not a surprise when you consider that many birds have not walked on land for months, even years, without actually "landing," only leaving the skies to float on water far out in the ocean.

True to the Galápagos tradition, like boobies and frigates, the albatross has an entertaining mating ritual. The couples perform an elaborate courtship display, clacking their bills together, sky calling and dancing around in a synchronized, circular walk. They sometimes do this for several hours, and the island turns into a kind of open-air avian disco. Albatross are not the faithful birds we once thought they were, however, and recent research has shown that some birds have several partners while others are monogamous. The courtship reaches its peak in April, and the first chicks arrive in June–July. They learn to fly before the end of the year and then migrate.

Galápagos Penguins

The last thing you'd expect to see on the equator is a penguin, and these endearing little birds are special in two ways—they are the only penguin found in the northern hemisphere (the Equator cuts across the north of Isabela), and at just 35 centimeters tall they are one of the smallest penguins in the world. They evolved from the Humboldt penguins that inhabit the coast of Chile, but have retained much of their original insulation. So while other species like iguanas and sea lions warm up on the rocks, the penguins struggle to cool down either by swimming or standing with their wings out. You're most likely to see them standing around on the rocks, but in the water they are quite a sight—streaking after fish at speeds up to 40 kilometers per hour.

The 1998 El Niño had a severe effect on penguin numbers, and there are only a few thousand left in the islands. The largest colonies are on Fernandina and Isabela, with much smaller colonies on Floreana and Bartolomé.

Flightless Cormorants

Flightless Cormorants are proof that evolution is not all about gaining skills but also about losing them. These birds spend so much time in water and with no predators to fear on land, they have lost their ability to fly. They have neither the chest muscles nor wingspan to take to the air, but instead have long necks,

© DR LOUISE WESTWOOD

Pelicans swoop into the ocean and fill their 14-liter beak pouches in search of lunch.

strong kicking legs, and webbed feet that make them experts at catching fish, eels, and even octopuses underwater. They also make their nests very close to the waterline, and many are washed away by high tides. You can only see these birds on Fernandina and western Isabela.

Endemic Gulls

There are over 35,000 **swallow-tailed gulls** nesting throughout the archipelago. These attractive birds sport a black head, a distinctive red eye ring, a white and gray body, and red feet. Unlike most gulls, swallow-tails feed nocturnally, heading out at dusk and helping to point boat captains toward land at dawn. The **lava gull** is thought to be the rarest gull in the world, with only 400 mating pairs nesting exclusively in the Galápagos. Their dark gray plumage makes them difficult to pick out from the lava rocks they inhabit.

Other Seabirds

Elsewhere in the world, the sight of a pelican swooping into the sea to catch fish is considered an impressive sight. Here in the Galápagos, **brown pelicans** don't get as much attention as the more colorful and rarer birdlife in the archipelago. They are amazing creatures, though, filling their enormous 14-liter beak pouches on impact with the ocean, filtering out the fish, and gulping them down.

Red-billed tropic birds feeds far out to sea and returns to their nests on windy cliff-sides. They have a gray-and-white body and long, flowing white pintails capped by a distinctive red bill and a black mask.

COASTAL AND LAND BIRDS

While they don't get nearly as much attention as their seafaring cousins, the islands' land and coastal birds are still fascinating, not least to Charles Darwin himself. One of the many mysteries of the Galápagos is how land birds that cannot fly over the sea could have arrived here, and the only conclusion is that they were blown all the way from the mainland by storms.

Darwin's Finches

These tiny birds are arguably the most important species in the Galápagos from a scientific viewpoint. The 13 species of finches, with their varied beak shapes, were the most important inspiration for Charles Darwin's development of his theory of evolution.

The key to the finches' survival, as Darwin noted, is the beak. Short, thick beaks enable **ground finches** to crack hard seeds, while longer, slimmer bills allow other species to probe crevices for insects and eat cacti or flowers. The finches obviously came from a common ancestor, but they are subtly different according to which island or even which part of the island they inhabit.

Finches are remarkably resourceful birds and are one of the few species to use tools to find prey. **Woodpeckers** and **mangrove finches** use a cactus spine or small twig to get at grubs burrowed deep in tree branches.

The **sharp-billed ground finch** is the most unusual species, and it is slightly sinister. It is

The many varieties of finches inspired Darwin's theory of evolution.

© DR. LOUISE WESTWOOD

THE GALÁPAGOS ISLANDS

nicknamed the "vampire finch" for its habit of pecking at the base of a booby's tail until it can drink a trickle of blood. The boobies offer little resistance, perhaps because the pecking also helps to remove parasites. This species also rolls other birds' eggs until they break and then eats the contents.

Herons and Egrets

There are five species of herons, all prolific hunters of small lizards, rodents, insects, and fish. They stand motionless as statues and spear their prey with their long beaks. The largest is the **great blue heron,** which stands 1.5 meters tall, while the smaller **yellow-crowned night heron** feeds by night. The only endemic species is the small gray **lava heron** that hunts in rock pools.

Greater Flamingos

Their distinctive pink make these birds an attractive sight in the lagoons around the archipelago. They feed on shrimp by filtering the salty lagoon water, and they actually turn pink from their original white because of their shellfish diet. The best places to see them are Punta Cormorant on Floreana, Red Beach on Rabida, Puerto Villamil on Isabela, along with Cerro Dragón and Bachas Beach on Santa Cruz.

Mockingbirds

There are four species of mockingbirds endemic to the Galápagos, feeding mainly on insects and small reptiles. The **Galápagos mockingbird** is the most common, found on Isabela, Floreana, Santa Cruz, Santiago, and Santa Fé. San Cristóbal is home to the **Chatham mockingbird,** and on Española there is the **Hood mockingbird** with its long curved beak. Floreana is home to the much rarer **Charles mockingbird.** Sadly, though, mockingbirds are increasingly endangered due to introduced species, such as rats and cats, that hunt the chicks. Adults also need their wits about them to avoid the Galápagos hawk. They are slowly being reintroduced to Floreana following a large-scale extermination of invasive species.

The Galápagos Hawk

Out of the water, this fearless bird is the largest natural predator on the islands. It eats everything from baby iguanas and lizards to small birds, rodents, and insects as well as scavenging on dead animals. It also has a highly unusual mating system known as cooperative polyandry: up to four males mate with a single female, then help to incubate and raise the young.

Other Land Birds

Other notable species include the beautiful but easily startled **Galápagos dove** (*Zenaida galapagoensis*), which has pink, gray, and white plumage, red feet, and a blue eye ring. The male **vermillion flycatcher** deserves special mention for its fiery red plumage, and the **yellow warbler**'s sunshine plumage is as beautiful as its songs.

MARINE LIFE

The temperatures of the waters around the Galápagos are the foundation on which most life is built, and they are as diverse as the wildlife, varying from a bone-chilling 15°C to near–thermal bath comfort of 30°C. With such a wide range of temperatures and profundities, some 300 fish species inhabit the waters, which makes the Galápagos a wonderful snorkeling and diving destination. You can often find yourself staring into a school of fish that seems to go on forever.

Choosing highlights among such an array of fish is tricky, but top of the list has to be the multicolored **parrotfish;** the **clownfish** of *Finding Nemo* fame; the **moorish idol,** with its long dorsal fin over a body banded with black, yellow, and white; and the orange, black, and white **harlequin wrasse,** which can spontaneously change sex from female to male.

Nobody expects crabs to be a highlight of a Galápagos trip, but you'll be surprised at how eye-catching some of the invertebrate species are. Most colorful is the bright-red **Sally Lightfoot crab,** so named for its fast movement across water over short distances. Other invertebrate species of note include **pencil-spined sea urchins,** many neon-colored species of **starfish,** and the increasingly rare **sea cucumbers,** which have been harvested for their medicinal benefits and are an endangered species.

Sharks

While there are few natural predators on land in the Galápagos, underwater it's a different story. The cold waters are ideal for sharks, so sea lions have to be careful when swimming too far out. Luckily for humans, these sharks are mainly harmless. The most common are the docile **white-tipped sharks** and **black-tipped sharks,** who eat plankton and small fish. They tend to rest under rocks and in caves but are also commonly seen swimming close to shore. They are found all over the archipelago, but you are most likely to encounter them in the waters around Española, Floreana, North Seymour, Bartolomé, Las Tintoneras (Isabela), and León Dormido–Kicker Rock (San Cristóbal). The larger **Galápagos shark** is another species that can be seen in these areas.

For the more adventurous, look out for scary-looking **hammerhead sharks.** Large schools of 30–40 of these incredible creatures are commonly encountered when diving, although they can occasionally be seen while snorkeling at León Dormido or off the north shore of Floreana. The largest shark in the archipelago is the huge **whale shark,** up to 20 meters long, found only on the outlying islands of Darwin and Wolfe, visited mainly by dedicated dive boats.

Rays

Encountering a school of rays gliding along flapping their wings like underwater birds is unforgettable, and the Galápagos is filled with these beautiful creatures. When they swim, it's a highlight of any snorkeling or diving excursion, and they can also be viewed from boats on occasion. The most common are **stingrays,** whose wings can span up to 1.8 meters, but be careful of the sting, which can whip up if you startle them. They are also found resting on sandy beaches, so watch where you step. More

spectacular are the brightly colored **golden rays,** the massive **manta rays,** which are an incredible six meters across, and the rarer **spotted eagle rays,** found mainly in deeper waters.

FLORA

With such a bewildering array of wildlife and rugged volcanic landscapes to keep visitors busy, the plants of the Galápagos don't get much attention, and you're more likely to notice the absence of vegetation than its presence in often barren terrain. However, the rainy season leads to an explosion of greenery on the larger islands, and there is much to admire in the hills.

The Galápagos has 550 native species of plants, about one-third of them endemic. Their habitat is spread across three diverse areas: the coastal or littoral area, where fresh highland water meets salt water; the dry semideserts of the dry areas; and the lush, humid, misty highland area.

The coastal areas' flora is dominated by tangled **mangroves,** consisting of trees and plants that can only grow in brackish waters. They weave themselves into the sand and send up small breathing roots called pneumatophores. The archipelago has four types: the red mangrove is the most common, with larger, pointier, shinier leaves. There is also the white mangrove, the black mangrove, and the less common button mangrove.

In the dry areas, the lifeless-looking *palo santo* tree blankets the landscape. They may not look like much, but the smell of the wood is famously aromatic, used throughout Ecuador both as incense in churches and to repel mosquitoes. The trees were given their name, which translates as "holy wood," for their habit of flowering near Christmas.

Even more prevalent in dry areas are various species of cacti. The prickly pear cactus *Opuntia* has evolved into 14 separate species throughout the archipelago. True to the Galápagos tradition, the species have evolved according to which predator they have to repel. On islands with large populations of land iguanas and tortoises, the cacti are taller and thicker with stronger spines, growing up to 12 meters high. On islands with no large predators, *Opuntia* cacti grow low to the ground, and their spines are soft enough for birds to nest and pollinate the cactus in return. Other Galápagos cactus species include the endemic lava cactus, often the first thing to grow in new lava flows, and the more impressive candelabra cactus, whose branches stretch up to seven meters across.

The highlands of Santiago, Santa Cruz, San Cristóbal, and Floreana contain the richest variety of plant life. Here you'll find dense forests of *lechoso* trees, a world away from the barren lowlands below. There are 90 species of ferns, some of which grow up to three meters. Orchids, an endemic species of mistletoe, the purple and pink **cacotillo,** and purple-and-white **passionflowers** bring splashes of color to the highlands. Darwin had a flower named after him, of course—**Darwin's aster,** whose tiny white blossoms can be seen in highland grass.

Santa Cruz and Nearby Islands

Santa Cruz (pop. 15,000) is the economic, tourism, and geographic center of the Galápagos. It's the best base to explore surrounding islands on day tours and to pick up last-minute deals. As for the island itself, many of its attractions can be seen independently, which is not the case in the rest of the archipelago.

Puerto Ayora is the archipelago's largest port and tourism hub, with the widest selection of hotels and restaurants. On the edge of town is **Charles Darwin Research Station,** the most convenient place to view giant tortoises up close, including the famous Lonesome George. A 45-minute walk west of Puerto Ayora is the sandy expanse of **Tortuga Bay,** the longest beach in the Galápagos. Another short hike from town are the brackish waters of **Las Grietas,** fissures in the lava rocks that make for a relaxing, cool dip. In the verdant highlands of Santa Cruz, there are several attractions that make an interesting day trip: **Los Gemelos** (The Twins) are two 30-meter-deep craters with abundant birdlife. East of Bellavista are the **lava tunnels** formed by the solidified outer skin of a molten lava flow. The biggest highland attraction is the huge **El Chato Tortoise Reserve** where these giant creatures roam in their natural habitat. On the north side of the island, **Bachas Beach** is a frequent stop on tours to nearby Seymour Norte, Plazas, or on the way from the airport.

The beach still contains wreckage of U.S. military barges from World War II as well as populations of Sally Lightfoot crabs and flamingos in nearby lagoons. Less frequently visited are the lagoons of **Black Turtle Cove** and **Cerro Dragón.**

PUERTO AYORA AND VICINITY

If you're expecting to come to the Galápagos and stay in a deserted island paradise far from humans, Puerto Ayora will come as something of a surprise. With a permanent population of about 12,000 and thousands more temporary residents and visitors, this is the bustling hub of the archipelago. While conservationists may wish the port away, blaming its expansion for the islands' environmental problems, it's hard not to like Puerto Ayora. Set in a sheltered bay lined with cacti and filled with dozens of anchored yachts, it's a pleasant place to be based for a few days. The facilities here are the best in the archipelago: hotels of all levels, from budget to seriously overpriced; a wide selection of good restaurants; reputable tour operators; and gift shops galore. If you're traveling independently, it makes the most sense to stay here to pick up day tours or last-minute cruises.

Note that Puerto Ayora has its drawbacks, however—there's too much traffic, especially the countless white-truck taxis shuttling

around town. There are also problems with the town's water supply, and the construction of a decent sewage-treatment facility is long overdue. The water supply is unfortunately no cleaner than in mainland Ecuador—so don't drink it.

Entertainment and Events

The downstairs disco **La Panga** (Av. Darwin, tel. 5/252-6266, 8 P.M.–2 A.M. daily) and upstairs bar **Bongo Bar** are the best places to have a big night out. La Panga often has a $10 cover charge on weekends and pumps out mainly electronic music. There are a few mellower

bars around town, notably **Limón y Café** (Av. Darwin and 12 de Febrero, tel. 5/252-7010, 7 P.M.–2 A.M. daily) to shoot pool and relax over a beer.

Shopping

You're never more than a few meters from a souvenir store in Puerto Ayora, and most sell postcards and the obligatory Galápagos-branded T-shirts and hats. Some stores also sell collectable stamps, handicrafts, wood-carvings, ceramics, and jewelry. Note that you should steer clear of buying anything made of endangered black coral or turtle shells. For completely guilt-free shopping, the Charles Darwin Center has two gift shops with profits going to the national park and the Darwin Foundation.

Recreation and Tours

Puerto Ayora is the best place to pick up day tours around Santa Cruz and to nearby islands. The cheapest tours are the bay tour ($25 pp), which takes in La Lobería, where you can snorkel with sea lions; Playa de los Perros, where marine iguanas and various birds are seen; Las Tintoreras, channels where sharks are often found; and the lava rock fissures of Las Grietas. The highlands tour ($80) goes to El Chato Giant Tortoise Reserve, the nearby lava tunnels, and the Los Gemelos collapsed craters. If you get a group together, you can share the bill. Alternately, see these sights independently with a taxi driver (about $30).

For visits to nearby islands, the cheaper tours (from $75 pp per day) go to Floreana or Santa Fé. Tours to Plaza Sur, Seymour Norte, and Bartolomé (about $125 pp) cost double that—a deliberate price hike imposed by the national park to restrict visitor numbers to these busy sites.

The tours listed above can all be booked with dozens of operators, mostly through offices on the main street, Avenida Charles Darwin. All operators do last-minute deals, and you can save up to 50 percent off the original price (and even greater savings when compared with prices quoted in the United States). The low seasons in May–June and September–October are the best times to find cut-price deals, but you may get lucky at any time of year. It's worth shopping around and hanging around for a few days to browse. Recommended agencies for day tours and last-minute cruises include **Galápagos Voyager** (Av. Charles Darwin at Colono, tel. 5/252-6833), **Metropolitan Touring** (Finch Bay Hotel, tel. 5/252-6297, www.metropolitan-touring.com), **Moonrise Travel** (Av. Charles Darwin, tel. 5/252-6348, www.galapagosmoonrise.com), and **We Are the Champions Tours** (Av. Charles Darwin, tel. 5/252-6951, www.wearethechampionstours.com).

Diving tours can be booked at specialist diving operators. Day tours are becoming more popular among divers because live-aboard trips are very expensive. Note that although you can learn to dive on the Galápagos, it's an expensive place to do so, and the strong currents and predominance of drift dives mean it is better suited to more experienced divers. La Lobería, Punta Estrada, and Punta Carrión are popular dive sites near Puerto Ayora. Academy Bay and Gordon Rocks are definitely for more experienced divers. Day tours (about $200 pp) have two dives per day.

Accommodations

The expansion of Puerto Ayora has led to increased opportunities for budget travelers. The town now has every conceivable level of accommodations, and you can pay anything from $20 pp per night to over $200 pp. Note, though, that many of the budget hotels have problems with their water supply, which often has a distinctly unappealing color.

One of the cheapest deals in town is **Hotel España** (Thomas de Berlanga and 12 de Febrero, tel. 5/252-6108, www.hotelespana-galapagos.com, $20 s, 30 d), with adequate guest rooms set around a colorful courtyard with hammocks. Next door, **Hotel Gardner** (Thomas de Berlanga and 12 de Febrero, tel. 5/252-6108, www.hotelgardnergalapagos.com, $25 s, $35 d, air-conditioning $5 extra, breakfast included) is worth the extra few dollars for its elegantly decorated, spacious guest rooms and friendly service. Other good budget options include the more basic guest rooms of **Hotel Sir Francis Drake** (Padre Julio Herrera, tel. 5/252-6221, $25 s, $40 d), **Hotel Lirio del Mar** (Islas Plaza and Thomas de Berlanga, tel. 5/252-6212, $20 s $30 d) and **Hotel Salinas** (Naveda and Thomas de Berlanga, tel. 5/252-6107, $18–30 pp), which has a small garden, communal cable TV, and a restaurant. Choose from simple double guest rooms downstairs to better-quality guest rooms upstairs with air-conditioning. For a family atmosphere, try the **Bed and Breakfast Peregrina** (Av. Charles Darwin and Indefatigable, tel. 5/252-6323,

THE GALÁPAGOS ISLANDS

$32s, $52d, breakfast included). There's a shady terrace, a garden, and laundry service.

Mid-range and pricier hotels all include breakfast. **Hotel Castro** (Los Colonos and Malecón, tel. 5/252-6173, $40 s $60 d) is recommended as a clean, quiet place with fans, a terrace, a restaurant, and a bar. Around the corner, **Estrella del Mar** (12 de Febrero, tel. 5/252-6427, $46 s, $66 d) is often recommended for its ocean views. **(Hotel Las Palmeras** (Thomas de Berlanga and Islas Plaza, tel. 5/252-6139, www.hotelpalmeras. com.ec, $65 s, $85 d) is one of the best mid-range options, with plushly decorated guest rooms and a large pool on the terrace. **Hotel Casa Natura** (Petrel and Isla Floreana, tel. 2/246-9846, www.vianatura.com, $125 d) is a friendly new hotel 10 minutes out of town with comfortable guest rooms, a filling buffet breakfast, and a small pool at the back.

The other hotels in and around Puerto Ayora are mostly top-end venues that fill with tour groups. You are better off booking most of these through a tour rather than individually. The most characterful has to be the **Red Mangrove Inn** (Av. Charles Darwin and Las Fragatas, tel./ fax 5/252-6564, www.redmangrove.com, $234 s, $290 d). Opened in 1994, this cozy hotel has walls decorated with batiks and tiles made by the previous owner. The dining room opens onto a deck, and the hot tub overlooks Darwin Bay. Mountain bikes, sea kayaks, and windsurfing equipment are available on request. The owners also offer tours of Santa Cruz. The Red Sushi restaurant is highly recommended for its Japanese and local seafood specialties.

The German-owned **Hotel Silberstein** (Av. Charles Darwin and Los Piqueros, tel./fax 5/252-6277, www.hotelsilberstein.com, $137 s, $201 d) is an elegantly designed Mexican-style villa with charming arches, a tropical courtyard, a swimming pool terrace, and spacious guest rooms with solar-heated water.

Across the harbor, accessible by water taxi, **Angermeyer's Waterfront Inn** (tel. 9/472-4955, www.angermeyer-waterfront-inn.com, $175 d) has a fantastic location overlooking the bay.

The two top hotels on the islands are out of town. A water-taxi ride and a short walk away is the **(Finch Bay Eco Hotel** (tel. 2/250-8810, ext. 2810, www.finchbayhotel.com, $250 d), the highlight of which is the private beach for sunbathing and snorkeling. The hotel also has its own water treatment plant and solar-heated water. It is the most ecologically sound hotel on the islands. To escape from Puerto Ayora and blow your budget completely, head up to Santa Rosa in the highlands to the **(Hotel Royal Palm Galápagos** (tel./fax 5/252-7408, www. royalpalmhotel.net, $420 d), a palatial spread with villas and suites commanding spectacular views of the highlands. There's a gourmet restaurant, a piano bar, a pool, a spa, a gym, tennis courts, and a private art gallery.

Food

There are basically two classes of restaurant in town—the economical places where the locals eat and the upscale, more expensive places for tour groups. For those on a budget, head to the string of small kiosks along Binford east of Baltra and eat dinner alfresco in the pedestrianized street. It gets very busy in the evening with locals wolfing down cheap, tasty specialties. **Servisabroson** (Binford, tel. 5/252-7461, lunch and dinner daily, entrées $4–7) is just one of the popular ones where *encocado* (fish in coconut sauce) is a particular favorite. For spicy soups and noodles, try the inexpensive Chinese **Chifa Asia** (Binford, no phone, lunch and dinner daily, $4–5).

Opposite the ferry docks, **(El Descanso del Guia** (Av. Charles Darwin, tel. 5/252-6618, breakfast, lunch, and dinner daily, entrées $3–4) is the preferred choice of guides, as its name (Guide's Rest) suggests. Fill up on breakfast, or chicken, fish, and meat staples washed down by a wide range of fresh juices for lunch. The two-course set meals are a great value and good quality. For seafood, try **Restaurant Salvavidas** (Av. Charles Darwin, tel. 5/252-6400, lunch and dinner daily, entrées from $4.50), also by the docks, deemed the best seafood place in town by locals and well-known for its octopus, lobster, and steamed shrimp.

For Italian cuisine, head to the **Hernan Café** (Baltra and Av. Charles Darwin, tel. 5/252-6573, breakfast, lunch, and dinner daily, entrées $6–12) on the corner facing the park. As well as the unusual decor—walls of lava stone and lamps made of dried cacti—the food is varied and very good quality, with big breakfasts, pizzas, and a range of pasta, fish, and meat dishes. Indulgent desserts and fresh coffee complete the menu. Another good Italian option is **La Dolce Italia** (Av. Charles Darwin, tel. 9/455-4668, 11 A.M.–3 P.M. and 6–10 P.M. daily, entrées $9–15) farther down. The excellent pizza and pasta, imaginative nautical decor, and friendly Sicilian owner make this an attractive option, and they even deliver to docked boats. For healthy organic breakfasts, salads, and cakes early on and burgers and seafood later, try the outdoor patio of **Tintorera** (Floreana and Av. Charles Darwin, tel. 9/338-0560, breakfast, lunch, and dinner daily, entrées $4–12). ◖ **The Rock** (Av. Charles Darwin and Naveda, tel. 5/252-7505, lunch and dinner daily, entrées $6–10) is a new restaurant that has quickly become popular. Named after the first ever Galápagos bar set up on Baltra in the 1940s, it serves up a feast of international food from Mexican quesadillas to teriyaki fish fillets along with plenty of juices, shakes, and cocktails to wash it all down.

For a more upscale atmosphere, ◖ **La Garrapata** (Av. Charles Darwin and Thomas de Berlanga, tel. 5/252-6264, lunch and dinner Mon.–Sat., entrées $7–15, set lunch $4) is the town's longest-operating quality restaurant with an attractive open-air setting and a mix of Ecuadorian meat and seafood specialties as well as a wide range of Italian pasta. The town's newest gourmet restaurant, ◖ **Il Giardino** (Av. Charles Darwin and Binford, tel. 5/252-6627, 8:30 A.M.–11:30 P.M. Tues.–Sun., entrées $6–10) does Mediterranean specialties such as gazpacho soup, homemade paninis, crepes, and delicious ice creams and sorbets afterward.

If you're staying in one of the top hotels, you won't need to go far for a great dinner—the restaurants at the Red Mangrove, Royal Palm Hotel, and Angermeyer Point are all renowned.

◖ **Red Sushi** (Red Mangrove Inn, Av. Charles Darwin, tel. 5/252-6564, lunch and dinner daily, entrées $10–20) does excellent Japanese specials that include sashimi and teppanyaki.

Information and Services

The **Cámara de Turismo** (Av. Charles Darwin and 12 de Febrero, tel. 5/252-6206, www.galapagostour.org) and the **Galápagos National Park Office** (tel. 5/252-6189 or 5/252-6511, www.galapagospark.org), near the Darwin station, both offer maps and information in English.

Banco del Pacífico (Av. Charles Darwin) has an ATM and changes traveler's checks, but lines are often long. **Banco de Bolivariano** also has an ATM next to the supermarket opposite the ferry dock. Internet access is available around town, but it's slow. Both **Porta** and **Movistar** offer cell phone coverage in large areas of the islands.

There are plenty of laundries, including **Monyfri Laundry** (12 de Noviembre), **Laundry Lava Flash** (Bolívar and Naveda), and **Lavandería Peregrina** (Av. Charles Darwin and Indefatigable), attached to the Peregrina guesthouse.

Getting There and Around

CITTEG, based at the new bus terminal two kilometers north of town, sends buses to the airport 7 A.M.–9:30 A.M. The trip costs $1.80 pp one-way and takes under an hour. If you miss the last bus at 9:30 A.M., a taxi ($15) is the only way to the airport.

There are daily services on small *lanchas* (speed-boat ferries) connecting Santa Cruz with San Cristóbal (2 hours) and Isabela (2.5 hours). Both routes cost $25 pp one-way. There is only one service per day; the ferries leave Isabela at 6 A.M. and San Cristóbal at 7 A.M., and depart Puerto Ayora for both islands at 2 P.M. If passenger numbers are larger, two boats run, and they can get booked up, so reserve one day in advance (there are a couple of kiosks opposite the dock). It can be a bumpy ride, particularly in the afternoon, so don't eat a big meal beforehand.

THE GALÁPAGOS ISLANDS

White *camionetas* (pickup trucks) are available for hire all around town, and most destinations cost $1. You can also negotiate prices to go into the highlands (usually $30 for a half-day). **Water taxis** wait at the dock to shuttle passengers to boats waiting in the harbor ($0.60 pp daytime, $1 at night).

If you're in a hurry and can afford the extra cost, take an interisland flights with **EMETEBE** (Los Colonos and Av. Charles Darwin, top fl., tel. 5/252 6177). Small eight-seater planes fly half-hour routes between San Cristóbal, Baltra, and Isabela several times per week. Prices are from $160 one-way, $260 round-trip, plus $15 taxes. **TAME** (tel. 5/252-6527) has an office at Avenida Charles Darwin and 12 de Febrero, and **Aerogal** (tel. 5/244-1950) has an office at Rodríguez Lara and San Cristóbal.

Charles Darwin Research Station

About 15 minutes' walk east of town is the headquarters of the Charles Darwin Foundation (tel. 5/252-6146, www.darwinfoundation.org, 7 A.M.–6 P.M. daily). The station was opened in the 1960s as a research and breeding center for endangered native species. There's an information center, a small museum, and a tortoise breeding and rearing center, where endangered subspecies are hatched and cared for until they can be released into the wild.

The highlight of the visit is the giant walk-in tortoise enclosure, where you can meet the giants face to face. There are 11 different subspecies, and the most famous resident is **Lonesome George,** the last surviving member of the Pinta Island subspecies. He has been here since 1971 and attempts to mate him with females of other subspecies have failed, so his species may die with him.

Note that the station is on every tour itinerary, so it's a good idea to get here early to avoid the crowds. A small beach just outside the station is open 7 A.M.–6 P.M. daily.

Tortuga Bay

Galápagos tours are often quite hectic, so you may welcome the chance to lie on a pristine

beach for a few hours. Luckily, one of the most beautiful beaches in the Galápagos is only a 45-minute walk from Puerto Ayora. Take Binford out of town to the west, up the steps, and past the National Park guard post. Follow the paved path through cacti forest straight to the beach. There are actually two very different beaches—the first is one of the longest in the archipelago, but the sea is a little rough, so for a calmer experience, walk to the right to the very end and turn inland to find a smaller shallow lagoon where marine turtles come to lay their eggs. You're unlikely to see the turtles, so content yourself with sunbathing and swimming. Note that the beach closes at 5 P.M., so you should set out earlier than 3 P.M. to have enough time to enjoy it. There are no facilities here, so bring water (and be sure to take the bottle back with you).

Las Grietas

Another nearby excursion within walking distance of the port is Las Grietas, where fissures

Visit Las Grietas for a relaxing dip in the brackish waters.

in the lava rocks have created two layers of water—saline and fresh. It's a beautiful, sheltered place for a swim, but come early to avoid the crowds. Take a water taxi ($0.50) across the bay to the dock of Angemeyer Point restaurant and walk past the Finch Bay Hotel to Playa de los Alemanes, a small sandy beach. Then walk up a path strewn with lava rocks to the steps leading down to Las Grietas. The hike from the dock takes about half an hour, and good walking shoes are recommended for the rocky part.

SANTA CRUZ HIGHLANDS

The reputation of the Galápagos for barren landscapes certainly doesn't apply to the highlands of Santa Cruz, and it's worth venturing inland to 600 meters elevation to experience a very different environment to the coast—misty forests and green pastures. Seven kilometers above Puerto Ayora are the small towns of **Bellavista** and **Santa Rosa,** where several trails lead into the hills. The peaks of **Media Luna,** five kilometers from Bellavista, can be climbed in 4–5 hours, and three kilometers beyond them is **Cerro Crocker,** a journey of 7–8 hours. Hiring a guide is advised but not required.

West of Santa Rosa, the biggest draw of the highlands is **El Chato Tortoise Reserve** ($3), which fills the entire southwest corner of the island. Here you can see the giants in their natural habitat on guided hikes through the forest. There's a slightly dubious photo op at the end of the tour where visitors wear the heavy shell of a dead tortoise.

A few kilometers up from Santa Rosa, on either side of the road, are **Los Gemelos,** 30-meter-deep craters formed when caverns left empty by flowing lava collapsed on themselves. The view is impressive into the now verdant craters where Galápagos hawks, barn owls, and vermillion flycatchers flit through damp *Scalesia* forests.

East of Bellavista, you can visit two sets of **lava tunnels** ($3), formed by the solidified outer skin of a molten lava flow. Entered through collapsed roof sections, the wide tunnels feel like mine shafts and stretch for nearly one kilometer. It's quite wet and muddy, so sneakers are preferable to sandals. The tunnels are on private land.

Steve Devine's Butterfly Farm ($4), between Bellavista and Santa Rosa, is another popular stop on tours of the highlands. This cattle ranch is run by a former American GI. Giant tortoises graze in the wet grass among the cattle, and there are abundant butterflies and birds, including yellow warblers and vermillion flycatchers. There's a restaurant and café if you want to stop for lunch.

All of these highland attractions can be seen on a guided tour organized with any operator in Santa Cruz. Costs average $80 for groups up to 14. Alternately, pay a taxi driver in the port about $30 for a half day to visit some of the attractions independently.

OTHER SANTA CRUZ SITES
Bachas Beach

This beach is named for the remains of wrecked U.S. military barges dating to World War II, whose rusty metal parts are still visible. The white-sand beach is often covered in Sally Lightfoot crabs, and it is also a sea turtle nesting site, while the lagoons behind the beach are home to flamingos. Las Bachas is often combined with other excursions, such as North Seymour, or can be seen on the way to or from the airport due to its proximity to Baltra.

Black Turtle Cove

Just west of the canal between Santa Cruz and Baltra, this shallow mangrove lagoon extends far inland. There is no landing site, so visitors are restricted to a slow tour on a *panga* (small boat). Above water there is abundant birdlife: Herons, gulls, frigate birds, and boobies all nest in the tangled branches of red and white mangroves. Beneath the surface, spotted eagle rays and golden rays glide by, and green sea turtles are commonly seen. You may also be lucky enough to see white-tipped sharks resting in the shallows.

Cerro Dragón

This new visitor site on the west side of the

island has a dry or wet landing, depending on the tide. There are two lagoons that are sometimes filled with flamingos and a two-kilometer trail through a forest of *palo santo* and *Opuntia* cacti leads to the top of Cerro Dragón, which commands good views. This is a good spot to see groups of land iguanas, which gave the hill its name.

DAPHNE MAJOR

Off the north coast of Santa Cruz, about 10 kilometers west of Seymour Norte, the two small islands of Daphne are not included on most itineraries, and access is restricted. The larger island Daphne Major is an important research site, but if you can get permission to come here and negotiate a very tricky landing, there is a steep trail to the 120-meter-high summit of a sunken crater, where masked and blue-footed boobies nest. Farther along the trail, red-billed tropic birds can also be seen.

SANTA FÉ

This small island is midway between Santa Cruz and San Cristóbal, about 1.5 hours from each. Landing on the island has recently been restricted to cruise tours. There's a wet landing on the northeast side and trails through a forest of *Opuntia* cacti, which grow up to 10 meters high. The trail is rocky in places, and you have to cross a steep ravine, so bring good walking shoes. The highlight is the yellowish Sante Fé iguana, endemic to the island, and you may be lucky enough to see Galápagos hawks in the forest. For day tours (about $60 pp), you are not allowed to land, so the highlight is the snorkeling—marine turtles, manta rays, white-tipped reef sharks, and sea lions can be seen in the shallow waters.

◖ SEYMOUR NORTE

This tiny island off the north coast of Santa Cruz is the best place to see large colonies of blue-footed boobies and magnificent frigate birds. You can decide for yourself which has the most interesting mating ritual—the boobies marching around displaying their blue feet or the frigates inflating their red chests

© DR LOUISE WESTWOOD

Seymour Norte is a prime spot to see blue-footed boobies.

to the size of a basketball. The 2.5-kilometer trail loops around the island and takes over an hour. At the end, you can appreciate the amazing sight of marine iguanas, sea lions, and red Sally Lightfoot crabs sharing the rocky beaches. Note that this is a very popular island and gets rather crowded, so the national park has raised the price of day trips, which average $125 pp from Puerto Ayora.

PLAZA SUR

Off the east coast of Santa Cruz are the two tiny islands of Plazas. You can only visit the south island, which at just two square kilometers is one of the smallest visited islands in the archipelago. Conversely, however, the island boasts one of the largest sea lion colonies in the Galápagos, about 1,000 individuals, and it's a great place to observe a colony up close. It's fascinating to watch them lounging around, yawning, and tending to their young. Keep your distance from the large males, though, who can get very irritable.

The trail climbs through a colorful landscape past a small colony of land iguanas to the cliffs on the far side of the island, which are teeming with birdlife—red-billed tropic birds, boobies, frigates, and swallow-tailed gulls. There is also a small sea lion bachelor colony separated from the main colony, plotting their next challenge to the dominant males below. Like Seymour Norte, Plazas is a busy visitor site, and prices have been raised to $125 pp for day tours.

San Cristóbal

The most easterly island in the Galápagos, San Cristóbal is the administrative center of the province, and its port, Puerto Baquerizo Moreno, is the capital. It's not as busy as Santa Cruz and retains the feel of a more modest tourism hub. The island has a troubled history, though, having been the site of a large penal colony in the late 19th century inland at the small town of El Progreso. These days, it is a pleasant enough place with some fantastic visitor sites, and it makes a slightly cheaper, quieter alternative base to Puerto Ayora, although excursion options are more limited. San Cristóbal is also leading the way in the archipelago's renewable energy drive, with 60 percent of its energy coming from wind and solar power. The hope is to eliminate diesel completely from the island in the next five years.

Near Baquerizo Moreno are several short walks to interesting sites. Northeast of the center is **The Interpretation Center,** which has arguably the best exhibition in the archipelago on the islands' history and ecology. Beyond this are walks to **Las Tijeretas,** renowned for frigate birds, and **Playa Cabo de Horno,** a good spot for snorkeling. On the opposite side of town you can walk among a large sea lion colony at **La Lobería.** Farther afield, the most popular boat trips are to **Isla Lobos,** excellent for snorkeling with sea lions, and **Kicker Rock,** also known as León Dormido, one of the best snorkeling and dive sites in the entire archipelago, with large populations of sharks as well as rays and turtles. At the northeastern end of the island, **Punta Pitt** has large colonies of red-footed, blue-footed, and masked boobies. In the highlands, an interesting day trip takes in the freshwater **Laguna El Junco,** the beach of **Puerto Chino,** and the large giant tortoise reserve of **La Galapaguera.**

PUERTO BAQUERIZO MORENO

The capital of Galápagos Province has a different feel to Puerto Ayora on Santa Cruz. It's smaller, cheaper, and not completely dependent on tourism—fishing and administration are also important employment sources in the town. The port has a very pleasant waterfront walkway where sea lions are often seen lounging lazily. The beach just west of the center is the sleeping area for an entire colony, and hundreds of them congregate here at night.

Sights

Baquerizo Moreno has several sights within walking distance that can be visited independently. A 10-minute walk northeast of the center along Alsacio Northia leads to the small, popular Mann Beach, which gets busy on weekends. Opposite the beach is a branch of the University of San Francisco de Quito.

Walk a little farther up to reach the **Interpretation Center** (tel. 5/252-0358, 8 A.M.–5 P.M. daily, free), which provides an in-depth overview of the islands' history, development, and environmental problems. It's better than the smaller exhibition in the Charles Darwin Center in Puerto Ayora.

Past the center, there is a forked path leading up to **Las Tijeretas,** also known as Frigate Bird Hill for its abundance of nesting frigates. The views are very impressive to the bay below, which is a good spot for snorkeling, although the entry, via the rocks, can be a bit tricky. The other path leads down to **Playa Cabo de**

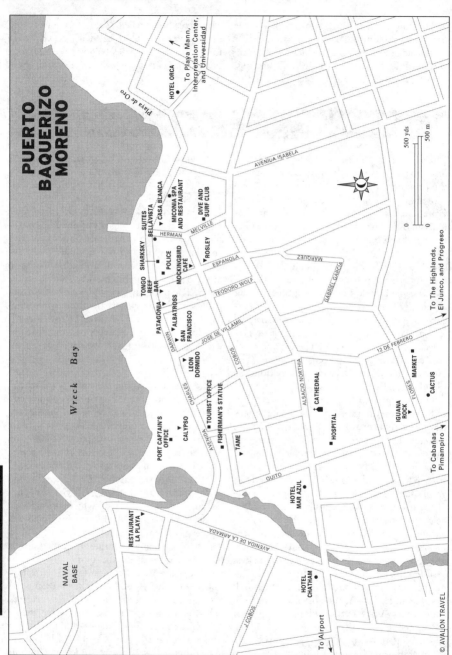

PUERTO BAQUERIZO MORENO

Wreck Bay

NAVAL BASE

Playa de Oro

HOTEL ORCA

To Playa Mann, Interpretation Center, and Universidad

AVENIDA ISABELA

CASA BLANCA

SUITES BELLAVISTA

MICONIA SPA AND RESTAURANT

DIVE AND SURF CLUB

HERMAN

MELVILLE

TONGO

SHARKSKY

ROSLEY

POLICE

MOCKINGBIRD CAFÉ

ESPANOLA

REEF BAR

PATAGONIA

ALBATROSS

SAN FRANCISCO

DARWIN

TEODORO WOLF

JOSE DE VILLAMIL

MARQUEZ

GABRIEL GARCIA

To The Highlands, El Junco, and Progreso

LEON DORMIDO

CHARLES

J. COBOS

12 DE FEBRERO

PORT CAPTAIN'S OFFICE

CALYPSO

AVENIDA

TOURIST OFFICE

FISHERMAN'S STATUE

ALSACIO NORTHIA

CATHEDRAL

MARKET

FLORES

CACTUS

IGUANA ROCK

TAME

HOSPITAL

QUITO

HOTEL MAR AZUL

To Cabañas Pimampiro

RESTAURANT LA PLAYA

AVENIDA DE LA ARMADA

J. COBOS

HOTEL CHATHAM

To Airport

500 yds
500 m
0
0

© AVALON TRAVEL

© BEN WESTWOOD

Puerto Baquerizo Moreno, the administrative center of the Galápagos Islands

Horno, also known as Playa de Amor, which has equally good snorkeling and a quiet stretch of beach frequented by sea lions and backed by mangroves.

On the opposite end of town, it's a half-hour walk or a taxi ride ($2) to **La Lobería,** a rocky beach where a large colony of sea lions laze around. There is also a colony of marine iguanas, as well as good surfing here most of the year.

Entertainment

Baquerizo Moreno comes alive at night, and you may be astonished at how many children and teenagers fill the waterfront on weekends. Nightlife options are restricted, though. The best place to go at night is three blocks inland at **Iguana Rock** (José Flores and Quito, 8 P.M.–2 A.M. Mon.–Sat.), where you can shoot pool and dance. There are various impromptu discos inland away from the center on weekends; just ask around or watch for fliers.

Recreation and Tours

There are some excellent day tours on San Cristóbal, all of which can be booked with tour operators. Most are either on Avenida Charles Darwin at the shore or along Española. You can also rent snorkeling gear, surfboards, and bicycles to get around. Recommended operators include **Sharksky** (Española, tel. 5/252-1188, www.sharksky.com), **Chalo's Tours** (Española, tel. 5/252-0953, chalotours@hotmail.com), and **Galakiwi** (Av. Charles Darwin, tel. 5/252-1562, www.southernexposuretours.co.nz). For scuba diving, all of the above organize tours, often on the same boats as snorkeling tours, or head to the **Dive and Surf Club** (Herman Melville, tel. 9/409-5450, www.divesurfclub.com). The most popular day trips are to León Dormido and Isla Lobos ($60 pp); a day tour of the highlands costs $60 pp, or you can hire a taxi to save money ($30).

Accommodations

Puerto Baquerizo Moreno has fewer accommodations than Puerto Ayora, but there are plenty of budget options. It lacks a large selection of top-end hotels, which is not necessarily

THE GALÁPAGOS ISLANDS

a bad thing because tour groups prefer to stay in Santa Cruz, keeping San Cristóbal quieter.

Along the *malecón,* the cheapest options with basic guest rooms are **Hostal San Francisco** (Malecón, tel. 5/252-0304, $10–12 pp) and **Hostal Albatross** (tel. 5/252-0264, $10 pp) right next door. For a little more money, a far better option is the family-run **☾ Hostal León Dormido** (José de Villamil and Malecón, tel. 5/252-0169, $20 pp), which has well-maintained guest rooms with private baths, fans, and TVs, a cozy lounge area, and a small coffee shop.

For more comfort, try the air-conditioned waterfront guest rooms of **Suites Bellavista** (Malecón and Melville, tel. 5/252-0352, $50 s or d). Some guest rooms have great views of the harbor. The most elegant place to stay on the waterfront without breaking the bank is the Moorish white **Casa Blanca** (Malecón and Melville, tel. 5/252-0392, www.casablanca-galapagos.com, $30 s, $50 d), which has rustic guest rooms with air-conditioning, wide balconies, and an art gallery downstairs.

Inland, another good mid-range option is the friendly **Los Cactus** (near the telephone office at Juan José Flores and Quito, tel. 5/252-0078, $25 s, $35 d, breakfast included). There are 13 guest rooms with private baths, hot water, air-conditioning, TVs, and Wi-Fi. On the road to the airport, the remodeled **Hotel Chatham** (Northia and Armada Nacional, tel. 5/252-0137, chathamhotel@hotmail.com, $42 s, $72 d, breakfast included) has guest rooms with air-conditioning, hot water, TVs, private baths, and a small pool.

The port has a few top-end hotels, though not as many as Puerto Ayora. **Miconia** (Av. Charles Darwin, tel. 5/252-0608, www.miconia.com, $87 s, $161 d), along the north end of the *malecón,* is one of the best. There's a pool, a jetted tub, a gym, and Wi-Fi. The restaurant has a good reputation and is open to nonguests.

Food
The cafés along the waterfront, including **Patagonia, Tongo Reef Bar,** and the café

below **Casa Blanca,** all serve up sandwiches and burgers for about $3, but if you want something more filling, it can be surprisingly difficult to find a good budget meal. **Rosley** (corner of Española and Ignacio Hernández, no phone, lunch and dinner daily, entrées $3) is the best set-meal joint in town, serving up an excellent-value two-course lunch and dinner popular with locals. Opposite, the **Mockingbird Café** (Española and Ignacio Hernández, tel. 5/252-0092, breakfast, lunch, and dinner daily, entrées from $2.50) is a good place to check your email accompanied by coffee, a milk shake, or a brownie. Most of the cheaper joints in town cater for locals and don't really advertize set menus, but ask around and you may be lucky.

If you don't mind spending upward of $10 on dinner, there are plenty of upscale options in town, mainly at the west end of the *malecón.* One of the most popular is **La Playa** (De la Armada, tel. 5/252-0044, lunch and dinner daily, entrées $7–12), which specializes in mouthwatering seafood dishes such as *ceviche* and breaded sea bass. Nearby is the more formal **Miramar** (Av. Charles Darwin, 6–11 P.M. daily, entrées $8–15), with views worthy of its name. Its location, right next to a beach filled with snoozing sea lions, is as good as the menu, which has a wide range of international and seafood dishes, including fish in coconut sauce and a long list of cocktails. The restaurant at **Hotel Miconia** (Av. Charles Darwin, tel. 5/252-0608, breakfast, lunch, and dinner daily, entrées $10) is also a good upscale option. Italian pizza and pasta are the main specialties, but the fried fish is also good.

Information and Services
The **CAPTURGAL tourist information office** (Ignacio Hernández, tel. 5/252-1124) and the **Municipal tourist office** (Darwin and 12 de Febrero, tel. 5/252-0119, www.sancristobal-galapagos.com) are both open 8 A.M.–noon and 2–5 P.M. Mon.–Fri. Telephone cabins are at several locations. Internet access can be found at the **Mockingbird Café** (Española and Ignacio Hernández, tel. 5/252-0092) and at

several offices along the waterfront. The **post office** is at the western end of Avenida Charles Darwin, past the municipal building.

Getting There and Around

Buses leave from the *malecón* half a dozen times daily for El Progreso in the highlands, or take a **taxi** (about $3). The interisland *lanchas* (speed-boat ferries) depart at 7 A.M. each morning to Santa Cruz (2 hours, $25 pp). For Isabela (2.5 hours, $25 pp), continue from Santa Cruz at 2:30 P.M.

EMETEBE (tel./fax 5/252-0615) has flights leaving most mornings at 8 A.M. for Baltra (30 minutes, $160 one-way) and Isabela (45 minutes, $160 one-way). San Cristóbal's **airport** is at the end of Alsacio Northia past the radio station; take a taxi ($2).

MARINE SITES

San Cristóbal has some excellent sites, and most are reachable on day trips from Baquerizo Moreno. They are usually quieter than many of the sites from Puerto Ayora because fewer visitors base themselves on San Cristóbal. Playa del Amor and **La Lobería** can all be visited independently, but the best marine sites require a boat trip.

◖ Isla Lobos and Kicker Rock (León Dormido)

Isla Lobos is a tiny rocky island 30 minutes north of Baquerizo Moreno by boat. Walking on the island is prohibited, so just jump straight in for excellent snorkeling with sea lions. This site is commonly combined with one of the Galápagos's most famous landmarks, Kicker Rock, also known as León Dormido (Sleeping Lion). Some people think it looks like a foot; others see the shape of a lion. Whichever name you prefer, this is one of the best snorkeling and dive sites in the archipelago. The sheer-walled volcanic tuff cone has been eroded in half with a narrow channel in between. This is a prime spot to see sharks—white-tipped reef sharks are commonly seen in and around the channel, while divers can go deeper to see awesome

© BEN WESTWOOD

THE GALÁPAGOS ISLANDS

Kicker Rock, also known as León Dormido, is one of the top snorkeling and diving sites on the islands.

schools of hammerheads. Sea turtles and a wide range of rays are also common. Boats are not allowed in the channel, so wait at either end while you snorkel or dive. Day trips often stop at the long white beach of **Cerro Brujo** afterward for more relaxing swimming, snorkeling, and sunbathing.

Punta Pitt

On the northeastern tip of San Cristóbal, the farthest site from the port is Punta Pitt. A wet landing is followed by a long and fairly strenuous hike (2 hours round-trip) past an olivine beach through thorny scrub and past tuff cones. The rewards are panoramic views and, more importantly, the only red-footed booby colony in the archipelago outside Genovesa, and the only spot where you can see all three booby species together. There are also populations of frigate birds, storm petrels, and swallow-tailed gulls. From here you can continue hiking for about two hours to reach the giant tortoise reserve at La Galapaguera.

SAN CRISTÓBAL HIGHLANDS

Avenida 12 de Febrero climbs north out of Baquerizo Moreno to El Progreso, a notorious former penal colony that's now a quiet farming village. There's not much to see, but for a unique experience, visit the **Casa del Ceibo** (near the main street, tel. 5/252-0248, $15 pp), a small house in a huge kapok tree. A maximum of two people can stay overnight here.

Tracks continue north from here to the settlement of Soledad, near an overlook at the southern end of the island, and east to Cerro Verde and Los Arroyos. About 10 kilometers east of Progreso, on the way to Cerro Verde, is a turnoff to the right along a steep dirt track to the **Laguna El Junco,** one of the few freshwater lakes in the Galápagos. At 700 meters elevation, the collapsed caldera is fed by rainwater and shelters wading birds, frigates, and seven species of Darwin's finches. It's also a good place to observe the typical highland tree ferns. A narrow trail encircles the rim and has spectacular panoramic views.

The road from Cerro Verde continues across the island to **Puerto Chino,** an isolated beach on the south coast. It's possible to camp here with permission from the national park office at the port.

A few kilometers inland from Puerto Chino is **La Galapaguera,** a giant tortoise reserve where San Cristóbal tortoises reside in 12 hectares of dry forest.

Most of these highland sights can be visited on a guided tour ($50 pp), or save money by sharing a taxi (from $30).

Santiago and Nearby Islands

SANTIAGO

Stepping onto the Galápagos's fourth-largest island, Santiago, also known as San Salvador, is rather like stepping back to the beginning of time. The effects of a long history of volcanic eruptions are everywhere on this island: Blackened lava dominates the landscape, and small plants and cacti are the first signs of life sprouting from the ashes. In recent years, though, destruction of a different kind has occurred on the island. Feral goats, introduced in the 1880s, grew to number over 100,000 in less than a century. A large-scale effort by the National Park Service and the Charles Darwin Research Center, however, had successfully eradicated the goats by 2006. Santiago cannot be visited on day trips at present and must be visited as part of a cruise tour.

The most popular sites on and near Santiago include the black lava trails of **Sullivan Bay,** the colonies of sea lions, seals and marine iguanas at **James Bay,** the famous **Pinnacle Rock** on Bartolomé (the most photographed site in the archipelago), and the bachelor sea lion colony and pelicans on **Rábida** island.

Sullivan Bay

One of the most popular sites on Santiago is this bay, on the east side of the island. An eruption in 1897 left the area covered in mesmerizing patterns of black lava, known as *pahoehoe* (a Hawaiian word for "rope") because of its tendency to buckle when it cools. The lava's glassy, almost ceramic feel comes from its high silicate content. The walk is a natural trail over 1.5 kilometers and takes about 1.5 hours. It is very uneven, so bring good walking shoes.

Buccaneer Cove

A freshwater source made this cove a haven for pirates in the 17th and 18th centuries. A few years back, divers found evidence in the shape of ceramic jars on the seabed, still intact and filled with wine and marmalade. Few tours stop here, but many boats sail slowly past to allow passengers to appreciate the steep cliffs and dark-red volcanic sand beach.

James Bay

On the western side of Santiago, a very popular visitor site is **Puerto Egas,** named after the owner of a salt mine that operated on the island in the 1960s. The long black-lava shoreline is home to a small colony of sea lions and large populations of marine iguanas.

A two-kilometer, three-hour loop trail leads inland past the rusted remains of the salt mine and a rather makeshift soccer field built by cruise-ship crews. Look to the skies and you may be lucky enough to see Galápagos hawks, circling in search of prey in the shape of Galápagos doves and mockingbirds.

Farther down the trail are the famous fur-seal grottoes, where the ocean fills a series of pools and underwater caverns occupied by seals, sea lions, and bright-red Sally Lightfoot crabs. There are great snorkeling opportunities here.

A second, lesser-used path, frequented by Darwin's finches and Galápagos doves, rises up 300 meters to **Volcán Sugarloaf.** At the north end of James Bay, five kilometers from Puerto Egas, is **Espumilla Beach,** another good spot for swimming and snorkeling. Sea turtles can sometimes be spotted and come ashore at night to lay their eggs. A two-kilometer trail leads inland through the mangroves to a lagoon populated by Galápagos flamingos, herons, and other wading birds.

◖ BARTOLOMÉ ISLAND

This tiny island off the southeast coast of Santiago is one of the most photographed sights in the archipelago. A wooden staircase leads 114 meters up to a summit with a breathtaking view—and for once this is no exaggeration. In the foreground the mangroves are flanked on either side by twin half-moon beaches. Rising up behind is the famous 40-meter Pinnacle Rock, a jagged lava formation, which has endured years of erosion as well as the U.S. Air Force using it as target practice in World War II. The blackened lava fields of Santiago in the background complete a perfect photograph.

After you've taken in the view, head to the mangrove-fringed beach below. There is excellent snorkeling with a small colony of sea lions as well as the chance to see the increasingly rare Galápagos penguins. Out of the water, a trail winds through the mangroves to the beach on the other side. Swimming is not allowed here, but look closely and you may glimpse stingrays, white-tipped sharks, and sea turtles that come ashore at night to lay their eggs. In the mangroves, bird-watchers should keep their eyes open for Galápagos hawks, herons, and oystercatchers. Bartolomé is included on many cruise itineraries, but as a day trip it has become more expensive and will set you back $125 pp with tour operators in Puerto Ayora.

RÁBIDA ISLAND

About five kilometers south of Santiago, this small island, also known as Jervis, is the exact geographic center of the Galápagos archipelago. There's a wet landing onto a rust-colored beach filled with dozens of sea lions stretched out; this is a great spot to walk among a colony and listen to their snorts and snoring. It's also an excellent place for snorkeling, but note that the male sea lion population is quite large (it's mainly a bachelor colony), so be careful. The beach is also one of the best places in the archipelago to see brown pelicans nesting. Chicks have a high mortality rate, so don't be surprised to stumble across numerous corpses, but there are plenty of live ones filling the skies, crying to their parents who are busy dive-bombing the oceans in search of the family lunch.

A 750-meter trail leads up to the island's 367-meter-high volcanic peak, which is covered in fragrant *palo santo* trees. There are good views over the steep cliffs on the other side. On the trail, look out for Galápagos hawks perched watchfully on tree branches, as well as Galápagos flamingos and yellow-crowned night herons stabbing at fish and shrimp in the salt ponds.

SOMBRERO CHINO

This tiny island off the southeastern tip of Santiago, just south of Bartolomé, is a volcanic cone with the rough shape of a "Chinese hat" (hence the name). Most cruise tours simply pass it to admire the shape because landing access is restricted to boats carrying 12 people or fewer. There's a small sea lion colony, marine iguanas, excellent snorkeling, and a short 700-meter trail across the island, which takes half an hour and commands impressive views.

Western Islands

Isabela and Fernandina are the youngest islands in the archipelago and have the most dramatic volcanic landscapes. They are also less visited than the central and southern islands, which only adds to their appeal.

From Isabela's port, **Puerto Villamil,** there are several sites close to town, notably the **Tortoise Breeding Center** (the largest in the archipelago) and the islets of **Las Tintoreras,** which offer great snorkeling with reef sharks. In the highlands, one of the best hikes in the Galápagos is to the steaming sulfur mines of **Sierra Negra,** Isabela's highest volcano, which boasts the second-largest crater in the world. Marine sites only accessible to cruise boats include *panga* rides into the mangroves of **Punta Moreno** to see penguins and **Elizabeth Bay** to see flightless cormorants. **Urbina Bay** contains a fascinating raised coral reef, and **Tagus Cove** is notable for the graffiti left by generations of pirates as well as a hike to the deep blue saline **Darwin Lake.**

West of Isabela is the archipelago's youngest and most volcanically active island, **Fernandina.** There is one visitor site at **Punta Espinosa,** which has a large population of nesting flightless cormorants as well as the largest colony of marine iguanas in the archipelago and a large sea lion colony.

ISABELA ISLAND

Isabela is by far the largest island in the Galápagos and accounts for half of the archipelago's total land mass at nearly 4,600 square kilometers. At 100 kilometers long, it's four times the size of Santa Cruz, the next largest island. The landscape is dominated by six intermittently active volcanoes—from north to south: Wolf (1,646 meters) and Ecuador (610 meters), which both straddle the equator, Darwin (1,280 meters), Alcedo (1,097 meters), Sierra Negra (1,490 meters), and Cerro Azul (1,250 meters), which was the latest to erupt, in May 2008.

The island's only port, Puerto Villamil, where most of the population of 2,000 lives, is slowly turning into a tourism hub, though on a much smaller scale than Puerto Ayora and Puerto Baquerizo Moreno. There are plenty of visitor sites near the port as well as excursions inland to the volcanoes, but many of the best coastal sites are on the western side of Isabela, only accessible to cruises.

As the giant of the archipelago, it's only fitting that Isabela has one of the largest populations of giant tortoises, which feed on the abundant vegetation in the highlands. There are five separate subspecies here, one for each volcano (excluding tiny Volcán Ecuador). The slopes of Volcán Alcedo have the biggest population—more than 35 percent of all the tortoises in the archipelago.

The west coast of the island has large populations of whales and dolphins as well as flightless cormorants, which dive down into the cool waters in search of fish and no longer need their wings. Isabela also has the largest populations of Galápagos penguins, although numbers fell dramatically as a result of the 1998 El Niño.

The tortoise population here has suffered considerably. Whalers used to hunt them, and more recently thousands of feral goats have eaten their vegetation; cows and donkeys trample on their eggs. Volcanic eruptions and a fire started by people that raged for five months in 1984 have also ravaged the landscapes. Things are improving, though, particularly after 100,000 goats were successfully eradicated in a huge government operation in the past decade, mainly employing Australian hunters in helicopters.

History
Whalers and pirates began visiting Isabela in the 18th century, hunting in the waters off the west coast and stopping over to gather tortoises as food for long voyages. The names of many of these ships are still carved into the rocks at Tagus Cove.

In 1946 it was the humans' turn to endure hardships on the island when a penal colony was built on the Sierra Negra's southern slopes. The best evidence of the brutal regime is the lava-rock *muro de las lagrimas* (wall of tears), which still stands near Puerto Villamil, a thoroughly pointless construction project built by luckless convicts over many years. Food supplies were scarce in those days, and usually consumed by the guards, leaving many convicts to starve to death. The notorious jail was closed in 1959.

PUERTO VILLAMIL AND VICINITY
About 2,000 people live in this small port on the southeast tip of Isabela. As well as fishing and a developing tourism industry, the locals have worked on all manner of projects—from sulfur mining in the nearby Sierra Negra volcano to lime production and coffee farming. The town is quite charming and a far more laid-back base than the two larger ports in the archipelago. With a small selection of hotels and restaurants and nearby beaches as well as lagoon and highland hikes, there's plenty to keep you busy for a few days.

Recreation and Tours
At the western edge of town is a set of lagoons with sizeable populations of flamingos that flock here to mate. **Poza de los Diablos** (Devil's Pool) is actually the largest lagoon in the entire archipelago. Wooden walkways take you past the lagoons before joining a trail through a forest.

Continue along the trail for 20 minutes (or take a taxi for $2) to reach the **Centro de Crianza** (Tortoise Breeding Center), a more impressive tortoise breeding center than the one at Charles Darwin Station on Santa Cruz. There are some 850 tortoises separated into eight enclosures as well as an information center documenting the life cycle of these fascinating creatures. It has an excellent program to boost the populations of Isabela's five subspecies.

Continue along the coast to the west another half an hour to reach the **Wall of Tears,** built by a penal colony in the 1940s. It's just a wall, but the brutal story behind it is interesting. The wall is 100 meters long and seven meters high and served no real purpose except punishment, which only adds to the tragedy of the men who suffered and died building it. There is a set of steps up to an impressive view of the wall and surrounding landscape. It's quite a walk to the wall (about an hour from town), so it's best done out of the heat of the day, or consider taking a taxi ($5) or a guided tour ($20 pp). You may be tempted to go swimming to cool off on the way back, and there is good surfing on the beaches west of the port.

Southeast of town is the best spot for snorkeling in a set of islets, **Las Tintoreras,** named after the reef sharks that frequent them. You can also spot sea lions, turtles, penguins, and white-tipped sharks, resting in the canals or under rocks. There is also a short trail around the islets, where Sally Lightfoot crabs scuttle. The islets are reachable from a jetty, but you must be accompanied by a guide. A tour ($25 pp) lasts 1–2 hours.

There are a couple of tour operators on the main plaza. The best is **Nautilus** (Antonio Gil and Las Fragatas, tel. 5/252-9076, www.nauti lustour.com). Tours are available to the Wall of Tears and various sites west of town ($20 pp), snorkeling at Las Tintoreras ($20 pp), and hiking to Sierra Negra (from $40 pp, depending on the group size).

Accommodations

There are fewer hotels here than in Baquerizo Moreno and Puerto Ayora, but prices are lower, and because the port is relatively quiet, it's possible to negotiate because hotels don't fill up that often. Accommodations on the beach are slightly pricier than inland. The best option for those on a tight budget is the informal **Posada del Caminante** (near Cormoran, tel. 5/252-9407, $15 s, $20 d) a 15-minute walk inland. Most guest rooms have kitchens, and there's a communal fridge and free laundry. In the center, the best-value budget hotels are **Rincon de George** (16 de Marzo and Antonio Gil, tel. 5/252-9214, $20 s, $30 d) and next door, **Hostal Villamil** (tel. 5/252-9180, $20 s, $30 d). Both offer comfortably furnished guest rooms with firm beds, hot water, and air-conditioning. The owner of Rincon de George is a registered tour guide. On the beach, you can find great ocean views and decent guest rooms at **The Dolphin House** (Antonio Gil, tel. 5/252-9138, $30 s, $45 d, breakfast included), but beware of the pair of roosters that are guaranteed to wake you up before dawn. Opposite is another attractive mid-range choice, **Volcano Hotel** (Antonio Gil, tel. 5/252-9034, $25 s, $40 d), with colorful guest rooms that have recently been renovated.

A mid-range option a few blocks inland that is popular with tour groups, **San Vicente** (Cormorant and Las Escalacias, tel. 5/252-9140, $30 s, $60 d, breakfast included) has comfortable guest rooms, private baths, air-conditioning, and hot water.

Puerto Villamil is beginning to cater to luxury land-based tours, and some top-end hotels have opened in the past few years. The swankiest hotel on the beach is the ideally located British-run **Albermarle** (Antonio Gil, tel. 5/252-9489, www.hotelalbemarle.com, $150 s or d, breakfast included). This two-story Mediterranean-style villa has guest rooms with stylish stone baths, high ceilings, and modern amenities. At the east end of town, the homey **Casa Marita** (Antonio Gil tel. 5/252-9301, www.casamaritagalapagos.com, $65 s, $100 d) has uniquely decorated guest rooms and suites. There's a jetted tub, a bar, a restaurant, and hammocks in the garden. Farther along, walking out of town toward the tortoise breeding center is the newest top-end hotel, **Iguana Crossing** (Antonio Gil, tel. 5/252-9484, www.iguanacrossing.com.ec, $200 s or d), which has immaculate guest rooms, a beautiful pool facing the beach, a spa, and a gourmet restaurant.

Food

Restaurant options in town are rather limited, mostly concentrated along the main road, Antonio Gil, parallel to the beach. Most of these do set menus for $4, although you often have to ask for it as they prefer to push the pricier menu items. The best restaurant in the center is probably **La Choza** (Antonio Gil, no phone, lunch and dinner daily, entrées $8–15), which serves oversize portions of barbecued meats in a rustic thatched hut. Farther along, **El Encanto de la Pepa** (Antonio Gil, no phone, lunch and dinner daily, entrées $5–7) is another good option, particularly for *ceviche*, breaded shrimp, and grilled fish. A cheaper option is **Tres Hermanos** (Antonio Gil, no phone, breakfast, lunch, and dinner daily, entrées $3–6), which offers set meals, snacks, and burgers. After dinner there is very little nightlife, but a good place for a drink is **Bar Beto** (Antonio Gil, no phone, 7 P.M.–midnight

Mon.–Sat.), a beach bar at the western edge of town. The cocktails are rather pricey, but the beer goes down well with the sea view.

Information and Services
The local **iTur tourist office** (16 de Marzo and Las Fragatas, tel. 5/301-6648) is two blocks inland. The **National Park office** (Antonio Gil and Piqueros, tel. 5/252-9178) is one block from the main plaza. Note that there is no bank or ATM on Isabela; some top-end hotels accept credit cards, but you need to bring enough cash for the duration of your stay.

Getting There and Around
Buses leave daily into the highlands, but you're better off exploring on a guided tour. **Taxis** can be picked up from near the main plaza and will take you around town for $1 and to nearby visitors sites for a little more. **EMETEBE** (Antonio Gil, tel. 5/252-9255) has flights to San Cristóbal and Baltra ($160 pp one-way). *Lanchas* (speed-boat ferries) shuttle to Puerto Ayora (2.5 hours, $30 pp one-way) at 6 A.M. daily from the main dock.

◖ Sierra Negra and the Highlands
The best excursion to take from Puerto Villamil and perhaps the most impressive geological sight in the entire archipelago is the hike up to the active **Sierra Negra,** Isabela's oldest and highest volcano. The last eruption was in 2005 and took geologists by surprise, so you can't trek right to the crater. However, there are two excellent treks—the shorter is to **Volcán Chico,** a fissure of lava cones northwest of the main crater. On this side, there is less mist and rain, offering spectacular views over the north of Isabela and across to Fernandina. This trek takes about four hours and is usually a combination of hiking and horseback riding. The longer trek is to **Las Minas de Azufre** (Sulfur Mines). It takes about 6–7 hours in total and is tougher, particularly in the rainy season, when it gets very muddy. Your toil will be rewarded, however, with fantastic views of the crater, which at 10 kilometers in diameter is the second-largest in the world after

Ngorongoro in Tanzania. The hike culminates in a dramatic descent into the yellow hills of the sulfur mines that spew out choking gas (hold your breath). Both treks can be booked with the tour operators in the port, but note that the longer trek is less common, so booking ahead is essential. **Nautilus** (Antonio Gil and Las Fragatas, tel. 5/252-9076, www.nautilus-tour.com) charges $40 pp. Wilmer Quezada is a particularly good local guide (tel. 8/687-8626 or 5/252-9326).

Marine Sites
All of the following visitor sites are off-limits to land-based visitors and are only accessible to cruise tours.

PUNTA MORENO
North of Cerro Azul, this site is reachable via a *panga* ride along the sea cliffs and into a grove of mangroves, where penguins and great blue herons are often seen. A two-kilometer hike inland along a *pahoehoe* lava flow leads to a handful of brackish ponds frequented in season by flamingos and white-cheeked pintails. There are impressive views of three of Isabela's volcanoes. Wear comfortable shoes because the lava rocks are difficult to negotiate in places.

ELIZABETH BAY
North of Punta Moreno, Elizabeth Bay has no landing site, so it can only be explored by *panga*. There are small populations of flightless cormorants, penguins, and marine iguanas in the bay. Farther in there is a set of shallow lagoons where you can see rays, turtles, and occasionally white-tipped sharks.

URBINA BAY
This bay was created by remarkable geological activity in 1954. A volcanic eruption lifted a chunk of seabed, including a coral reef, six meters above the water's surface. It's a somewhat surreal experience to see the coral littered with bones and shells of marine life. Flightless cormorants, pelicans and both land and marine iguanas can be seen here, and there are rays and turtles in the bay.

TAGUS COVE

This is the best place to see how humans have left a mark—literally—on the Galápagos islands. The rocks above this popular anchorage in the Bolívar Channel are covered in graffiti. It's a strange but interesting sight, with the oldest readable record from whalers dating from 1836.

The two-kilometer hike from the cove to the interior is quite strenuous but worth the effort. A dry landing leads to a trail through a steep gully to a wooden staircase and then along a gravel track. At the top is an impressive view over deep-blue **Darwin Lake.** This eroded crater is 12 meters deep, and the waters have a high salt content, so it's largely lifeless. Scientists have concluded that seawater seeped in through the porous lava rocks beneath the surface. The small, round pebbles covering the trails began as raindrops that collected airborne volcanic ash and hardened before hitting the ground. The trail leads to the lower lava slopes of Volcán Darwin, and there are spectacular views over the entire island of Isabela.

After the hike, there is a *panga* ride, and you can cool off with some good snorkeling along the rocky northern shore. Highlights include sea turtles, Galápagos penguins, flightless cormorants, and sea lions.

OTHER SITES

There are various other sites on Isabela, most of which have restricted access. Just north of Tagus Cove is **Punta Tortuga,** a beach surrounded by mangroves. Farther north, **Punta Vicente Roca** has good snorkeling and diving but no landing site at the base of small Volcán Ecuador. At Isabela's northern tip, **Punta Albermarle** was a U.S. radar base during World War II. There is no landing site, but there is plenty of birdlife to see from the boat, including flightless cormorants and penguins.

On the east side of Isabela, there is a landing site at **Punta García,** one of the few places on this side where flightless cormorants can be seen. This is the beginning for the trail up to **Volcán Alcedo,** famous for its seven-kilometer-wide crater. The ascent takes 6–7 hours over 14 kilometers. Along the way is a fascinating landscape of steaming fumaroles, ancient craters, lava flows, abundant birdlife, and hundreds of giant tortoises living on the volcano's slopes. Special permits must be obtained for this hike, which involves a time-consuming bureaucratic process, and it's not included on most itineraries.

FERNANDINA ISLAND

Fernandina is special even by Galápagos standards. The westernmost island in the archipelago is one of the few that have escaped the invasion of introduced species, and the island's pristine ecosystem has been preserved. This island is also less visited than most of the others due to its remote location, and it retains the air of a land that time forgot.

At under 1 million years old, Fernandina is the youngest volcanic island in the archipelago and also the most active. Volcán La Cumbre has erupted several times in recent years, most spectacularly in 1968 when the caldera collapsed more than 300 meters, and most recently in April 2009.

Punta Espinosa

Fernandina only has one visitor site, on the island's northeast corner, across from Isabela's Tagus Cove. A dry landing among the mangroves leads 250 meters to a sandy point partly covered by rough lava from recent flows. Nearby is the dramatic sight of the largest colony of marine iguanas in the archipelago sunning themselves on the rocks.

There is a large sea lion colony, and this is also one of the biggest nesting sites of flightless cormorants. Watch out for males returning from fishing to bring lunch to their mates, who sit in a tangled nest of seaweed and twigs near the water's edge.

A longer 750-meter trail leads over jagged lava spotted with lava cacti (bring sturdy shoes). Brilliant vermillion flycatchers often sit in the mangrove branches. The tour usually ends with a *panga* ride out into the strait, where schools of dolphins are often seen.

Southern Islands

South of Santa Cruz, Floreana can be visited both on day trips and on cruises. The island has a fascinating history, beautiful landscapes in the highlands, a rather quirky post office, and excellent snorkeling. Española is no longer reachable on day trips, so you need to be on a cruise tour to see its albatross breeding site.

Floreana's best sites include **Punta Cormorant,** which has populations of flamingos and other wading birds, the centuries-old post box at **Post Office Bay,** and excellent snorkeling spots at the submerged volcanic cone of **Devil's Crown** as well as **Enderby** and **Champion Island.**

On Española's west side, **Punta Suárez** shouldn't be missed—it's the biggest breeding site in the world for waved albatross and a great place to see them taking off, landing, and performing their dancing mating ritual. On the northeast side of the island, there are opportunities to snorkel with sea lions, reef sharks, and marine turtles at **Gardner Bay.**

FLOREANA ISLAND

As the lush hills of Floreana come into view, it's difficult to believe that such a serene island could have such a troubled history. The population of the island today stands at less than 200 residents, but Floreana was actually the first island in the archipelago to be populated.

History

In the 18th century, whalers and pirates were drawn to a rare springwater supply in the hills as well as fresh meat in the form of the island's giant tortoises. Rats, cats, and goats were introduced onto Floreana, causing untold damage and decimating the tortoise population. The whalers would spend so long at sea that they decided to set up a post office on the island as the only means of communicating with their families. You can still see evidence of the early settlers in carvings in the rocks in caves in the highlands.

In 1807, Floreana had its first permanent resident, Irishman Patrick Watkins. He was marooned here and lived for two years by growing vegetables. Eventually he stole a ship's longboat and left with a small crew, but he arrived alone in Guayaquil weeks later. Nobody knows what became of his crew.

After Ecuador's independence in 1830, Floreana was named after the country's first president, Juan José Flores, and it became a penal colony. Soon afterward, in 1841, Herman Melville, author of *Moby Dick,* visited the island and wrote about its history, increasing worldwide interest.

In the 1930s, the arrival of several German settlers looking for an escape to paradise further disturbed Floreana's tiny community. First a reclusive dentist, Dr. Friedrich Ritter, arrived with his lover, followed by the Wittmer family, and finally a troublesome woman, who claimed to be a baroness, arrived with three lovers. The story of deaths and disappearances that ensued is a tale worthy of a Hollywood movie and has been recounted in several books.

Nowadays, Floreana is a comparatively quiet island. While the archipelago's three other ports have developed rapidly, Puerto Velasco Ibarra has a population of less than 200. Of the invasive species, goats have been eradicated, but rats are far more difficult to remove, and the endemic mockingbird is just one species that is now endangered as a result. The tortoise population, which was hunted to extinction on Floreana in the 19th century, has been boosted by a breeding center for reintroduced tortoises in the highlands. There are day trips daily from Santa Cruz; very few visitors stay on the island, although there are a couple of hotels.

Puerto Velasco Ibarra

This tiny port, with less than 200 inhabitants, lives in comparative isolation from the rest of the islands. There are few basic services here, which is why most visits are confined to day trips. There are no banks, limited electricity, and the only mail service is through the Post Office Bay barrel.

DEATH IN PARADISE

By the early 20th century, the world woke up to the wonders of the Galápagos, and it was only a matter of time before Europeans were attracted to escape to a place depicted in books and newspapers as a slice of Pacific paradise. A certain Dr. Friedrich Ritter, an eccentric German doctor with a love of nudism, was so enchanted that in 1929 he set off for Floreana with his lover, Dora Strauch, a former patient disabled by multiple sclerosis. Not a man to do things by halves, he foresaw a problem with the lack of dental facilities on the islands, and removed all his teeth, replacing them with metal dentures before traveling.

The couple arrived in Floreana and lived a quiet, nude life of gardening. When Ritter sent dispatches about their experiences back to Germany, however, others inevitably thought it would be a good idea to join them. Visitors came and went, but most were deterred by the challenges of setting up life on such a remote island. The Wittmer family was different, though— father Heinz, pregnant wife Margaret, and their sickly 12-year-old son Harry arrived in 1932. Margaret wrote of the "Herculean task" that confronted them in building a life on Floreana, and their second son, Rolf, was born in a cave, the first recorded birth in the archipelago. Ritter, however, infamously unsociable and a misogynist, was none too pleased at the new arrivals and steadfastly refused to help them, keeping his food supplies to himself.

Shortly afterward, an Austrian woman in her early 40s stepped off a boat wearing riding breeches and carrying a pearl-handled revolver. She called herself Baroness Eloise Wagner von Bosquet and was accompanied by two men— Robert Philipsson, whom she referred to initially as her husband, and her lover, Rudolf Lorenz. As soon as she arrived, the baroness began causing trouble. She seemed to regard the island as her own and began rifling through the post and supplies, taking what she liked. She bathed naked in the island's only drinking water supply and began charging the other islanders for supplies that she had ordered. The baroness also made no secret of her desire to open a luxury hotel on Floreana and charmed the governor of the islands into giving her 10 square kilometers of land for the construction. United by their dislike of the baroness, Dr. Ritter and the Wittmer family developed closer contacts, and Ritter made formal complaints about her to the Ecuadorian government, but to no avail. By this time, the residents on the islands were well-known to the world's media, and luxury yachts began stopping off to see what all the fuss was about.

There are a couple of hotels on the island, and it's possible that in the next decade Floreana may develop further, but that's anybody's guess. The **Pensión Wittmer** (tel. 5/252-0150 or 5/252-9506, $30 s, $50 d) has guest rooms and bungalows overlooking the beach with fans, private baths, and hot water. Three meals cost an additional $20 pp. **Red Mangrove Lava Lodge** (Floreana tel. 5/252-4905, Santa Cruz tel. 5/252-6564, www.redmangrove.com, $168 s, $186 d, breakfast included) has been built recently—10 oceanfront pine cabins sleep 2–3 with private baths and porches overlooking a black lava beach.

Buses leave for the highlands early every morning. The island's only water source, **Asilo de la Paz,** is eight kilometers into the highlands, a half-hour drive or a three-hour walk. If you decide to stay on the island, you can sometimes hitch a ride back to Puerto Ayora with one of the day tours.

Punta Cormorant

The visit to this site on the north side of Floreana starts with a wet landing on a green-tinged beach, colored by olivine minerals. A 720-meter trail leads up to a saltwater lagoon, which is a good spot to see flamingos and other wading birds such as white-cheeked pintails, stilts, and gallinules. Along the trail, Floreana's comparatively lush surroundings can be appreciated. Among the vegetation is abundant

Meanwhile, the baroness's love triangle started to deteriorate. Lorenz, initially the baroness's favorite, was jilted and demoted to servant, and the baroness took up with Philipsson while eagerly pursuing other men who visited Floreana. Lorenz, humiliated by his treatment and bearing scars from beatings, told residents that the baroness's title was bogus, her marriage a sham, and that she had previously worked as a nightclub dancer and even a spy.

Events took a turn for the worse in March 1934 when the island experienced a severe drought. The baroness announced abruptly that she was leaving for Tahiti with Philipsson, as if it were a day trip rather than a 5,000-kilometer voyage. No boat was sighted, and nobody saw her leave the island, but the Baroness nor Philipsson were ever seen again. Dora Strauch later recalled hearing a bloodcurdling scream in the middle of the night. Lorenz's behavior became increasingly erratic after the baroness's disappearance, while Dr. Ritter seemed strangely calm.

To this day, what happened to the baroness remains a mystery. If she was indeed murdered, Lorenz is generally agreed to be the prime suspect, while Dr. Ritter didn't entirely escape suspicion. Neither lasted long enough to defend themselves, though. Lorenz finally raised enough money in July to take a boat to San Cristóbal with a Norwegian captain Nuggerud, but they never made it. Four months later, their bodies washed up on remote Marchena in the north, and evidence suggested that they had starved to death. Witter's demise in November 1934 was equally mysterious. According to Dora Rauch, she accidentally poisoned their chickens with pork meat. Not wanting to waste the chicken meat, she killed them and boiled them, thinking that this would destroy the poison. Despite being a vegetarian, Witter apparently ate it and fell gravely ill from food poisoning. He died a few days later, allegedly cursing his lover with his dying breath.

Dora Strauch returned to Germany and wrote a book titled *Satan Came to Eden*. She died in 1942. The Wittmers continued to live on the island, and Margaret's son Rolf opened a successful tour company; later the family opened a small hotel, both of which still operate today. Margaret wrote a book that included the events of the 1930s titled *Floreana: A Woman's Pilgrimage to the Galápagos*. She lived to age 95, dying in 2000.

Whether Hollywood will wake up to Floreana's remarkable story of death and intrigue remains to be seen.

birdlife, including yellow warblers and flycatchers. Beyond the lagoon is a beautiful white-sand beach, nicknamed Flour Beach for its incredibly fine sand. Stingrays and spotted eagle rays are common near the beach, and sea turtles nest here November–February. There are signs to keep you out of their nesting areas, but you may be lucky enough to see them swimming. Note that snorkeling and swimming are not allowed. The only drawback of this site is its perplexing name—there are no flightless cormorants here.

Post Office Bay

This is one of the quirkiest sites in the Galápagos. You wouldn't imagine that a mailbox would be of much appeal, but it has an interesting history and is also a bit of lighthearted fun. Back in 1793, whalers began the practice of leaving mail in a barrel for homeward-bound ships to collect. Crews would then hand-deliver the letters to their destination in a remarkable act of camaraderie. These days, the tradition has been carried on, mainly by visitors. Leave a postcard for a fellow national to collect, and take one home with you. Tradition dictates that you should deliver it in person, but paying the postage is probably preferable these days to turning up on a stranger's doorstep. The barrel has evolved into a wooden box on a pole surrounded by an assortment of junk. The visit lands you directly on the brown-sand beach. Just a few meters beyond the barrel is a lava tunnel, which you often need to wade through water to reach, and the rusted remains of a Norwegian fishing operation dating back to the 1920s. There is also a soccer field used by boat crews, who may invite you to join in a game. Be aware that there are sizeable populations of introduced wasps here, and their sting is painful, so be careful.

🄲 Corona del Diablo (Devil's Crown)

Offshore from Post Office Bay, the jagged peaks of this submerged volcanic cone poke out of the water and supply its name, Devil's Crown. Its nooks and crannies offer some of the best snorkeling in the islands, either outside the ring or in the shallow inner chamber, which is reached through a side opening. There is a rich variety of tropical fish—parrotfish, angelfish, and damselfish—and you can occasionally see sea lions and sharks. Note that the current can be quite strong on the seaward side.

Enderby and Champion Island

These two sites are very popular with snorkelers and divers. Enderby is an eroded tuff cone where you can snorkel with playful sea lions, and Champion Island is a small offshore crater, a popular nesting sight for boobies. Landing is not allowed, but the snorkeling is good.

ESPAÑOLA ISLAND

The southernmost island in the Galápagos is also the oldest. The island's reputation as one of the top spots for bird-watching has led to day trips from San Cristóbal and Santa Cruz being phased out, and you now need to be on a cruise to come here. The waved albatross that nest here April–November are the island's main draw. Witness these enormous birds taking off and landing and enjoy their amusing mating dance.

Gardener Bay

On the northeast side of Española, this beautiful crescent beach is reached by a wet landing. There are no hikes, so the main draw is the excellent snorkeling. Highlights include frolicking with playful sea lions (there's a colony here) as well as spotting stingrays or occasionally white-tipped sharks. The beach is an important nesting site for marine turtles,

Corona del Diablo is an excellent snorkeling and dive site.

so you might be lucky enough to see them. **Turtle Rock,** a short *panga* ride offshore, is another good snorkeling spot with a rich variety of bright tropical fish such as Moorish idols, damselfish, and parrotfish.

On the beach, you can walk among the sea lion colony, although try to give the males a wide berth. At the east end, there are marine iguanas and Sally Lightfoot crabs, and you can often see the endemic Hood mockingbirds.

◖ Punta Suárez

On the western tip of Española, Punta Suárez is one of the top visitor sites in the Galápagos. A wet landing leads to a trail toward the cliffs on the south side of the point. Along the way, there is a large blue-footed booby colony, and you need to watch your step as these tame birds remain utterly unconcerned by your presence and sit in the middle of the trail.

The best is yet to come. If you visit April–November, farther along the trail is the biggest breeding site of waved albatross in the world.

Seeing these birds taking off from the cliffs with their 2.5-meter wingspans is quite a sight. Seeing them land is also impressive but rather less elegant as they often fall over, being somewhat unsteady on their feet after long flights. If you're lucky, you can witness the entertaining courtship as the couple dance around each other clacking and calling skyward.

This site is teeming with birdlife, and aside from the boobies and albatross, you can see Galápagos hawks, Galápagos doves, swallow-tailed gulls, oystercatchers, red-billed tropic birds, and finches. The views of the cliffs below are equally impressive, with waves crashing onto rocks and water spurting high into the air through blowholes. The rocks are often covered in marine iguanas sunning themselves; these iguanas are more colorful than those found on other islands, with turquoise tinges to their backs and legs, perhaps the result of eating algae endemic to Española.

The entire trail is about 1,600 meters long and takes about two hours.

Northern Islands

Genovesa, Darwin, and Wolf are the remotest islands that can be visited in the archipelago, and most boats need to travel overnight. However, each have their unique attractions: **Genovesa** for its birds, particularly red-footed boobies at **Darwin Bay Beach** and **Prince Philip's Steps. Darwin** and **Wolf** rank among the best dive sites in the world.

GENOVESA

Genovesa, also known as Tower Island and even Booby Island, is famed for its abundant birdlife, notably red-footed boobies, but it takes some getting to—about eight hours overnight, so stock up on seasickness tablets.

Darwin Bay Beach

After passing rocks decorated with graffiti from visiting ships, you'll reach a wet landing onto the beach. A 1.5-kilometer trail leads

inland to the saltbushes filled with the nests of red-footed boobies and frigate birds. Masked boobies and swallow-tailed gulls also nest here, and you may also spot storm petrels and short-eared owls.

Another branch of the trail leads over rough rocks next to a series of tidal pools, where you can see yellow-crowned night herons half-asleep by day. Other species to watch for include mockingbirds, Galápagos doves, and Darwin's finches. The *Opuntia* cacti you see on the trail are noticeably softer than on other islands; scientists believe this is because the plants don't need to defend themselves against giant tortoises (there has never been a tortoise population on the island).

Prince Philip's Steps

Named in honor of a royal visit in the 1960s, this site (also known as El Barranco), near the

THE GALÁPAGOS ISLANDS

tip of Darwin Bay's eastern arm, is limited to boats of 16 people or fewer. A *panga* ride along the bottom of the cliffs provides glimpses of frigate birds and red-billed tropic birds before a steep-railed stairway leads to a dramatic 1.5-kilometer trail along the top of the cliffs. Masked and red-footed boobies nest here with frigate birds lurking nearby ready to scavenge. The *panga* ride and hike take about two hours.

WOLF AND DARWIN ISLANDS

These tiny islands, around 220 kilometers northwest of the main island group, are hidden jewels visited only by diving tours. It takes a full night to get here, but the rewards are rich indeed—these islands rank among the best diving in the world. The waters around Wolf and Darwin attract whale sharks June–November. Other shark species commonly seen are hammerheads, Galápagos sharks, and reef sharks. Manta rays, dolphins, and turtles also abound.

MARCHENA AND PINTA ISLANDS

Midway between Wolf and Genovesa in the far north of the archipelago, these two medium-sized islands are closed to visitors, although diving is possible in the waters off the coast of Marchena. Pinta is famous as the original home of Lonesome George, and giant tortoises are currently being reintroduced on the island. Marchena has a 343-meter volcano at its center that erupted in 1991.

BACKGROUND

The Land

The old adage "small is beautiful" applies perfectly to Ecuador. There are few places in the world where such a rich variety of breathtaking landscapes are packed into such a diminutive area. The second-smallest Spanish-speaking country in South America (only Uruguay, the Guyanas, and Suriname are smaller) extends over 269,178 square kilometers on the northwestern shoulder of the continent. Ecuador is roughly the size of Colorado and actually slightly bigger than Britain, a fact that most locals are reluctant to believe.

From a tourism point of view, its comparative small size is a huge asset. While larger Latin American countries have diverse landscapes spread over vast areas that involve long journeys, you can get from one end of Ecuador to the other in a day. And what a day it is—moving from Pacific beaches up through Andean foothills past snowy volcanic peaks and down again to cloud forests and swaths of rainforest on the edge of the Amazon. The locals are proud to call their country "three countries in one" (or four if you include the Galápagos Islands), and from a geographical point of view, it is no exaggeration. Colombia lies to the north and Peru to the east and south, and the Equator, which gave the country its name, passes through just north of Quito.

GEOGRAPHY
The Sierra

Although the Andes and their foothills fill only about one-quarter of Ecuador's land area, they certainly pack a punch with 10 peaks over 5,000 meters and another dozen over 4,000 meters. Two parallel mountain ranges run north–south—the Cordillera Occidental (Western Range) and the wider and higher Cordillera Oriental (Eastern Range). Between them is one of the most spectacular drives on the continent, along the Panamericana south of Quito, through the aptly named Avenue of the Volcanoes.

The 10 main intermountain basins, called *hoyas,* are where about half of Ecuador's population lives. All of the main cities in the Sierra—from north to south, Tulcán, Ibarra, Otavalo, Quito, Latacunga, Ambato, Riobamba, Cuenca, and Loja—sit at 2,000–3,000 meters above sea level. The foothills, called *nudos,* climb up to dramatic Andean grassland, *páramo,* which surrounds the icy peaks. West of the Cordillera Occidental the land drops down dramatically to cloud forests with rivers rushing down to the coastal plains. East of the Cordillera Oriental is an even more dramatic descent to the lush, humid Amazon basin.

The Coast

The coastal lowlands stretch from the foothills of the Andes to 2,237 kilometers of Pacific coastline. The seemingly endless agricultural plains are punctuated by low mountain chains such as the Mache and Chindul on the central coast and the Colonche near Guayaquil. None climb higher than 1,000 meters. The north is lusher and wetter, with tropical rainforests inland from the beaches. These blend into tropical dry forest in the center of Manabí Province, although most of this has sadly been destroyed. Farther south, the landscapes become more barren, fading into dry, thorny scrublands. Mangroves used to line much of the coast, and while many have given way to the ravages of shrimp farming, there are still pockets that have escaped. The entire coastline is lined with sandy beaches, most of which are exposed to strong Pacific currents, heaven for surfers but less ideal for swimmers.

Two main rivers carve through the lowlands. To the north, Río Esmeraldas flows 320 kilometers to the Pacific. Farther south, Río Babahoyo and Río Daule merge into Río Guayas, which flows for 60 kilometers into the

Gulf of Guayaquil. It is the widest river on the Pacific coast of the Americas.

Isla Puná in the Gulf of Guayaquil is the largest island in Ecuador outside the Gálapagos. There are other, far smaller islands lining the coast, the best known being Isla de la Plata in Manabí and the rather run-down island of Muisne in Esmeraldas.

Around half of the country's population lives on the coast. Guayaquil, with a population of well over 3 million and rising, is by far the biggest city, and Portoviejo, Manta, Machala, and Santo Domingo all have populations over 200,000.

The Oriente

While only 5 percent of the population lives here, Ecuador's slice of Amazon rainforest makes up half of the country's land area. It used to be far more before Peru annexed a huge section following the 1941 war, a long-running dispute that was only settled in 1998. East of the Andes, the land slopes down to secondary rainforest and then large swathes of primary rainforest that stretch to the Colombian and Peruvian borders and over 2,000 kilometers to the Atlantic coast of Brazil. The region's pristine environment has been affected by oil exploration, but the jewel in the crown, Yasuní National Park, remains protected as one of the world's biodiversity hot spots.

There is a cluster of population areas, but only Lago Agrio has more than 50,000 people. In descending order come Puyo, Coca, Tena, and Macas, the last two being the most scenic towns. East of these towns, the rivers are the main mode of transportation. In the north, Río Coca and Río Aguarico feed into Río Napo, Ecuador's longest river at 855 kilometers. Río Pastaza drains Pastaza Province and lies just north of Río Zamora, which becomes Río Santiago in Peru.

GEOLOGY

It comes as no surprise that a country that boast an Avenue of Volcanoes has a violent geological heritage. The country sits right on the Pacific Rim of Fire where two tectonic plates—the

IS SHE GONNA BLOW?

Ecuador and the Galápagos are home to more than 30 active or dormant volcanoes, 10 of which have erupted in the past decade. The following is a list of the country's most active peaks with dates of the most recent eruption.

ON THE ECUADORIAN MAINLAND

- Antisana: 1802
- Cayambe: 1786
- Chacana: 1760
- Cotopaxi: 1907
- Guagua Pichincha: 1999
- Reventador: 2008
- Sangay: 2009
- Sumaco: 1933
- Tungurahua: 2011

IN THE GALÁPAGOS

- Alcedo (Isabela): 1995
- Cerro Azul (Isabela): 2008
- Darwin: 1813
- La Cumbre (Fernandina): 2009
- Pinta: 1929
- Sierra Negra (Isabela): 2005
- Santiago: 1904
- Wolf: 1982

Nazca Plate and the American Plate—grind together. The result is a volcanologist's dream that sometimes becomes a nightmare for the local population.

About 65 of Ecuador's peaks began as **volcanoes,** and at least six have been recently active. Cotopaxi, one of the world's highest

MOUNTAIN HIGHS

A variety of high-altitude climbing options will keep mountaineers plenty busy in Ecuador. Beginners will find the country an excellent training ground for higher, more difficult ascents elsewhere, and there are certainly enough challenging climbs for seasoned veterans as well.

Several peaks, such as Pasochoa, Fuya Fuya, and Guagua Pichincha, are good starters for acclimating and getting into shape with minimum special equipment or training. Slightly higher training climbs include Rumiñahui and Iliniza Sur. Modest technical gear will do for the big three – Chimborazo, Cotopaxi, and Cayambe. El Altar is considered the most difficult ascent in the country. Sangay and Tungurahua and currently off-limits due to volcanic activity.

When planning your adventure, remember that many major peaks have roads leading close to or part way up their bases. The ascents themselves can be straightforward, but the conditions and routes vary drastically from year to year, even day to day. Never underestimate the mountains. Although climatic conditions will differ among regions, December–January are generally the best months to climb.

An experienced and responsible guide can make the difference between success and failure – and life and death. Always go with a licensed and qualified guide. For more information on guided hikes, contact **ASEGUIM,** the Ecuadorian Mountain Guide Association (tel. 2/223-4109, 3-6 P.M. Mon., Tues., and Thurs., www.aseguim.org). Also see each chapter's individual city listings for more information on local guides.

The following chart shows the heights of many of Ecuador's loftiest peaks. These figures come from the most trustworthy source – the 1979 Instituto Geográfico Militar (IGM) surveys.

Mountain	Height (meters)	Volcanic Activity	Glacier/Snow
Chimborazo	6,310	No	Glacier
Cotopaxi	5,897	Yes	Glacier
Cayambe	5,790	Yes	Glacier
Antisana	5,704	Yes	Glacier
El Altar	5,319	Yes	Glacier
Iliniza Sur	5,263	No	Glacier
Sangay	5,230	Yes	Glacier

active volcanoes, last erupted strongly in 1877 and has destroyed nearby Latacunga on a number of occasions. It was largely quiet in the 20th century, but climbers that reach the summit can sometimes see smoke coming from the crater. Antisana, El Altar, and the Pichinchas were all active in the 20th century. The most recent eruptions include Guagua Pichincha, which showered Quito in ash in 1999. Reventador, the aptly named "Exploder," duly exploded in 2002 in Ecuador's biggest eruption in decades. Sangay is one of the most active volcanoes on earth, with a constant pool of lava burbling in its crater. By far the show-stealer in the past decade has been Tungurahua ("throat of fire" in Kichwa) which awoke from an 80-year sleep in 1999, forcing an evacuation of nearby tourist town Baños. It has since erupted in 2006, 2008, and 2010 and remains highly volatile. Luckily for Baños, the town lies on the opposite side to the crater, and even in a full-scale eruption, a showering of ash is the worst it has experienced—so far.

The position of Baños just eight kilometers

Mountain	Height (meters)	Volcanic Activity	Glacier/Snow
Iliniza Norte	5,126	No	Rare
Carihuairazo	5,020	No	Glacier
Tungurahua	5,016	Yes	Glacier
Cotacachi	4,939	No	Rare
Sincholagua	4,893	No	Rare
Quilindaña	4,878	No	Rare
Guagua Pichincha	4,794	Yes	Rare
Corazón	4,788	No	Rare
Chiles	4,768	No	Rare
Rumiñahui	4,712	No	Rare
Rucu Pichincha	4,700	No	Rare
Sara Urcu	4,676	No	Rare
Imbabura	4,630	No	Rare
Atacazo	4,410	Yes	Rare
Fuya Fuya	4,262	No	No
Cerro Negro	4,260	No	No
Pasochoa	4,200	No	No

from Tungurahua is indicative of a recurrent problem in the Andes. Population areas have been built too close to active volcanoes and remain vulnerable to lava flows and mudslides. Even when towns such as Latacunga were destroyed three times in the 18th and 19th centuries, they were rebuilt in the same precarious position.

As destructive as volcanic eruptions are earthquakes. In 1987 an earthquake in the northern Oriente killed hundreds of people and caused $1 billion in damage, including the destruction of 40 kilometers of oil pipeline. In 1998 a quake of magnitude 7.1 devastated the coastal city of Bahía de Caráquez.

On a smaller scale but equally deadly are **landslides,** sometimes triggered by volcanic eruptions or earthquakes and more commonly by heavy rain. Avalanches of melted ice, snow, mud, and rocks can reach 80 kilometers per hour when careening downhill, and there are landslides every year in the Andes and the foothills. Thirty-nine people were killed in a landslide near Papallacta in 2001, and five people were killed in the Pastaza Valley outside Baños in 2010.

CLIMATE

There are not four seasons here on the equator; instead, Ecuador has four radically different geographical zones, each with its own climate. At high elevations, temperature fluctuations are such that you can be sweltering at midday and freezing cold the same evening. On the coast December April you could be sunbathing under clear blue skies in the morning and later flee a torrential downpour that stops as suddenly as it starts.

In the highlands, the temperature averages 15°C but varies widely through the day—it can gets quite hot at midday due to the elevation and correspondingly cold at night, particularly above 2,500 meters. The driest, warmest season is June–September, and the coldest is December–February, when temperatures sometimes drop to 0°C at night.

The Sierra

The Andes climate is often vaunted as ideally "springlike," but this is an oversimplification. You will likely wake up to a chill in the air, but it can heat up quickly at midday and plunge to wintry temperatures at night. At this elevation, cloud cover makes a huge difference, so be prepared by carrying 2–3 layers of clothes. Daytime temperatures average 15–20°C, occasionally peaking at 25°C, with nights falling to 7–8°C, but sometimes dropping to 0°C.

The rainy season runs for over half the year, October–May. It's far less dramatic than on the coast, with regular showers, most commonly in the afternoon and evening. The driest, warmest season runs June–September.

The Coast

There's a far more dramatic difference in the seasons on the coast, where the climate is clearly defined by two contrasting ocean currents. The Equatorial Counter Current from the north brings heat, humidity, and heavy rain December–April. Flooding is common in rural and urban areas, and some roads become impassable. The sun quickly burns through, and it gets very hot, averaging 30–35°C, getting even hotter inland in cities like Guayaquil and Portoviejo, the hottest city in Ecuador.

Every few years, the rainy season is made far worse by the famous **El Niño** climate pattern, which in Ecuador brings abnormal amounts of rain. Flooding wreaks havoc throughout the coastal provinces and disturbs wildlife dependent on stable ocean temperatures.

After May, the Humboldt Current comes up from the south, bringing cooler, dry weather and hardly any rain June–November. The weather can still be hot but averages 25–30°C and gets cooler at night, when you may require a light sweater. The cloudy, windy conditions verge on depressing in the beach resorts in July–August.

The Oriente

It's not called the rainforest for nothing, so come prepared to get wet. In the Oriente, it's not a question of whether it will rain, but rather how much. The wettest period is June–August, while September–December is drier. Daily highs average 30°C, with the nighttime lows reaching 20°C. Rain usually arrives in the afternoon, so tours tend to start early with this in mind. However, the coming of the rains in the rainforest is, for many people, a highlight of their visit. An eerie calm falls on the forest as the sky darkens and a low rumble quickly erupts into a deluge, which often stops as quickly as it starts, before the clouds clear and the sun breaks through again before sunset.

The Galápagos

The climate in the Galápagos more or less mirrors that of the coast, with the two ocean currents pulling the strings. December–April, seas are calmer and the weather mostly sunny and hot, with rain falling mainly in the highlands of the larger islands. June–November, the weather is cooler, and the sea becomes rougher and colder for swimming. The temperature peaks at over 30°C in March and cools to the low 20s in August.

ENVIRONMENTAL ISSUES
Problems

Ecuador has one of the highest rates of deforestation in Latin America. The nation has lost 4 million hectares in the past 20 years, according to the United Nations, accounting for nearly 30 percent of its total forested areas. The problem is most acute in the Oriente, with virgin rainforest particularly under threat.

Pressure from the highest population density in South America is the clearest engine for deforestation. More and more people need land for cultivation and cattle grazing, as well as wood for cooking, heating, and building. A short-term economic vision encourages Amazonian settlers to "improve" their land by clearing and planting it. Timber harvesters are paid on the basis of sheer volume, not on the amount of useful wood cut. The problem is compounded by the poor quality of the shallow soil below the rainforest. After a few years of slashing and burning, the soil becomes useless, and further deforestation is carried out to farm more land.

Reforestation also causes problems. In the highlands, many native plant species have been replaced by fragrant stands of eucalyptus brought from Australia in the 19th century for timber. The fast-growing trees, whose long, shallow roots suck up lots of water, have spread like weeds.

Oil exploration has been mainland Ecuador's biggest ecological disaster in recent years, and negligent extraction practices resulted in millions of liters of oil leaking into the environment in the 1970s and 1980s. Entire ecosystems were destroyed, local indigenous communities were displaced, and the water supplies were poisoned, resulting in rising cancer rates and lawsuits, the most famous of which, against Chevron-Texaco, is ongoing after nearly 20 years of legal wrangling.

Mining is another problem threatening many of the primary western cloud forests, and increasing state control of the industry has done little to improve the situation as the government looks to fund its rising budget. The search for copper and other precious metals has caused rifts in local communities as proposals for huge strip mines come with offers of schools and dubious employment benefits. The use of chemicals in the extraction processes will pollute many of the pristine water sources in these areas.

Meanwhile, the Galápagos Islands are in danger of being loved to death. Organized tourism, which began with 4,500 visitors in 1970, has spiraled out of control to more than 160,000 in 2010. Immigration rates have also soared, putting increased pressure on the fragile ecosystem. More traffic, more hotels and houses, more boats using poor-quality fuel, and, of course, a glut of invasive species—everything from fire ants to goats—all contributed to the islands being placed on the UNESCO List of World Heritage in Danger in 2007. In 2010, after a concerted government effort to address the problems, the islands were removed from the list, despite opposition from environmentalists and scientists. Although progress has been made, the ecological situation in the Galápagos remains extremely fragile.

Solutions

Even in the face of all these problems, there is hope. Reforestation programs in the Andes have planted hillsides with fast-growing Monterey pines. Debt-for-nature swaps, in which foreign conservation groups buy off part of the country's foreign debt in exchange for the protection of threatened areas, are another positive move. Environmental groups can also outbid logging companies for forest concessions—an expensive but effective arrangement. Private investors and organizations such as the nonprofit Fundación Jatun Sacha have small reserves dotted around the country that protect pockets of forest from commercial pressures.

By far the biggest project aimed at conservation is the government's Yasuní-ITT initiative to persuade the international community to pay hundreds of millions of dollars to prevent exploitation of oil reserves below Yasuní National Park. It's an innovative idea, but in the present economic climate, collecting foreign donations has proved very difficult.

SUSTAINABLE DEVELOPMENT

Both economists and settlers have recently begun to realize that a tract of forest can be more valuable left alone than stripped for lumber and agriculture. The key is renewable rainforest products, which can bring in as much or more money over the long haul than logging, farming, oil drilling, or cattle ranching can in the short term. Along the way, environmentalists must debunk the age-old belief that the only good forest is a cleared forest, and make sure that the profits go directly back to the people who generate them so that they'll continue what they're doing.

Conservation International's Tagua Initiative is an excellent model of sustainable development. The oblong white seeds of the *tagua* palm (which resemble Brazil nuts) are soft enough to carve when raw but become as hard as ivory when dried. They once accounted for one out of every five buttons used in the United States, but demand plummeted after the advent of plastics. Today, the Tagua Initiative is trying to resurrect this trade in Peru, Bolivia, Colombia, and Ecuador, where artisans are being trained to carve buttons, jewelry, and figurines from the seeds for export. One community in Ecuador employs more than 1,000 workers and exports enough raw material for the production of 25 million buttons.

Other sustainable rainforest-friendly products include chocolate, manioc, quinine, and natural rubber from trees. In this age of patent medicine, the health benefits alone from rainforest products can be worth their weight in gold. It's almost a cliché to say that a cure for cancer may be hiding in the last representative of a rainforest plant species right in the path of a bulldozer, but with all the medicines that have been found here already, it is probably true. International pharmaceutical companies send expeditions into the rainforest to tap the wealth of native healing knowledge, and even cosmetics firms are studying the possible uses of local fruits in their shampoos.

Agroforestry, in which native species are left growing among introduced food crops, anchors the soil and ensures a wider mix of nutrients for all plants involved. Indigenous people have been doing this for years—just visit any Achuar *chakra*—but modern colonists still often try to grow just one crop, quickly exhausting the soil's supply of key nutrients.

ECOTOURISM

Defined by the Ecotourism Society as "responsible travel that conserves natural environments and sustains the well-being of local people," ecotourism has been a rising wave in travel since the 1990s. There's a difference between ecotourism and simple "nature tourism," in which the natural world is used only as a draw; true ecotourism promotes conservation to travelers and locals alike, educating and inspiring both to continue conservation efforts even after the tour.

Some purists claim that even ecotourism is too much, arguing that any amount of traffic erodes trails, compacts soils, leaves litter, and disturbs animals. The Galápagos are a good example of both the pluses and the minuses of ecotourism in Ecuador. Thousands of visitors flood in to gaze at the wildlife, funding conservation efforts and maintaining a certain level of protection for the islands, while on the other hand, tourism pollutes the environment with increased infrastructure.

The Ecuadorian Ecotourism Association, **ASEC** (Baquerizo Moreno and Tamayo, Quito, tel. 2/250-7204, www.ecoturismo.org.ec) can provide a list of eco-friendly tour operators in Ecuador. Also try the award-winning **Planeta. com,** a great starting point for information on ecotourism in Latin America.

PARKS AND RESERVES

Ecuador's 40 national parks, reserves, refuges, and recreation areas cover 19 percent of the country, which is a very heartening statistic for environmentalists. However, the reality is that most of these areas are understaffed and underfunded. While many areas remain pristine and unspoiled, illegal encroachment by poachers as well as mining and oil companies is a very real threat.

Ecuador's biggest protected areas in the Oriente are Yasuní National Park and the

Cuyabeno Reserve. In the mountains, Sangay, Cayambe-Coca, and Cotacachi-Cayapas are the largest, while Cotopaxi is the most popular mainland national park. On the coast, national parks are fewer and smaller, with Machalilla the most popular. Of course, Ecuador's most-visited national park lies 1,000 kilometers off the coast in the Galápagos archipelago.

A host of private reserves, often associated with private lodges, have their own legal right to administer the land, buy more, and interact with local communities.

Flora and Fauna

Ecuador's status as one of the world's most biodiverse countries is particularly astonishing considering its size. This nation, which covers less than 0.005 percent of the planet's surface, boasts 10 percent of all plant species on earth (25,000), more than the total found in North America, and one-sixth of all birds (more than 1,600 species). The vast majority of this diversity is found in the Oriente, which makes up nearly half of Ecuador's territory.

Unfortunately, though, not enough people are impressed by Ecuador's biodiversity to consider it worth preserving. The tropical dry forest that once dominated the coastal regions has been decimated by logging to make way for plantations and shrimp farms, and oil exploration has already done untold damage to the rainforest and continues to threaten further destruction. However, money talks as much as government protection, and ecotourism, if properly organized, remains one of the most effective ways to preserve Ecuador's amazing natural beauty.

THE COAST

The coast is the agricultural breadbasket of Ecuador, and its natural ecology has been the most disturbed of all the regions. The coast used to be covered in **tropical dry forests** extending up to Colombia and Panama, but now only small pockets—less than 5 percent—remain, having given way to rice fields, plantations, shrimp farms, and the timber industry. Northwestern Ecuador falls within the Chocó bioregion, which contains some of the most biologically diverse forests on earth, in part because they acted as warmer refuges during various ice ages, saving countless species of plants and animals from extinction. They're also incredibly wet, thanks to the union of the warm Panama Current just offshore. Up to one-fifth of the plants in some areas are endemic and found nowhere else in the world.

Farther south, there are stretches of tropical dry forests from the central coast of Ecuador to the Peruvian border, a region with well-defined wet and dry seasons. Machalilla National Park and the Chongón Hills west of Guayaquil shelter some of the largest tracts of this increasingly rare ecosystem.

Plant life consists of species more suited to the desert: water-stingy varieties include the *palo santo* tree common in the Galápagos, ceiba and balsa trees, and the *tagua* palm, whose nuts can be carved like ivory. Birds such as the vermilion flycatcher, Pacific pygmy owl, and long-tailed mockingbird make their homes among the dry hills, accompanied by armadillos, opossums, and small cats called oncillas.

Large, tangled groves of **mangroves** grow in brackish conditions where fresh water meets the ocean. The red mangrove is the most common, each with an extensive network of stilt limbs sent up from roots and down from branches. Mangroves are good colonizers, providing homes for seabirds in their branches and sea creatures among the roots. Once again, protected areas such as Manglares Churute near Guayaquil are all that stands between this ecosystem and the spread of civilization. Here, the main threat is the shrimp industry, which bulldozes mangrove swamps to build shrimp ponds.

Birdlife

The mangroves and forests that remain on the coast are a haven to a plethora of birdlife, and many of the same species are found here as on the Galápagos Islands. Magnificent frigate birds can be observed inflating their red chests at several locations, including Isla Corazón and the mangroves near Bahía de Caráquez, Isla de la Plata in Machalilla National Park, and Puerto el Morro near Playas in Guayas. Blue-footed boobies and masked boobies can be seen at Isla de la Plata, which has been nicknamed "the poor man's Galápagos."

Marine Life

With a shortage of sheltered bays, snorkeling opportunities are limited on the coast. The best spots to observe abundant tropical fish, including parrot fish, clown fish, and countless other species, are off Machalilla National Park and Isla de la Plata. Of more interest are the larger inhabitants of the oceans. Humpback whales are seen in large numbers off the coast from Salinas up to Atacames June–September. The best place to watch them is around Puerto López in Machalilla National Park. Farther south in the estuaries of the Gulf Of Guayaquil, dolphins are frequently observed. The best spot is Puerto del Morro.

CLOUD FORESTS

The rainforest's lofty cousin covers the transition zone between the coast and the high Andes and on the eastern slopes down to lowland rainforest. Nicknamed the *cejas de las montañas* ("eyebrows of the mountains"), cloud forests have a delicate, misty appearance, with moss-draped trees set along cold rushing streams. Annual precipitation comes in the form of clouds and fog as often as it does in raindrops, which can be an annoyance for bird-watchers. The upshot is that this region is far more comfortable, with cooler temperatures, than the Amazon rainforest.

Flora

Cloud-forest vegetation is similar to that of the rainforest but sparser and more sturdy. Up to 60 percent of all plants are **epiphytes,** which live off airborne moisture and nutrient particles as they grow far above the soil, depending on other plants for structural support. Many of these are **orchids,** which thrive at moist moderate-to-high elevations. The largest family of flowering plants, with more than 30,000 identified species, are orchids, which range from tiny buds to eight-centimeter flowers suspended on branches of up to three meters. The woody trunks of **tree ferns** reach heights of 5–8 meters, topped by a crown of giant fronds. Huge stands of **bamboo** go to seed and die all at once, and every available surface is covered with **mosses, lichens,** and **brackens.**

Fauna

The bright-red feathers of the **Andean cock-of-the-rock** make it a birder's favorite. These birds prefer vertical cliffs and gather in courtship clearings called leks. **Golden-headed quetzals** have bright turquoise plumage and live in tree cavities next to vivid **tanagers** and top-heavy **toucans.** Dozens of species of **hummingbirds** have the best names of all: collared Inca, gorgeted sunangel, booted racket tail, and the green violetear, to name a few. Temperatures in the cloud forest fall too low for most large mammals, but there are still a few around. **Mountain tapirs,** one of three Ecuadorian species, have elongated snouts that betray their relationship to the rhinoceros. It's rare to see them, but their tracks are easy to spot in the mud (look for three toes on the rear foot and four on the front).

The **Andean spectacled bear,** named for white patches around its eyes, is the only bear native to South America. Males can grow two meters long and range through the cloud forest and *páramo* from Venezuela to Bolivia. Ecuador has one of the largest populations of this highly endangered animal, which is poached for its meat and supposed medicinal value—the paws are said to protect one from evil, and its fat is used as a healing ointment.

PÁRAMO

These high-elevation grasslands stretch between the temperate montane valleys and the inhospitable snows of the highest peaks. Chill mists, dark lakes, and tussocks of sharp grasses make the *páramo* a surreal and beautiful environment to explore. This landscape, with rivers carving their way through and serene lakes drawing a variety of birdlife, is among the most stunning in the country. Some of the most impressive can be found in the areas around Otavalo and Ibarra in the northern Sierra, Cotopaxi National Park and the Quilotoa Loop in the central Sierra, and Cajas and Podocarpus National Park in the Southern Sierra.

Flora

Thick, waxy leaf skins covered with fine insulating hairs help the low, spongy ground cover to survive high levels of ultraviolet light and wet, often freezing conditions. Plants stick low to the ground to escape the wind and temperature variations, and often grow their leaves in a circle to ensure none shade any of the others.

The distinctive **frailejón** is characteristic of the northern *páramo* near the Colombian border. With its crown of yellow leaves covered with insulating down, the plant is actually a member of the sunflower family. *Frailejones* range through the Andes from Ecuador to Venezuela, just as their namesake friars did in colonial times. At higher elevations, *frailejones* grow closer together for mutual protection against the elements.

The thistle-like **chuquiragua,** regarded as the national flower, has jagged leaves and orange flowers and is used by *indígenas* as a liver, kidney, and urinary-tract cleanser. Its name means "sword of blood" in Kichwa, and it is one of the few flowers found at this elevation. The **lycopodium** club moss (*Lycopodium crassum*) also brightens the dreary landscape with its tubular red-and-orange stalks. **Caspivela** plants have flat, bushy branches that resemble evergreens. Also called candlewood, this waxy bush is so flammable that it will burn in the rain.

Fauna

Hummingbirds (*colibrís* in Spanish) are characteristic of Ecuador's higher elevations, although they are also found on the coast and in the rainforest. Blurring wing beats allow them to hover and move backward, and at night most can enter a hibernation-like state called torpor, in which their body temperature and metabolism drop significantly. Their iridescent feathers were once sewn into cloaks for Inca rulers. Listen for the buzz of the buff-colored tawny-bellied hermit or the endemic Ecuadorian hillstar (*Oreotrochilus chimborazo*), with its blue head and white breast. The sword-billed hummingbird totes a 10-centimeter snout.

Torrent ducks, white-capped dippers, and **torrent tyrannulets** gather near running water. **Andean lapwings** have an unmistakably grating call and a gaudy, white-and-brown striped wing pattern. Cotopaxi National Park is the best place to see the **carunculated caracara,** the largest member of the falcon family, with its bright red face, yellow bill, and black body.

Cotopaxi is also a good place to spot the **Andean condor,** which is related to the

© QUITO TURISMO

Seeing a condor is a highlight of a visit to the Andes.

California condor and equally endangered. Actually a vulture (*Vultur gryphus*), the condor is the world's largest flying bird, with a wingspan of more than three meters. Mature condors have glossy black plumage with white upper flight feathers, a fuzzy white neck ruff, and a hooked beak. The red head and neck are naked of feathers to keep the bird clean as it digs into a tasty mess of carrion, its meal of choice. A mere 50 mating pairs remain alive because of habitat destruction and a mistaken fear among *campesinos* that the giant scavengers will carry off livestock and children. Other locations to spot condors include Antisana Reserve, Cajas National Park, Papallacta Pass, and at the Parque Condor refuge center near Otavalo.

South America's high-elevation relatives of the camel—**llamas, vicuñas,** and **alpacas**—were once domesticated by the Incas for meat, wool, and hauling cargo. Since the arrival of the Spanish, these animals were hunted into extinction in the Ecuadorian wilds, but reintroduction programs using animals from Chile and Bolivia have been highly successful in the Chimborazo Fauna Reserve and Cotopaxi National Park.

Chances are slim that you'll spot an **Andean deer, puma,** or small *páramo* **cat.**

RAINFORESTS

Although deforestation and oil exploration have seriously reduced Ecuador's tract of Amazon rainforest, there are still vast areas of primary rainforest stretching east to the Colombian and Peruvian borders. You may find that the landscapes are different from what you had imagined and not quite as impenetrable, with little undergrowth below the high, closed canopy. It's cooler underneath the canopy, with regular torrential downpours cooling things down further, although in the midday sunshine it can turn into an outdoor sauna.

Daytime in the rainforest is also surprisingly quiet, with the calls of birds one of the very few sounds emanating from the endless green. The most dramatic sounds come from the sudden rainstorms that disappear as quickly as they

© BEN WESTWOOD

Pumas are very shy and rarely seen.

arrive. At night, however, it's a different story, with the constant hum of insects making you glad to pull down the mosquito net.

Rainforests are defined by low elevation (up to 1,000 meters), high temperatures (25–28°C), and daily rainfall that varies widely over the year. The annual norm is 200–300 centimeters of rain. The result is a warm, humid environment as perfect for unbridled growth as any on earth. Among the oldest of all ecosystems, rainforests are also among the least known because of difficult access and scientific interest that has only recently blossomed. Large percentages of Ecuador's Amazonian plants and animals were only discovered within the last few decades. Large areas of the rainforest are flooded, and the only way to travel is on water—from the wide expanses of the Río Coca, Río Aguarico, and Río Napo to the countless tributaries that lead deeper into the forest beyond.

Species Richness

Scientists are just beginning to understand the incredible biological diversity of the Amazon forests, where 3,000 different types of beetles have been found in study plots of 12 square meters, and 87 species of frogs and toads were found in one hectare. Aside from having nearly ideal conditions for life, rainforests have also had time on their side. In some cases, plants and animals have had hundreds of millions of years to evolve into each one's particular "niche," a vague ecological term that essentially means an individual's role in the overall grand production of life—the space it occupies, the food it consumes, the ecological room it needs. Over the eons, species become more and more specialized, leaving room for other species to find equally narrow but slightly different niches often only a few millimeters to one side.

The theory of Pleistocene forest refugia holds that during cool, dry periods far in the past, isolated patches of rainforest served as islands in the middle of huge expanses of grasslands. These refuges eventually reconnected, complete with thousands of new, unique species that had evolved in isolation. Most of eastern Ecuador falls within the Napo Refuge, which has been one of the largest and most stable refugia throughout history, and thus one of the most biologically diverse.

Shallow Basement

It is well documented that for all the richness that lies in the rainforest, the soil underneath is surprisingly thin and poor. Unfortunately, those who clear the land for agriculture seem slow to realize this. In contrast with temperate forests and their rich, deep layers of humus, rainforests have most of their nutrients suspended in the vegetation itself—in both living and dead matter—instead of the ground. In fact, less than 1 percent of forest nutrients are thought to penetrate deeper than five centimeters into the soil. As a result, when rainforests are cleared, the thin topsoil washes away in a few years to reveal an impenetrable layer of clay on which little can grow.

Death takes on a whole new importance in an ecosystem where so little is siphoned away through the ground. Countless bacteria, fungi, and insects are crucial in breaking down dead matter quickly enough to return the nutrients to the pool of life. Thriving fungi give the rainforest its characteristic rich, organic odor.

Hydrology

Black-water rivers, unique to tropical forests, get their tealike color from tannins, substances used in winemaking and leather tanning, which seep out of the tropical forests. Even algae can't grow in these highly acidic waters. Sediment from the Andes gives **white-water rivers** their milky appearance and neutral pH.

Oxbow lakes are formed when a bend of a meandering lowland river is cut off from the main flow. The resulting U-shaped *cocha* (lake) slowly fills in with a succession of plants until it becomes indistinguishable from the rest of the forest.

Flora

Ecuador is home to more than 20,000 species of vascular plants, more than in all of North

America, and most of them live in the Amazon. Although temperate forests in North America may contain six tree species in abundance, a 10-square-meter plot of rainforest may shelter 25 different species.

Primary forest, undisturbed by humans, has a high, tight canopy layer that blocks out most sunlight, keeping undergrowth to a minimum. This is where you'll find the best example of **emergent trees,** up to 50 meters tall and five meters across at the base. Roots like rocket fins keep the towering giants upright—most of the time—and were used by indigenous people to signal over long distances (bang on one to see how). King of the rainforest trees is the towering **ceiba** (kapok), which grows up to 50 meters tall and is often used to build observation towers around. The smooth branches look more like upside-down roots, each covered with characteristically thick, smooth, oval leaves with tapered ends to shed heavy rainfall.

Each large tree in the rainforest supports a veritable zoo of aerial plant life, starting with huge, woody **lianas** that climb host trees to reach the sun. One kind of liana, contrary to all plant logic, initially grows toward darkness to find the base of the largest nearby tree to start climbing. Large lianas can loop several trees together, so that if one tree falls, several neighbors follow.

Epiphytes, aerial plants that get all their nutrients and water from the air, include **bromeliads,** which resemble the tops of pineapples (they're in the same taxonomic family). Inside each bromeliad's leafy crown, a small puddle of rainwater can support hundreds of insects, amphibians, and even other epiphytes. Epiphytes grow aerial roots to trap dust and falling debris for food, which can accumulate up to 50 centimeters thick on the tops of larger branches.

Supporting so much life has its drawbacks. **Strangler figs** of the *Ficus* genus are called *matapalos* ("tree killers") in Spanish for good reason. Starting as a small airborne seed, the fig eventually sends down woody roots that can encircle the host tree completely and squeeze it

to death. By then the fig, a tree in its own right, has established roots of its own. Their wood isn't good for lumber, so figs are often the only trees left standing in cleared plots, but birds and animals love the sweet fruit.

All this added weight can easily cause even a large tree to collapse, so the hosts have developed several defensive strategies. Some trees shed their outer bark periodically, leaving a smooth surface that epiphytes can't cling to. Other plants produce repulsive chemicals. Nonetheless, **tree falls** are surprisingly common, even if no one is around to hear them, and actually serve a crucial role in the life of the forest. Every large tree in a patch of forest can fall in as little as 100 years, each one producing a vital light gap that allows smaller plants to spurt upward in the hope of becoming canopy members themselves.

Translated as "vine of death" in Kichwa, **ayahuasca** is a type of vine well known to almost all the indigenous groups of the Amazon. *Banisteriopsis caapi* can grow up to eight centimeters in diameter and sprouts white, yellow, or red flowers. Its hallucinogenic properties come from an orchestra of alkaloids that give ayahuasca its intense yellow-brown color when cut. In carefully controlled ceremonies, community members use the vine to speak with dead ancestors, discover the causes of sickness, and communicate with the forest itself.

Other survival tactics are more ingenious. One type of tree has worked out an arrangement with a particular type of ant that clears the branches and the surrounding forest floor of competing plants and attacks any creature foolish enough to take a bite of a leaf. In return, the ants, which apparently taste like lemon, get to make their home in special hollow stems. Stinging spines on the roots and trunks of other trees discourage larger creatures from climbing, scratching, or otherwise hurting the tree.

Chemical defenses often have beneficial side effects for humans. An incredible array of **medicinal plants,** long known to native people, have only recently begun to be appreciated by modern science. Many substances you are already familiar with were discovered this way—among them nicotine, caffeine, strychnine, Novocain, and quinine, the first effective medicine against malaria.

Pollination strategies can be just as complex. Because other plants of the same species may be situated kilometers away, wind and luck may not be enough to get seeds or pollen to a receptive host. Large, white nocturnal flowers attract bats with their rich pollen, and hummingbirds love small, reddish flowers filled with sugar-rich nectar. In both cases, pollen (microscopic male seeds) is attached to the unwary creature and transported to the next plant. Seeds hidden inside tasty fruit are designed to pass unharmed through the digestive systems of monkeys, rodents, fish, and birds, growing wherever they are dispersed—some won't germinate otherwise.

Insects are the most common pollinators and are deceived no end by plants, often gaining little or nothing in return. Some orchids have parts that mimic female tachinid flies to lure males, or provide fragrances that male orchid bees collect and store to lure females. Fig wasps lay their eggs in fig flowers, from which the larvae eventually eat their way out and emerge covered in pollen. Some flowers smell like rotting meat to attract scavengers, whereas others mimic a mammalian ear, down to reddish veins and a musky odor, to lure mosquitoes.

Birds

It's said that 80 percent of the animals in the rainforest live above eye level, and most of that, it seems, is on the wing. Birds are by far the most abundant animal life you'll see: Ecuador alone has nearly 1,600 identified species, compared to 700 in the United States and Canada combined. You'll have the best luck spotting them along the borders of clear-cut areas and rivers, near a fruiting tree, at a salt lick, or from the lodge's canopy towers and during forest hikes. Different species often forage together in mixed flocks for added protection from predators.

Of the thousands of different species, a few stand out. **Hoatzins** are unmistakable, with

their Mohawk crest, ungainly body, and prehistoric squawk. The smell of decomposing leaves, which is used to deter predators, gives these birds the nickname "stinky turkeys." They have been called a missing link between birds and reptiles, since chicks are born with claws at the outer joints of their wings to help them climb back into the nest after they fall or jump out to escape predators. The hoatzin is one of the few birds that actually eat leaves, which it digests in a large, heavy crop that makes it almost impossible for the bird to fly gracefully.

The liquid call of an **oropendola** is unmistakable—like a large drop of water falling into a deep well—and it's one of the most attractive sounds in the rainforest. Their long woven nests are commonly seen dangling from tree branches. Oropendola chicks are a favorite prey of botfly larvae, so the birds often hang their nests near the nests of wasps to help keep the flies away. Parasitic species such as cuckoos lay their eggs in other birds' nests, leaving the unwitting parents to raise chicks that are often larger than they are.

Every species of **kingfisher** found in South America lives in Ecuador, including the ringed, green, Amazon, and the rare green-and-rufous American pygmy. **Harpy eagles** use their daggerlike claws to snatch monkeys out of tree branches. These eagles, which are South America's largest bird of prey, are revered by indigenous people.

Twenty species of **toucans** have huge, hollow bills for reaching and opening fruit and seeds in the canopy. Forty-five species of **macaws,** including the blue-and-yellow and the chestnut-fronted, mate for life. One of the rainforest's most spectacular sights is to see hundreds of these birds flocking to drink at clay licks, the most famous being in Yasuní National Park near Napo Wildlife Center.

Mammals

Some visitors are a little disappointed at the lack of large mammals in the Amazon. If you're looking for size, you're on the wrong continent. Large mammals are so rare here mainly because so many plant defenses have prevented the evolution of large herbivores that would have served as prey. Seventeen species of **monkeys** belong to the arboreal New World group (Platyrrhini), as opposed to the ground-dwelling Catarrhini of the Old World, which include us. **Capuchins** have white-and-black coats and faces like angry little old men. **Red howlers** are named after the roaring call—audible for kilometers—that males produce with a specialized bone in their throat. They sound very scary, as if an unseen monster is lurking somewhere in the tree. While they are very territorial, they are also one of the most affectionate monkeys, frequently seen on trees grooming and embracing one another. **Squirrel monkeys** follow larger species to fruiting trees and lack a prehensile tail. At the bottom of the scale are silky-furred **pygmy marmosets,** who eat tree sap and are among the smallest primates in the world.

Adorably lethargic **sloths** come in two- and three-toed varieties. Both hang from branches with their long claws and move so slowly that algae grow in their dense hair. A host of insect species also nest in sloth fur, including one type of moth that only lays its eggs in sloth feces (carefully buried at ground level once a week). More than 100 species of **bats** flit through Ecuador's rainforests in search of insects, small animals, fruit, and blood.

You will be extremely lucky to see any of the other mammals. Piglike **tapirs** and **peccaries** root among leaves for tasty morsels but are easily startled. Even more interesting is the incredible **capybara,** the largest rodent in the world, which has to be seen to be believed—it looks as though Harry Potter has put a magical enlargement spell on a regular rodent.

The big cats are here, but they don't laze around in prides like African lions in the savanna, and with good reason—humans have long hunted them for their coats. The **jaguar,** worshipped as a god of the rainforest by many indigenous groups, is the only member of the *Panthera* genus found in the Americas and the third-largest cat in the world after the tiger and lion. It is highly endangered and remains extremely elusive. Smaller cats such as the

© BEN WESTWOOD

Capybaras are the largest rodents in the world.

aquatic **jaguarundi** and the **ocelot** are also rarely seen.

Beneath the waters, pink **river dolphins** are a pleasant surprise. These descendants of Pacific species were cut off from their ancestors by the upward thrust of the Andes. They often feed where rivers join to produce clashing currents that confuse fish.

Reptiles and Amphibians

More than 400 species of **frogs and toads** fill the night with their sounds, giving Ecuador the highest frog and toad diversity per unit area of any country in the world, and almost as many species as the entire United States contains. Poison-arrow frogs raise their tadpoles in cups of water trapped in bromeliads. Their neon reds, blues, and greens warn potential predators of some of the most potent toxins in the animal kingdom. Indigenous hunters use the frogs' secretions on their arrow and dart points to bring down large game.

Semiaquatic **anacondas** can grow up to seven meters long (although five meters is more common). They are constrictors and squeeze the life out of their prey, feeding mainly on fish, rodents, and occasionally small caimans. Contrary to popular belief, they rarely attack larger animals. There are countless other snake species, but they are very hard to spot, which is no bad thing because many have deadly venom. Flashlight beams on night-time canoe rides will catch the glittering eyes of **caimans.** The smaller white species are mainly harmless, feeding mainly on crustaceans and small fish. The large black caiman are aggressive and will attack if provoked.

Fish

Amazon catfish, called *bagre* in Ecuador, are the largest freshwater fish in the world, often topping 200 kilograms. Fear of **piranhas** shouldn't keep you out of the water completely; these small fish do have a potent set of choppers, but they rarely attack an animal that isn't bleeding already, and some species feed solely on fruit. Tales of "feeding frenzies" probably come from occasions when large groups of piranhas, trapped in small pools of water, are

driven wild by the scent of blood. Fishing for piranha is a common activity on a rainforest tour and gives you a chance to bite back at dinner if you catch one.

Watch out for **stingrays,** which hide in muddy shallows and can inflict an excruciating sting with a barb on the end of their whip-like tail. Shuffle your feet when you can't see the bottom. Even more fearsome is the *candirú* **catfish,** a narrow little fish with a propensity for warm, dark openings. After following a warm water current into the gills of fish, they attach themselves to feed by extending a sharp dorsal spine. A stream of urine can attract them, and a urethra can be mistaken for a gill in muddy water (there was an infamous incident involving a luckless Brazilian man in 1997), so don't swim naked.

Insects

Some estimates say insects make up 80 percent of all animal species in Ecuador. Because they reproduce so often, insects can evolve quickly: Scientists estimate that the thousands of species they've already cataloged are still only a small fraction of what's out there. Insects are also easier to spot than most other creatures—just turn on a light after dark and you'll be swarmed within minutes.

Some insect species have evolved close relationships with certain plants to the point where each couldn't survive without the other, an arrangement called **obligatory mutualism.** *Heliconius* butterflies live months instead of weeks when they eat the nutritious vine pollen of the cucumber vine (*Psiguria*), which in turn gets cross-pollinated as the insects travel from one plant to the other. **Leafcutter ants** live in huge colonies of up to several million individuals. Small bits of leaves carried back to the nest are chewed up, fertilized with ant feces, and set in carefully tended gardens to grow a particular type of fungus the ants then eat. The fungus can't survive on its own, and the ants can't eat anything else.

Other times, the relationship isn't as mutually beneficial. The same *Heliconius* butterflies love the vine leaves of the passionflower, which tries to discourage them by growing barbed hairs, changing the shape of its leaves, and sprouting warts that deceive female butterflies into thinking that another butterfly has already laid eggs on the leaves. The butterflies keep adapting, covering the lethal hairs with soft webs and learning to detect the plant by its scent instead of its appearance. The result is the continual evolution of new species of butterfly and plant. Electric-blue **morpho butterflies** are one of the most eye-catching creatures in the forest, drifting lazily through patches of light on their way down forest trails or waterways.

The papery nests of **termites** are a common sight, made of digested wood cemented together with droppings. Termites play a crucial recycling role in the rainforest by digesting dead wood with the help of microbes. Inexorable columns of **army ants** are followed by antbirds, which eat the insects the army ants scare up. The nastiest of the Amazon ant species are the three-centimeter **conga ants,** which are known locally as *veinte-quatros* ("twenty-fours") for the day-long pain of their potent bite, so keep your distance.

History

EARLIEST CULTURES

If you've ever noticed the similarities in features of American indigenous people and Asians, you're not imagining it—most experts agree that the Americas were first colonized by nomadic hunter-gatherers who wandered across the Bering Strait from Siberia about 18,000 years ago. They gradually moved south, reaching South America a few thousands years later.

Close to the Panamanian isthmus, Ecuador was one of the first areas to be settled. In fact, the oldest pottery yet found in all of the Americas was unearthed in Ecuador, dating to the **Paleo-Indian period** (11,000–4000 B.C.), when small family groups roamed the area.

Coastal

The earliest Ecuadorian culture, **Las Vegas,** can be traced to the Santa Elena Peninsula as long ago as 9000 B.C. The culture developed cultivation of corn, pumpkins, and beans around 6000 B.C. The best-known remains are the skeletons called the Lovers of Sumpa, housed in a museum in Santa Elena.

By 3500 B.C., the Valdivia culture had developed, with organized settlements in Manabí, Santa Elena, and Guayas Provinces. They developed more sophisticated farming and trade, and they used pottery, large amounts of which have been excavated in the past century. The shiny red shell of the spiny oyster (*Spondylus calcifer*) was especially valued as a symbol of fertility and used as currency. The coastline today has been renamed the Spondylus Route, and the oysters are often sold as necklaces and used in cooking, although they are increasingly endangered.

The Valdivia were followed by the **Machalilla** culture (1500–800 B.C.), who practiced skull deformation as a sign of status, were more skilled at fishing, and increased trade with other cultures. They were followed by the **Chorerra** (900–300 B.C.), who produced beautiful ceramics.

The period of **Regional Development** (300 B.C.–A.D. 700) saw more coastal cultures building *tolas,* huge pyramids of earth topped with wooden temples. Hierarchical societies, such as the **Jama-Coaque** and **Bahía** in Manabí and the **Guangala** in Guayas, grew into communities of thousands clustered around ceremonial centers like San Isidro and Isla de la Plata. The **La Tola** culture, which spread from La Tola Island in northern Esmeraldas into southern Colombia, was the first in history to work platinum, a complex technique requiring temperatures of 1,000°C that wasn't discovered in Europe until the 19th century. Bizarrely beautiful feline images became a trademark of the La Tola, and their sun-mask emblem is the symbol of the Banco Central.

Coastal cultures reached their peak during the period of **Integration** (A.D. 700–1460). The **Manteña-Huancavilca** civilization, stretching from the Bahía de Caráquez to the Peruvian border, counted 20,000 members by the time the Spanish arrived. Master seafarers took advantage of favorable winds and currents as they piloted balsa rafts as far as Mexico to trade precious metals, mother-of-pearl, textiles, and ceramic figurines.

Andean

Coastal merchants found a new market for salt in three major kingdoms that had developed in the Sierra. The **Cara** got their start on the coast around A.D. 900, conquering the Bahía de Caráquez area before following Río Esmeraldas upstream to settle near Quito. The Shyris family dynasty ruled this sun-worshiping culture, built observatories to track the seasons, and believed that people inhabited the moon. Around A.D. 1300, a prince of the Puruh, a famous warrior culture, married a Shyris princess to unite the groups into the **Quitu** kingdom, from which the city Quito took its name. This culture dominated the Sierra until the arrival of the Incas and spawned many of today's indigenous groups, including the Otavaleños.

A loosely organized federation of 25 tribes formed the **Cañari** nation in the southern Sierra and coastal lowlands. These ferocious fighters would prove to be the Incas' toughest opponents in centuries to come. Even after many of them were relocated to Peru, the rest allied with the Spanish to fight against their former Inca overlords. According to oral history, the Cañari sacrificed 100 children every year to the god of corn and buried their chiefs with an entire retinue of wives and servants put to death for the purpose.

The Oriente

With a lack of major archaeological sites and an environment better suited to burying the past than preserving it, the Amazon region was once thought to be historically infertile. Historians have started to change their tune, however, theorizing that large settlements well into the thousands populated the rainforest and the eastern slopes of the Andes almost as early as the coast and Sierra were originally settled. Manioc root, still a rainforest staple, is known to have been domesticated at least 8,000 years ago and may have been instrumental in supporting Andean and coastal societies, along with corn imported from Central America. Clay pottery began to make an appearance around 4000 B.C.

THE RISE AND FALL OF THE INCAS
Conquest

The empire of the "Children of the Sun" began ignominiously near the shores of cold Lake Titicaca, between Peru and Bolivia, in the 11th century. Soon the Inca empire began to expand from its capital in Cuzco, Peru. By the 14th and 15th centuries, the empire they called Tawantinsuyu stretched from northern Chile to the edge of Ecuador.

In 1463 the ruling Inca, Topa Inca Yupanqui, began the push into Ecuador from Peru. As they advanced into the Sierra, Inca armies met fierce resistance from local tribes. Spears, slingshots, and war clubs flew in screaming melees where combatants wore cloth armor or nothing at all. The Cara put up 17 years of resistance, but the final victory of the Inca was brutal when thousands of Cara warriors were killed in 1495 at the edge of a lake north of Ibarra. The carnage turned the lake red with blood, hence its name, Lago Yahuarcocha (Bloody Lake). A new northern Inca outpost called Tomebamba, decked out in enough splendor to rival Cuzco itself, was built on the ruins of the Cañari capital in present-day Cuenca.

By 1500, Ecuador was under the control of Huayna Capac, the son of Topa and a Cañari princess. Huayna grew up in Ecuador and spent much of his time suppressing local uprisings.

Life Under the Incas

Ecuador's new overlords ruled for less than half a century but made their mark with surprising speed. From his base in Cuzco, the Inca emperor, revered as a living god, imposed an iron fist on the Quitosuyo (as the section of the empire from Ecuador to Cuzco was known). Ongoing local resistance made military rule a necessity, and workers built fortifications called *pucarás* at dozens of strategic lookouts, bridges, and mountain passes. Populations that refused to pay tribute to the divine authority of the Incas were moved in their entirety as far as Chile, and correspondingly, groups from as far away as Bolivia, such as the Saraguro, were moved to Ecuador in a concerted effort to displace and demoralize disobedient subjects. The *mita* system of collective work and annual tribute fueled the empire's expansion and filled the coffers in Cuzco with riches.

The Incas imposed the Quechua language (not to be confused with the Quechua people, who spoke and continue to speak their own language) on conquered cultures. Agriculture was collectivized under the watchful eye of the state, as new crops such as sweet potatoes and peanuts were introduced to Ecuador and grown on terraced fields watered by complicated systems of irrigation.

Records were kept through an intricate system of knotted, colored cords called *quipus,* which could be used to keep track of populations, seasons, and food supplies. Buildings in the famous Inca masonry style—blocks weighing tons fitted perfectly together—housed collections of intricately woven textiles, utensils made of precious metals, and musical instruments made of clay, shells, and human bones.

An incredible network of roads, perhaps the Incas' most impressive achievement, tied everything together and remains the core of the Ecuadorian Sierra's modern road network. Eight meters wide and paved with stone, the highways boasted trees planted for shade and a ditch of fresh water running alongside. Teams of runners could make the 2,000-kilometer journey from Cuenca to Quito along the Capacñan (Inca Highway) in eight days, crossing suspension bridges over at least 100 rivers and resting in roadhouses along the way.

The Inca Civil War

Huayna Capac, along with his eldest son, Ninan Cuyochi, died suddenly of disease (probably smallpox) in 1526, leaving a power vacuum. Two of his other sons tried to claim power: Huáscar, in Cuzco, and Atahualpa, whose mother was a Quitu princess, in Quito. Civil war began almost immediately, but Atahualpa quickly gained the upper hand because most of his father's armies had been based in the north. The two armies clashed in a huge battle at Ambato in which 30,000 soldiers died and Atahualpa drove south, finally defeating and imprisoning Huáscar. However, no sooner had Atahualpa claimed victory in 1532 than news arrived of a mysterious band of tall bearded white men landing on the coast, frightening the locals and making their way inland.

THE CONQUISTADORES ARRIVE
The Spanish Conquest Begins

Most conquistadores (literally, "conquerors") were low-ranking Spanish noblemen heading to the New World for wealth, fame, and adventure. Francisco Pizarro, the central figure in the conquest of the Incas, was an illiterate and illegitimate fortune-seeker from the Extremadura region of southern Spain. A decade after he accompanied Vasco Núñez de Balboa across the Panamanian isthmus to discover the Pacific Ocean, Pizarro received permission from the Spanish crown to explore the west coast of South America with fellow adventurer Diego de Almagro.

In 1526, while Pizarro was exploring Panama and Colombia, his main pilot, Bartolomé Ruiz sailed down the Ecuadorian coast on a reconnaissance mission and captured a Manta merchant vessel laden with gold and jewels. This news convinced Pizarro that the region contained untold riches. Following several largely unsuccessful voyages, Pizarro returned to Spain to plead for money and authority from King Charles I. He arrived again in the New World with the title of Governor and Captain-General of Peru. In 1532, he landed in Tumbes in northern Peru with Almagro (who was jealous of Pizarro's title and authority), 180 men, 27 horses, his brothers Gonzalo and Juan

Pizarro, and two half-brothers. The Incas initially greeted Pizarro's party with a mix of wonder and fear, but the rumors of the white men's acts of plundering on the fringes of the empire quickly spread, and things turned hostile. Pizarro relocated to the island of Puná in the Gulf of Guayaquil, where he met even fiercer resistance that resulted in a full battle on the island. This was the first test, and the Spanish, despite being hopelessly outnumbered, massacred the locals with superior fighting skills and firepower that included muskets and cavalry. Over 400 natives died, but just three Spaniards did. Pizarro sailed back to Tumbes and decided to move inland in the hope of avoiding further battles and finding the riches he craved.

Atahualpa's Fate

The undisputed Inca leader, after capturing his half-brother Huáscar, decamped to Cajamarca in the mountains of northern Peru to rest. As Pizarro was heading inland, he was alerted to the whereabouts of Atahualpa, and a meeting was arranged. The ensuing scene on November 15, 1532, would have been fascinating to witness: Two leaders meeting in the sunbaked central plaza under the eyes of dozens of Spanish soldiers and thousands of Inca warriors, with tension resonating in the air. Atahualpa, considered a living god by his people and with an army of thousands at his disposal, made the fatal mistake of underestimating a band of less than 200 Spaniards. Accounts of the events that followed differ, but most witnesses agree that Atahualpa refused the Spanish chaplain's order to submit to Spain and the Roman Catholic god, throwing a Bible to the ground in disgust. At a prearranged signal, Spanish soldiers fired cannons and charged their horses into the heart of the astonished Inca garrison. Within two hours, 7,000 Inca soldiers lay dead, the Sun King had been taken captive, and the fate of South America's greatest empire had been sealed. Among the Europeans, only Pizarro was wounded as he rushed to grab Atahualpa.

During the nine months of his imprisonment, Atahualpa learned Spanish, chess, and cards while retaining most of his authority. Attendants still dressed and fed him, burning everything he touched. Thinking that Pizarro planned to depose him in favor of Huáscar, Atahualpa ordered his captive half-brother killed. When it became clear that his own life hung in the balance, Atahualpa offered to buy his freedom with the wealth of his entire kingdom. He is said to have reached high on the wall of a room five meters wide by seven meters long, offering to fill it once with gold and twice with silver. The ransom—one of the largest the world has ever known—was assembled and was on its way to the capital when Pizarro went back on his word, fearful of the Inca leader's power. Atahualpa was put on trial for polygamy, idolatry, and crimes against the crown and was sentenced to be burned at the stake. He reacted with horror at this news because he believed that such a fate would prevent his body from passing into the afterlife. He agreed to be baptized and was strangled with a garrote on July 26, 1533, in Cajamarca. The ransom, quickly hidden en route from Cuzco, has never been found.

The Conquest Is Completed

In November 1533, just four months after Atahualpa's death, Cuzco fell to Pizarro and Hernando de Soto, and the Inca empire was finished. The victors were welcomed as liberators by many indigenous groups, who had resented and fought against the yoke of the Incas. A few battles remained to be fought: In May 1534, Sebastián de Benalcázar (Pizarro's second in command) found himself facing 50,000 Inca warriors under the guidance of Rumiñahui, the greatest Inca general, who had deserted and burned Quito rather than surrender it to the invaders. Benalcázar, aided by Cañari soldiers, defeated "Stone Face," whose capture, torture, and execution signaled the end of organized indigenous military resistance.

By 1549, fewer than 2,000 Spanish soldiers had defeated an estimated 500,000 indigenous people. Although these numbers seem unbelievable, they can be explained by a combination of battle tactics, epidemiology, and luck.

FRANCISCO DE ORELLANA

One of the most remarkable journeys in the history of the Americas almost ended before it began. In 1539, Francisco de Orellana, the former governor of Guayaquil and a relative of the influential Pizarro family, was assisting Gonzalo Pizarro in leading a few hundred Spanish soldiers, thousands of indigenous people, and an ark's worth of dogs, horses, and food animals in an exploration of the upper Amazon. Half of the party, including 2,000 *indígenas*, perished during the grueling journey over the Eastern Cordillera without ever seeing the rainforest. The rest survived by eating their horses, then their saddles, and many poisoned themselves eating forest roots.

When the group finally stumbled across the Río Napo, Pizarro ordered Orellana to build a boat to carry the weakest members and explore downriver in search of food. Two months' labor produced a large raft, which was pushed from the muddy shore on January 1, 1542. Within minutes, the strong brown current had swept the raft and its crew of 57 Spaniards and several hundred *indígenas* out of sight. Foremost on every Spanish mind was the legendary golden city of El Dorado, along with a fabled land of spices peopled by the Canelos, the "Cinnamon People."

The group passed quietly along the first part of the river, through what would become Ecuador. Native villages received the explorers with peaceful offers of food, and the Spanish planted crude crosses to claim the land for the king. Within a month, the party had reached the Río Napo's confluence with the Río Aguarico.

Aboard the new raft, Orellana's group began to fight for their lives as they entered a region of increasingly hostile locals. Orellana was skilled at picking up languages and saved his own life on many occasions with careful diplomacy and presenting European clothing as gifts to community chiefs.

By June 3, the exhausted survivors were amazed to reach the great joining of waters (today near Manaus in Brazil), where the coffee-black Río Negro (named by Orellana) joins the lighter Río Marañon, and the two flow side by side for kilometers without mixing.

An attack shortly after the meeting of the rivers sparked another legend. The Spanish soldiers described being attacked by a native group that included tall, light-skinned women armed with bows and arrows. The chronicler of the journey, Gaspar de Carvajal, who lost an eye in the attack, described how the Spanish boats looked like porcupines after so many arrows rained down. The defenders dubbed the fierce females "Amazonas" after the mythical women warriors of Greek legend. Just as the story stuck in the world's collective imagination for centuries, the name stuck to the river as well. One theory is that these "women" were actually male Yagua warriors, who had long hair and wore grass skirts.

On August 26, 1542, the waters suddenly spread to the horizon, and a tang of salt drifted in on the breeze. The straggling band had finally reached the Atlantic Ocean, becoming the first Europeans, and most likely the first human beings, to travel the entire length of the world's longest river – a trip that was not repeated for more than a century.

After skirting the coast north of the Margarita Islands off what would become Venezuela, Orellana rested and dispersed his group before leaving in May 1543 for Spain. King Charles I was delighted with Orellana's tale, making him governor of the territories he had discovered and authorizing (though not financing) him to lead a follow-up colonization expedition. In 1545, Orellana left Spain with a ragtag force, paid for out of his own pocket and consisting of 300 men on four small ships. By the time the expedition reached the mouth of the Amazon six months later, one boat had been lost and more than 200 of the crew had died or deserted. Some of the crew managed to reach Venezuela, but Francisco de Orellana died of fever in November 1546, aged just 35, somewhere in the lower delta of the river that made him famous.

The river was originally named Orellana by the explorer himself, but the name Amazonas replaced it in later years.

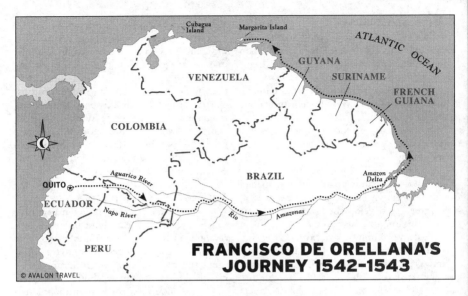

FRANCISCO DE ORELLANA'S JOURNEY 1542-1543

© AVALON TRAVEL

In the 16th century, Spanish soldiers were among the best in the world, almost invulnerable to attack from the ground when mounted on their fierce war horses in full battle armor. A dozen mounted soldiers could hold off and even defeat hundreds of Inca foot soldiers. In addition, European diseases, to which the indigenous people had no immunity, killed them by the thousands.

As much as anything, the incredible timing of the conquest sealed the Incas' fate. If the Spanish had arrived as little as a year or two earlier or later, things might have worked out quite differently. As it happened, though, they showed up exactly at the moment of the Incas' greatest vulnerability; the Inca empire had been split by a civil war, and many local groups were itching to throw off their newly acquired masters. The conquistadores, especially Pizarro, manipulated the situation brilliantly, installing puppet rulers to pacify the masses, and always acting with brutal decisiveness.

The End of the Conquistador Era

Victory did little to dampen the Spanish conquerors' lust for power, and they quickly began fighting among themselves. In 1538, Diego de Almagro contested Pizarro's right to govern the new territory of Peru. Almagro was defeated, tried, and sentenced to death in Lima, garroted in the same way as Atahualpa. Francisco himself was stabbed to death in his palace in 1541 by the remaining members of Almagro's rebel army, led by his son.

The Spanish crown tried to restore order by imposing the New Laws of 1542, aimed at controlling the unruly conquistadores and ending the enslavement of the indigenous peoples, already a widespread practice. A new viceroy, Blasco Núñez Vela, was sent to oversee the budding colonies in 1544, but Gonzalo Pizarro (Francisco's brother) organized resistance and fought and killed Núñez in the battle of Añaquito near Quito in 1544. Pizarro, in turn, was defeated by royal troops near Cuzco in 1548 and beheaded on the field of battle.

THE COLONIAL PERIOD

From 1544 to 1720, Ecuador existed as part of the Viceroyalty of Peru, one of the divisions of Spain's New World colonies. During two centuries of relative peace, settlers replaced the conquistadores, and female immigrants evened the balance of the sexes.

Farms and Slaves

Without the mineral wealth of Peru or Bolivia, Ecuador had to earn its keep from its soil. Soon the rich volcanic earth of the Andean highlands bore bumper crops of wheat, corn, and potatoes, which thrived in the mild climate. Cattle, horses, and sheep grazed on endless fields of grass.

The most common form of land tenure was the *encomienda* system, in which Spanish settlers were given the title to tracts of the best land, along with the right to demand tribute from any indigenous people who happened to live there. In exchange, the *encomendero* agreed to develop the land and convert its inhabitants to Christianity. The Spanish crown strove to impose strict rules governing the treatment of the *indígenas,* but the system was hard to regulate and usually resulted in virtual slavery. By the early 17th century, about 500 *encomenderos* controlled vast tracts of the Sierra.

Another important source of income was textile *obrajes* (workshops), where *indígenas* were forced to turn out cotton and wool cloth from dawn to dusk, often chained to their looms. Agriculture along the coast was hampered by rampant tropical diseases like malaria and yellow fever and a subsequent lack of natives to enslave. Bananas, cacao, and sugarcane filled lowland plantations, and shipping and trade kept ports such as Guayaquil in business. The coast north of the Manta area received most of the few African slaves that were imported to Ecuador, and the biggest community grew in Esmeraldas following a shipwreck in 1553, where they intermarried with indigenous people and occasionally escaped into fortified communities of runaways.

A sweltering climate, impassable terrain, and fierce indigenous groups kept most settlers out of the Oriente except a few brave (and often martyred) missionaries.

The Holy Scorecard

The Roman Catholic Church was a cornerstone of life during the colonial period for indigenous people and immigrants alike. By a majority vote, the Vatican had decided that indigenous people actually did have souls, making their conversion a worthwhile endeavor. Every town had a church operated either by Franciscans, Jesuits, or Dominicans, all competing for souls like sports teams vying for points. A strict tithing system made the church the largest landowner in the colonies. Jesus and the Virgin Mary were blended with the old gods of the sky and mountains in ceremonies in remote villages.

The Racial Pot Simmers

Over everything lay the subtle but pervasive gauze of race. Europeans born in Spain (*peninsulares*) or the New World (criollos) stood at the top of the social ladder. They ran the sweatshops and owned the haciendas (farm estates), raking in money as others labored in the sun.

Mixed-blood mestizos were in the middle, keeping the urban machinery going as shopkeepers, craftspeople, and skilled laborers. This middle class, aspiring to wealth and status as they looked down on the native masses, was politically unstable and easily provoked by fiery rhetoric—a ready source of fuel for the spark of independence.

The indigenous people that remained after the Spanish conquest made up most of colonial society, numbering 750,000–1 million by the 16th century. Countless numbers had died of imported diseases like smallpox, measles, cholera, and syphilis, to which they had no natural immunity, especially on the coast. Others were forced onto *reduciones,* hastily assembled townships that made it easier for the Spanish to collect taxes and demand labor.

Forced labor systems had *indígenas* working months to build roads and buildings. The debts they accumulated along the way far outweighed the pittance they earned, if anything, resulting in a system of peonage in which debt was handed down from generation to generation. Some *indígenas,* luckily, were left more or less alone, since much of the land they inhabited was inaccessible or otherwise of little interest to the Spanish.

INDEPENDENCE FROM SPAIN
First Sparks

Just as things had settled into a comfortable pattern in the colonies, a series of events unfolded that would eventually shake the continent to its foundation. Scientific visitors started to bring news of the outside world and new ideas in science and philosophy. From 1736 to 1745, the French mission to measure the shape of the earth at the Equator spread ideas of rational science and personal liberty, courtesy of the Enlightenment. Revolutions in the United States (1776) and France (1789) set the stage for the wars of independence in South American countries, and in the early 19th century, German explorer and scientist Alexander von Humboldt helped diffuse the latest scientific findings, which further fueled the fire.

In Ecuador, the physician and writer Eugenio Espejo was born in 1747, growing up to become a liberal humanist who demanded freedom and a democratic government for the colonies. Thrown in jail repeatedly and even exiled for his books and articles, Espejo died of dysentery he contracted in a Quito prison in 1795 and is hailed as one of the fathers of independence. Elsewhere in the country, uprisings among both *indigenas* and mestizos protested colonial treatment at the hands of Spain and its regime in the New World.

The final straw came in July 1808 when Napoleon invaded Spain, deposed King Ferdinand VII, and installed his brother Joseph Bonaparte on the throne. Monetary demands on the colonies—always a source of friction—skyrocketed as Spain sought funds to fight for the deposed Ferdinand, and the colonists decided enough was enough.

Early Uprisings

On August 10, 1809, a group of Quito's elite jailed the president of the Quito *audiencia* (colonial government) and seized power in the name of the deposed king of Spain. Ironically, the Quiteño Rebellion, the first declaration of independence in the Spanish colonies, took place in support of the Spanish king and ended abruptly. All the main players were executed by troops loyal to Bonaparte.

Ecuador's independence struggle is depicted on the main clock tower in Loja.

EL LIBERTADOR

Revered and despised, triumphant and frustrated, El Libertador (The Liberator) embodied all the contradictions and potential of the continent he helped set Latin America free from the colonial clutches of Spain. One thing is true: Whether as the heroic liberator of South America or the tyrannical despot chasing an impossible vision of continental unity, Simón Bolívar made his mark on history. At his death, his dream remained only half fulfilled: He had freed his beloved land, but he couldn't unify it.

Born in Caracas on July 24, 1783, to a wealthy family of planters, Simón Antonio de la Santisima Trinidad Bolívar y Palacios saw both his parents die before his 10th birthday. Relatives and friends helped raise him in the cultured circles of the New World's upper class.

Bolívar's early teenage years were spent in military school, where his records reveal his innate martial talent. His studies continued in Europe; he divided his time between aristocratic parties and studies of history, art, and the classics. His attention was soon captured by the rising star Napoléon Bonaparte, who had just crowned himself emperor of France for life. As he soaked up the rhetoric of philosophers such as Rousseau and Voltaire, advocating the sacred duty of a monarch to protect the common man by means of the law, Bolívar was solidifying his own ideas for South America.

From his European experiences, Bolívar came to believe that the best way to organize the struggling republics would be through a strongly centralized, even dictatorial government. At the helm would preside a lifetime ruler with limitless power who would labor for the greatest good, instead of abusing his position – in other words, a "moralistic monarch."

By 1807, Bolívar was back at his estate in Caracas and a member of the growing independence struggle. Napoléon's deposition of Ferdinand VII of Spain gave the revolutionaries their chance: Venezuela proclaimed its independence on July 5, 1811, and declared war on Spain soon after. Although the campaign did not fare well initially, Bolívar soon established his military reputation. Two years later, ecstatic crowds greeted him in Caracas, where he was formally titled El Libertador and given complete dictatorship over the country.

Spain struck back with crushing force, occupying Caracas in 1814. Ironically, the defeat of his political role model at the battle of Waterloo provided crucial aid to Bolívar's revolution. Having declared "war to the death," Bolívar quickly snapped up the surplus arms and soldiers and turned them to his cause. Mean-

In December 1811, a junta declared the *audiencia* independent and sent troops off to fight the Spanish, who routed them at Ibarra in 1812.

The Battle for Independence

As the independence struggle faltered in Ecuador, Simón Bolívar's struggle in Venezuela resulted in a final victory over the Spanish at the Battle of Boyacá in 1819. Bolívar's success inspired antiroyalist forces in Guayaquil, and a bloodless military coup was carried out on October 9 by forces led by José Joaquín de Olmedo. At the same time, a two-pronged independence movement was heading toward Ecuador: Venezuelan Simón Bolívar led the armies to the north in Colombia and Venezuela, and Argentine José de San Martín from Peru to the south.

However, the revolutionary forces suffered some early defeats as they tried to take the highlands and were beaten back to the coast after a rout by royalist forces at the Battle of Huachi near Ambato in November 1820. The cause was boosted in May 1821, when brash young general Antonio José de Sucre arrived in Guayaquil on Bolívar's orders and reinforcements were sent by San Martín from Peru. Royalists inflicted a second defeat at Ambato in September 1821, and Sucre decided to change his tactics. Instead of trying

while, he was busy organizing the Congress of Angostura, which in 1819 made his dream of Gran Colombia real, with Bolívar as dictatorial president.

Nowhere else did Bolívar's contradictions seem more apparent than in his political philosophy. The same man who admired the United States so much that he described the North American democracy as "a government so sublime that it might more nearly benefit a republic of saints," also wrote to a friend how he was "convinced that our America can only be ruled through a well-managed, shrewd despotism." Perhaps Bolívar was demonstrating a ruthless practicality. Latin America, in his eyes, was simply not ready for democracy. "Do not adopt the best system of government," he said, "but the one that is most likely to succeed."

Spain's hold over Venezuela had finally been broken, but the battle for a united South America was far from won. Even before Bolívar freed Ecuador and Peru, finally eliminating the Spanish threat to the New World, his dream of Gran Colombia began to falter. Bolívar knew the worst was yet to come – and it was in peace that the newly freed nations would eventually disappoint him. His noble-minded revolution soon dissolved into a bloody struggle between disparate political, regional, and racial factions. In a last-ditch attempt to reconcile the warring populations, Bolívar organized a peace congress in Panama in 1826. His effort was in vain – only four countries showed up.

Bolívar became depressed by his failure to build a united continent, and in April 1830 he resigned as leader of Gran Colombia, declaring: "America is ungovernable; all who served the revolution have plowed the sea." It was an ominous prediction of the chaos that would grip much of the continent during the 19th century. Bolívar planned to go into exile but lost his final battle with tuberculosis, dying at age 47 on December 17, 1830, in a small town on the Colombian coast. He never answered the question of whether a South America unified under a monarch would have prospered, or if he simply would have recreated in the New World the system he fought to dispel. Shortly before he died, the fiery general seethed with bitterness at what he saw as the betrayal of both himself and his dream: "There is no good faith in America, nor among the nations of America. Treaties are scraps of paper; constitutions, printed matter; elections, battles; freedom, anarchy."

Even on his deathbed, though, his thoughts were full of hope for his beloved federation: "Colombians! My last wishes are for the happiness of our native land."

---

to march to Quito via Guaranda, he decided to head south and take Cuenca first, cutting supply lines for royalist forces. Marching with a multinational force of 3,000 men, mostly Peruvians, his force outnumbered the royalists, who fled north, and Cuenca was taken in February 1822 without a single shot being fired. Sucre moved north to Latacunga, and royalists retreated farther to positions in the hills around Quito.

Knowing that the royalists held strong positions, Sucre decided to head for Quito via an arduous climb over the Pichinchas to the southwest of the city. Royalists attacked in the early morning of May 24, 1822, and the ensuing Battle of Pichincha lasted three hours and cost 600 lives. The patriots very nearly lost before reinforcements arrived, and the royalists retreated and surrendered formally two days later. Simón Bolívar arrived in Quito three weeks later and arranged his famous meeting with José de San Martín in Guayaquil on July 26, 1822, commemorated in the city's famous monument on the waterfront.

A pair of additional victories in Peru sealed South America's independence. The Battle of Junín on August 7, 1823, was fought by so many cavalrymen that it was called the "Battle of the Centaurs." The night before the Battle of Ayacucho in 1824, men from both sides crossed into the opposing camps to bid farewell to friends and brothers. The next day, fewer than 6,000 patriots defeated more than 9,000 royalists, who had them outgunned by a factor of 10. Spain was beaten and withdrew its administrative apparatus from the Americas, with its tail between its legs. It was arguably the end of Spain as a truly global power.

Bolívar's grand plan for a united South America soon succumbed to regional rivalries, and he resigned as leader of Gran Colombia in April 1830. In August, Ecuador withdrew from Gran Colombia and became fully independent.

EARLY YEARS OF THE REPUBLIC

Ecuador's childhood as a nation was marked by power struggles among criollo elites, in particular aristocratic conservatives from Quito and free-enterprise liberals from Guayaquil. Meanwhile, the new republic had little effect on most of the country—the poor, in other words, stayed poor.

Juan José Flores held power 1830–1845, either directly as president or through puppet figures. Most of his power came from Quito, but widespread discontent by 1845 forced him to flee the country. The 1845–1860 period saw 11 governments and three constitutions come and go as the economy stagnated and the military's influence in politics grew. By 1860 the country was on the brink of chaos, split by provincial rivalries and tension over border disputes with Peru and Colombia.

The Moreno Era

In 1860 a new player rose to the top. Gabriel García Moreno embodied devout Sierra conservatism—so much so that some historians have dubbed his regime a theocracy. He grew up during the chaos of the preceding decades and was determined to impose religious and political order on Ecuador.

Conservatives loved him, citing his many social programs as proof that he saved the country from disaster. An improved school system now accepted women and *indígenas,*

new roads connected the coast to the highlands and Quito to the rest of the country, hospitals and railroads were built, and exports jumped from $1 million to $10 million between 1852 and 1890. Moreno was deeply religious, and he established Roman Catholicism as the official state religion, with membership a prerequisite for citizenship and voting. Free speech was tightly controlled and political opposition squelched. He even renamed army battalions "Guardians of the Virgin" and "Soldiers of the Infant Jesus."

Not surprisingly, Moreno's firm stance made him many enemies among liberals, and in 1875, six years after establishing the official Conservative Party, he was hacked to death on the steps of the presidential palace. His last words were reportedly "God doesn't die." His death divided the nation with deep mourning among conservatives and celebration among liberals. Writer Juan Montalvo rejoiced from his European exile: "My pen has killed him."

INTO THE 20TH CENTURY

Two decades of jousting between the Liberal and Conservative Parties ended with the ascension to power of General José Eloy Alfaro. In two terms as president, 1897–1901 and 1906–1911, Alfaro embodied the Radical Liberal Party as much as Moreno typified conservatism. Alfaro toppled the Catholic Church from its domination of daily life by seizing church lands, instituting freedom of religion, secularizing marriage and education, and legalizing divorce. He also completed the Quito–Guayaquil railroad and rode triumphantly aboard it in 1908. However, as with Moreno, Alfaro made many enemies and became a hated figure for conservatives. He lost power in a coup in 1911 and soon afterward was arrested and brought to Quito. An angry mob broke into the prison where he was held and shot him dead, dragging his body through the streets and burning it in Parque El Ejido. It was a barbaric end for the "old fighter," who is considered the hero of Ecuador's liberal revolution and particularly revered by the current president Rafael Correa.

Crisis and War

After Alfaro's death, Ecuador stood on the brink of civil war, and a severely weakened state meant that the real power was held by the land-owning elite. The 1920s saw a prolonged economic and political crisis, and between 1925 and 1948, Ecuador had no fewer than 22 heads of state, each of whom tried to ride out the economic slumps that culminated in the 1929 Wall Street crash, which caused exports to fall by two-thirds. In 1934 the celebrity of José María Velasco Ibarra began, who said, "Give me a balcony, and I will become president." He was elected over and over. The first to appeal to both liberals and conservatives, Ibarra was nonetheless overthrown four times during his five terms between 1934 and 1961.

The border between Ecuador and Peru, outlined only roughly by the colonial *audiencia* in Quito, had been a bone of contention since Ecuador became a country. Boundary talks broke down into skirmishes, and in 1941 Peru launched an all-out invasion of Ecuador's southern and easternmost provinces, taking advantage of the rest of the world's focus on World War II. Fearing a coup, president Carlos Alberto Arroyo del Río kept the best troops in Quito during the border fighting, but a cease-fire was arranged within two months. The January 1942 Protocol of Peace, Friendship, and Boundaries, also known as the Río Protocol, quickly became a national disgrace for Ecuadorians. Not only did Ecuador have to sign away more than 200,000 square kilometers of territory rich in oil and gold deposits to its hated larger neighbor, but the country also lost the Amazon river port of Iquitos, its main river access to the Atlantic, in the bargain. Ecuadorians quickly looked for someone to blame beyond the guarantor countries of the United States, Chile, Argentina, and Brazil, who were more interested in their own much larger war.

Postwar Ecuador: Instability and Military Rule

A period of relative political stability in the mid-20th century proved too good to last.

Ecuador sided with the Allies in World War II, during which the United States built a naval base in the Galápagos and tried to kick all German settlers off the archipelago. After the war, Ecuador enjoyed a resurgence of democracy and its attendant freedoms. Even old Velasco Ibarra was finally able to finish a full term—his third—in 1952.

When a wave of disease ravaged Central America's banana crop, Ecuador stepped in to supply the huge U.S. demand with the help of the United Fruit Company. Exports jumped from $2 million in 1948 to $20 million in 1952, and Ecuador's position as world banana king became official.

By the late 1950s, however, the banana boom was over. Ibarra, who was reelected in 1960, began a proud Ecuadorian political tradition by renouncing the Río Protocol in his inaugural address, to the delight of the crowd. His left-leaning policies proved ill-timed, however, coming at the height of the Cold War. A gunfight in the congressional chamber proved how bad things had gotten at the top. In November 1961 the military removed Ibarra from power; two years later it replaced his successor with a four-man junta.

Ecuador's first experiment with outright military rule was short-lived, barely managing to pass the well-intentioned but ultimately ineffectual Agrarian Reform Law of 1964 before succumbing to concerns over another economic slump. Ibarra was reelected in 1968 for the fifth time with barely a third of the popular vote. For two years he enjoyed military support as he dismissed Congress and the Supreme Court, suspended the Constitution, and dictated harsh but necessary economic measures designed to get the country back on its feet.

By 1972—the same year in which Ecuador was found to have the third-largest petroleum reserves in Latin America—another military junta was back in power. In response to widespread concern that the newfound wealth would be squandered by a corrupt civilian government, the junta instituted a firm strategy of modernization. Industrialization leapt forward, and the middle class grew in numbers and power, but further attempts at land reform met the stone wall of the landholding elite. Not surprisingly, the poor suffered from the oil-boom inflation without reaping the attendant benefits.

The Return to Democracy

Coups in 1975 and 1976 caused splits within the military, and they sought to return Ecuador to civilian rule. In January 1978 a national referendum voted for a new constitution, universal suffrage, and guaranteed civil rights. The following year, highly popular and charismatic left-winger Jaime Roldós Aguilera took office in a landslide election victory. He found himself at the wheel of a country unfamiliar with democracy, but with a government budget and per capita income increased more than 500 percent by the oil windfall. His center-left government began programs of improving rural literacy and housing. Roldós championed human rights, formed a friendship with the Sandinista government in Nicaragua, challenged the oil contracts negotiated with foreign companies, and turned down an invitation to Ronald Reagan's inauguration. Tragedy struck in May 1981 when Roldós and his wife were killed in a mysterious plane crash. Left-wing Panamanian leader Omar Torrijos died in a similar plane crash a few months later, and a common view is that they were both assassinated by a right-wing conspiracy. You can read about these theories in John Perkins's 2004 book *Confessions of an Economic Hitman.*

The early 1980s brought a succession of crises. Border fighting with Peru flared up in January 1981, December 1982, and January 1983, and the disastrous 1982–1983 El Niño climate pattern caused $640 million in damage from drought and floods, ruining rice and banana crops along the coast. Sudden declines in petroleum reserves left the country with a foreign debt of $7 billion by 1983, when inflation hit an all-time high of 52.5 percent.

Conservative León Febres Cordero beat out eight other candidates for the presidency in 1984. A pro-U.S. foreign policy, neoliberal plans to roll back state control, and strong-arm tactics that led to accusations of human rights abuses brought him into conflict with Congress and the country. In January 1987, Cordero was kidnapped by air force troops under orders from a mutinous general in prison. Only by granting the general amnesty was he able to secure his own release after 11 hours in captivity, a move widely perceived as cowardly by Ecuadorians. That same month, an earthquake in Napo Province killed hundreds and ruptured the all-important oil pipeline, causing Ecuador to suspend interest payments on its $8.3 billion foreign debt.

In 1988, social democrat Rodrigo Borja Cevallos won the presidency and introduced more gradual reforms, including a literacy program and legislation to protect civil liberties. His tenure was plagued by high inflation and a general strike by indigenous groups, which resulted in the granting of territorial rights for Huaorani groups in the Oriente.

Like a pendulum, Ecuadorian voters swung back to the right, and in 1992, Christian Socialist Sixto Durán Ballén assumed the presidency. Further economic austerity measures, including a privatization law that left 100,000 public employees without jobs, helped curb inflation but prompted widespread demonstrations and a general strike in May 1993. Ballén's administration was also clouded by a scandal involving vice president and economic guru Alberto Dahik, who fled to Costa Rica in a private plane after being accused of embezzling millions of dollars in state funds. A government cover-up, which involved the seizure of Central Bank vaults that held incriminating microfilm, led to the resignation of ministers and the impeachment of one Supreme Court judge.

Meanwhile, the political turmoil was compounded when tensions with Peru erupted into outright war in January 1995. Six weeks of combat over the headwaters of Río Cenepa ended only after the intervention of a multinational team of observers. Even though Ecuador claimed victory, the fighting cost Ecuador $250 million in damage plus untold losses in commerce and tourism.

El Loco

Desperate times led the voters to desperate choices. In 1996, the same year Jefferson Pérez became Ecuador's first-ever Olympic medalist by winning a gold medal in speed walking in Atlanta, Abdalá Bucaram decided to run for president for the second time. The grandson of a Lebanese immigrant, he had carved out a successful political career as founder of the Partido Roldista Ecuatoriano (PRE), named after his brother-in-law Jaime Roldós. Bucaram had been mayor of Guayaquil and built a reputation for his eccentric style and rousing speeches. His nickname was "El Loco" (The Crazy One), and he was an energetic campaigner who often used to sing at political gatherings. He was seen as a political outsider, an image that he exploited to perfection, marketing himself as the people's hero who would lead them out of poverty. He defeated favorite and current Guayaquil Mayor Jaime Nebot by only 200,000 votes in the 1996 election.

From the start, it was clear that El Loco wasn't firing on all cylinders. His inaugural address was described as a two-hour "hysterical diatribe." One day he was raising money for charity by shaving his mustache on live TV; the next he was having lunch with Ecuadorian-American Lorena Bobbitt, who infamously cut off her husband's penis in 1993. The president released an album titled *A Madman in Love* and crooned at beauty contests. More importantly, he outraged his supporters by introducing austerity measures that led to skyrocketing utility bills, and he was accused of large-scale corruption. A general protest strike paralyzed the country, and on February 6, Congress determined that he was unfit to govern on grounds of "mentally incapacity" by a 44–34 vote. Bucarám holed up in the presidential palace for days before finally fleeing to exile in Panama, allegedly with suitcases filled with public money, a mere six months after taking power. He has always protested his innocence of any wrongdoing and has tried several times to return. His son continues to be an important politician in Ecuador.

Vice president Rosalía Arteaga became Ecuador's first woman leader for a matter of hours before the male-dominated Congress reacted with horror and put a man back into the post: Congress leader Fabián Alarcón. He repealed the austerity measures and muddled through for another year or so until another election was called.

Economic Crises and Dollarization

After the pantomime of Bucaram's brief presidency, Ecuadorians thought that things couldn't get much worse, but how wrong they were. A second El Niño hit the country badly in 1998, washing out roads, devastating the country's farming and fishing industries, and killing off wildlife in the Galápagos. In August, an earthquake of magnitude 7.1 hit near Bahía de Caráquez, knocking out water and electricity supplies and even more roads.

Meanwhile, Ecuadorians made what seemed to be a sensible choice by electing former Quito mayor and Harvard graduate Jamil Mahuad to the presidency by a margin of less than 5 percent in a hotly contested election against billionaire Álvaro Noboa. Things began well when Mahuad finally laid to rest the long-standing border dispute with Peru a few months after taking office. However, the rising cost of El Niño, depressed oil prices, and plummeting confidence of foreign investors led to Ecuador's worst economic crisis in modern times. The country's currency, the sucre, fell dramatically from 6,000 to the U.S. dollar in early 1999 to 25,000 in January 2000. The economy shrank by more than 7 percent, and inflation rocketed to 60 percent. Mahuad pressed ahead with deeply unpopular economic austerity measures, and in a disastrous decision, froze more than $3 billion of bank deposits, preventing millions of Ecuadorians from making withdrawals. Worse news came when Ecuador became the first country to default on its Brady bonds. Filanbanco, the country's largest bank, then folded, taking $1.2 billion in public funds with it.

Mahuad likened the situation to the sinking of the *Titanic* in a state-of-the-nation speech.

Typically, the captain goes down with the ship, and some 10,000 mostly indigenous protestors made sure he did by shutting down much of the country in a general strike on January 21, 2000. Mahuad's last-ditch policy was to freeze the sucre at 25,000 to the U.S. dollar and adopt the greenback as Ecuador's official currency, but opponents charged that this would worsen poverty and have a catastrophic effect on those who had their savings in sucres. Hundreds of indigenous protestors occupied the Congress and Supreme Court buildings in Quito and declared a new government. Violent protests in Guayaquil followed, and Mahuad was deposed by a three-man military junta in a bloodless coup. Mahuad handed over the reins to his vice president, Gustavo Noboa, a university professor from Guayaquil. Noboa pressed ahead with the dollarization plan and introduced austerity measures to obtain $2 billion in aid from the International Monetary Fund. By 2001, the economy had begun to stabilize, but by then 500,000 Ecuadorians had already emigrated to North America and Europe in search of a better life.

In 2002 the leader of the coup that disposed Mahaud was himself elected president, again pushing billionaire Álvaro Noboa into second place. Colonel Lucio Gutiérrez campaigned on an outsider platform that painted him as a friend of the downtrodden. His ascent was seen as one more signal of a general leftward political shift in Latin America, but it didn't last long. As soon as he got into power, Gutiérrez's policies moved markedly to the right. He befriended U.S. President George Bush and introduced austerity measures to finance the country's massive debt. He then fired the entire Supreme Court and announced plans to allow his old ally Abdalá Bucaram to return. Thousands of protestors flooded into the streets again, and after he lost the support of the army in April 2005, Gutiérrez was forced to flee in fear for his life, leaving by helicopter from the roof of the presidential palace in Quito. On the positive side, the country's economy grew by 7 percent in 2004, in part due to higher oil prices, which

helped the government post a fiscal surplus for the first time in decades.

Rafael Correa and 21st-Century Socialism

Alfredo Palacio took over from Gutiérrez and managed the country ably until the next election in 2006. This time, a young populist left-winger named Rafael Correa, who served briefly as finance minister under Palacio, entered the fray. Correa, a middle class Guayaco with a doctorate in economics, described himself as a "Christian socialist" and a "humanist." He founded his own political movement, Alianza PAIS, championed the rights of the poor, and used a pun on his name, which translates as "belt," to promise to "whip" the political and economic elite. He even introduced Ecuador to a new word: *pelucón* (bigwig), in reference to the richer classes. Correa came second in the first round of elections but won the second round, inflicting a third straight defeat on Álvaro Noboa.

Correa took office in January 2007 and quickly began rebuilding the political structure, mindful that Ecuador had gone through presidents like hot dinners—he was the seventh in 10 years. He pushed through a referendum to replace Congress, which he lambasted as corrupt, with a new constituent assembly. The new body was tasked with drafting a new constitution, which was approved by referendum with nearly 65 percent support in September 2008. The new constitution was the first in the world that protected the rights of the environment (*la pacha mama*), and also guaranteed rights to clean water, health care, pensions, and free state education, including at the university level. Crucially and controversially, Correa consolidated his position by including in the Constitution increased presidential powers, the right of the president to be reelected, and a clause stipulating that any assembly vote to remove him would result in an immediate election.

In his economic policies, Correa vowed to end "the long dark night of neoliberalism." He renegotiated oil contracts, declared Ecuador's national debt "illegitimate," and increased government spending on health, education, and roads. He expelled the World Bank representative and allowed the country to default on its debt in December 2008, buying it back at 30 percent of its value five months later. It may have been an economic masterstroke, but the uncertainty over Correa's unpredictability did little to encourage foreign investors.

In foreign policy, Correa has had a topsy-turvy relationship with both the United States and Colombia. His friendship with Venezuelan President Hugo Chávez didn't endear him to either country, and he followed through on his election promise to refuse the renewal of the U.S. military base in Manta, which some commentators have blamed for an increase in organized crime on the coast. Far more serious was the situation with Colombia, when Colombian President Álvaro Uribe ordered an attack on a FARC guerrilla camp two kilometers inside Ecuadorian territory near Lago Agrio. Tensions were high for many months, although with the election of Uribe's successor, Juan Manuel Santos, diplomatic ties have been fully restored.

Correa has also made no secret of the fact that he is no friend of the private media in Ecuador, branding them his "biggest enemy." His government has spent millions of dollars on publicity while attempting to introduce controls on private media. There have been frequent clashes, and Correa has accused one of the country's biggest TV stations, Teleamazonas, of lying and forced its temporary closure in December 2009.

Correa became the first Ecuadorian president in 30 years to be reelected, in April 2009, taking 52 percent of the vote, far ahead of his nearest rival, former president Lucio Gutiérrez, who had 28 percent. However, later that year his popularity fell following a national energy shortage caused by a lack of water in the country's main hydroelectric plants. There was also a scandal involving his elder brother, Fabricio, who had received multimillion-dollar government contracts, and upon losing the contracts campaigned for his own brother's removal from office.

On September 30, 2010, Ecuador was plunged into an astonishing and unforeseen crisis when proposed budget cuts to the police sparked a nationwide police protest that left the country without any law enforcement for an entire day. As robberies mounted, Correa went to negotiate with the renegade police officers in Quito, but he was attacked with tear gas, kidnapped, and held in a police hospital. The nation held its breath as the military attacked the hospital and fought a fierce battle with police rebels to free Correa. Eight people were killed. Correa reacted swiftly, purging the police force and introducing a state of emergency. His popularity has soared since, and the crisis, if anything, has strengthened his position, even though many Ecuadorians considered the president to be at least partly to blame.

Correa's latest project was a referendum in May 2011 to amend the constitution to implement a stricter penal system, regulate the judiciary, and ban financial institutions from owning media. Other proposed measures included the prohibition of casinos and blood sports, particularly controversial because of the popularity of bullfighting in the Sierra. The 10 proposals were narrowly approved by popular vote, but most received less than 50 percent support. It remains to be seen if they will be ratified by an increasingly divided National Assembly.

Whether or not Ecuador has entered a long era of political life with Rafael Correa at the helm is impossible to say, but he is the most consistently popular and longest-serving president of the past 30 years, and he has already brought sweeping social, political, and economic changes to the country.

Government and Economy

POLITICS

For much of its history, Ecuador has been anything but politically stable. The first 160 years after independence saw 86 governments and 17 constitutions come and go. Of the few administrations that resulted from popular election, not many were free of fraud. Citizens became understandably disenchanted with the system. At the same time, Ecuador has managed to avoid many of the pitfalls its neighbors have fallen into. Democracy has been in place in name since 1948, and in reality since the end of military rule in 1979. Ecuador was one of the first countries in Latin America to return to democracy after a wave of dictatorships in the 1960s and 1970s, and the political system seems more entrenched every day. However, the military is never far away from the political arena, and military-backed coups have removed several presidents, including Jamil Mahuad in 2000 and Lucio Gutiérrez in 2005, while current president Rafael Correa was kept in power and rescued by his own military in 2010.

The traditional rivalry between liberal trade-happy coastal residents and conservative landholding Sierra elites has spilled over into politics, and the presidency has historically alternated between the two interests. Sometimes the transition isn't smooth: In 1988 outgoing president León Febres Cordero, a Guayaco, refused to hand over the presidential sash to his successor, Rodrigo Borja, from Quito.

There are many reasons for Ecuador's history of political instability: Regionalist feelings are very strong, which is never a recipe for unity, and the enormous number of political parties has also made matters worse. The people are very passionate and very vocal in voicing their displeasure with the government, and general strikes and mass protests have played a key role in bringing down presidents. Ecuador's Congress members have also been quick to blame the president for the country's political ills and are more interested in saving their own skins than backing the head of state.

Another factor is Ecuador's compulsory voting system: Nonvoters are fined and lose some of their citizenship rights. The system usually hands election wins to a populist who promises to end poverty single-handedly, and then quickly loses support when he fails to deliver (as happened with Abdalá Bucaram and Lucio Gutiérrez).

However, current president Rafael Correa has bucked this trend in many ways. He has reduced political instability by forming a new political party, Alianza PAIS, which now dominates the National Assembly. He has increased presidential powers and, most importantly, followed through on every election promise he made in his first election win. Confidence in the political system is at an all-time high, but the kidnapping of Correa in September 2010 serves as a warning that any political stability that may have been achieved in the past few years could be swept away without the backing of the military, who still wield enormous, if unseen, power in Ecuador.

Organization

Under the 2008 Constitution, Ecuador is a representative democracy with compulsory suffrage for all literate citizens over age 18. People aged 16–17 have the option to vote. An executive branch consists of 15 ministers, a vice president, and a president elected by majority vote every four years. Presidents must be elected by at least a 50 percent majority, leading to frequent runoff elections. Under the new Constitution, presidents can now stand for reelection.

The National Assembly of Ecuador replaced the National Congress in 2009 following the approval of the new Constitution. It has 124 seats filled by national and provincial deputies who serve four-year terms. The regional voting system gives less populated provinces, such as those in the Oriente and the Galápagos, disproportionate representation, since each deputy needs fewer votes to be elected. The National

Assembly in turn appoints justices to form the judiciary branch of the Corte Suprema (Supreme Court).

Twenty-four *provincias* (provinces)—the newest, Santo Domingo de los Tsáchilas and Santa Elena, were formed in 2007—are ruled by governors who oversee 219 *cantones* (counties) and around 1,000 *parroquias* (parishes).

Parties
Ecuador used to have some 35 different political parties, which only contributed to instability. The recent domination of President Correa's party, Allianza PAIS, has changed things. The government party holds just under half of all seats, but at the time of this writing, its lack of an overall majority means that building coalitions is important. The party is also very broad and cannot rely on all its members to tow the government line. Ten other parties hold seats in the assembly, but only two hold more than 10 seats: former president Lucio Gutiérrez's Partido Sociedad Patriótica (PSP) and the long-standing right-wing Partido Social Cristiano (PSC), created by the late president León Febres Cordero. Billionaire Álvaro Noboa's party holds seven seats at present. Abdalá Bucharam's son (with the same name) heads the left-wing Partido Roldosista Ecuatoriano (PRE) and frequently supports the current government. Pachakutik, the mostly indigenous political party, is an important political force, although it only holds four assembly seats at present. It helped overthrow Jamil Mahuad and elect Lucio Gutiérrez, and it can organize nationwide strikes involving thousands of members.

ECONOMY
Ecuador's economy balances among relatively small agricultural enterprises, businesses in the Sierra, and huge export projects along the coast. Oil supplies half of the country's export earnings, and bananas, cut flowers, shrimp, coffee, and cacao are the other main exports. Trade is mainly with North and South America, although exports to Asia have increased recently. Natural resources abound, but a large foreign debt and high inflation have historically blighted the country's economic development.

After the economic crisis a decade ago, the Ecuadorian economy has recovered well, posting annual growth of 5 percent 2002–2006, peaking at 7 percent because of high oil prices in 2007, and growth remains high. However, as with many developing countries, Ecuador's wealth is concentrated with a few people at the top of the social ladder with little trickling down to the rest. President Correa has been trying to change this and succeeded in reducing the national debt, but it still remains at $14 billion, 23 percent of GDP. Inflation has also fallen to a historic low of 3.3 percent in 2010. However, there is still a long way to go. According to government statistics, the monthly cost of basic food for a family (known as *la canasta básica*) stood at $544 in 2010, while the average family income is just $448. A minimum wage has been introduced and increased to $264 monthly, but it's still very low. Unemployment may be relatively low at 6 percent, but this doesn't tell the whole story. Informal craftspeople and vendors make up close to 40 percent of the workforce, and the real problems are underemployment, low pay, and high prices, which go all the way back to dollarization a decade ago. The number living below the poverty line is still 35 percent (more than 5 million people) in 2010, a slight reduction from previous years.

Agriculture
The conquistadores never realized it, but Ecuador's true wealth lies in its soil and the people who work it. Agriculture is the primary industry in the Sierra, followed by livestock trading and crafts. Despite agrarian reform laws established in 1964 and 1974, the land remains unevenly distributed. Tiny farms of less than two hectares can't support families, leading many people to emigrate to the cities and the coast in search of work.

The rich river flood plains on the coast have seen their share of booms and busts. At the turn of the 20th century, cacao beans provided funds

Ecuador's economy is dominated by crops such as bananas.

The biggest industrial moneymaker is, of course, oil—the "black gold" that brought the Oriente into the national economy and Ecuador to the attention of the world. Modern drilling in the Amazon had to wait for decades after the invention of the internal combustion engine because most of the Oriente was still inaccessible, but major strikes in 1967 near Lago Agrio got the sticky black ball rolling. In 1971 a pipeline was built from Lago Agrio through Quito to Esmeraldas, and Ecuador began to export petroleum. One year later, Ecuador was found to have the third-largest reserves in Latin America, and a symbolic barrel of oil was paraded around the country. Ecuador joined the Organization of Petroleum Exporting Countries (OPEC) in 1974, and the economic focus of the country began to shift away from agriculture. The government's coffers filled, allowing the construction of new roads and factories. Foreign countries began to see Ecuador as a creditworthy nation, and export earnings quintupled 1971–1975, although little of the money made its way to the country's poor, and poverty levels actually worsened in the 1980s.

At present, oil still accounts for nearly half of Ecuador's export earnings and supplies a third of public money, but such a dependence on oil makes the country vulnerable to fluctuations in world oil prices. Far worse is the environmental damage to the Amazon's fragile ecosystems and indigenous communities, and lawsuits are ongoing. Current reserves will not last long, and pressure to drill in new territories is building, especially under Yasuní National Park, which has huge untapped reserves.

After oil, mining is Ecuador's other main industry, and gold mines in the southern highlands and Oriente, especially in Zamora-Chinchipe Province, are very lucrative, although the amount of gold left is far less than what was taken by foreign companies and Spanish colonizers in past centuries. As with oil, pressure to mine previously protected areas is increasing, and the government is facing stiff resistance from indigenous groups to mine on their territory.

for the Quito–Guayaquil railroad, and coffee and rice took off in the 1930s. Today, coffee is the nation's second-most-valuable crop, grown on 20 percent of all farms. Rich shrimp farms along the coast have made Ecuador one of the world's largest shrimp exporters. The banana boom came in the 1940s, becoming Ecuador's leading export crop by 1947, and one Ecuadorian in 10 is still dependent in some way on the banana industry. Flower exports exploded in the 1990s and are now the country's fourth-largest export.

Industry

One-quarter of Ecuador's gross national product (GNP) has some catching up to do—the country's economy is still dominated by the export of raw materials and the import of finished products—but the situation is better than in many other developing countries. The government has recently increased import duties as a protectionist measure while boosting manufacturing. Factories process food and manufacture textiles, wood products, chemicals, plastics, metal goods, and timber.

People and Culture

DEMOGRAPHY

Ecuador's population currently stands at 14.4 million. It doesn't seem like that many people for a country slightly larger than Britain, which packs 62 million into almost the same amount of space. However, with the amount of comparatively inhospitable mountain and rainforest terrain, two-thirds of the population live in densely populated urban areas, and Ecuador actually has one of the highest population densities in South America (21 people per square kilometer). Driving through endless plantations, hills, and rainforest makes this hard to believe, but once you arrive in the major cities, the problems are clear to see. Beyond the colonial churches, leafy parks, and shopping malls are ramshackle shantytowns plagued by a serious lack of basic amenities.

Ecuador's population continues to grow at over 1 percent per year, and large families are still considered normal, not least because the predominant Roman Catholic religion frowns on birth control. Women still tend to marry young and have children quickly. The effect of this is a very young population—35 percent are under age 15, while only 4.5 percent are over 65. In direct contrast to the aging populations of North America and Europe, the pressure in Ecuador is already showing on the education system and job market.

However, things are beginning to change, albeit slowly. While many of their mothers didn't work, most young women expect to work nowadays, and particularly in the wealthier classes, many are marrying later and having fewer children. The steep rise in the cost of living as a result of dollarization a decade ago may also be a factor in the recent tendency toward smaller families.

At the other end of the life cycle, death rates are decreasing. Life expectancy stands at a respectable 75 years, and infant mortality has been cut by more than half in the last three decades to just 2 percent, according to the World Bank.

Distribution

The population is split roughly equally between the coast and the mountains, about 45 percent in each region, with the remaining 5 percent residing in the Oriente, easily the most sparsely populated region. The majority of the population used to live in the mountains until large-scale economic migration through the 20th century saw millions of people flood to the coast in search of work in the plantations, farms, and factories. This coastal shift was also an urban shift, with the rural population declining and correspondingly rapid growth of urban slums, especially in Guayaquil, where the population has doubled in the past 20 years to over 3.3 million. Guayacos commonly refer to the dwellers in slums on the outskirts of town as *invasores* (invaders).

Racial Breakdown

Ecuador remains deeply divided along racial lines. The largest racial group is mestizo—people of mixed Spanish and indigenous heritage—although you'll rarely hear anyone refer to themselves by this word. Indigenous people make up 25 percent, mainly living in the mountains. White people of Hispanic descent (5–7 percent) dominate Ecuador's wealthy classes. A small Afro-Ecuadorian population, concentrated mainly in Esmeraldas, Quito, and Guayaquil, makes up 3 percent, with immigrants from the Middle East, Asia, Europe, and elsewhere in Latin America rounding out the numbers (including this author).

While racism is deeply entrenched, the younger generation is more open-minded, and the current government has gone further than previous administrations to open high-profile positions of power to both indigenous people and Afro-Ecuadorians.

Emigration and Immigration

There are estimated to be at least 1.5 million Ecuadorians living abroad, mainly in the United States and Spain, which both have populations of more than 400,000 Ecuadorians. The economic crises have driven 1 million people to leave the country since 1999, though nobody knows the true number because so many left illegally. In recent years, most of these emigrants have become legal residents after amnesties in both Spain and the United States.

The Ecuadorian family economy depends heavily on money sent back from abroad; remittances are valued at $1.7 billion annually and are therefore the second largest contributor to the local economy after oil. The current government has launched a repatriation program to lure Ecuadorians home, offering incentives such as waiving duties on shipping and providing cheap loans to start new businesses. So far it has not been very successful.

Ironically, while emigration levels have been high, in recent years immigration has also increased markedly, with large numbers of Colombians and Peruvians arriving in Ecuador. There is also an increasing Chinese population, and you'll notice that even small towns have a Chinese-run restaurant.

Ecuador is also growing in popularity as a retirement destination for North Americans. *International Living* magazine has voted Ecuador the top retirement destination two years running, citing low housing prices, the stability of the U.S. dollar, a favorable climate, friendly locals, and diverse travel opportunities as reasons to come here. Vilcabamba, Cuenca, and small towns near Quito such as Tumbaco and Cotacachi are listed as popular retirement destinations, and the beaches of Santa Elena and Manabí are also growing in popularity.

INDIGENOUS GROUPS
The Sierra
Most of Ecuador's indigenous population inhabits the northern and central Andes. About 800,000 of the **Runa,** or "the people," as the Quechua-speaking descendants of the Incas call themselves, live in tightly knit communities where kinship bonds are paramount, and everyone helps in voluntary communal work events called *mingas*. The *cabildo* (town hall), which

> ## INDIGENOUS MARKET DAYS
>
> - **Sunday:** Cajabamba, Cañar, Cayambe, Chordeleg, Chugchilán, Cuenca, Gualaceo, Machachi, Pujilí, Quito (Parque El Ejido), Santo Domingo, Saraguro, Sigchos
> - **Monday:** Ambato
> - **Tuesday:** Latacunga
> - **Wednesday:** Pujilí, Otavalo
> - **Thursday:** Guamote, Saquisilí, Tulcán
> - **Friday:** Latacunga
> - **Saturday:** Guaranda, Latacunga, Otavalo, Peguche, Riobamba, Zumbahua

is run by the *alcalde* (mayor), keeps things running smoothly. Artisanal work and subsistence agriculture bring in the most money, with private and community-owned plots planted with maize, barley, and potatoes. Festivals of Roman Catholic patron saints are combined with ancient Inca harvest ceremonies.

Imbabura Province is home to the famously successful **Otavaleños** as well as smaller groups of **Caranquis** and **Natabuelas.** Traditional dress persists here, with different groups represented by different colors and patterns. Cotopaxi Province is home to special celebrations of Corpus Christi along with important pilgrimages to sanctuaries in Baños and El Quinche.

Chimborazo Province has more highland *indígenas* than any other province, while Cañar is home to the ancient **Cañari** people, and Loja to the successful cattle-raising **Saraguros,** brought from Bolivia in the 15th century by the Incas.

The Coast
The **Tsáchilas,** also known as Los Colorados

(colored ones) because of the traditional red dye in their hair, inhabit the western foothills of the Andes and give the city its name: Santo Domingo de los Colorados. A handful of small communities contain about 2,000 members who make their living farming tropical crops and raising livestock. Modern clothing and hairstyles have mostly replaced the traditional dress and red hair-painting. They are famous for their knowledge of natural medicine—the governor general is also the head *pone* (curer), who is adept in the use of medicinal plants as well as ceremonies to drive away evil spirits, attract good fortune, and look into the future.

The tropical river country of the western Cotacachi-Cayapas Ecological Reserve is home to the **Chachis,** also called the Cayapas. Tradition holds that they came from Quito in a series of migrations under pressure from Spanish settlers. Today, the Chachis number about 4,000 and practice slash-and-burn agriculture, fishing, and hunting. Traditional open-sided one-room homes covered by thatched roofs are built by entire communities.

About 1,600 **Awá-Kwaiker** live between the Río Mira and Río San Juan in Carchi Province near Colombia as well as in Imbabura Province. The Awá owe their continued existence to a flagship program begun by Ecuador and Colombia in 1986 in which three protected areas, including 100,000 hectares in Ecuador, are being managed for environmental and cultural longevity.

The Oriente

Of the 17 distinct ethnic groups that lived in the Amazon before European contact, only eight are left today. Animistic religions practiced in the Oriente center around the idea of transmigration of souls from one form to another—the animal you kill today was probably a person in another life, and you may come back as a plant, so treat them all with equal respect. Shamans serve as intermediaries between the terrestrial and spiritual world, curing diseases, overseeing initiation ceremonies, and preserving oral traditions. Crafts include basket-weaving, pottery, and colorful ornaments of wood, feathers, beads, and insect parts. Foreign demand for animal parts has encouraged some native groups to kill endangered species.

Although contacted much later than groups in the highlands and coast, Oriente indigenous communities have had to deal with tens of thousands of settlers because of a huge push from the Ecuadorian government to populate the area, along with the pollution and development that have accompanied oil exploration. Disease, clear-cutting, and slaughter of game animals are all part of the mess, which has encouraged the formation of strong-willed indigenous groups to fight for their rights.

Lowland Quechuas, or Kichwas, are the largest group of Amazonian *indígenas,* numbering 30,000–40,000. Two distinct subgroups, the Napu (Quijos) and the Canelos, fill western Napo and northern Pastaza Provinces. Patrilineal groups of extended families called *ayllus* live in widely dispersed permanent settlements that raise cattle and grow crops in communal (*llactas*) and family (*carutambo*) plots. Men hunt, fish, clear the land, and tend the cattle, while women weed, harvest, and care for the home (*huasi*) and garden plot (*chakra*).

Women also make the famous lowland Kichwa pottery, an art that is passed down from mother to daughter. One subgroup, the Sarayacu, is especially well-known for creating striking white, red, and black images of gods such as Quilla Runa, the moon, who was banished to the sky for committing incest with his sister; and Pasu Supai Huarmi, the beautiful forest goddess with long dark hair, black lips, and teeth stained red from drinking the blood of her enemies.

The second-largest indigenous group in the Ecuadorian Amazon is made up of two related tribes. United by language to each other and groups across the border in Peru, the **Shuar-Achuar** once sent fear into the hearts of children worldwide when they were known as the Jivaro, headhunters who shrunk the heads of their enemies. For centuries, the two closely related groups have earned their tough reputation by protecting their rugged, isolated territory between the Río Pastaza and Río Marañón

© BEN WESTWOOD

Shuar tribes believed that the ceremonial process of creating shrunken heads trapped the souls of enemies.

east of Cuenca. Their resistance started in 1527, when they sent Huayna Capac packing after his attempt to invade the Amazon; the Inca leader was forced to buy time with gifts as he fled. Soon after the first contact with the Spanish, the Achuar decided that the Europeans' desire for gold was a disease. After capturing the town of Logroño, they poured molten gold down the governor's throat to satisfy his thirst for the metal.

Salesian missionaries helped the Shuar-Achuar found the first ethnic federation in the Ecuadorian Amazon in 1964. Today, the groups, under the Shuar Federation and the Organization of Ecuadorian Achuar Nationalities, are among the best organized in the country. One reason for this was the ongoing border war with Peru, which pitted indigenous battalions against members of their own tribes across the border. They are still not to be trifled with: A survey of the Achuar in 1993 found that 50 percent of tribe members' male ancestors had died from gunshot blasts, usually administered by other members. This gave them one of the highest murder rates of any population group in the world and still helps explain the traditional Achuar greeting, *Pujamik* ("Are you living?").

Many Shuar-Achuar live in the traditional oval house called the *jea,* separated into male (*tankamash*) and female (*ekent*) zones. Crops such as yucca, papaya, sweet potato, and pineapple fill the gardens. The ceremonial process of creating *tsantsas* (shrunken heads) has faded, although the occasional unlucky sloth is still targeted. The fine-tuned Achuar calendar predicts everything from the rainy season to the breeding time of rainforest insects. It's timed around the movement of the Pleiades, which the Shuar-Achuar view as seven mythical orphans called the Musach, who fled their despotic father for the heavens. The Río Pastaza serves as the axis of the traditional Shuar worldview of the world as hemispheres of earth and sky surrounded by water.

The **Huaorani,** or Waorani, entered the headlines for their fight against oil exploration. They were one of the last groups contacted in the Ecuadorian Amazon, and they remain one of the least Westernized. Most of the tribe's 1,300 or so members live in a special reserve created for them in the shadow of Yasuní National Park from the Río Napo to the Río Curaray. The Huaorani have started to abandon their nomadic ways and to settle in small enclaves grouped by clan.

Men once wore only a *komi,* a small cord tying the penis to the belly, but Western clothing has become popular. Both sexes still stretch their earlobes with balsa plugs, called *dicago,* up to five centimeters around. The Huaorani have a reputation for defending their isolated autonomy with a fierceness equaled only perhaps by the Shuar. They speared five Summer Institute of Linguistics missionaries to death in 1956, and as recently as 1987, a Roman Catholic bishop visiting the tribe on a government-sponsored mission to open the way for the oil companies was found with 17 spears in his body.

About 1,000 **Siona-Secoya** live a

seminomadic existence along Río Aguarico, Río Eno, Río Shushufindi, and Río Cuyabeno in Sucumbíos and eastern Napo Provinces. The two groups, related in language and history to neighboring tribes across the border in Colombia, merged during the 20th century but have recently begun to maintain distinct ethnic identities. After oil exploration began to devastate their territory, the Sionas and Secoyas sued Texaco (now Chevron) in 1993 for more than $1 billion for environmental abuses. The case was unsuccessful in U.S. courts but was transferred to Ecuadorian courts in 2003. Chevron were ordered to pay $9 billion in January 2011, but a lengthy appeals process means it could take years for the tribes to see any money, if they ever do.

The **Cofán** are one of the smallest remaining groups, with about 1,500 members left (down from 20,000 at the time of the Spanish conquest). They live along the Río Bermejo in western Sucumbíos Province. Randy Borman, the son of an American missionary couple, grew up among the Cofán and has become their de facto head, leading them in their fight against oil exploration and encroachment by settlers.

Recent anthropological studies have shown that the **Zapara,** once thought extinct, have actually partially integrated with some of the **Lowland Kichwas** living in isolated parts of the central rainforests. Funding from international nongovernmental organizations is helping to preserve their language and culture.

RELIGION

Since the first conquistador planted a cross in honor of God and the king of Spain, Roman Catholicism has been a linchpin of Latin American culture, and Ecuador is no exception—around 95 percent of the population consider themselves Catholic.

Catholicism has played a central role in Ecuador's history, and after the conquest many of the local indigenous people were pressured into converting for fear of what their new masters would do if they refused. However, many of the old traditions prevailed, and while the

Spanish built churches directly on top of Inca temples, the best example of the religious mix can be seen in the fusion of indigenous and Catholic celebrations. For example, Inti Raymi, the festival of the summer solstice, is merged into the Catholic celebrations of Saint John the Baptist. La Mama Negra celebration in Latacunga exhibits an even more complex racial mix, blending together Afro-Ecuadorian, indigenous, and Catholic beliefs. In modern Ecuador, many indigenous people still defend their beliefs proudly and appear to see no conflict between calling themselves Catholics while also consulting shamans.

Belief in fate is pervasive in Ecuador: The expression *así es la vida* (such is life) is ubiquitous and has led to a certain acceptance that life is hard and there's not much to be done about it. However, things are changing. One of the most significant shifts occurred in the 1960s, when a wave of liberation theology swept through Latin America. Priests who once encouraged the poor to accept their lot in life and hope for better treatment in heaven began to urge them to improve their current situation instead. Missionaries instituted literacy campaigns and helped fight for land reforms and social justice, to the horror and opposition of the more conservative elements of society. In the present day, President Rafael Correa has also made the clear connection between religious belief and social reform, referring to himself as a "Christian socialist," and his moral indignation at the supposed greed of Ecuador's super-rich has endeared him to the masses while making him a hated figure to much of the economic elite.

The domination of Roman Catholicism is not total, however. Evangelical Protestantism continues to make inroads, as do sects such as Mormons and Jehovah's Witnesses, particularly in Guayaquil. North American missionaries have been instrumental in the growth of these religions both in urban and rural areas, although they still only account for less than 5 percent of the population.

Note that religious belief is very strong in Ecuador, and atheism is considered unusual and indeed frowned upon by most locals. If you're not religious, it's preferable to avoid the subject than to engage in spiritual debates, which could become heated.

LANGUAGE

Spanish is Ecuador's official tongue and is spoken by the vast majority of the population. Many residents of the Sierra still speak dialects of Kichwa (the language of the Inca), and in the farther reaches of the Oriente, several indigenous languages are still in use, but most indigenous people have a good knowledge of Spanish. In the highlands, they tend to speak relatively slowly and clearly, making cities like Quito, Baños, and Cuenca popular for studying Spanish. On the coast, the people speak noticeably faster. The easiest way to distinguish between the coastal and mountain accents is the pronunciation of the letter *s*. In the mountains it is pronounced very strongly (*"mas-s-s o menos-s-s"*) and on the coast it often disappears completely (*"ma' o meno'"*). Wherever you are in Ecuador, you will notice that the accent, as in all of Latin America, is markedly different to Castilian Spanish from Spain.

English is spoken mainly by highly educated people and those working in tourism, so don't expect to bark requests at locals and receive a favorable response. On the established tourist trail, you will find tour operators and guides who speak English and a select few who speak other European languages, but most of the time independent travelers will struggle to communicate without some knowledge of Spanish. So don't be lazy—learn some Spanish before you come to Ecuador! Nine times out of 10, even a modest knowledge of Spanish is enough to get by as a traveler. Ecuadorians are patient with foreigners and appreciate any efforts you make to speak their language.

EDUCATION

The education system in Ecuador has improved markedly in recent years but still has serious problems. The good news is that Ecuador actually has one of the highest youth literacy rates in South America—estimated at 95 percent, helped by government programs in rural areas where Spanish is often secondary to indigenous languages such as Kichwa. In theory, schooling from ages 6 to 14 is free and compulsory, but in practice many poorer children either do not attend or lack money for essential school supplies—even pens and paper as well as books. (This makes pencils and pens a good present to hand out to begging children, if you must give something.) However, investment in education has increased under Rafael Correa's government, and regulations have been introduced to require that teachers have the correct qualifications and to pay them accordingly.

The real problems begin in secondary school, which at present has an enrollment rate of less than 65 percent. Many families see little point in their children continuing education beyond age 14 if they are most likely to do manual work or street vending to contribute to the family income. State high schools are blighted by administrative and infrastructural problems, although government investment is improving the situation gradually. The best schools are nearly all private and cost anywhere from $150 to $500 per month, an impossible level for most Ecuadorians, who earn a minimum wage of $240 per month. These schools exist only in urban centers and deliver bilingual education; English is increasingly important.

At the university level, the situation has become a little fairer in recent years. The current government ordered all state universities to eradicate fees for poorer students, while the middle classes make small contributions according to their family's salary level. Many of the best universities in Ecuador are actually state institutions, including Escuela Politécnica del Litoral in Guayaquil and Escuela Politécnica Nacional in Quito. Loja, Cuenca, and Ambato also have very good universities. There are reputable Roman Catholic universities in Quito and Guayaquil, the latter attended by President Correa. The best private institutions include San Francisco de Quito and Universidad de Especialidades Espíritu Santo (UEES) in Samborondón, outside

Guayaquil, both of which have scholarship programs for less wealthy students. Despite the improvements in higher education, many of the wealthiest students still study in North America and Europe.

Unfortunately, it's not only the education that is important, but the connections, and many people still secure employment through their personal relationships and family name.

ARTS AND ENTERTAINMENT
Visual Arts

Early colonial sculptors and painters remained anonymous, remembered only for their gloomy but heartfelt images of the Virgin and Gothic-style saints. Indigenous influences began to emerge with the onset of the Renaissance and baroque styles, allowing artists like Gaspar Sangurima, Manuel Chili (a.k.a. Caspicara), and Miguel de Santiago more freedom for personal expression in their works.

The Quito School, spanning the 17th and 18th centuries, was one of colonial South America's most productive artistic centers and became famous for its mastery of polychrome carvings (decorative coloring) of the Virgin Mary, Jesus, and numerous saints. It was particularly well-known for its use of realism, emphasizing the suffering of Christ and even using real human hair. The use of the color red was predominant.

The 19th century and independence brought "popular" art to the fore, and the Quito school's influence faded, as it was synonymous with Spanish rule. Concerned with the secular as much as the holy, it consisted of intense colors and naturalistic images of landscapes and common people. This was followed in the 20th century by the reverberations of impressionism and cubism.

Powerful representations of the dignity and suffering of Ecuador's original inhabitants dominated the work of Ecuadorians Eduardo Kingman (1913–1999), Camilo Egas (1889–1962), Olga Fisch (1901–1990), and Manuel Rendón (1894–1982).

Oswaldo Guayasamín (1919–1999) is probably Ecuador's most famous modern artist.

TIGUA HIDE PAINTINGS

The brightly colored paintings created by the artists of the Tigua Valley are some of Ecuador's most distinctive (and portable) souvenirs. The paintings typically depict scenes of village life, such as *campesinos* tilling their fields as llamas look on and condors fly over a snow-covered volcano in the background.

This style of painting began as a way to decorate small drums used in traditional festivals. In the early 1970s, local artist Julio Toaquiza began to paint the Andean scenes on small canvases of sheep hide stretched over a wooden frame. Julio taught his family the skill and watched as the craft acquired a life of its own. Today more than 200 artists turn out the paintings in a handful of communities nestled in the Andes west of Latacunga. The Toaquiza family painters are still considered to be the best. Orlando Quindigalle in Pujilí is also renowned.

The original bright enamel paints have since been supplanted to an extent by more durable oils and acrylics. Many of the larger frames are works of art in themselves, covered with intricate patterns. The frame can often determine the overall quality of the work – when purchasing a painting, look for even, straight frames with taut hides.

Tigua paintings can be found all over Ecuador, but the best selection and prices are at the source. There's an artists' cooperative in the small community of **Tigua-Chimbacucho,** 52 kilometers west of Latacunga on the road to Quevedo, as well as a few artists in **Quilotoa** and **Pujilí** who sell their paintings at their residences.

In Quito, the **Tianguez** shop (Plaza de San Francisco, tel. 2/223-0609, www.tianguez.org, 9 A.M.-6 P.M. daily), run by the Fundación Sinchi Sacha, has a good selection. It is located below the Iglesia San Francisco.

His tortured, distorted figures, heavily influenced by cubism, led people to call him an "Americanista Picasso." The painting *La Ternura,* depicting an indigenous mother embracing her child, is particularly moving, and his final magnum opus, *La Capilla del Hombre* (Chapel of Man) is a highlight of any visit to Quito.

A school of "naive" painting, centered in the Tigua Valley in the central Andes, began with images painted on ceremonial drums. Now the miniature paintings are made on animal skin stretched over a wood frame. Quality varies widely, but the better ones are true works of art—vibrantly detailed depictions of everyday life in the *campo.*

Music and Dance

The haunting melodies and wistful lyrics of the Ecuadorian Andes are played by groups throughout the highlands, from brass bands to guitar trios and lone crooners on street corners. The music can be extremely beautiful, although there is an obsession with churning out the same old songs for visitors such as "El Condor Pasa," made famous by Simon and Garfunkel in the 1960s. Flutes were considered holy by the Inca, who provided the original set of instruments and tunes for modern-day Andean music. The *quena,* a vertical flute once made from condor leg bones, is used to play the melody, along with panpipes such as the *rondador* and *zampoña.* Bass drums made from hollow logs or clay are used to keep the beat, with the help of various rattles and bells.

The colonial Spanish tried their best to suppress indigenous music, but in the end only succeeded in adding a host of new instruments. Relatives of the guitar include the 10-stringed *charango,* originally from Bolivia and made from armadillo shells. The *charango* is strummed lustily next to *bandolinas* (15 strings) and familiar-looking *guitarras* with six nylon strings. Violins, clarinets, accordions, harmonicas, mandolins, and brass instruments were used to join in the fun along the way.

Along the northern coast, you'll find some of the most African-influenced music on the continent. Rhythms like marimba and the Caribbean-flavored *cumbia* from Colombia make it almost impossible not to move your hips while listening, especially to bands along the northern coast and in the valley of Río Chota in the northern Sierra.

Along the southern coast, centered around Guayaquil, the poignant acoustic guitar–based love songs of *pasillo,* which has its origins in waltz, were made famous throughout South America by Julio Jaramillo in the 1950s and 1960s.

In the latter 20th century, salsa and merengue began to dominate, and they remain extremely popular across the generations. Merengue is the faster of the two but actually simpler to dance to, while mid-tempo salsa has a more complex rhythm. If you are in Ecuador for an extended period, consider taking classes, as dancing is very important at social occasions and a good way to meet people. Locals will be delighted to see you try.

International rock and pop are also very popular in Ecuador, and many top music acts come to Quito to perform. Heavy rock is particularly popular, and Quito, and to a lesser extent Guayaquil, have a thriving *rockero* scene. There is also a particular obsession with dubious 1980s pop music, noticeable if you turn on the English-language radio stations.

In the past 10 years, the booming beats of *reggaetón* have started to dominate the party scene, particularly in teenage discos and on the beach. It originated in the Caribbean as an electronic Spanish form of reggae but owes as much to hip-hop. *Reggaetón* is famous (or infamous) for its explicit lyrics, gyrating dance moves, and repetitive beat; you'll either love it or hate it.

Literature

Cumandá, a romantic drama set in the rainforest written by Juan León Mera, is one of Ecuador's most famous books from the late 19th century. Writers of the early 20th century mainly focused on realistic social themes of injustice and race. Jorge Icaza's *Huasipungo* (*The Villagers,* 1934) is considered one of Ecuador's best novels, vividly portraying the hardships of everyday life in an indigenous village. Other important writers formed part of the Grupo de Guayaquil who jointly wrote *Los Que Se Van.* The avant-garde movement in the 1930s was led by Pablo Palacios, who dealt with challenging subjects such as mental illness (from which he himself suffered). One of his most widely read works is *Un Hombre Muerto a Puntapiés* (*The Man Who Was Kicked to Death*).

Liberal essayist Juan Montalvo wrote the philosophical work *Los Siete Tratados* and *Capitulos Que Se Le Olviadaron a Cervantes* (*Chapters Cervantes Forgot to Write*), and was exiled for his liberal views by conservative President Gabriel García Moreno. José Joaquín de Olmedo eulogized the struggles for independence in *The Victory of Junín* and *Song of Bolívar.* Adalberto Ortiz's *Juyungo* (1942) deals with the lives of poor blacks in Esmeraldas. Jorge Carrera Andrade, from Cuenca, is one of the country's best-known poets with his *Place of Origin.* Alejandro Carrión Aguirre, a journalist and novelist, was another well-respected

20th century writer. The bilingual selection *Ten Stories from Ecuador,* available at the Libri Mundi bookstore in Quito, gives good insight into modern Ecuadorian writers. Current writers, such as Abdón Ubidia, whose *Wolf's Dream* is available in English, or Gabriela Aleman, who was voted one of "Latin America's 40 most promising writers under 40," help keep Ecuador well-represented on bookshelves. However, a lack of publishers, abuse of copyright, and the rise of the Internet has made it harder than ever for Ecuadorian writers to make a living in their own country.

Holidays, Festivals, and Events

Ecuadorians like to celebrate, and there are 10 official public holidays—from historical commemorations of famous generals, battles, independence anniversaries, and religious celebrations. In addition, most cities celebrate their foundation, and it seems that every month part of Ecuador is celebrating something.

Many of the better festivals are worth scheduling a visit around, especially La Mama

© CHRIS O'CONNELL

Good Friday celebrations in Quito involve painstaking reenactments.

PUBLIC HOLIDAYS AND MAJOR FESTIVALS

- **January 1:** New Year's Day – the morning after becomes six mornings after, with post-holiday festivities that include dancing and fireworks lasting until Epiphany.

- **January 6:** Epiphany or Día de los Reyes (Day of the Kings) – celebrated in the highlands with parades, the baking of sweet bread, and ritual burning of Christmas trees.

- **February or March** (weekend closest to new moon): Carnival – the country's biggest party, with national holidays on Monday and Tuesday tacked onto the weekend, when water-throwing is ubiquitous. Guaranda and Ambato hold the biggest highland celebrations, and the beaches are packed.

- **March or April** (40 days after Ash Wednesday): Easter Week – religious parades nationwide; the best is in Quito on Good Friday and includes purple-robed penitents.

- **May 1:** Labor Day – workers' parades around the country.

- **May 24:** Battle of Pichincha – commemorates the decisive Battle of Liberation above Quito in 1822 that resulted in independence from Spain.

- **May or June** (9th Thursday after Easter): Corpus Christi – honors the Eucharist, particularly celebrated by indigenous people in the Central Sierra.

- **June 21-29:** Inti Raymi – the preconquest celebration of the summer solstice combines with the San Juan parades (June 24) as well as San Pedro and San Pablo (June 29) and is celebrated particularly fervently in Otavalo and Cayambe.

- **July 24:** Simón Bolívar's Birthday – Continent-wide celebration of the man who dreamed of a united South America.

- **July 25:** Foundation of Guayaquil – one of the city's biggest celebrations, tacked onto Bolívar's birthday.

- **August 10:** Independence Day – commemorates the country's first (failed) uprising against the Spanish in 1809.

- **August 15:** The festival of La Virgen del Cisne (Virgin of the Swan) – celebrated in Loja with an extraordinary 72-kilometer procession.

- **September 1-15:** Fiesta del Yamor – Imbabura's biggest festival, celebrating the fall equinox with bullfights, dancing, and *yamor*, a nonalcoholic corn drink.

Negra, Inti Raymi, and the biggest parties of the year at Carnival and New Year. Most major holidays consist of up to a week of blowing off steam and generally celebrating life, along with the only acceptable occasion for cross-dressing in this macho culture. Parades march to the beat of brass bands as entire towns dance in the street. Special food is cooked, fireworks set off, and beauty queens selected between serious religious processions and private celebrations in homes. Hotels and restaurants often fill to overflowing and jack up their prices. During national holidays, it can be difficult to find a room or space on a bus—or even to find a bus. Most businesses close on the public holidays, so make reservations and exchange money beforehand.

The Catholic Church's most festive season revolves around **Easter,** which technically occurs on the Sunday after the full moon of the vernal equinox. **Carnival,** in February or March, is the huge party before the 40 days of fasting and penance known as **Lent,** which begins on **Ash Wednesday. Semana Santa** (Holy Week) occurs just before Easter. **Palm Sunday** kicks things off, with parishioners bringing palm fronds or corn stalks to church. Four days later, **Holy Thursday,** similar to the Day of the Dead

- **Third week of September:** Feria Mundial del Banano – Machala's biggest celebration of the yellow fruit that dominates its economy. The focal point is the beauty pageant to select the Banana Queen.

- **September 24:** Mama Negra de la Merced – the more religious of Latacunga's two festivals, with processions to honor the Virgin Mary.

- **October 9:** Independence of Guayaquil – parades and fireworks.

- **October 12:** Columbus Day – celebrates the "discovery" of the New World under the name Día de la Raza (Day of the Race), particularly celebrated in Guayas, Los Rios, and Manabí.

- **October 31:** Halloween – a big night nationwide with costumed revelers going trick-or-treating and partying hard.

- **November 2:** All Souls' Day – better known as Day of the Dead. Families bring food, flowers, and offerings to the graves of loved ones. Don't miss the delicious *colada morada*, a sweet purple fruit drink.

- **November 3:** Foundation of Cuenca – the city's biggest celebration, which merges with the previous holiday.

- **Week before November 11:** La Mama Negra – the more raucous secular festival in Latacunga, with colorful costumes, parades, and the arrival of a blackened man in woman's clothing throwing milk and water, culminating in Latacunga's Independence Day on November 11.

- **December 6:** Foundation of Quito – the capital's biggest party with parades, dances, and bullfights.

- **December 24:** Christmas Eve – masses and parades, particularly famous in Cuenca. Most locals celebrate Christmas with gifts at midnight.

- **December 25:** Christmas Day – the morning after, but highlights include Paseo de los Niños (Children's Parade).

- **December 28:** All Fools' Day – masquerades and clowns.

- **December 28-31:** New Year's Eve – life-size effigies of prominent figures of the outgoing year, called Años Viejos (Old Years), are ridiculed and burned at midnight. Expect a lot of smoke and fumes in Guayaquil and Quito. Minor roads are blocked with revelers after 4 P.M. Travelers need lots of small change to give donations to revelers.

in November, precedes the solemn processions on **Good Friday** and elaborate nighttime masses on **Holy Saturday.** Businesses not closed already will close on Saturday. Easter morning mass signifies the end of the deprivations of Lent and the holiday cycle.

FOOD AND DRINK

Ecuador isn't known for gourmet food, but it does have a wide range of tasty dining options beyond the famous roasted guinea pig. "Traditional" Ecuadorian cuisine (*comida típica*) borrows from the country's indigenous and Spanish heritage, and often caters to the poor majority with dishes that can be described in two words: cheap and filling. For the most part, *comida típica* isn't health food—animal fats are used to add flavor to soups, fried food is the norm, often on top of a mountain of rice, and there's a notable lack of vegetables. You wouldn't expect to come to the Equator and put on weight, but it can happen if you don't choose carefully. Being vegetarian can also be tricky, although in most tourist towns there are vegetarian restaurants and natural food stores. The best local food is the seafood on the coast, which competes with anywhere else in the world.

Dozens of restaurants in every town offer

A GUIDE TO SOUTH AMERICAN FRUIT

- **babaco:** Resembles a skinnier green-yellow papaya and has pronounced ridges that form a star in cross-section. Soft, juicy flesh is lightly sweet with a citrus tang.

- **banana:** The many varieties include *guineos* (familiar, long, and yellow), *magueños* (red and stubby), and *oritas* (finger bananas).

- **cherimoya:** Also known as custard apple or sweetsop; fist-sized with green, dimpled skin and sweet flesh.

- **granadilla:** Smooth, round crust 6-8 centimeters in diameter, with yellow, red, or green colors and a short stem. Crack it open to enjoy the delicious insides with a disgusting texture.

- **guanabana:** Football-sized and vaguely pear-shaped, dark green outside, with stubby spines. Spongy, white flesh has a lung-like consistency; almost artificially sweet.

- **mango:** Smooth and fist-sized, in yellow, orange, and green colors. Ripe when soft. Peel off the skin to uncover the stringy flesh around a large seed. Sweet, tart, and a delicious mess: slice off sections of skin, eat from those, and then suck on the stone for good measure.

- **maracuyá:** (passion fruit): Pale yellow baseball-sized rind is similar to granadilla, but crust is tougher, and orange insides are more tangy.

- **mora:** South American native in the blackberry family; delicious source of ice cream and juices.

- **naranjilla:** Yellow-orange, bright, and shiny, 5-7 centimeters in diameter, with a stem. Tart citrus taste is best in juice. Grown only in Ecuador and Colombia.

- **papaya:** Dark greenish-orange skin, 20-30 centimeters in diameter, 20-100 centimeters long, heavy, and slightly soft when ripe. Inside is smooth, pink-orange flesh great for *batidos* (milkshakes). Scoop out seeds and cut off the skin to eat. Skin has a peppery taste.

- **plátanos:** These green cooking plantains look like large bananas. *Verde* taste more like a potato, and *maduro* are closer to bananas.

- **taxo:** Elongated yellow-orange fruit 10 centimeters long, with peach-like skin. Soft when ripe. Tightly packed flesh packets with orange seeds inside. Sweet and tangy, similar to maracuyá.

- **tomate del arbol:** The tree tomato is sweet, but still definitely a tomato. Good in juice.

- **tuna:** Cactus fruit (prickly pear) is 2-4 centimeters long and green, yellow, and red, with spine stumps. Mildly sweet.

- **uvilla:** Small, round, yellow-orange fruit comes wrapped in its own papery protection and looks like a Chinese lantern. A specialty in the Chota Valley.

- **zapote:** Solid and fist-sized, with brown peach-fuzz skin and an acorn-like stem cap. Bright orange pulp surrounds 4-5 large seeds. Lightly sweet vegetable taste. Suck the stringy pulp off the seed, then go floss.

cheap two-course set meals with a drink for $1.50–3. The bargain-basement prices often reflect the quality of the food, although the better establishments often serve up great meals, so take your time to browse, and the advantage is that you can see exactly what they're serving as locals gobble it down.

If you tire of rice and beans—and you certainly will at some point—Ecuador's tourist towns and larger cities have a wide range of international cuisine, and much of it is top-notch. Italian food is particularly good here, as is Mexican. Chinese restaurants are called *chifas* and most serve *chaulafan* (fried rice) and *tallarines* (noodles), mixed with meat or vegetables, but Asian food is very hit-and-miss, and the quality is variable. Many of the best restaurants are attached to high-level hotels and charge prices comparable to those in the United States.

If you're staying in Ecuador for a while, it makes sense to do your own cooking, but don't forget to be vigilant with hygiene. Food from outdoor markets and supermarkets can be less expensive and better tasting, provided you have access to a kitchen or at least a knife and a plate. Prepare fruits and vegetables by peeling and washing them in purified water or with a concentrated food bactericide like Vitalin, available in supermarkets.

Food poisoning and diarrhea are unfortunately common among visitors to Ecuador. The likeliest culprits are unpeeled raw fruit and vegetables, salads, ice, pork, and shellfish. Needless to say, always buy bottled water and never drink from the faucet. It's also best to avoid buying food from vendors on public transportation—you have no idea how fresh or clean the food is, however tasty it looks.

Eating Out

A restaurant filled with locals usually means the food is good. A set meal (*menú del día*) is the cheapest and most filling option for budget travelers in any restaurant.

Breakfast (*desayuno*) isn't big, often just enough to hold you over to lunch. For $2–3 you can get a continental breakfast consisting of *tostada* (toast) or simply piping fresh *pan* (bread) with *mantequilla* (butter) and *mermelada* (jam), *café* (coffee), and *jugo* (juice) to wash it down. A *desayuno Americano* (American breakfast) adds *huevos* (eggs) served *fritos* (fried), *tibios* (soft boiled), or *revueltos* (scrambled). A bowl of fruit, yogurt, and granola is another popular breakfast option. Locals, particularly on the coast, often eat *bolón,* a fried ball of green plantains filled with cheese or bacon. In the southern Sierra, *tigrillos* (mashed plantains with cheese and egg) are a specialty.

At lunch (*almuerzo*), the largest meal of the day, locals either come home or eat out with their friends and relax during the hottest part of the early afternoon. Set lunches (*almuerzos*) include a *sopa* (soup), a *segundo* (main dish, usually some sort of meat or fish with rice, occasionally with vegetables or salad), a glass of juice, and sometimes a small *postre* (dessert). Dinner (*cena*) tends to be smaller and eaten from 7 P.M. on, although many Ecuadorians will eat out as late as 10 P.M. A set evening meal is called a *merienda* and follows a similar format to lunch.

Ecuadorians are not big on desserts, but there are great bakeries and ice cream places in most tourist towns. The ice cream is particularly good in the highlands. Traditional desserts include flan (a sweet custard made with eggs) and *dulce tres leches* (sweet three milks), a cake made with evaporated milk, condensed milk, and cream.

Snacks

Inexpensive, carbohydrate-rich foods like rice, potatoes, plantains, yucca, and corn are staples for most of the country. Grains include wheat, barley, and native quinoa, which was once sacred to the Inca and is now being recognized globally as an incredibly nutritious food with many of the same complete proteins as meat. Grains are popular in soups.

Many of these carbs are made into tasty, filling snacks. Plantains can be mashed into tortillas or fried for breakfast with cheese and bacon as *bolón;* the sweeter *maduros* are either fried or baked and served with cheese. *Choclo* (corn) is grilled and eaten whole with fresh cheese or mashed up and steamed in plantain leaves to make delicious sweet *humitas,* a popular option served with coffee for breakfast or as an afternoon snack. Other specialties found mainly in the southern Sierra are tamales (corn dough steamed with chicken, meat, or cheese) and *quimbolitos* (sweet steamed pudding with raisins).

Pastries such as empanadas are often filled with meat, cheese, and vegetables. *Yucca,* a root vegetable similar to parsnip, can be mashed into tortillas, or the starch is used to make bread, a popular snack usually served with

GOING BANANAS

To most of us a banana is simply a yellow fruit that makes a handy snack, but to many Ecuadorians it is a way of life, playing an essential economic and nutritional role. Ecuador is the world's largest banana exporter, distributing over $2 billion worth of fruit annually. Production of "green gold" centers around the coastal provinces of Guayas, Manabí, and El Oro, whose capital, Machala, hosts a Banana Fair every September in which local women compete for the coveted if slightly bizarre title of Banana Queen.

Peel away the skin and the banana plant can be used in a variety of different ways. The banana's cousin, the plantain, is most useful in cookery. When green (verde), they taste similar to a potato and can be mashed into empanadas (similar to potato cakes) or bolón (a fried ball filled with cheese and bacon) for breakfast. For lunch they are fried into circular patacones to accompany seafood as an alternative to french fries. As a snack they are sliced and fried into chifles, similar to potato chips. The riper plantains are called maduros (literally "ripe ones") and are similarly versatile. They too can be sliced into sweet chifles or fried or baked and served whole as a tasty side dish, often with cheese. Both varieties of plantains are a useful ingredient in soups, particularly maduro, which adds essential sweetness to coastal soups such as biche.

If this is all too complicated, you can always stick to the basics and simply peel back a guineo (banana) and munch away. After all, there are plenty to go around.

yogurt in fast-food joints. *Salchipapas* are a less authentic but hugely popular fast food: french fries topped by chunks of hot dog and smothered with ketchup, mayonnaise, or mustard.

Staples

Rice and beans are the most common ingredients of any meal. Beans are usually cooked in a sauce and served as *menestra,* which can also be made with lentils. Meats include *lomo* (beef, also called *res* or simply *carne,* "meat") and *chancho* (pork), served *a la parilla* (roasted) or *asada* (grilled). A very common sight in markets is a whole roasted pig (*hornado*). *Chorizo* is a spicy pork sausage, *chuletas* are pork chops, and *hamburguesas* are, obviously, burgers. Note that your burger will often come drenched in mayonnaise unless you specify otherwise. Set meals often include a *seco,* literally a "dry" stew, but in practice it usually has a sauce made of tomatoes, onion, and coriander. Choose among beef, *pollo* (chicken), or *chivo* (goat). If you choose the right place, it will be delicious, but in bargain joints, you'll get a greasy chicken leg on a mound of rice. *Estofado* is another type of stew, made with either chicken or meat and usually containing potatoes and carrot. *Bistec* is a version of beefsteak, usually cooked with tomato and onions.

Throughout Ecuador, piping hot *sopa* (soup), *caldo* (broth), and *crema* (cream soup) are popular. Watch out for *caldo de pata* (cow's hoof soup, also made with pig's trotters).

It's easy to remember the name of the hot pepper sauce that sits on almost every table in the country: *Ají* ("ahee!") is also the sound you'll make when you put too much of it on your food. It comes in handy to flavor up bland dishes.

Specialties

Fanesca, a whole grain dish including everything from peanuts and fish to squash and onions, is eaten at Easter and is a leading contender for the Ecuadorian national dish.

Specialties from the mountains include thick *locros,* made with potatoes, corn, and cheese. *Locro de papa,* served with avocado, is particularly good. *Yaguarlocro,* on the other hand, is for the more adventurous, made with blood sausage. *Llapingachos* are fried potato cakes that originated in Peru, usually served with a

© QUITO TURISMO

Fanesca is a traditional Easter dish made with fish and vegetables.

peanut sauce. Pork is very popular in the mountains, and along with the traditional roasted *hornado,* there is *fritada* (chunks of pork served with *mote,* a type of grain) and *chugchucara,* a regional variation found in Latacunga. You might want to go on a diet afterward to give your arteries a rest. For something healthier, try the fresh river fish, the most common of which are *trucha* (trout) and tilapia.

The most famous specialty in the Sierra is *cuy* (guinea pig), which are quite a sight in markets roasted whole on a spit. The meat tastes somewhere between smoked pork and chicken.

The coast is where you mouth really starts to water. The fish and shellfish here are delicious. The most popular fish on the coast is *corvina* (white sea bass), followed by *dorado.* Fish is usually offered *frito* (fried), *apanada* (breaded and fried), *al vapor* (steamed), or *a la plancha* (filleted and baked, literally "on the board"). *Camarones al ajillo* (shrimp in garlic sauce) is popular nationwide, and for good reason. Other shellfish include *cangrejo*

(crab), *calamare* (squid), *ostione* (oyster), and *langosta* (lobster or jumbo shrimp). *Patacones,* small pieces of plantain mashed flat and fried crispy, usually accompany seafood dishes and originally hail from Colombia. Salads accompanying seafood tend to come with a dressing made from lemon juice and salt.

On the north coast, one of the best dishes is *encocado,* seafood cooked with sweet coconut milk. Fish soup is excellent all along the coast, but an even more delicious version, *biche,* is made with sweet plantains and corn, found mainly in the central province of Manabí.

Ceviche is one of Ecuador's most famous dishes and consists of seafood (often raw), onions, and coriander marinated in lemon or lime juice, served with a dish of popcorn on the side. When shrimp is used in seviche, it's cooked beforehand, but those made with raw *pescado* (fish) or *concha* (clams) may pose a health risk. If you prefer your seafood soup hot, then try *encebollado,* a fish and onion soup served by street vendors as well as restaurants and renowned locally to stave off a hangover.

Another interesting coastal specialty is *cazuela*, a seafood broth made with plantains and flavored with peanuts.

The Amazon region is not renowned for its food, but as in the mountains the fresh river fish is good, including trout and tilapia. In the region around Coca, *maito* is a particularly delicious white fish. On rainforest trips, you might be treated to piranha (more bones than meat, but still tasty). The small heart of the *chonta* palm, called *palmito*, makes a tasty side dish, even though it kills the entire plant to harvest it. Most are grown on farms. The more adventurous can try *guanta*, an Amazonian rodent, which, like many unusual meats, is reported to taste similar to chicken.

Drinks

One of the highlights of a trip to Ecuador is the vast range of fresh fruit available, which locals make into *jugos* (juices), *batidos* (milkshakes), and *yogur* (yogurt). They're often made very sweet, and you can ask for less sugar (*menos azúcar*). A juice is usually included with a set meal. *Colada* is another popular drink, made with fruit and oats. The best is the purple *colada morada* served around the Day of the Dead (Nov. 2).

Coffee is good when it's pure (*café pasado*), but many places only have instant available. Check before ordering breakfast or go to a specialist coffee shop, which are more common in tourist towns. The best regions for fresh coffee are in the southern highlands around Zaruma and Loja.

Tea is becoming more readily available in tourist areas. The most common flavors are *manzanilla* (chamomile), *menta* (mint), *anis* (aniseed), *cedrón* (lemongrass), and *horchata*, a red-colored specialty popular around Loja that uses over a dozen herbs. Note that English tea is known as *té negro* (black tea), and you need to order milk separately, which often causes confusion.

Chilean **wines** yield the best value for the money because Ecuadorian vintages tend to be poor. Local **beers** include Pilsner (small or large bottles), weaker Pilsener Light (small bottles) and stronger Club Verde (small bottles and cans), but beer connoisseurs will be disappointed. U.S. and European imports of both wine and beer are available but very expensive. Microbreweries are slowly appearing, including the Turtle's Head in Quito.

Chicha is a fermented Sierra homebrew made with corn, yeast, and sugar. In the Oriente, it's still made the old-fashioned way: Women chew up yucca, spit it into water, and wait a day or so for the enzymes in the saliva to start fermentation. You may well be offered some on a rainforest trip, and it's rude to refuse, so down the hatch it goes.

Whisky is very popular in Ecuador, but the more traditional sugarcane liquor, known as *aguardiente* or simply *trago*, is the alcohol of choice in most of rural Ecuador. Heated and mixed with cinnamon and sugar, the potent concoction is called *canelazo*. With honey and *naranjilla*, a relative of the tomato, it becomes an *hervida*, served hot at fiestas. In any form, it can leave you howling at the moon. If you get too *borracho* (drunk) the night before, you may wake up *chuchaqui*, a Quechua word meaning "hungover" that proves even the Incas knew the perils of the morning after.

ESSENTIALS

Getting There

BY AIR

A wide range of airlines offer flights into Ecuador's two international airports, located in Quito and Guayaquil. Tracking down the cheapest fare is more problematic than finding flights.

General Suggestions

Make your reservations as early as possible, and reconfirm your flight or make sure your travel agency does it for you. Otherwise, you may lose your seat. As with most destinations around the world, airlines routinely overbook flights.

It may be less expensive to fly to other cities in South America than directly to Ecuador, depending on where you're coming from and how much time you have to complete the trip to Ecuador overland. Caracas, Venezuela, is the cheapest city in South America to fly to from the United States, and Lima, Peru, is a travel hub for the northwestern part of South America.

Published fares to Latin America can vary much more than flights within the United States—up to 30–40 percent from airline to airline. Comparing prices among various airlines certainly pays off. Flights to Latin America are slightly cheaper if you buy them ahead of time, because prices tend to rise close to high season as availability decreases. Planes

may be full for months in advance of the peak season during the North American summer and December–January. Ask about "open-jaw" flights, meaning you can fly out of a different city than you flew into, but don't consider one-way tickets unless you plan on staying more than a year. It's usually much cheaper to book a round-trip ticket and change your return date if necessary, rather than buying a return ticket once you're in Latin America, where ticket prices are much higher. Tickets valid for 30 days, called "bulk tickets," are almost always the cheapest. Stopovers are common among Latin American airlines, and you can make savings by taking an indirect route.

The travel agency **eXito** (U.S. tel. 800/655-4053, www.exitotravel.com) specializes in flying to Latin America and has useful information on its website. It organizes guided tours in Ecuador, Peru, and Bolivia, sells air passes, and can set you up with language schools in many different countries.

Charter operators and consolidators, called "bucket shops" in the United Kingdom, are legal discount ticket brokers who often advertise in the classifieds and travel sections of major city newspapers. In exchange for a lower price, you may have to buy your ticket quickly before the specific fare is sold out, or put up with a narrow travel window.

Student, Teacher, and Youth Fares

If you're under 26 or enrolled in some sort of school, you're eligible for a host of discounts. **STA Travel** (U.S. tel. 800/781-4040 or 800/385-9808, www.statravel.com) is the world's largest youth and student travel organization, with offices in 85 countries. Customers have access to worldwide emergency assistance, and STA issues the handy **International Student Identity Card** (ISIC) for $22, which can save you a great deal on airfare, lodging, and activities in Ecuador and other countries. The ISIC carries basic accident and sickness insurance coverage, as well as access to a 24-hour travelers' assistance hotline offering legal and emergency medical services. Teachers can purchase an **International Teacher Identity Card** (ITIC), and nonstudents under 26 are still eligible for an **International Youth Travel Card** (IYTC)—both offer similar discounts and insurance for the same price. The cards are also available directly from the **International Student Travel Confederation** (www.isic.org), a worldwide network of organizations devoted to promoting travel, study, and work exchange opportunities for students, young people, and academics.

Air Passes

Ask a travel agent about the **All America Airpass** (www.allairpass.com), which covers 15 airlines flying to and within Latin America. Choose from an unlimited combination of flights throughout the region, with fares that depend on the route and carrier. LAN (www.lan.com), an alliance of LAN Chile and LAN Peru, is part of the **One World Visit South America Air Pass** (www.oneworld.com), good for travel in Argentina, Brazil, Bolivia, Chile, Colombia, Ecuador, and Peru. Other airlines participating in the One World program include American Airlines, British Airways, Iberia, and Qantas.

Baggage Restrictions

These restrictions vary by airline, usually two checked bags per person, weighing 20–25 kilograms each. Fees for more luggage add up quickly, so weigh your baggage before you go to the airport if possible and ensure it's evenly distributed (you may be charged if one bag is over the limit even though the other bag is far lighter). A customs duty is sometimes charged when leaving Ecuador with any checked bags beyond the first two.

Leaving Ecuador

A $44 **exit tax** is levied at Mariscal Sucre International Airport in Quito (leaving from Guayaquil costs $27). The current **duty-free** allowance includes one liter of alcohol, 200 cigarettes or 50 cigars, and a "reasonable quantity" of perfume and gifts totaling no more than $200.

To and From the United States

American Airlines (Quito tel. 2/226-0900, U.S. tel. 800/433-7300, www.aa.com) has daily flights to Ecuador from most major U.S. cities via Miami or New York. **Continental** (U.S. tel. 800/222-333, www.continental.com) shuttles its planes through Houston and New York, and some stop over in Panama. **Delta** (U.S. tel. 800/101-060, www.delta.com) has daily flights from its Atlanta hub. All these airlines offer quality service and can bring you to either Quito or Guayaquil. Newer routes are offered by **Copa** (www.copaair.com) through Panama and by **Lacsa/TACA** (www.taca.com) through Costa Rica. **Aerogal** (www.aerogal.com.ec) and **LAN** (www.lan.com) are competing with new flights to Miami. The trip takes about four hours from Miami and five hours from Houston and Atlanta. Round-trip prices vary, but expect to pay $500–800 for a round-trip ticket. Shop around because prices vary greatly.

To and From Canada

Most flights from Canada connect through gateway cities in the United States. Air Canada and American Airlines fly from Toronto and Montreal via New York and Miami to Quito. **Travel Cuts** (www.travelcuts.com) is Canada's discount student travel agency, with more than 60 offices throughout the country.

To and From Europe

Of the major European carriers, only **KLM** (www.klm.com) and **Iberia** (www.iberia.com) fly their own planes to Ecuador. KLM go from Amsterdam and Iberia from Madrid. **Air Comet** and **Air Europa** are new competition from Europe. The others make connections in Caracas, Bogotá, Miami, or New York. Flights take 15–17 hours and costs vary widely from $1,000 upward.

A competitive discount travel market in the United Kingdom keeps prices reasonable. Good reports have come in on **Journey Latin America** (12–13 Healthfield Terrace, Chiswick, London W4 4JE, UK tel. 20/8747-3108, UK fax 20/8742-1312, www.journeylatinamerica.co.uk) and **Trailfinders** (63 Conduit St., London W1S 2GB, www.trailfinders.com).

To and From Australia and New Zealand

There are no direct flights to Ecuador from Australia and New Zealand. The best route is with Qantas/LAN Chile via Santiago or via Buenos Aires with Aerolíneas Argentinas. Travel times are a minimum of 24 hours and cost nearly A$2,000.

To and From Latin America

Although major airlines connect Quito and Guayaquil with most other capitals in South America, it's usually cheapest to cross borders by bus because international flights are highly taxed. For prices and flight times, check in the various capitals for the national airline or a branch of an Ecuadorian airline in: **Argentina** (Aerolíneas Argentinas), **Bolivia** (Boliviana de Aviación), **Brazil** (Gol), **Chile** (LAN Chile), **Colombia** (Avianca and TAME Calí), **Peru** (LAN Peru), and **Venezuela** (Santa Bárbara).

Airlines that offer flights within Central America and the Caribbean include Lacsa/TACA in **Costa Rica,** Cubana in **Cuba,** and Copa in **Panama.** The least expensive air route between Central and South America is via Colombia's tiny Caribbean island of San Andrés, connecting to Cartagena and beyond.

BY CAR OR MOTORCYCLE

To drive a vehicle into Ecuador, you'll need your passport, your driver's license from your home state, and full registration papers in the driver's name. An international driving license is also helpful. If someone else holds the title, bring a notarized letter signed by the owner authorizing you to use the vehicle. At present, a *libreta de passage* (*Carnet de Passages en Douane*) is not required to enter the country, but be sure to double-check, because this requirement tends to change from year to year. Hold on to all documents you are given so you can leave with a minimum of hassle.

Until the Pan-American Highway (Panamericana) penetrates the rainforests of the Darién Gap between Panama and Colombia, driving from Central to South America will remain impossible. Shipping companies in Panama City will transport your vehicle around the gap by ferry, and some go all the way to Ecuador.

Drivers should carry a driver's license from their home country along with the title to the vehicle and a temporary import permit given at the border (if applicable). This should be enough to satisfy any official. Guard all of these documents carefully.

BY SEA

One interesting way to get to Ecuador is on a **freighter.** Few people know that these floating warehouses usually carry passengers along with cargo, and those who have taken freighters comment on the first-class service (amenities often include TVs and video players, a swimming pool, and officers-mess dining) and the chance to stop in different countries along the way. The biggest drawbacks are the itineraries, which can change at the last minute, and being cooped up on a ship for weeks at a time.

The **Travltips Cruise & Freighter Travel Association** (P.O. Box 580188, Flushing, NY 11358, U.S. tel. 800/872-8584, www.travl-tips.com) publishes a newsletter on worldwide freighter travel. **Freighter World Cruises** (180 South Lake Ave., Suite 335, Pasadena, CA 91101-2655, U.S. tel. 626/449-3106 or 800/531-7774, www.freighterworld.com) is a freighter travel agency.

Getting Around

BY CAR OR MOTORCYCLE

Driving in Ecuador should not be undertaken lightly. Although many roads have been improved in recent years, the range of hazards still includes huge potholes, ice at higher elevations, cows on the low roads, and a frightening lack of road signs and traffic lights.

On the whole, Latin Americans drive much more aggressively than most North Americans. Vehicles spend more time passing each other than in the travel lane, turn signals are unheard of, and red *pare* (stop) signs seem to elicit the same response as a matador's cape. It's even worse for pedestrians, and you are often taking your life in your hands crossing busy roads.

Drive defensively and anticipate bad judgment from other drivers. Avoid driving at night or in heavy rain. A 4WD vehicle is ideal, especially those that run on diesel, because diesel is the cheapest and most accessible fuel. For driving in bad weather on the coast and in the Oriente, extra tire traction is essential. Two-wheel-drive automobiles should have high clearance. When preparing your vehicle, the more problems you're able to diagnose and

fix yourself, the easier life on the road will be. Take every tool and spare part you can, and know how to use them. Security is equally important: Two antitheft devices, the more visible the better, are a good idea.

Fines for speeding and other motoring offences have increased recently. Beware of unscrupulous traffic police looking to make a quick buck, and don't give them an excuse to fine you.

Police and military checkpoints, especially in the Oriente, are common. As a gringo in a rental or foreign car, you may just be waved through, but be prepared to stop and show your passport and documents. Gasoline ranges from unfiltered fuel siphoned out of drums in the Oriente to quality high-octane unleaded. With so many trucks hammering the highways, diesel is common.

Roads

The Pan-American Highway (Panamericana, or just "Pana") is the country's main artery, running through the Andes from Tulcán to Machala. Side branches lead east and west: the

Oriente can be reached from Julio Andrade, Quito, Baños, Riobamba, Guamote, Azogues, Cuenca, or Loja, and roads run to the coast from Ibarra, Quito, Aloag, Ambato, Riobamba, Latacunga, Cuenca, Alausí, Cañar Tarqui, and Loja. There are key routes running east of Quito to Lago Agrio and Coca, and south to Tena, Puyo, and Macas. A route from Baños goes to Puyo and Tena. Most of these roads have improved considerably in the past few years thanks to multimillion-dollar investment from the government. This is good for travelers, but the environmental cost could be high, particularly with expansion into the Oriente.

Road numbers exist but are seldom used or even indicated. Most secondary roads are dirt tracks. Towns of any significant size will most likely have paved roads, smaller towns may have cobbled roads, and remote villages have only dirt roads.

Safety and Security

In case of an accident, keep a level head and don't leave the scene or move anything or anyone, especially if they are damaged or hurt. Summon an ambulance or doctor if someone is injured, and wait for the police to arrive. Gather any and all relevant information about the other car and witnesses, and get a copy of the *denuncia* (report) for insurance and possible legal tangles. Be warned that drivers are often assumed guilty until proven innocent, and may be put in jail until things are sorted out.

In case of a breakdown or flat, try to flag down help or a ride to the nearest repair shop (*mecánica automotriz*). Hundreds of *vulcanizadoras* (tire repair shops) line major roads, most no more than a wooden shack with an old tire hanging out front. It's fascinating to watch tires be repaired with brute force and the most basic of tools.

Try not to drive at night, if possible. Road hazards materialize out of the darkness, and thieves have been known to stop vehicles with roadblocks. To discourage robberies, never leave anything of value in a parked car, take everything with you, and leave the glove compartment open and empty.

Street parking spaces may have a self-appointed guardian, often a scruffy child who will look after your vehicle for $0.50. You might not have much choice in the matter, so it's best to go along with it.

Car Rental

You'll have to shell out as much or more than you would back home to enjoy the freedom of driving yourself around Ecuador. Drivers must be at least 25 years old and have a credit card. A hefty deposit is charged on the card to ensure that the car is returned in one piece. Prices vary widely, but don't expect to pay much less than you would in the United States—$50 per day or $300 per week for a small car, rising to $80 per day, $500 per week for a larger 4WD vehicle. The deductible on the insurance is very high, usually $1,000 for damage and $3,000 for theft. During the tourist high season, cars are more expensive and harder to come by without reservations.

Before driving your rental car off the lot, check the vehicle carefully inside and out, recording all dings and blemishes on the checkout form. Try to spot any missing parts, such as a radio antenna or windshield wipers; once you leave the lot, the company may hold you responsible for any lost article not noted on the form. Make sure a jack and inflated spare tire are included, and check fluid and pressure levels.

Rental agency branches overseas often have nothing in common with their namesake agencies back home, so be sure to get everything about the rental in writing, including prices, insurance, taxes, discounts, and where and when you're supposed to return the vehicle. Read the contract carefully so you'll notice any extra charges that happen to turn up on the final bill.

Taxis

Cabs in Ecuador are cheap by most standards. In smaller towns they seldom charge more than $1–2 for short trips. Taxi drivers are legally required to use a meter in the larger cities, although you'll often hear that *"el métro está roto"*

("The meter is broken"), or simply *"no hay"* ("There isn't one"), even if this is obviously untrue. In that case, either pass on this taxi or negotiate the fare in advance. As a general rule, it's a good idea to ask a local or foreign resident what the approximate fare should be and suggest this fare to the driver rather than asking him how much it will be. Night and weekend trips are usually more expensive. Rip-offs are more common in Quito and Guayaquil.

In more remote areas, hiring a pickup truck is often the only way to get around in the absence of frequent buses, but again try to find out the approximate price.

Longer trips of a half day or full day can be an economical, efficient alternative to renting a car, especially if a group of people splits the cost. You'll find that some drivers are also knowledgeable, friendly local guides.

Safety in taxis is a serious issue, as robberies and "express kidnappings" (a robbery using a car in which the victim is driven around, often to cash machines) have been reported. It's best to order a cab from a reputable company, ideally suggested by your hotel owner or tour operator. If not, ensure you check the cab has an orange license plate and the taxi number on the side of the car and on the windshield.

Hitchhiking

It's hardly recommended as a safe or reliable alternative to waiting for the bus, but occasionally, hitching may be the only option. Even though *ir al dedo* ("thumbing it") means the same in Latin America as it does elsewhere, here you'll have to wave down passing cars for them to stop. Truck drivers, often bored and lonely, are a good bet. But for this reason (among many others), women alone or even in a group should not consider hitchhiking. Use your own judgment when deciding to get in. It's common to offer a token sum for the service: just ask *"¿Le debo algo?"* ("Do I owe you anything?") when you're dropped off.

BY BICYCLE

Crossing Ecuador by bike will put you in intimate contact with the land, people, and weather. Along the way, you'll experience well-paved highways, muddy tracks, and cobblestone roads populated by drivers whose idea of sharing the road is less than ideal.

Mountain bikes are the best for the terrain even though they're heavier and less aerodynamic. Touring bikes are more delicate, but also more comfortable over long distances. Their higher speed can be a blessing until the first major pothole warps your wheel.

Toe clips, bar ends, and a big granny gear make high-elevation grinds less of an ordeal. To carry your gear, you'll need to invest in panniers (bags that attach to special frames on your bicycle) or a tow-behind trailer. Other extras to include are two water-bottle cages, a quality pump, an odometer, a rearview mirror, a U-lock, and a flashing red taillight or three. Also consider an ultrasonic dog zapper, fenders, a dust mask, and a tube or two of Slime to protect tubes against punctures.

Carry as many lightweight tools and replacement parts as you think are practical—the only ones available regularly in Ecuador are tubes, spokes, and cables. Although there are *talleres de bicicletas* (bike repair shops) in most moderate to large towns, mechanics may lack the experience to repair complicated modern mechanisms.

Of course, you can make your life easier by hiring a bike, but make sure you check it thoroughly (especially the brakes). If you're uncertain about striking out on your own, there are plenty of guided tours, especially in the Andes and foothills. The best operators are in Quito, Riobamba, Otavalo, and Baños.

Safety and Security

Always yield to traffic, whether you have a choice or not. Paved shoulders are rare, so be ready for the unexpected, which could pop out in the road ahead of you at any moment: people, cars, animals, potholes, oil slicks, or debris. Buy a good, comfortable helmet and *always* wear it.

Lock both tires and the frame to a solid object every time you park, and keep a photo of the bike, its serial number, and a photocopy of your bill of sale in a safe place in case of theft. Because panniers are the most visible and accessible target for thieves, lock them securely or take them with you. Always take bicycles inside at night to avoid losing parts or the entire bike. Avoid riding after dark completely.

Transporting Bicycles

Most airlines will accept bicycles as checked baggage. Bike stores will usually give you a box that new bicycles come in. Take off the wheels and pedals, deflate your tires to keep them from exploding, and pad your bike well before entrusting it to the baggage handlers.

Lock your bike to the roof rack on buses, and remove anything that can be taken or shaken off. Some buses may have room inside in the back for the entire bike, but this is rare.

Resources

Tour operators in various cities offer guided trips lasting from one to several days. The bikes supplied are often high-quality imports, and support vehicles and guides take some of the burden off novice riders. The Mountaineers publish two excellent books on cycling in Latin America: *Latin America by Bike* by Walter Sienko, and *Two Wheels and a Taxi* by Virginia Urrutia.

BY BUS

Love it or hate it (and you'll probably experience both emotions), bus travel in Ecuador cannot be avoided, unless you have a very big budget. Ecuador's network of bus routes ties the country together like a spiderweb, allowing the poorest citizen down the farthest dirt lane to reach the big city with relatively little expense and inconvenience. Bus travel is how most people get around here, and if you want to do any traveling on your own, you'll get to know Ecuador's buses well.

Most cities have a *terminal terrestre* (bus terminal), either in the center or, increasingly, on the outskirts of town. Failing that, there is usually a park or intersection from which buses come and go. Some companies also have their own office or terminal for arrivals and departures. With so many people to carry, long-distance schedules are strict and competitive. Local schedules are looser, allowing drivers to leave early if the bus is full or circle around to gather up more people before they depart.

Comfort levels vary as widely as the buses themselves. Usually, the longer the trip, the better the bus—all the way up to sleek, ultramodern vehicles with air-conditioning, toilets, reclining seats, and attendants. Some luxury routes depart in the evening and drive by night, saving you money on a hotel room but leaving your neck bent at strange angles by morning (an inflatable travel pillow makes it easier). Accidents and thefts are also more common at night, so take this into account.

Shorter trips are handled by shoddier buses. Smaller *colectivos* and *busetas* make inner-city runs, and *camionetas* (pickups) and *rancheros* (wooden buses with open sides) ply rural areas. Drivers load buses to capacity, and then some—you may find yourself crammed among crates of chickens, sacks of quinoa, and the obligatory motion-sick child.

Whatever bus you're on, don't expect peace and quiet, although this is not necessarily a bad thing. If you're lucky, the stereo will pump out a mix of salsa, merengue, and *cumbia,* which add a perfect soundtrack to the scenery. However, you may be less lucky and be subjected to booming techno, when foam earplugs can be worth their weight in gold. Most buses have video players and TVs, but movie selection tends to revolve around badly dubbed action movies at high volume, and you'll become well acquainted with the acting talents of Jean-Claude Van Damme, Sylvester Stallone, and Arnold Schwarzenegger.

Long-distance buses stop for meals, and vendors climb aboard in most towns selling sodas, ice cream, and snacks. You're safe with most sealed products, but fresh pastries, snacks, and homemade juices should be avoided as a potential health risk.

Ecuador's buses are the livelihood of many thousands of vendors, selling everything from food to medical products and pirated DVDs.

Although this can be an annoyance, it can also be entertaining, and remember that these people make a living from it, so perhaps giving a quarter for a few candies is not unreasonable. Most vendors have a set routine, and you'll be amazed at how much time and effort they put into their sales pitch. First they greet all the passengers, thank God for the beautiful day, and give a long apology for disturbing their journey. This may be followed by a tale of woe about their current economic situation. Then they give a detailed description of the product, its contents, benefits, and instructions for use. The vendor then walks through the bus handing a product to every passenger, emphasizing that this is by no means an indication of intent to purchase (you can refuse to take it or give it back later). The vendor will then try to surprise you with a very reasonable offer (most products are sold for $0.25–2) and then go back through the bus collecting sales. You'll notice that locals are very tolerant of the vendors and frequently make purchases, sometimes out of sympathy.

If you're unlucky on a bus, you'll have to disembark to pass a landslide or washed-out bridge on foot to another bus waiting on the other side, especially during the rainy season. Keep an eye on your bus at military checkpoints, where you have to get off and register with the authorities in person, to make sure it doesn't leave without you. Be especially careful of thieves and pickpockets in terminals and on buses, especially on popular tourist routes out of Quito terminals, where you can pretty much guarantee there will be a thief on the bus. Keep your belongings hidden about your person and stow belongings in front of you between your legs rather than under the seat or in the overhead compartment (both places are easy pickings for thieves). Try to avoid the cramped back seats in older buses, whose rear suspensions are often shot. To get off along the way, yell *¡Pare!* (Stop), *¡A la esquina!* (At the corner), or simply *¡Gracias!* (Thanks).

Baggage

If your luggage is small enough, it's best to keep it inside the bus with you. Don't let the bus company charge you for the extra seat your backpack may take up—it's their responsibility to find a place for bags, even if they have to put them on the roof. If yours does wind up on the roof, get out the protective covering and lock everything to the roof rack.

Cost

On average, buses cost about $1 per hour. Prices climb slightly higher for longer luxury rides. It's possible to buy tickets a day or so ahead of time to reserve a seat, and this is strongly recommended on public holidays and on weekends during high season (especially on beach routes). Watch for a "gringo tax," charged when buying your ticket on the bus itself—pay attention to how much everyone else is charged, or ask at the station for the correct price. Cheaper fares usually mean older, less comfortable buses. You should pay less if you're only going part of the way—something you may need to remind the ticket collector. Don't forget to collect your *cambio* (change), even if you have to wait until the collector has gathered enough coins from everyone else. Try to carry change and small notes to avoid problems.

International Buses

A few companies run buses as far as Lima or Bogotá, but it's always cheaper to take an Ecuadorian bus to the border, cross overland, and get on a Peruvian or Colombian bus on the other side.

BY TRAIN

Latin America is a gold mine of classic railroads, and Ecuador is back on train lovers' list after a multimillion-dollar plan to revitalize its entire rail network, which had been left in disrepair for decades.

The famous Nariz del Diablo (Devil's Nose) ride south of Riobamba remains the most impressive and exhilarating, carving its way through a series of tight switchbacks in the mountainside. The route south of Quito to Latacunga is already running, and the entire two-day route from Durán near Guayaquil to Quito will be ready by 2014; renovation of the northern section will follow that.

For years, the roof was considered by many

THE TRACKS OF TIME:
THE GUAYAQUIL-QUITO RAILROADS

Ecuador's rail network stands as a metaphor for travel around this fascinating nation: There may be inevitable delays and periods of frustration, but ultimately the results are spectacular.

Arch-conservative President Gabriel García Moreno first launched the construction of a train line between Guayaquil and Quito in 1873. Only 91 kilometers were completed between Yaguachi and Milagro on the coast before García Moreno's assassination in 1875. No further work was done for 20 years until the project was resurrected by President Eloy Alfaro after the liberal revolution of 1895. American engineer Archer Harman and some 4,000 Jamaican workers joined an Ecuadorian workforce, but work was beset with engineering problems because of the rapidly changing terrain leading up 3,000 meters into the Andes. The workforce also struggled with disease and heat exhaustion, and many died, including Harman's older brother and chief engineer, John Harman. The railroad gained a reputation as being "the most difficult in the world" not least because it came up against a vertical section of rock known as *La Nariz del Diablo* (Devil's Nose), 130 kilometers east of Guayaquil. The solution was ingenious: A complicated set of tight zigzags carved into the rock allowed the train to climb by going forward and backward. This section was completed in 1902, and the 446-kilometer line finally reached Quito in 1908, inaugurated by a triumphant Eloy Alfaro. The bitter irony for Alfaro was that, three years later, after he had lost power in a coup d'état, he was arrested and embarked on his final journey on the same railroad he had constructed before his brutal assassination in Quito.

After Alfaro's death, construction continued on a northern section of the railroad, but at a much slower pace. It took until 1928 for the line from Quito to Ibarra to be completed, and until 1953 for the entire 370-kilometer line to reach San Lorenzo on the coast.

The toil of thousands of workers over decades was undone during the 20th century, however, when maintenance and administration of the train line was seriously neglected. It fell into disrepair, and by the 1990s only small sections at La Nariz del Diablo and north of Ibarra were running.

All this changed in 2008: Current President Rafael Correa, for whom Eloy Alfaro is a hero, announced ambitious government plans to revitalize the entire rail network, relaunching the two-day route from Durán, near Guayaquil, to Quito by 2014 and subsequently renovating the northern section.

For more information and reservations, visit www.ferrocarrilesdelecuador.gob.ec. At the time of writing, the following sections are running. Fares and times are for a one-way trip unless otherwise indicated:

- Ibarra-Salinas: 1.5 hours, $7.50

- Quito-Latacunga, via Machachi and Boliche: 4 hours, $10

- Alausí-Sibambe via La Nariz del Diablo: 2.5 hours, $20, round-trip only

- Durán-Yaguachi: 1 hour, $10

---

travelers to be the best seat, but following the death of two Japanese visitors in 2007, railroad authorities have forbidden roof riding.

At the time of this writing, the following sections are running. Prices and durations are for the single fare unless otherwise indicated. For further information and reservations, visit www.ferrocarrilesdelecuador.gob.ec.

- Ibarra–Salinas: 1.5 hours, $7.50
- Quito–Latacunga (via Machachi and Boliche): 4 hours, $10
- Alausí–Sibambe (La Nariz del Diablo): 2.5 hours, $20 (round-trip only)
- Durán–Yaguachi: 1 hour, $10

BY AIR

Flights within Ecuador that originate in Quito and Guayaquil are relatively cheap and convenient; many travelers prefer them to long bus rides. Another option is to fly one-way and take the bus the other way.

Reserving seats can be a chore: Flights are often overbooked, and delays are common, though thankfully less so than outright cancellations. Reconfirmation is essential. On some flights, seats aren't even reserved, turning boarding into a first-come, first-served elbow-fest.

Tickets, payable up front and refundable only with time and patience, cost more for foreigners than for Ecuadorians to the Galápagos and the Amazon. Most flights within mainland Ecuador cost $60–80 one-way. It'll cost you $310–410 to get to the Galápagos, depending on the time of year and whether you fly from Quito or Guayaquil. Students under age 26 can get discounts on high-season prices—apply weekdays at the main TAME office on Colón in Quito.

TAME (tel. 2/397-7100, www.tame.com.ec), Ecuador's national airline, offers reasonably priced flights from Quito to Coca, Cuenca, Esmeraldas, the Galápagos, Guayaquil, Lago Agrio, Loja, Machala, Tulcán, and Cali, Colombia. There are flights from Guayaquil to Coca, Cuenca, the Galápagos, Quito, Loja, and Cali. Prices start at about $60 one-way.

Icaro (tel. 2/244-8626 or 2/245-0928), Aerogal (tel. 2/294-2800), and Air Cuenca (tel. 7/408-4410 or 7/408-3381) all serve Quito, Guayaquil, and Cuenca and are sometimes a bit cheaper. A new option is Chilean airline LAN (tel. 2/299-2300, www.lan.com), which offers flights among Quito, Guayaquil, Cuenca, and the Galápagos. A few smaller air companies, such as SAEREO and VIP, have limited national flights.

Visas and Officialdom

TOURIST VISAS

Most travelers entering Ecuador are given a stamp in their passport and a stamped **tourist card** (also called a T-3). The duration of the visa is 90 days. If you overstay your visa without extending it, you'll have to pay a $200 fine.

To enter Ecuador, all travelers must have a passport that is valid for more than six months from the date of entry, a return ticket, and "proof of economic means to support yourself during your stay," which is loosely defined and may just involve showing a sheaf of traveler's checks to the immigration authority. The latter two requirements are seldom invoked, and only then by a harried border official to someone who really annoys them. Hold onto your stamped visa card because you'll need to turn it in when you leave.

Tourist visas may be extended beyond the original 90 days to a maximum of 180 days. However, this is at the discretion of the immigration official, and it's not made easier by the fact that you cannot do it in advance but must go to the immigration office the day before your visa expires. Extensions beyond 90 days are handled in Quito at the Ministry of Foreign Relations (**Ministerio de Relaciones Exteriores** Carrión E1-76 at 10 de Agosto, Quito, tel. 2/299-3200, www.mmrree.gob.ec, 8:30 A.M.–1:30 P.M. Mon.–Fri.) In Guayaquil the office is opposite the bus terminal on Avenida Benjamín Rosales.

VISAS FOR LONGER STAYS

Other visas are divided into immigrant (10-1 to 10-VI) and nonimmigrant (12-1 to 12-10). A study visa is 12-V (up to one year), work is 12-VI (very complicated to get and of variable length), volunteering is 12-VII (up to two years), cultural exchange is 12-VIII (often used for teaching, up to one year), business is 12-IX (variable), and tourism is 12-X (90 days); the last can be bolted onto to the end of another visa to extend your stay after completing your work or studies. Costs vary from $30 for a tourism visa to $200 for a work visa.

It's more complicated to sort out a visa while in Ecuador, so you're much better off dealing with this at home. Ecuadorian law states that a tourist visa cannot be changed to any other type of visa inside the country, which makes things very complicated, and you may require legal advice, which can be costly.

To obtain a visa, call the Ecuadorian consulate nearest you to check on what you'll need (everything from bank statements to police certificates) and follow the instructions. Start this process early, because it may take a while. For initial questions, check with the U.S. National Passport Information Center (U.S. tel. 877/487-2778). If you're pressed for time, try an expeditor service, such as **A Briggs Passport and Visa Expeditors** (1054 31st St. NW, Suite 270, Washington, DC 20007, U.S. tel. 800/806-0581, U.S. fax 202/464-3006, www.abriggs.com) or **Travisa** (1731 21st St. NW, Washington, DC 20009, U.S. tel. 202/463-6166 or 800/222-2589, U.S. fax 202/293-1112, www.travisa.com).

If you're staying longer than six months, you'll need a **censo,** the temporary residence card that can save you lots of money entering Ecuador's national parks (the Galápagos are $25 with a *censo,* as opposed to $100 for nonresidents). To get one, register your visa in Quito at the Central Office of the **Ministerio de Relaciones Exteriores** (Carrion E1-76 at 10 de Agosto, Quito, tel. 2/299-3200, www.mmrree.gob.ec, 8:30 A.M.–1:30 P.M. Mon.–Fri.) and pay the $10 fee at the bank indicated. Then get your *censo* on the ground floor of the **Dirección Nacional de Migración** (Amazonas and República, tel. 2/281-5417),

In Guayaquil, the Ministry of Foreign Relations office is in Kennedy Norte (Francisco de Orellana at Justino Cornejo, Gobierno del Litoral, tel. 4/268-2523, 8:30 A.M.–1:30 P.M. Mon.–Fri.). In Cuenca, go to Edificio

Centro Comercial Astudillo (Ordoñez Lazo at Cipreses, tel. 7/285-0085 or 7/285-0086, 8:30 A.M.–1:30 P.M. Mon.–Fri.).

Note that there is a **30-day time limit** from when you enter Ecuador in which you must obtain your *censo;* otherwise there is a fine of $200.

If the visa is for more than one year of residence, a *cedula* is then issued at **Registro Civil** (Amazonas and Naciones Unidas, Quito).

Because visa rules change often, including which office handles what, it's a good idea to check in at the Quito clubhouse of the South American Explorers (SAE, corner of Plaza and Washington, Quito, tel. 2/222-5228, www.saexplorers.org, 9 A.M.–5 P.M. Mon.–Fri.) for an update.

LEAVING ECUADOR

Tourists with 90-day visa cards simply turn them in at the border and get an exit stamp in their passports. Those with longer visas must present their *censo* and their passports at the airport when leaving.

CUSTOMS

It's prohibited to bring firearms, ammunition, or illegal drugs into Ecuador. Importing plants or animals requires prior permission from the Ministerio de Agricultura y Ganadería (Ministry of Agriculture and Livestock). Exportation of any kind of plant or animal product or archaeological artifact is forbidden. Check with your country's customs office for details of what you can bring home legally.

BORDER TOWNS

The major crossing points into and out of Ecuador are at **Huaquillas, Macará,** and **Zumba** on the Peruvian border, and **Tulcán** on the Colombian border. It's also possible to cross at other points along the border, such as at Nuevo Rocafuerte in the Oriente, and Morona on the Río Santiago, but there is little regular traffic.

Conduct and Customs

Ecuadorians are renowned for their laid-back attitude, which contrasts strongly with North American and European reliance on rules, regulations, and schedules. The pervasive feeling is *así es la vida* ("that's life") and helps to explain why Ecuadorians seem to smile through frustrations that can leave many of us gringos shaking with anger.

This relaxed demeanor shows itself in so many aspects of life in Ecuador. Punctuality—or rather lack of it—is one of the most famous traits, and you need to accept that people will arrive late for social gatherings, and even scheduled departures will be late (although you need to arrive on time just in case). There's no point blowing your top about it; try adapting and go with the flow—after all, does it really matter that much if things don't begin on time?

Bureaucracy is where things get more frustrating, particularly if you need to sort out something important, such as immigration. Complex regulations are arbitrarily enforced by low-ranking officials, and this can be the biggest downside of South American culture. There seem to be rules for everything, many of them senseless in their inefficiency; there is a preoccupation with stamping documents officially and having countless copies made, and above all, there is very little trust. The hefty bureaucracy has been set up primarily to reduce corruption, but ironically it probably increases it. You are presented with two choices: follow the procedures and wait, often for days or even weeks, present everything you need, only to be told you need something else; the alternative taken by many locals is to come to some kind of "arrangement." Bear in mind that bribing a public official is a criminal offence, so it's best to get someone local to talk on your behalf. The best thing you can do is smile, ask what can be done *("¿Pues, qué podemos hacer?"),* and you might be surprised to find that things shift in your favor. Most Ecuadorians wearily accept that giving a "tip" for a faster service is normal.

GREETINGS AND GENERAL POLITENESS

Latin Americans are much more physical in day-to-day interactions than their northern neighbors. Men give a firm handshake to other men both when arriving and leaving; women give one or two pecks on the cheek when being introduced to another woman, and usually to another man. Verbal greetings are essential; *"Hola"* ("Hello") is often followed by *"Como está?"* ("How are you?"), even if you don't know the person. It's normal to begin any conversation with *"Buenos días/tardes/noches,"* and even complete strangers will greet each other in this way, unprompted. If you see someone eating, it's polite to say *"Buen provecho"* ("enjoy your meal"), again even among strangers. This use of physical and verbal greetings is all part of the Latin American concern for appearances. It is frowned upon to be rude in public, and foreigners often acquire a reputation for being unfriendly, bordering on rude, if they don't use greetings properly. Using greetings is also a quick way to make friends.

HOSPITALITY

Ecuadorians love to be hospitable, and this is particularly gratifying for visitors. Don't be surprised if you are quickly invited to functions and parties, and you shouldn't feel like you're putting them to any trouble. On the contrary, they will be delighted to host you and will probably be disappointed if you decline. Any get-together quickly expands into a full-blown party, celebrated long and hard into the night. Note that if an Ecuadorian uses the word *invite* (invite), this usually means that he or she will pay. Equally, if you invite someone, you will be expected to pay. This is particularly true across the genders; men are expected to pay for women. If your hosts want to pay for you, it's best to let them, and return the favor on another occasion. You could offer to split the bill, but refusing to let them pay for you could actually cause offence by implying that they can't afford it.

GENDER AND SEXUALITY

Latin American culture is very sexually polarized. Men tend to be the traditional heads of the household, and women manage the home and raise the children. Recently, though, Latin American women have begun to assert themselves and claim new freedoms in work and daily life.

The challenges that women face are clear: Female beauty is overwhelmingly emphasized, and women are expected to spend a lot of time on their appearance. This extends beyond clothing and makeup to a national obsession with plastic surgery. Women also receive lower salaries than men and none at all for housework, and male dominance runs through society from top to bottom. Women find themselves in a split position in Latin society—both elevated on a platform as the saintly wife-mother figure, and looked down upon and protected as the "weaker sex." Most daughters are expected to live with their parents until marriage.

Feminism came late to Ecuador: In 1979, President Jaime Roldós Aguilera's wife, Martha Bucaram, was one of the first prominent Ecuadorian feminists and the first woman to serve in the country's cabinet. Since then, things have slowly begun to change. Many young women now expect equal rights, and the present government has appointed more women to ministerial positions than previous administrations. There has also been a well-received television campaign against spousal violence, and even an amusing media discussion about a woman's right to have an orgasm.

Feminism's greatest enemy is, of course, machismo, which manifests itself in ways ranging from subtle to blatant. Whistles and catcalls are seen as harmless, but men find themselves feeling they have to prove their manhood in their posturing, driving, and womanizing. Add in the Latin preoccupation with appearances, and it's no surprise that there is enormous hypocrisy when it comes to sexuality. Men boast about their sexual conquests, and there is a notable lack of shame (replaced by pride) about cheating on a partner. Many women, on the other hand, feel compelled to maintain an illusion of virginity, and it's no surprise that clandestine "motels," usually in seedier areas of towns, are the most common secret meeting points for lovers.

Dealing with machismo as a foreigner can be tricky. Realize that it's a part of the culture, but don't let it pass unchallenged. In some ways, getting used to it is easier for foreign men, who may be delighted to meet beautiful young women accustomed to the submissive role in the relationship (as long as the man pays for everything). Foreign women, on the other hand, can face continual frustration when dating a local man raised with deep-rooted macho attitudes. Don't be afraid to confront locals about sexism, but bear in mind that making an Ecuadorian look bad in public is not to be done lightly and will likely lead to resentment.

Machismo extends to negative attitudes toward gay people, and even though gay civil marriage is now permitted in Ecuador, homophobia is pervasive here. Gay travelers need to bear in mind that being open about their sexuality can lead to anything from embarrassment to religious rants and even violence. There is a burgeoning gay community, however, and Quito has the biggest gay scene in the country, with an annual pride parade and several gay bars. There are also a few gay bars in Guayaquil and Cuenca.

RACISM AND REGIONALISM

Ecuador is far from being a racially equal society, and a look back at history reveals why. The power held by many of the richest families in the country can be traced right back to colonial times, when the landowning elite first establishing dominance over the local indigenous people. White Ecuadorians are fiercely proud of the heritage, and they dominate the country's economy and media. This leaves the mestizo (mixed race) majority often feeling a sense of inferiority, which shows itself in the explosion in popularity of plastic surgery (the nose is the most common feature to be altered to try to look more "white"). Many indigenous people, however, think differently and are very proud of their racial heritage, content to stay within their communities. However, as globalization penetrates every corner of the country, the younger generation increasingly casts off the ponchos for jeans and T-shirts. Ecuador's Afro-Ecuadorian population is the poorest ethnic group, concentrated mainly in impoverished Esmeraldas Province, in the Chota Valley in Imbabura, and in urban areas of Guayaquil and Quito. Unlike many indigenous people who have grown wealthy from their trades, Afro-Ecuadorians have found it hard to make progress. However, there are signs that things are changing: The domination of Afro-Ecuadorian football players on Ecuador's national team, Miss Ecuador 2010 Lady Mina, and Governor Roberto Cuero of Guayas are all examples of high-profile successes from Ecuador's black community.

Regional prejudice in Ecuador is just as visible as racism and equally damaging. The rivalry is fiercest between the mountains and the coast, particularly between Guayaquil and Quito. Many *costeños* from the coast view *serranos* from the mountains as uptight, conservative, two-faced, and hypocritical, and they resent paying taxes to Quito. *Serranos,* on the other hand, see *costeños* as brash, loud, uncultured gossips who waste their money on frivolity. Some of the stereotypes may have an element of truth in them, but you should take Ecuadorians as you find them: There are plenty of liberal-minded people in Quito and plenty of archconservatives in Guayaquil. It can be a touchy subject for locals, however, and reactions vary from good-natured jokes to deep resentment.

Sports and Recreation

MOUNTAINEERING

There aren't many countries where you can leave the capital, climb an ice-capped volcano, and be back in your hotel the next day. In Ecuador, you can do that with eight of the country's 10 highest peaks, including one higher than 6,000 meters, as long as you're fit, acclimated, and lucky with the weather. It's a great country to gain experience in high-altitude mountaineering without the usual toll in sweat and tears. Guiding services are numerous, and competition keeps prices down. With plenty of easy routes, several difficult ones, and even a few new routes waiting to be tackled, Ecuador is a climber's playground.

Beginning mountaineers will find the country an excellent training ground for higher, more difficult ascents elsewhere, but there's still enough challenging climbing to keep veterans busy for years. Most of the major peaks along the Avenue of the Volcanoes have roads leading close to or even partway up their bases, and the ascents themselves are usually straightforward. Modest technical gear will do for the big three—Chimborazo, Cotopaxi, and Cayambe—whose

huts and summits overflow with climbers during busy weekends in the peak season. Other peaks aren't as welcoming. El Altar, probably the most difficult in the country, wasn't climbed until 1963, and volcanoes such as Tungurahua, Sangay, and Reventador are far too active to climb. Even the "easy" ones can turn deadly in an instant. An avalanche on Easter Sunday 1996 buried the shelter on Cotopaxi, killing 11 visitors. Never underestimate the mountains.

In the end, though, there is no substitute for **up-to-the-minute information** and the services of a **trained guide.** An overwhelming majority of climbers killed in Ecuador were climbing without a locally trained guide. Conditions and routes vary drastically from year to year, or even day to day. If you're hesitant, be sensible and hire a qualified guide—or at the very least, arm yourself with the latest reports on the mountain you plan to tackle. Remember: Many climbers fall victim to not knowing when to turn back.

Climbing Weather

Although climatic conditions differ among

regions, December–January are generally the best months to climb. February–May are the wettest months in the Western Cordillera, with heavy rain and snow. In the Western Cordillera, June–September tend to be dry, clear, and therefore very good months for climbing. Warm air from the Oriente brings heavy precipitation June–August to the Eastern Cordillera, including El Altar, Antisana, Sangay, Tungurahua, and Cayambe. This side of the Andes is driest in December–January, and occasionally passable as early as October and as late as February.

Training Climbs

Several peaks are good starters for acclimating and getting into shape with a minimum of special equipment or training. Pasochoa, Rucu Pichincha, Imbabura, Cotacachi, Corazón, and Atacazo can all be done in a day. Iliniza Norte requires a night in the refuge but can often be done in hiking boots. Rumiñahui occasionally requires snow-climbing equipment and may involve spending the night on the way up, depending on whether you have your own transportation or not. Tungurahua is off-limits until it stops erupting.

Equipment

Specialized mountain gear, such as hard plastic boots, crampons, rope, helmets, and ice axes, can be rented from various shops in Quito. An ice hammer, ice screws, and snow stakes are necessary for the glaciated peaks. Refuges make tents unnecessary, but bring your own sleeping pad and a 20°C sleeping bag, although some tour operators can provide them. For warmth, a down jacket can't be beat when combined with a balaclava, gloves, and thermal underwear. Waterproof outer layers, gaiters, and dark climbers' glasses with side light-guards complete the outfit.

Because snow climbing is done at night, when the snow is hardest, a headlamp is essential, as are ski poles for balance and support. All huts have stoves for cooking. Your medical kit should include a low-reading thermometer for hypothermia, glacier cream or zinc oxide for the high-altitude sun, and inflatable splints or at least ACE bandages for falls and sprains. Topographical maps are available in Quito from the Instituto Geográfico Militar (IGM, Senierges and Paz y Miño, tel. 2/250-2091, 8 A.M.–4 P.M. Mon.–Fri.).

Guides

An experienced, responsible guide can make the difference between success and failure— and life and death—in the thin air and unpredictable conditions of Ecuador's highest peaks. It's easy to underestimate the task at hand or overestimate your own abilities, twin errors that kill novice and veteran climbers alike around the world. A guide is essential for your first few ascents of snow-capped mountains.

Guided climbs typically include any necessary equipment, transportation to the base, meals in a hut, and a guide who will take you to the peak or decide if conditions merit a hasty retreat. For all that, you'll pay $160 pp and up, depending on the mountain, the season, and how many people are in your group. Pay less, and you're probably looking at less experienced guides and lots of extra costs, like equipment rental.

Always go with a licensed and qualified guide. Several organizations handle licensing, including groups set up by the tourism board, university groups, and **ASEGUIM,** the Ecuadorian Mountain Guide Association (Pinto and Juan León Mera, 3rd Fl., tel. 2/222-2954, fax 2/223-4109, 3–6 P.M. Mon.–Tues. and Thurs., www.aseguim.org). A ratio of 2–3 clients per guide is recommended, although larger groups allow more of a chance to rearrange rope teams if some people need to turn back.

The most up-to-date information is available from the South American Explorers' Quito clubhouse, climbing clubs in Quito, or tour operators and guides themselves. See individual city listings for local guides (nationwide operators are listed in the *Quito* chapter), and see *Suggested Reading* for recommended climbing guidebooks.

HIKING AND CAMPING

With boots, a backpack, a tent, and a sleeping bag, you're ready to explore just about any part

Ecuador offers hiking opportunities that suit all levels of experience.

of Ecuador's spectacular countryside. Even if all you brought is tough footwear, it's amazing how much lies within reach of a day hike, even near major cities. Longer trips can bring you to places accessible only on foot in the high Andes and remote rainforest.

Parks and reserves are the most popular areas for camping, and the only ones with organized, maintained campsites. Park entrance fees range $5–20 on the mainland and $100 for the Galápagos. Information is available from many branches of the Ecuadorian National Park agency or from local guide companies.

Outside the reserves, you'll have to find your own campsites, often on private property. This is usually no problem, but you must ask permission first. Camping near a house may discourage thieves. Avoid military zones, especially in the Oriente and along the coast, and always keep valuables close at hand. You may be able to find shelter in a *tambo,* one of many small thatched huts used by *campesinos* for emergency shelter in the Andes, but secure permission from the owner beforehand.

Bring everything you think you may need from home; camping and hiking equipment in Ecuador tends toward high prices and low quality (good hiking boots like Hi-Tec and Timberland are available at various shopping centers in Quito and Guayaquil). Water purification is essential, either through a filter or iodine tablets. Even day hikers should always carry 1–2 liters of water, snacks, warm and waterproof layers of clothing, a flashlight, at least a minimal first-aid kit, a map, and a compass. Never leave for a trip without telling someone where you're going, your approximate route, and when you expect to be back; don't forget to confirm your safe return.

RAFTING AND KAYAKING

White-water sports are very popular in Ecuador, and the terrain is perfect, with rivers rushing down either side of the Andes to the coastal plains to the west and Amazon basin to the east. There are many stretches of Class 3, Class 4, and even Class 5 rivers, and the spectacular scenery through green foliage and precipitous gorges makes these trips as beautiful as they are exciting.

Guides in Quito, Baños, the Quijos Valley, and Tena can take you on day trips or week-long expeditions. With some experience and your own equipment, you may be able to kayak down some of the country's best runs on your own, although never underestimate the power of the rivers. The upper sections of many rivers in the Andes offer difficult, technical Class 5 runs best left to expert kayakers. As they flow downward and pick up volume, the flows become mellower, but the rapids can still be continuous, requiring sustained effort to manage the hours of Class 3 and Class 4 white water. The eastern slopes of the Andes are less polluted and more remote than the western slopes.

Most of the better companies have applied international standards to the training of their guides, and have Class 3 certification or higher from the International Rafting Federation (IRF, www.internationalrafting.com). Trip leaders should have Wilderness Advanced First Aid qualifications. The Ministry of Tourism now requires all rafting companies to be certified. When shopping around, look for experienced guides and new equipment in good condition. Ask about guides' rafting, rescue, and first-aid training as well as Ministry of Tourism certification, and make sure each trip has safety and first-aid equipment. Safety kayakers and on-river emergency communications are recommended on many rivers.

The more reliable companies in the country tend to be run by foreign or foreign-trained Ecuadorian guides, such as the British-run **River People** (15 de Noviembre and 9 de Octubre, Tena, tel. 6/288-8384, www.riverpeoplerafting.com) in Tena and **Yacu Amu** (Foch 746 at Amazonas, Quito, tel. 2/290-4054, www.yacuamu) in Quito. **Ríos Ecuador** (Tarqui, Tena, tel. 6/228-8672, www.riosecuador.com) is Yacu Amu's branch in Tena.

Rivers

The **Río Blanco,** northwest of Quito, is the most frequently run in Ecuador, in part because it's so close to the capital. Many of the 100 kilometers of raftable white water in the Blanco Valley can be done in a day trip, which often starts in the Toachi. After navigating the technical Class 3–4 run, including the notorious El Sapo Canyon, rafters enter the lower Río Blanco to ride its big Class 3 rapids. The upper Río Blanco offers 47 kilometers of sustained Class 3–4 rapids in four hours. If they're still hungry for more, kayakers can take on Río Mindo (Class 3–4), Río Saloya (4–5), Río Pilatón (4–5), and the upper Río Toachi (4–5), depending on the time of year and their ability.

Within a 30-minute drive of the town of El Chaco, east of Quito, the "white-water playground" of the **Río Quijos** offers everything from Class 3 white water near the Antisana Reserve to steep Class 4–5 streams as it drops through narrow rock canyons. Rafters, including the world's top racers, head for the main Río Quijos (Class 3–5), and kayakers tackle the Papallacta (Class 5), Cosanga (Class 3–4), and Oyacachi (Class 4) tributaries.

As it runs from Puerto Libre to Lumbaquí, the upper **Río Aguarico** has large Class 2–3 rapids within two hours of Lago Agrio. To the south, the clear **Río Due** tributary flows off Volcán Reventador in Class 3–4 rapids.

Near Tena, the **Río Napo** and its tributaries offer enough variety to let you paddle a different river every day for a week. The most popular trip in the area is the Class 3 Upper Napo, but the Class 4 **Río Misahualli Bajo** is more exhilarating. It's subject to sudden, extreme changes in water level, but still draws paddlers with its rainforest setting around Casanova Falls. For seekers of nonstop Class 4 action, trips on the steeper and more technical Río Misahualli Alto are also offered during the rainy season, April–September.

Kayakers have a longer list of possibilities, and dozens of new rivers have been opened for kayak trips in recent years on both the western and eastern flanks of the Andes. Note that kayaking on Class 4 rivers and above requires prior experience and is not advisable for novices. Most operators offer courses. The best stretches include **Ríos Misahualli, Jondachi, Anzu, Piatua,** and **Hollin,** which tend to stick around Class 4–5 when there's enough water to ride. The **Río Patate** is run out of Baños, but pollution, the eruption of Volcán Tungurahua, and the death of four tourists here in the late 1990s have lessened its popularity. Some expert kayakers have called the **Río Topo** (Class 5) the best steep creek run in Ecuador, as well as the magnificent Namangosa Gorge of the **Río Upano** (Class 4) near Macas in the southern Oriente, lined with primary rainforest and 100-meter waterfalls.

Most rafting specialists also offer kayaking. For further information, www.kayakecuador.com is a useful website.

When to Go
The Ríos Toachi, Blanco, and Upper Napo are run year-round. The commercial companies run the bigger rainforest rivers (Ríos Quijos, Lower Misahualli, Upano) during the dry season, October–February, when air temperatures are comfortable and water levels are reasonable but still challenging. The rainy season, March–September, brings high flows and continuous white water that are more suited to expert kayakers.

SURFING
With 2,237 kilometers of Pacific coastline, Ecuador offers plenty of action for surfers, and there are several world-class breaks along the coast. Starting in the south, a popular spot is Playas in Guayas Province. In Santa Elena, Salinas is comparatively sheltered and a good place for beginners. Farther north, the backpacker party town of Montañita is still the biggest surfer hangout in the country, despite losing a sizable chunk of its beach during the 1997–1998 El Niño climate pattern. All these towns get jam-packed in high season (December–April), so consider heading farther north. Canoa in Manabí Province is a mellower resort, although it is developing fast; Manta and nearby Crucita, a paragliding hub, also see some action. In Esmeraldas Province, Mompiche is developing into a pleasant little resort with one of the longest left point breaks in South America (500 meters on good days).

The best months for large swells and little wind are December–May. Warm shore currents mean wetsuits aren't necessary, but footwear is a good idea to protect your feet against lava rocks and spiny creatures. A few shops rent and sell boards, but bring your own if you have one. Some breaks in Guayas province are on military land; if you're polite and show your passport, you shouldn't have a problem.

FISHING
Take some fishing tackle on your hikes into the high Sierra, and with minimal effort and luck, you'll reel in some of the rainbow trout that have been introduced throughout the highlands, with an as-yet-unknown impact on native ecosystems. In the Oriente, a simple line and hook baited with meat can be enough to catch the infamous piranha, although these fish are very adept at biting chunks out of the bait and leaving you feeling foolish. It'll take a bit more to bring in a 90-kilogram *bagre* (catfish) from the muddy rivers, but the delicious meat makes it worth it. Expensive deepsea charters off the central and southern coast yield black marlin, sailfish, tuna, and bonito. Salinas is a popular base.

BIRDING
Ecuador is one of the premier countries for birding in the world, hands down. With almost 1,600 recorded species of birds—twice as many as all of Europe—Ecuador has the highest avian diversity of any region its size on the continent. An incredible range of habitats shelter many species found nowhere else.

There are so many birds in Ecuador that every region in the country has an abundance of species. You can even come across hummingbirds in the urban sprawl of Guayaquil. The best regions for seeing the widest variety of colorful species are the Oriente and the western slope of the Andes, particularly the area around Mindo. The northern lowlands near the Hacienda Tinalandia and the Río Palenque Science Center are also excellent, and southwest

Ecuador, including Podocarpus National Park, is rich in endemic and endangered species.

Many parks and lodges offer checklists for nearby species. Guides to Ecuadorian birds are listed in *Suggested Reading*. Greenfield and Ridgely's two-volume illustrated *Birds of Ecuador* is considered the birding bible here.

Some of the tour companies listed in the *Quito* chapter have birding tours, particularly those that operate in the Mindo area. However, most organized tours from Quito are expensive. For better value, you can hire a guide locally, although this is subject to availability. In Quito, Swede Jonas Nilsson and American Charlie Vogt run **Andean Birding** (Salazar Gómez E14-82 at Eloy Alfaro, Quito, tel./fax 9/418-4592, www.andeanbirding.com). They promote responsible tourism, contributing a portion of their profits to conservation and ornithological research. Birding trips of 7–14 days start at $900 pp.

Several foreign tour companies also focus on birds. The leading agency is **Victor Emanuel Nature Tours** (2525 Wallingwood Dr., Suite 1003, Austin, TX 78746, U.S. tel. 512/328-5221 or 800/328-8368, U.S. fax 512/328-2919, www.ventbird.com), which offers highly regarded birding tours throughout Ecuador from $2,500 pp. **Wings** (1643 N. Alvernon Way, Suite 105, Tucson, AZ 85712, U.S. tel. 888/293-6443, 520/320-9868, or 520/320-9373, www.wingsbirds.com) has been leading international birding tours (from $2,750 pp) for almost 30 years. **Field Guides Inc.** (9433 Bee Cave Rd., Bldg. 1, Suite 150, Austin, TX 78733, U.S. tel. 512/263-7295 or 800/728-4953, U.S. fax 512/263-0117, www.fieldguides.com) offers a range of tours from $2,750 pp.

RAINFOREST TOURS

Ecuador's relatively small size means that you can get to the Oriente far more easily than elsewhere in South America—a half-hour flight or a seven-hour bus ride from Quito followed by two hours in a boat places you in the middle of primary rainforest. Secondary rainforest surrounded by indigenous communities is even closer.

There is a wide range of tours available. At the top end, expect to pay $600–1,000 for a 4–5-day tour to the best lodges, which are mainly concentrated east of Coca near Yasuní National Park. Add on $65 one-way or $130 round-trip to fly into Coca. These lodges include Sacha, La Selva, Napo Wildlife Center, Sani, Yachana, and Amazon Dolphin Lodge. There are also two *flotel* cruise boats offering similar prices on the Río Napo, the *Manatee* and *La Misión*. Farther south, the best lodge is Kapawi, which costs $800–1,000 pp, plus $306 for flights.

If your budget doesn't stretch that far, don't worry. The other options to experience primary rainforest are either farther north or southwest of Coca. To the north, travel via Lago Agrio, which you should spend as little time in as possible due to security problems, to Cuyabeno Reserve. Here, camping lodges charge as little as $200 for five days, while more comfortable lodges charge $300–600.

Between Coca and Tena, you'll find pockets of primary rainforest near Limoncocha Reserve, where tours cost from $45 pp per day. East of Misahuallí there are several lodges in primary rainforest charging $50–70 pp per day.

Plenty of community rainforest tours operate out of Puyo and Tena, but bear in mind that this is mainly secondary rainforest. Rates are about $40 pp per day. Community tours deeper in the rainforest to visit the Huaorani people are far more expensive. A four-day tour including a return flight from Shell costs $800 pp.

Farther south in Macas, there are great opportunities to visit local Shuar communities from $50 pp per day.

In general, you get what you pay for: Smaller operators and freelance guides are more flexible and cheaper, and they may surprise you with their expertise; larger, more expensive companies have the facilities, training, and staff to correct problems or solve them before they occur. A good guide makes all the difference. Check to see if guides are licensed and speak your language, or at least one you can understand. Most travelers book Amazon tours in Quito, Baños, Tena, or online.

When to Go

Although it rains just about every day in the Amazon, June–August has the most precipitation, making many roads impassable. Less rain falls September–December. No matter when you go, don't make any important plans (especially connecting flights) for the first day or two after you're due back, since the vagaries of climate can easily cause delays.

What to Take

Leave your hiking boots at home—*botas de caucho* (rubber boots) are essential in the sodden rainforest. Most good tours provide them, but check before departure. They're available at hardware stores in larger cities. Note that if you need an unusually large size (U.S. size 10 and up for men), you should bring your own. Bring waterproof clothes and a raincoat, ideally lightweight, and resealable ziplock bags will protect your things from rain and dampness. Long sleeves and long pants are preferable to avoid mosquito bites. It's also essential to bring insect repellent with a high a percentage of DEET (see *Health and Safety*). However, DEET can irritate skin, so don't use it long-term. Bring after-bite lotion and, of course, sunblock—the sun is very strong when it's not raining. As far as equipment goes, a camera and a flashlight for night walks are essential, and binoculars are preferable for spotting wildlife. Hanging mosquito screens for beds *(mosquiteros)* are available in most rainforest cities, although most lodges provide them.

Bring your passport for frequent military checkpoints, and make sure you have enough cash, since it's hard to find places in the Oriente to exchange traveler's checks, and the rates are bad.

Activities

Every tour includes guided hikes along forest paths, ideally with an indigenous guide to spot and explain different species of plants and animals along the way. Often the sound of branches shaking overhead is your clue to troops of capuchin, squirrel, or *saki* monkeys moving through the treetops. A good guide and a pair of binoculars can help you to spot the countless birds species in the trees. Viewing the forest from above on an observation tower is another unforgettable experience, and great for spotting birdlife as well as monkeys sunning themselves on the treetops after the rains.

Canoe trips are another staple of rainforest tours. On large water stretches, you may hear the huff of pink river dolphins surfacing to breathe, or spot the dark head of a river otter. Nocturnal hikes will show you how much more active and noisy the forest is after dark. Visits to tarantula holes are not as scary as they sound (these spiders are mainly harmless). Listen for the soft, quick fluttering of bats swerving to miss your flashlight beams. Along the shore, your light might catch the iridescent eyes of caimans.

A visit to an indigenous village can easily be the high point of a tour. Some tours are based around cultural encounters, but even if it's only for an afternoon, the chance to see how people eke out a living in the rainforest is not to be missed. Rest assured that they'll be as curious about you as you are about them. Try your hand at hitting a piece of fruit with a blowgun. You may be invited to lend a hand in the manioc field, learn how to thread a bead necklace, or get your face painted and watch a traditional dance, complete with macaw feathers and gourd rattles.

It's up to you how large a grain of salt to take it all with. Many of them probably wouldn't be dressing up and dancing if you weren't there, and the crafts are often made solely for the tourist trade. In the end, your presence makes a real difference to the economy of these communities.

OTHER RECREATION

Ecuador's diverse topography makes **cycling** an arduous but rewarding way to experience the country. Downhill rides either side of the Andes are understandably the most popular, including spectacular rides in the Intag Valley northwest of Quito, the ride from Baños to Puyo, and riding down the flanks of Volcán Cotopaxi. Various tour companies and private operators in major cities rent bikes and organize cycling trips in the Sierra.

Before the introduction of cars and trains, everyone who could afford it got around on **horseback.** Today, many people still do, and renting horses on your own or on a guided trip is a great way to see the countryside up close. Guided horseback tours cost approximately $25–50 pp for four hours.

The vertical landscapes are conducive to **paragliding,** a sport that has recently taken off both in the Sierra and along the coast. Ibarra and the hills close to Baños are popular venues, and Crucita, on the coast, is also good. Tandem flights are offered for beginners.

The incredible marine life of the Galápagos makes the islands among the world's best spots for **scuba diving,** but it's not the cheapest or easiest place to learn. A few agencies in Puerto Ayora offer diving certification, but Puerto López near Machalilla National Park on the coast is a cheaper option. The Galápagos Islands also have the best **snorkeling** in the world. On the mainland, snorkeling sites are few, but Isla de la Plata is one of the good spots.

SPECTATOR SPORTS

Soccer (*fútbol*) is a Latin American passion and Ecuador's national game, far more popular than all other sports combined. Informal matches pop up on makeshift fields in the most improbable places: at the edge of a steep

ECUADOR'S LOVE OF SOCCER

Like most countries in South America, Ecuadorians are crazy about soccer (known as football in most countries worldwide). This love affair has resulted in substantial on-field success in recent years, seemingly disproportionate to Ecuador's relatively small size.

In the 20th century, Ecuador's teams achieved very little, but this all changed in 2001 when a successful qualifying campaign, including a famous victory over Brazil, catapulted them to their first-ever participation in the FIFA World Cup. This achievement was celebrated wildly across the country for days and ranked as the best moment in Ecuador's history in a survey by news magazine *Vistazo*, a reflection of the nation's obsession with the Beautiful Game.

The national team plays in Quito at an elevation of 2,800 meters, a huge advantage over teams from lower elevations, and their home record was a big factor in their success. However, the team also contained some fantastic players, mainly of Afro-Ecuadorian origin, including Ulises de la Cruz and Agustín Delgado, one of South America's best goal-scorers at the time. In the World Cup itself, Ecuador didn't perform particularly well and was eliminated in the first round, although they scored a victory over Croatia in the final match.

Four years later, Ecuador repeated their achievement of qualifying for the 2006 World Cup in Germany, and this time they were a force to be reckoned with. They beat Poland and Costa Rica and qualified for the second round, only to be eliminated by England. After the tournament, many of the team's best players retired, and it has struggled since then, failing to qualify for the 2010 World Cup despite beating highly rated Argentina in Quito.

As well as the success of the national team, Ecuador's clubs have also recorded considerable success in recent years. In Guayaquil, Barcelona is the most supported club in the country and reached the final of the coveted Copa de Libertadores in 1998. Liga de Quito went one better in 2008 and won the cup to become club champions of South America. In 2009, Antonio Valencia became the first Ecuadorian to play for Manchester United, one of the world's most famous soccer clubs.

During important matches, both at club and national level, it seems like much of Ecuador closes down for a few hours, and people crowd around the television, often at full volume. Attending a match is an incredible experience, as the fervor of supporters knows no bounds. Win or lose, it's a great excuse for a party.

© CHRIS O'CONNELL

Bullfighting is a popular but controversial tradition in Ecuador.

drop-off in the Sierra, for instance, or on a patch of cleared rainforest with bamboo goalposts in the Amazon. Players on local teams compete fiercely for the chance to rise into the big leagues and play internationally.

Ecuavolley, the local version of volleyball, is another popular sport, both on the beach and on concrete courts. **Basketball** is also popular, while **tennis** and **golf** are confined to the wealthier classes.

There are several sports that horrify animal rights activists, and indeed at the time of this writing President Correa is trying to ban any sport that involves cruelty to animals. However, **cockfighting** (*pelea de gallos*) remains very popular, particularly in the highlands. Fiestas are the best times to catch **bullfights** (*corrida de toros*), which are held in *plazas de toro* (bullrings) throughout the highlands. Quito has the largest arena.

Tips for Travelers

OPPORTUNITIES FOR STUDY AND EMPLOYMENT
Language and Cultural Studies

Intensive Spanish instruction attracts students of all ages to Ecuador for anywhere from a week to a year. A host of schools, both foreign and national, offer language courses and programs in ecology, literature, and Latin American culture. Optional excursions to the Galápagos, the Amazon, or out into the Andes are part of some curricula. Prices for Spanish classes start from $5 per hour. A few schools also offer Kichwa classes. Homestays can also be arranged for as little as $10 per day. It's cheaper to arrange a course locally, but to book from abroad, contact Amerispan (www.amerispan.com) or CESA Languages Abroad (www.cesa-languages.com).

Ask beforehand if insurance and airfare are included in the price. Are there any prerequisites, such as a minimum grade point average or previous Spanish instruction? How large are the classes? What is the refund policy? Can

WHAT TO TAKE

Pack light and leave room for souvenirs. In terms of clothing, bring enough for a week and pack appropriately for where you're heading: sandals, shorts, and sunblock for the beach; warm and waterproof layers for the Sierra; long sleeves, sunglasses, and a hat for sun protection anywhere. For footwear, bring a comfortable pair of shoes or sneakers, and broken-in hiking boots if you plan to trek.

You can rent and buy camping equipment, mountaineering boots, and rubber boots (for the rainforest) in Ecuador. And don't forget your camera – Ecuador is one of the most photogenic places you'll ever visit.

Bring small-denomination U.S. dollar bills, traveler's checks, and a credit card as backup.

VOLUNTEERING IN ECUADOR

Charities and nongovernmental organizations offer a range of conservation and cultural opportunities, accepting volunteers for various lengths of time. Duties vary from the mundane to the fascinating – before you sign up, try to get a description of what you'll be doing. You may be asked to contribute some money toward room and board.

ORGANIZATIONS BASED IN ECUADOR

- **AmaZOOnico** (tel. 9/980-0463, www. amazoonico.org): working with animal rehabilitation.

- **Bospas Fruit Forest Farm** (El Limonal, Imbabura, tel. 6/264-8692, www.bospas.org): organic family farm in northwest Ecuador.

- **Bosque Nublado Santa Lucia** (tel. 2/215-7242, www.santaluciaecuador.com): forestry and teaching at a community-owned cloud forest reserve in northwest Ecuador.

- **Charles Darwin Foundation** (6 de Diciembre N36-109 at Pasaje California, Quito, tel. 2/224-4803, Santa Cruz tel. 5/252-6146, cdrs@fcdarwin.org.ec, www.darwinfoundation.org): placements in conservation and environmental science on the Galápagos.

- **Ecuador Volunteer** (Yanez Pinzón N25-106 at Colón, Quito, tel. 2/255-7749): authorized to find a wide variety of placements throughout the country.

- **Fundación Jatun Sacha** (Pasaje Eugenio de Santillán N34-248 at Maurián, Rumipamba, tel. 2/243-2240, www.jatunsacha.org): placements at seven biological stations in the Oriente, the Andes, the coast, and the Galapágos.

- **Fundación Natura** (Elia Liut N45-10 at Telégrafo Primero, Quito, tel. 2/331-7489, www. fnatura.org): placements in reforestation, conservation, and research.

- **Fundación Sobrevivencia Cofán** (tel. 2/247-4763, kimreyanna@gmail.com, www.cofan. org): placements in Cofán communities.

- **Rio Muchacho Organic Farm** (Guacamayo Tours, Bolívar and Arenas, Bahía de Caráquez, tel. 5/269-1412 or 5/261-6384, www.riomuchacho.com): placements working on the community farm.

ORGANIZATIONS BASED IN NORTH AMERICA AND EUROPE

- **Earthwatch Institute** (114 Western Ave., Boston, MA 02134, U.S. tel. 800/776-0188, www.earthwatch.org): placements worldwide with research scientists.

- **JustAct** (3307 26th St., San Francisco, CA 94110, U.S. tel. 415/431-4204, U.S. fax 415/431-5953, www.justact.org): placements in sustainable and self-reliant communities around the world.

- **Rainforest Concern** (8 Clanricarde Gardens, London, UK W2 4NA, UK tel. 207/229-2093, www.rainforestconcern.org): helping to protect endangered rainforests worldwide.

- **Volunteers for Peace** (1034 Tiffany Rd., Belmont, VT 05730-0202, U.S. tel. 802/259-2759, U.S. fax 802/259-2922, www.vfp.org): runs 2,800 low-cost volunteer programs in more than 90 countries.

- **World Teach** (www.worldteach.org): teaching positions in impoverished communities throughout the world.

- **WWOOF** (www.wwoof.org): an international organization encouraging the exchange of work for room and board on organic farms around the world.

- **Year Out Group** (www.yearoutgroup. org): British organization of gap-year specialists.

TEACHING ENGLISH

If you're interested in supporting yourself during an extended stay in Ecuador, teaching your native language is one of the surest ways to do it (it has been this author's main income in Ecuador for many years). Demand for teachers is high, so getting a position can be easier than you think. It's also possible to receive Spanish instruction in exchange for teaching English: Check the bulletin boards at the South American Explorers' Quito clubhouse and the Catholic University language department in Quito. There are also opportunities to teach French, German, Dutch, and Chinese at international schools associated with these countries.

Requirements vary from school to school. Teachers who can speak Spanish are usually preferred, and you may be asked to provide an English teaching certificate – the most internationally recognized is the Cambridge CELTA (Certificate of English Language Teaching to Adults), and if you have a bachelors or masters in education from a North American or European university, even better. However, many institutions will take on unqualified native English speakers as long as they have a college education and a good level of Spanish, but pay rates are lower.

A CV or résumé listing any previous teaching experience is standard, as is a personal interview. The pay is enough to live on modestly – but some teachers have reported problems getting paid, so it's a good idea to go with a reliable recommended institute like those listed below.

Teacher training ranges from plenty to next to nothing, and contracts can be on a day-to-day basis or last six months to a year. Private lessons offer higher wages and more flexible hours. Outside Quito and Guayaquil, salaries for teaching English tend to be very low. You're better off organizing a rural placement with a voluntary organization than trying to do it independently.

IN QUITO
Language Institutes and Universities

- **Centro de Educación Continua of the Escuela Politécnica Nacional** (Ed. Araucaria, Reina Victoria and Baquedaño, tel. 2/250-0068, fax 2/235-3605, www.epn.edu.ec): requires BA degree; teaching experience preferred.

- **The Experiment in International Living** (Hernando de la Cruz N31-120 at Mariana de Jesús, tel. 2/255-1937, fax 2/223-3528, www.eilecuador.org): Teaching English as a Second Language (TESOL) degree preferred, but inexperienced conversation teachers accepted.

- **Fulbright Commission** (Almagro 961 at Colón, tel. 2/256-3095, fax 2/250-8149, www.fulbright.org.ec): native speakers with TESOL certification and experience preferred.

- **Princeton International Language Insti-**

you transfer credit to a college back home? Past participants are your best source for firsthand recommendations; most programs will supply you with a list. The *Quito* chapter has a list of Spanish schools based in the capital.

Working in Ecuador

Teaching English is the most common job for foreigners. Regardless of your position, you may need a work visa, although many employers organize a cultural visa where you agree to give free classes in exchange for an "allowance." This is just a way around the red tape, which is considerably greater for a work visa. Your employer should send you all the documentation, but bear in mind that it is much easier to arrange nontourist visas from abroad than to switch to this visa once you are in Ecuador. The best places to look for teaching jobs in Ecuador are ESL-dedicated websites. Examples are www.tefl.com, www.eslcafe.com, www.esljobs.com, www.totalesl.com, www.eslemployment.com, and www.teachabroad.com.

tute (Colón 1133 at Amazonas, tel. 2/252-8291, tel./fax 2/254-7944, princetonec@hotmail.com): native speakers with TESL preferred.

• **South American Spanish Institute** (Amazonas N-2659 at Santa María, tel. 2/254-4715, fax 2/222-6348, www.southamerican.edu.ec): six-month or one-year contracts offered.

• **Southern Cross** (Alfaro N39-125 at Manuel Guzman, tel. 2/292-1831, www.southerncross.com.ec): British-run school that employs mainly British teachers with a bachelor's degree and teaching qualifications.

• **Universidad de San Francisco** (Diego de Robles and Vía Interoceanica, tel. 2/297-1700, www.usfq.edu.ec): bachelor's and master's degrees required.

High Schools

These international or bilingual schools offer extended contracts and may require teachers to instruct in other subjects besides languages.

• **Academia Cotopaxi** (De las Higuerrillas and De las Alondras, Monteserrin, tel. 2/246-7411, fax 2/244-5195, www.cotopaxi.k12.ec): teaching certificate, BA degree, and three years' international teaching experience required.

• **Colegio Albert Einstein** (Diego de Contreras Km. 4.5, tel. 2/247-7901, tel./fax 2/247-0144, www.einstein.k12.ec): September–July contract.

• **Colegio Americano de Quito** (Manuel Benigno Cueva N80-190, Urb. Carcelén, tel. 2/247-2974, fax 2/247-2972, www.fcaq.k12.ec): one-year contracts for qualified teachers with bachelor's degrees.

IN GUAYAQUIL

English teachers can also get reasonably well-paid work in Guayaquil.

• **CELEX** (Malecón and Loja, tel. 4/253-0555, www.celex.espol.edu.ec): The English department of the highly rated Politécnica university requires a bachelor's degree and teaching qualifications, and prefers a master's degree.

• **Southern Cross** (Luis Orrantia González, Kennedy Norte, Guayaquil, tel. 4/268-4404, www.southerncross.com.ec): British-run school that employs mainly British teachers with bachelor's degrees and teaching qualifications.

• **UEES** (Vía la Puntilla Km. 2.5, Samborondón, near Guayaquil, tel. 4/283-5630): one of Guayaquil's best-paid institutions. Master's degree essential for teaching English or business.

ACCOMMODATIONS

The entire spectrum of accommodations is represented in Ecuador, from luxury international hotels to bug-infested cells. In general, the cheapest are called *residencial, pensión,* or *hostal. Hosterías* tend to be larger, swankier, rural accommodations, as are haciendas (country estates). A hotel officially should be good quality, but in practice this word is applied loosely to every range of accommodations. Here are a few tips to have the best stay possible:

• Prices vary depending on the time of year, so be aware of national holidays and high season, when prices rise sharply, before planning your trip.

• Prices are not usually fixed in cheaper hotels, so bargaining is possible, especially if you're staying a few nights.

• Check the prices of *dobles* (two single beds) and *matrimoniales* (one double bed). If the latter is cheaper, consider sharing the bed.

• Always ask to see the room before paying

(*"Puedo ver la habitación por favor?"*). Check the mattress quality, signs of mustiness, and the cleanliness of the bathroom.

- Consider the location of the accommodations. If it is central on a busy street, ask for a back room (*"Una habitación atras"*).

- A 22 percent tax is levied in more expensive hotels (included in the prices quoted in this book), along with a 10–20 percent surcharge for paying by credit card.

- Electric showers in less expensive places can be dangerous if improperly wired; *don't* turn them on or off when you're soaking wet. Remember that *C* stands for *caliente* (hot) and *F* means *frío* (cold).

- The plumbing in Ecuador can't handle toilet paper, so be sure to throw it in the garbage instead of flushing it down the toilet.

- Most mid-range and some budget hotels offer TV. If you like relaxing in your room, then it's worth asking beforehand if it has cable (pronounced "kahbleh"), which has English-language movies, comedies, and dramas. National TV is generally of poor quality.

- There are motels in every town (and on highways), mainly used by lovers rather than travelers. Most are not called "motel" but "*residencial*" or "hotel." They are generally identifiable by tacky names, surly service, a lack of business cards, and frequent comings and goings. Accommodations listed in this book are not considered motels, although some of the cheapest hotels are used for this purpose.

- If you find yourself stuck in the middle of nowhere without camping gear, you might be able to wrangle a spare room in a private house, school building, or community center. Police officers (*policía*), the local mayor (*alcalde*), the town headman (*jefe*), and the village priest (*cura*) are good people to ask. Inquire around for *"la posada,"* which can mean simply a place to sleep.

Homestays

One of the best ways to get to know Ecuador and its culture is by staying with a local family.

By stepping outside the normal world of hotels, restaurants, and branching out beyond the same conversations with fellow travelers, you can gain firsthand knowledge of the country as well as improve your Spanish far more quickly.

Many Spanish schools in Ecuador set up students with local families; many of these are listed in the *Quito* chapter. Check with **South American Explorers** (SAE, Jorge Washington 311 at Plaza, Quito, tel./fax 2/222-5228, www.saexplorers.org, 9:30 A.M. 5 P.M. Mon.–Wed. and Fri., 9:30 A.M.–8 P.M. Thurs., 9:30 A.M.–noon Sat.) for a recent list of families offering homestay arrangements.

Haciendas

Throughout the Sierra, you'll find these relics of former huge estates that often date back to the 16th and 17th centuries, when Spanish conquistadores carved up the country. Recent land reforms have broken up most of the largest estates, which once served as social, political, and commercial centers for entire provinces. Nowadays, flower farms, organic gardens, and computer technology have infiltrated the sprawling grounds, but legions of caretakers and housekeepers are still needed to keep everything running smoothly.

If you can afford it, staying in a hacienda is an experience not to be missed. The settings are invariably the most beautiful around, and accommodations and service are of the highest quality. Home-cooked meals by a roaring fire, thick whitewashed walls hung with antique portraits and worn leather saddles, and lush flower gardens all create the feeling of stepping back in time. Hiking, horseback riding, and shopping for locally made crafts are among the many recreational opportunities. Reservations can be made directly through the haciendas or through tourism agencies.

ACCESS FOR DISABLED TRAVELERS

Travelers with disabilities shouldn't expect many concessions. Wheelchair ramps are rare on buildings and sidewalks, disabled toilets are rare, Braille is nonexistent, and guide dogs need at least a rabies vaccine to enter the country. International airports and top-class hotels are the few places where disabled travelers can expect reasonable facilities. Otherwise, you may find that you are seriously restricted. For more information, contact **Mobility International, USA** (45 W. Broadway, Suite 202, Eugene, OR 97401, U.S. TTY tel. 514/343-1284, U.S. fax 514/343-6812, www.miusa.org) and the online **Global Access Disabled Traveler Network** (www.globalaccessnews.com).

Travelers with disabilities have a range of options for travel-planning assistance, including the **Information Center for Individuals with Disabilities** (P.O. Box 750119, Arlington Heights, MA 02475, U.S. fax 781/860-0673, www.disability.net) and the **Access-Able Travel Source** (www.access-able.com). Health escorts can be arranged through **Travel Care Companions** (Box 21, Site 9, RR 1, Calahoo, Alberta, Canada T0G 0J0, Canada tel. 888/458-5801 or 780/458-2023, www.travelcarecompanions.com).

WOMEN TRAVELING ALONE

Whistles, comments, honks, and catcalls are an ingrained part of Latin American culture. Thanks to pop culture stereotypes, foreign women, especially blonds, get the most attention. Follow the lead of Ecuadorian women and simply ignore it. After all, a response is what they're after; if you react rudely, you may make the situation worse.

Physical boundaries are a different story. Pinches and outright grabs should be dealt with immediately and unequivocally. Just make sure there are other people around. Also on that note: don't go anywhere alone at night.

This doesn't mean that women can't travel alone; many do, with no problems at all, despite repeated disbelief from Ecuadorians. You just need to take extra care.

TRAVELING WITH CHILDREN

Children are considered life's greatest reward in Latin America, so parents traveling with children will enjoy compliments and assistance across the continent. Foreigners traveling with children will receive particular attention. Sometimes it will feel too much, but 90 percent of the time it's just good-natured. Be wary of safety issues, though, not just with strangers but also with a lack of safety regulations; most children's fun parks in Ecuador would have U.S. lawyers in convulsions. Products for children and babies are available in department stores in larger cities. Discounts for infants are common in top-class hotels, and most attractions have reduced child rates.

GAY AND LESBIAN TRAVELERS

Ecuador is still by and large a homophobic culture, and many gay people are either in the closet or keep their sexuality well-guarded. However, things have changed in recent years. The 2008 Constitution guarantees civil rights to gays and lesbians and allows civil marriage. Despite this, gay and lesbian travelers are advised to keep a low profile.

The best way to join the community is to meet someone already inside. There are several websites that can help, including www.gayecuador.com, www.quitogay.net, and http://quito.queercity.info. These websites have chat rooms and listings for events, bars, and other hangouts. Note that for safety reasons, many places are members-only. Quito has the most developed gay scene, with several bars in the New Town, while Cuenca and Guayaquil also have gay bars. Visiting these alone is not recommended, and take a taxi at night.

SENIOR TRAVELERS

Age is respected in Ecuador, but there aren't any senior associations or travel organizations in the country. Make sure you can handle the physical demands of tours and lodges (some of the Galápagos hikes are steep and strenuous), and bring along a printed medical history and enough prescription medications for the entire trip, plus extra.

AARP (U.S. tel. 888/687-2277, www.aarp.org) offers a Purchase Privilege Program for discounts on airfares, car rentals, and hotels. **Road Scholar** (U.S. tel. 800/454-5768, www.roadscholar.org), formerly Elder Hostel, is a 25-year-old nonprofit that offers educational adventures for adults older than 55.

Health and Safety

BEFORE YOU GO

Travelers to tropical (i.e. northern) South America must take a number of specific health concerns into consideration. There are diseases here you've probably never heard of, although most are rare and preventable. Don't worry, though—with proper precautions, you shouldn't have any serious problems.

Major hospitals and those attached to universities in your home country usually have **traveler's clinics** or **occupational medicine clinics** that can recommend and administer pretravel shots. The *International Travel Health Guide* (see *Suggested Reading* in the *Resources* chapter) has a list of clinics in the United States. Also check with your local Department of Public Health for an **immunization clinic.** If you're sufficiently informed, you might just be able to walk in with a list of the shots and pills you want.

Note that regulations on medications are very loose in Ecuador. The upside is that you can walk into a pharmacy and get hold of a range of medicines without a prescription, but the downside is that supplies are often low, and beware of unqualified pharmacists trying to sell you expensive medication. Make sure you know exactly what you're taking before it goes in your mouth (a quick Internet search can help).

Vaccinations

Vaccinations are recorded on the **Yellow Card,** an international certificate of vaccination that you should bring with you to Ecuador. You may be asked to show this document to prove your immunizations, especially in the case of a yellow fever outbreak. Get these vaccinations as soon as possible, since some shot series take a few months to take effect. Your doctor should know which ones not to mix with others (especially immunoglobulins) so as not to decrease their effectiveness. See your doctor at least 4–6 weeks before you leave to allow time for immunizations to take effect.

Viral hepatitis A: This viral infection of the liver is contracted mainly from contaminated food and water. The vaccination is strongly recommended, and a booster after 6 or 12 months guarantees protection for over 10 years. Get the first shot before you leave, and it is possible to get a follow-up shot from a good private clinic in Ecuador.

Typhoid fever: This dangerous gut infection is also acquired from food and water. The vaccination is strongly recommended and can be administered as a live oral vaccine or through two injections taken at least four weeks apart.

Yellow fever: This vaccination is necessary when entering Ecuador from Peru or Colombia (both officially infected countries), but it is a good idea in any case because it's a dangerous disease.

Hepatitis B: This is a less common disease for travelers because it's contracted through sexual contact or exposure to infected blood. The vaccination is recommended for longer-term travel (more than six months) and if you are likely to come into close contact with locals (for example, working in medicine). This disease is more insidious than others, and you can be a carrier for years without symptoms, and it can cause serious liver damage. The complication is that you need three vaccinations spaced a month apart.

Routine immunizations: Any trip is a good time to update the following: diphtheria-tetanus, influenza, measles, mumps, poliomyelitis, and pneumococcus.

Other Concerns

Travelers who plan to spend extended periods in remote areas and come into frequent contact with animals should also consider a vaccine against **rabies.** Although **cholera** is a problem, the vaccine against it isn't recommended, because it's only partially effective, short-lived, and possibly dangerous.

Try to get a **dental checkup** before you leave on a long trip, stock up on any prescription medication you require (including oral contraceptives), and bring copies of prescriptions for eyewear and birth control pills (just in case).

WHILE ON THE ROAD

The best you can do to keep healthy while traveling—besides taking any prescriptions you brought along—is to wash your hands often, pay attention to what you eat and drink, and be on the lookout for any unusual symptoms. Buying alcohol-based hand gel is very useful, and a basic first-aid kit is a must. In the end, nothing can take the place of qualified medical attention, both at home and in Ecuador.

Sunburn

It's easy to forget the amazing power of the equatorial sun when you're shivering in the Andes, but unexposed parts of your body can fry just as badly under a sweater as under a swimsuit. The sun is fiercely strong all over the country—at high elevations particularly so, and on the coast, the reflection off the sea and sand means you will burn in under half an hour without protection. Sunscreen (SPF 30 and above), lip balm, and proper clothing—especially a wide-brimmed hat—will help protect you. A good pair of sunglasses with UV protection is also essential.

Diseases from Food and Water

If you're going to get sick while traveling, it will probably be from contaminated water or food. As a tropical country, Ecuador is full of bacteria and parasites, particularly in the lowlands, rainforest, and coast. Minimize your chances of getting sick by remembering this mantra: cook it, peel it, wash it, or forget it. Get in the habit of washing your hands at least 2–3 times a day, preferably before every meal and certainly after every restroom visit.

Let's start with the drinks. Obviously, drink only bottled water and never from the faucet. This becomes more complicated when ordering drinks made with water. To minimize the risks, buy bottled fruit juices (Deli is a good local brand) or sodas. However, you're bound to want to try the freshly made juices and shakes,

which can be a risk because they are occasionally mixed with unpurified water or unpasteurized milk. Avoid the cheaper, dirtier joints. Ice cubes are a particular risk, so ask for drinks *"sin hielo"* (without ice). When outdoors, purify water with a camping filter, by boiling (a few minutes is sufficient), or with a chemical treatment. Iodine tablets like Potable Aqua or two drops of tincture of iodine per liter will kill any bacteria in 10 minutes.

Regarding food, the biggest culprits are shellfish, pork, and other undercooked or poorly prepared meats. Food poisoning from these can be particularly dangerous. Be careful with salads and unpeeled fruits—some restaurants wash their fruit and vegetables in purified or chemically treated water and will definitely advertise this, while others use any water available, or none at all. Even though it is handy and often tasty, food from street vendors should be avoided; eat it at your own risk.

No one is safe from **traveler's diarrhea,** although most cases are mild. Bloody stool or anything beyond mild diarrhea, gas, cramps, nausea, or fever may be cholera or amoebic dysentery, which require medical attention. Ease a low-grade case of the runs with Imodium A-D (loperamide) or Pepto-Bismol, but bear in mind that these medicines are often short-term solutions. Drink plenty of water and noncaffeinated fluids like fruit juice and ginger ale. Oral rehydration solutions are very handy, and if you haven't bought any, they're easy to make (one teaspoon salt and 2–3 tablespoons sugar or honey in a liter of water will work). More serious cases may require a doctor's appointment and antibiotics.

Cholera is an intestinal infection caused by bacteria. Luckily, the risk is low, and symptoms are often mild. About 5 percent of sufferers lose enough liquids through severe diarrhea and vomiting to require medical attention. Otherwise, a rehydration mixture should help.

Typhoid fever is also a bacterial infection courtesy of *Salmonella* Typhi, all too common in the coastal region. Early symptoms resemble the flu: fever, chills, aches, and loss of appetite.

Diarrhea, constipation, and rashes are less common. Seek medical attention, since one-quarter of all cases may be fatal.

Hepatitis A, which attacks the liver, is transmitted by contaminated food or water or contact with an infected person. It is the most common type of hepatitis and is present in Ecuador's rural areas. Symptoms appear 2–6 weeks after exposure and include nausea, vomiting, aches, fatigue, fever, loss of appetite, dark urine, and jaundice (yellowing of the whites of the eyes). Once you catch it, there's no cure; the best treatment is resting, drinking lots of fluids, and avoiding fats, alcohol, and unnecessary medications.

Diseases from Insects

Ecuador has its fair share of biting insects, and mosquitoes, of course, cause the most problems, both in the rainforest and on the coast. The strongest repellents include DEET (applied to the skin), permethrin (sprayed on clothing), and pyrethrin (sprayed on surfaces). Higher percentages of the chemicals on a small area are more effective, but also more toxic to humans. Camping stores and mail-order catalogs carry mosquito netting, which is also available in Ecuador at fabric stores.

As well as using repellant, there are various things you can do to minimize bites. Wear long sleeves and long pants, and wear closed shoes, ideally with socks in the evenings (if it's not too hot) because ankles and feet are particularly popular with mosquitoes. Wear light-colored clothing and avoid black and dark colors, which attract mosquitoes. Note that perfume attracts mosquitoes, while oils such as eucalyptus, citronella, and lavender can act as repellants.

Malaria is present on the northern coast and in the Oriente in Ecuador. It is caused by *Plasmodium* parasites, spread by the bite of *Anopheles* mosquitoes. The *P. falciparum* species kills around 3 million people worldwide each year, but fortunately for travelers to Ecuador, it's rare in South America, and the nonlethal *P. vivax* strain is more common. Consult your doctor before traveling. The cautious route is

to take medication, and Malarone is the most recommended; avoid Lariam (mefloquine) completely due to potentially dangerous side effects. In practice, though, few travelers going to the rainforest for a short trip bother with medication, and cases of malaria in Ecuador among visitors are actually comparatively rare. If you are unlucky, symptoms don't necessarily appear right away, but they are unmistakable: dark urine and alternating cycles of chills and fever. A prophylactic drug regimen suppresses the symptoms, but nothing can kill the parasites but your own immune system.

Yellow fever is also spread by mosquitoes. Symptoms include jaundice, fever, headaches, chills, and vomiting. No treatment exists, but the disease is rarely fatal. Even so, seek medical attention. It's advisable to get the vaccination before you arrive in Ecuador.

Dengue fever, transmitted by *Aedes* mosquitoes, is most common in coastal urban areas, and there is no vaccine. The mosquito lives mainly in dirty water and bites during the day. Flulike symptoms, such as nausea, bad headaches, joint pain, and sudden high fever are often misdiagnosed as other tropical diseases. Severe cases leading to shock syndrome or hemorrhagic fever are rare, but if you have already had dengue fever, a second case can be more dangerous. The only treatments known so far are rest, fluids, and fever-reducing medications. Medical attention is strongly recommended, if only for diagnosis.

Chagas' disease is caused by the *Trypanosoma cruzi* parasite found in the bite of the nocturnal reduviid, or "kissing" bug, common to rural coastal regions. The insect usually bites near the mouth (hence the name) after dropping from the ceiling. Only a small percentage of victims show symptoms beyond a hard swelling around the bite area. Even if you escape the fever, swollen lymph nodes, vomiting, diarrhea, and rash, you're not in the clear yet. Over decades, the untreated disease attacks the heart, making it one of the leading causes of heart disease in Latin America. So if you show symptoms, it's best to get a course of strong antiparasitic medicine. Apply insect repellent and use netting when camping along the coast, especially inside adobe buildings with thatched roofs. Seek medical attention if symptoms develop; a vaccine is being developed.

Leishmaniasis arrives aboard tiny *Phlebotomus* sand flies. One of the world's most common parasitic diseases, it occurs throughout Ecuador. Small, itching red bites develop into skin lesions that affect the mucous membranes. Once the disease spreads to the internal organs, death follows quickly. Netting must be extra-fine (more than 10 holes per square centimeter) to keep these flies out. Keep an eye on any particularly annoying insect bites, and see a doctor if they don't heal.

Onchocerciasis, also known as "river blindness," occurs near rivers in Esmeraldas Province. Tiny roundworms spread by the bite of a black fly cause itching, rash, and inflammation of the eye. Less than 10 percent of cases result in blindness. No vaccine is available, but a simple complete blood count (CBC) test reveals the disease.

Other Diseases

Human immunodeficiency virus (HIV) is transmitted by direct contact with the bodily fluids of an infected person, most often through blood transfusions, intravenous injections, or sexual contact. It's a serious problem in Latin America, but easy to prevent: do not have unprotected sex, share needles, or accept a blood transfusion that isn't 100 percent safe. To be extra careful, take and use your own syringes. There is no cure yet for HIV or the AIDS virus. Other types of **sexually transmitted diseases (STDs)** such as chlamydia, gonorrhea, syphilis, and herpes reveal themselves through various types of genital pain, discharge, and sores. These are even more common than HIV—another reason to practice safe sex. Some can be treated by antibiotics. Note that condoms are of variable quality in Ecuador, so it's best to buy a recognized brand or bring them from abroad.

Hepatitis B, like its cousin hepatitis A, is a viral infection of the liver, but it is spread through the exchange of body fluids, such as the blood or semen of an infected person. Chances of complete recovery and subsequent lifetime immunity are excellent. Practice the same precautions as you would to prevent contracting HIV, and seek medical attention in cases of infection.

Once commonly spread by body lice, **typhus** is on the way out worldwide. Symptoms include pounding headaches, a dark rash on the upper body, fever, and delirium. Medical facilities should have tetracycline drugs to cure it.

Animals

Any mammal bite leads to a risk of contracting **rabies,** which is fatal if left untreated. Immediately wash the wound with soap and hot water, and disinfect it with alcohol or iodine. Bats and monkeys are common carriers, but treat any dog bite as a possible risk, and see a doctor in all cases.

The most dangerous creatures to humans frequent the water. Portuguese man-of-war jellyfish, sea wasps, and stingrays can each inflict a painful, even fatal sting requiring quick medical attention. Male sea lions are the most dangerous animals in the Galápagos—don't approach one, and back off if it looks like it wants you to.

Ecuador's collection of potentially harmful **arthropods,** including scorpions, centipedes, black widows, and brown recluse spiders, ranges from one end of the country to the other. Pay attention to any bites to see if unusual symptoms develop. **Poisonous snakes** are more frightened of you than you are of them, but there are some potentially fatal species such as the coral and fer-de-lance. Baby snakes can be more dangerous because they often inject more poison. If you are bitten, try to identify the snake and apply pressure to the bite (but not a tourniquet, as this can increase the likelihood of amputation). Keep the bite area below the level of your heart if possible. Avoid overexertion, and find a doctor.

Mountain Health

High-altitude illnesses can be prevented by proper acclimation. Spend several days in

Quito and climb a few 4,000-meter peaks before tackling any higher ones, eat a diet high in carbohydrates, drink plenty of fluids, and avoid caffeine and alcohol. Altitude sickness can strike even the prepared and experienced, so mountaineers should be able to recognize the symptoms. The biggest problem in Ecuador is travelers who decide spontaneously to climb peaks without proper preparation. Unfortunately, unscrupulous operators may sell you a climbing package without bothering to ask you about acclimation. As a general rule, above 4,000 meters, you need at least a day to fully adjust for every additional 500 meters in elevation, so going straight from Quito (2,800 meters) to climb peaks over 5,000 meters such as Cotopaxi, Chimborazo, and Cayambe is a bad idea.

About one in four climbers suffers some degree of **acute mountain sickness (AMS),** known locally as *soroche,* which feels like the world's worst hangover: headache, nausea, fatigue, insomnia, and loss of appetite. The drug Diamox (acetazolamide) can lessen the odds of getting AMS, and analgesics can handle some of the aches. **Pulmonary edema** occurs when fluids start accumulating in the lungs, causing shortness of breath and a rattling cough that eventually brings up blood. **Cerebral edema** is fluid in the brain, which is accompanied by severely impaired mental functioning and poor judgment. Each of these conditions is less common than the one before it, and all should be treated by immediate descent to a lower elevation. Edemas require medical attention.

Hypothermia occurs when your body loses more heat than it can produce. Wet clothing, wind, and an exposed head are the most common culprits. Always be prepared in the Andes, even on short hikes, with raingear and warm layers for your body, head, and hands. Watch your companions during climbs for signs of dropping body temperature. Severe shivering reveals mild cases, in which body temperature doesn't drop below 33°C. Get the person warm and dry, and encourage him or her to move around to generate heat. Shivering actually ceases as body temperature drops, followed by loss of coordination, impaired judgment, fatigue, and eventually death.

Pain in the extremities isn't necessarily the surest indicator of **frostbite,** when part of the body becomes frozen. Numbness is often the first symptom, followed by the area becoming hard and white, then black. Often the area has become wet or the person is exhausted. Keep extremities warm and moving, especially the toes, fingers, ears, nose, and cheeks. A little numbness is normal, but if it lasts longer than half an hour, you'll want to loosen tight clothing, stamp your feet, or warm your chilly parts against a friend's body. Do not rub afflicted areas with snow. If frostbite has taken hold, special rapid rewarming techniques become necessary. There's no particular hurry to start this excruciating process, since frostbitten fingers and toes can, in effect, hibernate for days.

You'd be surprised at all the places sunlight bouncing off the snow can cause **sunburn** (inside your nose, for one). Spread high-SPF sunscreen, glacier cream, or zinc oxide everywhere you can reach. Reflected sunlight can also cause agonizing **snow blindness,** a temporary condition that only dark glacier goggles with side baffles can prevent. The goggles are a good investment if you plan to do several high-elevation snow climbs; you can buy them in Quito. **Cavities** can hurt like hell at high elevation because of a pressure difference between the inside of the tooth and the outside.

If Something Happens

Because many locals can't afford the services of a doctor, **pharmacists** *(farmacéuticos)* tend to be more proactive in Latin America. Provided you speak some Spanish, they can usually be trusted to recommend treatments and medicines for minor ailments that require a prescription back home. However, if your problem is more serious, you need the expertise of a doctor. If you are hospitalized, try to talk to an English-speaking doctor before agreeing to any procedures. Be ready to pay up front, even if you have insurance coverage. Make sure to get a detailed, comprehensive receipt—in English, if possible—for insurance reimbursements.

POST-TRAVEL REMINDERS

If you're taking any medical regimens, such as malaria pills, make sure to continue taking them for as long as you're supposed to, even after you return home. Pay close attention to your health for at least six months after your trip, since many exotic diseases have long incubation periods. Symptoms may resemble other illnesses, such as the flu, causing doctors unfamiliar with tropical medicine to misdiagnose. If you have any mysterious symptoms, tell your doctor where you've been—a fever in particular should call for a blood test. A posttravel checkup with blood and stool exams is a good idea in any case, as well as tests for STDs, particularly HIV, if you've had sexual contact with unfamiliar partners during your travels.

RESOURCES

The **U.S. Centers for Disease Control and Prevention** (U.S. tel. 877/394-8747, www.cdc.gov/travel) has an extensive website with up-to-date information on health issues around the world. The **Pan American Health Organization** (PAHO, 525 23rd St. NW, Washington, DC 20037, U.S. tel. 202/974-3000, www.paho.org) is the Americas branch of the World Health Organization. PAHO's website has country health profiles for travelers and information on many health topics.

The nonprofit **International Association for Medical Assistance to Travelers** (1623 Military Rd., Suite 279, Niagara Falls, NY 14304-1745, U.S. tel. 716/754-4883, info@iamat.org, www.iamat.org) is one of the best general travelers health resources. For free or a small donation, the organization sends information on health risks abroad, including an immunization chart and a membership card that allows you access to its worldwide list of English-speaking doctors who operate for a fixed fee.

The **Traveler's Emergency Network** (P.O. Box 668, Millersville, MD 21108, U.S. tel. 800/275-4836, U.S. fax 888/258-2911, www.tenweb.com) has membership programs starting at $139 pp per year that offer worldwide medical assistance, 24-hour medical consultation, referral to English-speaking doctors, and emergency sickness or injury evacuation.

Travel Medicine (351 Pleasant St., Suite 312, Northampton, MA 01060, U.S. tel. 800/872-8633, www.travmed.com) and **Chinook Medical Gear** (P.O. Box 1736, Edwards, CO 81632, U.S. tel. 800/766-1365, U.S. fax 970/926-9660, chinook@vail.net, www.chinookmed.com) both sell medical supplies and books for travelers.

Excellent travel health books include *CDC Health Information for International Travel* (Mosby, 2009), *Travel Health Guide* by Mark Wise (Firefly, 2010), Avalon Travel Publishing's own *Staying Healthy in Asia, Africa, and Latin America,* by Dirk Schroeder (5th ed., 2000) and *A Comprehensive Guide to Wilderness & Travel Medicine,* by Eric A. Weiss (Adventure Medical Kits, 2005).

CRIME

Quantifying danger is very difficult, but two facts are true about Ecuador: Firstly, it's not as dangerous as other Latin American countries, but secondly, it is more dangerous than it used to be. The overall crime rate in South America is high: Murder rates are 26 per 100,000, and while Ecuador reports less than 20, that's still substantially higher than the United States (which hovers around 5 per 100,000). However, the vast majority of incidents of violence are within dangerous slums among rival gangs. Over 1 million visitors come to Ecuador every year, and the vast majority of visits are trouble-free, but the economic crisis and rising food prices have led to higher crime rates, so you need to take certain precautions to keep yourself out of harm's way.

Common Crimes and Danger Spots

The most serious crime is a big increase in so-called "express kidnappings" (*secuestro express*). This is a kidnapping that takes place in a car or taxi; the victim is kept at gunpoint in the car, robbed, and often driven to ATMs to withdraw as much money as possible before being released, usually in a remote location. Wealthier Ecuadorians are the most common targets, but foreigners in Quito, Guayaquil, and Manta have been targeted. Unless you have your own car, taxis are the biggest threat. Never take an unmarked cab, and look for the company name and registered number on the side of the cab as well as the ID on the inside of the windshield. It's better to ask your hotel owner to order a cab from a recommended company.

Longer-term kidnappings and ransom demands do happen, but they are far less common following a concerted effort by the Colombian and Ecuadorian governments to improve security in the border area. However, outside of Tulcán, the border remains unsafe, and you should avoid it completely, especially San Lorenzo in Esmeraldas and north of Lago Agrio in Sucumbíos.

Armed robbery is also on the rise, particularly in Quito, Guayaquil, Manta, and Esmeraldas Province. The tourist area of Mariscal Sucre in Quito is a particularly hot spot, although at the time of this writing, police and army patrols have increased following pressure from local businesses. Quito's Old Town at night is also not particularly safe, and the area around El Panecillo is dangerous during the day as well (always take a taxi up to the statue). Walking alone at night is the biggest risk. Take a marked taxi, preferably with advanced booking, when going out at night. If you are confronted by an armed thief, the most important thing is to give them your valuables without discussion or resistance; most thieves don't want things to escalate and simply want to take the money and run, so don't give them a reason to harm you.

By far the biggest problem for visitors in Ecuador is sneak theft. While this is the lesser evil because no physical harm is likely to come to you, that's little consolation if you lose large amounts of money or camera equipment. The most common thefts take place on public buses, trolleybuses in Quito and Guayaquil, crowded tourist spots like markets and plazas, and from hotel rooms, usually cheaper accommodations.

Staying Safe

As simple as it sounds, the best defense is to keep one eye open at all times and to look like you know what you're doing. Some people use the traffic light system. When outside a completely secure environment, such as your hotel, it's a good idea to switch from green to a cautionary yellow. This should switch to red if you see anything suspicious, particularly at night, in crowded areas or on public transportation. Insecurity attracts criminals, and inattentiveness gives them a window of opportunity. You won't be able to prevent all crimes, but you can cut down the odds drastically. Pay attention to your gut instincts: If something tells you not to walk down that dim alley, don't. Be on your guard at night, when taking taxis and when using public transportation. Lock expensive items in the lockbox (*caja fuerte* or *caja de seguridad*) available in most hotels, along with your passport, tickets, and money. Get a receipt for the exact contents.

Make copies of your passport, plane tickets, and traveler's checks. Keep one copy of these at home, along with a list of expensive items you're bringing and their model and serial numbers, and take one copy with you separate from the originals. Find out if and what your insurance covers while abroad, and how to file a claim. Leave extraneous valuables at home, especially jewelry.

Some travelers carry an emergency wad of money in their shoes or sewn into a piece of clothing. Velcro strips sewn across pockets will slow down pickpockets. A small canister of mace or pepper spray may give you added confidence. Although you can't fly with one, you can buy canisters at *ferreterías* (hardware stores) in major cities. Take a few practice squirts outside.

Money and Valuables

Money is what most thieves are after, and the best defense is not to carry large amounts. It's a bad idea to carry all your money in one place. Leave most of it locked in a secure place, and keep a few dollars separate from the rest. If you are carrying large amounts of money, it's a very bad idea to carry it physically separate from your body (i.e. in your backpack). Never carry your wallet in your back pocket or a loose pocket (traditional Ecuadorian pants and sweaters are notorious for having loose pockets). Most secure is a pouch worn under or as part of your clothing, like a money belt or nylon leg or neck pouch. One trick is to wear a neck pouch with the string around your waist and the pouch down the front of your pants—nobody's going to try to get in there surreptitiously. It's a good idea to have a small purse with small denominations so that you don't reveal the whereabouts of your main source of money when paying small amounts like bus fares and snacks.

Try to insist that all credit-card imprints are made in front of you. Tear up any incomplete or void imprints yourself, and make sure you know the whereabouts of all carbons.

Luggage

Small locks for outside pockets and zip closures are available in most stores at home, or in Ecuador on the street and in hardware stores. Cable locks are useful for securing your bag to the roof of a bus, or to something hefty in your room while you go out. These locks won't stop a determined thief, but they will at least slow things down long enough to prevent a casual theft. Never keep valuables in your bag if you are stowing it, regardless of whether it's in the luggage compartment, above your head, or below your seat. Bag slashers operate not only in crowded areas but also on public transportation, and many of them are shameless: They will sit directly behind you and try to get into your bag as you sit with it stowed by your legs. It's best to keep day packs in front of you in plain sight, securely held in place with one arm. Keep hold of a strap when you put a bag down, and never leave anything hanging on the back of a chair. When sightseeing, never set your camera down.

One of the best ways to secure your belongings is with a **Pacsafe** from Outpac Designs (U.S. tel. 800/873-9415, www.pac-safe.com). These lightweight but sturdy steel-mesh sacks fit snugly over backpacks and duffel bags and lock closed, making it impossible for someone to open your bag without a key. You can use them to lock your bags to anything sturdy as well. Outpac also makes the Travel Safe, a small, lockable nylon pouch reinforced with steel mesh.

Where and When to Be Careful

Walk briskly and look like you know where you're going (or better yet, *actually* know where you're going), particularly after coming out of a bank or money-exchange office. Everyone should be exceptionally vigilant after dark. For women, certain precautions can decrease your odds of assault: Travel by day as much as possible, travel with men or in a group, and avoid situations where you could be cornered in an out-of-the-way spot.

Pickpocketing is the most common crime against visitors by far, and don't underestimate how skilled these people are. They are professional thieves, and if their activities weren't so annoying, you'd have to applaud them for their adept skills. Airports, bus stations, public buses, trolleybuses, markets, and busy tourist sights are their favorite haunts. When visiting tourist sights, keep your money hidden away, and keep you camera on your person with the strap. When visiting markets, consider leaving your camera behind: After all, do you really need to take photos of markets?

By far the worst place for pickpockets is public transportation. On short rides, particularly on the electric buses in Quito and Guayaquil, the services are crawling with pickpockets, and it's a safe bet that they will make a beeline for a foreign visitor. If you are going sightseeing, you should consider avoiding these services completely. If you do use them, take minimum valuables and leave your camera behind. The crowded spaces are perfect for them to snatch something from your pocket in a flash, and they will often use diversionary tactics—one will engage you in conversation while the other robs you. Blocking tactics are also used. Two people will block the way so you have to push past them, allowing them to frisk your pockets (the author is writing, sadly, from personal experience).

Longer bus rides make vigilance harder—you can't sit for hours constantly watching for thieves, but by keeping all valuables about your person and out of sight, and by holding on to your bag placed in front of you, the risk of being robbed is considerably reduced.

Use your judgment if someone other than a good friend offers you food or drink; druggings are known to happen, particularly to young female visitors. If you decide not to accept what someone offers, the best strategy is to feign illness or allergy. Traveling in pairs, of course, is preferable.

Robbery, assault, and rape have occurred in the backcountry, especially on popular climbs like Pichincha. There have also been reports of occasional assaults in the lakes around Otavalo. Try to go in a group, and never leave gear unattended in mountain huts. Avoid any deserted beach areas after dark.

Drugs

Even though Ecuador's drug problem is not as serious as in Peru or Colombia, controlled substances still top the list of things you don't want to get mixed up in as a foreigner. Most of the foreigners in jail in Ecuador are there for drug offenses. Drug sales are often setups, and police can be in cahoots with informants. If you're caught, don't expect much support from your embassy or the Ecuadorian legal system. Jails are often hellholes, the judicial process can take years, and penalties are steep. Steer clear.

Officialdom

Being stopped and asked to show your papers is often a new experience for foreigners, but it happens occasionally in Ecuador—just smile and comply. Police searches of cars and hotel rooms can happen. Make sure you're present, and request a *testigo* (witness). Because civil servants are paid next to nothing, corruption does occur among police. Some are even outright criminals, or criminals posing as police or drug enforcement agents. Be wary of anyone posing as a plainclothes police officer. Insist

on seeing his identification—for more than a brief flash—and don't go anywhere with him if none is produced, especially not into a vehicle. Even if everything seems on the level, insist on walking to the nearest police station in public.

If Something Happens

In the police station, you'll have to fill out a *denuncia* to report a crime. Get a receipt, for insurance purposes if nothing else, and ask for temporary identification papers if yours were stolen. Your embassy may be able to help arrange the wiring or emergency funds, or even (in rare cases) a reimbursable loan in the interim. The embassy can also help find a lawyer if you're thrown in jail.

In the unfortunate event of rape, women's health clinics (*clínicas de la mujer*) in larger cities can provide specialized treatment and gather evidence for the police report. Don't expect too much help from local police, but fill out a report as soon as possible in any case. A high dose of oral contraceptives (also known as the morning-after pill) lowers the odds of an unwanted pregnancy and is available at most *farmacias*. Every woman's emotional response to such a traumatic event will be different. For some, continuing their travels may be the best antidote, whereas others may prefer to end the trip early.

Traveler's checks and credit cards each have their own emergency numbers in case of loss or theft. Notify your travel insurance carrier, if applicable. In the case of a lost airline ticket, you'll probably have to buy a new one and wait until you get home to be reimbursed for the old one. Ask at the local airline branch for details. Your embassy or consulate will tell you what to do in case your passport goes missing.

Resources for Travelers

The U.S. Department of State's **Bureau of Consular Affairs** (2201 C St. NW, Washington, DC 20520, U.S. tel. 202/647-5225, www.travel.state.gov) publishes *Travel Advisories* on individual countries, available by mail, fax, or on its website. The British

Foreign Office (www.fco.gov.uk/travel) publishes its own advisories on its website. Publications such as *A Safe Trip Abroad, Travel Warning on Drugs Abroad,* and *Tips for Travelers to Central & South America* are available online as well. U.S. citizens can register with the Department of State for free before leaving home (http://travelregistration.state.gov/ibrs), so that their information is on file in case of an emergency.

Information and Services

MONEY
Currency
In September 2000, Ecuador officially laid the beleaguered old *sucre* to rest and replaced it with the **U.S. dollar.** In the short term, the devaluation of the *sucre* and its subsequent replacement was a financial disaster for millions of Ecuadorians who saw the value of their savings plummet, while prices of basic food skyrocketed. Once one of the cheapest Latin American countries for traveling, Ecuador is now in the middle of the price list—cheaper than Colombia and considerably cheaper than Brazil and Chile, but more expensive than Bolivia and Peru. The biggest plus for visitors is that there's no need to worry about exchanging money.

Outside major cities, **cash** is the easiest—and often only—form of money to use. Ecuador's coins are equivalent to U.S. cents (100 in one dollar): nickels ($0.05), dimes ($0.10), quarters ($0.25), and half dollars ($0.50), although they have different symbols and faces than their U.S. counterparts. Note that U.S. coins are often rejected, so it's best only to bring banknotes. Finding small change is always a problem; bring small bills, as most places don't accept bills over $20, and even $20 can cause problems in smaller towns, so ensure you have a few $5 and $10 bills. Keep an eye out for **counterfeit** bills, which can often be spotted by their smoothness (real bills are printed with faint impressions), limpness (real bills are crisp), and sloppy presidential portraits. Keep your bills in good condition; any note with small tears is often rejected as potentially fake.

You could carry the bulk of your money in **traveler's checks,** which can be refunded if lost or stolen, but they are becoming steadily more difficult to change outside major cities, and commissions are usually charged. U.S. dollars are best; Canadian dollars, British pounds, Japanese yen, and euros are very difficult to change. American Express and Visa traveler's checks are the most widely accepted, but Thomas Cook and Citibank checks also pass. Always try to have some cash on you—the farther you get from Quito and Guayaquil, the more commission you pay to change traveler's checks, especially on weekends. Commissions are often 2–5 percent and sometimes depend on the amount changed.

Be sure to keep the serial numbers of traveler's checks and the number to call in a separate place in case your checks are lost or stolen. Exchange houses (*casas de cambio,* an almost extinct species in Ecuador nowadays) and some banks change traveler's checks to cash dollars, but few businesses will let you pay with traveler's checks—usually only those near the high end. Most tellers are very picky with signatures, so if your chicken scratch doesn't match the one on the check, it may be rejected. If this happens with American Express checks, the office in Quito will issue you new ones immediately.

Credit cards are accepted in many higher-end shops, hotels, restaurants, and travel agencies, but there is often a surcharge up to 10 percent. It's generally best to pay with cash whenever possible and save your credit cards for emergencies or ATM use. MasterCard and Visa are the most widely accepted, and cardholders can draw cash advances. American Express, Diner's Club, and Discover are much harder to use.

FOREIGN TOUR COMPANIES

- **Cheeseman's Ecology Safaris** (20800 Kittredge Rd., Saratoga, CA 95070, U.S. tel. 408/867-1371 or 800/527-5330, U.S. fax 408/741-0358, www.cheesemans. com): smaller, more intimate trips led by a husband-and-wife biology professor–wildlife photographer and birder team.

- **Holbrook Travel** (3540 NW 13th St., Gainesville, FL 32609, U.S. tel. 800/451-7111, www. holbrooktravel.com): Galápagos tours, field courses, and custom tours.

- **Journey Latin America** (12-13 Healthfield Terrace, Chiswick, London, UK W4 4JE, UK tel. 20/8747-8315, www.journeylatinamerica.co.uk): UK-based operator specializing in trips all over Latin America, including the Ecuadorian Sierra, the Amazon, and the Galápagos.

- **Mountain Travel-Sobek** (1266 66th St., Emeryville, CA 94608, U.S. tel. 888/831-7526 or 510/594-6000, www.mtsobek.com): Adventure tours range from Galápagos cruises to hiking the haciendas in the Sierra.

- **Myths and Mountains** (976 Tee Court, Incline Village, NV 89451, U.S. tel. 800/670-MYTH – 800/670-6984, U.S. fax 775/832-4454, www.mythsandmountains. com): Educational tourism combines classroom and hands-on study of religion, folk medicine, crafts, and natural history with fieldwork in indigenous communities in the Sierra and Oriente.

- **Nature Expeditions International** (7860 Peters Rd., Suite F-103, Plantation, FL 33324, U.S. tel. 954/693-8852 or 800/869-0639, U.S. fax 954/693-8854, www.naturexp.com): educational adventure travel for older active guests. Tours of the Galápagos and the Sierra from $2,650 pp.

- **Wilderness Travel** (1102 9th St., Berkeley, CA 94710, U.S. tel. 800/368-2794, U.S. fax 510/558-2489, www.wildernesstravel. com): tours of the Sierra, including haciendas, along with visits to the Galápagos and destinations in Peru.

- **Wildland Adventures** (3516 NE 155th St., Seattle, WA 98155-7412, U.S. tel. 206/365-0686 or 800/345-4453, U.S. fax 206/363-6615, www.wildland.com): an award-winning ecotourism company offering visits to La Selva, the Galápagos, and highland haciendas.

Note that interest rates on **cash advances** are often compounded daily, and they may even carry a maintenance fee. These are available in Ecuador only at the credit-card company's head offices, listed in the *Quito* chapter. American Express members can buy AmEx traveler's checks at the office in Quito, using a personal check from your bank account, for a 1 percent fee (gold card members don't even need the personal check).

Keep the customer service number in a separate place from any credit card, in case the card is lost or stolen. Just because an establishment sports a credit-card sticker doesn't mean it necessarily takes them; always ask.

Automated teller machines (ATMs) are becoming more and more common in Ecuador. Almost all credit cards can now issue you a personal identification number (PIN) so you can use the card to withdraw cash advances at ATMs. (Ask for a four-digit PIN, since five-digit ones don't work in Ecuador.) Machines accept ATM cards on the Plus and Cirrus networks, as well as MasterCard and Visa cards that have been assigned a PIN—call your card issuer for information on setting this up. Most ATMs have a daily withdrawal limit of $300–500 or less, which you can sometimes subvert by visiting multiple machines. Don't count on getting more than $500 in a single day. Check with your bank about any transaction charge. Cash advances are available from the main office of Banco del Pacifico in Quito and other cities. Note that in small towns, there is usually only one ATM that all too often runs out of money, so you should always have enough cash for a couple of days—as a general rule, keep a minimum of $50 cash on you at all times.

Money transfers are probably the least cost-effective way to get funds, but in a pinch, they're often the only fast and sure way to get your hands on cash. Ask at your home bank about direct bank-to-bank transfers. Find out before your trip which banks in Ecuador, if any, your bank deals with, and how long the transaction takes. **Western Union** has offices all over the country.

Tipping

A *propina* (tip) isn't required or expected, but it usually doesn't take much out of your pocket and can make someone's day. Better restaurants add 10 percent for *servicio* (service) and the 12 percent *IVA* (value-added tax); if they don't charge for service, consider leaving it anyway. Remember that most waiters earn minimum wage or even worse if their employer has hired them informally. For cheaper restaurants, porters, hairdressers, and guides, 5–10 percent will do. See the *Galápagos Islands* chapter for advice on tipping naturalist guides in the islands.

Taxes

Shops, hotels, and restaurants must charge a 12 percent **IVA** (value-added tax), which should be noted separately on the *cuenta* (bill). On leaving the country, you'll be slapped with an **airport departure tax** ($44 in Quito, $27 in Guayaquil).

Budgeting

No longer the travel steal it once was, Ecuador is still a comparatively inexpensive place to visit. Serious budget travelers can get by for under $25 pp per day by taking advantage of cheap buses, $5–8 hotel rooms, and $2–3 set meals. A more comfortable budget of $25–35 per day will get a better room, better meals, the odd taxi, and a *cerveza* or two when the day is done. Planning $50 pp per day and upward

allows you to factor in quality hotels, domestic flights, and day tours.

COMMUNICATIONS AND MEDIA
Mail

With the arrival of the Internet and email, "snail mail" systems around the world are shrinking in volume and rising in price. Airmail postcards and letters under 20 grams cost about $1.55 to North and South America, $1.80 to Europe, and $2.40 elsewhere. For mail weighing 20–100 grams, you will pay $3.71 to North and South America, $4.29 to Europe, and $5.28 to anywhere else. Don't mail any objects of value, as things go missing quite often from Ecuador's postal system, especially incoming packages. It's better to use a private courier company like DHL or FedEx.

The regular mail service is notoriously unreliable, and packages are routinely opened by customs, ostensibly checking for contraband. The South American Explorers' Quito clubhouse, American Express, and various Spanish schools can receive and hold mail for members.

Telecommunications

Compared to the postal service, the national telephone system functions well under the national phone company. It's currently called Andinatel in the Andes and Pacifictel along the coast. Almost every town has its own office, but service varies; domestic calls are no problem, but international calls may be impossible. Some offices will charge you for calls if the phone rings more than eight times, even if no one answers. Connections to the Galápagos and some parts of the Oriente and the coast are sometimes congested and tenuous at best. New *cabinas* have sprung up in towns and villages all over the country: **Allegro, Movistar,** and **Claro** (formerly Porta) provide excellent service, meaning that it is no longer necessary to search out the Andinatel or Pacifictel office to make a call in any city or town.

Per-minute local calls cost about $0.10, domestic calls $0.20, while calling North

TELEPHONE PREFIXES

Prefixes listed by province, with major cities in parentheses:

Prefix	Region
1	services
2	Pichincha (Quito), Santo Domingo de los Tsáchilas (Santo Domingo)
3	Bolívar (Guaranda), Cotopaxi (Latacunga), Chimborazo (Riobamba), Pastaza (Puyo), Tungurahua (Ambato, Baños)
4	Guayas (Guayaquil), Santa Elena (Salinas)
5	Los Ríos, Manabí (Manta, Portoviejo, Bahía de Caráquez), Galápagos (Puerto Ayora, Baquerizo Moreno)
6	Carchi (Tulcán), Esmeraldas (Atacames), Imbabura (Otavalo, Ibarra), Napo (Tena), Orellana (Coca), Sucumbíos (Lago Agrio)
7	Azuay (Cuenca), Cañar (Azogues), El Oro (Machala), Loja (Loja), Morona Santiago (Macas), Zamora-Chinchipe (Zamora)
8 and 9	cell phones

dial 0 followed by the regional prefix code and the seven-digit phone number. Drop the 0 within the same region. Cellular phones are everywhere; their numbers begin with 9 or 8, and you can choose between Movistar and Claro (formerly Porta). For directory information, dial 104; for help with domestic long distance, dial 105; and for international long distance, dial 116 or 117. Numbers beginning with 800 are toll-free.

If you bring your own cell phone from home, you can use it if it has roaming service, but this is expensive. It is better to take it into a service shop and purchase a chip for local use at minimal cost (about $5).

Although it's possible to call other countries through the normal telephone network, Internet phone connections are so much cheaper that it's almost not worth it. It will cost you about $1 per minute to talk on a normal connection through the national telephone system or one of the pay-phone companies. Different countries have different codes for reaching an international operator. All codes are preceded by 999. Codes for some countries include: Canada, 175; Italy, 164/174; Spain, 176; United Kingdom, 178; Switzerland, 160; France, 180; United States, 170 for MCI, 171 for Sprint/NYNEX, 119 for AT&T USA Direct.

To call Ecuador from the United States, dial the international access code (011), the country code for Ecuador (593), the provincial code (2–7) or cell phone code (8 or 9), and the seven-digit local number—that's 15 digits in all. **Language Line** (U.S. tel. 877/886-3885, www.languageline.com) has translators available around the clock for a moderate per-minute charge.

Two competing cellular companies, Movistar and Claro (formerly Porta), offer public pay phones. Claro seems to have better coverage in the mountains, and each system takes its own type of calling card (*tarjeta telefónica*), which you can buy in various denominations just about anywhere. Phones display the amount left on your card; domestic calls cost about $0.17 per minute.

America costs from $0.20–0.30, Europe from $0.40, and Australia $0.80. Calls cost up to 20 percent less on weekdays after 7 P.M. and from 7 A.M. Saturday to 7 A.M. Monday. Calls from hotels are always more expensive, and many businesses will let you use their phone for domestic calls for a small charge. Hotel management will sometimes try to charge you, even if you use a calling card or call collect.

To make long-distance calls within Ecuador,

Internet

Internet access has exploded in Ecuador in recent years. Instantaneous and inexpensive, email (*correo electrónico*) and Skype make it easy to keep in touch with friends back home. Most Internet cafés are open 8 A.M.–10 P.M. daily and charge $1 or less per hour for Internet access. Almost all cafés offer Internet phone services that allow you to dial phone numbers worldwide and talk through the computer using a microphone and headset. This setup is cheaper than normal long-distance calls ($0.10–0.20 per minute from Ecuador to the United States). Most Internet cafés also have instant messaging programs with webcams, scanners, printers, fax services, and word-processing programs. If you plan to use the Internet to stay in touch, you can set up a free email account through services like Hotmail (www.hotmail.com), Yahoo (http://mail.yahoo.com), or Gmail (www.google.com/gmail). Digital photographers can burn images onto CDs for $2–3 at many Internet cafés or carry a flash drive.

Since Internet cafés open and close with surprising speed, it doesn't make much sense to list specific ones in cities outside Quito. Rest assured that in pretty much any town, you'll find an Internet café within a block or two. In addition, many hotels and restaurants have Wi-Fi service included, so travelers can use their own laptops.

Newspapers and Magazines

Local publications include national Spanish-language newspapers, such as Quito-based *Hoy* and *El Comercio,* Guayaquil-based *El Universo,* and government-owned *El Telégrafo.* The gutter press is dominated by *Extra,* which mixes nauseating images of violence with nudity and gossip. International editions of *Time* and *Newsweek,* along with the foreign edition of the *Miami Herald,* are available in larger cities. It's often easier to keep up-to-date online.

Television and Radio

Latin American television comprises three elements: soccer, slapstick, and soap operas.

Telenovelas are archetypal Latin soap operas in which poor Cinderellas from the *barrio* struggle for love against the wickedness of the rich. There's a lot of crying, screaming, and over-acting. Most educated Ecuadorians admit that there's nothing worth watching on their national TV network. If TV is important to you for relaxation between traveling, it's worth asking at hotels if your room has *TV cable* or *TV nacional; TV cable* will have several English-language movie channels as well as U.S. comedies and dramas.

Radio helps to keep people in touch in the remoter parts of the country. Stations broadcast music, news, and educational programming in Spanish and indigenous languages.

MAPS AND VISITOR INFORMATION

Maps

International Travel Maps (530 W. Broadway, Vancouver, BC V5Z 1E9, Canada, tel. 604/879-3621, Canada fax 604/879-4521, www.itmb.com) has 150 of its own maps and distributes 23,000 more by other publishers. Its 1:700,000 Ecuador map (C$13.95) is the best available. In the United States, maps of Ecuador and South America are available from **Maplink** (30 South La Patera Lane, Unit 5, Santa Barbara, CA 93117, U.S. tel. 805/692-1394, U.S. fax 805/692-6787, www.maplink.com). In Ecuador, the best resource is the **Instituto Geográfico Militar** (IGM, Senierges and Paz y Miño, tel. 2/397-5100, www.igm.gob.ec, 8 A.M.–4 P.M. Mon.–Fri.) near Parque El Ejido in Quito. Otherwise, you can pick up useful city, town, and regional maps at tourist offices across the country.

Travel Resources

The **South American Explorers** organization has its headquarters in the United States (126 Indian Creek Rd., Ithaca, NY 14850, U.S. tel. 607/277-0488, www.samexplo.org) and clubhouses in Quito, Cusco, and Lima. See *Information* in the *Quito* chapter for more details. For useful travel books and websites, see the *Resources* chapter.

BETTER LATE THAN NEVER

Ecuador is officially on eastern standard time (five hours earlier than UTC or Greenwich Mean Time), but in reality the country operates in its very own time zone, known locally as *hora Ecuatoriana*.

Imagine you arrange to meet some locals for a drink at 8 P.M. In most other countries you might aim to arrive between 8 and 8:30. Leave it later than 9, and a call or text message might be required. In Ecuador, most locals would arrive at 10, maybe even later. So why not simply arrange to meet at 10? It's best not to ask.

Even by Latin American standards, Ecuadorians' inability to keep track of time is infamous. In 2003 a citizens group went so far as to launch a campaign to improve the nation's punctuality, claiming that lateness cost about $2 billion annually (nobody knows how they worked out that figure). Jefferson Pérez, Ecuador's Olympic champion race walker, led his compatriots to synchronize their watches to inaugurate the punctuality campaign, and the government backed it by distributing posters to schools and businesses. However, the effort was somewhat undermined by the fact that President Lucio Gutiérrez himself was notoriously tardy, and the campaign soon fizzled out.

As a visitor to Ecuador, you can either tear your hair out about people's lateness or just accept it. Arrive an hour late and you'll still be early, so bring a book or a friend and plenty of patience. In many years of living in Ecuador, I've worked out that on social occasions, arriving 1-2 hours later than the expressed time is considered normal, and arriving right on time can actually be slightly rude because it's unexpected. Group invitations are commonly made deliberately earlier than the expected time of arrival, so a dinner party set for 7 P.M. means come between 8 and 9 P.M.

However, it's worth noting that when it comes to traveling around, Ecuadorians laid-back attitude to time evaporates completely. Locals seem to undergo a personality change when they hit the road, and everybody is in an incredible hurry to arrive as quickly as possible. Be a split-second late at the change of a red light and you'll be deafened by a chorus of beeps; keep somebody waiting by sticking to the speed limit on a highway and it's even worse. Surely they're not in such a hurry because they don't want to be late? As the saying goes, time waits for no one.

ELECTRICITY

As in North America, electricity in Ecuador is 100 volts, 60 hertz alternating current. Flat-prong outlets seldom have the third grounding hole. Plug in expensive electronic equipment, such as computers, using a 3-to-2-prong adapter and surge protector available at U.S. hardware stores.

Power outages are common, even in major cities. Electricity is often shut off in rural areas after dark, and far-flung lodges usually operate on electric generators or solar panels, limiting usage even further. Note that you should take extra care with electric showers as some are poorly wired.

TIME

The Ecuadorian mainland is five hours earlier than UTC or Greenwich Mean Time, the same as North American eastern standard time. The Galápagos Islands are one hour earlier than the mainland, which is six hours earlier than UTC or Greenwich Mean Time, the same as North American central standard time. Because days and nights on the equator are the same duration year-round, daylight saving time is not used in Ecuador.

BUSINESS HOURS

Hours of operation change with amazing rapidity, often at the whim of employees or owners. Long lunch breaks are the norm, and they last longer (up to three hours) in hotter areas, such as the coastal region. A good strategy is to come 10–20 minutes before something reopens after the lunch break to guarantee your spot at the front of the line.

Typical business hours are 8 or 9 A.M.–5 or 6 P.M. Monday–Friday, with a lunch break 12:30–2 P.M. Business hours on Saturday are often half days ending at noon or 1 P.M. Banks operate 9 A.M.–1 P.M. Monday–Friday, and some reopen 2–4 P.M. and on Saturday mornings. Government offices and embassies often close by early afternoon. You're best off getting any money and administrative matters done in the morning. Restaurants tend to stay open later, in typical Latin American fashion. Dinner usually starts at 9 P.M.

LAUNDRY

Self-service laundry machines are few and far between. Many inexpensive hotels, though, have a *pila* (scrubbing board) and a clothesline out back. Water basins are often used for drinking water, so scoop water out instead of washing directly in the basin. Hotels generally frown on guests washing clothes in sinks. Packets of *detergente* are available at general stores.

Laundry services wash clothes by the piece or by the kilogram. This can be expensive in high-end hotels, and it may take a day or two for everything to air dry. Laundromats (*lavanderías*) are more popular among budget travelers, and you can usually get a decent load washed for $2–3, usually by the end of the day or the next morning. Dry cleaning (*lavaseco*) is available in larger cities.

RESOURCES

Glossary

abrazo a platonic hug

adobe sun-dried mud brick building

aguardiente sugarcane alcohol

aguas termales hot springs

almuerzo lunch

artesanías handicrafts

barrio district, often a poor neighborhood

batido fruit shake

botas de caucho rubber boots

brujo/a witch, practitioner of magic

buseta minibus

cabaña cabin

camioneta truck, often public transport

campesino/a rural resident

campo countryside

canelazo hot, sweet alcoholic drink made with sugarcane

cangil popcorn

¡carajo! strong expression of frustration, mildly offensive

caramba mild expression of surprise

centro comercial (CC) shopping mall

cerveza beer

chicha fermented maize drink

chifa Chinese restaurant

chifles chips made with crispy fried plantains

chiva open-top bus used for parties

cholo originally coastal fishermen, but also used as a derogatory term for lower class, un-educated people

choza thatched hut, sometimes converted into tourist accommodations

colectivo public bus or truck

cordillera mountain range

costeño person from the coast

criollo originally a person of pure Spanish descent born in the colonies but now applied to anything traditional, especially food

curandero/a medicinal healer

cuy roasted guinea pig

ejecutivo executive or first-class, particularly on buses

fanesca a fish stew dish served during Lent

finca small farm

¡fuchi! exclamation indicating a bad smell

gringo term for North Americans, but applied to most white foreigners; not particularly de-rogatory

guácala exclamation indicating that you don't like something, most commonly food

hacienda farm or country estate

helado type of sorbet; *helados de paila* is an Ecuadorian specialty

hostería inn

IGM (Instituto Geográfico Militar) Ecuadorian Military Geological Institute

indígena indigenous person (note that *indio* is considered insulting)

invierno "winter" or rainy season (relatively hot and wet)

lancha small boat

lavandería self-service laundry

lavaseca dry cleaner

maíz corn

malecón riverside or seaside promenade

menestra lentils or beans cooked in sauce to accompany rice

menú del día set menu of the day

merienda supper, also used for cheap set-menu dinners

mestizo person of mixed indigenous and European blood

minga community voluntary work

monos monkeys – slightly derogatory term used for people from Guayaquil

mosquitero hanging mosquito screen for beds

municipio town hall or city hall

obraje textile workshop

panadería bakery

Panamericana Panamerican highway

panga small boat

páramo high-elevation grasslands

parrillada restaurant specializing in grilled meat

paseo stroll or walk, often in the evening

pasillo Ecuador's national music

pelucón literally bigwig; mildly derogatory expression coined by *peña* bar with traditional live music

plata silver, slang for money

propina tip

quinoa grain native to the Andes

quinta fine country house

ranchero wooden bus with open sides, also known as *chiva*

salchipapas french fries topped with chunks of hot dog

salsateca Latin dance club

selva rainforest

serrano person from the Sierra or mountains

soroche altitude sickness

SS HH sign for public restroom (*servicios higiénicos*)

tambo a small, thatched hut used for emergency shelter in the Andes

tarabita a small cable car

terminal terrestre bus terminal

tienda shop

tróle trolley or electric bus

tsantsa shrunken head

verano "summer," a drier and cooler season

Spanish Phrasebook

An important barrier to breach if you're in Ecuador for an extended period is the language, and your Ecuadorian adventure will be far more fun if you use a little Spanish. It's really not as difficult as you imagine if you put your mind to it. Ecuadorians, although they may smile at your funny accent, will appreciate your halting efforts to break the ice and transform yourself from a foreigner into a potential friend. It will also empower you to be more in control of your travels.

Spanish commonly uses 30 letters: the familiar English 26, plus four straightforward additions: *ch, ll, ñ,* and *rr,* which are explained under *Consonants.*

PRONUNCIATION

Once you learn them, Spanish pronunciation rules – in contrast with English – don't change. Spanish vowels generally sound softer than in English. The capitalized syllables below are stressed.

Vowels

a as 'ah' in "hah": *agua* AH-gwah (water), *pan* PAHN (bread), *casa* KAH-sah (house)

e as 'e' in "bet:" *mesa* MEH-sah (table), *tela* TEH-lah (cloth), *de* DAY (of, from)

i as 'ee' in "need": *diez* DEE-ehss (10), *comida* ko-MEE-dah (meal), *fin* FEEN (end)

o two sounds: either the short "o" sound in British English "hot": *comer* KO-mare (eat); or like a longer "oh," as in *poco* POH-koh (a bit). *Ocho* has both sounds: O-choh (eight).

u as 'oo' in "cool": *uno* OO-noh (one) and *usted* oos-TEHD (you); when it follows a *q,* the **u** is silent; when it follows an *h* or has an umlaut (ü), it's pronounced like "w."

Consonants

b, f, k, l, m, n, p, q, s, r, t, v, w, x, y, z, and ch

pronounced almost as in English; **h** is used, but is silent – not pronounced at all. **D** is very similar to English but softer (between "d" and "th").

c as 'k' in "keep": *casa* KAH-sah (house); when it precedes *e* or *i*, **c** is pronounced as 's' in "sit": *cerveza* sayr-VAY-sah (beer), *encima* ehn-SEE-mah (on top of).

g as 'g' in "gift" when it precedes *a, o, u,* or a consonant: *gato* GAH-toh (cat), *hago* AH-goh (I do, make); otherwise, **g** is pronounced as 'h' in "hat": *giro* HEE-roh (money order), *gente* HEHN-tay (people).

j as 'h' in "has": *jueves* HOOAY-vays (Thursday), *mejor* meh HOR (better)

ll as 'y' in "yes": *toalla* toh-AH-yah (towel), *ellos* AY-yohs (they, them), *llamas* YAH-mahs (llamas)

ñ as 'ny' in "canyon": *año* AH-nyo (year), *señor* SEH-nyor (Mr., sir)

rr like a Scottish rolled "r." This distinguishes *perro* (dog) from *pero* (but) and *carro* (car) from *caro* (expensive). Many foreigners have particular trouble with this sound. If you do, try to use a different word, e.g. *auto* for car.

Note: the one small but common exception to all of the above is the pronunciation of **y** when used as the Spanish word for "and," as in "Ron y Kathy" (Ron and Kathy). In such cases, pronounce it as 'ee' in "keep": Ron "ee" Kathy.

Stressed Syllables

The rule for putting relative stress on syllables within a word, is straightforward. If a word ends in a vowel, an *n*, or an *s*, stress the next-to-last syllable; if not, stress the last syllable.

Pronounce *gracias* GRAH-seeahs (thank you), *orden* OHR-dayn (order), and *carretera* kah-ray-TAY-rah (highway) with stress on the next-to-last syllable.

Otherwise, accent the last syllable: *venir* veh-NEER (to come), *ferrocarril* feh-roh-cah-REEL (railroad), *edad* eh-DAHD (age).

Exceptions to the accent rule are always marked with an accent sign: (á, é, í, ó, or ú), such as *teléfono* teh-LAY-foh-noh (telephone), *jabón* hah-BON (soap), and *rápido* RAH-pee-doh (rapid).

BASIC AND COURTEOUS EXPRESSIONS

Most Spanish-speaking people consider formalities important. When approaching anyone for information or any other reason, do not forget the appropriate salutation – good morning, good evening, and so on. Standing alone, the greeting hola (hello) can sound brusque.

Hello. *Hola.*

Good morning. *Buenos días.*

Good afternoon. *Buenas tardes.*

Good evening. *Buenas noches.*

How are you? (formal) *¿Cómo está usted?*

How are you? (informal) *¿Qué tal?* or *¿Qué fue?*

Very well, thank you. *Muy bien, gracias.*

OK; good. *Bien.*

So-so. *Más o menos.*

Not OK; bad. *Mal.*

And you? *¿Y usted?*

Thank you. *Gracias.*

Thank you very much. *Muchas gracias.*

You're very kind. *Muy amable.*

You're welcome. *De nada.*

Goodbye. *Ciao* ("chow") or *Adios.*

See you later. *Hasta luego.*

please *por favor*

yes *sí*

no *no*

I don't know. *No sé.*

Just a moment, please. *Momentito, por favor.*

Excuse me, please. (when you're trying to get attention) *Disculpe* or *Con permiso* (for moving past someone)

Sorry (when you've made an error) *Disculpe* or *Lo siento* (stronger and more formal)

Pleased to meet you. *Mucho gusto* or *Encantado* (more formal and stronger)

How do you say...in Spanish? *¿Cómo se dice...en español?*

What is your name? *¿Cómo se llama usted?*

Do you speak English? *¿Habla usted inglés?*

Is English spoken here? (Does anyone here speak English?) *¿Se habla inglés?*

I don't speak Spanish well. *No hablo bien el español.*

I don't understand. *No entiendo.*

My name is... *Me llamo...*

Would you like... *¿Quisiera usted...*

Let's go to... *Vamos a...*

TERMS OF ADDRESS

When in doubt, use the formal *usted* (you) as a form of address.

I *yo*
you (formal) *usted*
you (familiar) *tu*
he/him *él*
she/her *ella*
we/us *nosotros*
you (plural) *ustedes*
they/them *ellos* (all males or mixed gender); *ellas* (all females)
Mr., sir *señor*
Mrs., Madam *señora*
Miss, young woman *señorita*
wife *esposa*
husband *esposo*
friend *amigo* (male); *amiga* (female)
boyfriend/girlfriend *novio* (male); *novia* (female; this also can imply engagement)
son; daughter *hijo; hija*
brother; sister *hermano; hermana* or *ñaño; ñaña* (less formal, originally from Quechua).
father; mother *padre; madre*
grandfather; grandmother *abuelo; abuela*

TRANSPORTATION

Where is...? *¿Dónde está...?*
How far is it to...? *¿A cuánto está...?*
from...to... *de...a...*
How many blocks? *¿Cuántas cuadras?*
Where (Which) is the way to...? *¿Dónde está el camino a...?*
the bus station *la terminal de autobuses*
the bus stop *la parada de autobuses*
Where is this bus going? *¿Adónde va este autobús?*
the taxi stand *la parada de taxis*
the train station *la estación de ferrocarril*
the boat *el barco*
the airport *el aeropuerto*
I'd like a ticket to... *Quisiera un boleto a..* (*un ticket* is also common)
first (second) class *primera (segunda) clase*
round-trip *ida y vuelta*
reservation *reservación*
baggage *equipaje*
Stop here, please. *Pare aquí, por favor.*

the entrance *la entrada*
the exit *la salida*
the ticket office *la oficina de boletos*
(very) near; far *(muy) cerca; lejos*
to; toward *a*
by; through *por*
from *desde*
the right *la derecha*
the left *la izquierda*
straight ahead *derecho; recto*
in front *en frente*
beside *al lado*
behind *atrás*
the corner *la esquina*
the stoplight *el semáforo*
a turn *una vuelta*
right here *aquí*
somewhere around here *por acá*
right there *allí*
somewhere around there *por allá*
street; avenue *calle; avenida*
highway *carretera; Pana*
bridge; toll *puente; peaje*
address *dirección*
north; south *norte; sur*
east; west *oriente (este); occidente (oeste)*

ACCOMMODATIONS

hotel *hotel*
Is there a room available? *¿Hay una habitación libre?*
May I (may we) see it? *¿Puedo (podemos) verlo?*
What is the rate? *¿Cuál es el precio?*
Is that your best rate? *¿Es su mejor precio?*
Is there something cheaper? *¿Hay algo más económico?*
Does it include breakfast? *¿Incluye el desayuno?*
I'm leaving today. *Me voy hoy dia.*
a single room *una habitación sencilla* or *individual*
a double room with two beds *una habitación doble*
a double room with a double bed *una habitación matrimonial*
with private bath *con baño privado*
with shared bath *con baño compartido*

hot water *agua caliente*
shower *ducha*
bath *tina*
towels *toallas*
soap *jabón*
toilet paper *papel higiénico*
blanket *corbija; manta*
sheets *sábanas*
air-conditioned *aire acondicionado*
fan *ventilador*
key *llave*
manager *gerente*
discount *descuento*

FOOD
I'm hungry *Tengo hambre.*
I'm thirsty. *Tengo sed.*
menu *carta; menú*
order *orden*
glass *vaso*
fork *tenedor*
knife *cuchillo*
spoon *cuchara*
teaspoon *cucharita*
napkin *servilleta*
alcoholic drink *bebida* or *trago*
soft drink *refresco*
soda *cola*
coffee *café*
tea *té*
bottled carbonated water *agua con gas*
bottled noncarbonated water *agua sin gas*
beer *cerveza*
wine *vino*
milk *leche*
juice *jugo*
cream *crema*
sugar *azúcar*
cheese *queso*
snack *bocadillos*
breakfast *desayuno*
lunch *almuerzo*
daily lunch special *el menú del día*
dinner *cena*
the check *la cuenta*
eggs *huevos*
bread *pan*
salad *ensalada*

fruit *fruta*
mango *mango*
watermelon *sandía*
papaya *papaya*
banana *plátano*
apple *manzana*
orange *naranja*
lime *limón*
fish *pescado*
shellfish *mariscos*
shrimp *camarones*
meat (without) *(sin) carne*
chicken *pollo*
pork *chancho*
beef; steak *res; bistec; lomo*
bacon; ham *tocino; jamón*
fried *frito*
roasted *asada*
barbecue; barbecued *ala parrilla; al carbón*

SHOPPING
money *dinero*
money-exchange bureau *casa de cambio*
I would like to exchange traveler's checks. *Quisiera cambiar cheques viajeros.*
What is the exchange rate? *¿Cuál es el tipo de cambio?*
How much is the commission? *¿Cuánto cuesta la comisión?*
Do you accept credit cards? *¿Aceptan tarjetas de crédito?*
money order *giro*
How much does it cost? *¿Cuánto cuesta?*
What is your final price? *¿Cuál es su último precio?*
expensive *caro*
cheap *barato; económico*
more *más*
less *menos*
a little *un poco*
too much *demasiado*

HEALTH
Help me, please. *Ayúdeme por favor.*
I am ill. *Estoy enfermo.*
Call a doctor. *Llame un doctor.*
Take me to... *Lléveme a...*
hospital *hospital; clínica*

drugstore *farmacia*
pain *dolor*
fever *fiebre*
headache *dolor de cabeza*
stomachache *dolor de estómago*
burn *quemadura*
cramp *calambre*
nausea *náusea*
vomiting *vomitar*
medicine *medicina*
antibiotics *antibióticos*
pill, tablet *pastilla*
aspirin *aspirina*
ointment or cream *crema*
bandage *venda*
Band-Aid *curita*
cotton *algodón*
sanitary napkins use brand name, e.g. *Kotex*
birth control pills *pastillas anticonceptivas*
condoms *preservativos; condones*
toothbrush *cepillo de dientes*
dental floss *hilo dental*
toothpaste *pasta de dientes*
dentist *dentista*
toothache *dolor de muelas*

POST OFFICE AND COMMUNICATIONS

long-distance telephone *teléfono larga distancia*
I would like to call... *Quisiera llamar a...*
collect *por cobrar*
person-to-person *persona a persona*
credit card *tarjeta de crédito*
post office *correo*
general delivery *lista de correo*
letter *carta*
stamp *estampilla; timbre*
postcard *tarjeta*
airmail *correo aereo*
registered *registrado*
money order *giro*
package; box *paquete; caja*
string; tape *piola; cinta*

AT THE BORDER

border *frontera*
customs *aduana*

immigration *migración*
tourist card *tarjeta de turista*
inspection *inspección; revisión*
passport *pasaporte*
profession *profesión*
marital status *estado civil*
single *soltero*
married; divorced *casado; divorciado*
widowed *viudado*
insurance *seguros*
title *título*
driver's license *licencia de conducir*

AT THE GAS STATION

gas station *gasolinera*
gasoline *gasolina*
high-quality gasoline *super*
low-quality gasoline *extra*
diesel *diesel*
fill it, please *lleno, por favor*
tire *llanta*
tire repair shop *vulcanizadora*
air *aire*
water *agua*
oil (change) *aceite (cambio)*
grease *grasa*
My...doesn't work. *Mi...no sirve.*
battery *batería*
radiator *radiador*
alternator *alternador*
generator *generador*
tow truck *grúa*
repair shop *taller mecánico*
tune-up *afinación*
auto parts store *repuestos*

VERBS

Verbs are the key to getting along in Spanish. They employ mostly predictable forms and come in three classes, which end in *ar, er,* and *ir,* respectively:
to buy *comprar*
I buy; you (he/she/it) buys *compro; compra*
We buy; you (they) buy *compramos; compran*
to eat *comer*
I eat; you (he/she/it) eats *como; come*
We eat; you (they) eat *comemos; comen*

to climb *subir*
I climb; you (he/she/it) climbs *subo; sube*
We climb; you (they) climb *subimos; suben*
to do or make *hacer*
I do or make; you (he/she/it) does or make *hago; hace*
We do or make; you (they) do or make *hacemos; hacen*
to go *ir*
I go; you (he/she/it) goes *voy; va*
We go; you (they) go *vamos; van*
to go (walk) *andar*
to love *amar*
to work *trabajar*
to want *querer*
to need *necesitar*
to read *leer*
to write *escribir*
to repair *reparar*
to stop *parar*
to get off (the bus) *bajar*
to arrive *llegar*
to stay (remain) *quedar*
to stay (lodge) *hospedar*
to leave *salir* (regular except for *salgo*, "I leave")
to look at *mirar*
to look for *buscar*
to give *dar* (regular except for *doy*, "I give")
to carry *llevar, cargar*
to have *tener* (irregular but important: *tengo, tiene, tenemos, tienen*)
to come *venir* (similarly irregular: *vengo, viene, venimos, vienen*)
Spanish has two forms of "to be." Use *estar* **when speaking of location or a temporary state of being: "I am at home."** *"Estoy en casa."* **"I'm sick."** *"Estoy enfermo."* **Use** *ser* **for a permanent state of being: "I am a doctor."** *"Soy doctora." Estar* **is regular, except for** *estoy,* **"I am."** *Ser* **is very irregular:**
to be *ser*
I am; you (he/she/it) is *soy; es*
We are; you (they) are *somos; son*

NUMBERS
0 *cero*

1 *uno*
2 *dos*
3 *tres*
4 *cuatro*
5 *cinco*
6 *seis*
7 *siete*
8 *ocho*
9 *nueve*
10 *diez*
11 *once*
12 *doce*
13 *trece*
14 *catorce*
15 *quince*
16 *dieciseis*
17 *diecisiete*
18 *dieciocho*
19 *diecinueve*
20 *veinte*
21 *veinte y uno* or *veintiuno*
30 *treinta*
40 *cuarenta*
50 *cincuenta*
60 *sesenta*
70 *setenta*
80 *ochenta*
90 *noventa*
100 *ciento*
101 *ciento y uno* or *cientiuno*
200 *doscientos*
500 *quinientos*
1,000 *mil*
10,000 *diez mil*
100,000 *cien mil*
1,000,000 *millón*
half *medio* or *la mitad*
one-third *un tercio*
one-quarter *un cuarto*

TIME
What time is it? *¿Qué hora es?*
It's 1 o'clock. *Es la una.*
It's 3 in the afternoon. *Son las tres de la tarde.*
It's 4 A.M. *Son las cuatro de la mañana.*
6:30 *seis y media*
quarter to 11 *un cuarto para las once*

quarter past 5 *las cinco y cuarto*
an hour *una hora*
a minute *un minuto*
a second *un segundo*

DAYS AND MONTHS
Monday *lunes*
Tuesday *martes*
Wednesday *miércoles*
Thursday *jueves*
Friday *viernes*
Saturday *sábado*
Sunday *domingo*
today *hoy*
tomorrow *mañana*
yesterday *ayer*
January *enero*
February *febrero*

March *marzo*
April *abril*
May *mayo*
June *junio*
July *julio*
August *agosto*
September *septiembre*
October *octubre*
November *noviembre*
December *diciembre*
a week *una semana*
a month *un mes*
after *después*
before *antes*

Courtesy of Bruce Whipperman, author of *Moon Pacific Mexico.* Amended for Ecuadorian usage by Ben Westwood.

Suggested Reading

The titles below are all available on Amazon.com, either new or used, in the case of many that are out of print. In Ecuador, the Libri Mundi bookstore is the best source, or try secondhand bookshops on Mariscal Sucre in Quito.

TRAVEL AND MEMOIRS

Bemelmans, Ludwig. *The Donkey Inside.* New York: Paragon House, 1990. Out of print. The French author of the famous *Madeline* series for children traveled in Ecuador in the late 1930s and early 1940s. Subtle, always perceptive and sympathetic, and at times biting characterizations of Ecuadorians and their attitudes.

Lourie, Peter. *Sweat of the Sun, Tears of the Moon.* Lincoln: University of Nebraska Press, 1998. Firsthand account of an obsession with the treasure in the Llanganates.

Michaux, Henri. *Ecuador: A Travel Journal.* Evanston, IL: Marlboro Press/Northwestern, 2001. Out of print. A short, quirky account of the Belgian-born author's travels in Ecuador in 1927. An interesting and very philosophical read, at times even spiritual.

Poole, Richard. *The Inca Smiled: The Growing Pains of an Aid Worker in Ecuador.* Oxford, UK: Oneworld Publications, 1997. Out of print. The story of a British volunteer in Ecuador in the 1960s, with interesting takes on the Andean indigenous personalities and Third World development.

Theroux, Paul. *The Old Patagonian Express: By Train Through the Americas.* Boston: Hougton Mifflin, 1997. The author travels from Canada to the tip of Chile by train. One chapter is on the Quito–Guayaquil line, even though he didn't ride it.

Thomsen, Moritz. *Living Poor: A Peace Corps Chronicle.* Seattle: University of Washington Press, 1969. Out of print. Describing two years on a farm in Esmeraldas in the 1960s, this is said to be one of the best books on the Peace Corps experience. The narrative continues in *The Farm on the River of Emeralds* (Boston: Houghton Mifflin, 1978) and *The Saddest Pleasure: A Journey on Two Rivers* (St. Paul, MN: Graywolf Press, 1990). All are eloquent and wrenching.

HISTORY AND CULTURE

Buchanan, Christy, and Cesar Franco. *The Ecuador Cookbook: Traditional Vegetarian and Seafood Recipes.* Christy Buchanan, 1998. A bilingual cookbook that uses easy-to-find ingredients.

De las Casas, Bartolomé. *A Short Account of the Destruction of the Indies.* New York: Penguin, 1999. Originally written as a plea to Prince Philip of Spain in the 16th century, this is a searing indictment of European cruelty toward the indigenous peoples of the New World.

Crowder, Nicholas. *Culture Shock: Ecuador! A Survival Guide to Customs and Etiquette.* Singapore: Marshall Cavendish, 2009. An entertaining, humorous book concentrating on cultural differences and how to adapt to them.

Cuvi, Pablo. *Crafts of Ecuador.* Quito: Dinediciones, 1994. Beautifully photographed book on Ecuadorian crafts.

De la Torre, Carlos. *The Ecuador Reader: History, Culture and Politics.* Durham, NC: Duke University Press, 2008. An excellent collection of writings from authors, politicians, and journalists.

Hemming, John. *The Conquest of the Incas.* San Diego: Harcourt Brace, 1973. Probably the best account of the Spanish arrival in the New World and its aftermath. A long but surprisingly readable account, exhaustively researched.

Honigsbaum, Mark. *Valverde's Gold.* London: Picador, 2005. Investigation into the legend of the lost Inca gold in the Llanganates.

Perkins, John. *Confessions of an Economic Hitman.* London: Ebury Press, 2005. Explosive account of the economic pressure applied to South American governments in the 1970s and 1980s. Claims that Ecuadorian president Jaime Roldós Aguilera was assassinated in a right-wing conspiracy.

LITERATURE

Adoum, Jorge Enrique, ed. *Poesía Viva del Ecuador, Siglo XX.* Quito: Grijalbo, 1990. Out of print. In Spanish. Collection of 20th-century Ecuadorian poetry.

Beardsell, Peter R. *Winds of Exile: The Poetry of Jorge Carrera Andrade.* Oxford: Dolphin, 1977. Out of print.

Burroughs, William S. *Queer.* New York: Viking Penguin, 1996. A companion piece to Burroughs's first novel, *Junky* (1953), *Queer* describes a fictional addict's sexual escapades during a "hallucinated month of acute withdrawal" in Guayaquil and Mexico City.

Carvalho-Neto, Paulo. *Cuentos Folklóricos del Ecuador, Sierra y Costa, Vol. I–III.* Quito: Ediciones Abya-Yala. In Spanish. Folklore from the Andes and the coast.

Cuvi, Pablo, et al. *Ten Stories from Ecuador (Diez Cuentistas Ecuatorianos).* Quito: Ediciones Libri Mundi, 1990. A bilingual selection of modern Ecuadorian authors.

Izaca, Jorge Juan. *Huasipungo: The Villagers.* Carbondale, IL: Southern Illinois University Press, 1973. Landmark novel about peasant life in Ecuador that caused a furor when it was originally published in the 1930s. Brutally honest.

Mera, Juan León. *Cumandá: The Novel of the Ecuadorian Jungle.* 1879; reprint Bloomington, IN: AuthorHouse, 2007. One of Ecuador's most famous novels is a romantic drama set in 19th-century Oriente. The English translation by Colombian Noe Vaca and the original Spanish version are both available.

Spindler, Frank, trans. *Selections from Juan Montalvo*. Tempe, AZ: Center for Latin American Studies, Arizona State University, 1984. Out of print.

Vonnegut, Kurt Jr. *Galápagos*. New York: Delta, 1999. The emperor of irony's take on what would happen if the only people to survive a worldwide epidemic were the passengers on a Galápagos cruise ship.

THE AMAZON

Emmons, Louise. *Neotropical Rainforest Mammals*. Chicago: University of Chicago Press, 1997. This scientific field guide has become the standard for studying these types of mammals.

Forsyth, Adrian, and Ken Miyata. *Tropical Nature: Life and Death in the Rainforests of Central and South America*. New York: Touchstone, 1987. A great introduction for the nonscientist, this book makes tropical ecology fascinating and understandable.

Kane, Joe. *Savages*. New York: Vintage Departures, 1996. Firsthand account of the Huaorani's fight against oil exploration, missionaries, and environmentalists.

Kricher, John. *A Neotropical Companion*. Princeton, NJ: Princeton University Press, 1999. Another good introduction to tropical ecology.

Montgomery, Sy. *Journey of the Pink Dolphins: An Amazon Quest*. New York: Simon & Schuster, 2009. An exhaustive, lyrical account of the author's many trips to the Amazon in search of the elusive pink river dolphins. Contains color photos and discussions of the people, flora and fauna, politics, and ecology.

Sawyer, Suzana. *Crude Chronicles*. Durham, NC: Duke University Press, 2004. Passionate account of indigenous resistance to oil exploration in the Ecuadorian Amazon.

THE GALÁPAGOS

Angermeyer, Johanna. *My Father's Island: A Galápagos Quest*. New York: Viking, 1990. Out of print. Life in the Galápagos through much of the 20th century.

Bassett, Carol Ann. *Galápagos at the Crossroads: Pirates, Biologists, Tourists and Creationists Battle for Darwin's Cradle of Evolution*. Washington, DC: National Geographic, 2009. Provocative analysis of the islands' environmental problems.

Castro, Isabel. *A Guide to the Birds of the Galápagos Islands*. Princeton, NJ: Princeton University Press, 1996. Presents every species to have been recorded within the archipelago, including accidentals and vagrants, with 32 color plates.

Darwin, Charles. *On the Origin of Species by Means of Natural Selection, or the Preservation of Favoured Races in the Struggle for Life*. New York: Signet Classics, 2003. The book that shook the world—and, as a bonus, it's one of the few groundbreaking scientific works that's truly readable.

Darwin, Charles. *The Voyage of the Beagle*. New York: Penguin, 1999. A classic of early travel literature written by a wide-eyed, brilliant young man setting out to see the whole world. You can almost witness his theories being born.

Darwin, Charles, and Mark Ridley, ed. *The Darwin Reader*. New York: W. W. Norton, 1996. Selections from Darwin's works, including *The Voyage of the Beagle* and *On the Origin of Species*.

De Roy, Tui. *Spectacular Galápagos: Exploring an Extraordinary World*. Westport, CT: Hugh Lauter Levin Associates, 1999. Text and breathtaking photographs by one of the islands' foremost advocates. De Roy lived in the Galápagos for 35 years and also wrote *Galápagos: Islands Born of Fire* (Oxford, UK: Warwick, 2000).

Jackson, Michael. *Galápagos: A Natural History.* Calgary: University of Calgary Press, 1994. This definitive guide to the islands is a must-read for every visitor.

McMullen, Conley. *Flowering Plants of the Galápagos*. Ithaca, NY: Cornell University Press, 1999.

Weiner, Jonathan. *The Beak of the Finch: A Story of Evolution in Our Own Time*. New York: Vintage Books, 1995. Describes the work of Rosemary and Peter Grant, who have studied 20 generations of finches on Daphne Major over two decades.

Wittmer, Margaret. *Floreana: A Woman's Pilgrimage to the Galápagos*. Wakefield, RI: Moyer Bell, 1990. Firsthand account of early Floreana settlers, including Margaret's account of the mysterious events of the 1930s.

BIRDING

Fjeldsa, Jon, and Niels Krabbe. *Birds of the High Andes*. Copenhagen: Apollo Books, 1990. Covers birds the length of the Andes above 2,000 meters. More than 880 pages and beautiful plates.

Ridgely, Robert, and Paul Greenfield. *The Birds of Ecuador: A Field Guide*. Ithaca, NY: Comstock, 2001. The bible of birding in Ecuador, with 800 pages of color plates and descriptions of Ecuador's 1,600 species.

Rodner, Clemencia, Miguel Lentino, and Robin Restall. *A Checklist of the Birds of Northern South America*. New Haven, CT: Yale University Press, 2001. Covers Ecuador, Colombia, and Venezuela.

Wheatley, Nigel. *Where to Watch Birds in South America*. Princeton, NJ: Princeton University Press, 2000. Site-specific; includes maps.

CLIMBING

Brain, Yossi. *Ecuador: A Climbing Guide*. Seattle: The Mountaineers, 2000. The most up-to-date and detailed guide to climbing Ecuador's major peaks.

Kunstaetter, Robert, and Daisy Kunstaetter. *Trekking in Ecuador*. Seattle: The Mountaineers, 2002. Details on short and long foot journeys throughout the country.

Rachowiecki, Rob, and Mark Thurber. *Climbing and Hiking in Ecuador*. Bucks, England: Bradt, 2004. A wide-ranging book that covers mountaineering and hikes of various lengths throughout the country.

HEALTH

Bezruchka, Stephen, MD. *The Pocket Doctor*. Seattle: The Mountaineers, 1999. A handy travel health reference.

Forgey, William, MD. *Travelers' Medical Resource*. Merrillville, IN: ICS Books, 1990. Comprehensive, and includes a toll-free computer database update service.

Rose, Stuart, and Jay Stephen Keystone. *International Travel Health Guide*. Northampton, MA: Travel Medicine, 2005. Excellent comprehensive guide.

Wise, Mark. *International Travel Health Guide*. Northampton, MA: Travel Medicine, 2005. Excellent comprehensive guide.

Internet Resources

GENERAL ECUADOR WEBSITES

EcuadorExplorer.com
www.ecuadorexplorer.com
Complete online guide.

Ecuador.com
www.ecuador.com
News, features, and cultural and business information.

Ecuador Travel
www.ecuador.travel
Ministry of Tourism site.

Exploring Ecuador
www.exploringecuador.com
Tourism, business, arts, cultural organizations, and news.

Ecuaroads
www.ecuaworld.com/ecuaroads
Road trips through Ecuador.

The Best of Ecuador
www.thebestofecuador.com
Complete online guide.

QUITO

InQuito
www.inquito.com
Online guide to Quito in English, German, and French.

Quito Official Travel Information
www.quito.com.ec
City tourist office's website, with comprehensive information.

THE GALÁPAGOS ISLANDS

International Galápagos Tour Operators Association
www.igtoa.org

Charles Darwin Foundation
www.darwinfoundation.org
Website of the Charles Darwin Foundation and the Charles Darwin Research Station.

Galápagos Conservation Trust
www.savegalapagos.org

Discover Galápagos
www.discovergalapagos.com
Natural history, conservation issues, and travel information.

NEWS AND MEDIA

El Comercio
www.elcomercio.com
Quito-based national daily newspaper, in Spanish.

El Universo
www.eluniverso.com
Guayaquil-based national daily newspaper, in Spanish.

Hoy
www.hoy.com.ec
Quito-based national daily newspaper, in Spanish.

Miami Herald
www.miami.com/mld/miamiherald/news/world/americas
Coverage of Latin America.

South America Daily
www.southamericadaily.com

GOVERNMENT

British Foreign Office Travel Advice
www.fco.gov.uk/travel
Click on "Ecuador" in the "Country" menu.

CIA World Factbook: Ecuador
www.cia.gov/library/publications/
the-world-factbook
Click on "Ecuador" on the map.

**Ecuadorian Embassy
in Washington, DC**
www.ecuador.org

**Ecuador's Ministry of
External Relations**
www.mmrree.gob.ec
Up-to-date information on visa and immigration issues.

Presidency of Ecuador
www.presidencia.gov.ec
The latest news and views from Ecuador's government.

**U.S. Department of State Ecuador
Country Profile**
http://travel.state.gov
Click on "Ecuador" in the "Country" menu.

U.S. Embassy in Ecuador
www.usembassy.org.ec

WEATHER AND THE NATURAL WORLD
Weather.com
www.weather.com
Five- and 10-day forecasts throughout Ecuador.

**Instituto Geofísico-Escuela
Politécnica Nacional**
www.igepn.edu.ec
Local volcano watchers provide daily updates, seismograms within 15 minutes of events, and photos.

**Smithsonian Institution
Global Volcanism Program**
www.volcano.si.edu
Includes recent worldwide activity.

LANGUAGE
SpanishDICT.com
www.spanishdict.com
Online Spanish dictionary.

Learn Spanish
www.studyspanish.com
Free, award-winning online tutorial.

THE ENVIRONMENT
Fundación Sinchi Sacha
www.sinchisacha.org
Helps the indigenous population of Ecuador by encouraging self-directed development and fair trade.

Fundación Natura
www.fnatura.org
Ecuador's largest environmental organization.

Jocotoco Foundation
www.fjocotoco.org
Purchases land to preserve avifauna and biodiversity.

OTHER WEBSITES
Cultures of the Andes
www.andes.org
Kichwa language links, songs, and pictures.

Human Rights Watch
www.hrw.org/americas
Information on human rights issues in Ecuador.

Index

List of Maps

Acknowledgments

I would like to thank many friends and colleagues around Ecuador who gave their time, local knowledge, expertise, and photography to this project: Udy Brill, Chris O'Connell, Vicente Muñoz, Brian Stefanelli, and Dr. Louise Westwood. Special thanks to Luz Elena Coloma and Maria Gabriela Torres at Quito Turismo, Peter Andrew at Madre Tierra, Esteban Velásquez at Via Natura, Nicola Mears at Rio Muchacho, Peter Stromberg at Surf Shak, Tracy Wilson at Touch the Jungle, Patrick Pecaut at La Barquita, Manuel Sibaja at Mindo Canopy Adventures, Diego Falconi at Casa Mojanda, and Irina Gomez at Gobierno Provincial de Imbabura.

Thanks to the following companies and organizations: Runa Tupari in Otavalo, Amarongachi Tours in Tena, Cuidad Alfaro in Montecristi, Napo Wildlife Center, and Ferrocarriles del Ecuador.

Thanks to the previous writers, Julian Smith and Jean Brown, for giving me an excellent starting point for this edition, and I'd particularly like to thank University Especialidades Espíritu Santo (UEES) for giving me the time to complete this project.

Last but not least, I'd like to thank my family: my parents for the education, my wife for the support, and my children for putting up with the phrase "Daddy's working" all too often. Special thanks also to my sister Lucinda, who many years ago let me tag along on a trip to Thailand, where I first developed a passion for travel writing.

www.moon.com

DESTINATIONS | ACTIVITIES | BLOGS | MAPS | BOOKS

MOON.COM is ready to help plan your next trip! Filled with fresh trip ideas and strategies, author interviews, informative travel blogs, a detailed map library, and descriptions of all the Moon guidebooks, Moon.com is all you need to get out and explore the world—or even places in your own backyard. While at Moon.com, sign up for our monthly e-newsletter for updates on new releases, travel tips, and expert advice from our on-the-go Moon authors. As always, when you travel with Moon, expect an experience that is uncommon and truly unique.

KEEP UP WITH MOON ON FACEBOOK AND TWITTER
JOIN THE MOON PHOTO GROUP ON FLICKR

MAP SYMBOLS

▦ Expressway	◖ Highlight	✗ Airfield	⚓ Golf Course
▦ Primary Road	○ City/Town	✗ Airport	🅿 Parking Area
▦ Secondary Road	◉ State Capital	▲ Mountain	▲ Archaeological Site
┅ Unpaved Road	✪ National Capital	✛ Unique Natural Feature	⛪ Church
┄ Trail	★ Point of Interest		
┈ Ferry	• Accommodation	🌊 Waterfall	⛽ Gas Station
┅ Railroad	▼ Restaurant/Bar	▲ Park	🗺 Glacier
▦ Pedestrian Walkway	■ Other Location	▣ Trailhead	🗺 Mangrove
▦ Stairs	▲ Campground	✗ Skiing Area	🗺 Reef
			🗺 Swamp

CONVERSION TABLES

$°C = (°F - 32) / 1.8$
$°F = (°C \times 1.8) + 32$
1 inch = 2.54 centimeters (cm)
1 foot = 0.304 meters (m)
1 yard = 0.914 meters
1 mile = 1.6093 kilometers (km)
1 km = 0.6214 miles
1 fathom = 1.8288 m
1 chain = 20.1168 m
1 furlong = 201.168 m
1 acre = 0.4047 hectares
1 sq km = 100 hectares
1 sq mile = 2.59 square km
1 ounce = 28.35 grams
1 pound = 0.4536 kilograms
1 short ton = 0.90718 metric ton
1 short ton = 2,000 pounds
1 long ton = 1.016 metric tons
1 long ton = 2,240 pounds
1 metric ton = 1,000 kilograms
1 quart = 0.94635 liters
1 US gallon = 3.7854 liters
1 Imperial gallon = 4.5459 liters
1 nautical mile = 1.852 km

**MOON ECUADOR &
THE GALÁPAGOS ISLANDS**

Avalon Travel
a member of the Perseus Books Group
1700 Fourth Street
Berkeley, CA 94710, USA
www.moon.com

Editor: Erin Raber
Series Manager: Kathryn Ettinger
Copy Editor: Christopher Church
Graphics and Production Coordinator: Darren Alessi
Cover Designer: Darren Alessi
Map Editor: Mike Morgenfeld
Cartographers: Chris Henrick, Kaitlin Jaffe
Indexer: Judy Hunt

ISBN: 978-1-59880-354-9
ISSN: 1095-886X

Printing History
1st Edition – 1998
5th Edition – January 2012
5 4 3 2

Front color photos: Page 4 © Ben Westwood; page
5 © Tracy Wilson/Touch the Jungle; page 6 (inset)
© Quito Turismo, (bottom) © Ben Westwood; page
7 (top left) © Chris O'Connell, (top right) © Mindo
Canopy Adventure, (bottom left and right) © Chris
O'Connell; page 8 © Mindo Canopy Adventure; page
10 © Peter Stromberg; page 11 © Carolina Westwood;
page 12 © Chris O'Connell; page 13 © Ben Westwood;
pages 14 and 15 © Chris O'Connell; page 16 © Ben
Westwood; pages 17 and 18 © Dr. Louise Westwood;
page 20 © Vicente Muñoz

Printed in Canada by Friesens

KEEPING CURRENT

If you have a favorite gem you'd like to see included in the next edition, or see anything
that needs updating, clarification, or correction, please drop us a line. Send your
comments via email to feedback@moon.com, or use the address above.